T0235253

Lecture Notes in Computer Science 9723

Commenced Publication in 1973
Founding and Former Series Editors:
Gerhard Goos, Juris Hartmanis, and Jan van Leeuwen

More information about this series at http://www.springer.com/series/7410

Joseph K. Liu · Ron Steinfeld (Eds.)

Information Security and Privacy

21st Australasian Conference, ACISP 2016
Melbourne, VIC, Australia, July 4–6, 2016
Proceedings, Part II

 Springer

Editors
Joseph K. Liu
Monash University
Melbourne, VIC
Australia

Ron Steinfeld
Monash University
Melbourne, VIC
Australia

ISSN 0302-9743   ISSN 1611-3349 (electronic)
Lecture Notes in Computer Science
ISBN 978-3-319-40366-3   ISBN 978-3-319-40367-0 (eBook)
DOI 10.1007/978-3-319-40367-0

Library of Congress Control Number: 2015940421

LNCS Sublibrary: SL4 – Security and Cryptology

Printed on acid-free paper

This Springer imprint is published by Springer Nature
The registered company is Springer International Publishing AG Switzerland

Preface

This volume contains the papers presented at ACISP 2016: the 21st Australasian Conference on Information Security and Privacy held during July 4–6, 2016, in Melbourne.

This year we received a record high number of submissions: 176. Each submission was reviewed by an average of 2.9 Program Committee members. The committee decided to accept 52 full papers and eight short papers. In addition, we also included eight invited papers in order to widen the coverage to different areas of cyber security such as smart cities security and bitcoin security. We would like to extend our sincere thanks to all authors who submitted their papers to ACISP 2016.

The program included two excellent and informative keynote addresses. One of them was from Prof. Elisa Bertino, of Purdue University in the USA. Another was from Prof. Chris Mitchell, of Royal Holloway, University of London in the UK. Furthermore, our program also included eight invited talks from eight international well-known researchers in cyber security. They were Prof. Ed Dawson from Queensland University of Technology, Australia; Prof. Willy Susilo from University of Wollongong, Australia; Prof. Xun Yi from RMIT, Australia; Prof. Yu Yu from Shanghai Jiao Tong University, China; Prof. Wenlei Zhou from Deakin University, Australia; Dr. Surya Nepal from Data61, Australia; Prof. Jinjun Chen from University of Technology Sydney, Australia; and Dr. Jonathan Oliver from Trend Micro, Australia.

We would like to thank the 86 Program Committee members (from 22 different countries) as well as the external reviewers for their volunteer work of reading and discussing the submissions. We also deeply thank the general chair, Prof. Yang Xiang, publication co-chairs, Dr. Dong Seong Kim and Dr. Kaitai Liang, publicity chair, Dr. Nalin Asanka, and the Web chair, Dr. Yu Wang. This conference would not have been successful without their great assistance. Last but not least, we would like to thank EasyChair for providing a user-friendly interface for us to manage all submissions and proceeding files.

July 2016

Joseph K. Liu
Ron Steinfeld

Organization

Program Committee

Cristina Alcaraz	University of Malaga, Spain
Myrto Arapinis	University of Edinburgh, UK
Claudio Ardagna	Università degli Studi di Milano, Italy
David Aspinall	University of Edinburgh, UK
Giuseppe Ateniese	Sapienza University of Rome, Italy
Man Ho Au	Hong Kong Polytechnic University, HKSAR China
Joonsang Baek	Khalifa University of Science, Technology and Research, UAE
Zubair Baig	Edith Cowan University, Australia
Lynn Batten	Deakin University, Australia
Colin Boyd	Norwegian University of Science and Technology (NTNU), Norway
Serdar Boztas	RMIT University, Australia
Alvaro Cardenas	University of Texas at Dallas, USA
Aniello Castiglione	University of Salerno, Italy
Jinjun Chen	University of Technology Sydney, Australia
Liqun Chen	Hewlett-Packard Laboratories, UK
Xiaofeng Chen	Xidian University, China
Ray Cheung	City University of Hong Kong, HKSAR China
Kim-Kwang Raymond Choo	University of South Australia, Australia
Christophe Doche	Macquarie University, Australia
Ernest Foo	Queensland University of Technology, Australia
Steven Galbraith	Auckland University, New Zealand
David Galindo	SCYTL Secure Electronic Voting, Spain
Felix Gomez Marmol	NEC Laboratories Europe, Germany
Swee-Huay Heng	Multimedia University, Malaysia
Andreas Holzer	University of Toronto, Canada
Xinyi Huang	Fujian Normal University, China
Mitsugu Iwamoto	University of Electro-Communications, Japan
Sanjay Jha	University of New South Wales, Australia
Akinori Kawachi	The University of Tokushima, Japan
Dong Seong Kim	University of Canterbury, New Zealand
Howon Kim	Pusan National University, South Korea
Steve Kremer	Inria Nancy - Grand Est, France
Marina Krotofil	European Network for Cyber Security, The Netherlands

Noboru Kunihiro	The University of Tokyo, Japan
Miroslaw Kutylowski	Wroclaw University of Technology, Poland
Junzuo Lai	Jinan University, China
Gaëtan Leurent	Inria, France
Jin Li	Guangzhou University, China
Yingjiu Li	Singapore Management University, Singapore
Zhen Li	Institute for Infocomm Research, Singapore
Kaitai Liang	Aalto University, Finland
Joseph Liu	Monash University, Australia
Shengli Liu	Shanghai Jiao Tong University, China
Zhe Liu	University of Waterloo, Canada
Javier Lopez	University of Malaga, Spain
Jiqiang Lu	Institute for Infocomm Research, Singapore
Rongxing Lu	Nanyang Technological University, Singapore
Kazuhiko Minematsu	NEC Corporation, Japan
Chris Mitchell	Royal Holloway, University of London, UK
Yi Mu	University of Wollongong, Australia
Udaya Parampalli	The University of Melbourne, Australia
Mathias Payer	Purdue University, USA
Christian Payne	Murdoch University, Australia
Thomas Peyrin	Ingenico, Singapore
Josef Pieprzyk	Queensland University of Technology, Australia
Michalis Polychronakis	Columbia University, USA
Kui Ren	State University of New York at Buffalo, USA
Reza Reyhanitabar	NEC Laboratories Europe, Germany
Carsten Rudolph	Monash University, Australia
Sushmita Ruj	Indian Statistical Institute, India
Joerg Schwenk	Ruhr-Universität Bochum, Germany
Jun Shao	Zhejiang Gongshang University, China
Taeshik Shon	Ajou University, South Korea
Haya Shulman	Technische Universität Darmstadt, Germany
Anna Squicciarini	Penn State University, USA
Ron Steinfeld	Monash University, Australia
Chunhua Su	Osaka University, Japan
Willy Susilo	University of Wollongong, Australia
Shaohua Tang	South China University of Technology, China
Juan Tapiador	Universidad Carlos III de Madrid, Spain
Mahesh Tripunitara	University of Waterloo, Canada
Craig Valli	Edith Cowan University, Australia
Frederik Vercauteren	K.U. Leuven - ESAT/COSIC, Belgium
Triet D. Vo-Huu	Northeastern University, USA
Petros Wallden	The University of Edinburgh, UK
Cong Wang	City University of Hong Kong, HKSAR China
Yu Wang	Deakin University, Australia
Sheng Wen	Deakin University, Australia
Qianhong Wu	Beihang University, China

Guomin Yang	University of Wollongong, Australia
Yanjiang Yang	Huawei, Singapore
Wun-She Yap	Universiti Tunku Abdul Rahman, Malaysia
Xun Yi	RMIT University, Australia
Yong Yu	University of Electronic Science and Technology, China
Tsz-Hon Yuen	Huawei, Singapore
Aaram Yun	Ulsan National Institute of Science and Technology, South Korea

Additional Reviewers

Alamer, Ahmed
Aono, Yoshinori
Behnia, Rouzbeh
Boura, Christina
Chattopadhyay, Anupam
Chen, Wei
Cheng, Yao
Chin, Ji-Jian
Cui, Hui
Dai, Tianxiang
El Ioini, Nabil
Gaudenzi, Filippo
Ghodosi, Hossein
Ghosh, Satrajit
Gotfryd, Karol
Guasch, Sandra
Han, Shuai
Hanzlik, Lucjan
He, Kai
He, Shuangyu
Higo, Haruna
Hirano, Takato
Hongjun, Wu
Imine, Abdessamad
Jahan, Mosarrat
Javali, Chitra
Kim, Jun Young
Kluczniak, Kamil
Koshiba, Takeshi
Lauer, Sebastian
Li, Fagen
Liang, Zhi
Liu, Weiran

Liu, Ximeng
Luykx, Atul
Majcher, Krzysztof
Morozov, Kirill
Murphy, Sean
Myers, David
Nieto, Ana
Nishimaki, Ryo
Nuida, Koji
Peikert, Chris
Peters, Thomas
Rahman, Anisur
Reparaz, Oscar
Roenne, Peter
Saito, Teruo
Sakzad, Amin
Schneider, Thomas
Sengupta, Binanda
Seo, Hwajeong
Shani, Barak
Shibutani, Kyoji
Sinha Roy, Sujoy
Späth, Christopher
Sun, Li
Sun, Shifeng
Szepieniec, Alan
Tan, Hailun
Tan, Syhyuan
Tso, Raylin
Velichkov, Vesselin
Vivek, Srinivas
Vizár, Damian
Wang, Jianfeng

Wang, Qin
Wei, Xiaochao
Yau, Wei-Chuen
Ye, Jun
Yu, Xingjie
Yu, Zuoxia

Zhang, Lei
Zhao, Chuan
Zhao, Minghao
Zheng, Haibin
Zhong, Lin
Zhou, Xiuwen

Contents – Part II

Signature and Key Management

One-Round Strong Oblivious Signature-Based Envelope 3
  Rongmao Chen, Yi Mu, Willy Susilo, Guomin Yang, Fuchun Guo,
  and Mingwu Zhang

Proxy Signature with Revocation 21
  Shengmin Xu, Guomin Yang, Yi Mu, and Sha Ma

On the Relations Between Security Notions in Hierarchical Key
Assignment Schemes for Dynamic Structures 37
  Arcangelo Castiglione, Alfredo De Santis, Barbara Masucci,
  Francesco Palmieri, and Aniello Castiglione

Public Key and Identity-Based Encryption

Content-Based Encryption 57
  Xiaofen Wang and Yi Mu

Provably Secure Threshold Paillier Encryption Based on Hyperplane
Geometry 73
  Zhe Xia, Xiaoyun Yang, Min Xiao, and Debiao He

Identity-Based Group Encryption 87
  Xiling Luo, Yili Ren, Jingwen Liu, Jiankun Hu, Weiran Liu,
  Zhen Wang, Wei Xu, and Qianhong Wu

Edit Distance Based Encryption and Its Application 103
  Tran Viet Xuan Phuong, Guomin Yang, Willy Susilo, and Kaitai Liang

Proxy Re-encryption with Delegatable Verifiability 120
  Xiaodong Lin and Rongxing Lu

Efficient Completely Non-Malleable and RKA Secure Public Key
Encryptions 134
  Shi-Feng Sun, Udaya Parampalli, Tsz Hon Yuen, Yu Yu, and Dawu Gu

Searchable Encryption

Verifiable Searchable Encryption with Aggregate Keys for Data Sharing in
Outsourcing Storage   153
    Tong Li, Zheli Liu, Ping Li, Chunfu Jia, Zoe L. Jiang, and Jin Li

Public Key Encryption with Authorized Keyword Search   170
    Peng Jiang, Yi Mu, Fuchun Guo, and Qiaoyan Wen

Linear Encryption with Keyword Search   187
    Shiwei Zhang, Guomin Yang, and Yi Mu

Broadcast Encryption

Generic Anonymous Identity-Based Broadcast Encryption
with Chosen-Ciphertext Security   207
    Kai He, Jian Weng, Man Ho Au, Yijun Mao, and Robert H. Deng

Anonymous Identity-Based Broadcast Encryption with Revocation for File
Sharing   223
    Jianchang Lai, Yi Mu, Fuchun Guo, Willy Susilo, and Rongmao Chen

Mathematical Primitives

Partial Key Exposure Attacks on RSA with Multiple Exponent Pairs   243
    Atsushi Takayasu and Noboru Kunihiro

A New Attack on Three Variants of the RSA Cryptosystem   258
    Martin Bunder, Abderrahmane Nitaj, Willy Susilo, and Joseph Tonien

Generalized Hardness Assumption for Self-bilinear Map with Auxiliary
Information   269
    Takashi Yamakawa, Goichiro Hanaoka, and Noboru Kunihiro

Deterministic Encoding into Twisted Edwards Curves   285
    Wei Yu, Kunpeng Wang, Bao Li, Xiaoyang He, and Song Tian

Symmetric Cipher

Improved Rebound Attacks on AESQ: Core Permutation of CAESAR
Candidate PAEQ   301
    Nasour Bagheri, Florian Mendel, and Yu Sasaki

Efficient Beyond-Birthday-Bound-Secure Deterministic Authenticated
Encryption with Minimal Stretch   317
    Christian Forler, Eik List, Stefan Lucks, and Jakob Wenzel

Improved (related-key) Attacks on Round-Reduced KATAN-32/48/64
Based on the Extended Boomerang Framework   333
    Jiageng Chen, Je Sen Teh, Chunhua Su, Azman Samsudin,
    and Junbin Fang

Authenticated Encryption with Small Stretch (or, How to Accelerate
AERO)   347
    Kazuhiko Minematsu

Impossible Differential Cryptanalysis of 14-Round Camellia-192   363
    Keting Jia and Ning Wang

Automatic Differential Analysis of ARX Block Ciphers with Application to
SPECK and LEA   379
    Ling Song, Zhangjie Huang, and Qianqian Yang

On the Security of the LAC Authenticated Encryption Algorithm   395
    Jiqiang Lu

Linear Hull Attack on Round-Reduced Simeck with Dynamic
Key-Guessing Techniques   409
    Lingyue Qin, Huaifeng Chen, and Xiaoyun Wang

Short Papers-Public Key and Identity-Based Encryption

Reducing the Key Size of the SRP Encryption Scheme   427
    Dung Hoang Duong, Albrecht Petzoldt, and Tsuyoshi Takagi

Short Papers-Biometric Security

Biometric Access Control with High Dimensional Facial Features   437
    Ying Han Pang, Ean Yee Khor, and Shih Yin Ooi

Security Analysis on Privacy-Preserving Cloud Aided Biometric
Identification Schemes   446
    Shiran Pan, Shen Yan, and Wen-Tao Zhu

Short Papers-Digital Forensics

Interest Profiling for Security Monitoring and Forensic Investigation   457
    Min Yang, Fei Xu, and Kam-Pui Chow

Short Papers-National Security Infrastructure

Pseudonymous Signature on eIDAS Token – Implementation Based
Privacy Threats   467
    Mirosław Kutyłowski, Lucjan Hanzlik, and Kamil Kluczniak

Short Papers-Mobile Security

A Feasible No-Root Approach on Android.   481
    Yao Cheng, Yingjiu Li, and Robert H. Deng

Short Papers-Network Security

Improved Classification of Known and Unknown Network Traffic Flows
Using Semi-supervised Machine Learning   493
    Timothy Glennan, Christopher Leckie, and Sarah M. Erfani

Short Papers-Pseudo Random/One-way Function

A Noiseless Key-Homomorphic PRF: Application on Distributed Storage
Systems.   505
    Jhordany Rodriguez Parra, Terence Chan, and Siu-Wai Ho

Author Index   515

Contents – Part I

Invited Papers

I Know Where You All Are! Exploiting Mobile Social Apps
for Large-Scale Location Privacy Probing 3
    Shuang Zhao, Xiapu Luo, Bo Bai, Xiaobo Ma, Wei Zou, Xinliang Qiu,
    and Man Ho Au

MUSE: Towards Robust and Stealthy Mobile Botnets via Multiple Message
Push Services 20
    Wei Chen, Xiapu Luo, Chengyu Yin, Bin Xiao, Man Ho Au,
    and Yajuan Tang

A Survey on the Cyber Attacks Against Non-linear State Estimation in
Smart Grids 40
    Jingxuan Wang, Lucas C.K. Hui, S.M. Yiu, Xingmin Cui, Eric Ke Wang,
    and Junbin Fang

Towards Bitcoin Payment Networks 57
    Patrick McCorry, Malte Möser, Siamak F. Shahandasti, and Feng Hao

Statistical Disclosure Control for Data Privacy Using Sequence of
Generalised Linear Models. 77
    Min Cherng Lee, Robin Mitra, Emmanuel Lazaridis, An Chow Lai,
    Yong Kheng Goh, and Wun-She Yap

Energy-Efficient Elliptic Curve Cryptography for MSP430-Based Wireless
Sensor Nodes 94
    Zhe Liu, Johann Großschädl, Lin Li, and Qiuliang Xu

National Security Infrastructure

A Comparison Study of Wireless Network Security in Several Australasian
Cities and Suburbs 115
    Alastair Nisbet and Andrew Woodward

On the Guessability of Resident Registration Numbers in South Korea 128
    Youngbae Song, Hyoungshick Kim, and Jun Ho Huh

Social Network Security

Towards Privacy-Preserving Data Mining in Online Social Networks:
Distance-Grained and Item-Grained Differential Privacy.   141
    Shen Yan, Shiran Pan, Yuhang Zhao, and Wen-Tao Zhu

Bitcoin Security

Fair Client Puzzles from the Bitcoin Blockchain   161
    Colin Boyd and Christopher Carr

Statistical Privacy

Privacy-Preserving k-Nearest Neighbour Query on Outsourced Database   181
    *Rui Xu, Kirill Morozov, Yanjiang Yang, Jianying Zhou,
    and Tsuyoshi Takagi*

Reversible Data Hiding for Encrypted Images Based on Statistical Learning . . .   198
    Zhen Li and Wei Wu

Network Security

An Ensemble Learning Approach for Addressing the Class Imbalance
Problem in Twitter Spam Detection.   215
    Shigang Liu, Yu Wang, Chao Chen, and Yang Xiang

Smart City Security

Putting the User in Control of the Intelligent Transportation System   231
    *Catalin Gosman, Tudor Cornea, Ciprian Dobre, Florin Pop,
    and Aniello Castiglione*

Digital Forensics

Exploring the Space of Digital Evidence – Position Paper   249
    Carsten Rudolph

Lightweight Security

Towards Lightweight Anonymous Entity Authentication for IoT
Applications   265
    *Yanjiang Yang, Haibin Cai, Zhuo Wei, Haibing Lu,
    and Kim-Kwang Raymond Choo*

Hybrid MQ Signature for Embedded Device   281
    Shaohua Tang, Bo Lv, and Wuqiang Shen

Secure Batch Processing

Batch Verifiable Computation with Public Verifiability for Outsourcing
Polynomials and Matrix Computations.   293
    Yujuan Sun, Yu Yu, Xiangxue Li, Kai Zhang, Haifeng Qian,
    and Yuan Zhou

Accelerating Oblivious Transfer with Batch Multi-exponentiation   310
    Yang Sun, Qianhong Wu, Jingwen Liu, Jianwei Liu, Xinyi Huang,
    Bo Qin, and Wei Hu

Pseudo Random/One-way Function

CTM-sp: A Family of Cryptographic Hash Functions from Chaotic Tent
Maps.   329
    Xun Yi, Xuechao Yang, Yong Feng, Fengling Han,
    and Ron van Schyndel

One-Key Compression Function Based MAC with Security Beyond
Birthday Bound   343
    Avijit Dutta, Mridul Nandi, and Goutam Paul

Cloud Storage Security

Towards Efficient Fully Randomized Message-Locked Encryption   361
    Tao Jiang, Xiaofeng Chen, Qianhong Wu, Jianfeng Ma, Willy Susilo,
    and Wenjing Lou

Secure and Traceable Framework for Data Circulation.   376
    Kaitai Liang, Atsuko Miyaji, and Chunhua Su

Public Cloud Data Auditing with Practical Key Update and Zero
Knowledge Privacy.   389
    Yong Yu, Yannan Li, Man Ho Au, Willy Susilo,
    Kim-Kwang Raymond Choo, and Xinpeng Zhang

Password/QR Code Security

Exploiting the Error Correction Mechanism in QR Codes for Secret Sharing   409
    Yang-Wai Chow, Willy Susilo, Guomin Yang, James G. Phillips,
    Ilung Pranata, and Ari Moesriami Barmawi

Password Requirements Markup Language.   426
    Moritz Horsch, Mario Schlipf, Johannes Braun,
    and Johannes Buchmann

Functional Encryption and Attribute-Based Cryptosystem

Leakage-Resilient Functional Encryption via Pair Encodings   443
   Zuoxia Yu, Man Ho Au, Qiuliang Xu, Rupeng Yang, and Jinguang Han

Secret Handshakes with Dynamic Expressive Matching Policy   461
   Lin Hou, Junzuo Lai, and Lixian Liu

Ciphertext-Policy Attribute-Based Encryption with Key-Delegation Abuse
Resistance   477
   Yinhao Jiang, Willy Susilo, Yi Mu, and Fuchun Guo

Chosen Ciphertext Secure Attribute-Based Encryption with Outsourced
Decryption   495
   Cong Zuo, Jun Shao, Guiyi Wei, Mande Xie, and Min Ji

Accountable Large-Universe Attribute-Based Encryption Supporting Any
Monotone Access Structures.   509
   Yinghui Zhang, Jin Li, Dong Zheng, Xiaofeng Chen, and Hui Li

A Cloud-Based Access Control Scheme with User Revocation and
Attribute Update   525
   Peng Zhang, Zehong Chen, Kaitai Liang, Shulan Wang, and Ting Wang

Author Index   541

Signature and Key Management

One-Round Strong Oblivious Signature-Based Envelope

Rongmao Chen[1,2]($\boxtimes$), Yi Mu[1]($\boxtimes$), Willy Susilo[1], Guomin Yang[1],
Fuchun Guo[1], and Mingwu Zhang[3]

[1] Centre for Computer and Information Security Research School of Computing
and Information Technology, University of Wollongong, Wollongong, Australia
{rc517,ymu,wsusilo,gyang,fuchun}@uow.edu.au
[2] College of Computer, National University of Defense Technology, Changsha, China
[3] School of Computers, Hubei University of Technology, Wuhan, China
csmwzhang@gmail.com

Abstract. Oblivious Signature-Based Envelope (OSBE) has been
widely employed for anonymity-orient and privacy-preserving applications. The conventional OSBE execution relies on a secure communication channel to protect against eavesdroppers. In TCC 2012, Blazy,
Pointcheval and Vergnaud proposed a framework of OSBE (BPV-OSBE)
without requiring any secure channel by clarifying and enhancing the
OSBE security notions. They showed how to generically build an OSBE
scheme satisfying the new strong security in the standard model with
a common-reference string. Their framework requires 2-round interactions and relies on the smooth projective hash function (SPHF) over
special languages, i.e., languages from encryption of signatures. In this
work, we investigate the study on the strong OSBE and make the following contributions. First, we propose a generic construction of *one-round
yet strong* OSBE system. Compared to the 2-round BPV-OSBE, our
one-round construction is more appealing, as its non-interactive setting
accommodates more application scenarios in the real word. Moreover,
our framework relies on the regular (identity-based) SPHF, which can
be instantiated from extensive languages and hence is more general. Second, we also present an efficient instantiation, which is secure under the
standard model from classical assumptions, DDH and DBDH, to illustrate the feasibility of our one-round framework. We remark that our
construction is the first one-round OSBE with strong security.

Keywords: Oblivious signature-based envelope · Smooth projective
hash function · Privacy

1 Introduction

In 2003, Li et al. [25] introduced a new primitive namely Oblivious Signature-
Based Envelope (OSBE), which can be regarded as a nice way to ease the asym-
metrical aspect of several authentication protocols. One motivating scenario for

© Springer International Publishing Switzerland 2016
J.K. Liu and R. Steinfeld (Eds.): ACISP 2016, Part II, LNCS 9723, pp. 3–20, 2016.
DOI: 10.1007/978-3-319-40367-0_1

OSBE is as follows: Alice is a regular entity without any specific affiliation. She wants to send a private message to another party (named Bob) if that party possesses certain credentials, e.g., a certificate produced by an authority. For example, Alice might be a potential informant and Bob might be an agent of Central Intelligence Agency (CIA). However, due to the sensitive nature of CIA, Bob is unwilling, or not allowed, to reveal his credentials. In this case, Alice and Bob are stuck and no session could be established. OSBE protocols can well deal with the aforementioned scenario since it allows Alice to send an envelope, which encapsulates her private message, to Bob in such a way that Bob will be able to open the envelope and obtain the private message if and only if Bob has possessed a credential, e.g., a signature on an agreed-upon message from CIA. In the process, Alice cannot determine whether Bob does really belong to CIA (*obliviousness*) and no other party learns anything about Alice's private message (*semantic security*).

Three OSBE protocols were presented in [25]: RSA-OSBE, Rabin-OSBE and BLS-OSBE. The last two protocols are one-round and derived from Identity-Based Encryption [8,17] while RSA-OSBE is 2-round with some interesting properties. Although these protocols satisfy the security requirements of the aforementioned scenario, they implicitly require a secure channel during the execution to protect against eavesdroppers. The reason is that an adversary may eavesdrop and replay a part of a previous interaction to impersonate a CIA agent. Particularly, the Certification Authority who has the signing key can reveal Alice's private message by eavesdropping on the communication between Alice and Bob. To eliminate the dependency on the secure channel for the OSBE, in TCC 2012, Blazy et al. [7] clarified and enhanced the security models of the OSBE by considering the security for both the sender and the receiver against the authority. Their new strong notion, namely *semantic security w.r.t. the authority*, requires that the authority who plays as the eavesdropper on the protocol, learns nothing about the private message of the sender. They showed how to generically build a 2-round OSBE scheme that can achieve the defined strong security in the standard model with a *common-reference string* (CRS), as well as an efficient instantiation (BPV-OSBE) in the standard model from the classical assumption.

Motivations. Although the work in [7] can achieve stronger security than the conventional OSBE protocols, we remark that their 2-round framework has some limitations as follows.

- From a practical point of view, the 2-round OSBE framework requires the receiver to send his obfuscated certificate/signature to the sender first and thereafter the sender sends its envelope to the receiver. Despite that this setting is reasonable in the interaction case, it might be unsuitable for some application scenarios. For example, in the aforementioned scenario, as an informant, Alice would prefer to send her envelope directly to the CIA agent, i.e., Bob, without contacting him in advance, as Alice might be also unwilling to reveal her identity. However, no one-round OSBE protocol with the strong security exists in the literature. It is thus desirable to propose an OSBE protocol that is *one-round* yet with strong security.

- Theoretically, the main idea of the generic construction in [7] is to use the smooth projective hash function (SPHF) on the *special* language defined by the encryption of valid signatures. Precisely, the framework requires the underlying encryption scheme to be semantically secure and the signature scheme to be existentially unforgeable. Although these schemes are quite common in reality, the framework does require them to be of some additional properties when it comes to instantiations. This is essentially due to the complex special language construction for the SPHF. For example, in the instantiation (BPV-OSBE) shown in [7], a linear encryption and a re-randomizable signature is used as the building blocks to achieve the strong security. Therefore, in some sense, the framework is somewhat not general due to the above instantiating limitation.

Based on the aforementioned observations, we can conclude that designing a *one-round* yet *general* OSBE framework with *strong security* is of practical and theoretical importance. In this paper, we are interested in such an OSBE protocol that is secure in the standard model from classical assumptions.

Table 1. Comparisons with existing OSBE protocols

Protocols	Round	Comp.	Comm.	Security			Assumptions
				O.A.	S.S.	S.S.A.	
RSA-OSBE [25]	2	4E+4M	$2\mathbb{Z}_N+P$	$\checkmark$	$\checkmark$	$\times^*$	R.O, CDH
Rabin-OSBE [25]	1	$4|P| \cdot$ E	$2|P| \cdot \mathbb{Z}_N$	$\checkmark$	$\checkmark$	$\times$	R.O., QR
BLS-OSBE [25]	1	3E+2P	$\mathbb{G}_1+2P$	$\checkmark$	$\checkmark$	$\times$	R.O., BDH
BPV-OSBE [7]	2	12E+8M+6P	$6\mathbb{G}_1+P$	$\checkmark$	$\checkmark$	$\checkmark$	CDH, DLin
Our protocol	1	5E+3M+2P	$2\mathbb{G}_1+3\mathbb{G}_T+P$	$\checkmark$	$\checkmark$	$\checkmark$	DDH, DBDH

[a] We use E to denote exponentiation, M the multiplication, P the pairing computation, P the private message.

[b] For the column of **Security**, O.A. denotes the security of *obliviousness w.r.t the authority*, S.S. denotes the security of *semantic security* and S.S.A. denotes the strong security of *semantic security w.r.t. the authority*.

[c] For the column of **Assumption**, R.O. denotes the *random oracle assumption*.

Our Contributions. In this work, we make the following contributions.

- *A Generic One-Round OSBE with Strong Security.* We propose a generic construction of one-round OSBE system of the strong security with a CRS. Compared to the 2-round framework in [7], our one-round construction is more appealing, as its non-interactive setting can accommodate more application scenarios in the real word. Moreover, our framework relies on the regular (IB-)SPHF, which can be instantiated from extensive languages and hence is more general than the work in [7] where special languages, i.e., languages from encryption of signatures are needed for instantiations.

- *An Efficient Instantiation from Classical Assumptions.* An efficient instantiation secure in the standard model from classical assumptions, DDH and DBDH, is presented to illustrate the feasibility of our generic construction. As shown in Table 1, our one-round protocol is of the same strong security as the BPV-OSBE [7] while the protocols in [25] are under the random oracle model and fail to achieve the *semantic security w.r.t. the authority*. It is worth noting that, as remarked in [7], the authority in the 2-round RSA-OSBE protocol can break the scheme by generating the RSA modulus $N = pq$ dishonestly. In terms of the efficiency, the communication complexity of our protocol is comparable to that of the BPV-OSBE [7] while our computation (include both the sender and the receiver) is much more efficient.

Technique Overview. Our central idea is to utilize the *conjunction* of an SPHF and an identity-based SPHF (IB-SPHF) for the protocol construction. The definition of an SPHF [19] requires the existence of a domain $\mathcal{X}$ and an underlying $\mathcal{NP}$ language $\mathcal{L}$, where elements of $\mathcal{L}$ form a subset of $\mathcal{X}$, i.e., $\mathcal{L} \subset \mathcal{X}$. The key property of SPHF is that the hash value of any word $W \in \mathcal{L}$ can be computed by using either a secret hashing key, or a public projection key with the witness to the fact that $W \in \mathcal{L}$ (*correctness*). However, the projection key gives almost no information about the hash value of any point in $\mathcal{X} \setminus \mathcal{L}$ (*smoothness*). Moreover, we say that the subset membership problem is hard if the distribution of $\mathcal{L}$ is computationally indistinguishable from $\mathcal{X} \setminus \mathcal{L}$. Similarly, an IB-SPHF [4,9] has the above properties except that its underlying language is usually associated with the identity which also acts as the public projection key. The secret (identity) hashing key is then derived based on the identity using a master secret key. The IB-SPHF system has formed the backbone of many IBE schemes [9,16,18,21,22], which, as shown in [8], give rise to the signature scheme. The master secret key plays as the signing key and each message is viewed as an identity. The signature is the private key corresponding to the identity.

    Our construction deserves further interpretation. Precisely, the receiver owns a hashing key pair (hk, hp) belonging to the SPHF system while the authority has a master key pair (msk, mpk) belonging to the IB-SPHF system. The authority can use msk to issue the receiver a valid signature on any agreed-upon message (denoted as M), which is viewed as the identity in the IB-SPHF system. The CRS in our system contains both hp and mpk. To send a message P, the sender firstly samples two distinct words for the SPHF and the IB-SPHF respectively and derives the hash value of each word using hp and M (the identity) with their witnesses to conceal P into the envelope. The sender then sends the two words with the concealed P to the receiver. Upon receiving the message, the receiver uses hk and the valid signature (i.e., identity private key) of M to compute the hash value of the words and thereafter reveals P. One can note that the correctness of our framework relies on the correctness of the underlying SPHF and IB-SPHF. The obliviousness is clear in our one-round framework since the sender does not receive any information from the receiver. The semantic security is guaranteed by the smoothness and the hard subset membership problem of the IB-SPHF while the semantic security w.r.t. the authority is due to the underlying SPHF system.

Organization. The rest of this paper is organized as follows. We review some primitives, including the definition of SPHF and IB-SPHF in Sect. 2, and introduce a generic construction of one-round strong OSBE with formal security analysis in Sect. 3. An efficient instantiation of our framework is then given in Sect. 4. We then conclude our work in Sect. 5.

2 Preliminaries

2.1 Notations and Assumptions

Through this paper, ℓ denotes the security parameter. For a finite set Ω, $\omega \xleftarrow{\$} \Omega$ denotes that ω is selected uniformly from Ω while $\omega \xleftarrow{R} \Omega$ denotes that ω is picked randomly from Ω. Let X and Y be two random variables over a finite domain Ω, the *statistical distance* between X and Y is defined as $\mathsf{SD}(X,Y) = \frac{1}{2}\sum_{\omega \in \Omega}|\Pr[X = \omega] - \Pr[Y = \omega]|$. We say that X and Y are ϵ-*statistically indistinguishable* if $\mathsf{SD}(X,Y) \leq \epsilon$ and for simplicity we denote it by $X \overset{s}{\equiv} Y$.

Definition 1 (Decisional Diffie-Hellman (DDH) Assumption). *Let $\mathbb{G}$ be a general cyclic group of prime order p and $g_1, g_2 \in \mathbb{G}$ the generators of $\mathbb{G}$. Given (g_1, g_2), we say that the decisional Diffie-Hellman assumption holds on $\mathbb{G}$ if for any PPT adversary $\mathcal{A}$,*

$$\mathsf{Adv}_{\mathcal{A}}^{\mathsf{DDH}}(\ell) = |\Pr[\mathcal{A}(g_1^{r_1}, g_2^{r_1}) = 1] - \Pr[\mathcal{A}(g_1^{r_1}, g_2^{r_2}) = 1]| \leq \mathsf{negl}(\ell)$$

where the probability is taken over the random choices $r_1, r_2 \xleftarrow{R} \mathbb{Z}_p$ and the bits consumed by the adversary $\mathcal{A}$.

Let $\mathbb{G}_1, \mathbb{G}_T$ be two multiplicative groups with the same prime order p. Let g be the generator of $\mathbb{G}_1$ and I be the identity element of $\mathbb{G}_T$. A symmetric bilinear map is a map $e : \mathbb{G}_1 \times \mathbb{G}_1 \to \mathbb{G}_T$ such that $e(u^a, v^b) = e(u, v)^{ab}$ for all $u, v \in \mathbb{G}_1$ and $a, b \in \mathbb{Z}_p$. It is worth noting that e can be efficiently computed and $e(g, g) \neq I$. We assume the existence of a group-generation algorithm $\mathcal{BG}(1^\ell)$ which takes as input 1^ℓ and outputs a tuple $(\mathbb{G}_1, \mathbb{G}_T, g, e(\cdot, \cdot), p)$ where $\mathbb{G}_1, \mathbb{G}_T$ are of prime order p.

Definition 2 (Decisional Bilinear Diffie-Hellman (DBDH) Assumption). *Let $(\mathbb{G}_1, \mathbb{G}_T, g, e(\cdot, \cdot), p) \leftarrow \mathcal{BG}(1^\ell)$. Given $D = (g, g^x, g^y, g^z)$, we say that the decisional bilinear Diffie-Hellman assumption holds on $\mathbb{G}$ if for any PPT adversary $\mathcal{A}$,*

$$\mathsf{Adv}_{\mathcal{A}}^{\mathsf{DBDH}}(\ell) = |\Pr[\mathcal{A}(D, e(g, g)^{xyz}) = 1] - \Pr[\mathcal{A}(D, e(g, g)^r) = 1]| \leq \mathsf{negl}(\ell)$$

where the probability is taken over the random choices $x, y, z, r \xleftarrow{R} \mathbb{Z}_p$ and the bits consumed by the adversary $\mathcal{A}$.

2.2 Smooth Projective Hash Functions

Smooth projective hash function (SPHF) is originally introduced by Cramer and Shoup [19] and extended for constructions of many cryptographic primitives [1–3,5,6,10,11,20,23,24]. We start with the original definition.

An SPHF is based on a domain $\mathcal{X}$ and an $\mathcal{NP}$ language $\mathcal{L}$, where $\mathcal{L}$ contains a subset of the elements of the domain $\mathcal{X}$, i.e., $\mathcal{L} \subset \mathcal{X}$. An SPHF system over a language $\mathcal{L} \subset \mathcal{X}$, onto a set $\mathcal{Y}$, is defined by the following five algorithms (SPHFSetup, HashKG, ProjKG, Hash, ProjHash):

$(\mathsf{param}, \mathcal{L}) \leftarrow \mathsf{SPHFSetup}(1^\ell)$: The SPHFSetup algorithm takes as input a security parameter ℓ and generates the *global parameters* param and the description of an $\mathcal{NP}$ language $\mathcal{L}$. All other algorithms HashKG, ProjKG, Hash, ProjHash implicitly include $(\mathcal{L}, \mathsf{param})$ as input.

$\mathsf{hk} \leftarrow \mathsf{HashKG}$: The HashKG algorithm generates a *hashing key* hk;

$\mathsf{hp} \leftarrow \mathsf{ProjKG}(\mathsf{hk})$: The ProjKG algorithm derives the *projection key* hp from the hashing key hk;

$\mathsf{hv} \leftarrow \mathsf{Hash}(\mathsf{hk}, W)$: The Hash algorithm takes as input a word W and the hashing key hk, outputs the hash value $\mathsf{hv} \in \mathcal{Y}$;

$\mathsf{hv} \leftarrow \mathsf{ProjHash}(\mathsf{hp}, W, w)$: The ProjHash algorithm takes as input the projection key hp and a word W with the witness w to the fact that $W \in \mathcal{L}$, outputs the hash value $\mathsf{hv} \in \mathcal{Y}$.

An SPHF should satisfies the following properties.

Correctness. Formally, for any word $W \in \mathcal{L}$ with w the witness, we have $\mathsf{Hash}(\mathsf{hk}, W) = \mathsf{ProjHash}(\mathsf{hp}, W, w)$.

Smoothness. For any $W' \in \mathcal{X} \backslash \mathcal{L}$, the following two distributions are statistically indistinguishable, i.e.,$\mathcal{V}_1 \overset{\$}{\equiv} \mathcal{V}_2$, where $\mathcal{V}_1 = \{(\mathcal{L}, \mathsf{param}, W', \mathsf{hp}, \mathsf{hv}) | \mathsf{hv} = \mathsf{Hash}(\mathsf{hk}, W')\}$, and $\mathcal{V}_2 = \{(\mathcal{L}, \mathsf{param}, W', \mathsf{hp}, \mathsf{hv}) | \mathsf{hv} \overset{\$}{\leftarrow} \mathcal{Y}\}$. Precisely, the quantity of $\mathsf{Adv}_{\mathsf{SPHF}}^{\mathsf{smooth}}(\ell) = \sum_{v \in \mathcal{Y}} | \Pr_{\mathcal{V}_1}[\mathsf{hv} = v] - \Pr_{\mathcal{V}_2}[\mathsf{hv} = v] |$ is negligible.

For cryptographic purposes, we normally requires the $\mathcal{NP}$ language $\mathcal{L}$ to be membership indistinguishable, which is formally defined as follows.

Definition 3 (Hard SMP for SPHF). *The subset membership problem (SMP) is hard on $(\mathcal{X}, \mathcal{L})$ for an SPHF that consists of (SPHFSetup, HashKG, ProjKG, Hash, ProjHash), if for any PPT adversary $\mathcal{A}$,*

$$\mathsf{Adv}_{\mathcal{A}, \mathsf{SPHF}}^{\mathsf{SMP}}(\ell) = \Pr \left[b' = b : \begin{array}{l} (\mathsf{param}, \mathcal{L}) \leftarrow \mathsf{SPHFSetup}(1^\ell); \\ \mathsf{hk} \leftarrow \mathsf{HashKG}; \mathsf{hp} \leftarrow \mathsf{ProjKG}(\mathsf{hk}); \\ b \overset{R}{\leftarrow} \{0, 1\}; \\ W_0 \overset{\$}{\leftarrow} \mathcal{X} \backslash \mathcal{L}; W_1 \overset{\$}{\leftarrow} \mathcal{L}; \\ b' \leftarrow \mathcal{A}(\mathsf{param}, \mathcal{L}, \mathsf{hk}, \mathsf{hp}, W_b) \end{array} \right] - \frac{1}{2} \leq \mathsf{negl}(\ell),$$

2.3   Identity-Based Smooth Projective Hash Function

The paradigm of IB-SPHF firstly appeared in [9], where the IB-SPHF is viewed as an SPHF with trapdoor. It was later shown as an identity-based key encapsulation mechanism (IB-KEM) with some special algebraic properties in [4]. IB-SPHF and its extensions have been well applied for cryptographic constructions [12–16].

It is worth noting that most, if not all, IB-SPHF systems require the underlying language $\mathcal{L}$ to depend on the projection key, i.e., the identity. To encompass a broad class of IB-SPHF systems, we associate the language to the identity and refer $\mathcal{L}_{\mathsf{ID}} \subset \mathcal{X}_{\mathsf{ID}}$ to the language for an identity ID. An IB-SPHF system over $\mathcal{L}_{\mathsf{ID}} \subset \mathcal{X}_{\mathsf{ID}}$, onto a set $\mathcal{Y}$, is defined by the following algorithms (IB-SPHFSetup, IB-HashKG, IB-Hash, IB-ProjHash):

$(\mathsf{param}, \mathcal{L}_{\mathsf{ID}}, (\mathsf{msk}, \mathsf{mpk})) \leftarrow \mathsf{IB\text{-}SPHFSetup}(1^{\ell})$: The IB-SPHFSetup algorithm takes as input a security parameter ℓ and generates the *global parameters* param with the description of an $\mathcal{NP}$ language $\mathcal{L}_{\mathsf{ID}}$. It outputs the *master public key* mpk and the *master secret key* msk. The master public key defines an *identity set* $\mathcal{ID}$. All other algorithms IB-HashKG, IB-Hash, IB-ProjHash implicitly include $(\mathcal{L}_{\mathsf{ID}}, \mathsf{param}, \mathsf{mpk})$ as input.

$\mathsf{hk}_{\mathsf{ID}} \leftarrow \mathsf{IB\text{-}HashKG}(\mathsf{ID}, \mathsf{msk})$: For any identity $\mathsf{ID} \in \mathcal{ID}$, the IB-HashKG algorithm uses the master secret key msk to generates an *identity hashing key* $\mathsf{hk}_{\mathsf{ID}}$;

$\mathsf{hv} \leftarrow \mathsf{IB\text{-}Hash}(\mathsf{hk}_{\mathsf{ID}}, W)$: The IB-Hash algorithm takes as input a word W and the identity hashing key $\mathsf{hk}_{\mathsf{ID}}$, outputs the hash value $\mathsf{hv} \in \mathcal{Y}$;

$\mathsf{hv} \leftarrow \mathsf{IB\text{-}ProjHash}(\mathsf{ID}, W, w)$: The IB-ProjHash algorithm takes as input the identity ID and a word W with the witness w to the fact that $W \in \mathcal{L}_{\mathsf{ID}}$, outputs the hash value $\mathsf{hv} \in \mathcal{Y}$.

The properties of IB-SPHF are similar to that of an SPHF system, i.e.,

- *Correctness.* For any values of $\mathsf{msk}, \mathsf{mpk}$ produced by IB-SPHFSetup and $\mathsf{ID} \in \mathcal{ID}$ and word $W \in \mathcal{L}_{\mathsf{ID}}$ with w the witness, we have $\mathsf{IB\text{-}Hash}(\mathsf{hk}_{\mathsf{ID}}, W) = \mathsf{IB\text{-}ProjHash}(\mathsf{ID}, W, w)$.
- *Smoothness.* For any $\mathsf{ID} \in \mathcal{ID}$ and any $W' \in \mathcal{X}_{\mathsf{ID}} \backslash \mathcal{L}_{\mathsf{ID}}$, the following two distributions are statistically indistinguishable, i.e., $\mathcal{V}_1 \overset{\$}{\equiv} \mathcal{V}_2$, where $\mathcal{V}_1 = \{(\mathcal{L}, \mathsf{param}, \mathsf{mpk}, W', \mathsf{ID}, \mathbb{HK}, \mathsf{hv}_{\mathsf{ID}}) | \mathsf{hv}_{\mathsf{ID}} = \mathsf{IB\text{-}Hash}(\mathsf{hk}_{\mathsf{ID}}, W')\}$, and $\mathcal{V}_2 = \{(\mathcal{L}, \mathsf{param}, \mathsf{mpk}, W', \mathsf{ID}, \mathbb{HK}, \mathsf{hv}_{\mathsf{ID}}) | \mathsf{hv}_{\mathsf{ID}} \overset{\$}{\leftarrow} \mathcal{Y}\}$. Here $\mathbb{HK}$ is the set of identity hashing key for any identity $\mathsf{ID}' \in \mathcal{ID}$ and $\mathsf{ID}' \neq \mathsf{ID}$. Precisely, the quantity of $\mathsf{Adv}^{\mathsf{smooth}}_{\mathsf{IB\text{-}SPHF}}(\ell) = \sum_{v \in \mathcal{Y}} | \Pr_{\mathcal{V}_1}[\mathsf{hv} = v] - \Pr_{\mathcal{V}_2}[\mathsf{hv} = v]|$ is negligible.

Definition 4 (Hard SMP for IB-SPHF). *The subset membership problem (SMP) is hard on* $(\mathcal{X}_{\mathsf{ID}}, \mathcal{L}_{\mathsf{ID}})$ *for an* IB-SPHF *which consists of* (IB-SPHFSetup, IB-HashKG, IB-Hash, IB-ProjHash), *if for any PPT adversary* $\mathcal{A}$,

$$\mathsf{Adv}^{\mathsf{SMP}}_{\mathcal{A},\mathsf{IB\text{-}SPHF}}(\ell) = \Pr\left[b' = b : \begin{array}{l} \mathsf{hk}_{\mathsf{ID}} \leftarrow \mathsf{IB\text{-}HashKG}(\mathsf{ID},\mathsf{msk}); \\ b \xleftarrow{R} \{0,1\}; \\ W_0 \xleftarrow{\$} \mathcal{L}_{\mathsf{ID}}; W_1 \xleftarrow{\$} \mathcal{X}_{\mathsf{ID}} \backslash \mathcal{L}_{\mathsf{ID}}; \\ b' \leftarrow \mathcal{A}^{\mathcal{O}_{\mathsf{reveal}}(\cdot)}(\mathsf{param},\mathcal{L}_{\mathsf{ID}},\mathsf{mpk},\mathsf{ID},W_b) \end{array} \right] -1/2 \le \mathsf{negl}(\ell),$$

where $\mathsf{msk},\mathsf{mpk}$ *is produced by* $\mathsf{IB\text{-}SPHFSetup}$ *and* $\mathcal{O}_{\mathsf{reveal}}(\cdot)$ *is an oracle that on input of any* $\mathsf{id} \in \mathcal{ID}$, *returns* $\mathsf{hk}_{\mathsf{id}} \leftarrow \mathsf{IB\text{-}HashKG}(\mathsf{id},\mathsf{msk})$.

3   A One-Round Framework for Strong OSBE

In this section, we first briefly introduce the Oblivious Signature-Based Envelope, as well as the formal security models. We then show the first generic construction of one-round OSBE with strong security.

3.1   Oblivious Signature-Based Envelope

An OSBE protocol involves two parties, i.e., a sender $\mathcal{S}$ and a recipient $\mathcal{R}$. $\mathcal{S}$ wants to send a private message P to the recipient $\mathcal{R}$ so that R can receive P if and only if he/she possesses a certificated/signature on a predefined message M. The formal definition is as follows. We mainly follow the definition in [25] to accommodate our generic one-round construction which is introduced in Sect. 3.2. We remark that the new framework captures all the required properties defined in [7, 25].

Definition 5 (Oblivious Signature-Based Envelope). *An OSBE scheme is defined by an algorithm* $\mathsf{OSBESetup}$ *and an interactive protocol* $\mathsf{OSBEProtocol} < \mathcal{S}, \mathcal{R} >$.

- $\mathsf{OSBESetup}(1^{\ell})$: *The* $\mathsf{OSBESetup}$ *algorithm takes as input the security parameter* ℓ, *generates the global parameters* param, *and the master key pair* $(\mathsf{mpk},\mathsf{msk})$ *for the authority. The receiver* $\mathcal{R}$ *is issued a certificate/signature* σ *on* M *by the authority.*
- $\mathsf{OSBEProtocol} < \mathcal{S}(M,P), \mathcal{R}(M,\sigma) >$: *The* $\mathsf{OSBEProtocol}$ *is an interactive protocol between the sender* $\mathcal{S}$ *with a private message* P, *and the receiver* $\mathcal{R}$ *with a certificate/signature* σ. *At the end of the protocol,* $\mathcal{R}$ *receives* P *if* σ *is a valid certificate/signature on* M, *otherwise it learns nothing.*

The *correctness* of an OSBE scheme requires that at the end of $\mathsf{OSBEProtocol}$, the authorized receiver $\mathcal{R}$ (who has a valid certificate/signature σ on M) can output P.

Security Notions for Strong OSBE. According to the original definition [25], in additional to the *correctness*, an OSBE scheme must satisfy *obliviousness* and *semantic security*. In this work, we are interested in the strong OSBE scheme that should also satisfy another two security properties—*obliviousness w.r.t. the authority* and *semantic security w.r.t. the authority*, which are defined in [7].

Obliviousness (w.r.t. the Authority). Below we first briefly describe the notions of *obliviousness* and *obliviousness w.r.t the authority*. The *obliviousness* requires that the sender S should not be able to distinguish whether R uses a valid certificate/signature or not during the protocol execution. The *obliviousness w.r.t. the authority* requires that the above indistinguishability should also hold to the authority who plays as the sender or just eavesdrops on the protocol. One can easily notice that the latter notion is stronger than the former one and both of them can be trivially achieved in one-round OSBE schemes, since S receives no information from R.

We now formally introduce the security notions of *semantic security* and *semantic security w.r.t. the authority*.

Semantic Security. This security is against the malicious receiver. Roughly speaking, it requires that at the end of the protocol, R learns nothing about the private input P of S if it does not use a valid certificate/signature on the predefined message M. The formal security game between the challenge C and the adversary A is defined as follows.

Setup. C runs OSBESetup(1^ℓ) and sends A the global parameters param.

Query. A can issues the following two queries:

- Sign-Query. On input of M, C returns the valid signature σ_M of M to A.
- Exec-Query. On input of (M, P), C first generates σ_M of M, runs OSBEProtocol $< S(M, P), R(M, \sigma_M) >$ and returns the transcript to A.

Challenge. A chooses a predefined message M^* which has not been queried for signature by A, with two challenge message P_0, P_1 and sends them to C. C randomly chooses a bit $b \xleftarrow{\$} \{0, 1\}$ and runs OSBEProtocol $< S(M^*, P_b), A >$.

Query. A continues the query defined above, except that it cannot query M^* for signature.

Guess. Finally, A outputs b' as its guess on b and wins the game if $b' = b$.

We define the advantage of A in the above game as $\mathsf{Adv}^{\mathsf{SS}}_{A,\mathsf{OSBE}}(\ell) = \Pr[b = b'] - \frac{1}{2}$.

Semantic Security w.r.t. the Authority. This security is against the malicious authority. Roughly speaking, it requires that at the end of the protocol, the authority who plays as the eavesdropper on the protocol, learns nothing about the private input P of S. The formal security game between the challenge C and the adversary A is defined as follows.

Setup. $\mathcal{C}$ runs $\mathsf{OSBESetup}(1^\ell)$ and sends $\mathcal{A}$ the global paramters param with the master secret key msk.

Query. $\mathcal{A}$ issues an Exec query with chosen input (M, P, σ_M). To answer this query, $\mathcal{C}$ runs $\mathsf{OSBEProtocol} < \mathcal{S}(M, P), \mathcal{R}(M, \sigma_M) >$ and returns the transcript to $\mathcal{A}$.

Challenge. $\mathcal{A}$ chooses a predefined message M^* with two challenge message P_0, P_1 and sends them to $\mathcal{C}$. $\mathcal{C}$ randomly chooses a bit $b \xleftarrow{\$} \{0, 1\}$ and runs $\mathsf{OSBEProtocol} < \mathcal{S}(M^*, P_b), \mathcal{R}(M^*, \sigma_{M^*}) >$ which $\mathcal{A}$ can access to its interaction transcript.

Query. $\mathcal{A}$ continues the Exec query as defined above.

Guess. Finally, $\mathcal{A}$ outputs b' as its guess on b and wins the game if $b' = b$.

We define the advantage of $\mathcal{A}$ in the above game as $\mathsf{Adv}_{\mathcal{A},\mathsf{OSBE}}^{\mathsf{SS-Authority}}(\ell) = \Pr[b = b'] - \frac{1}{2}$.

Definition 6 (Secure OSBE). *An OSBE scheme is secure if it is oblivious w.r.t. the authority and for any probabilistic polynomial-time adversaries $\mathcal{A}$, both $\mathsf{Adv}_{\mathcal{A},\mathsf{OSBE}}^{\mathsf{SS}}(\ell)$ and $\mathsf{Adv}_{\mathcal{A},\mathsf{OSBE}}^{\mathsf{SS-Authority}}(\ell)$ are negligible in ℓ.*

Remark. One may note that our security notions appear to be different from [7], where the adversary can access several queries in addition to the original models [25]. The reason is that our defined OSBE scheme follows the original one while the work in [7] revised the OSBE framework to accommodate its proposed construction. However, we insist that our models are essentially as strong as the notions defined in [7]. The *enhanced* semantic security (denoted sem) in [7] allows the adversary to obtain several interactions between the server and the receiver with a valid certificate/signature while the adversary in our notion is provided with the access to a so-called Exec oracle which returns the transcript of the honest interaction with adaptively chosen input (M, P) from the adversary. It is worth noting that we put no restriction on the Exec query input (M, P) from $\mathcal{A}$. In particular, $\mathcal{A}$ can make query with input the challenge messages, i.e., $M = M^*$ and $P = P_0/P_1$. Moreover, the Sign query through which $\mathcal{A}$ can obtain the signature of any non-challenge predefined message is also defined in both our model and the experiment in [7]. Similarly, the adversary in our defined notion of *semantic security w.r.t. the authority* can also query the Exec oracle for the transcripts of any specified interaction. We therefore remark that our defined models capture the same security properties as those do in [7].

3.2   The Proposed Generic Construction

We present a generic construction of OSBE from the conjunction of an SPHF and an IB-SPHF. Let SPHF = (SPHFSetup, HashKG, ProjKG, Hash, ProjHash) be a smooth projective hash function over $\mathcal{L} \subset \mathcal{X}$ and IB-SPHF = (IB-SPHFSetup, IB-HashKG, IB-Hash, IB-ProjHash) be an identity-based smooth projective hash function over $\mathcal{L}_{\mathsf{ID}} \subset \mathcal{X}_{\mathsf{ID}}$. Suppose both systems are onto the same set $\mathcal{Y}$. We additionally use a key derivation function KDF for the generation of a pseudo-random bit-string as the encryption key for the private message. The generic construction of an one-round OSBE protocol on a predefined message M and a private message p is as follows.

- OSBESetup(1^ℓ) : The OSBESetup takes as input a security parameter ℓ.
  - It first generates the individual parameters as SPHFSetup(1^ℓ) $\rightarrow$ (param$_1$, $\mathcal{L}$), IB-SPHFSetup(1^ℓ) $\rightarrow$ (param$_2$, $\mathcal{L}_{\mathsf{ID}}$, (msk, mpk)). The master key pair (msk, mpk) is for the authority.
  - It generates a key pair (hk, hp) for the SPHF system as HashKG $\rightarrow$ hk, ProjKG(hk) $\rightarrow$ hp. The hash key pair (hk, hp) is produced for the receiver.
  - The authority issues a signature $\sigma = \mathsf{hk}_M$ (by viewing M as the identity) as IB-HashKG(msk, M) $\rightarrow \mathsf{hk}_M$. A valid receiver is then given the signature σ.

  The output *global parameters* param = (param$_1$, param$_2$, $\mathcal{L}$, $\mathcal{L}_{\mathsf{ID}}$, mpk, hp). All the algorithms involved in the protocol OSBEProtocol implicitly include param as input.
- OSBEProtocol $< \mathcal{S}(M, P), \mathcal{R}(M, \sigma) >$: The OSBEProtocol executes as follows:
  - $\mathcal{S}$ picks $W_1 \leftarrow \mathcal{L}, W_2 \leftarrow \mathcal{L}_M$ with w_1, w_2 the witnesses respectively and computes

  $$V = \mathsf{ProjHash}(\mathsf{hp}, W_1, w_1) \oplus \mathsf{IB\text{-}ProjHash}(M, W_2, w_2),$$

  $$Q = P \oplus \mathsf{KDF}(V).$$

  $\mathcal{S}$ then sends (W_1, W_2, Q) to $\mathcal{R}$;
  - Upon receiving (W_1, W_2, Q), $\mathcal{R}$ computes,

  $$V' = \mathsf{Hash}(\mathsf{hk}, W_1) \oplus \mathsf{IB\text{-}Hash}(\mathsf{hk}_M, W_2),$$

  $$P' = Q \oplus \mathsf{KDF}(V').$$

3.3   Security Analysis

We show that the generic construction is secure under our defined models.

Theorem 1 (Correctness). *The generic OSBE construction is correct.*

Proof. Due to the correctness of SPHF and IB-SPHF, we have that

$$\mathsf{ProjHash}(\mathsf{hp}, W_1, w_i) \oplus \mathsf{IB\text{-}ProjHash}(M, W_2, w_2) = \mathsf{Hash}(\mathsf{hk}, W_1) \oplus \mathsf{IB\text{-}Hash}(\mathsf{hk}_M, W_2),$$

i.e., $V = V'$ and thus $P' = P \oplus \mathsf{KDF}(V) \oplus \mathsf{KDF}(V') = P$.

Theorem 2 (Obliviousness w.r.t. the Authority). *The generic OSBE construction is oblivious w.r.t. the authority.*

Proof. This property is trivial since the protocol is one-round and the server $\mathcal{S}$ receives no information from the receiver $\mathcal{R}$ during the protocol execution.

Theorem 3 (Semantic Security). *The generic OSBE construction is semantically secure if the* SMP *is hard on* $(\mathcal{X}_M, \mathcal{L}_M)$ *for* IB-SPHF *(and under the pseudo-randomness of* KDF*).*

Proof. Let $\mathcal{A}$ be an adversary against the *semantic security* of our construction with advantage $\mathsf{Adv}^{\mathsf{SS}}_{\mathcal{A},\mathsf{OSBE}}(\ell)$. We define a sequence of games between the challenger $\mathcal{C}$ and $\mathcal{A}$ as follows.

Game $\mathcal{G}_0$. In this game, $\mathcal{C}$ simulates as follows.

- **Setup.** $\mathcal{C}$ runs OSBESetup(1^ℓ) and outputs the global parameter param with the receiver secret key hk to $\mathcal{A}$. $\mathcal{C}$ keeps the master secret key msk itself.
- **Query.** $\mathcal{C}$ answers the query as follows.
  - Sign-Query. On input of M from $\mathcal{A}$, $\mathcal{C}$ computes IB-HashKG$(\mathsf{msk}, M) \to \mathsf{hk}_M$, and then returns hk_M to $\mathcal{A}$;
  - Exec-Query. On input of (M, P) from $\mathcal{A}$, $\mathcal{C}$ randomly picks $W_1 \xleftarrow{\$} \mathcal{L}, W_2 \xleftarrow{\$} \mathcal{L}_M$ with w_1, w_2 the witnesses respectively. $\mathcal{C}$ then computes $V = \mathsf{ProjHash}(\mathsf{hp}, W_1, w_1) \oplus \mathsf{IB\text{-}ProjHash}(M, W_2, w_2), Q = P \oplus \mathsf{KDF}(V)$ and then sends (W_1, W_2, Q) to $\mathcal{A}$;
- **Challenge.** $\mathcal{A}$ chooses a predefined message M^* that is not issued to the Sign oracle, with two challenge message P_0, P_1 and sends them to $\mathcal{C}$. $\mathcal{C}$ randomly chooses a bit $b \xleftarrow{\$} \{0, 1\}$ and picks $W_1^* \leftarrow \mathcal{L}, W_2^* \leftarrow \mathcal{L}_{M^*}$ with w_1^*, w_2^* the witnesses respectively and computes

$$V^* = \mathsf{ProjHash}(\mathsf{hp}, W_1^*, w_1^*) \oplus \mathsf{IB\text{-}ProjHash}(M^*, W_2^*, w_2^*), Q^* = P_b \oplus \mathsf{KDF}(V^*).$$

  $\mathcal{C}$ then sends (W_1^*, W_2^*, Q^*) to $\mathcal{A}$;
- **Query.** $\mathcal{C}$ simulates as defined above.
- **Output.** Finally, $\mathcal{A}$ outputs b' as its guess on b.

We define the advantage of $\mathcal{A}$ in game $\mathcal{G}_0$ as $\mathsf{Adv}^{\mathcal{G}_0}_{\mathcal{A},\mathsf{OSBE}}(\ell)$. One can note the definition of game $\mathcal{G}_0$ is exactly the original model of semantic security and thus we have $\mathsf{Adv}^{\mathcal{G}_0}_{\mathcal{A},\mathsf{OSBE}}(\ell) = \mathsf{Adv}^{\mathsf{SS}}_{\mathcal{A},\mathsf{OSBE}}(\ell)$.

Game $\mathcal{G}_1$. Let game $\mathcal{G}_1$ be the same game as $\mathcal{G}_0$, except that in the challenge stage, instead of choosing $W_2^* \xleftarrow{\$} \mathcal{L}_{M^*}$, $\mathcal{C}$ chooses $W_2^* \xleftarrow{\$} \mathcal{X}_{M^*} \backslash \mathcal{L}_{M^*}$ and computes V^* as $V^* = \mathsf{ProjHash}(\mathsf{hp}, W_1^*, w_1^*) \oplus \mathsf{IB\text{-}Hash}(\mathsf{hk}_{M^*}, W_2^*)$. Due to the *hard subset membership problem* and the *correctness* of IB-SPHF, we have $|\mathsf{Adv}^{\mathcal{G}_1}_{\mathcal{A},\mathsf{OSBE}}(\ell) - \mathsf{Adv}^{\mathcal{G}_0}_{\mathcal{A},\mathsf{OSBE}}(\ell)| \leq \mathsf{Adv}^{\mathsf{SMP}}_{\mathcal{A},\mathsf{IB\text{-}SPHF}}(\ell)$.

Game $\mathcal{G}_2$. Let game $\mathcal{G}_2$ be the same game as $\mathcal{G}_1$, except that in the challenge stage, $\mathcal{C}$ computes V^* as $V^* = \mathsf{ProjHash}(\mathsf{hp}, W_1^*, w_1^*) \oplus r$, where $r \xleftarrow{\$} \mathcal{Y}$. Due to the *smoothness* of IB-SPHF, we have $|\mathsf{Adv}^{\mathcal{G}_2}_{\mathcal{A},\mathsf{OSBE}}(\ell) - \mathsf{Adv}^{\mathcal{G}_1}_{\mathcal{A},\mathsf{OSBE}}(\ell)| \leq \mathsf{Adv}^{\mathsf{smooth}}_{\mathsf{IB\text{-}SPHF}}(\ell)$.

Game $\mathcal{G}_3$. Let game $\mathcal{G}_3$ be the same game as $\mathcal{G}_2$, except that $\mathcal{C}$ computes $Q^* = P_b \oplus R$ where $R \xleftarrow{\$} \{0, 1\}^l$. Due to the pseudo-randomness of KDF, we have $|\mathsf{Adv}^{\mathcal{G}_3}_{\mathcal{A},\mathsf{OSBE}}(\ell) - \mathsf{Adv}^{\mathcal{G}_2}_{\mathcal{A},\mathsf{OSBE}}(\ell)| \leq \mathsf{Adv}^{\mathsf{PR}}_{\mathcal{A},\mathsf{KDF}}(\ell)$.

Game $\mathcal{G}_4$. Let game $\mathcal{G}_4$ be the same game as $\mathcal{G}_3$, except that $\mathcal{C}$ computes $Q^* \xleftarrow{\$} \{0,1\}^l$. One can note that $\mathsf{Adv}^{\mathcal{G}_3}_{\mathcal{A},\mathsf{OSBE}}(\ell) = \mathsf{Adv}^{\mathcal{G}_4}_{\mathcal{A},\mathsf{OSBE}}(\ell)$. It is easy to see that $\mathcal{A}$ can only wins with probability at most $1/2$ as Q^* is independent of b and hence we have $\mathsf{Adv}^{\mathcal{G}_4}_{\mathcal{A},\mathsf{OSBE}}(\ell) = 0$.

Therefore, from game $\mathcal{G}_0, \mathcal{G}_1, \mathcal{G}_2, \mathcal{G}_3$ and $\mathcal{G}_4$, we have that $\mathsf{Adv}^{\mathsf{SS}}_{\mathcal{A},\mathsf{OSBE}}(\ell)$ is negligible, which completes the proof. □

Theorem 4 (Semantic Security w.r.t. the Authority). *The generic OSBE construction is semantically secure w.r.t. the authority if the SMP is hard on $(\mathcal{X}, \mathcal{L})$ for SPHF (and under the pseudo-randomness of KDF).*

Proof Let $\mathcal{A}$ be an adversary against the *semantic security w.r.t. the authority* of our construction with advantage $\mathsf{Adv}^{\mathsf{SS-Authority}}_{\mathcal{A},\mathsf{OSBE}}(\ell)$. We define a sequence of games between the challenger $\mathcal{C}$ and $\mathcal{A}$ as follows.

Game $\mathcal{G}_0$. In this game, $\mathcal{C}$ simulates as follows

- **Setup.** $\mathcal{C}$ runs $\mathsf{OSBESetup}(1^\ell)$ and outputs the global parameter param with the master secrete key msk to $\mathcal{A}$. $\mathcal{C}$ keeps the hashing key hk itself.
- **Query.** On input of (M, P, σ_M) from $\mathcal{A}$ for an Exec query, $\mathcal{C}$ randomly picks $W_1 \xleftarrow{\$} \mathcal{L}, W_2 \xleftarrow{\$} \mathcal{L}_M$ with w_1, w_2 the witnesses respectively and computes $V = \mathsf{ProjHash}(\mathsf{hp}, W_1, w_1) \oplus \mathsf{IB\text{-}ProjHash}(M, W_2, w_2), Q = P \oplus \mathsf{KDF}(V)$. $\mathcal{C}$ then sends (W_1, W_2, Q) to $\mathcal{A}$;
- **Challenge.** $\mathcal{A}$ chooses a predefined message M^* with two challenge message P_0, P_1 and sends them to $\mathcal{C}$. $\mathcal{C}$ randomly chooses a bit $b \xleftarrow{\$} \{0,1\}$ and picks $W_1^* \leftarrow \mathcal{L}, W_2^* \leftarrow \mathcal{L}_{M^*}$ with w_1^*, w_2^* the witnesses respectively, computes $V^* = \mathsf{ProjHash}\ (\mathsf{hp}, W_1^*, w_1^*) \oplus \mathsf{IB\text{-}ProjHash}(M^*, W_2^*, w_2^*), Q^* = P_b \oplus \mathsf{KDF}(V^*)$. $\mathcal{C}$ then sends (W_1^*, W_2^*, Q^*) to $\mathcal{A}$;
- **Query.** $\mathcal{C}$ simulates as defined above.
- **Output.** Finally, $\mathcal{A}$ outputs b' as its guess on b.

We define the advantage of $\mathcal{A}$ in game $\mathcal{G}_0$ as $\mathsf{Adv}^{\mathcal{G}_0}_{\mathcal{A},\mathsf{OSBE}}(\ell)$. One can note the definition of game $\mathcal{G}_0$ is exactly the original model of semantic security and thus we have $\mathsf{Adv}^{\mathcal{G}_0}_{\mathcal{A},\mathsf{OSBE}}(\ell) = \mathsf{Adv}^{\mathsf{SS-Authority}}_{\mathcal{A},\mathsf{OSBE}}(\ell)$.

Game $\mathcal{G}_1$. Let game $\mathcal{G}_1$ be the same game as $\mathcal{G}_0$, except that in the challenge stage, instead of choosing $W_1^* \xleftarrow{\$} \mathcal{L}$, $\mathcal{C}$ chooses $W_1^* \xleftarrow{\$} \mathcal{X} \backslash \mathcal{L}$ and computes $V^* = \mathsf{Hash}(\mathsf{hk}, W_1^*) \oplus \mathsf{IB\text{-}ProjHash}(M^*, W_2^*, w_2^*)$. Due to the *hard subset membership problem* and the *correctness* of SPHF, we have $|\mathsf{Adv}^{\mathcal{G}_1}_{\mathcal{A},\mathsf{OSBE}}(\ell) - \mathsf{Adv}^{\mathcal{G}_0}_{\mathcal{A},\mathsf{OSBE}}(\ell)| \leq \mathsf{Adv}^{\mathsf{SMP}}_{\mathcal{A},\mathsf{SPHF}}(\ell)$.

Game $\mathcal{G}_2$. Let game $\mathcal{G}_2$ be the same game as $\mathcal{G}_1$, except that in the challenge stage, $\mathcal{C}$ computes V^* as $V^* = r \oplus \mathsf{IB\text{-}ProjHash}(M^*, W_2^*, w_2^*)$, where $r \xleftarrow{\$} \mathcal{Y}$. Due to the *smoothness* of SPHF, we have $|\mathsf{Adv}^{\mathcal{G}_2}_{\mathcal{A},\mathsf{OSBE}}(\ell) - \mathsf{Adv}^{\mathcal{G}_1}_{\mathcal{A},\mathsf{OSBE}}(\ell)| \leq \mathsf{Adv}^{\mathsf{smooth}}_{\mathsf{SPHF}}(\ell)$.

Game $\mathcal{G}_3$. Let game $\mathcal{G}_3$ be the same game as $\mathcal{G}_2$, except that $\mathcal{C}$ computes $Q^* = P_b \oplus R$ where $R \xleftarrow{\$} \{0,1\}^l$. Due to the pseudo-randomness of KDF, we have $|\mathsf{Adv}^{\mathcal{G}_3}_{\mathcal{A},\mathsf{OSBE}}(\ell) - \mathsf{Adv}^{\mathcal{G}_2}_{\mathcal{A},\mathsf{OSBE}}(\ell)| \leq \mathsf{Adv}^{\mathsf{PR}}_{\mathcal{A},\mathsf{KDF}}(\ell)$.

Game $\mathcal{G}_4$. Let game $\mathcal{G}_4$ be the same game as $\mathcal{G}_3$, except that $\mathcal{C}$ computes $Q^* \xleftarrow{\$} \{0,1\}^l$. One can note that $\mathsf{Adv}^{\mathcal{G}_3}_{\mathcal{A},\mathsf{OSBE}}(\ell) = \mathsf{Adv}^{\mathcal{G}_4}_{\mathcal{A},\mathsf{OSBE}}(\ell)$. It is easy to see that $\mathcal{A}$ can only wins with probability at most $1/2$ as Q^* is independent of b and hence we have $\mathsf{Adv}^{\mathcal{G}_4}_{\mathcal{A},\mathsf{OSBE}}(\ell) = 0$.

Therefore, from game $\mathcal{G}_0, \mathcal{G}_1, \mathcal{G}_2, \mathcal{G}_3$ and $\mathcal{G}_4$, we have that $\mathsf{Adv}^{\mathsf{SS\text{-}Authority}}_{\mathcal{A},\mathsf{OSBE}}(\ell)$ is negligible, which completes the proof.   □

Based on the results of **Theorems** 1, 2, 3 and 4, we then have the following conclusion.

Theorem 5. *The generic OSBE construction is secure if both* SPHF *and* IB-SPHF *are over hard subset membership problem (and under the pseudorandomness of* KDF*).*

4   An Efficient Instantiation

In this section, we present a concrete OSBE protocol based on the DDH assumption and DBDH assumption.

4.1   Instantiating the Building Blocks

Due to the space limitation, we briefly describe the instantiations of SPHF and IB-SPHF from the DDH assumption and DBDH assumption respectively and refer the reader to the full version for more details.

DDH-*Based* SPHF. We first introduce the Diffie Hellman language $\mathcal{L}_{\mathsf{DH}}$ as follows. Let $\mathbb{G}$ be a group of prime order p and g_1, g_2 be the generators of $\mathbb{G}$.

$$\mathcal{L}_{\mathsf{DH}} = \{(u_1, u_2) | \exists r \in \mathbb{Z}_p, \text{s.t.}, u_1 = g_1^r, u_2 = g_2^r\}$$

One can see that the witness space of $\mathcal{L}_{\mathsf{DH}}$ is $\mathbb{Z}_p$ and $\mathcal{L}_{\mathsf{DH}} \subset \mathbb{G}^2$. Below we show an concrete SPHF (denoted by $\mathcal{SPHF}_{\mathsf{DH}}$) over the language $\mathcal{L}_{\mathsf{DH}} \subset \mathcal{X}_{\mathsf{DH}} = \mathbb{G}^2$ onto the group $\mathcal{Y} = \mathbb{G}$.

$\mathsf{SPHFSetup}(1^\ell)$: Set $\mathsf{param} = (\mathbb{G}, p, g_1, g_2)$;

HashKG : Pick $(\alpha_1, \alpha_2) \xleftarrow{\$} \mathbb{Z}_p^2$. Output $\mathsf{hk} = (\alpha_1, \alpha_2)$;

$\mathsf{ProjKG}(\mathsf{hk})$: Compute $\mathsf{hp} = g_1^{\alpha_1} g_2^{\alpha_2}$;

$\mathsf{Hash}(\mathsf{hk}, W)$: For a word $W = (u_1, u_2)$, output $\mathsf{hv} = u_1^{\alpha_1} u_2^{\alpha_2}$;

$\mathsf{ProjHash}(\mathsf{hp}, W, w)$: For a word $W = (g_1^r, g_2^r)$, output $\mathsf{hv} = \mathsf{hp}^r = (g_1^{\alpha_1} g_2^{\alpha_2})^r$.

DBDH-*Based* IB-SPHF. We introduce the language for our instantiated IB-SPHF, which can be viewed as the backbone of the IBE scheme in [16]. Let $(\mathbb{G}_1, \mathbb{G}_T, g, e(\cdot, \cdot), p) \leftarrow \mathcal{BG}(1^\ell)$, $u, h \in \mathbb{G}_1, \alpha, \beta \in \mathbb{Z}_p$. For any $\mathsf{ID} \in \mathcal{ID}$, the associated language $\mathcal{L}_{\mathsf{ID}} \subset \mathcal{X}_{\mathsf{ID}}$ are,

$$\mathcal{L}_{\mathsf{ID}} = \{(u_1, u_2, u_3) | \exists z \in \mathbb{Z}_p, \text{s.t.}, u_1 = g^z, u_2 = (u^{\mathsf{ID}} h)^z, u_3 = e(g, g)^{\beta z}\}$$
$$\mathcal{X}_{\mathsf{ID}} = \{(u_1, u_2, u_3) | \exists z_1, z_2 \in \mathbb{Z}_p, \text{s.t.}, u_1 = g^{z_1}, u_2 = (u^{\mathsf{ID}} h)^{z_1}, u_3 = e(g, g)^{\beta z_2}\}$$

One can see that the witness space is $\mathbb{Z}_p$ and $\mathcal{L}_{\mathsf{ID}} \subset \mathbb{G}_1 \times \mathbb{G}_1 \times \mathbb{G}_T$. Below we show the resulted IB-SPHF (denoted by $\mathcal{IB\text{-}SPHF}$) over the language $\mathcal{L}_{\mathsf{ID}} \subset \mathcal{X}_{\mathsf{ID}}$ onto the group $\mathcal{Y} = \mathbb{G}_T$.

IB-SPHFSetup(1^ℓ) : Let $(\mathbb{G}_1, \mathbb{G}_T, g, e(\cdot,\cdot), p) \leftarrow \mathcal{BG}(1^\ell)$. Pick $u, h \xleftarrow{\$} \mathbb{G}_1, \alpha, \beta \xleftarrow{\$} \mathbb{Z}_p$, set param $= (\mathbb{G}_1, \mathbb{G}_T, g, e(\cdot,\cdot), p, u, h)$, msk $= (\alpha, \beta)$, mpk $= (e(g,g)^\alpha, e(g,g)^\beta)$. The identity set is $\mathcal{ID} = \mathbb{Z}_p$.

IB-HashKG(ID, msk) : For ID $\in \mathbb{Z}_p$, choose $t, r \xleftarrow{\$} \mathbb{Z}_p$. Output hk$_{\mathsf{ID}}$ = $(sk_1, sk_2, sk_3) = (g^\alpha g^{-\beta t}(u^{\mathsf{ID}}h)^r, g^{-r}, t)$;

IB-Hash(hk$_{\mathsf{ID}}$, W)   : For a word $W = (u_1, u_2, u_3)$, output hv$_{\mathsf{ID}}$ = $e(u_1, sk_1)e(u_2, sk_2)u_3^{sk_3}$;

IB-ProjHash(ID, W, w) : For a word $W = (u_1, u_2, u_3) = (g^z, (u^{\mathsf{ID}}h)^z, e(g,g)^{\beta z})$, outputs hv$_{\mathsf{ID}}$ = $e(g,g)^{\alpha z}$.

4.2 Concrete OSBE Protocol

Using $\mathcal{SPHF}_{\mathsf{DH}}$ and $\mathcal{IB\text{-}SPHF}$ as instantiation blocks, below we show the resulted OSBE protocol, where a sender $\mathcal{S}$ wants to send a private message $P \in \{0,1\}^l$ to a recipient $\mathcal{R}$ in possession of a signature (i.e., the identity hashing key) on a message M.

- OSBESetup(1^ℓ) : Let $\mathbb{G}$ be a group of prime order p and g_1, g_2 the generators of $\mathbb{G}$ and set param$_1 = (\mathbb{G}, p, g_1, g_2)$. Let $(\mathbb{G}_1, \mathbb{G}_T, g, e(\cdot,\cdot), p) \leftarrow \mathcal{BG}(1^\ell)$, pick $u, h \xleftarrow{\$} \mathbb{G}_1, \alpha, \beta \xleftarrow{\$} \mathbb{Z}_p$, set param$_2 = (\mathbb{G}_1, \mathbb{G}_T, g, e(\cdot,\cdot), p, u, h)$ and set msk $= (\alpha, \beta)$, mpk $= (e(g,g)^\alpha, e(g,g)^\beta)$.

  - Pick $(\alpha_1, \alpha_2) \xleftarrow{\$} \mathbb{Z}_p$, compute hk $= (\alpha_1, \alpha_2)$, hp $= g_1^{\alpha_1} g_2^{\alpha_2}$. Set (hk, hp) as the receiver key pair.
  - For any predefined message $M \in \mathbb{Z}_p$, choose $t, r \xleftarrow{\$} \mathbb{Z}_p$ and compute its signature as $\sigma = $ hk$_M = (sk_1, sk_2, sk_3) = (g^\alpha g^{-\beta t}(u^M h)^r, g^{-r}, t)$

- OSBEProtocol $< \mathcal{S}(M, P), \mathcal{R}(M, \sigma) >$:
  - $\mathcal{S}$ picks $W_1 = (\widehat{u_1}, \widehat{u_2}) = (g_1^r, g_2^r)$, $W_2 = (u_1, u_2, u_3) = (g^z, (u^M h)^z, e(g,g)^{\beta z})$ and computes

    $$V = (g_1^{\alpha_1} g_2^{\alpha_2})^r \cdot e(g,g)^{\alpha z}, Q = P \oplus \mathsf{KDF}(V).$$

    $\mathcal{S}$ then sends (W_1, W_2, Q) to $\mathcal{R}$;
  - Upon receiving (W_1, W_2, Q), $\mathcal{R}$ computes,

    $$V' = (\widehat{u_1}^{\alpha_1} \widehat{u_2}^{\alpha_2}) \cdot (e(u_1, sk_1)e(u_2, sk_2)u_3^{sk_3}),$$

    $$P' = Q \oplus \mathsf{KDF}(V').$$

One should note that in the above concrete protocol, we requires the language used in our $\mathcal{SPHF}_{\mathsf{DH}}$ works on the $\mathbb{G}_T$, i.e., the DDH assumption is on $\mathbb{G} = \mathbb{G}_T$.

The *correctness* of the above protocol is guaranteed by the correctness of $\mathcal{SPHF}_{\mathsf{DH}}$ and $\mathcal{IB\text{-}SPHF}$ while the *oblivious w.r.t. the authority* is clear due to the one-round execution. Based on the **Theorem** 5, we have the following conclusion.

Theorem 6. *The instantiated OSBE protocol is secure under the* DDH, DBDH *assumptions (and the pseudo-randomness of* KDF*).*

Efficiency. Our one-round protocol requires only one flow from the sender $\mathcal{S}$ during the execution. Precisely, in addition to the l-bit string (i.e., Q) for the masked $P \in \{0,1\}^l$, the communication in our protocol consists of 2 elements in $\mathbb{G}_1$ and 3 elements in $\mathbb{G}_T$ and hence is slightly higher than the BPV-OSBE protocol [7], where 6 elements in $\mathbb{G}_1$ are needed per execution. It is worth noting that by using a hash function $H : \mathbb{G} \to \mathbb{G}_T$ on the computation of V, i.e., letting $V = H((g_1^{\alpha_1} g_2^{\alpha_2})^r) \cdot e(g,g)^{\alpha z}$, we can reduce the communication cost of our protocol, as the language used by the $\mathcal{SPHF}_{\mathsf{DH}}$ is now on the smaller group $\mathbb{G}$, instead of $\mathbb{G}_T$. Regarding the computation cost, we remark that our protocol is much more efficient that the BPV-OSBE protocol. Particularly, our protocol mainly requires 5 exponentiation, 3 multiplication and only 2 pairing computation in total per execution while the BPV-OSBE protocol needs 12 exponentiation, 8 multiplication and 6 pairing computation.

5   Conclusion

In this work, we mainly improved the work from TCC 2012 [7] and presented a generic construction of one-round OSBE system that is strongly secure with a common reference string. Compared to the 2-round framework in [7], our one-round construction is more appealing due to the fact that its non-interactive setting accommodates more application scenarios in the real word. Moreover, our framework relies on the (IB-)SPHF, which can be instantiated from extensive languages and hence is more general than the work in [7] where special languages, i.e., languages of ciphertexts from signatures are needed for instantiations. An efficient instantiation, which is secure under the standard model from classical assumptions, DDH and DBDH, is also shown to illustrate the feasibility of our one-round framework.

Acknowledgements. We would like to thank the anonymous reviewers for their invaluable comments on a previous version of this paper. The work of Guomin Yang is supported by the Australian Research Council Discovery Early Career Researcher Award (Grant No. DE150101116) and the National Natural Science Foundation of China (Grant No. 61472308). The work of Mingwu Zhang is supported by the National Natural Science Foundation of China (Grant No. 61370224).

References

1. Abdalla, M., Benhamouda, F., Blazy, O., Chevalier, C., Pointcheval, D.: SPHF-friendly non-interactive commitments. In: Sako, K., Sarkar, P. (eds.) ASIACRYPT 2013, Part I. LNCS, vol. 8269, pp. 214–234. Springer, Heidelberg (2013)
2. Abdalla, M., Benhamouda, F., Pointcheval, D.: Disjunctions for hash proof systems: new constructions and applications. In: Oswald, E., Fischlin, M. (eds.) EUROCRYPT 2015. LNCS, vol. 9057, pp. 69–100. Springer, Heidelberg (2015)
3. Abdalla, M., Chevalier, C., Pointcheval, D.: Smooth projective hashing for conditionally extractable commitments. In: Halevi, S. (ed.) CRYPTO 2009. LNCS, vol. 5677, pp. 671–689. Springer, Heidelberg (2009)
4. Alwen, J., Dodis, Y., Naor, M., Segev, G., Walfish, S., Wichs, D.: Public-key encryption in the bounded-retrieval model. In: Gilbert, H. (ed.) EUROCRYPT 2010. LNCS, vol. 6110, pp. 113–134. Springer, Heidelberg (2010)
5. Benhamouda, F., Blazy, O., Chevalier, C., Pointcheval, D., Vergnaud, D.: New techniques for SPHFs and efficient one-round PAKE protocols. In: Canetti, R., Garay, J.A. (eds.) CRYPTO 2013, Part I. LNCS, vol. 8042, pp. 449–475. Springer, Heidelberg (2013)
6. Blazy, O., Chevalier, C., Vergnaud, D.: Mitigating server breaches in password-based authentication: secure and efficient solutions. In: CT-RSA, pp. 3–18 (2016)
7. Blazy, O., Pointcheval, D., Vergnaud, D.: Round-optimal privacy-preserving protocols with smooth projective hash functions. In: Cramer, R. (ed.) TCC 2012. LNCS, vol. 7194, pp. 94–111. Springer, Heidelberg (2012)
8. Boneh, D., Franklin, M.: Identity-Based Encryption from the Weil Pairing. In: Kilian, J. (ed.) CRYPTO 2001. LNCS, vol. 2139, pp. 213–229. Springer, Heidelberg (2001)
9. Boneh, D., Gentry, C., Hamburg, M.: Space-efficient identity based encryption without pairings. In: Proceedings of 48th Annual IEEE Symposium on Foundations of Computer Science (FOCS 2007), October 20–23, 2007, Providence, RI, USA, pp. 647–657 (2007)
10. Chen, R., Mu, Y., Yang, G., Guo, F., Wang, X.: A new general framework for secure public key encryption with keyword search. In: Foo, E., Stebila, D. (eds.) ACISP 2015. LNCS, vol. 9144, pp. 59–76. Springer, Heidelberg (2015)
11. Chen, R., Mu, Y., Yang, G., Susilo, W., Guo, F.: Strongly leakage-resilient authenticated key exchange. In: CT-RSA, pp. 19–36 (2016)
12. Chen, Y., Zhang, Z., Lin, D., Cao, Z.: Anonymous identity-based hash proof system and its applications. In: Takagi, T., Wang, G., Qin, Z., Jiang, S., Yu, Y. (eds.) ProvSec 2012. LNCS, vol. 7496, pp. 143–160. Springer, Heidelberg (2012)
13. Chen, Y., Zhang, Z., Lin, D., Cao, Z.: Identity-based extractable hash proofs and their applications. In: Bao, F., Samarati, P., Zhou, J. (eds.) ACNS 2012. LNCS, vol. 7341, pp. 153–170. Springer, Heidelberg (2012)
14. Chen, Y., Zhang, Z., Lin, D., Cao, Z.: Generalized (identity-based) hash proof system and its applications. IACR Cryptology ePrint Archive 2013, 2 (2013)
15. Chen, Y., Zhang, Z., Lin, D., Cao, Z.: CCA-secure IB-KEM from identity-based extractable hash proof system. Comput. J. 57(10), 1537–1556 (2014)
16. Chow, S.S.M., Dodis, Y., Rouselakis, Y., Waters, B.: Practical leakage-resilient identity-based encryption from simple assumptions. In: Proceedings of the 17th ACM Conference on Computer and Communications Security, CCS 2010, Chicago, Illinois, USA, 4–8 October 2010, pp. 152–161 (2010)

17. Cocks, C.: An identity based encryption scheme based on quadratic residues. In: Honary, B. (ed.) Cryptography and Coding 2001. LNCS, vol. 2260, pp. 360–363. Springer, Heidelberg (2001)

18. Coron, J.: A variant of Boneh-Franklin IBE with a tight reduction in the random oracle model. Des. Codes Crypt. **50**(1), 115–133 (2009)

19. Cramer, R., Shoup, V.: Universal hash proofs and a paradigm for adaptive chosen ciphertext secure public-key encryption. In: Knudsen, L.R. (ed.) EUROCRYPT 2002. LNCS, vol. 2332, pp. 45–64. Springer, Heidelberg (2002)

20. Gennaro, R., Lindell, Y.: A framework for password-based authenticated key exchange. In: EUROCRYPT, pp. 524–543 (2003)

21. Gentry, C.: Practical identity-based encryption without random oracles. In: Vaudenay, S. (ed.) EUROCRYPT 2006. LNCS, vol. 4004, pp. 445–464. Springer, Heidelberg (2006)

22. Gentry, C., Peikert, C., Vaikuntanathan, V.: Trapdoors for hard lattices and new cryptographic constructions. In: Proceedings of the 40th Annual ACM Symposium on Theory of Computing, Victoria, British Columbia, Canada, May 17–20, 2008, pp. 197–206 (2008)

23. Halevi, S., Kalai, Y.T.: Smooth projective hashing and two-message oblivious transfer. J. Cryptology **25**(1), 158–193 (2012)

24. Katz, J., Vaikuntanathan, V.: Round-optimal password-based authenticated key exchange. In: Ishai, Y. (ed.) TCC 2011. LNCS, vol. 6597, pp. 293–310. Springer, Heidelberg (2011)

25. Li, N., Du, W., Boneh, D.: Oblivious signature-based envelope. In: PODC, pp. 182–189 (2003)

Proxy Signature with Revocation

Shengmin Xu[1], Guomin Yang[1(✉)], Yi Mu[1], and Sha Ma[1,2]

[1] Centre for Computer and Information Security Research,
School of Computing and Information Technology, University of Wollongong,
Wollongong, NSW, Australia
{sx914,gyang,ymu,sma}@uow.edu.au
[2] College of Mathematics and Informatics, South China Agricultural University,
Guangzhou 510640, Guangdong, China

Abstract. Proxy signature is a useful cryptographic primitive that allows signing right delegation. In a proxy signature scheme, an original signer can delegate his/her signing right to a proxy signer (or a group of proxy signers) who can then sign documents on behalf of the original signer. In this paper, we investigate the problem of proxy signature with revocation. The revocation of delegated signing right is necessary for a proxy signature scheme when the proxy signer's key is compromised and/or any misuse of the delegated right is noticed. Although a proxy signature scheme usually specifies a delegation time period, it may happen that the original signer wants to terminate the delegation before it is expired. In order to solve this problem, in this paper we propose a new proxy signature scheme with revocation. Our scheme utilises and combines the techniques in the Naor-Naor-Lotspiech (NNL) framework for broadcast encryption, the Boneh-Boyen-Goh (BBG) hierarchical identity-based encryption and the Boneh-Lynn-Shacham (BLS) short signature scheme and thereby constructing an efficient tree-based revocation mechanism. The unrevoked proxy signer only needs to generate evidences for proving that he/she is a valid proxy signer once in per revocation epoch, and the verifier does not need a revocation list in order to verify the validity of a proxy signature.

Keywords: Proxy signature · Revocation · Hierarchical structure

1 Introduction

Mambo, Usuda and Okamoto introduced the concept of proxy signatures in 1996 [16,17]. In a proxy signature scheme, an original signer is allowed to delegate his signing power to a designated person called the proxy signer, and then the proxy signer is able to sign the message on behalf of the original signer.

There are four types of delegation in proxy signature. Mambo et al. [16] proposed three of them in their seminal work: full delegation, partial delegation and delegation by warrant. In the full delegation, the original signer just gives his signing key to the proxy signer as the proxy signing key. Thus, the proxy signer has the same signing ability as the original signer so that the real

© Springer International Publishing Switzerland 2016
J.K. Liu and R. Steinfeld (Eds.): ACISP 2016, Part II, LNCS 9723, pp. 21–36, 2016.
DOI: 10.1007/978-3-319-40367-0_2

signer of a signature is indistinguishable. To overcome this drawback, partial delegation was proposed, in which the original signer and the proxy signer work together to derive the proxy signing key that consists of partial private keys of the original signer and the proxy signer. Partial delegation is further classified into proxy-unprotected delegation and proxy-protected delegation [11]. In proxy-unprotected partial delegation, the original signer can derive the proxy signing key without the interaction with the proxy signer, but the proxy signer cannot derive the proxy signing key without the help from the original signer. In the case of proxy-protected partial delegation, the proxy signing key needs the contribution of both the proxy signer and the original signer. However, in the partial delegation, the proxy signer has unlimited signing ability. To conquer this problem, delegation by warrant has been proposed. The original signer signs a warrant that certifies the legitimacy of the proxy signer. Kim et al. [10] later proposed a new type of proxy delegation called partial delegation with warrant combining advantages of partial delegation and delegation with warrant.

Besides, proxy signature can be categorized into proxy multi-signature scheme and multi-proxy signature scheme. In a proxy multi-signature scheme [13,22], a designed proxy signer can generate the signature on behalf of two or more original signers. In the case of multi-proxy signature scheme [12,21], it allows a group of original signers to delegate the signing capability to a designated group of proxy signers.

1.1 Motivation of This Work

In this paper, we focus on proxy signature with revocation. Although there are many research works on proxy signature, only few of them deal with proxy revocation. It is necessary to address the problem of proxy revocation in proxy signature when the proxy signer is compromised. Moreover, in reality, the proxy signer may also misuse the delegated signing right. In such situations, the original signer should have a way to revoke the signing right delegated to the proxy signer even when the delegation has not expired. One straightforward solution to address this problem is to let the original signer publish a revocation/black list and a verifier needs to check the list before verifying a proxy signature. One limitation of such an approach is that the verifier needs to obtain the latest revocation list before verifying a proxy signature. Another problem brought by this approach is that a proxy signature generated before the proxy signer is revoked also becomes invalid. Ideally, such proxy signatures should still be considered valid since the proxy signer is not revoked when the signature is generated.

In [20], Sun suggested that the revocation problem can be solved by using a timestamp and proposed a proxy signature which allows the verifier to trace the proxy signer. However, the proposed scheme has some security issues. As pointed out in [4], an attacker can easily forge a proxy signature.

Another solution proposed in the literature to address the problem is utilising a trusted third party. Das et al. [4] and Lu et al. [15] proposed some proxy signature schemes with revocation where a trusted third party called the authentication server (AS) is used to provide the immediate revocation. However, a trusted third party is a very strong assumption. Hence, such a solution is not very practical in real applications.

The third solution that has been proposed by Seo et al. [19] and Liu et al. [14] is to use a third party called SEcurity Mediator (SEM) which is a partially trusted online server. In such a solution, the original signer divides the delegation into two parts and gives these two parts to the proxy signer and the SEM, respectively. When the proxy signer wants to generate a proxy signature, he/she must get the assistance from the SEM. Thus, the SEM works as a certifier to authenticate the signing ability of every proxy signer. Such a solution is not practical either since whenever the proxy signer wants to generate a proxy signature, he/she needs to contact the SEM which is a bottleneck of the system.

1.2 Our Result

In this paper, we introduce a novel proxy signature scheme with revocation. Compared with the previous solutions, our scheme has the following advantages.

- Our scheme does not need any third party. In addition, the verifier does not need to obtain the revocation list in order to verify a proxy signature. Instead he/she only needs to know the current revocation epoch in order to verify a proxy signature.
- The original signer can revoke a set of proxy signers in each revocation epoch. An unrevoked proxy signer only needs to generate once in each revocation epoch a proof which shows his/her valid proxy signing right.
- Our scheme explicitly includes the revocation epoch in signature verification, and hence, the verifier only denies signatures generated by a proxy signer after his/her proxy signing right is revoked. The signatures generated before revocation will remain valid.

1.3 Outline of Paper

The rest of this paper is organized as follows. Some preliminaries are presented in Sect. 2. The formal security models for our scheme is described in Sect. 3. The proposed proxy signature with revocation scheme is detailed in Sect. 4. We analyze the proposed scheme in Sect. 5. Finally, some concluding remarks are given in Sect. 6.

2   Preliminaries

In this section, we provide some background knowledge used in this paper.

2.1   Bilinear Map

Let $\mathbb{G}$ and $\mathbb{G}_T$ denote two cyclic multiplicative groups of prime order p and g be a generator of $\mathbb{G}$. The map $e : \mathbb{G} \times \mathbb{G} \to \mathbb{G}_T$ is said to be an admissible bilinear map if the following properties hold.

1. Bilinearity: for all $u, v \in \mathbb{G}$ and $a, b \in \mathbb{Z}_p$, $e(u^a, v^b) = e(u, v)^{ab}$.
2. Non-degeneration: $e(g, g) \neq 1$.
3. Computability: it is efficient to compute $e(u, v)$ for any $u.v \in \mathbb{G}$.

We say that $(\mathbb{G}, \mathbb{G}_T)$ are bilinear groups if there exists a bilinear map $e : \mathbb{G} \times \mathbb{G} \rightarrow \mathbb{G}_T$ as above.

2.2 Complexity Assumptions

Definition 1 (*Computational Diffie-Hellman (CDH) problem*). *Given* $g, g^a, g^b \in \mathbb{G}$ *for some unknown* $a, b \in \mathbb{Z}_p$, *the computational Diffie-Hellman (CDH) problem is to compute* $g^{ab} \in \mathbb{G}$.

Definition 2 (*Computational Diffie-Hellman (CDH) assumption*). *The* (t, ϵ)-*CDH assumption holds in group* $\mathbb{G}$ *if no algorithm with running time* t *has probability at least* ϵ *in solving the CDH problem.*

2.3 Digital Signature Scheme

A digital signature scheme consists of three algorithms [6]:

Key generation $\mathcal{G}(1^k)$: it inputs a security parameter k and outputs in polynomial time a pair (pk, sk) of matching public and secret keys.

Signature $\mathcal{S}_{sk}(m)$: it produces a signature $\sigma \leftarrow \mathcal{S}_{sk}(m)$ for a message m using the secret key sk.

Verification $\mathcal{V}_{pk}(m, \sigma)$: it tests whether σ is a valid signature for message m using the public key pk. The algorithm outputs either 1 (valid) or 0 (invalid).

2.4 Security Model for Existential Unforgeability

The de facto security notion is existential unforgeability under adaptive chosen message attacks [6] which is defined using the following game.

Setup: The challenger runs $\mathcal{G}$. It gives the adversary the resulting public key pk and keeps the private key sk to itself.

Signing Query ($\mathcal{O}_{\mathcal{EU}_S}$): The adversary issues signing queries $m_1, ..., m_q$. To each query m_i, the challenger responds by running $\mathcal{S}$ to generate a signature σ_i of m_i and sending σ_i to the adversary. These queries may be asked adaptively so that each query m_i may depend on the replies to $m_1, ..., m_{i-1}$. A database $D_{\mathcal{EU}_S}$ to record the messages have been signed.

Output: Finally the adversary outputs a pair (m^*, σ^*). The adversary wins if σ^* is a valid signature of m^* according to $\mathcal{V}$ and m^* is not among the messages $D_{\mathcal{EU}_S}$ appeared during the query phase.

Definition 3. *A signature scheme is (t, q, ϵ) existentially unforgeable under adaptive chosen message attacks if no t-time adversary $\mathcal{A}_{\mathcal{EU}}$ making at most q signing queries has advantage at least ϵ in the above game. For any PPT adversary $\mathcal{A}_{\mathcal{EU}}$ involved in the experiment hereafter, we have $\mathsf{Adv}_{\mathcal{A}_{\mathcal{EU}}}^{eu-cma}(\lambda) = \Pr[\mathsf{Expt}_{\mathcal{A}_{\mathcal{EU}}}^{eu-cma}(\lambda) = 1] \in \mathsf{negl}(\lambda)$.*

Experiment $\mathsf{Exp}_{\mathcal{A}_{\mathcal{EU}}}^{eu-cma}(\lambda)$	Oracle $\mathcal{O}_{\mathcal{EU}_S}(m)$
$(pk, sk) \leftarrow Gen(1^\lambda); D_{\mathcal{EU}_S} \leftarrow \emptyset$	$\sigma \leftarrow Sign(sk, m)$
$\sigma \leftarrow \mathcal{A}_{\mathcal{EU}}^{\mathcal{O}_{\mathcal{EU}_S}}(m)$	$D_{\mathcal{EU}_S} \leftarrow D_{\mathcal{EU}_S} \cup m$
$(m^*, \sigma^*) \leftarrow \mathcal{A}_{\mathcal{EU}}(pk, \mathcal{O}_{\mathcal{EU}_S})$	Return σ
If $Ver(pk, m^*, \sigma^*) = 1$, and	
$m^* \notin D_{\mathcal{EU}_S}$ return 1 else return 0	

2.5 Boneh-Lynn-Shacham Short Signature Scheme

BLS Short Signature Scheme was proposed in [3]. We use this short signature as a primitive to provide authentication in our hierarchical revocation algorithm. Some details of the BLS short signature are given below.

Keygen: The public key is $(\mathbb{G}, \mathbb{G}_T, q, g, y, \mathcal{H}_1)$ and secret key is s, where $y = g^s$ and $\mathcal{H}_1 : \{0,1\}^* \to \mathbb{G}$ is a hash function.

Sign: The signature for message m is $\sigma = h^s$, where $h = \mathcal{H}_1(m)$.

Verify: Check whether the equation $e(\sigma, g) = e(\mathcal{H}_1(m), y)$ holds.

This scheme has been proven to be secure against adaptive chosen-message attacks in the random oracle model assuming the CDH problem is hard.

2.6 Boneh-Boyen-Goh Hierarchical Identity-Based Encryption

Hierarchical identity-based encryption (HIBE) is a generalization of identity-based encryption and mirrors an organizational hierarchy. An identity at level k of the hierarchy tree can issue private keys to its descendant identities, but cannot decrypt messages intended for other identities. Boneh et al. [2] described the first HIBE scheme where the size of ciphertext does not depend on the depth of the receiver in the hierarchy. This HIBE scheme will be modified as an important part in our hierarchical revocation algorithm. The BBG HIBE scheme, which has five algorithms, is reviewed below.

Setup: The master public key is $(\mathbb{G}, \mathbb{G}_T, g, g_1, g_2, \{h_i\}_{i=0}^\ell)$ and master secret key is g_2^α, where ℓ is the number of levels in the hierarchy, $g_1 = g^\alpha$ and $\alpha \in \mathbb{Z}_p$ is a random number and $h_0, h_1, ..., h_\ell \in \mathbb{G}$.

Keygen: Given master secret key msk and an identity $id = (I_1, ..., I_k)$, it will choose a random numbers $r \in \mathbb{Z}_p$ and generate the private key $d_{id} = (D_1, D_2, K_{k+1}, ..., K_\ell)$. D_1 and D_2 are decryption keys. $(K_{k+1}, ..., K_\ell)$ is the delegation part and it is used to derive decryption keys for descendant identities.

$$D_1 = g_2^\alpha \cdot (h_0 \cdot \prod_{i=1}^k h_i^{I_i})^r, \quad D_2 = g^r, \quad K_i = h_i^r \text{ for } i = k+1, ..., \ell.$$

Derive: Given the private key d_{id} and an identity $id' = (I_1, ..., I_k, I_{k+1})$ that is the descendant of $id = (I_1, ..., I_k)$, it chooses a random number $r \in \mathbb{Z}_p$ and outputs a private key $d_{id'} = (D_1', D_2', K_{k+2}', ..., K_\ell')$ for id'.

$$d_{id'} = (D_1 \cdot K_{d+1}^{I_{k+1}} \cdot (h_0 \cdot \prod_{i=1}^{k+1} h_i^{I_i})^{r'}, D_2 \cdot g^{r'}, K_{k+2} \cdot h_{k+2}^{r'}, ..., K_\ell \cdot h_\ell^{r'}).$$

Encrypt: Given the master public key mpk, an identity $id = (I_1, ..., I_d)$ and a message m, it outputs a ciphertext $C = (C_0, C_1, C_2)$ by choosing a random number $s \in \mathbb{Z}_p$ and computing the following elements

$$C_0 = m \cdot e(g_1, g_2)^s, \ C_1 = g^s, \ C_2 = (h_0 \cdot h_1^{I_1} \cdots h_d^{I_d})^s.$$

Decrypt: It returns $M = C_0 \cdot e(C_1, D_1)^{-1} \cdot e(C_2, D_2)$.

This scheme has been proven to be selective-ID secure in the standard model and fully secure in the random oracle model.

2.7   Naor-Naor-Lotspiech Framework for Broadcast Encryption

Naor et al. [18] introduced a subset cover framework for broadcast encryption. This framework is based on complete subtree (CS) method and subset difference (SD) method. Halevy and Shamir [7] proposed a new method called layered subset difference (LSD) to improve the key distribution in the SD method. Later, Dodis and Fazio [5] pointed out that HIBE schemes can base on the above methods. In this section, we will briefly introduce the SD method.

The SD method works like a white list and we call it a revocation list in this paper. Each user is assigned to a leaf node in the tree and given the private keys of all co-path nodes from the root to the leaf. Let $\mathcal{N}$ denote all the users and $\mathcal{R}$ the revoked users. This method will group the valid users $(\mathcal{N} \setminus \mathcal{R})$ into m sets $S_{k_1, u_1}, ..., S_{k_m, u_m}$. Each valid user belongs to at least one set, the number of set m satisfies $m \leq 2|\mathcal{R}| - 1$. Let T_{x_j} denote the subtree rooted at x_j.

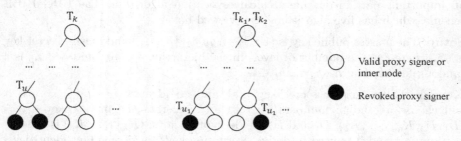

Valid proxy signer or inner node

Revoked proxy signer

All revoked users are under a subtree   Revoked users are under different subtrees

Fig. 1. The SD method

The subset S_{k_i,u_i} is defined as follows. T_{k_i} is called the primitive root. T_{u_i} is called the secondary root, and T_{u_i} is a descendant of T_{k_i}. The valid users in the set S_{k_i,u_i} consists of the leaves of T_{k_i} that are not in T_{u_i}. Thus, each user may belong to more than one set.

3   Formal Definitions and Security Models

In this section, we will introduce the syntax of a hierarchical revocation algorithm and a proxy signature with revocation and their formal security models. Here, we provide the details of some notations that will be used in this section.

- $\mathcal{N}$ is the set of proxy signers, and $|\mathcal{N}|$ is the number of proxy signer.
- $\mathcal{R}$ is the set of revoked proxy signers, and $|\mathcal{R}|$ is the number of revoked proxy signer. $\mathcal{R}_t$ is the set of revoked proxy signers in the revocation epoch t.
- $\ell \in \mathbb{Z}$ is the maximum level of the tree and $|\mathcal{N}| \leq 2^{\ell}$.
- $id \in \{0,1\}^{\leq \ell}$ is the label value for each node in the tree.
- $prefix(id) \in \{0,1\}^{\leq \ell}$ is the set of label values which are the prefix of id.
- $w \in \mathbb{Z}$ is a warrant for signing right delegation.
- $d_{id_i} = (D_{i,1}, D_{i,2}, K_{i,1}, ..., K_{i,\ell-|id_i|+1})$ is the hierarchical private key for id_i.

3.1   Hierarchical Revocation Scheme

This hierarchical revocation scheme is derived from the Boneh-Boyen-Goh hierarchical identity based encryption scheme (BBG HIBE) [2] and is an essential part of our proxy signature with revocation scheme. This scheme keeps a white list to reject all the revoked proxy signers and the size of this revocation list is $O(|\mathcal{R}|)$ since we use the Subset Difference (SD) method in the Naor-Naor-Lotspiech framework [18]. This scheme can be described using the following algorithms.

Setup$(1^{\lambda}, 1^{\ell})$: Given a security parameter λ and a maximum level ℓ of the complete binary tree, it outputs the system parameter $param$, the master secret key msk and the master public key mpk.

Keygen(w_i, pk_i, msk, id): Given a proxy signer's warrant w_i and his/her public key pk_i, master secret key msk, the master public key mpk and the label value id in the tree, it outputs a hierarchical private key d_{id}, where d_{id} includes the decryption key and delegation key as shown in the HIBE scheme reviewed above.

Derive(mpk, id, d_{id}, id'): Given master public key mpk, a label value id and its hierarchical private key d_{id} and a label value id', which is a descendant of id in the tree structure, it outputs another hierarchical private key $d_{id'}$ for id'.

Encode(mpk, id, id'): Given master public key mpk, a label value id and another label value id' which is a descendant of id, it outputs a encoding value C.

Verify$(mpk, w_i, pk_i, id, C, d_{id'})$: Given master public key mpk, a proxy signer's warrant w_i and his/her public key pk_i, a label value id, an encoding value C (with regards to id and id') and a hierarchical private key $d_{id'}$, it outputs either 1 or 0.

Security Model for Hierarchical Revocation Algorithm. We propose a security notion called key robustness to define the security of our hierarchical revocation algorithm. The security model is defined using the following game:

Setup: The challenger runs *Setup*. It gives the adversary the resulting of master public key mpk and keeps the master private key msk to itself.

Keygen Query $(\mathcal{O}_{\mathcal{A}_{\mathcal{G}}})$: The adversary issues up to q_G key generations queries $\{(id_i, w_i, pk_i)\}_{i=1}^{q_G}$. To each (id_i, w_i, pk_i), the challenger responds by running *Keygen* to generate a result d_{id_i} for (id_i, w_i, pk_i) and sending d_{id_i} to the adversary. These queries may be asked adaptively so that each query (id_i, w_i, pk_i) may depend on the replies to $(id_1, w_1, pk_1), ..., (id_{i-1}, w_{i-1}, pk_{i-1})$. A database $D_{\mathcal{A}_{\mathcal{G}}}$ records all the messages that have been queried.

Output: Finally the adversary outputs $(id^*, id^{*\prime}, w^*, C^*, pk^*, d_{id^{*\prime}}^*)$ such that C^* is an encoding with regards to id^* and $id^{*\prime}$. The adversary wins if $(id^{*\prime}, w^*, pk^*)$ or $(prefix(id^{*\prime}), w^*, pk^*)$ has not appeared in any *Kengen queries*, and $(mpk, w^*, pk^*, id^*, C^*, d_{id^{*\prime}}^*)$ can pass the verification.

In the random oracle model, we have an additional oracle called hash oracle:

Hash Query $(\mathcal{O}_{\mathcal{A}_{\mathcal{H}}})$: The adversary issues hash queries $\{(id_i, w_i, pk_i)\}_{i=1}^{q_H}$. To each (id_i, w_i, pk_i), the challenger responds by returning a random element in the range of the hash function $\mathcal{H}_1$. The same result is returned if the same input is queried for more than one time.

Definition 4. *A hierarchical revocation scheme is (t, q_H, q_G, ϵ) key robust if no t-time adversary $\mathcal{A}$ making at most q_H hash queries and q_G keygen queries has advantage at least ϵ in the above game. For any PPT adversary $\mathcal{A}$ involved in the experiment hereafter, we have* $\mathsf{Adv}_{\mathcal{A}}^{key-robust}(\lambda) = \Pr[\mathsf{Expt}_{\mathcal{A}}^{key-robust}(\lambda, \ell) = 1] \in \mathsf{negl}(\lambda)$.

Oracle $\mathcal{O}_{\mathcal{A}_{\mathcal{H}}}(id, w, pk)$	Oracle $\mathcal{O}_{\mathcal{A}_{\mathcal{G}}}(id, w, pk)$
Return $\mathcal{H}_1(id, w, pk)$	$D_{\mathcal{A}_{\mathcal{G}}} \leftarrow D_{\mathcal{A}_{\mathcal{G}}} \cup (id, w, pk)$
	Return $keygen(w, pk, msk, id)$

Experiment $\mathsf{Expt}_{\mathcal{A}}^{key-robust}(\lambda, \ell)$

$\quad (mpk, msk) \leftarrow Setup(1^\lambda, 1^\ell); D_{\mathcal{A}_{\mathcal{G}}} \leftarrow \emptyset$

$\quad H_i \leftarrow \mathcal{A}^{\mathcal{O}_{\mathcal{A}_{\mathcal{H}}}}(id_i, w_i, pk_i); d_{id_i} \leftarrow \mathcal{A}^{\mathcal{O}_{\mathcal{A}_{\mathcal{G}}}}(id_i, w_i, pk_i)$

$\quad (id^*, id^{*\prime}, w^*, C^*, pk^*, d_{id^{*\prime}}^*) \leftarrow \mathcal{A}(mpk, \mathcal{O}_{\mathcal{A}_{\mathcal{H}}}, \mathcal{O}_{\mathcal{A}_{\mathcal{G}}})$

$\quad$ If $Verify(mpk, w^*, pk^*, id^*, C^*, d_{id^{*\prime}}^*) \to 1$, $(id^{*\prime}, w^*, pk^*) \notin D_{\mathcal{A}_{\mathcal{G}}}$, and $(prefix(id^{*\prime}), w^*, pk^*)^* \notin D_{\mathcal{A}_{\mathcal{G}}}$ return 1 else return 0

3.2 Proxy Signature with Revocation

In our scheme, there are two parties: an original signer $\mathcal{O}$ and a group of proxy signers $\mathcal{P}_i$ for $i = 1, ..., |\mathcal{N}|$. A proxy signature scheme with revocation can be described as a collection of the following algorithms:

Setup$(1^\lambda, 1^\ell)$: Given a system security parameter λ and a maximum level of the complete binary tree that defines the maximum number of the proxy signers $|\mathcal{N}| = 2^\ell$, it outputs the system parameters $\mathcal{Y}$.

Keygen$(1^\lambda, \mathcal{Y})$: Given a system security parameter λ and the system parameters $\mathcal{Y}$, it outputs a pair of public and secret key (pk, sk). The original signer runs this algorithm to generate its own public pk_o and security key sk_o. The proxy signers runs this function to generate its own public pk_i and security key sk_i.

Delegation$(\mathcal{Y}, w_i, pk_i, pk_o, sk_o)$: Given a system parameters $\mathcal{Y}$, the warrant w_i and public key pk_i of the proxy signer $\mathcal{P}_i$ and the public key pk_o and secret key sk_o of original signer, it generates the delegated information I_i.

Revocation$(\mathcal{Y}, sk_o, t, \mathcal{R}_t)$: Given a system parameters $\mathcal{Y}$, the secret key sk_o of original signer, the current revocation epoch t and the set of revoked proxy signers $\mathcal{R}_t$, it outputs a revocation list RL_t under the revocation epoch t.

Sign$(\mathcal{Y}, RL_t, sk_i, I_i, M)$: Given a system parameters $\mathcal{Y}$, the revocation list RL_t under revocation epoch t, the secret key sk_i and delegated information I_i of proxy signer $\mathcal{P}_i$ and a message M, it outputs a proxy signature σ.

Verify$(\mathcal{Y}, t, pk_i, pk_o, M, \sigma)$: Given a system parameter $\mathcal{Y}$, the revocation epoch t, public key pk_i of proxy signer, public key pk_o of original signer, the message M and the proxy signature σ, it outputs either 1 or 0.

Security Models for Proxy Signature with Revocation. To define the unforgeability of our proxy signature scheme with revocation, according to the classification of Huang et al. [8] and their continuing work [9], we divide the adversaries into the following four types[1]:

1. *Type I*: This type of adversary $\mathcal{A}_\mathcal{I}$ has public parameter $\mathcal{Y}$, public key of original signer pk_o, and public keys of all proxy signers $\{pk_i\}_{i=1}^{|\mathcal{N}|}$.
2. *Type II*: This type of adversary $\mathcal{A}_{\mathcal{II}}$ has public parameter $\mathcal{Y}$, public key of original signer pk_o, public keys of all proxy signers $\{pk_i\}_{i=1}^{|\mathcal{N}|}$, and the secret key of original signer sk_o.
3. *Type III*: This type of adversary $\mathcal{A}_{\mathcal{III}}$ has public parameter $\mathcal{Y}$, public key of original signer pk_o, public keys of all proxy signers $\{pk_i\}_{i=1}^{|\mathcal{N}|}$, and secret keys of all proxy signers $\{sk_i\}_{i=1}^{|\mathcal{N}|}$.
4. *Type IV*: This type of adversary $\mathcal{A}_{\mathcal{IV}}$ has public parameter $\mathcal{Y}$, public key of original signer pk_o, public keys of all proxy signers $\{pk_i\}_{i=1}^{|\mathcal{N}|}$, and the secret key and delegated information of all revoked proxy signers $\{sk_i, I_i\}_{i \in \mathcal{R}}$[2].

One can find that if our proxy signature scheme is secure against *Type II* (or *Type III* or *Type IV*) adversary, our scheme is also unforgeable against *Type I* adversary. Below we give the formal security models.

Security Model for Adversary $\mathcal{A}_{\mathcal{II}}$. Adversary $\mathcal{A}_{\mathcal{II}}$ represents original signer, who wants to generate a valid proxy signature without knowing the secret key of the proxy signer. The security model is defined using the following game:

---

[1] In all the security models, we assume that there is only one set of revoked signers $\mathcal{R}_{t_i}$ for each revocation epoch t_i.

[2] For achieving the backward security [1], we needs the time stamp server to generate the time certificate for each proxy signature.

Setup: The challenger generates $|\mathcal{N}| + 1$ public key and secret key pairs and assigns them to the original signer and proxy signers. Then it gives the adversary the system parameter $\mathcal{Y}$, the public keys of original signer pk_o and proxy signers $\{pk_i\}_{i=1}^{|\mathcal{N}|}$, secret key of original signer sk_o, and keeps the secret keys of all proxy signers $\{sk_i\}_{i=1}^{|\mathcal{N}|}$ to itself.

Signing Query ($\mathcal{O}_{\mathcal{II}_S}$): The adversary issues signing queries $\{(w_i, pk_i, M_i, t_i, \mathcal{R}_{t_i})\}_{i=1}^{q}$ where $pk_i \notin \mathcal{R}_{t_i}$. The challenger responds by running *Delegation* algorithm to get delegated information I_i, *Revocation* algorithm to get revocation list RL_{t_i}, and *Sign* algorithm to get the proxy signature σ_i. After that, the challenger sends σ_i to the adversary. These queries may be asked adaptively so that each query $(w_i, pk_i, M_i, t_i, \mathcal{R}_{t_i})$ may depend on the replies to all previous queries. A database $D_{\mathcal{II}_S}$ records all the information of queries. If $pk_i \in \mathcal{R}_{t_i}$, the challenger rejects the query.

Output: Finally, the adversary outputs $(w^*, pk^*, M^*, t^*, \mathcal{R}_{t^*}, \sigma^*)$. The adversary wins if pk^* is one of the proxy signer public keys that have been given, $(w^*, pk^*, t^*, \mathcal{R}_{t^*}, M)$ does not appear in $D_{\mathcal{II}_S}$, and $(\mathcal{Y}, t^*, pk^*, pk_o, M^*, \sigma^*)$ can pass the verification.

Definition 5. *A proxy signature scheme is (t, q, ϵ) existentially unforgeable under Type-II adaptive chosen message attacks if no t-time adversary $\mathcal{A}_{\mathcal{II}}$ making at most q signing queries has advantage at least ϵ in the above game. For any PPT adversary $\mathcal{A}_{\mathcal{II}}$ involved in the experiment hereafter, we have $\mathsf{Adv}_{\mathcal{A}_{\mathcal{II}}}^{\mathsf{eu-cma}}(\lambda) = \Pr[\mathsf{Expt}_{\mathcal{A}_{\mathcal{II}}}^{\mathsf{eu-cma}}(\lambda, \ell) = 1] \in \mathsf{negl}(\lambda).$*

Oracle $\mathcal{O}_{\mathcal{II}_S}(w, pk, M, t, \mathcal{R}_t)$
   $I \leftarrow Delegation(\mathcal{Y}, w, pk, pk_o, sk_o); RL_t \leftarrow Revocation(\mathcal{Y}, sk_o, t, \mathcal{R}_t)$
   $\sigma \leftarrow Sign(\mathcal{Y}, RL_t, sk, I, M); D_{\mathcal{II}_S} \leftarrow D_{\mathcal{II}_S} \cup (w, pk, M, t, \mathcal{R}_t)$
   Return σ

Experiment $\mathsf{Exp}_{\mathcal{A}_{\mathcal{II}}}^{\mathsf{eu-cma}}(\lambda, \ell)$
   $(\mathcal{Y}, pk_o, sk_o, \{pk_i, sk_i\}_{i=1}^{|\mathcal{N}|}) \leftarrow Setup(1^\lambda, 1^\ell); D_{\mathcal{II}_S} \leftarrow \emptyset$
   $\sigma \leftarrow \mathcal{A}_{\mathcal{II}}^{\mathcal{O}_{\mathcal{II}_S}}(w, pk, M, t, \mathcal{R}_t)$
   $(w^*, pk^*, M^*, t^*, \mathcal{R}_{t^*}, \sigma^*) \leftarrow \mathcal{A}_{\mathcal{II}}(\mathcal{Y}, pk_o, sk_o, \{pk_i\}_{i=1}^{|\mathcal{N}|}, \mathcal{O}_{\mathcal{II}_S})$
   If $Verify(\mathcal{Y}, t^*, pk^*, pk_o, M^*, \sigma^*) = 1$, $pk^* \in \{pk_i\}_{i=1}^{|\mathcal{N}|}$, and
   $(w^*, pk^*, M^*, t^*, \mathcal{R}_{t^*}) \notin D_{\mathcal{II}_S}$ return 1 else return 0

Security Model for Adversary $\mathcal{A}_{\mathcal{III}}$. Adversary $\mathcal{A}_{III}$ represents proxy signers, who want to generate the proxy signature without knowing the delegated information. The security model is defined using the following game:

Setup: The challenger generates $|\mathcal{N}| + 1$ public key and secret key pairs and assigns them to original signer and proxy signers. Then it gives the adversary the system parameter $\mathcal{Y}$, the public keys of original signer pk_o and proxy signers $\{pk_i\}_{i=1}^{|\mathcal{N}|}$, secret keys of proxy signers $\{sk_i\}_{i=1}^{|\mathcal{N}|}$, and keeps the secret key of original signer sk_o to itself.

Delegation Query $(\mathcal{O}_{III_D})$: The adversary issues up to q_D delegation queries. To each (w_i, pk_i), the challenger responds by running *Delegation* algorithm to gain the delegated information I_i and the challenger sends I_i to the adversary. These queries may be asked adaptively. A database D_{III_D} records all the delegation queries.

Revocation Query $(\mathcal{O}_{III_R})$: The adversary issues up to q_R revocation queries $(t_i, \mathcal{R}_{t_i})$. To each query, the challenger responds by executing *Revocation* algorithm to get the revocation list RL_{t_i} for revocation epoch t_i. Then the challenger sends RL_{t_i} to the adversary. These queries may be asked adaptively. Notice that we assume there is only one $\mathcal{R}_{t_i}$ for each t_i.

Signing Query $(\mathcal{O}_{III_S})$: The adversary makes up to q_S signing queries to the challenger. For each $(w_i, pk_i, M_i, t_i, \mathcal{R}_{t_i})$ where $pk_i \notin \mathcal{R}_{t_i}$, the challenger gains the delegated information I_i by running *Delegation* algorithm, runs the *Revocation* algorithm to get the revocation list RL_{t_i}, and executes the *Sign* algorithm to acquire the proxy signature σ_i. These queries may be asked adaptively. A database D_{III_S} records all the signing queries.

Output: Finally, the adversary outputs $(w^*, pk^*, M^*, t^*, \mathcal{R}_{t^*}, \sigma^*)$. The adversary wins if pk^* is one of the proxy signer's public keys given, (w^*, pk^*) has not been queried to *Delegation* oracle, $(w^*, pk^*, M^*, t^*, \mathcal{R}_{t^*})$ has not been queried to *Signing* oracle, and $(\mathcal{Y}, t^*, pk^*, pk_o, M^*, \sigma^*)$ can pass verification.

Definition 6. *A proxy signature scheme is $(t, q_D, q_R, q_S, \epsilon)$ existentially unforgeable under Type-III adaptive chosen message attacks if no t-time adversary $\mathcal{A}_{III}$ making at most q_D delegation queries, q_R revocation queries and q_S signing queries has advantage at least ϵ in the above game. For any PPT adversary $\mathcal{A}_{III}$ involved in the experiment hereafter, we have $\mathsf{Adv}_{\mathcal{A}_{III}}^{\mathsf{eu-cma}}(\lambda) = \Pr[\mathsf{Expt}_{\mathcal{A}_{III}}^{\mathsf{eu-cma}}(\lambda) = 1] \in \mathsf{negl}(\lambda)$.*

Oracle $\mathcal{O}_{III_D}(w, pk)$	Oracle $\mathcal{O}_{III_S}(w, pk, M, t, \mathcal{R}_t)$
$\quad I \leftarrow Delegation(\mathcal{Y}, w, pk, pk_o, sk_o)$	$\quad I \leftarrow Delegation(\mathcal{Y}, w, pk, pk_o, sk_o)$
$\quad D_{III_D} \leftarrow D_{III_D} \cup (w, pk)$	$\quad RL_t \leftarrow Revocation(\mathcal{Y}, sk_o, t, \mathcal{R}_t)$
$\quad$ Return I	$\quad \sigma \leftarrow Sign(\mathcal{Y}, RL_t, sk, I, M)$
Oracle $\mathcal{O}_{III_R}(t, \mathcal{R}_t)$	$\quad D_{III_S} \leftarrow D_{III_S} \cup (w, pk, M, t, \mathcal{R}_t)$
$\quad RL_t \leftarrow Revocation(\mathcal{Y}, sk_o, t, \mathcal{R}_t)$	$\quad$ Return σ
$\quad$ Return RL_t	

Experiment $\mathsf{Expt}_{\mathcal{A}_{III}}^{\mathsf{eu-cma}}(\lambda, \ell)$

$\quad (\mathcal{Y}, pk_o, sk_o, \{pk_i, sk_i\}_{i=1}^{|\mathcal{N}|}) \leftarrow Setup(1^\lambda, 1^\ell); D_{III_D}, D_{III_S} \leftarrow \emptyset$

$\quad I_i \leftarrow \mathcal{A}_{III}^{\mathcal{O}_{III_D}}(w_i, pk_i); RL_{t_i} \leftarrow \mathcal{A}_{III}^{\mathcal{O}_{III_R}}(t_i, \mathcal{R}_{t_i})$

$\quad \sigma_i \leftarrow \mathcal{A}_{III}^{\mathcal{O}_{III_S}}(w_i, pk_i, M_i, t_i, \mathcal{R}_{t_i})$

$\quad (w^*, pk^*, M^*, t^*, \mathcal{R}_{t^*}, \sigma^*) \leftarrow \mathcal{A}_{III}(\mathcal{Y}, pk_o, \{pk_i, sk_i\}_{i=1}^{|\mathcal{N}|}, \mathcal{O}_{III_D}, \mathcal{O}_{III_R}, \mathcal{O}_{III_S})$

$\quad$ If $Verify(\mathcal{Y}, t^*, pk^*, pk_o, M^*, \sigma^*) = 1, pk^* \in \{pk_i\}_{i=1}^{|\mathcal{N}|}$,

$\quad (w^*, pk^*) \notin D_{III_D}$, and $(w^*, pk^*, M^*, t^*, \mathcal{R}_{t^*}) \notin D_{III_S}$ return 1 else return 0

Security Model for Adversary $\mathcal{A}_{IV}$. Adversary $\mathcal{A}_{IV}$ represents proxy signers, who want to generate the proxy signature when they have been revoked. The security model is defined using the following game:

Setup: The challenger generates $|\mathcal{N}| + 1$ public key and secret key pairs and assigns them to the original signer and proxy signers. Then it gives the adversary the system parameter $\mathcal{Y}$, the public keys of original signer pk_o and proxy signers $\{pk_i\}_{i=1}^{|\mathcal{N}|}$, secret keys of proxy signers $\{sk_i\}_{i=1}^{|\mathcal{N}|}$, and keeps the secret key of original signer sk_o to itself.

Delegation Query ($\mathcal{O}_{\mathcal{IV}_D}$): The adversary issues up to q_D delegation queries. To each (w_i, pk_i), the challenger responds by running *Delegation* algorithm to gain the delegated information I_i and the challenger sends I_i to the adversary. These queries may be asked adaptively.

Revocation Query ($\mathcal{O}_{\mathcal{IV}_R}$): The adversary issues up to q_R revocation queries $(t_i, \mathcal{R}_{t_i})$. To each query, the challenger responds by executing *Revocation* algorithm to get the revocation list RL_{t_i} for revocation epoch t_i. Then the challenger sends RL_{t_i} to the adversary. These queries may be asked adaptively. A database $D_{\mathcal{IV}_R}$ records all the queries. Notice that we assume there is only one $\mathcal{R}_{t_i}$ for each t_i.

Signing Query ($\mathcal{O}_{\mathcal{IV}_S}$): The adversary sends up to q_S signing queries to the challenger. For each $(w_i, pk_i, M_i, t_i, \mathcal{R}_{t_i})$ where $pk_i \notin \mathcal{R}_{t_i}$, the challenger gains the delegated information I_i by running *Delegation* algorithm, runs the *Revocation* algorithm to get the revocation list RL_{t_i}, and executes the *Sign* algorithm to acquire the proxy signature σ_i. These queries may be asked adaptively. A database $D_{\mathcal{IV}_S}$ records all the signing queries.

Output: Finally, the adversary outputs $(w^*, pk^*, M^*, t^*, \mathcal{R}_{t^*}, \sigma^*)$. The adversary wins if $pk^* \in \mathcal{R}_{t^*}$, $(w^*, pk^*, M^*, t^*, \mathcal{R}_{t^*})$ has not been queried to *Sign* oracle, and $(\mathcal{Y}, t^*, pk^*, pk_o, M^*, \sigma^*)$ can pass the verification.

Definition 7. *A proxy signature scheme is $(t, q_D, q_R, q_S, \epsilon)$-strongly existentially unforgeable under an adaptive chosen message attack if no t-time adversary $\mathcal{A}_{\mathcal{IV}}$ making at most q_D delegation queries, q_R revocation queries and q_S signing queries has advantage at least ϵ in the above game. For any PPT adversary $\mathcal{A}_{\mathcal{IV}}$ involved in the experiment hereafter, we have* $\mathsf{Adv}_{\mathcal{A}_{\mathcal{IV}}}^{\mathsf{eu-cma}}(\lambda) = \Pr[\mathsf{Expt}_{\mathcal{A}_{\mathcal{IV}}}^{\mathsf{eu-cma}}(\lambda) = 1] \in \mathsf{negl}(\lambda)$.

Oracle $\mathcal{O}_{\mathcal{IV}_D}(w, pk)$	Oracle $\mathcal{O}_{\mathcal{IV}_S}(w, pk, M, t, \mathcal{R})$
$\quad I \leftarrow Delegation(w, \mathcal{Y}, pk, pk_o, sk_o)$	$\quad I \leftarrow Delegation(\mathcal{Y}, w, pk, pk_o, sk_o)$
$\quad$ Return I	$\quad RL_t \leftarrow Revocation(\mathcal{Y}, sk_o, t, \mathcal{R}_t)$
Oracle $\mathcal{O}_{\mathcal{IV}_R}(t, \mathcal{R}_t)$	$\quad \sigma \leftarrow Sign(\mathcal{Y}, RL_t, sk, I, M)$
$\quad RL_t \leftarrow Revocation(\mathcal{Y}, sk_o, t, \mathcal{R}_t)$	$\quad D_{\mathcal{IV}_S} \leftarrow D_{\mathcal{IV}_S} \cup (w, pk, M, t, \mathcal{R}_t)$
$\quad D_{\mathcal{IV}_R} \leftarrow D_{\mathcal{IV}_R} \cup (t, \mathcal{R}_t)$	$\quad$ Return σ
$\quad$ Return RL_t	

Experiment $\mathsf{Expt}_{\mathcal{A}_{\mathcal{IV}}}^{\mathsf{eu-cma}}(\lambda, \ell)$

$\quad (\mathcal{Y}, pk_o, sk_o, \{pk_i, sk_i\}_{i=1}^{|\mathcal{N}|}) \leftarrow Setup(1^\lambda, 1^\ell); D_{\mathcal{IV}_R}, D_{\mathcal{IV}_S} \leftarrow \emptyset$

$\quad I_i \leftarrow \mathcal{A}_{\mathcal{IV}}^{\mathcal{O}_{\mathcal{IV}_D}}(w_i, pk_i)$

$\quad RL_{t_i} \leftarrow \mathcal{A}_{\mathcal{IV}}^{\mathcal{O}_{\mathcal{IV}_R}}(t_i, \mathcal{R}_{t_i})$

$\quad \sigma_i \leftarrow \mathcal{A}_{\mathcal{IV}}^{\mathcal{O}_{\mathcal{IV}_S}}(w_i, pk_i, M_i, t_i, \mathcal{R}_{t_i})$

$\quad (w^*, pk^*, M^*, t^*, \mathcal{R}_{t^*}, \sigma^*) \leftarrow \mathcal{A}_{\mathcal{IV}}(\mathcal{Y}, pk_o, \{pk_i, sk_i\}_{i=1}^{|\mathcal{N}|}, \mathcal{O}_{\mathcal{IV}_D}, \mathcal{O}_{\mathcal{IV}_R}, \mathcal{O}_{\mathcal{IV}_S})$

$\quad$ If $Verify(\mathcal{Y}, t^*, pk^*, pk_o, M^*, \sigma^*) = 1$, $pk^* \in R_{t^*}$,

$\quad\quad (w^*, pk^*, M^*, t^*, \mathcal{R}_{t^*}) \notin D_{\mathcal{IV}_S}$ return 1 else return 0

4   The Proposed Scheme

In this section, inspired by the BBG HIBE scheme [2], the NNL framework for broadcast encryption [18] and the BLS short signature [3], we will construct a hierarchical revocation scheme. Based on this revocation scheme, we will then build our proxy signature scheme with revocation.

4.1   Hierarchical Revocation Scheme

Our hierarchical revocation scheme consists of the following algorithms.
Setup$(1^\lambda, 1^\ell) \rightarrow (param, msk, mpk)$:

- Set system parameter $param = (e, \mathbb{G}, \mathbb{G}_T, g, p)$.
- The original signer $\mathcal{O}$ has $(pk_o, sk_o) = (g^{x_o}, x_o)$ and each proxy signer $\mathcal{P}_i$ has $(pk_i, sk_i) = (g^{x_i}, x_i)$, where $x_i \in \mathbb{Z}_p^*$. For each $\mathcal{P}_i$, assign a warrant w_i.
- Set master secret key $msk = sk_o$ and master public key $mpk = (pk_o, \{h_i\}_{i=0}^\ell)$, where $h_0, h_1, ..., h_\ell \in \mathbb{G}$.
- Select a injective function $\mathcal{H} : \{0,1\}^{\leq \ell} \rightarrow \mathbb{Z}_p^*$ and a hash function $\mathcal{H}_1 : \{0,1\}^* \rightarrow \mathbb{G}$.

Keygen$(w_i, pk_i, msk, id) \rightarrow d_{id}$:

$$d_{id} = (D_1, D_2, K_2, ..., K_{\ell-|id|+1})$$
$$= (\mathcal{H}_1(id, w_i, pk_i)^{sk_o} \cdot (h_0 \cdot h_1^{\mathcal{H}(id)})^r, g^r, h_2^r, ..., h_{\ell-|id|+1}^r).$$

Derive$(mpk, id, d_{id}, id' = (id, I_1, ..., I_d)) \rightarrow d_{id'}$:

$$d_{id'} = (D_1', D_2') = (D_1 \cdot \prod_{i=1}^d K_{i+1}^{\mathcal{H}(I_i)}, D_2)$$
$$= (\mathcal{H}_1(id, w_i, pk_i)^{sk_o} \cdot (h_0 \cdot h_1^{\mathcal{H}(id)} \cdot h_2^{\mathcal{H}(I_1)} \cdots h_{d+1}^{\mathcal{H}(I_d)})^r, g^r).$$

Encode$(mpk, id, id' = (id, I_1, ..., I_d)) \rightarrow C$: $C = h_0 \cdot h_1^{\mathcal{H}(id)} \cdot h_2^{\mathcal{H}(I_1)} \cdots h_{d+1}^{\mathcal{H}(I_d)}$.

Verify$(mpk, w_i, pk_i, id, C, d_{id'}) \rightarrow \{0,1\}$: Parse $d_{id'} = (D_1', D_2')$, return 1 if following equation is true: $e(g, D_1') = e(pk_o, \mathcal{H}_1(id, w_i, pk_i)) \cdot e(C, D_2')$.

4.2   Proxy Signature with Revocation

Our proxy signature with revocation scheme consists of the following algorithms.

Setup$(1^\lambda, 1^\ell)$: $\lambda \in \mathbb{N}$ is a security parameter and $N = 2^\ell$ is the maximum number of proxy signer. Generate a bilinear map $(e, \mathbb{G}, \mathbb{G}_T, p, g)$. Choose randomly $\{h_i\}_{i=0}^\ell$ from $\mathbb{G}$. Choose a injective functions $\mathcal{H} : \{0,1\}^{\leq \ell} \rightarrow \mathbb{Z}_p^*$ and two hash functions $\mathcal{H}_i : \{0,1\}^* \rightarrow \mathbb{G}$ $(i = 1, 2)$. The system parameter $\mathcal{Y} = ((e, \mathbb{G}, \mathbb{G}_T, p, g), \{h_i\}_{i=0}^\ell, \mathcal{H}, \mathcal{H}_1, \mathcal{H}_2)$.

Keygen$(1^\lambda, \mathcal{Y})$: original signer $\mathcal{O}$ and each proxy signer $\mathcal{P}_i$ run the key generation algorithm to generate their own public key and secret key pair. $\mathcal{O}$ generates $(pk_o, sk_o) = (x_o, g^{x_o})$ and $\mathcal{P}_i$ generates $(pk_i, sk_i) = (x_i, g^{x_i})$.

Delegation$(\mathcal{Y}, w_i, pk_i, pk_o, sk_o)$: $\mathcal{O}$ generates the delegated information I_i to $\mathcal{P}_i$.

- A warrant w_i is an explicit description of the delegation relation.
- $\mathcal{O}$ assigns to $\mathcal{P}_i$ an availabel leaf v_i of label $\langle v_i \rangle$. Let $x_0 = \epsilon, x_1, ..., x_{\ell-1}, x_\ell = v_i$ be the path from the root ϵ of T to v_i. For $j = 0$ to ℓ, $\mathcal{O}$ does the following. Consider the sub-tree T_{x_j} rooted at node x_j. Let copath_{x_j} be the co-path from x_j to v_i. For each node $\omega \in \mathsf{copath}_{x_j}$, since x_j is an ancestor of ω, $\langle x_j \rangle$ is a prefix of $\langle \omega \rangle$ and we denote by $\omega_{\ell_1}...\omega_{\ell_2} \in \{0,1\}^{\ell_2 - \ell_1 + 1}$, for some $\ell_1 \le \ell_2 \le \ell$, the suffix of $\langle \omega \rangle$ coming right after $\langle x_j \rangle$. Choose a random $r \in \mathbb{Z}_p^*$ and compute

$$d_w = (D_{\omega,1}, D_{\omega,2}, K_{\omega,\ell_2-\ell_1+3}, ..., K_{\omega,\ell})$$
$$= (\mathcal{H}_1(x_j, \omega_i, pk_i)^{sk_o} \cdot (h_0 \cdot h_1^{\mathcal{H}(\langle x_j \rangle)} \cdot h_2^{\mathcal{H}(\langle \omega_{\ell_1} \rangle)} \cdots h_{\ell_2-\ell_1+2}^{\mathcal{H}(\langle \omega_{\ell_2} \rangle)})^r,$$
$$g^r, h_{\ell_2-\ell_1+3}^r, ..., h_\ell^r).$$

$\mathcal{P}_i$ gains the delegated information $I_i = (w_i, \langle v_i \rangle, \{\{d_\omega\}_{\omega \in \mathsf{copath}_{x_j}}\}_{j=0}^\ell)$.

Revocation$(\mathcal{Y}, sk_o, t, \mathcal{R}_t)$:

- Using the SD covering algorithm, find a cover of unrevoked user set $\mathcal{N} \setminus \mathcal{R}_t$ as the union of disjoint subsets of the form $S_{k_1,u_1}, ..., S_{k_m,u_m}$, with $m \le 2 \cdot |\mathcal{R}| - 1$.
- For $i = 1$ to m, do the following.
  1. Consider S_{k_i,u_i} as the difference between sub-trees rooted at an internal node x_{k_i} and one of its descendants x_{u_i}. The label of x_{u_i} can be written as $\langle x_{u_i} \rangle = \langle x_{k_i} \rangle \| u_{i,\ell_{i,1}}...u_{i,\ell_{i,2}}$. Then, compute an encoding of S_{k_i,u_i} as a group element:

$$C_i = h_0 \cdot h_1^{\mathcal{H}(\langle x_{k_i} \rangle)} \cdot h_2^{\mathcal{H}(u_{i,\ell_{i,1}})} \cdots h_{\ell_{i,2}-\ell_{i,1}+2}^{\mathcal{H}(u_{i,\ell_{i,2}})}.$$

  2. $\mathcal{O}$ generates a signature $\Theta_i = Sign_{sk_o}(C_i, g^t) = \mathcal{H}_2(C_i, g^t)^{sk_o}$.

Return the revocation list RL_t which is defined to be

$$RL_t = (t, \mathcal{R}_t, \{\langle x_{k_i} \rangle, \langle x_{u_i} \rangle, (C_i, \Theta_i)\}_{i=1}^m).$$

Sign$(\mathcal{Y}, RL_t, sk_i, I_i, M)$: Proxy signer only needs to generate the HIBE decryption key once in each revocation epoch.

- Using RL_t, determine the set S_{k_l,u_l}, with $l \in \{1, ..., m\}$, that contains the leaf v_i (this subset must exist since $pk_i \notin \mathcal{R}_t$) and let x_{k_l} and x_{u_l} denote the primary and secondary roots of S_{k_l,u_l}. Since x_{k_l} is an ancestor of x_{u_l}, we can write $\langle x_{u_l} \rangle = \langle x_{k_l} \rangle \| u_{l,\ell_1}...u_{l,\ell_2}$, for some $\ell_1 < \ell_2 < \ell$ and with $u_{l,\kappa} \in \{0,1\}$ for each $\kappa \in \{\ell_1, ..., \ell_2\}$. The proxy signer $\mathcal{P}_i$ computes an HIBE decryption key of the form

$$(D_{l,1}, D_{l,2}) = \left((\mathcal{H}_1(x_{k_l}, w_i, pk_i)^{sk_o} \cdot (h_0 \cdot h_1^{\mathcal{H}(\langle x_{k_l} \rangle)} \cdot h_2^{\mathcal{H}(u_{l,\ell_1})} \cdots h_{\ell_2-\ell_1+2}^{\mathcal{H}(u_{l,\ell_2})})^r, g^r\right).$$

Note that $(D_{l,1}, D_{l,2})$ can be reused in whole revocation epoch.

– Compute $\sigma_m = Sign_{sk_i}(M, \Omega)$ where $\Omega = (w_i, x_{k_l}, x_{u_l}, D_{l,1}, D_{l,2}, C_l, \Theta_l)$.

Return the proxy signature $\sigma = (\Omega, \sigma_m)$.

Verify$(\mathcal{Y}, t, pk_i, pk_o, M, \sigma)$: Verifier checks the proxy signature.

1. Check σ_m: If $Verify_{pk_i}((M, \Omega), \sigma_m) = 0$, return 0.
2. Check Θ_l: If $Verify_{pk_o}((C_l, g^t), \Theta_l) = 0$, return 0.
3. Check C_l: If $e(g, D_{\ell_1}) = e(pk_o, \mathcal{H}_1(x_{k_l}, w_i, pk_i)) \cdot e(C_\ell, D_{\ell_2})$, return 1. Otherwise, return 0.

5   Security Analysis

The proposed schemes is secure against Type-II/III/IV adversaries in the random oracle model. Please refer to the full version of the paper for the full proofs.

Theorem 1. *The hierarchical revocation scheme is key robust assuming that the CDH assumption holds in $\mathbb{G}$.*

Theorem 2. *The proxy signature with revocation scheme is secure against Type-II/III/IV adversaries.*

6   Conclusions

In this paper, we proposed a new solution for proxy signature with revocation. Compared with the previous approaches, our solution does not require any third party. In addtion, the verifier does not need to access the latest revocation list in order to verify a proxy signature. We also built a novel hierarchical revocation scheme, which is of independent interest. We proved the security of the hierarchical revocation scheme and the proxy signature scheme with revocation against various types of adversaries.

Acknowledgement. The last author of this work is supported by the National Natural Science Foundation of China (No. 61402184).

References

1. Ateniese, G., Song, D., Tsudik, G.: Quasi-efficient revocation of group signatures. In: Blaze, M. (ed.) FC 2002. LNCS, vol. 2357, pp. 183–197. Springer, Heidelberg (2003)
2. Boneh, D., Boyen, X., Goh, E.-J.: Hierarchical identity based encryption with constant size ciphertext. In: Cramer, R. (ed.) EUROCRYPT 2005. LNCS, vol. 3494, pp. 440–456. Springer, Heidelberg (2005)
3. Boneh, D., Lynn, B., Shacham, H.: Short signatures from the weil pairing. In: Boyd, C. (ed.) ASIACRYPT 2001. LNCS, vol. 2248, pp. 514–532. Springer, Heidelberg (2001)

4. Das, M.L., Saxena, A., Gulati, V.P.: An efficient proxy signature scheme with revocation. Informatica **15**(4), 455–464 (2004)
5. Dodis, Y., Fazio, N.: Public key broadcast encryption for stateless receivers. In: Feigenbaum, J. (ed.) DRM 2002. LNCS, vol. 2696, pp. 61–80. Springer, Heidelberg (2003)
6. Goldwasser, S., Micali, S., Rivest, R.L.: A digital signature scheme secure against adaptive chosen-message attacks. SIAM J. Comput. **17**(2), 281–308 (1988)
7. Halevy, D., Shamir, A.: The LSD broadcast encryption scheme. In: Yung, M. (ed.) CRYPTO 2002. LNCS, vol. 2442, pp. 47–60. Springer, Heidelberg (2002)
8. Huang, X., Mu, Y., Susilo, W., Zhang, F., Chen, X.: A short proxy signature scheme: efficient authentication in the ubiquitous world. In: Enokido, T., Yan, L., Xiao, B., Kim, D.Y., Dai, Y.-S., Yang, L.T. (eds.) EUC-WS 2005. LNCS, vol. 3823, pp. 480–489. Springer, Heidelberg (2005)
9. Huang, X., Susilo, W., Mu, Y., Wu, W.: Proxy signature without random oracles. In: Cao, J., Stojmenovic, I., Jia, X., Das, S.K. (eds.) MSN 2006. LNCS, vol. 4325, pp. 473–484. Springer, Heidelberg (2006)
10. Kim, S., Park, S., Won, D.: Proxy signatures, revisited. In: Information and Communications Security, pp. 223–232 (1997)
11. Lee, B., Kim, H.-S., Kim, K.: Secure mobile agent using strong non-designated proxy signature. In: Varadharajan, V., Mu, Y. (eds.) ACISP 2001. LNCS, vol. 2119, pp. 474–486. Springer, Heidelberg (2001)
12. Lee, B., Kim, H., Kim, K.: Strong proxy signature and its applications. In: Proceedings of SCIS, vol. 1, pp. 603–608 (2001)
13. Li, X., Chen, K., Li, S.: Multi-proxy signature and proxy multi-signature schemes from bilinear pairings. In: Liew, K.-M., Shen, H., See, S., Cai, W. (eds.) PDCAT 2004. LNCS, vol. 3320, pp. 591–595. Springer, Heidelberg (2004)
14. Liu, Z., Yupu, H., Zhang, X., Ma, H.: Provably secure multi-proxy signature scheme with revocation in the standard model. Comput. Commun. **34**(3), 494–501 (2011)
15. Lu, E.J.-L., Hwang, M.-S., Huang, C.-J.: A new proxy signature scheme with revocation. Appl. Math. Comput. **161**(3), 799–806 (2005)
16. Mambo, M., Usuda, K., Okamoto, E.: Proxy signatures: delegation of the power to sign messages. IEICE Trans. Fundam. Electron. Commun. Comput. Sci. **79**(9), 1338–1354 (1996)
17. Mambo, M., Usuda, K., Okamoto, E.: Proxy signatures for delegating signing operation. In: Proceedings of the 3rd ACM Conference on Computer and Communications Security, pp. 48–57. ACM (1996)
18. Naor, D., Naor, M., Lotspiech, J.: Revocation and tracing schemes for stateless receivers. In: Kilian, J. (ed.) CRYPTO 2001. LNCS, vol. 2139, pp. 41–62. Springer, Heidelberg (2001)
19. Seo, S.-H., Shim, K.-A., Lee, S.-H.: A mediated proxy signature scheme with fast revocation for electronic transactions. In: Katsikas, S.K., López, J., Pernul, G. (eds.) TrustBus 2005. LNCS, vol. 3592, pp. 216–225. Springer, Heidelberg (2005)
20. Sun, H.-M.: Design of time-stamped proxy signatures with traceable receivers. In: IEE Proceedings-Computers and Digital Techniques, vol. 147, no. 6, pp. 462–466 (2000)
21. Tzeng, S.-F., Yang, C.-Y., Hwang, M.-S.: A nonrepudiable threshold multi-proxy multi-signature scheme with shared verification. Future Gener. Comput. Syst. **20**(5), 887–893 (2004)
22. Yi, L., Bai, G., Xiao, G.: Proxy multi-signature scheme: a new type of proxy signature scheme. Electron. Lett. **36**(6), 527–528 (2000)

On the Relations Between Security Notions in Hierarchical Key Assignment Schemes for Dynamic Structures

Arcangelo Castiglione, Alfredo De Santis, Barbara Masucci,
Francesco Palmieri, and Aniello Castiglione(✉)

Department of Computer Science, University of Salerno,
Via Giovanni Paolo II, 132, 84084 Fisciano, SA, Italy
{arcastiglione,ads,bmasucci,fpalmieri}@unisa.it, castiglione@ieee.org

Abstract. A *hierarchical key assignment scheme* distribute some private information and encryption keys to a set of classes in a partially ordered hierarchy, so that the private information of higher classes can be employed to derive the keys of classes lower down in the hierarchy. A hierarchical key assignment scheme for *dynamic structures* allows to make dynamic updates to the hierarchy, such as addition, deletion and modification of classes and relations among them, as well as the revocation of users.

In this work we analyze *security notions* for hierarchical key assignment schemes supporting dynamic structures. In particular, we first propose the notion of key recovery for those schemes. Furthermore, we extend to such schemes the strong key indistinguishability and strong key recovery security definitions proposed by Freire et al. for hierarchical key assignment schemes. Finally, we investigate the relations occurring between all the state-of-the-art security notions for hierarchical key assignment schemes supporting dynamic structures, showing implications and separations which hold between such notions. In detail, we prove that also in the case of dynamic structures, security with respect to strong key indistinguishability is *equivalent to the* one with respect to key indistinguishability.

Keywords: Access control · Key assignment · Dynamic structures · Dynamic adversary · Strong key recovery · Strong key indistinguishability

1 Introduction

The main aim of the *access control management* is to provide only authorized users with the access to certain resources. More precisely, based on their relative responsibilities and roles, the users of a system are usually grouped into *hierarchies*, characterized by some disjoint classes (*security classes*). Hierarchical structures find a natural way of application in many different areas.

The use of cryptography to deal with key management issues in hierarchical structures was first addressed by Akl and Taylor [2], which introduced a

© Springer International Publishing Switzerland 2016
J.K. Liu and R. Steinfeld (Eds.): ACISP 2016, Part II, LNCS 9723, pp. 37–54, 2016.
DOI: 10.1007/978-3-319-40367-0_3

hierarchical key assignment scheme where each class is provided with a key that can be employed, together with some public information generated by a *Trusted Authority (TA)*, to derive the key of any class lower down in the hierarchy. Following the seminal work due to Akl and Taylor, many schemes have been proposed in the literature, each providing different trade-offs for what concerns the quantity of public and private information, as well as the complexity of key derivation (e.g., [3,4,6,14,16,17,21,24,25,27,29,30,32–35,40]). Again, other schemes have been proposed, either supporting more general access control policies [18,20,31,41] or satisfying further time-dependent constraints [7,8,15,22,23,28,37–39,42]. However, it is important to remark that despite many schemes have been proposed in the literature, many of them are not provided with a formal security proof or have been broken by *collusive attacks* [7,19,36,43,44], when some classes collude to calculate a key to which they cannot access.

The first formalization of the security properties concerning hierarchical key assignment schemes was made by Atallah et al. [3], which introduced two distinct notions: security with respect to *key recovery* and against *key indistinguishability*. In particular, the first notion represents the fact that an adversary should not be allowed to compute a key to which it cannot access, whereas, the second one denotes that the adversary should not even be allowed to distinguish the real key from a random string having the same length. More precisely, the model proposed in [3] enables an adversary which intends to attack a given class in the hierarchy to access the private information relative to all the users which cannot access such a class, besides all the public information. Afterwards, several different schemes satisfying the security notions due to Atallah et al. have been proposed in [5,7,8,10,12,16,17,21,23–25].

Novel security notions for hierarchical key assignment schemes were introduced by Freire et al. [26]. More precisely, such notions, referred to as security with respect to *strong key recovery* and security against *strong key indistinguishability*, enable the adversary to compromise a wider set of classes and hence they represent an improvement of the model introduced in [3]. In detail, in the model proposed by Freire et al., the adversary, given a target class, can obtain the private information relative to all the users which cannot access such a class, besides the public information and encryption keys relative to the classes that precede the target class in the hierarchy. Finally, Freire et al. proved that the security provided by the notion of key recovery is weaker than the one provided by the notion of strong key recovery. Therefore, such notions *are separated*, that is, some schemes are secure with respect to key recovery but not with respect to strong key recovery. However, the authors left as an open question the problem of clarifying the relations between the notions of security with respect to key indistinguishability and with respect to strong key indistinguishability. The equivalence between the notions of security with respect to strong key indistinguishability and with respect to key indistinguishability has been recently proven in [11]. A similar result was previously shown for the *unconditionally secure setting* [9].

It is important to remark that all security models proposed so far consider an operational scenario which is *fixed and immutable*. More precisely, the adversary is not allowed to make any changes to the hierarchy, which is fixed and chosen at the time of the attack. It is easy to note that this fact represents an important limitation, since the existing models are not able to characterize the different scenarios which may arise in many operating environments.

For example, advances in wireless communication have allowed the development of *User-Centric Networks (UCNs)*, which are an abstraction of the *infrastructureless networks*. Again, since the *Internet of Things (IoT)* technology permits the transfer and sharing of data among things and users, in this highly dynamic sharing environment the access control is essential to ensure secure communication. Furthermore, in the context of the *smart cities*, IoT hubs act as data aggregators, where a hub can support not only access to infrastructure data, but also participatory sensing and crowd sourced data where city employees and citizens contribute directly to the data infrastructure of a city. Another possible operational scenario is given by *Vehicular Ad Hoc Networks (VANETs)*.

In order to overcome the above defined limitations, Castiglione et al. [13] have recently proposed a novel model for hierarchical key assignment schemes supporting dynamic updates. More precisely, they have extended the notions of security with respect to key indistinguishability provided by Atallah et al., to address the further challenges introduced by the updates to the hierarchy. Finally, they have proposed a construction which is secure with respect to key indistinguishability.

In this work we consider *security notions* for hierarchical key assignment schemes implementing dynamic structures and the purpose of this work is three-fold. In particular, we first propose the notion of key recovery for those schemes. Furthermore, we extend to such schemes the strong key indistinguishability and strong key recovery security definitions proposed by Freire et al. for hierarchical key assignment schemes. Finally, we investigate the relations between all the aforementioned security notions, by illustrating implications and separations occurring between them. In detail, we show that also for what concerns dynamic structures, the notion of security with respect to strong key indistinguishability *is equivalent* to that against key indistinguishability, thus demonstrating that the former notion is *not stronger* than the latter.

The paper is structured as follows: in Sect. 2 we introduce some notions concerning hierarchical key assignment schemes with dynamic updates which will be used later. In Sect. 3 we investigate the relations between all the security notions proposed for hierarchical key assignment schemes supporting dynamic structures, by showing implications and separations. Finally, in Sect. 4 we draw some conclusions.

2   Hierarchical Key Assignment Schemes for Dynamic Structures

Consider a set of users grouped into several disjoint classes, denoted as *security classes*, where a security class can denote a generic entity. A binary relation $\preceq$

which partially orders the set of classes V is defined based on some characteristics of each class in V. The poset $(V, \preceq)$ is referred to as *partially ordered hierarchy*. Given two classes u and v, the notation $u \preceq v$ indicates that the users in v can access u's data. It is easy to note that since v is allowed to access its own data, then $v \preceq v$, for any $v \in V$. The partially ordered hierarchy $(V, \preceq)$ is usually characterized by a directed graph $G^* = (V, E^*)$, in which each class represents a vertex in G^*, and there exist an edge from v to u if and only if $u \preceq v$. Let $G = (V, E)$ be the *minimal representation* of the graph G^*, i.e., the directed acyclic graph resulting from the *transitive and reflexive reduction* of the graph $G^* = (V, E^*)$. We remark that the graph G is characterized by the same transitive and reflexive closure of G^*, that is, there exist a path of length greater than or equal to zero from v to u in G if and only if there exist the edge (v, u) in E^*. Aho et al. [1] showed that every directed graph has a transitive reduction, which can be computed in polynomial time and is unique for directed acyclic graphs. From now on, let Γ denote a family of graphs characterizing partially ordered hierarchies, e.g., Γ could represent the family of the rooted trees [34], the family of the d-dimensional hierarchies [4], etc. Let Γ be a family of graphs characterizing partially ordered hierarchies and let $G = (V, E)$ be a graph in Γ. For any class $v \in V$, let A_v^G be the *accessible set* of v in G, i.e., the set $\{u \in V : \text{there is a path from } v \text{ to } u \text{ in } G\}$ of classes which can be accessed by v in G. Similarly, let F_v^G be the *forbidden set* of v in G, i.e., the set $\{u \in V : \text{there is no path from } u \text{ to } v \text{ in } G\}$ of classes which cannot access v in G.

A hierarchical key assignment scheme for a family Γ of partially ordered hierarchies, supporting dynamic updates, has been first introduced in [13] and is defined as follows.

Definition 1. *A hierarchical key assignment scheme for Γ, supporting dynamic updates, is a triple (Gen, Der, Upd) of algorithms with the following characteristics:*

1. *The information generation algorithm Gen, carried out by a Trusted Authority (TA), is probabilistic polynomial-time. It takes as inputs the security parameter 1^τ and a graph $G = (V, E)$ in Γ, and returns as outputs*
   (a) *a private information s_u, for any class $u \in V$;*
   (b) *a key $k_u \in \{0, 1\}^\tau$, for any class $u \in V$;*
   (c) *a public information pub.*
   Let (s, k, pub) be the output of the algorithm Gen on inputs 1^τ and G, in which s and k denote the sequences of private information and keys, respectively.
2. *The key derivation algorithm Der, executed by some authorized user, is deterministic polynomial-time. It takes as inputs the security parameter 1^τ, a graph $G = (V, E)$ in Γ, two classes $u \in V$ and $v \in A_u^G$, the private information s_u assigned to class u and the public information pub, and returns as output the key $k_v \in \{0, 1\}^\tau$ assigned to class v.*

It is required that for each class $u \in V$, each class $v \in A_u^G$, each private information s_u, each key $k_v \in \{0, 1\}^\tau$, each public information pub which can be computed by Gen on inputs 1^τ and G, it holds that

$$Der(1^\tau, G, u, v, s_u, pub) = k_v.$$

3. *The* update algorithm *Upd, carried out by the TA, is probabilistic polynomial-time. It takes as inputs the security parameter 1^τ, a graph $G = (V, E)$ in Γ, the tuple (s, k, pub) (generated either by Gen or by Upd itself), an update type up, a sequence of additional parameters params, and produces as outputs*
   (a) a updated graph $G' = (V', E')$ in Γ;
   (b) a private information s'_u, for any class $u \in V'$;
   (c) a key $k'_u \in \{0, 1\}^\tau$, for any class $u \in V'$;
   (d) a public information pub'.
   The sequence params, if not empty, is used to generate new keys and secret information as a consequence of the update type up. We denote by (s', k', pub') the sequences of private information, keys, and public information output by $Upd(1^\tau, G, s, k, pub, up, params)$.

The update types we consider are the following: *insertion of an edge, insertion of a class, deletion of an edge, deletion of a class, key replacement,* and *revocation of a user from a class.* Notice that some types of updates can be seen as a sequence of other types of updates. For example, the deletion of a class u can be performed by executing a sequence of edge deletions, one for each edge ingoing u and outgoing from u. On the other hand, the deletion of the edge (u, v) requires a key replacement operation for the class v. Finally, the revocation of a user from a class u requires a sequence of key replacement operations. In the above definition it is required that the updated graph G' still belongs to the family Γ of partially ordered hierarchies, i.e., only updates which preserve the partial order relation between the classes in the hierarchy are allowed.

Security with respect to Key Indistinguishability. The notion of security with respect to key indistinguishability has been extended in [13], to address the additional security challenges introduced by the algorithm Upd used for handling dynamic updates to the hierarchy. More precisely, in order to evaluate the security of a hierarchical key assignment scheme supporting dynamic updates, a *dynamic adaptive adversary* ADAPT attacking the scheme has been considered. Such an adversary can make three different types of operations: *performing a dynamic update, corrupting a class,* and *attacking a class.*

The first type of operation includes all kinds of updates described before. More precisely, consider an *updating oracle* $\mathcal{U}$, modeling the behavior of the *TA*, which performs the required updates on the hierarchy. At the beginning, the state of the updating oracle is represented by the tuple (G^0, s^0, k^0, pub^0), where (s^0, k^0, pub^0) is the output of algorithm *Gen* on inputs 1^τ and the initial graph G^0. For any $i \geq 0$, the $(i + 1)$-th adversary's query to the updating oracle consists of a pair $(up^{i+1}, params^{i+1})$, where up^{i+1} is an update operation on the graph G^i and $params^{i+1}$ is sequence of parameters associated to the update, which the oracle answers with the updated graph G^{i+1}, the public information pub^{i+1} associated to G^{i+1}, and with a sequence of keys, denoted by old_k^i, which have been modified as a consequence of the update, according to the specification of the algorithm Upd. More precisely, the updating oracle $\mathcal{U}_{(1^\tau, G^i, s^i, k^i, pub^i)}(\cdot, \cdot)$, given the query $(up^{i+1}, params^{i+1})$, runs algorithm $Upd(1^\tau, G^i, s^i, k^i, pub^i, up^{i+1}, params^{i+1})$ and returns G^{i+1}, pub^{i+1}, and old_k^i to the adversary. In the following, we denote by $\mathcal{U}^i(\cdot, \cdot)$ the oracle $\mathcal{U}_{(1^\tau, G^i, s^i, k^i, pub^i)}(\cdot, \cdot)$. Due to its adaptive nature, the adversary may require a polynomial number $m = poly(|V|, 1^\tau)$ of dynamic updates, where each update is decided on the basis of the answers obtained from the updating oracle at the previous steps.

The second type of operation is the *class corruption*, which can be performed in an adaptive order and for a polynomial number of classes. For any $i \geq 0$, consider a *corrupting oracle* $\mathcal{C}^i$, which provides the adversary with the private information held by the corrupted classes in the graph G^i. In particular, an adversary's query to the corrupting oracle $\mathcal{C}^i$ consists of a class v in the graph G^i, which the oracle answers with the private information held by class v in all graphs $G^0, G^1, \ldots, G^i$ (if v belongs to them).

Finally, the third type of operation is the *class attack*, where the adversary chooses an update index t and a class u in the hierarchy G^t and is challenged either in computing the key k_u^t or in distinguishing k_u^t from a random string in $\{0, 1\}^\tau$, depending on the security requirement.

In detail, Castiglione et al. have considered a *dynamic adaptive adversary* $\texttt{ADAPT} = (\texttt{ADAPT}_1, \texttt{ADAPT}_2)$ running in two stages [13]. In advance of the adversary's execution, the algorithm Gen is run on inputs 1^τ and G and outputs the tuple (s, k, pub), which is kept hidden from the adversary, with the exception of the public information pub. During the first stage, the adversary $\texttt{ADAPT}_1$ is given access to both updating and corrupting oracles for a polynomial number m of times. The responses obtained by the oracles are saved in some state information denoted as *history*.

After interacting with the updating and corrupting oracles, the adversary chooses an update index t and a class u in G^t, among all the classes in G^t which cannot be accessed by the corrupted classes. In particular, the chosen class u is such that, for any class v already queried to the corrupting oracle $\mathcal{C}^i(\cdot)$ and any $i = 0, \ldots, m$, v cannot access u in the hierarchy G^i. In the second stage, the adversary $\texttt{ADAPT}_2$ is given again access to the corrupting oracle and is then challenged either in computing the key k_u^t assigned to u or in distinguishing k_u^t from a random string $\rho \in \{0, 1\}^\tau$. Clearly, it is required that the key k_u^t on which the adversary will be challenged is not included in the sequence old_k^{t-1} of keys which have been updated in the graph G^t.

Definition 2 (IND-DYN-AD). *Let Γ be a family of graphs corresponding to partially ordered hierarchies, let $G = (V, E) \in \Gamma$ be a graph, and let (Gen, Der, Upd) be a hierarchical key assignment scheme for Γ supporting dynamic updates. Let $m = poly(|V|, 1^\tau)$ and let $\texttt{ADAPT} = (\texttt{ADAPT}_1, \texttt{ADAPT}_2)$ be a dynamic adaptive*

*adversary that during the first stage of the attack is given access both to the
updating oracle $\mathcal{U}^i(\cdot, \cdot)$ and the corrupting oracle $\mathcal{C}^i(\cdot)$, for $i = 1, \ldots, m$, and
during the second stage of the attack is given access only to the corrupting ora-
cle. Consider the following two experiments:*

$$\text{Experiment } \mathbf{Exp}_{\text{ADAPT}}^{\text{IND-DYN}-1}(1^\tau, G)$$
$$(s, k, pub) \leftarrow Gen(1^\tau, G)$$
$$(t, u, history) \leftarrow \text{ADAPT}_1^{\mathcal{U}^i(\cdot, \cdot), \mathcal{C}^i(\cdot)}(1^\tau, G, pub)$$
$$d \leftarrow \text{ADAPT}_2^{\mathcal{C}^i(\cdot)}(1^\tau, t, u, history, k_u^t)$$
$$\textbf{return } d$$

$$\text{Experiment } \mathbf{Exp}_{\text{ADAPT}}^{\text{IND-DYN}-0}(1^\tau, G)$$
$$(s, k, pub) \leftarrow Gen(1^\tau, G)$$
$$(t, u, history) \leftarrow \text{ADAPT}_1^{\mathcal{U}^i(\cdot, \cdot), \mathcal{C}^i(\cdot)}(1^\tau, G, pub)$$
$$\rho \leftarrow \{0, 1\}^\tau$$
$$d \leftarrow \text{ADAPT}_2^{\mathcal{C}^i(\cdot)}(1^\tau, t, u, history, \rho)$$
$$\textbf{return } d$$

*It is required that the class u output by ADAPT_1 is such that v cannot access u
in the graph G^i, for any class v already queried to the corrupting oracle $\mathcal{C}^i(\cdot)$.
Moreover, it is also required that ADAPT_2 never queries the corrupting oracle $\mathcal{C}^i(\cdot)$
on a class v such that v can access u in the graph G^t. The advantage of ADAPT
is defined as*

$$\mathbf{Adv}_{\text{ADAPT}}^{\text{IND-DYN}}(1^\tau, G) = |Pr[\mathbf{Exp}_{\text{ADAPT}}^{\text{IND-DYN}-1}(1^\tau, G) = 1]$$
$$- Pr[\mathbf{Exp}_{\text{ADAPT}}^{\text{IND-DYN}-0}(1^\tau, G) = 1]|.$$

*The scheme is said to be secure with respect to IND-DYN-AD if for each graph
$G = (V, E)$ in Γ, the function $\mathbf{Adv}_{\text{ADAPT}}^{\text{IND-DYN}}(1^\tau, G)$ is negligible, for each adaptive
adversary ADAPT whose time complexity is polynomial in τ.*

Notice that if the adversary ADAPT_1 never queries the updating oracle during the first stage of the attack, the above definition reduces to that of security
with respect to key indistinguishability against adaptive adversaries for hierarchical key assignment schemes with static hierarchies, referred to as IND-AD
in [8]. However, for such schemes, it has been shown that adaptive adversaries
are *polynomialy equivalent* to *static* ones, i.e., when the class to be attacked is
chosen in advance to the execution of the scheme.

Security with respect to Key Recovery. Now, we introduce the weaker requirement
of *security against key recovery*. As done before, we assume the existence of the
oracles $\mathcal{U}^i$ and $\mathcal{C}^i$. We require that the adversary will guess the key k_u^t with
probability only negligibly different from $1/2^\tau$.

Definition 3 (REC-DYN-AD). *Let Γ be a family of graphs corresponding to partially ordered hierarchies, let $G = (V, E) \in \Gamma$ be a graph and let (Gen, Der, Upd)
be a hierarchical key assignment scheme for Γ supporting dynamic updates. Let*

$m = poly(|V|, 1^\tau)$ and let $\mathtt{ADAPT} = (\mathtt{ADAPT}_1, \mathtt{ADAPT}_2)$ be a dynamic adaptive adversary that during the first stage of the attack is given access both to the updating oracle $\mathcal{U}^i(\cdot, \cdot)$ and the corrupting oracle $\mathcal{C}^i(\cdot)$, for $i = 1, \ldots, m$, and during the second stage of the attack is given access only to the corrupting oracle. Consider the following experiment:

$$
\begin{aligned}
&\text{Experiment } \mathbf{Exp}^{\mathtt{REC-DYN}}_{\mathtt{ADAPT}}(1^\tau, G) \\
&\quad (s, k, pub) \leftarrow Gen(1^\tau, G) \\
&\quad (t, u, history) \leftarrow \mathtt{ADAPT}_1^{\mathcal{U}^i(\cdot, \cdot), \mathcal{C}^i(\cdot)}(1^\tau, G, pub) \\
&\quad k_u^{t,*} \leftarrow \mathtt{ADAPT}_2^{\mathcal{C}^i(\cdot)}(1^\tau, t, u, history) \\
&\quad \textbf{return } k_u^{t,*}
\end{aligned}
$$

It is required that the class u output by $\mathtt{ADAPT}_1$ is such that v cannot access u in the graph G^i, for any class v already queried to the corrupting oracle $\mathcal{C}^i(\cdot)$. Moreover, it is also required that $\mathtt{ADAPT}_2$ never queries the corrupting oracle $\mathcal{C}^i(\cdot)$ on a class v such that v can access u in the graph G^t. The advantage of $\mathtt{ADAPT}$ is defined as

$$
\mathbf{Adv}^{\mathtt{REC-DYN}}_{\mathtt{ADAPT}}(1^\tau, G) = Pr[k_u^{t,*} = k_u^t].
$$

The scheme is said to be secure with respect to $\mathtt{REC-DYN-AD}$ if, for each graph $G = (V, E)$ in Γ, the function $\mathbf{Adv}^{\mathtt{REC-DYN}}_{\mathtt{ADAPT}}(1^\tau, G)$ is negligible, for each adaptive adversary $\mathtt{ADAPT}$ whose time complexity is polynomial in τ.

If the adversary $\mathtt{ADAPT}_1$ never queries the updating oracle during the first stage of the attack, the above definition reduces to that of security against key recovery in presence of adaptive adversaries for hierarchical key assignment schemes with static hierarchies, referred to as $\mathtt{REC-AD}$ in [8].

3 Relations Among Security Notions

As mentioned before, Freire et al. strengthened the security notions introduced in [3] to deal with a wider set of concrete attacks. More precisely, they enable the adversary to access the encryption keys for all the classes that precede the target class. In fact, such keys might leak due to usage, e.g., cryptanalysis or misuse and this may cause a compromise of the private information or encryption key for the target class. Therefore, the model proposed by Freire et al. provides the adversary with this further compromise capability.

In the following, we extend the security notions introduced by Freire et al. to hierarchical key assignment schemes supporting dynamic updates. In our model, the adversary can access the keys assigned to all the classes in the set P_u^t, which denotes the predecessors of class u in the graph G^t. Let $Keys_u$ be an algorithm that taken as input the encryption keys k^t assigned to the classes in G^t, extracts the keys k_v^t assigned to all the classes $v \in P_u^t$. We denote by $keys_{u,t}$ the output returned by $Keys_u(k^t)$.

Security with respect to Strong Key Indistinguishability. The next definition formalizes the *strong key indistinguishability* requirement for hierarchical key assignment schemes supporting dynamic updates.

Definition 4 (STRONG-IND-DYN-AD). *Let Γ be a family of graphs corresponding to partially ordered hierarchies, let $G = (V, E) \in \Gamma$ be a graph, and let (Gen, Der, Upd) be a hierarchical key assignment scheme for Γ supporting dynamic updates. Let $m = poly(|V|, 1^\tau)$ and let $\mathrm{ADAPT} = (\mathrm{ADAPT}_1, \mathrm{ADAPT}_2)$ be a dynamic adaptive adversary that during the first stage of the attack is given access both to the updating oracle $\mathcal{U}^i(\cdot, \cdot)$ and the corrupting oracle $\mathcal{C}^i(\cdot)$, for $i = 1, \ldots, m$, and during the second stage of the attack is given access only to the corrupting oracle. Consider the following two experiments:*

> Experiment $\mathbf{Exp}_{\mathrm{ADAPT}}^{\mathrm{STRONG-IND-DYN}-1}(1^\tau, G)$
> $(s, k, pub) \leftarrow Gen(1^\tau, G)$
> $(t, u, history) \leftarrow \mathrm{ADAPT}_1^{\mathcal{U}^i(\cdot, \cdot), \mathcal{C}^i(\cdot)}(1^\tau, G, pub)$
> $keys_{u,t} \leftarrow Keys_u(k^t)$
> $d \leftarrow \mathrm{ADAPT}_2^{\mathcal{C}^i(\cdot)}(1^\tau, t, u, history, keys_{u,t}, k_u^t)$
>   **return** d

> Experiment $\mathbf{Exp}_{\mathrm{ADAPT}}^{\mathrm{STRONG-IND-DYN}-0}(1^\tau, G)$
> $(s, k, pub) \leftarrow Gen(1^\tau, G)$
> $(t, u, history) \leftarrow \mathrm{ADAPT}_1^{\mathcal{U}^i(\cdot, \cdot), \mathcal{C}^i(\cdot)}(1^\tau, G, pub)$
> $keys_{u,t} \leftarrow Keys_u(k^t)$
> $\rho \leftarrow \{0, 1\}^\tau$
> $d \leftarrow \mathrm{ADAPT}_2^{\mathcal{C}^i(\cdot)}(1^\tau, t, u, history, keys_{u,t}, \rho)$
>   **return** d

We require that the class u output by ADAPT_1 is such that v cannot access u in the graph G^i, for any class v already queried to the corrupting oracle $\mathcal{C}^i(\cdot)$. Moreover, we also require that ADAPT_2 never queries the corrupting oracle $\mathcal{C}^i(\cdot)$ on a class v such that v can access u in the graph G^t. The advantage of ADAPT is defined as

$$\mathbf{Adv}_{\mathrm{ADAPT}}^{\mathrm{STRONG-IND-DYN}}(1^\tau, G) = |Pr[\mathbf{Exp}_{\mathrm{ADAPT}}^{\mathrm{STRONG-IND-DYN}-1}(1^\tau, G) = 1]$$
$$- Pr[\mathbf{Exp}_{\mathrm{ADAPT}}^{\mathrm{STRONG-IND-DYN}-0}(1^\tau, G) = 1]|.$$

The scheme is said to be secure with respect to STRONG-IND-DYN-AD *if for each graph $G = (V, E)$ in Γ, the function $\mathbf{Adv}_{\mathrm{ADAPT}}^{\mathrm{STRONG-IND-DYN}}(1^\tau, G)$ is negligible, for each adaptive adversary ADAPT whose time complexity is polynomial in τ.*

Security with respect to Strong Key Recovery. Now, we consider the weaker requirement of *security against strong key recovery* for hierarchical key assignment schemes supporting dynamic updates. As done before, we assume the existence of the oracles $\mathcal{U}^i$ and $\mathcal{C}^i$. We require that the adversary will guess the key k_u^t with probability only negligibly different from $1/2^\tau$.

Definition 5 (STRONG-REC-DYN-AD). *Let Γ be a family of graphs corresponding to partially ordered hierarchies, let $G = (V, E) \in \Gamma$ be a graph and let (Gen, Der, Upd) be a hierarchical key assignment scheme for Γ supporting dynamic updates. Let $m = poly(|V|, 1^\tau)$ and let $\text{ADAPT} = (\text{ADAPT}_1, \text{ADAPT}_2)$ be a dynamic adaptive adversary that during the first stage of the attack is given access both to the updating oracle $\mathcal{U}^i(\cdot, \cdot)$ and the corrupting oracle $\mathcal{C}^i(\cdot)$, for $i = 1, \ldots, m$, and during the second stage of the attack is given access only to the corrupting oracle. Consider the following experiment:*

$$\text{Experiment } \mathbf{Exp}_{\text{ADAPT}}^{\text{STRONG-REC-DYN}}(1^\tau, G)$$
$$(s, k, pub) \leftarrow Gen(1^\tau, G)$$
$$(t, u, history) \leftarrow \text{ADAPT}_1^{\mathcal{U}^i(\cdot, \cdot), \mathcal{C}^i(\cdot)}(1^\tau, G, pub)$$
$$keys_{u,t} \leftarrow Keys_u(k^t)$$
$$k_u^{t,*} \leftarrow \text{ADAPT}_2^{\mathcal{C}^i(\cdot)}(1^\tau, t, u, history, keys_{u,t})$$
$$\mathbf{return} \ k_u^{t,*}$$

It is required that the class u output by ADAPT_1 is such that v cannot access u in the graph G^i, for any class v already queried to the corrupting oracle $\mathcal{C}^i(\cdot)$. Moreover, it is also required that ADAPT_2 never queries the corrupting oracle $\mathcal{C}^i(\cdot)$ on a class v such that v can access u in the graph G^t. The advantage of ADAPT is defined as

$$\mathbf{Adv}_{\text{ADAPT}}^{\text{STRONG-REC-DYN}}(1^\tau, G) = Pr[k_u^{t,*} = k_u^t].$$

The scheme is said to be secure with respect to STRONG-REC-DYN-AD *if, for each graph $G = (V, E)$ in Γ, the function $\mathbf{Adv}_{\text{ADAPT}}^{\text{STRONG-REC-DYN}}(1^\tau, G)$ is negligible, for each adaptive adversary ADAPT whose time complexity is polynomial in τ.*

Following the same lines as Theorems 4.1, 4.2, 4.3, 4.4 and 4.5 in [11] the next results can be easily proven.

Theorem 1 (STRONG-IND-DYN-AD$\Rightarrow$STRONG-REC-DYN-AD). *Let Γ be a family of graphs characterizing partially ordered hierarchies. If a hierarchical key assignment scheme for Γ supporting dynamic updates is secure with respect to STRONG-IND-DYN-AD, then it is also secure with respect to STRONG-REC-DYN-AD.*

Theorem 2 (STRONG-REC-DYN-AD$\not\Rightarrow$STRONG-IND-DYN-AD). *Let Γ be a family of graphs characterizing partially ordered hierarchies. If there exists a hierarchical key assignment scheme for Γ supporting dynamic updates that is secure with respect to STRONG-REC-DYN-AD, then there exists a hierarchical key assignment scheme for Γ supporting dynamic updates which is secure with respect to STRONG-REC-DYN-AD but is not secure with respect to STRONG-IND-DYN-AD.*

Theorem 3 (STRONG-REC-DYN-AD$\Rightarrow$REC-DYN-AD). *Let Γ be a family of graphs characterizing partially ordered hierarchies. If a hierarchical key assignment scheme for Γ supporting dynamic updates is secure with respect to STRONG-REC-DYN-AD, then it is also secure with respect to REC-DYN-AD.*

Theorem 4 (REC-DYN-AD$\not\Rightarrow$STRONG-REC-DYN-AD). *Let Γ be a family of graphs characterizing partially ordered hierarchies. If there exists a hierarchical key assignment scheme for Γ supporting dynamic updates that is secure with respect to* REC-DYN-AD, *then there exists a hierarchical key assignment scheme for Γ supporting dynamic updates which is secure with respect to* REC-DYN-AD *but which is not secure with respect to* STRONG-REC-DYN-AD.

Theorem 5 (STRONG-IND-DYN-AD$\Rightarrow$IND-DYN-AD). *Let Γ be a family of graphs characterizing partially ordered hierarchies. If a hierarchical key assignment scheme for Γ supporting dynamic updates is secure with respect to* STRONG-IND-DYN-AD, *then it is also secure with respect to* IND-DYN-AD.

Following the lines of Theorem 4.6 in [11] we prove that the notion of security with respect to strong key indistinguishability is equivalent to the one of key indistinguishability, namely, STRONG-IND-DYN-AD is *not stronger* than IND-DYN-AD.

Theorem 6 (IND-DYN-AD$\Rightarrow$STRONG-IND-DYN-AD). *Let Γ be a family of graphs characterizing partially ordered hierarchies. If a hierarchical key assignment scheme for Γ supporting dynamic updates is secure with respect to* IND-DYN-AD, *then it is also secure with respect to* STRONG-IND-DYN-AD.

Proof. Let Γ be a family of graphs characterizing partially ordered hierarchies. Assume by contradiction that there exists a hierarchical key assignment scheme Σ for Γ supporting dynamic updates which is secure with respect to IND-DYN-AD but that is not secure with respect to STRONG-IND-DYN-AD.

As a consequence, there exists a graph $G = (V, E)$ in Γ and a dynamic adaptive adversary ADAPT $=$ (ADAPT$_1$, ADAPT$_2$) which distinguishes between experiments $\mathbf{Exp}_{\text{ADAPT}}^{\text{STRONG}-\text{IND}-\text{DYN}-1}(1^\tau, G)$ and $\mathbf{Exp}_{\text{ADAPT}}^{\text{STRONG}-\text{IND}-\text{DYN}-0}(1^\tau, G)$ with non-negligible probability. We remark that the only difference between such two experiments is the last input of ADAPT, corresponding to the real key k_u^t assigned by the scheme Σ to class u after the t-th update in the former experiment and to a random value $\rho \in \{0,1\}^\tau$ in the latter. Let $q(n, 1^\tau)$ be the running-time of ADAPT, where q is a bivariate polynomial. For any $i = 1, \ldots, q(n, 1^\tau)$, let $\mathbf{S}_i$ be an adversary which behaves as ADAPT$_1$ until the choice of the key to be attacked. If the chosen key is equal to k_i, then $\mathbf{S}_i$ continues to follow ADAPT$_2$, otherwise it outputs 0. The advantage of ADAPT can be written as

$$\mathbf{Adv}_{\text{ADAPT}}^{\text{IND}-\text{DYN}}(1^\tau, G) \leq \sum_{i=1}^{q(n,1^\tau)} Pr[\text{ADAPT}_1 \text{ chooses } k_i] \cdot \mathbf{Adv}_{\mathbf{S}_i}^{\text{IND}-\text{DYN}}(1^\tau, G).$$

Since $\mathbf{Adv}_{\text{ADAPT}}^{\text{STRONG}-\text{IND}-\text{DYN}}(1^\tau, G)$ is non-negligible, then there exists at least an index h, where $1 \leq h \leq q(n, 1^\tau)$, such that $\mathbf{Adv}_{\mathbf{S}_h}^{\text{STRONG}-\text{IND}-\text{DYN}}(1^\tau, G)$ is non-negligible.

We distinguish the two following cases:

- **Case 1:** $h \geq n + 1$. This case corresponds to the scenario where the key k_h chosen by the adversary either has been created, due to a class insertion operation, or has been modified, due to a key replacement operation.
- **Case 2:** $1 \leq h \leq n$. This case corresponds to the scenario where the key k_h chosen by the adversary has been assigned to some class in the initial graph G.

Analysis of Case 1 Assume that the key k_h chosen by the adversary either has been created or has been modified by the t-th update operation, which has assigned such a key to a certain class u in the graph G^t. Thus, attacking the key k_h corresponds to attacking the class u in the graph G^t obtained after the t-th update. Let P_u^t be the set of predecessor of class u in G^t. Let $(u_1, \ldots, u_m)$ be the output of a deterministic algorithm Alg which, on input the set of predecessors of u, finds a topological ordering of the classes in the subgraph of G^t induced by P_u^t.

We remark that the sequence $keys_{u,t}$, taken as input by ADAPT, in both the experiments $\mathbf{Exp}_{S_h}^{\texttt{STRONG-IND-DYN-1}}(1^\tau, G)$ and $\mathbf{Exp}_{S_h}^{\texttt{STRONG-IND-DYN-0}}(1^\tau, G)$ contains exactly the keys $k_{u_1}^t, \ldots, k_{u_m}^t$. Notice that if $m = 0$ the sequence $keys_{u,t}$ is empty, hence the experiments $\mathbf{Exp}_{S_h}^{\texttt{STRONG-IND-DYN-1}}(1^\tau, G)$ and $\mathbf{Exp}_{S_h}^{\texttt{STRONG-IND-DYN-0}}(1^\tau, G)$ correspond to $\mathbf{Exp}_{S_h}^{\texttt{IND-DYN-1}}(1^\tau, G)$ and $\mathbf{Exp}_{S_h}^{\texttt{IND-DYN-0}}(1^\tau, G)$, respectively. In this case, since S_h can distinguish between the above experiments with non-negligible probability, this implies that the scheme Σ is not secure with respect to IND-DYN-AD, thus leading to a contradiction.

Again, consider the case where $m > 0$. In the following we demonstrate how to transform the adversary S_h into a polynomial-time adversary S'_{u_ℓ}, where $u_\ell \in P_u^t$, which breaks the scheme Σ with respect to IND-DYN-AD, thus leading to a contradiction. More precisely, we create two sequences, referred to as $\mathbf{Exp}_{u,t}^{1,1}, \ldots, \mathbf{Exp}_{u,t}^{1,m+1}$ and $\mathbf{Exp}_{u,t}^{2,1}, \ldots, \mathbf{Exp}_{u,t}^{2,m+1}$, respectively, each composed of $m + 1$ experiments, all defined over the same probability space, in which the first experiment of the former sequence, that is $\mathbf{Exp}_{u,t}^{1,1}$, is equal to $\mathbf{Exp}_{S_h}^{\texttt{STRONG-IND-DYN-0}}$, whereas, the last experiment of the latter sequence, that is $\mathbf{Exp}_{u,t}^{2,m+1}$, is equal to $\mathbf{Exp}_{S_h}^{\texttt{STRONG-IND-DYN-1}}$. For any $q = 2, \ldots, m + 1$, the experiment $\mathbf{Exp}_{u,t}^{1,q}$ in the former sequence is defined as follows:

$$
\begin{aligned}
&\text{Experiment } \mathbf{Exp}_{u,t}^{1,q}(1^\tau, G) \\
&\quad (s, k, pub) \leftarrow Gen(1^\tau, G) \\
&\quad (t, u, history) \leftarrow \texttt{ADAPT}_1^{\mathcal{U}^i(\cdot, \cdot), \mathcal{C}^i(\cdot)}(1^\tau, G, pub) \\
&\quad keys_{u,t}^q \leftarrow Keys_u^q(k^t) \\
&\quad d \leftarrow \texttt{ADAPT}_2^{\mathcal{C}^i(\cdot)}(1^\tau, t, u, history, keys_{u,t}^q, \rho) \\
&\quad \textbf{return } d
\end{aligned}
$$

The algorithm $Keys_u^q$ returns as output the sequence $keys_{u,t}^q$, in which the first $q - 1$ values are chosen independently at random in $\{0,1\}^\tau$ and, if $q \leq m$, the other $m - q + 1$ values are set equal to the keys of the classes $u_q, \ldots, u_m$ in the graph G^t. Again, for any $q = 1, \ldots, m$, experiment $\mathbf{Exp}_{u,t}^{2,q}$ in the second sequence is defined as follows:

$$\begin{aligned}
&\text{Experiment } \mathbf{Exp}_{u,t}^{2,q}(1^\tau, G)\\
&\quad (s, k, pub) \leftarrow Gen(1^\tau, G)\\
&\quad (t, u, history) \leftarrow \mathtt{ADAPT}_1^{\mathcal{U}^i(\cdot,\cdot), \mathcal{C}^i(\cdot)}(1^\tau, G, pub)\\
&\quad keys_{u,t}^{m-q+2} \leftarrow Keys_u^{m-q+1}(k^t)\\
&\quad d \leftarrow \mathtt{ADAPT}_2^{\mathcal{C}^i(\cdot)}(1^\tau, t, u, history, keys_{u,t}^{m-q+2}, k_u^t)\\
&\quad \textbf{return } d
\end{aligned}$$

where $keys_{u,t}^{m-q+2}$ represents the sequence in which the first $m - q + 1$ values are chosen independently at random in $\{0,1\}^\tau$ and, if $q \geq 2$, the other $q - 1$ values are set equal to the keys of the classes $u_{m-q+2}, \ldots, u_m$ in the graph G^t.

Since S_h can distinguish with non-negligible probability between $\mathbf{Exp}_{u,t}^{1,1}$, which corresponds to $\mathbf{Exp}_{\mathsf{S}_h}^{\mathtt{STRONG-IND-DYN-0}}$, and $\mathbf{Exp}_{u,t}^{2,m+1}$, which corresponds to $\mathbf{Exp}_{\mathsf{S}_h}^{\mathtt{STRONG-IND-DYN-1}}$, then there exists at least a pair of adjacent experiments, in the sequence of $2m + 2$ experiments obtained by composing the two aforementioned sequences, which can be distinguished by S_h with non-negligible probability.

We first show that such a pair cannot consist of the two extremal experiments, namely, the last experiment of the first sequence, that is $\mathbf{Exp}_{u,t}^{1,m+1}$, and the first experiment of the second sequence, that is $\mathbf{Exp}_{u,t}^{2,1}$. Assume by contradiction that S_h is able to distinguish between $\mathbf{Exp}_{u,t}^{1,m+1}$ and $\mathbf{Exp}_{u,t}^{2,1}$ with non-negligible probability. Notice that the only difference between such two experiments is the last input of S_h, corresponding to a random value chosen in $\{0,1\}^\tau$ in experiment $\mathbf{Exp}_{u,t}^{1,m+1}$, and to the real key k_u^t in experiment $\mathbf{Exp}_{u,t}^{2,1}$. We show how to create another adversary S'_h breaking the security of the scheme Σ with respect to $\mathtt{IND-DYN-AD}$, by using the adversary S_h. The adversary S'_h, on inputs 1^τ, t, u, $history$, and a value α, which corresponds either to the key k_u^t or to a random value chosen in $\{0,1\}^\tau$, creates the sequence $keys_{u,t}^{m+1}$ needed for S_h choosing independently at random m elements in $\{0,1\}^\tau$. Then, S'_h returns the same output as $\mathsf{S}_h(1^\tau, t, u, history, keys_{u,t}^{m+1}, \alpha)$. Clearly, since S_h can distinguish between $\mathbf{Exp}_{u,t}^{1,m+1}$ and $\mathbf{Exp}_{u,t}^{2,1}$ with non-negligible probability, then S'_h can distinguish between $\mathbf{Exp}_{\mathsf{S}'_h}^{\mathtt{IND-DYN-AD-0}}$ and $\mathbf{Exp}_{\mathsf{S}'_h}^{\mathtt{IND-DYN-AD-1}}$ with non-negligible probability, thus breaking the security of the scheme Σ with respect to $\mathtt{IND-DYN-AD}$. Contradiction. Therefore, the pair of adjacent experiments that S_h can distinguish belongs either to the first sequence or to the second one.

Without loss of generality, assume that the pair of adjacent experiments which S_h can distinguish belongs to the first sequence and it is composed of $\mathbf{Exp}_{u,t}^{1,\ell}$ and $\mathbf{Exp}_{u,t}^{1,\ell+1}$, for some $\ell = 1, \ldots, m$. We remark that the views of S_h in the aforementioned adjacent experiments differ only in one value, corresponding to the key $k_{u_\ell}^t$ in $\mathbf{Exp}_{u,t}^{1,\ell}$ and to a random value chosen in $\{0,1\}^\tau$ in

$\mathbf{Exp}_{u,t}^{1,\ell+1}$. In the following we show how to create an adversary S''_{u_ℓ}, which by using the adversary S_h is able to break the security of the scheme Σ with respect to IND-DYN-AD. More precisely, we show that S''_{u_ℓ} can distinguish between the experiments $\mathbf{Exp}_{S''_{u_\ell}}^{\text{IND-DYN-AD-0}}$ and $\mathbf{Exp}_{S'_{u_\ell}}^{\text{IND-DYN-AD-1}}$ with non-negligible probability. The adversary S''_{u_ℓ}, on inputs 1^τ, t, u_ℓ, $history$ and a value α, which corresponds either to the key $k_{u_\ell}^t$ or to a random value chosen in $\{0,1\}^\tau$, constructs the inputs for S_h as follows:

- Extracts from $history$ the private information stored by corrupted classes. This can be done since $u_\ell \in P_u$, i.e., u_ℓ is a predecessor of u, hence the classes corrupted for u are also corrupted for u_ℓ, and their private information is stored in $history$.
- Uses the above private information and α to construct a sequence $keys_{u,t}^\alpha$, which corresponds either to $keys_{u,t}^\ell$ or to $keys_{u,t}^{\ell+1}$. More precisely, the first $\ell - 1$ elements of $keys_{u,t}^\alpha$ are chosen independently at random in $\{0,1\}^\tau$, the ℓ-th element corresponds to α, while the other $m - \ell$ elements, corresponding to the keys of classes $u_{\ell+1}, \ldots, u_m$ in G^t, are computed through the private information of these classes, which are stored in $history$.
- Furthermore, the final input for S_h is set equal to a random value ρ chosen in $\{0,1\}^\tau$.

Finally, S''_{u_ℓ} returns as output the same output as $S_h(1^\tau, t, u, history, keys_{u,t}^\alpha, \rho)$. It is easy to note that since S_h can distinguish between $\mathbf{Exp}_{u,t}^{1,\ell}$ and $\mathbf{Exp}_{u,t}^{1,\ell+1}$ with non-negligible probability, then S''_{u_ℓ} can distinguish between $\mathbf{Exp}_{S''_{u_\ell}}^{\text{IND-DYN-AD-0}}$ and $\mathbf{Exp}_{S''_{u_\ell}}^{\text{IND-DYN-AD-1}}$ with non-negligible probability, hence breaking the security of the scheme Σ with respect to IND-DYN-AD. Contradiction.

We remark that if the pair of adjacent experiments which can be distinguished belongs to the second sequence, namely, it is composed of $\mathbf{Exp}_{u,t}^{2,\ell}$ and $\mathbf{Exp}_{u,t}^{2,\ell+1}$, for some $\ell = 1, \ldots, m$, then the proof works similarly to the previous case.

Analysis of Case 2 As done for **Case 1**, we can show that no adversary S_h, where $1 \leq h \leq n$, distinguishes between experiments $\mathbf{Exp}_{S_h}^{\text{STRONG-IND-DYN-0}}$ and $\mathbf{Exp}_{S_h}^{\text{STRONG-IND-DYN-1}}$ with non-negligible probability.

To conclude, we have proven that no dynamic adaptive adversary ADAPT has non-negligible probability in distinguishing between experiments $\mathbf{Exp}_{\text{ADAPT}}^{\text{STRONG-IND-DYN-0}}$ and $\mathbf{Exp}_{\text{ADAPT}}^{\text{STRONG-IND-DYN-1}}$. Thus, the scheme is secure with respect to STRONG − IND − DYN.

In Fig. 1 we summarize implications and separations occurring between security notions for hierarchical key assignment schemes supporting dynamic updates. Notice that the relations represented by the arrows without label can be deduced trivially, due to the equivalence between STRONG-IND-DYN-AD and IND-DYN-AD security notions.

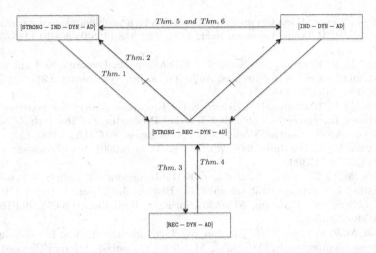

Fig. 1. Overview of the relations occurring between security notions for hierarchical key assignment schemes supporting dynamic updates.

4 Conclusions

In this paper we focused on hierarchical key assignment schemes for dynamic structures, i.e., supporting dynamic updates such as insertions/deletions of classes and relations between classes, as well as key replacements and user revocations.

In particular, we have first extended to the dynamic setting the existing security definitions for hierarchical key assignment schemes proposed by Freire et al., namely, security with respect to *strong key indistinguishability* and *strong key recovery*, by providing the adversary with further attack abilities.

Moreover, we have investigated the relations occurring between the security notions for hierarchical key assignment schemes for dynamic structures, by showing implications and separations which hold between those notions. More precisely, we have shown that also for what concerns dynamic structures, security with respect to strong key indistinguishability is equivalent to that with respect to key indistinguishability. Therefore, the notion of strong key indistinguishability is *not stronger* than the one with respect to key indistinguishability.

Acknowledgments. This work has been partially supported by the Italian Ministry of Research within PRIN project "GenData 2020" (2010RTFWBH).

References

1. Aho, A.V., Garey, M.R., Ullman, J.D.: The transitive reduction of a directed graph. SIAM J. Comput. **1**(2), 131–137 (1972). doi:10.1137/0201008

2. Akl, S.G., Taylor, P.D.: Cryptographic solution to a problem of access control in a hierarchy. ACM Trans. Comput. Syst. **1**(3), 239–248 (1983). doi:10.1145/357369. 357372
3. Atallah, M.J., Blanton, M., Fazio, N., Frikken, K.B.: Dynamic and efficient key management for access hierarchies. ACM Trans. Inf. Syst. Secur. **12**(3), 18 (2009). doi:10.1145/1455526.1455531
4. Atallah, M.J., Blanton, M., Frikken, K.B.: Key management for non-tree access hierarchies. In: Ferraiolo, D.F., Ray, I. (eds.) Proceedings of the 11th ACM Symposium on Access Control Models and Technologies, SACMAT 2006, Lake Tahoe, California, USA, 7–9 June 2006, pp. 11–18. ACM (2006). http://doi.acm.org/10. 1145/1133058.1133062
5. Atallah, M.J., Blanton, M., Frikken, K.B.: Incorporating temporal capabilities in existing key management schemes. In: Biskup, J., López, J. (eds.) ESORICS 2007. LNCS, vol. 4734, pp. 515–530. Springer, Heidelberg (2007). doi:10.1007/ 978-3-540-74835-9_34
6. Atallah, M.J., Frikken, K.B., Blanton, M.: Dynamic and efficient key management for access hierarchies. In: Atluri, V., Meadows, C., Juels, A. (eds.) Proceedings of the 12th ACM Conference on Computer and Communications Security, CCS 2005, Alexandria, VA, USA, 7–11 November 2005, pp. 190–202. ACM (2005). http:// doi.acm.org/10.1145/1102120.1102147
7. Ateniese, G., De Santis, A., Ferrara, A.L., Masucci, B.: Provably-securetime-bound hierarchical key assignment schemes. In: Juels, A., Wright, R.N., di Vimercati, S.D.C. (eds.) Proceedings of the 13th ACM Conference on Computer and Communications Security, CCS 2006, Alexandria, VA, USA, October 30–November 3 2006, pp. 288–297. ACM (2006). http://doi.acm.org/10.1145/1180405.1180441
8. Ateniese, G., De Santis, A., Ferrara, A.L., Masucci, B.: Provably-secure time-bound hierarchical key assignment schemes. J. Cryptology **25**(2), 243–270 (2012). doi:10. 1007/s00145-010-9094-6
9. Cafaro, M., Civino, R., Masucci, B.: On the equivalence of two security notions for hierarchical key assignment schemes in the unconditional setting. IEEE Trans. Dependable Sec. Comput. **12**(4), 485–490 (2015)
10. Castiglione, A., De Santis, A., Masucci, B.: Hierarchical and shared key assignment. In: 17th International Conference on Network-Based InformationSystems, NBIS 2014, pp. 263–270. IEEE (2014). http://dx.doi.org/10.1109/NBiS.2014.106
11. Castiglione, A., De Santis, A., Masucci, B.: Key indistinguishability vs. strong key indistinguishability for hierarchical key assignment schemes. IEEE Trans. Dependable Sec. Comput. (2015). http://dx.doi.org/10.1109/TDSC.2015.2413415
12. Castiglione, A., De Santis, A., Masucci, B., Palmieri, F., Castiglione, A., Li, J., Huang, X.: Hierarchical and shared access control. IEEE Trans. Inf. Forensics Secur. **11**(4), 850–865 (2016). doi:10.1109/TIFS.2015.2512533
13. Castiglione, A., De Santis, A., Masucci, B., et al.: Cryptographic hierarchical access control for dynamic structures. Manuscript Submitted for Publication in IEEE Transactions of Information Forensics and Security (2015)
14. Chen, T., Chung, Y.: Hierarchical access control based on chinese remainder theorem and symmetric algorithm. Comput. Secur. **21**(6), 565–570 (2002). doi:10.1016/ S0167-4048(02)01016-7
15. Chien, H.: Efficient time-bound hierarchical key assignment scheme. IEEE Trans. Knowl. Data Eng. **16**(10), 1301–1304 (2004). doi:10.1109/TKDE.2004.59

16. D'Arco, P., De Santis, A., Ferrara, A.L., Masucci, B.: Security and tradeoffs of the Akl-Taylor scheme and its variants. In: Královič, R., Niwiński, D. (eds.) MFCS 2009. LNCS, vol. 5734, pp. 247–257. Springer, Heidelberg (2009). doi:10.1007/978-3-642-03816-7_22

17. D'Arco, P., Santis, A.D., Ferrara, A.L., Masucci, B.: Variations on a theme by Akl and Taylor: security and tradeoffs. Theor. Comput. Sci. **411**(1), 213–227 (2010). doi:10.1016/j.tcs.2009.09.028

18. De Santis, A., Ferrara, A.L., Masucci, B.: Cryptographic key assignment schemes for any access control policy. Inf. Process. Lett. **92**(4), 199–205 (2004)

19. De Santis, A., Ferrara, A.L., Masucci, B.: Enforcing the security of a time-bound hierarchical key assignment scheme. Inf. Sci. **176**(12), 1684–1694 (2006). doi:10.1016/j.ins.2005.07.002

20. De Santis, A., Ferrara, A.L., Masucci, B.: Unconditionally secure key assignment schemes. Discrete Appl. Math. **154**(2), 234–252 (2006). doi:10.1016/j.dam.2005.03.025

21. De Santis, A., Ferrara, A.L., Masucci, B.: Efficient provably-secure hierarchical key assignment schemes. In: Kučera, L., Kučera, A. (eds.) MFCS 2007. LNCS, vol. 4708, pp. 371–382. Springer, Heidelberg (2007). doi:10.1007/978-3-540-74456-6_34

22. De Santis, A., Ferrara, A.L., Masucci, B.: New constructions for provably-secure time-bound hierarchical key assignment schemes. In: Lotz, V., Thuraisingham, B.M. (eds.) Proceedings of the 12th ACM Symposium on Access Control Models and Technologies, SACMAT 2007, Sophia Antipolis, France, 20–22 June 2007, pp. 133–138. ACM (2007). http://doi.acm.org/10.1145/1266840.1266861

23. De Santis, A., Ferrara, A.L., Masucci, B.: New constructions for provably-secure time-bound hierarchical key assignment schemes. Theor. Comput. Sci. **407**(1–3), 213–230 (2008). doi:10.1016/j.tcs.2008.05.021

24. De Santis, A., Ferrara, A.L., Masucci, B.: Efficient provably-secure hierarchical key assignment schemes. Theor. Comput. Sci. **412**(41), 5684–5699 (2011). doi:10.1016/j.tcs.2011.06.024

25. Freire, E.S.V., Paterson, K.G.: Provably secure key assignment schemes from factoring. In: Parampalli, U., Hawkes, P. (eds.) ACISP 2011. LNCS, vol. 6812, pp. 292–309. Springer, Heidelberg (2011). doi:10.1007/978-3-642-22497-3_19

26. Freire, E.S.V., Paterson, K.G., Poettering, B.: Simple, efficient and strongly KI-secure hierarchical key assignment schemes. In: Dawson, E. (ed.) CT-RSA 2013. LNCS, vol. 7779, pp. 101–114. Springer, Heidelberg (2013)

27. Harn, L., Lin, H.: A cryptographic key generation scheme for multilevel data security. Comput. Secur. **9**(6), 539–546 (1990). doi:10.1016/0167-4048(90)90132-D

28. Huang, H., Chang, C.: A new cryptographic key assignment scheme with time-constraint access control in a hierarchy. Comput. Stan. Interfaces **26**(3), 159–166 (2004). doi:10.1016/S0920-5489(03)00073-4

29. Liaw, H., Wang, S., Lei, C.: A dynamic cryptographic key assignment scheme in a tree structure. Comput. Math. Appl. **25**(6), 109–114 (1993). http://www.sciencedirect.com/science/article/pii/089812219390305F

30. Lin, C.H.: Dynamic key management schemes for access control in a hierarchy. Comput. Commun. **20**(15), 1381–1385 (1997). http://www.sciencedirect.com/science/article/pii/S014036649700100X

31. Lin, I.C., Hwang, M.S., Chang, C.C.: A new key assignment scheme for enforcing complicated access control policies in hierarchy. Future Gener. Comput. Syst. 19(4), pp. 457 – 462 (2003). http://www.sciencedirect.com/science/article/pii/S0167739X02002005. Selected Papers from the IEEE/ACM International Symposium on Cluster Computing and the Grid, Berlin-Brandenburg Academy of Sciences and Humanities, Berlin, Germany, 21–24 May 2002

32. MacKinnon, S.J., Taylor, P.D., Meijer, H., Akl, S.G.: An optimal algorithm for assigning cryptographic keys to control access in a hierarchy. IEEE Trans. Comput. **34**(9), 797–802 (1985). doi:10.1109/TC.1985.1676635

33. Min-Shiang, H.: A cryptographic key assignment scheme in a hierarchy for access control. Math. Comput. Model. **26**(2), 27–31 (1997). doi:10.1016/S0895-7177(97)00120-9

34. Sandhu, R.S.: Cryptographic implementation of a tree hierarchy for access control. Inf. Process. Lett. **27**(2), 95–98 (1988). doi:10.1016/0020-0190(88)90099-3

35. Shen, V.R.L., Chen, T.: A novel key management scheme based on discrete logarithms and polynomial interpolations. Comput. Secur. **21**(2), 164–171 (2002). doi:10.1016/S0167-4048(02)00211-0

36. Tang, Q., Mitchell, C.J.: Comments on a cryptographic key assignment scheme. Comput. Stan. Interfaces **27**(3), 323–326 (2005). doi:10.1016/j.csi.2004.07.001

37. Tzeng, W.: A time-bound cryptographic key assignment scheme for access control in a hierarchy. IEEE Trans. Knowl. Data Eng. **14**(1), 182–188 (2002). doi:10.1109/69.979981

38. Tzeng, W.: A secure system for data access based on anonymous authentication and time-dependent hierarchical keys. In: Lin, F., Lee, D., Lin, B.P., Shieh, S., Jajodia, S. (eds.) Proceedings of the 2006 ACM Symposium on Information, Computer and Communications Security, ASIACCS 2006, Taipei,Taiwan, 21–24 March 2006, pp. 223–230. ACM (2006). http://doi.acm.org/10.1145/1128817.1128851

39. Wang, S., Laih, C.: Merging: an efficient solution for a time-bound hierarchical key assignment scheme. IEEE Trans. Dependable Sec. Comput. **3**(1), 91–100 (2006). doi:10.1109/TDSC.2006.15

40. Wu, T., Chang, C.: Cryptographic key assignment scheme for hierarchical access control. Comput. Syst. Sci. Eng. **16**(1), 25–28 (2001)

41. Yeh, J., Chow, R., Newman, R.: A key assignment for enforcing access control policy exceptions. In: Proceedings of the International Symposium on Internet Technology, pp. 54–59 (1998)

42. Yeh, J.: An RSA-based time-bound hierarchical key assignment scheme for electronic article subscription. In: Herzog, O., Schek, H., Fuhr, N., Chowdhury, A., Teiken, W. (eds.) Proceedings of the 2005 ACM CIKM International Conference on Information and Knowledge Management, Bremen,Germany, 31 October–5 November 2005, pp. 285–286. ACM (2005). http://doi.acm.org/10.1145/1099554.1099629

43. Yi, X.: Security of chien's efficient time-bound hierarchical key assignment scheme. IEEE Trans. Knowl. Data Eng. **17**(9), 1298–1299 (2005). doi:10.1109/TKDE.2005.152

44. Yi, X., Ye, Y.: Security of tzeng's time-bound key assignment scheme for access control in a hierarchy. IEEE Trans. Knowl. Data Eng. **15**(4), 1054–1055 (2003). doi:10.1109/TKDE.2003.1209023

Public Key and Identity-Based Encryption

Content-Based Encryption

Xiaofen Wang[1,2]($\boxtimes$) and Yi Mu[2]($\boxtimes$)

[1] Center for Cyber Security and Big Data Research Center,
University of Electronic Science and Technology of China,
Chengdu 611731, Si Chuan, China
xfwang@uestc.edu.cn
[2] Centre for Computer and Information Security Research,
School of Computing and Information Technology, University of Wollongong,
Wollongong 2500, Australia
ymu@uow.edu.au

Abstract. Content-centric networks have demonstrated an entirely new type of network topology, which offers a new way to distribute information in the data-driven network. Unlike the TCP/IP network topology, which is address-driven, content-centric networks do not require any address. Based on the content-to-consumer paradigm, content-centric networking architecture was proposed for the content to be provided efficiently with great convenience to users. As the content-centric network is not address-driven, when a data packet is delivered it cannot be encrypted with any encryption key of a node. Therefore, data confidentiality in content-centric network is a challenging problem. Motivated to solve this problem, we introduce a new cryptosystem for content-based encryption, where the encryption key is associated with the content. We propose a content-based encryption scheme (CBE), which is proven to be semantically secure in the random oracle model. We apply the CBE to construct a secure content delivery protocol in a content-centric network.

Keywords: Content-centric network · Content-based encryption · Chosen plain-text security

1 Introduction

In the traditional TCP/IP network, which is address-centric, the data packets need to tell *where* the content is. Therefore, the IP packets contain two addresses, one for the source and the other for the destination host. All the traffic on the Internet rely on these IP addresses. To address the security of TCP/IP network, conventional cryptography can be applied. In case of public-key cryptography, each host is usually equipped with a pair of public and private keys. In traditional public key infrastructure (PKI), the public key of a host is accompanied with a certificate. To simplify certificate management in traditional PKI, identity-based infrastructure [1,4] can also be applied in a TCP/IP network, where the public key of a host can be its IP address. The problem for the TCP/IP networking is

© Springer International Publishing Switzerland 2016
J.K. Liu and R. Steinfeld (Eds.): ACISP 2016, Part II, LNCS 9723, pp. 57–72, 2016.
DOI: 10.1007/978-3-319-40367-0_4

that it assumes there is end-to-end physical connectivity. However, end-to-end connectivity may not ever exist and links (contacts) may not be suitable for schedules. Therefore, if the target provider is unreachable or unable to provide the requested content, then the content acquisition in TCP/IP network will fail.

When users acquire a content, which could be a file, a music, a video, etc., in a network, they concern *what* they receive, where the location of the content might not be important. To replace *where* with *what* and to overcome the inherent problem in the TCP/IP network, the content-to-consumer paradigm was presented to replace the host-to-host paradigm. Therefore, Content-centric Networking [8,9,13] or Information-centric Networking [2,11], a new communication architecture built on named data, was introduced. Content-centric network has no notion of host at its lowest level, while a packet "address" names content (not location). In a content-centric network, the content is delivered to the intended consumers regardless of their addresses [8,9,11,13]. Therefore, it offers great advantage for content acquisition, as in the content-centric network, the content-centric mechanism is employed to seek the target content, and any node which holds the requested contents can provide contents. This is a distinct feature compared with the TCP/IP network, since in the TCP/IP network, even if an intermediate node between the source node and the destination node possesses the requested content, it cannot provide the content because only the target provider node can provide it [10]. Therefore, the content acquisition cost and latency might be increased. In the content-centric network, the consumer node can acquire the content in an optimal manner. The content can be provided by a nearest node instead of a further node if both nodes possess the content. Therefore, the content-centric network can greatly reduce the cost of content transmission.

As the content-centric network is not address-driven, in a public-key setting, a content cannot be encrypted with the destination node's public key for the confidentiality of the content. Therefore, different from the TCP/IP networking, the traditional public key infrastructure cannot be used to best suit content-centric networking. The ID-based encryption [3,12] is unsuitable for the content-centric network either. In 1984, Shamir [12] asked for a public key encryption scheme in which the public key can be an arbitrary string. Their motivation was to simplify certificate management in traditional public key crypto-systems. Boneh and Franklin [3] proposed the first practical and provably secure ID-based encryption scheme. In an ID-based encryption, the user's identity is used as the public key, which is usually the IP address in a network protocol, and the corresponding private key is extracted from the identity. As in this content-to-consumer paradigm, there is no notion of host, which means no "IP address" is used, the ID-based encryption cannot be used for the content-centric network when a provider node encrypts the content. The conventional symmetric encryption is neither a good choice to provide the content's confidentiality in a content-centric network, since the content provider and the content consumer need to share the same symmetric key. The obvious issue is key distribution, which requires users' addresses.

In this paper, we propose a new notion of *content-based encryption*, where the encryption key is directly associated with the content itself, and the corresponding private decryption keys, generated by a trusted party, are provided for the valid users who are potential content receivers. Any user who wants to acquire the content needs to obtain one of the associated private keys of the content. With the content-based encryption key, the content provider can encrypt the content. The ciphertext is then relayed by intermediate nodes to the corresponding consumer who acquires the content. The consumer can decrypt it with his private decryption key.

To better illustrate the applicability of our scheme to the content-centric encryption, in the paper, we also construct a secure content delivery protocol tailored for the content-centric network. We describe how a content can be delivered by the content provider and acquired by the consumer and how the confidentiality of the content is achieved.

Besides the content-centric network, the content-based encryption can be used in many other content sharing applications, e.g. secure multimedia content dispatching and selling. The content owner encrypts the content under the content-based public key. The consumer who has got one of the corresponding private keys can decrypt it and retrieve the content.

As a note, we noticed that Zhao and Zhuo [14] proposed a content-based encryption scheme for wireless H.264 compressed videos. However it is not relevant to our notion of content-based encryption.

Our Contribution. We propose a new notion of *content-based encryption* for the content-centric network. In this new encryption paradigm, the public encryption key is directly associated with the content name itself and the private keys of the content are derived secretly from the content name. The content encrypted with the public key can be decrypted by any user who holds a valid content-based private key. We present a concrete content-based encryption scheme and prove its semantic security under the random oracle model. Significantly, we are able to show the application of the proposed content-based encryption scheme when the content is delivered in the content-centric network.

Organization. We provide the definitions of content-based encryption and its security notion in Sect. 2. In Sect. 3, we introduce the preliminaries and the hard problem assumption. We then present our first construction CBE and its security proof in Sect. 4. In Sect. 5, we present an application of our scheme to show how it works in the content-centric network. We conclude this paper in Sect. 6.

2   Definitions

A content-based encryption scheme $\mathcal{E}$ is specified by four algorithms, namely **Setup, Encrypt, Key-Extract**, and **Decrypt**:

Setup(1^λ): it takes as input the security parameter λ and returns the system parameters params and master-key MK. params are publicly known, while MK is only known to the Private Key Generator (PKG).

Encrypt(params, C, name): it is a randomized algorithm that takes as input the public parameters params, a content C and the unique name of the content name and outputs the ciphertext CT. Each content has a unique content name.

Key-Extract(params, MK, name): it is a randomized algorithm that takes as input params, master-key MK, the unique name of the content C and outputs a set of private keys SK_i, $i = 1, \ldots, \bar{n}$, for an integer $\bar{n}$.

Decrypt(params, CT, SK_i): it takes as input a ciphertext CT, a private key SK_i, and the public parameters params and outputs the content C.

In the following, we slightly modify the definition of semantic security (IND-CPA) for a public key encryption scheme [7] and define a new semantic security model in content-based encryption where the adversary can obtain the decryption key associated with any content wrt content name name$_j$ of her choice (other than the content name name being attacked).

We say that a content-based encryption scheme $\mathcal{E}$ is semantic secure against an adaptive chosen plaintext attack (IND-name-CPA) if no polynomially bounded adversary $\mathcal{A}$ has a non-negligible advantage against the challenger in the following IND-name-CPA game.

Setup: the challenger takes a security parameter λ as input and runs the **Setup** algorithm. It gives the adversary the resulting system parameters params and keeps the master-key MK to itself.

Phase 1: $\mathcal{A}$ adaptively issues queries $q_1, \ldots, q_m$ where query q_i is one of:

Key Extraction queries $\langle$name$_i\rangle$. The challenger responds by running algorithm **Key-Extract** to generate one private decryption key SK_i corresponding to the public key name$_i$. It sends SK_i to the adversary $\mathcal{A}$.

Challenge: once Phase 1 is over, it outputs two equal length contents C_0^*, C_1^* on which it wishes to be challenged. The only constraint is that the adversary did not make any key extraction query of their corresponding content names name$_0^*$ or name$_1^*$ in Phase 1. The challenger picks a random bit $b \in \{0,1\}$ and sets $CT^* = $ Encrypt(params, C_b^*, name$_b^*$). It sends the challenge ciphertext CT^* to the adversary $\mathcal{A}$.

Phase 2: $\mathcal{A}$ adaptively issues queries $q_{m+1}, \ldots, q_t$ key extraction queries as in Phase 1. The restriction is that the adversary cannot make any key extraction query for name$_b^*$ $(b = 0, 1)$.

Guess: finally, $\mathcal{A}$ outputs a guess $b' \in \{0, 1\}$ and wins the game if $b' = b$.

We refer to such an adversary $\mathcal{A}$ as an IND-name-CPA adversary. We define adversary $\mathcal{A}$'s advantage in attacking the scheme $\mathcal{E}$ as the following function of the security parameter λ: $\mathsf{Adv}_{\mathcal{E},\mathcal{A}}(\lambda) = \left| \Pr[b' = b] - \frac{1}{2} \right|$.

Definition 1. *A content-based encryption system $\mathcal{E}$ is semantically secure against an adaptive chosen plaintext attack if for any polynomial time IND-name-CPA adversary $\mathcal{A}$ the function $Adv_{\mathcal{E},\mathcal{A}}(\lambda)$ is negligible. As shorthand, we say that $\mathcal{E}$ is IND-name-CPA secure.*

3 Preliminaries

3.1 Bilinear Maps

Let $\mathbb{G}$ and $\mathbb{G}_T$ be two multiplicative cyclic groups of large prime order p. $e : \mathbb{G} \times \mathbb{G} \to \mathbb{G}_T$ is a bilinear map which satisfy the following properties:

- Bilinear. For all $u, v \in \mathbb{G}$ and $a, b \in \mathbb{Z}_p^*$, we have $e(u^a, v^b) = e(u, v)^{ab}$;
- Non-degenerate. $e(g, g) \neq 1$, if g is a generator of $\mathbb{G}$;
- Computable. For any $u, v \in \mathbb{G}$, $e(u, v)$ can be computed efficiently.

3.2 Complexity Assumptions

The security of our encryption system is based on the truncated decision augmented bilinear Diffie-Hellman exponent assumption (truncated decision ABDHE) [6]. The truncated decision n-ABDHE problem is defined as follows.

Let n be an integer and $(p, \mathbb{G}, \mathbb{G}_T, e)$ be a bilinear map group system. Let g, g' be the generators of $\mathbb{G}$. For some unknown $a \in \mathbb{Z}_p^*$, given a vector of $n + 3$ elements $(g', g'^{(a^{n+2})}, g, g^a, g^{(a^2)}, \ldots, g^{(a^n)}) \in \mathbb{G}^{n+3}$ and an element $Z \in \mathbb{G}_T$ as input, decide whether $Z = e(g', g)^{(a^{n+1})}$ or not.

We define an algorithm $\mathcal{B}$ that outputs $b \in \{0, 1\}$ has advantage ε in solving truncated decision n-ABDHE problem if

$$\left| \Pr\left[\mathcal{B}(g', g'^{(a^{n+2})}, g, g^a, g^{(a^2)}, \ldots, g^{(a^n)}, e(g', g)^{(a^{n+1})}) = 0 \right] \right.$$

$$\left. - \Pr\left[\mathcal{B}(g', g'^{(a^{n+2})}, g, g^a, g^{(a^2)}, \ldots, g^{(a^n)}, Z) = 0 \right] \right| \geq \varepsilon$$

where the probability is over the random choice of generators g, g' in $\mathbb{G}$, the random choice of a in $\mathbb{Z}_p^*$ and the random choice of Z in $\mathbb{G}_T$.

Definition 2. *We say that the truncated decision (t, ε, n)-ABDHE assumption holds in $\mathbb{G}$ if no t-time algorithm has advantage at least ε in solving the truncated decision n-ABDHE problem in $\mathbb{G}$.*

4 Construction for Chosen Plaintext Security

We propose a content-based encryption system CBE that is secure against the chosen plaintext attack. In the construction, we assume each content denoted by C is associated with a unique identifier denoted by name. The public encryption key of each content is name, and its private decryption keys are generated based on its name. For each content, there is a unique encryption key, but multiple private decryption keys.

Let $\mathbb{G}$ and $\mathbb{G}_T$ be groups of prime order p, and $e : \mathbb{G} \times \mathbb{G} \to \mathbb{G}_T$ be the bilinear map. The content-based encryption system CBE works as follows.

Setup. The PKG picks random generators $g, h, y \in \mathbb{G}$ and a random number $\alpha \in \mathbb{Z}_p^*$. It sets $g_1 = g^\alpha \in \mathbb{G}$. It also chooses two collision-resistant hash functions $H : \mathbb{G} \to \mathbb{Z}_p^*$ and $H_1 : \{0,1\}^* \to \mathbb{Z}_p^*$. The public parameters params and the master secret key MK are given by $\mathsf{params} = (g, g_1, h, y, H, H_1)$, $.$ $\mathsf{MK} = \alpha$.

Encrypt. To encrypt the content $\mathsf{C} \in \mathbb{G}_T$ using its unique identifier $\mathsf{name} \in \{0,1\}^*$, the sender generates a random number $z \in \mathbb{Z}_p^*$ and computes the ciphertext CT as follows: $U = (g_1 g^{-H_1(\mathsf{name})})^z$, $V = y^{-z}, W = e(g,g)^z$, $T = \mathsf{C} \cdot e(g,h)^{-z}$. The sender sends the ciphertext $CT = (U, V, W, T)$ to the users.

Key-Extract. For $i = 1, 2, \ldots, \bar{n}$, the PKG generates the secret key SK_i for a content C with the identifier name. The PKG generates a random number $r_i \in \mathbb{Z}_p^*$, and computes $R_i = g^{r_i}$, $t_i = H(R_i)$, $S_i = (hy^{r_i}g^{-t_i})^{\frac{1}{\alpha - H_1(\mathsf{name})}}$. For $i = 1, 2, \ldots, \bar{n}$, the PKG outputs the private decryption key $SK_i = (R_i, S_i)$, and sends it to the user U_i.

Decrypt. To decrypt the ciphertext $CT = (U, V, W, T)$, the user U_i who holds the decryption key $SK_i = (R_i, S_i)$, firstly computes $t_i = H(R_i)$ and decrypts the ciphertext to obtain the content: $\mathsf{C} = T \cdot e(U, S_i) \cdot e(V, R_i) \cdot W^{t_i}$.

Correctness. Assuming the ciphertext is well-formed for name:

$$e(U, S_i) \cdot e(V, R_i) \cdot W^{t_i}$$
$$= e(g^{z(\alpha - H_1(\mathsf{name}))}, (hy^{r_i}g^{-t_i})^{\frac{1}{\alpha - H_1(\mathsf{name})}}) \cdot e(y^{-z}, g^{r_i}) \cdot e(g,g)^{zt_i}$$
$$= e(g,h)^z \cdot e(g,y)^{zr_i} \cdot e(g,g)^{-zt_i} \cdot e(g,y)^{-zr_i} \cdot e(g,g)^{zt_i} = e(g,h)^z,$$

as required. Therefore, the content C can be recovered.

Remark. In our construction, the PKG generates multiple different secret keys corresponding to each content. These secret keys are securely distributed to multiple users (at registration, for example). An authorized user who holds a private decryption key can recover the content. In CBE, without the knowledge of the master key MK, the authorized users cannot collude to generate a new valid secret key of the same content.

CBE is proved IND-name-CPA secure under the truncated decision n-ABDHE assumption.

Theorem 1. *Assume the truncated decision (t, ε, n)-ABDHE assumption holds for $(\mathbb{G}, \mathbb{G}_T, e)$. The proposed CBE scheme is (t', ε', q_n) IND-name-CPA secure where $q_n = n - 1$, $t' = t - \mathcal{O}(t_{H_1} \cdot n^2) - \mathcal{O}(t_H \cdot n) - \mathcal{O}(t_{exp} \cdot n^2)$, $\varepsilon' = \varepsilon + \frac{1}{p}$, t_{H_1} is the time required to compute the hash H_1, t_H is the time required to compute the hash H, and t_{exp} is the time required to compute the exponentiation in $\mathbb{G}$.*

Proof. Assume that $\mathcal{A}$ is an adversary that (t', ε', q_n)-breaks the IND-name-CPA security of CBE above. We can then construct an algorithm, $\mathcal{B}$, that solves the truncated decision n-ABDHE problem, as follows. $\mathcal{B}$ takes as input a random truncated decision n-ABDHE challenge $(g', g'^{a^{n+2}}, g, g^a, \ldots, g^{a^n}, Z)$, where Z is either $e(g, g')^{a^{n+1}}$ or a random element of $\mathbb{G}_T$. $\mathcal{B}$ works as a challenger in the following procedure.

Setup. $\mathcal{B}$ generates a random polynomial $f(x) \in \mathbb{Z}_p[x]$ of degree n. It also randomly chooses $c, x^* \in \mathbb{Z}_p^*$. It sets $h = g^{f(a)}$ by computing from $g, g^a, \ldots, g^{a^n}$. $\mathcal{B}$ sets $g_1 = g^a$ and $y = g_1^c g^{-cx^*} = g^{c(a-x^*)}$. It sends the public key (g, g_1, h, y) to the adversary $\mathcal{A}$. Since g, a, c and $f(x)$ are uniformly chosen at random, h and y are uniformly random, and the public key has a distribution identical to that in the actual attack.

Hash Query. $\mathcal{B}$ can make hash queries of H_1 and H, and maintains two hash lists L_1 and L_2 correspondingly.

H_1-query: $\mathcal{B}$ maintains a list L_1 of a tuple (name_i, x_i). The list is initially empty. Upon receiving a hash query for name_i, $\mathcal{B}$ looks up the list L_1 to find the hash value x_i of name_i and returns x_i to $\mathcal{A}$. If name_i is not on the list L_1, $\mathcal{B}$ randomly chooses $x_i \in \mathbb{Z}_p^*$ and adds a new tuple (name_i, x_i) to L_1. Then $\mathcal{B}$ returns x_i.

H-query: $\mathcal{B}$ maintains a list L_2 of a tuple (r_i, R_i, t_i). The list is initially empty. Upon receiving a hash query for $R_i = g^{r_i}$, $\mathcal{B}$ looks up the list L_2 to find the hash value t_i of R_i and returns t_i to $\mathcal{A}$. If (r_i, R_i) is not on the list L_2, $\mathcal{B}$ randomly chooses $t_i \in \mathbb{Z}_p^*$ and adds a new tuple (r_i, R_i, t_i) to L_2. Then $\mathcal{B}$ returns t_i.

Phase 1. $\mathcal{A}$ makes key extraction queries. $\mathcal{B}$ responds to a key extraction query for name_i as follows. Firstly $\mathcal{B}$ looks up L_1 to find a corresponding x_i. If $x_i = a$, $\mathcal{B}$ uses a to directly solve the truncated decision n-ABDHE problem. Otherwise, $\mathcal{B}$ randomly chooses $r_i \in \mathbb{Z}_p^*$ and computes $R_i = g^{r_i}$. It makes an H-query to obtain $H(R_i) = t_i$. Then $\mathcal{B}$ sets $S_i = g^{\frac{f(a)+acr_i-x^*cr_i-t_i}{a-x_i}}$ by computing from $g, g^a, \ldots, g^{a^{n-1}}$. $\mathcal{B}$ sets the private decryption key for name_i as (R_i, S_i). This is a valid secret key for name_i, since $S_i = g^{\frac{f(a)+acr_i-x^*cr_i-t_i}{a-x_i}} = (hy^{r_i} g^{-t_i})^{\frac{1}{a-H(\text{name}_i)}}$, as required.

Challenge. $\mathcal{A}$ outputs two equal length contents $\mathsf{C}_0^*, \mathsf{C}_1^* \in \mathbb{G}_T$ with unique identifiers name_0^* and name_1^* correspondingly. If $x^* = a$, $\mathcal{B}$ uses a to solve the truncated decision n-ABDHE problem directly. Otherwise, $\mathcal{B}$ generates a bit $b \in \{0, 1\}$, and computes a secret key $(R_b = g^{r^*}, S_b = (hy^{r^*} g^{-t^*})^{\frac{1}{a-x^*}})$ for name_b^* as in Phase 1. Let $f_2(x) = x^{n+2}$ and let $F_2(x) = \frac{f_2(x)-f_2(x^*)}{x-x^*}$, which is a polynomial of degree $n + 1$. $\mathcal{B}$ sets $U^* = g'^{f_2(a)-f_2(x^*)}$, $V^* = g'^{-c(f_2(a)-f_2(x^*))}$, $W^* = Z \cdot e(g', \prod_{i=0}^n g^{F_{2,i}a^i})$, $T^* = \frac{\mathsf{C}_b^*}{e(U^*, S_b)e(V^*, R_b)W^{*t^*}}$, where $t^* = H(R_b)$ and $F_{2,i}$ is the coefficient of x^i in $F_2(x)$. It returns $CT^* = (U^*, V^*, W^*, T^*)$ to $\mathcal{A}$ as the challenge ciphertext.

Let $s = (\log g g')F_2(a)$. If $Z = e(g', g)^{a^{n+1}}$, then $U^* = g^{s(a-x^*)} = (g_1 g^{-H(\text{name}_b^*)})^s$, $V^* = y^{-s}$, $W^* = e(g, g)^s$ and $\mathsf{C}_b/T^* = e(U^*, S_b)e(V^*, R_b)$

$W^{t^*} = e(g,h)^s$ under randomness s. Since $\log g^{g'}$ is uniformly random, s is uniformly random. Therefore, (U^*, V^*, W^*, T^*) is a valid, appropriately distributed ciphertext to $\mathcal{A}$.

Phase 2. $\mathcal{A}$ makes key extraction queries. $\mathcal{B}$ responds as in Phase 1.

Guess. Finally, $\mathcal{A}$ outputs its guess b'. If $b' = b$, $\mathcal{B}$ outputs 0; otherwise, it outputs 1.

Perfect Simulation. When $Z = e(g^{(a^{n+1})}, g')$, the public key and challenge ciphertext issued by $\mathcal{B}$ come from a distribution identical to that in the actual construction. Now we will show that the secret keys issued by $\mathcal{B}$ are appropriately distributed. Let $\mathcal{I}$ be a set consisting of a, the hash value $H(\mathsf{name}^*_i)$, and the hash value $H(\mathsf{name}_i)$ queried by $\mathcal{A}$; observe that $|\mathcal{I}| \leq n + 1$. As $f(x)$ is a uniformly random polynomial of degree n, from $\mathcal{A}$'s view, the values $\{f(a_i) : a_i \in \mathcal{I}\}$ are uniformly random and independent. Therefore, the keys issued by $\mathcal{B}$ are appropriately distributed.

Probability Analysis. If $Z = e(g^{a^{n+1}}, g')$, then the simulation is perfect, and $\mathcal{A}$ will guess the bit b correctly with probability $\frac{1}{2} + \varepsilon'$. Otherwise, Z is uniformly random, thus the elements (U^*, V^*, W^*) are uniformly random and independently distributed in $\mathbb{G} \times \mathbb{G} \times \mathbb{G}_T$. In this case, the inequality $W^* \neq e(U^*, g)^{\frac{1}{a-x^*}}$ holds with probability $1 - \frac{1}{p}$. Since r^* is uniformly random and independent from $\mathcal{A}$'s view, t^* is random and independent. When the inequality $W^* \neq e(U^*, g)^{\frac{1}{a-x^*}}$ holds, the value of

$$e(U^*, S_b)e(V^*, R_b)W^{*t^*} = e(U^*, (hy^{r^*}g^{-t^*})^{\frac{1}{a-x^*}})e(V^*, g^{r^*})W^{*t^*}$$

$$= e(U^*, h^{\frac{1}{a-x^*}})e(U^*, y^{\frac{1}{a-x^*}})^{r^*}e(V^*, g^{r^*})(W^*/e(U^*, g)^{\frac{1}{a-x^*}})^{t^*}$$

is uniformly random and independent from $\mathcal{A}$'s view. Therefore,

$$T^* = \frac{\mathsf{C}^*_b}{e(U^*, S_b)e(V^*, R_b)W^{*t^*}}$$

is uniformly random and independent, and (U^*, V^*, W^*, T^*) can impart no information regarding the bit b.

Assume that no $H_1(\mathsf{name}_i)$ equals a (which would only increase $\mathcal{B}$'s success probability). If Z is randomly sampled from $\mathbb{G}_T$,

$$\left| \Pr[\mathcal{B}(g', g'^{(a^{n+2})}, g, g^a, g^{(a^2)}, \ldots, g^{(a^n)}, Z) = 0] - \frac{1}{2} \right| \leq \frac{1}{p}.$$

When $Z = e(g^{a^{n+1}}, g')$,

$$\left| \Pr[\mathcal{B}(g', g'^{(a^{n+2})}, g, g^a, g^{(a^2)}, \ldots, g^{(a^n)}, Z) = 0] - \frac{1}{2} \right| \geq \varepsilon'.$$

Thus, for uniformly random g, g', a and Z, we have

$$\left| \Pr[\mathcal{B}(g', g'^{(a^{n+2})}, g, g^a, g^{(a^2)}, \ldots, g^{(a^n)}, e(g', g)^{(a^{n+1})}) = 0] \right.$$
$$\left. - \Pr[\mathcal{B}(g', g'^{(a^{n+2})}, g, g^a, g^{(a^2)}, \ldots, g^{(a^n)}, Z) = 0] \right| \geq \varepsilon' - \frac{1}{p}.$$

Time-Complexity. In the simulation, to respond $\mathcal{A}$'s key extraction queries for $name_i$, $\mathcal{B}$ needs to make n H_1-hash query, 1 H-hash query and to compute $g^{\frac{f(a)+acr_i-x^*cr_i-t_i}{a-x_i}}$, where $\frac{f(a)+acr_i-x^*cr_i-t_i}{a-x_i}$ is a polynomial of degree $n-1$. Therefore, each key extraction query needs to compute $\mathcal{O}(n)$ exponentiations in $\mathbb{G}$. Since $\mathcal{A}$ makes at most $n-1$ such queries, $t = t' + \mathcal{O}(t_{H_1} \cdot n^2) + \mathcal{O}(t_H \cdot n) + \mathcal{O}(t_{exp} \cdot n^2)$, where t_{H_1} is the time required to compute the hash H_1, t_H is the time required to compute the hash H, and t_{exp} is the time required to compute the exponentiation in $\mathbb{G}$.

This concludes the proof of Theorem 1.

By applying a technique due to Fujisaki-Okamoto [5], we can easily convert the IND-name-CPA secure content-based encryption scheme CBE into a chosen ciphertext secure content-based encryption system in the random oracle model.

5   Securing Content-Centric Network

We apply our content-based encryption scheme to a content-centric network and demonstrate the applicability of our scheme for a real-world application.

5.1   Content-Centric Network Architecture

The content-centric network consists of a trusted third party (TTP) and three types of nodes as shown in Fig. 1:

- TTP: it provides the unique identifier for each content and acts as a private key generator (PKG) that generates the private decryption keys for the content;
- Provider node: it is a node which provides the content uniquely identified by its name to the other nodes in the network;
- Consumer node: it is a node which is authorized to obtain the content provided by the Provider node;
- Intermediate node: it is a node resided between a Provider node and a Consumer node, and it aims to forward an Interest sent by a Consumer node or a Data (here, we refer content as Data) returned by a Provider node.

In Fig. 1, an example of the content-centric network is presented, where C_1, C_2 and C_3 are the Consumer nodes; E_1, E_2, E_3, E_4 and E_5 are the Intermediate nodes; P_1 and P_2 are the Provider nodes. Note that a Provider node could also be an Intermediate node or a Consumer node for another content; a Consumer node could also be a Provider node or an Intermediate node for another content;

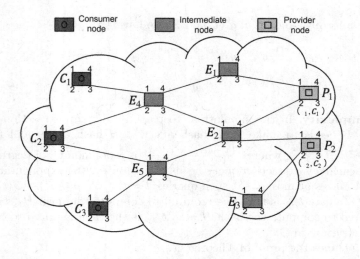

Fig. 1. Content-centric network architecture.

an Intermediate node could be a Provider node or a Consumer node for another content. Each node has multiple interfaces where the data comes or outputs. For simplicity, assume all the nodes including the Provider nodes, the Consumer nodes and the Intermediate nodes have four interfaces denoted as 1, 2, 3 and 4. Therefore, It allows multiple sources for data and can query them all in parallel.

The content-centric network communication is driven by the consumers of data. There are three content-centric network packet types, Route Establishing Request, Interest and Data. A Provider node which holds a content makes a Route Establishing Request to establish links among the nodes according to the content identifier. A Consumer node asks for an interested content by broadcasting its Interest over all available interfaces [9]. Any node which has received the Interest and has the data that satisfies it can respond with a Data packet (content chunk). Data is transmitted only in response to an Interest and consumes that Interest [9].

As shown in Fig. 2, the core content-centric network packet forwarding engine has three main data structures: FIB (Forwarding Information Base), CS (Content Store, i.e. buffer memory), and PIT (Pending Interest Table) [8]. The FIB is used to forward Interest packets toward content sources, i.e. the Provider nodes which have the matching Data. The CS is the same as the buffer memory of an IP router but it stores the received Data packet as long as possible. The PIT tracks Interests forwarded upstream toward content source(s), so returned Data can be sent downstream to its requester(s) [8]. After the PIT entries are used to forward a matching Data packet, they are erased immediately.

When an Interest arrives at an interface, if there is a matching entry in the CS, it will be returned from the same interface where the Interest comes. If there is no matching entry, the PIT is checked for an existing Pending Interest. If there is already a matching entry, the arrival Interface for the new Interest is added to the list in the corresponding PIT entry. If there is no already an

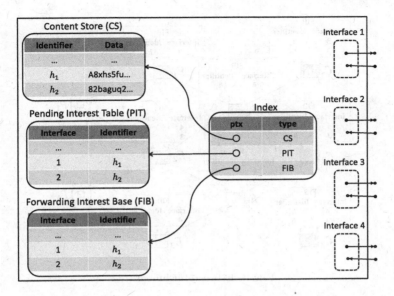

Fig. 2. Content-centric network forward engine model.

existing PIT entry, the FIB table is checked for forwarding information. If there is a corresponding entry, the Interest is forwarded accordingly, and the Interest and the arrival Interface are added to the PIT.

In content-centric network, the Data packet is not routed but simply follows the chain of PIT entries back to the original requester(s).

5.2 Secure Content Delivery in Content-Centric Network

The content-centric network presented in this section is built on our notion of content-based security for protection of the content. The proposed content-based encryption is applied to protect the content when it is acquired and transmitted over the content-centric network.

System Setup. To achieve the content confidentiality, the TTP executes the following steps to setup the system. It generates the master-key MK and the public system parameters params; chooses two collision-resistant hash functions $H_2 : \mathbb{Z}_p^* \to \{0,1\}^{l_1}$ and $H_3 : \mathbb{G}_T \to \{0,1\}^{l_2}$, where l_1, l_2 are positive integers. Then it publishes params and H_2, H_3, and keeps MK secret.

FIB Establishment. To establish the route among the three types of nodes, each node maintains a Forwarding Information Base (FIB) where each entry contains two fields: *Interface* and *Identifier*, as shown in Fig. 3. The routing establishment follows the next four steps:

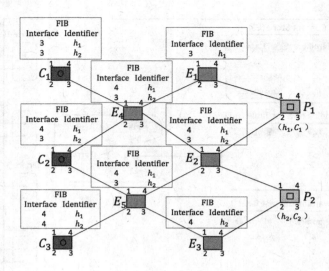

Fig. 3. FIB establishment.

1. If an original Provider node P_x wants to provide the content C_i, it sends the original name name_i of C_i and a unique tag ($\mathsf{tag}_i = H_3(C_i)$) to the TTP. The TTP computes $N_i = H_1(\mathsf{name}_i \| \mathsf{tag}_i)$. The public key of C_i is set as $PK_i = N_i$. Then the TTP publishes (N_i, name_i). The Provider node P_x computes the identifier $h_i = H_2(N_i)$, and randomly selects a secure symmetric key k_i to compute C_i's ciphertext $e_i = \mathsf{SEnc}(C_i, k_i)$ and $d_i = \mathsf{Encrypt}(k_i, PK_i)$ where SEnc is the symmetric encryption and $\mathsf{Encrypt}$ is the proposed content-based encryption.

2. The Provider node P_x generates a route establishing request $\mathsf{RER} = (h_i, T_i)$ where h_i is the header and T_i is the timestamp. P_x forwards the request RER to nearby nodes.

3. If an Intermediate node (or a Consumer node) receives this RER from interface j, the Intermediate node (or Consumer node) does the following operations:

   If there is no entry for h_i in the FIB of the Intermediate node (or Consumer node), it forwards the received request RER via each interface except the interface where RER arrived, and adds a new entry $[j, h_i]$ in its FIB where j is the interface the request arrived and h_i is the identifier; Otherwise, it discards the received RER;

4. Repeat Step 3 until all the Consumer nodes in the network receive the RER with identifier h_i and build an entry for h_i in their FIBs, as shown in Fig. 3.

Assume that in the content-centric network architecture, the Provider nodes can provide totally m pieces of contents. Each content C_i ($i \in [1, m]$) is uniquely identified by h_i. As shown in Fig. 3, the Provider node P_1 owns content C_1 and it provides (h_1, Data_1) where h_1 is the identifier of content C_1 with public key N_1, $\mathsf{Data}_1 = (e_1, d_1)$ is the ciphertext of content C_1. The Provider node P_2 owns content C_2 and it provides (h_2, Data_2) where h_2 is the identifier of content C_2 with public key N_2, $\mathsf{Data}_2 = (e_2, d_2)$ is the ciphertext of content C_2.

As shown in Fig. 3, P_1 forwards a Route Establishing Request message $\mathsf{RER}_1 = (h_1, T_1)$ where the header is h_1 from all its interfaces to its nearby nodes. P_2 forwards a Route Establishing Request message $\mathsf{RER}_2 = (h_2, T_2)$ where the header is h_2 from all its interfaces to its nearby nodes.

When the Intermediate node E_1 receives RER_1 from interface 3, it creates a new entry $[3, h_1]$ where 3 indicates the coming interface and h_1 is the identifier in its FIB, and then it forwards RER_1 from all its interfaces except interface 3. Similarly, when the intermediate node E_2 receives RER_1 from interface 4, it creates a new entry $[4, h_1]$ in its FIB, and then it forwards RER_1 from all its interfaces except interface 4.

When the intermediate node E_4 receives RER_1 from interface 4, it creates a new entry $[4, h_1]$ in its FIB, and then it forwards RER_1 from all its interfaces except interface 4. Then, when E_4 receives an RER_1 with the same identifier h_1 from interface 3, it discards this request, since there is already an entry for h_1 in its FIB.

When the Intermediate node E_5 receives RER_1 from interface 4, it creates a new entry $[4, h_1]$ in its FIB, and then it forwards RER_1 from all its interfaces except interface 4.

The Consumer nodes C_1, C_2 and C_3 receive the request RER_1 from interface 3, 4, 4, respectively, and they create entries $[3, h_1]$, $[4, h_1]$, $[4, h_1]$ in their FIBs, respectively. With the same approach, the Consumers nodes C_1, C_2 and C_3 receive the request RER_2 from interface 3, 3, 4, respectively, and they create entries $[3, h_2]$, $[3, h_2]$, $[4, h_2]$ in their FIBs, respectively.

Content Acquisition. As shown in Fig. 4, to support content acquisition, all the Intermediate nodes maintain two tables: a Pending Interest Table (PIT) and a Content Store (CS). In the PIT, each entry consists of two fields: *Interface* and *Identifier*. Differing from FIB, the interface in PIT is the interface where the Interest message comes, while the interface in FIB is the interface where the Route Establishing Request RER comes. In CS, each entry consists of two fields: *Identifier* and *Data*.

If a Consumer node C_y wants to acquire the content C_i identified by h_i, it firstly checks whether h_i is in its FIB. If there is an entry for h_i, it acquires the corresponding private decryption key $SK_{i,y}$ from the TTP. The private decryption key is generated according to the content-based encryption scheme in Sect. 4. After that the Consumer node C_y acquires the content C_i according to the following steps:

1. C_y checks the entry for h_i in its FIB. Assume the entry is $[k, h_i]$. C_y then forwards an interest message $\mathsf{Interest} = (h_i, T_i')$ where h_i is the header and T_i' is the timestamp from the interface k to the nearby nodes;
2. If a node receives this Interest from interface j, the node does the following operations:

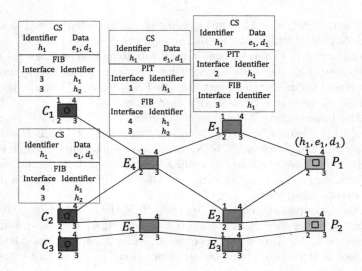

Fig. 4. Content acquisition.

- If there is no entry $[h_i, (e_i, d_i)]$ in the CS of the node, where h_i is the identifier and (e_i, d_i) is the data, the PIT is checked for an Interest entry with the same identifier. If there is already a matching entry, the arrival interface for the new Interest is added to the PIT list in the corresponding PIT entry. Otherwise, a new entry $[j, h_i]$ is added in the PIT where j is the interface the Interest comes and h_i is the identifier. The node forwards Interest from each interface except the interface where Interest comes, and then Step 2 is repeated;

- Otherwise, the node constructs a response data packet Data $= (h_i, e_i, d_i)$ where the header is h_i and the payload is (e_i, d_i), and forwards back Data from interface j;

3. If a node receives Data from the interface f, it checks if there is an entry for h_i in its CS. If no, creates a new entry $[h_i, (e_i, d_i)]$ and adds it to its CS. Otherwise, the new coming Data is not added to its CS. Then it checks its PIT. If there is an entry $[j, h_i]$ in its PIT, it forwards the response data packet Data back from the interface j according to the entry in PIT. After that it removes that entry in its PIT.

4. Repeat Step 3 until C_y receives the response data packet Data. Then, C_y decrypts d_i with the private decryption key $SK_{i,y}$ to obtain k_i, and decrypts e_i with k_i to obtain C_i.

Note that the response data packet Data includes two fields of CS entries, i.e. *Identifier* and *Data*.

In the following, we will give an example. Assume the Consumer node C_1 wants to acquire the content with identifier h_1. It firstly acquires the corresponding decryption key $SK_{1,1}$ securely from the TTP. It searches for the entry for h_1 in its FIB. If there is an entry $[3, h_1]$, C_1 forwards an interest message Interest $= (h_1, T_1')$ where the header is h_1 from interface 3. Node E_4 receives this Interest from interface 1. Since there is no entry $[h_1, e_1, d_1]$ in E_4's CS, E_4 cannot provide the data to C_1. E_4 creates an entry $[1, h_1]$ in its PIT. Then, E_4 checks the entry for h_1 in its FIB and finds the corresponding entry $[4, h_1]$. E_4 forwards this interest message Interest $= (h_1, T_1')$ via interface 4. The Intermediate node E_1 receives this interest message Interest via the interface 2. However, there is no entry $[h_1, e_1, d_1]$ in E_1's CS either. Therefore, E_1 also creates an entry $[2, h_1]$ in its PIT. Then, E_1 checks the entry for h_1 in its FIB and finds the corresponding entry $[3, h_1]$. E_1 forwards this interest message Interest $= (h_1, T_1')$ via interface 3. Finally, the Provider node P_1 receives the Interest from interface 1.

When P_1 receives the interest message Interest $= (h_1, T_1')$, it constructs the response data packet Data $= (h_1, e_1, d_1)$ where h_1 is the header and (e_1, d_1) is the payload. Then, it forwards this response data packet Data via interface 1. When E_1 receives this Data, it adds an entry $[h_1, e_1, d_1]$ in its CS where h_1 is the identifier and (e_1, d_1) is the ciphertext of the content C_1. E_1 forwards this response data packet Data from interface 2 based on its PIT, and then removes the entry $[2, h_1]$ from its PIT. When E_4 receives this response data packet Data, it also adds an entry $[h_1, e_1, d_1]$ in its CS. E_4 forwards Data from interface 1 based on its PIT, and then removes the entry $[1, h_1]$ from its PIT. Finally, the Consumer node C_1 receives this response data packet Data $= (h_1, e_1, d_1)$, and it decrypts d_1 with the secret key $SK_{1,1}$ to obtain the symmetric key k_1 and decrypts e_1 with k_1 to acquire the content C_1.

If the Consumer node C_2 wants to acquire the content with the identifier h_1, it firstly acquires the corresponding secret key $SK_{1,2}$ securely from the TTP. It searches for the entry with the identifier h_1 in its FIB. As there is an entry $[4, h_1]$ in its FIB, C_2 forwards an interest message Interest$' = (h_1, T_1'')$ where the header is h_1 via interface 4. Node E_4 receives this Interest$'$ from interface 2. Since there is already an entry $[h_1, e_1, d_1]$ in E_4's CS, it forwards the response data packet Data $= (h_1, e_1, d_1)$ via interface 2 directly. Then the Consumer node C_2 receives this response data packet Data $= (h_1, e_1, d_1)$, and it decrypts d_1 with the secret key $SK_{1,2}$ to obtain the symmetric key k_1 and decrypts e_1 with k_1 to acquire the content C_1.

As the content is encrypted with a symmetric key and the symmetric key is encrypted under the content-based encryption system, any node without a valid decryption key cannot decrypt the ciphertext and obtain the content. As the Intermediate nodes store the ciphertext of the content transmitted via them, if an Intermediate node wants to acquire the content it can directly decrypt the ciphertext when it has obtained a valid decryption key. If a nearby Intermediate node has stored the ciphertext, the Consumer node need not acquire the content from the Provider node, but from the Intermediate node directly instead.

6 Conclusion

We presented the notion of content-based encryption tailored for content-centric networks and also defined its security models. We proposed a content-based encryption scheme and proved that it is semantic secure in the random oracle model under the truncated decision ABDHE assumption. We applied our content-based encryption to protect the content delivered in the content-centric network.

Acknowledgment. The first author thanks the partial support from the National Natural Science Foundation of China (No. 61502086). We thank Xiaonan Wang for useful discussions about content-centric networks.

References

1. Abe, M., Cui, Y., Imai, H., Kiltz, E.: Efficient hybrid encryption from ID-based encryption. Des. Codes Crypt. **54**(3), 205–240 (2010)
2. Amadeo, M., Molinaro, A., Ruggeri, G.: E-CHANET: routing, forwarding and transport in information-centric multihop wireless networks. Comput. Commun. **36**(7), 792–803 (2013)
3. Boneh, D., Franklin, M.K.: Identity-based encryption from the weil pairing. SIAM J. Comput. **32**(3), 586–615 (2003)
4. Boyen, X., Waters, B.: Anonymous hierarchical identity-based encryption (without random oracles). In: Dwork, C. (ed.) CRYPTO 2006. LNCS, vol. 4117, pp. 290–307. Springer, Heidelberg (2006)
5. Fujisaki, E., Okamoto, T.: Secure integration of asymmetric and symmetric encryption schemes. J. Cryptology **26**(1), 80–101 (2013)
6. Gentry, C.: Practical identity-based encryption without random oracles. In: Vaudenay, S. (ed.) EUROCRYPT 2006. LNCS, vol. 4004, pp. 445–464. Springer, Heidelberg (2006)
7. Goldwasser, S., Micali, S.: Probabilistic encryption. J. Comput. Syst. Sci. **28**(2), 270–299 (1984)
8. Jacobson, V., Smetters, D.K., Thornton, J.D., Plass, M.F., Briggs, N.H., Braynard, R.: Networking named content. In: Proceedings of the 2009 ACM Conference on Emerging Networking Experiments and Technology, CoNEXT 2009, pp. 1–12, Rome, Italy, 1–4 December 2009
9. Jacobson, V., Smetters, D.K., Thornton, J.D., Plass, M.F., Briggs, N., Braynard, R.: Networking named content. Commun. ACM **55**(1), 117–124 (2012)
10. Lee, E., Lee, E., Gerla, M., Oh, S.: Vehicular cloud networking: architecture and design principles. IEEE Commun. Mag. **52**(2), 148–155 (2014)
11. Polyzos, G.C., Ahlgren, B., Jacobson, V., Koponen, T., Sitaraman, R.K., Trossen, D.: Information-centric networking: state 'of advance. In: 2011 ACM SIGCOMM Workshop on Information-Centric Networking, ICN 2011, pp. 25–25, Toronto, ON, Canada, 19 August 2011
12. Shamir, A.: Identity-based cryptosystems and signature schemes. In: Blakely, G.R., Chaum, D. (eds.) CRYPTO 1984. LNCS, vol. 196, pp. 47–53. Springer, Heidelberg (1985)
13. Zhang, L., Afanasyev, A., Burke, J., Jacobson, V., Claffy, K.C., Crowley, P., Papadopoulos, C., Wang, L., Zhang, B.: Named data networking. Comput. Commun. Rev. **44**(3), 66–73 (2014)
14. Zhao, Y., Zhuo, L.: A content-based encryption scheme for wireless H.264 compressed videos. In: Wireless Communications and Signal Processing (WCSP), 2012 International Conference, Proceedings, pp. 1–6, Huangshan, China, 25–27 October 2012

Provably Secure Threshold Paillier Encryption Based on Hyperplane Geometry

Zhe Xia[1], Xiaoyun Yang[1], Min Xiao[1], and Debiao He[2(✉)]

[1] Department of Computing, Wuhan University of Technology,
Wuhan 430070, China
xiazhe@whut.edu.cn
[2] State Key Laboratory of Software Engineering, Wuhan University,
Wuhan 430072, China
hedebiao@163.com

Abstract. In threshold encryption, the secret key is shared among a set of decryption parties, so that only a quorum of these parties can decrypt a given ciphertext. It is a useful building block in cryptology to distribute the trust of the secret key as well as increase availability. In particular, threshold Paillier encryption has been widely used in various security protocols, such as e-auction, e-voting and e-lottery. In this paper, we present the idea of designing provably secure threshold Paillier encryption using hyperplane geometry. Compared with the existing schemes that are based on polynomial interpolation, our work not only renovates the threshold Paillier cryptosystem using a different mathematical structure, but also enjoys some additional benefits: (1) our proposed method avoids the technical obstacle of computing inverses in the group whose order is unknown; (2) it gains computational advantages over Shoup's trick and it can be used as a general building block to design secure and efficient threshold cryptosystems based on factoring.

1 Introduction

Public key encryption is a key ingredient in cryptology. It allows anyone to encrypt some message using the public key, while only the party who possesses the corresponding secret key can recover the message. Paillier encryption [14] is an example of public key encryption that enjoys the additive homomorphic property: the encryption of the sum of multiple messages equals to the product of the encryption of individual ones, and the computation can be carried out with encrypted data without knowledge of the secret key. Hence, Paillier encryption can be found in many applications where computing with encrypted values is required.

However, in many cases, the ability to perform decryption gives too much power, and it is desirable to distribute this power. Threshold encryption is just a solution for these cases. In (t, n)-threshold encryption, the public key is made public and a trusted dealer shares the corresponding secret key among n decryption parties. A given ciphertext encrypted using the public key can only be decrypted if more than t of these parties work together. But less than t parties

© Springer International Publishing Switzerland 2016
J.K. Liu and R. Steinfeld (Eds.): ACISP 2016, Part II, LNCS 9723, pp. 73–86, 2016.
DOI: 10.1007/978-3-319-40367-0_5

are unable to perform the decryption. Moreover, threshold encryption can be used even if some parties are corrupted and they violate the protocol. A general requirement is that the minority corrupted parties are unable to prevent honest parties from recovering the plaintext. Hence, threshold encryption could not only prevent some dishonest parties from learning the underlying plaintext, but also increase the availability of the cryptosystem.

1.1   Previous Works

Threshold cryptosystem was first introduced by Desmedt and Frankel in [6]. In that paper, a threshold ElGamal encryption was proposed, and it was pointed out that designing threshold RSA encryption is much more difficult because of the "interpolating over $\mathbb{Z}_{\phi(N)}$ problem" (N is the RSA modulus and ϕ is the Euler's totient function). That is, anyone who wants to recover the plaintext by interpolating the decrypted shares will encounter the technical obstacle of computing inverses in the group whose order is unknown.

The first attempt to address this problem was also proposed by Desmedt and Frankel [7]. Their solution, followed by Santis et al. [18] and Gennaro et al. [11], extends the ring of integers modulo $\phi(N)$ to a different algebraic structure, so that the inverses can be disclosed safely. A different solution was proposed by Frankel et al. [10], followed by Rabin [16], and their strategy is to introduce an extra layer of secret sharing.

However, the above solutions to the "interpolating over $\mathbb{Z}_{\phi(N)}$ problem" are impractical, since they have introduced a lot of interaction and complexity. A much simpler and elegant solution to this problem was introduced by Shoup [19] in Eurocrypt 2000. His trick is to multiply a constant value $\Delta = n!$ with each of the Lagrange coefficient when interpolating the decrypted shares, where n is the number of decryption parties. Because Δ will be a multiple of the denominator in all Lagrange coefficients, there is no need to compute inverses in the group whose order is unknown. From then on, Shoup's trick [19] has become the de facto standard for designing threshold cryptosystems based on factoring. For example, Fouque et al. have extended the Pailler encryption [14] to its threshold version [9], and Damgård et al. have proposed a generalised threshold Paillier encryption [5], both works are based on Shoup's trick.

Nowadays, threshold Paillier encryption has become a popular building block in cryptology, and it has been widely used in various security protocols, such as e-auction, e-voting and e-lottery, in which computation needs to be performed with encrypted data and the power of the secret key needs to be distributed [1, 12, 13, 17].

1.2   Our Contributions

In this paper, we revisit the research of threshold Paillier encryption, and renovate this technique using a different mathematical structure. We show that provably secure threshold Paillier encryption also can be designed using hyperplane geometry. And compared with the existing solutions that are based on polynomial interpolation, our proposed scheme has two additional benefits: (1) it avoids the technical obstacle of computing inverses in the group whose order is unknown (2) it gains computational advantages over Shoup's trick and it can be used to reduce the computational cost in existing threshold cryptosystems based on factoring.

1.3   Outline of the Paper

The rest of this paper is organised as follows: the system model and security definitions are described in Sect. 2. Some basic tools are reviewed in Sect. 3. The proposed threshold Paillier encryption is described in Sect. 4, and its security analysis and efficiency analysis are presented in Sect. 5. Finally, we conclude in Sect. 6.

2   System Model and Security Definitions

A threshold encryption cryptosystem is consisted of the following five algorithms:

- KeyGen: the key generation algorithm takes as input a security parameter κ, the number of decryption parties n ($n \geq 1$), the threshold number t ($1 \leq t \leq n$) and a random string x. It outputs a public key pk, a set of secret key shares $\{s_1, s_2, \ldots, s_n\}$, and a number of verification keys $v, \{v_1, v_2, \ldots, v_n\}$.
- Enc: the encryption algorithm takes as input the public key pk, a random string x and a plaintext m. It outputs a ciphertext c.
- PartDec: the partial decryption algorithm takes as input the public key pk, a ciphertext c, an index i ($1 \leq i \leq n$) and the corresponding secret key share s_i. It outputs a decryption share c_i and a proof p_i that proves the validity of partial decryption.
- Veri: the verification algorithm takes as input a ciphertext c, an index i ($1 \leq i \leq n$), the verification keys v, v_i, the decryption share c_i and its proof p_i. It output 1 if the proof is valid, and otherwise $\perp$.
- Comb: the combining algorithm takes as input the public key pk and any subset of t valid decryption shares. It outputs the plaintext m.

2.1   System Model and Communication Model

There are three types of players in our proposed protocol: a trusted dealer $\mathcal{D}$, a set of n decryption parties and an adversary $\mathcal{A}$. We assume that all these players can be modelled as probabilistic polynomial time (PPT) Turing machines.

Among these n decryption parties, we assume that there exists t honest ones. The corrupted parties are controlled by the adversary $\mathcal{A}$, and these parties can be coerced by $\mathcal{A}$ to surrender their private information or violate the protocol in any way. Note that in order to prevent corrupted parties from decrypting the plaintext, it is required that $n - t < t$. In this paper, we assume that $n = 2t - 1$. Moreover, we assume that the adversary $\mathcal{A}$ is static: $\mathcal{A}$ chooses which parties to corrupt at the beginning of the protocol.

About the communication channels, we assume that there exists a private channel between the dealer and every decryption party. The adversary is unable to tamper or intercept the information send through this channel. And we assume that all players can access to some authenticated broadcast channel.

In a high level, our proposed protocol works as follows:

1. In the initialisation phase, the trusted dealer $\mathcal{D}$ uses the KeyGen algorithm to generate the public key, secret key shares and verification keys. The public key pk and all the verification keys $v, \{v_1, v_2, \ldots, v_n\}$ are made public through the broadcast channel. And $\mathcal{D}$ sends the secret key shares to the decryption parties using the private channels.
2. To encrypt a message, anyone can implement the Enc algorithm using the public key pk.
3. To decrypt a given ciphertext c, each decryption party uses her secret key share s_i and the PartDec algorithm to generate a decryption share c_i along with a proof p_i that proves the validity of c_i. Each party broadcasts the pair (c_i, p_i). Note that the proposed protocol is non-interactive, and we do not require that all parties broadcast this pair simultaneously.
4. Now, anyone can use the verification keys v, v_i and the Veri algorithm to check whether the partial decryption c_i is valid or not.
5. Finally, any subset of t valid decryption shares can be collected to recover the plaintext using the Comb algorithm.

2.2   Security Definitions

In order to provide a rigorous security analysis for our proposed protocol, we use the following security definitions:

Correctness: if there exists t honest decryption parties, a threshold encryption cryptosystem can decrypt a ciphertext and output the correct plaintext, even in the presence of some adversary who has full control of $t-1$ corrupt decryption parties.

Threshold Semantic Security: this definition was first defined by Fouque et al. in [9], and it is an extention of the semantic security definition for non-threshold encryption. Consider the following game G:

- G1: The adversary $\mathcal{A}$ chooses $t-1$ decryption parties to corrupt. $\mathcal{A}$ can force them to surrender their private information, and $\mathcal{A}$ has full control of their behaviour for the rest of the game.
- G2: The trusted dealer $\mathcal{D}$ runs the KeyGen algorithm to generate the keys. The public key pk and all verification keys $v, \{v_1, v_2, \ldots, v_n\}$ are broadcasteded, and each decryption party receives her secret key share. The adversary $\mathcal{A}$ learns the secret key shares hold by the corrupted parties.
- G3: The adversary $\mathcal{A}$ has access to a *partial decryption oracle*. For example, $\mathcal{A}$ can encrypt a message m and input its ciphertext c into the oracle. Then, the oracle returns n decryption shares of c, along with proofs of their validity. $\mathcal{A}$ can use this oracle as many times as she likes.

- G4: The adversary $\mathcal{A}$ issues two messages m_0 and m_1 in the message space, and sends them to an *encryption oracle*. This oracle randomly selects a bit b, encrypts the message m_b, and returns its ciphertext c to $\mathcal{A}$.
- G5: Again, the adversary $\mathcal{A}$ uses the *partial decryption oracle* as many times as she likes. The requirement is that $\mathcal{A}$ cannot use c to query the partial decryption oracle.
- G6: The adversary $\mathcal{A}$ outputs a bit b'.

The adversary's advantage is defined to be the absolute difference between $1/2$ and the probability that $b = b'$. A threshold encryption is said to be *threshold semantic secure* if for any PPT adversary $\mathcal{A}$, her advantage of running the game G is negligible.

3   Basic Tools

In this section, we briefly review some basic tools that are used in our proposed protocol.

3.1   Blakely's Secret Sharing

In (t, n) Blakely's secret sharing [2], the secret is treated as some coordinate of a point in a t-dimensional space. Each of the n parties is given a different t-dimensional hyperplane in the space. And all these hyperplanes intersect at this point. When t parties work together, they can solve a system of equations to retrieve the secret. But less than t parties are unable to learn any information about the secret. Blakely's secret sharing works as follows:

- **Initialisation phase:** to share a secret $z = a_1$, a dealer selects $t - 1$ random values $\{a_2, a_3, \ldots, a_t\}$. Then, the dealer generates an $n \times t$ matrix M and broadcasts it. It is required that any t rows of M will form a $t \times t$ invertible matrix $\mathsf{M}_{\mathcal{S}}$.
- **Share generation phase:** the dealer generates a linear system of equations $s_i = b_{i,1}a_1 + b_{i,2}a_2 + \ldots + b_{i,t}a_t$ for $i = 1, 2, \ldots, n$, where $b_{i,j}$ is the (i, j)-th entry of M. Then, the dealer sends these secret shares s_i to each party using the private channels.
- **Secret reconstruction phase:** if any subset of t parties reveal their secret shares, the secret z can be recovered. Without loss of generality, suppose the vector of secret shares $\bar{s} = [s_1, s_2, \ldots, s_t]$ is revealed. Then, the vector $\bar{a} = [a_1, a_2, \ldots, a_t]$ can be reconstructed as $\bar{a}^T = \mathsf{M}_{\mathcal{S}}^{-1} \cdot \bar{s}^T$. Note that to recover the secret $z = a_1$, only the first row of $\mathsf{M}_{\mathcal{S}}^{-1}$ needs to be computed.

3.2   Paillier Encryption

The Paillier encryption [14] works as follows: let $N = pq$ be an RSA modulus, where p, q are large primes. Let g be an integer of order a multiple of N modulo

N^2, i.e. $g = (1+N)^{\alpha}\beta^N$ for some $\alpha \in \mathbb{Z}_N$ and $\beta \in \mathbb{Z}_N^*$. The public key is (g, N), and the secret key is the Carmichael function $\lambda = \mathrm{lcm}((p-1), (q-1))$.

To encrypt a message $m \in \mathbb{Z}_N$, we randomly choose $x \in \mathbb{Z}_N^*$ and compute the ciphertext $c = g^m x^N \bmod N^2$. It is obvious that the Paillier encryption enjoys the additive homomorphic property. To decrypt c, we compute

$$m = \frac{L(c^{\lambda} \bmod N^2)}{L(g^{\lambda} \bmod N^2)} \bmod N$$

where the function $L(\cdot)$ takes as input from the set $S_N = \{u < N^2 | u \equiv 1 \pmod{N}\}$ and computes $L(u) = (u-1)/N$.

To see why the decryption works, we first show that for any value $a \in \mathbb{Z}_N^*$, we have $a^{\lambda} \equiv 1 \pmod{N}$. Suppose there exists a value t such that, for any value $a \in \mathbb{Z}_N^*$, we have $a^t \equiv 1 \pmod{N}$. This implies that $a^t \equiv 1 \pmod{p}$ and $a^t \equiv 1 \pmod{q}$. Because p and q are both primes, according to Fermat's little theorem, this holds only if $p-1$ and $q-1$ are both divisors of t. Therefore, the smallest t satisfying this requirement equals λ. For similar reasons, we also have $a^{\lambda N} \equiv 1 \pmod{N^2}$ for any value $a \in \mathbb{Z}_{N^2}^*$. Moreover, recall that $g = (1+N)^{\alpha}\beta^N$ for some $\alpha \in \mathbb{Z}_N$ and $\beta \in \mathbb{Z}_N^*$, the following two equations always hold:

$$L(g^{\lambda} \bmod N^2) = \frac{((1+N)^{\alpha\lambda}\beta^{N\lambda} \bmod N^2) - 1}{N} = \frac{(1+\alpha\lambda N) - 1}{N} \equiv \alpha\lambda$$
$$L(c^{\lambda} \bmod N^2) = L((g^m x^N)^{\lambda} \bmod N^2) = L(g^{m\lambda} \bmod N^2) = m\alpha\lambda$$

Hence, if given the secret key λ, the plaintext can be retrieved as

$$m = \frac{L(c^{\lambda} \bmod N^2)}{L(g^{\lambda} \bmod N^2)} \bmod N$$

The semantic security of the Paillier encryption is based on the *decisional composite residuosity assumption* (DCRA) that distinguishing N^{th} residues from non-N^{th} residues modulo N^2 is infeasible for PPT adversaries.

3.3   Proof of Equality of Discrete Logarithms

The Chaum-Pedersen protocol [4] can be used to prove the equality of discrete logarithms. Let p, q be two large primes such that $q|p-1$. We denote G_q as the subgroup of $\mathbb{Z}_p^*$ with order q. Let g and h be two generators of G_q. We can prove that the values $y \equiv g^x \pmod{p}$ and $t \equiv h^x \pmod{p}$ have the same exponent value x without revealing it. The proof works as follows:

- The prover $\mathcal{P}$ randomly chooses a value $r \in \mathbb{Z}_q$, she then sends $U \equiv g^r \pmod{p}$ and $V \equiv h^r \pmod{p}$ to the verifier $\mathcal{V}$.
- $\mathcal{V}$ sends a random challenge $e \in \mathbb{Z}_q$ back to $\mathcal{P}$.
- $\mathcal{P}$ computes $z = r + xe \bmod q$, and sends z to $\mathcal{V}$.
- $\mathcal{V}$ accepts the proof if $g^z \equiv Uy^e \pmod{p}$ and $h^z \equiv Vt^e \pmod{p}$. Otherwise, she rejects the proof.

The correctness of the above protocol is obvious. Special soundness holds because for two accepting conversations with the same first move (U, V, e_1, z_1) and (U, V, e_2, z_2), where $e_1 \neq e_2$, the witness x that satisfies $y \equiv g^x \pmod{p}$ and $t \equiv h^x \pmod{p}$ can be extracted as $x \equiv (z_1 - z_2)/(e_1 - e_2) \pmod{q}$. Honest verifier zero-knowledge holds because for any random values $e \in \mathbb{Z}_q$ and $z \in \mathbb{Z}_q$, the fabricated tuple $(g^z y^{-e}, h^z t^{-e}, e, z)$ will be an acceptable conversation, and its distribution is perfectly indistinguishable from a real proof.

The above protocol can be made non-interactive using Fiat-Shamir heuristics [8]. Moreover, as shown in [3,15], the proof of equality of discrete logarithms can be extended to work in the cyclic group of squares in $\mathbb{Z}_{N^2}^*$, where $N = pq$ is the RSA modulus.

4   Our Proposed Scheme

Our proposed threshold Paillier encryption based on hyperplane geometry works as follows:

Key Generation Algorithm KeyGen:
The trusted dealer $\mathcal{D}$ first chooses two large safe primes $p = 2p' + 1$ and $q = 2q' + 1$. Define $N = pq$ and $\lambda = p'q'$. $\mathcal{D}$ also chooses two random values $\alpha \in \mathbb{Z}_N$ and $\beta \in \mathbb{Z}_N^*$, and sets $g = (1 + N)^\alpha \beta^N \bmod N^2$. $\mathcal{D}$ then chooses a random value γ in $\mathbb{Z}_N$. Now, the public key pk is a triple (g, N, θ), where $\theta = \alpha\lambda\gamma \bmod N$, and the corresponding secret key is $\lambda\gamma$. Note that the use of safe primes ensures that $\gcd(N, \phi(N)) = 1$, where ϕ is the Euler's totient function. And this further implies that the function $f(x, y) = (1 + N)^x y^N \bmod N^2$ is a bijection from $\mathbb{Z}_N \times \mathbb{Z}_N^*$ to $\mathbb{Z}_{N^2}^*$.

As follows, $\mathcal{D}$ chooses an $n \times t$ matrix M:

$$M = \begin{pmatrix} b_{1,1} & b_{1,2} & \dots & b_{1,t} \\ b_{2,1} & b_{2,2} & \dots & b_{2,t} \\ \vdots & & \vdots & \\ b_{n,1} & b_{n,2} & \dots & b_{n,t} \end{pmatrix}$$

It is required that any t rows of M will form a $t \times t$ invertible matrix M_S. Moreover, $\mathcal{D}$ sets a_1 as the secret key $a_1 = \lambda\gamma$, and chooses $t - 1$ random values $\{a_2, a_3, \dots, a_t\}$. Then, $\mathcal{D}$ computes the secret shares $s_i = a_1 b_{i,1} + a_2 b_{i,2} + \dots + a_t b_{i,t}$ for $i = 1, 2, \dots, n$.

Finally, $\mathcal{D}$ selects the verification key v as a generator of Q_{N^2} which is a cyclic group of squares within $\mathbb{Z}_{N^2}^*$ and the order of Q_{N^2} is λN. The other verification keys are calculated as $v_i = v^{s_i} \bmod N^2$ for $i = 1, 2, \dots, n$.

Now, $\mathcal{D}$ broadcasts the public key $pk = (g, N, \theta)$, the matrix M, and the verification keys $v, \{v_1, v_2, \dots, v_n\}$. And $\mathcal{D}$ sends the secret key shares $\{s_1, s_2, \dots, s_n\}$ to the corresponding decryption parties privately.

Encryption Algorithm Enc:

To encrypt a message $m \in \mathbb{Z}_N$, anyone can randomly select $x \in \mathbb{Z}_N^*$ and compute the ciphertext $c = g^m x^N \bmod N^2$.

Partial Decryption Algorithm PartDec:

Given a ciphertext c, each decryption party partially decrypts it. For example, the ith party P_i uses her secret share s_i to compute the decryption share $c_i = c^{2s_i} \bmod N^2$. She also generates a non-interactive proof p_i to prove that c^2 and v have been raised to the same power s_i. The reason to use c^2 instead of c is to ensure that the value used is a square in $\mathbb{Z}_{N^2}^*$.

The proof works as follows: let H be some collision-resistant hash function. P_i randomly selects a value r, computes $c' = c^{2r}, v' = v^r$. Then, the proof p_i is a pair (z, e), where $e = H(c^2, v, c_i, v_i, c', v')$ and $z = s_i e + r$. P_i broadcasts the decryption share c_i as well as its proof p_i.

Verification Algorithm Veri:

To verify whether the proof p_i is valid, anyone can check the equation $e = H(c^2, v, c_i, v_i, c^{2z}c_i^{-e}, v^z v_i^{-e})$ using the verification keys v and v_i. If p_i is valid, c_i is a correct decryption share of c.

Combining Algorithm Comb:

Without loss of generality, we assume that the parties with indexes $1, 2, \ldots, t$ are honest and their published proofs are valid. If the corresponding rows are selected from the matrix M, we get a $t \times t$ matrix $\mathsf{M}_{\mathcal{S}}$:

$$\mathsf{M}_{\mathcal{S}} = \begin{pmatrix} b_{1,1} & b_{1,2} & \ldots & b_{1,t} \\ b_{2,1} & b_{2,2} & \ldots & b_{2,t} \\ \vdots & & \vdots & \\ b_{t,1} & b_{t,2} & \ldots & b_{t,t} \end{pmatrix}$$

Denote $\mathsf{M}_{\mathcal{S}}'$ as the adjoint matrix of $\mathsf{M}_{\mathcal{S}}$, with the (i, j)th entry as $d_{i,j}$. Then $d_{i,j}$ is the value $(-1)^{i+j}$ times the determinant of the matrix obtained by deleting the jth row and ith column of $\mathsf{M}_{\mathcal{S}}$. Note that the adjoint matrix can be computed without division. Hence, our proposed protocol could avoid the technical obstacle of computing inverses in the group whose order is unknown. Now, anyone can recover the plaintext m using these decryption shares $\{c_1, c_2, \ldots, c_t\}$ as:

$$m = L(\prod_{i=1}^{t} c_i^{d_{1,i}} \bmod N^2) \times \frac{1}{2\Omega\theta} \bmod N$$

where Ω is the determinant of $\mathsf{M}_{\mathcal{S}}$.

5   Security and Efficiency Analysis

In this section, we analyse the security properties and the computational cost of our proposed threshold Paillier encryption scheme.

5.1   Security Analysis

Correctness. We first show that the above protocol achieves the correctness property: if there exists t honest decryption parties, the correct plaintext will be recovered even in the presence of $t - 1$ corrupt decryption parties.

Note that the group Q_{N^2} is defined as the subgroup of the squares in $\mathbb{Z}_{N^2}^*$, and its order is λN. The number of generators of Q_{N^2} is $\phi(\lambda N)$, and the probability that a randomly chosen square in $\mathbb{Z}_{N^2}^*$ to be a generator of Q_{N^2} is extremely high, roughly $1 - 1/\sqrt{N}$. Hence, the proof of equality of discrete logarithms works with very high probability. In other words, if any corrupt decryption party publishes invalid decryption share, the validity proof cannot pass the verification algorithm Veri. Moreover, based on the assumption that t decryption parties are honest, there will exist at least t valid decryption shares. Without loss of generality, we denote $\{c_1, c_2, \ldots, c_t\}$ as a set of t valid decryption shares. Then, the plaintext m can be recovered because:

$$L(\prod_{i=1}^{t} c_i^{d_{1,i}} \bmod N^2) = L(c^{2\sum_{i=1}^{t} s_i \cdot d_{1,i}} \bmod N^2)$$

$$= L(c^{2\Omega\lambda\gamma} \bmod N^2)$$
$$= L((g^m x^N)^{2\Omega\lambda\gamma} \bmod N^2)$$
$$= L((1+N)^{2m\Omega\alpha\lambda\gamma} \cdot (\beta^{2m\Omega\gamma})^{\lambda N} \cdot (x^{2\Omega\gamma})^{\lambda N} \bmod N^2)$$
$$= L((1+N)^{2m\Omega\alpha\lambda\gamma} \bmod N^2)$$
$$= 2m\Omega\alpha\lambda\gamma$$
$$= m \cdot 2\Omega\theta$$

Hence, the combining algorithm Comb will return the correct plaintext m.

Threshold Semantic Security. We use reduction to show that the above protocol achieves threshold semantic security. Assume that there exists a PPT adversary $\mathcal{A}$ who can break the threshold semantic security of our proposed protocol with some non-negligible probability. Then, we prove that, using $\mathcal{A}$ as a subroutine, an attacker $\mathcal{B}$ can be constructed in polynomial time that breaks the semantic security of the original Paillier encryption [14]. In order to invoke $\mathcal{A}$ as a subroutine, the attacker $\mathcal{B}$ must simulate all information that $\mathcal{A}$ views in the threshold protocol. And $\mathcal{A}$ should not be able to distinguish between a simulated conversation and a real run of the protocol.

Theorem 1. *In the random oracle model, the threshold Paillier encryption based on hyperplane geometry achieves threshold semantic security against static adversaries under the decisional composite residuosity assumption.*

Proof. To break semantic security of the original Paillier encryption, the attacker $\mathcal{B}$ runs a game with the challenger. Firstly, $\mathcal{B}$ is given the public key (g, N). Then, $\mathcal{B}$ chooses two messages m_0 and m_1 from the plaintext space, and sends them to the challenger who then randomly chooses a bit b and returns the encryption of m_b to $\mathcal{B}$. $\mathcal{B}$ guesses which message has been encrypted. Now, we show that in order to invoke $\mathcal{A}$ as a subroutine, $\mathcal{B}$ can simulate $\mathcal{A}$'s view in the game G.

- G1: The adversary $\mathcal{A}$ chooses $t - 1$ decryption parties to corrupt. Without loss of generality, we denote these parties as $P_1, P_2, \ldots, P_{t-1}$.
- G2: The attacker $\mathcal{B}$ generates an $n \times t$ matrix M such that any t rows of M will form an invertable $t \times t$ matrix $M_{\mathcal{S}}$. The (i, j)th entry of M is denoted as $b_{i,j}$. $\mathcal{B}$ randomly chooses $\alpha' \in \mathbb{Z}_N$, $\beta' \in \mathbb{Z}_N^*$ and computes $g' = g^{\alpha'} \beta'^N \bmod N^2$. $\mathcal{B}$ also randomly selects $\theta \in \mathbb{Z}_N$ and $t - 1$ values $s_1, s_2, \ldots, s_{t-1}$ in the range $\{0, 1, \ldots \lfloor N^2/4 \rfloor - 1\}$. Moreover, $\mathcal{B}$ randomly selects a value $\omega \in \mathbb{Z}_N$ and sets $v = g'^{2\omega} \bmod N^2$. Hence, v is a square in $\mathbb{Z}_{N^2}^*$. For $i = 1, 2, \ldots, t - 1$, $\mathcal{B}$ computes $v_i = v^{s_i} \bmod N^2$. The other verification keys v_j, where $j = t, t+1, \ldots, n$, can be calculated as follows: define a $t \times t$ matrix A as

$$
A = \begin{pmatrix}
1 & 0 & \ldots & 0 \\
b_{1,1} & b_{1,2} & \ldots & b_{1,t} \\
b_{2,1} & b_{2,2} & \ldots & b_{2,t} \\
\vdots & & \vdots & \\
b_{t-1,1} & b_{t-1,2} & \ldots & b_{t-1,t}
\end{pmatrix}
$$

Hence, we have $A \cdot [a_1, a_2, \ldots a_t]^T = [a_1, s_1, \ldots s_{t-1}]^T$. Denote $\lambda_{i,j}$ as the (i, j)th entry of A^{-1}. For $k = 2, 3, \ldots, t$, we have

$$
v^{a_k} \equiv (v^{a_1})^{\lambda_{k,1}} \cdot \prod_{i=1}^{t-1} (v^{s_i})^{\lambda_{k,i+1}} \equiv (1 + 2w\theta N)^{\lambda_{k,1}} \cdot \prod_{i=1}^{t-1} v_i^{\lambda_{k,i+1}} \pmod{N^2}
$$

Therefore, for $j = t, t+1, \ldots, n$, we can compute

$$
v_j = (1 + 2\omega\theta N)^{b_{j,1}} \cdot \prod_{k=2}^{t} (v^{a_k})^{b_{j,k}} \bmod N^2
$$

Finally, the attacker $\mathcal{B}$ sends the matrix M, the public key (g', N, θ), the $t - 1$ secret key shares $s_1, s_2, \ldots, s_{t-1}$, and the verification keys $v, v_1, v_2, \ldots, v_n$ to the adversary $\mathcal{A}$.

- G3: $\mathcal{B}$ simulates the *partial decryption oracle* and answers $\mathcal{A}$'s decryption queries. If $\mathcal{A}$ encrypts a message m and asks $\mathcal{B}$ to decrypt its ciphertext $c = g'^m x^N \bmod N^2$. $\mathcal{B}$ will compute $c_i = c^{2s_i}$ for $i = 1, 2, \ldots, t - 1$. The other decryption shares c_j, where $j = t, t+1, \ldots, n$, can be calculated similarly as in the above step: for $k = 2, 3, \ldots, t$, we have

$$
c^{2a_k} \equiv (c^{a_1})^{2\lambda_{k,1}} \cdot \prod_{i=1}^{t-1} (c^{2s_i})^{\lambda_{k,i+1}} \equiv (1 + m\theta N)^{2\lambda_{k,1}} \cdot \prod_{i=1}^{t-1} c_i^{\lambda_{k,i+1}} \pmod{N^2}
$$

Therefore, we can compute

$$
c_j = (1 + m\theta N)^{2b_{j,1}} \cdot \prod_{k=2}^{t} (c^{2a_k})^{b_{j,k}} \bmod N^2
$$

for $j = t, t + 1, \ldots, n$. Next, $\mathcal{B}$ need to generate proofs for these decryption shares. If $\mathcal{B}$ knows s_i, the proof p_i is generated in the standard way as described in Sect. 3.3. Moreover, in the random oracle model, the attacker $\mathcal{B}$ has full control of the hash function, and $\mathcal{B}$ can answer a hash query using any value of her choice, as long as she returns consistent output if the same input is queries multiple times. Hence, $\mathcal{B}$ can fabricate the other proofs that she has no knowledge of their secret shares. This is done by defining the value of the random oracle at $H(c^2, v, c_i, v_i, c^{2z}c_i^{-e}, v^z v_i^{-e})$ to be e. Now, $\mathcal{B}$ returns the n decryption shares $(c_1, c_2, \ldots, c_n)$ along with their proofs $(p_1, p_2, \ldots, p_n)$ to $\mathcal{A}$.

- G4: In this step, $\mathcal{B}$ first waits for $\mathcal{A}$ to select two messages m_0 and m_1 from the plaintext space. Once receiving these two values, $\mathcal{B}$ forwards them to the challenger. The challenger then randomly selects a bit b, encrypts m_b using the original Paillier encryption and returns its ciphertext c to $\mathcal{B}$. Now, $\mathcal{B}$ computes $c' = c^{\alpha'} \bmod N^2$ and sends c' to $\mathcal{A}$.
- G5: This step is similar as in step G3. The additional requirement is that $\mathcal{A}$ is not allowed to use c' to query the *partial decryption oracle*.
- G6: $\mathcal{A}$ outputs a bit b', and $\mathcal{B}$ forwards b' to the challenger.

It is clear that the above simulation can be carried out in polynomial time. The remaining task is to prove that a simulated conversation is indistinguishable from a real run of the protocol. Because no information has been simulated in the steps G1 and G6, and the step G5 just repeats G3. We only need to show that the adversary $\mathcal{A}$ can not distinguish the simulated information from the step G2 to the step G4.

- **Indistinguishability of information in G2:** In this step, the same matrix M can be reused. Both g and g' are uniformly distributed within the set of elements whose order is a multiple of N. θ is uniformly distributed in $\mathbb{Z}_N$. Hence, the matrix M and public key (g', N, θ) follow exactly the same distribution as in the real protocol. The secret key shares are randomly distributed in $\{0, 1, \ldots, \mathbb{Z}_{\lambda N} - 1\}$ in the real protocol. In the simulation, they are randomly distributed in $\{0, 1, \ldots \lfloor N^2/4 \rfloor - 1\}$. Although there is some gap between these two sets, their statistical distance is $O(n^{-1/2})$ that cannot be distinguished by PPT adversaries. The simulated verification keys $v, v_1, v_2, \ldots, v_n$ are randomly distributed in the cyclic group of squares within $\mathbb{Z}_{N^2}^*$, and they cannot be distinguished from real ones. Hence, the simulated information in this step is statistically indistinguishable from a real run of the protocol.
- **Indistinguishability of information in G3:** In this step, the simulated decryption shares $(c_1, c_2, \ldots, c_n)$ follow the same distribution as those in the real protocol. Both of them are randomly distributed in the cyclic group of squares within $\mathbb{Z}_{N^2}^*$. Moreover, the simulated proofs $(p_1, p_2, \ldots, p_n)$ also follow the same distribution as those in the real protocol. Hence, the simulated information in this step is indistinguishable.
- **Indistinguishability of information in G4:** In this step, the ciphertext c and the modified ciphertext $c' = c^{\alpha'} \bmod N^2$ are both randomly distributed in $\mathbb{Z}_{N^2}$. Hence, they are indistinguishable.

5.2 Efficiency Analysis

In this part, we analyse the computational cost of our proposed protocol and compare it with some existing works in the literature that are based on polynomial interpolation, e.g. [5,9]. The analysis is divided into two parts. In general cases, we do not restrict the selection of the matrix M as long as any t rows of it can form an invertible matrix M_S. Moreover, we discuss the use of Vandermonde matrix. And we show that our work is more efficient than Shoup's trick in this special case.

- **In general cases:** In the KeyGen algorithm, the major difference between our work and the existing works is how to compute the secret shares. In [5,9], this is done by evaluating a $t-1$ degree polynomial. Using Horner's algorithm, its computational complexity is $O(t)$, where t is the threshold. In our work, the complexity of this task is also $O(t)$. In both our work and the existing works, the Enc, PartDec and Veri algorithms are similar. While in the Comb algorithm, [5,9] use polynomial interpolation, and their computational complexity is $O(t^2)$. In our work, the heavy load is to compute the adjoint matrix of a $t \times t$ matrix. More precisely, because only the first row of the adjoint matrix needs to be calculated, our computational complexity is also $O(t^2)$. Hence, our work is as efficient as the existing works in general cases.
- **Using Vandermonde matrix:** In this case, the technical details of our work will be very similar as in those existing work. When recovering the secret using the decryption shares, our work also can be considered as polynomial interpolation. The reason that our work avoids the "interpolating over $\mathbb{Z}_{\phi(N)}$ problem" is that a constant value Ω has been multiplied with each of the Lagrange coefficient during interpolating, where Ω is the determinant of the $t \times t$ matrix M_S. Note that in Vandermonde matrix, $\Omega = \prod_{i,j=1,i<j}^{t}(a_i - a_j)$. It is clear that Ω is a divisor of $\prod_{i,j=1,i<j}^{n}(a_i - a_j) = t!(n-t)!$. Since $t!(n-t)!$ further divides $\Delta = n!$, Ω is a non-trivial divisor of Δ. We have to note that during polynomial interpolation, the modulus of the exponent part is unknown, so the exponent value cannot be reduced. Therefore, compared with Shoup's trick [19], a smaller exponent value in our work not only saves some computational cost, but also requires less storage in the register during computation. Actually, Ω is the least common multiple of the denominator in the Lagrange coefficients. Hence, our work can be regarded as optimization of Shoup's trick and it also can be used to improve the existing threshold cryptosystems that are based on factoring.

6 Discussion and Conclusion

In this paper, we propose a threshold Paillier encryption cryptosystem using hyperplane geometry. We have proved that it is correct and it achieves threshold semantic security in the random oracle model. Compared with the existing schemes based on polynomial interpolation, our work does not suffer the technical obstacle of computing inverses in the group whose order is unknown. Moreover, it is more computationally efficient than Shoup's trick and it can be used as a general building block to design secure and efficient threshold cryptosystems based on factoring.

Acknowledgement. This work was partially supported by the National Natural Science Foundation of China (Grant No. 61501333, 61572379, 61370224), National Key Technology Support Program of China (Grant No. 2012BAH45B01), and Natural Science Foundation of Hubei Province of China (Grant No. 2015CFA069, 2015CFB257). We are also grateful to the anonymous reviewers for their valuable comments on the paper.

References

1. Baudron, O., Fouque, P.-A., Pointcheval, D., Stern, J., Poupard, G.: Practical multi-candidate election system. In: Proceedings of the 20th ACM Symposium on Principles of Distributed Computing (PODC 2001), pp. 274–283, New York, NY, USA (2001)
2. Blakley, R.: Safeguarding cryptographic keys. Proc. Nat. Comput. Conf. **48**, 313–317 (1979)
3. Camenisch, J.L., Michels, M.: A group signature scheme with improved efficiency. In: Ohta, K., Pei, D. (eds.) ASIACRYPT 1998. LNCS, vol. 1514, pp. 160–174. Springer, Heidelberg (1998)
4. Chaum, D., Pedersen, T.P.: Wallet databases with observers. In: Brickell, E.F. (ed.) CRYPTO 1992. LNCS, vol. 740, pp. 89–105. Springer, Heidelberg (1993)
5. Damgård, I., Jurik, M., Nielsen, J.B.: A generalisation of Paillier's public-key system with application to electronic voting (2003)
6. Desmedt, Y.G., Frankel, Y.: Threshold cryptosystems. In: Brassard, G. (ed.) CRYPTO 1989. LNCS, vol. 435, pp. 307–315. Springer, Heidelberg (1990)
7. Desmedt, Y.G., Frankel, Y.: Shared generation of authenticators and signatures. In: Feigenbaum, J. (ed.) CRYPTO 1991. LNCS, vol. 576, pp. 457–469. Springer, Heidelberg (1992)
8. Fiat, A., Shamir, A.: How to prove yourself: practical solutions to identification and signature problems. In: Odlyzko, A.M. (ed.) CRYPTO 1986. LNCS, vol. 263, pp. 186–194. Springer, Heidelberg (1987)
9. Fouque, P.-A., Poupard, G., Stern, J.: Sharing decryption in the context of voting or lotteries. In: Frankel, Y. (ed.) FC 2000. LNCS, vol. 1962, pp. 90–104. Springer, Heidelberg (2001)
10. Frankel, Y., Gemmell, P., MacKenzie, P.D., Yung, M.: Optimal-resilience proactive public-key cryptosystems. In: Proceedings of the 38th IEEE symposium on the Foundations of Computer Science (FOCS 1997), pp. 384–393 (1997)
11. Gennaro, R., Jarecki, S., Krawczyk, H., Rabin, T.: Robust and efficient sharing of RSA functions. In: Koblitz, N. (ed.) CRYPTO 1996. LNCS, vol. 1109, pp. 157–172. Springer, Heidelberg (1996)
12. Hazay, C., Nissim, K.: Efficient set operations in the presence of malicious adversaries. J. Cryptology **25**(3), 383–433 (2012)
13. Kissner, L., Song, D.: Privacy-preserving set operations. In: Shoup, V. (ed.) CRYPTO 2005. LNCS, vol. 3621, pp. 241–257. Springer, Heidelberg (2005)

14. Pieprzyk, J.P., Harper, G., Menezes, A., Vanstone, S.A., Paillier, P.: Public-key cryptosystems based on composite degree residuosity classes. In: Stern, J. (ed.) EUROCRYPT 1999. LNCS, vol. 1592, pp. 223–238. Springer, Heidelberg (1999)
15. Poupard, G., Stern, J.: Security analysis of a practical "on the fly" authentication and signature generation. In: Nyberg, K. (ed.) EUROCRYPT 1998. LNCS, vol. 1403, pp. 422–436. Springer, Heidelberg (1998)
16. Rabin, T.: A simplified approach to threshold and proactive RSA. In: Krawczyk, H. (ed.) CRYPTO 1998. LNCS, vol. 1462, pp. 89–104. Springer, Heidelberg (1998)
17. Ryan, P.Y.A., Bismark, D., Heather, J., Schneider, S., Xia, Z.: Prêt à voter: a voter-verifiable voting system. IEEE Trans. Inf. Forensics Secur. 4(4), 662–673 (2009)
18. De Santis, A., Desmedt, Y., Frankel, Y., Yung, M.: How to share a function securely. In: Proceedings of the 26th ACM Symposium on the Theory of Computing, pp. 522–533 (1994)
19. Shoup, V.: Practical threshold signatures. In: Preneel, B. (ed.) EUROCRYPT 2000. LNCS, vol. 1807, pp. 207–220. Springer, Heidelberg (2000)

Identity-Based Group Encryption

Xiling Luo[1,4,5], Yili Ren[1], Jingwen Liu[2], Jiankun Hu[3], Weiran Liu[1],
Zhen Wang[1], Wei Xu[2], and Qianhong Wu[1,6(✉)]

[1] School of Electronic and Information Engineering, Beihang University,
Beijing, China
qianhaong.wu@buaa.edu.cn
[2] Potevio Information Technology Co., Ltd., Beijing, China
[3] School of Engineering and IT, University of New South Wales, Sydney, Australia
[4] State Key Laboratory of Integrated Services Networks, Xidian University,
Xi'an, China
[5] Beijing Key Laboratory for Network-based Cooperative Air Traffic Management,
Beijing, China
[6] State Key Laboratory of Information Security,
Institute of Information Engineering, Chinese Academy of Sciences,
Beijing 100093, China

Abstract. Cloud computing makes it easy for people to share files anywhere and anytime with mobile end devices. There is a privacy issue
in such applications even if the files are encrypted. Specially, the public
keys or identities of the receivers will be exposed to the cloud server or
hackers. Group Encryption (GE) is designed to achieve anonymity of the
receiver(s). The existing GE schemes are all realized in the public key
infrastructure (PKI) setting, in which complicated certificates management is required to ensure security. It is observed that GE is especially
appealing to institutions which usually have their own closed secure user
management system. In this paper, we propose a new concept, referred
to as identity-based group encryption (IBGE), which realizes GE in the
identity-based cryptography setting. In the IBGE, a private key generator (PKG) designates each user a secret key associated with his identity;
and the user can register his identity as a group member to a group
manager without leaking his secret key. Then anyone can send confiden-
tial messages to the group member without leaking the group member's
identity. However, the group manager can trace the receiver if a dispute
occurs or the privacy mechanism is abused. Following this model, we propose the first IBGE scheme that is formally proven secure in the standard
model. Analysis shows that our scheme is also efficient and practical.

Keywords: Group encryption · Identity-based · Knowledge proof

1 Introduction

With cloud storage, now it is easy for people to share private files anywhere and
anytime with smart mobile devices. To protect the files, it is usually suggested that

J.K. Liu and R. Steinfeld (Eds.): ACISP 2016, Part II, LNCS 9723, pp. 87–102, 2016.
DOI: 10.1007/978-3-319-40367-0_6

one encrypts the files before uploading to the cloud. However, even with encryption, the receivers' identity information will be exposed to the cloud server and hackers, which may raise social engineering attacks. Many cryptographic schemes have been proposed to achieve user privacy. Among them, group signature [7] allows a sender to issue a signature on behalf of the group while concealing his identity within a group of legitimate users. Group signature schemes were introduced by Chaum and van Heyst [7] and developed by Boyen, Waters, Kiayias, Yung and Groth [6,12,15]. Group encryption [14] is the encryption analogue of group signatures and achieve different security goals. Specifically, a GE allows a sender to send a ciphertext to a receiver whose identity is hidden within a group of certified users. A group manager (GM) issues the certificates to these users and make them become the legitimate group members. In GE schemes, a public authority can identify the receiver if a need arises. GE schemes were motivated by multiple applications such as Ad-Hoc access structure group signature, secure oblivious retriever storage and anonymous trusted third parties. GE schemes were introduced by Kiayias, Tsiounis and Yung [14] and further developed in a line of works [9,16,21].

A majority of GE schemes are based on Public Key Infrastructure (PKI). This leads to some drawbacks of GE schemes. First, GE could be implemented in classified organizations. These organizations have their own closed secure user management system. They do not have to use a PKI as a component, which comes from an open environment. A problem of PKI-based GE schemes is obvious. If the Certificate Authority (CA) is occasionally offline, then the certificates can not be updated and the GE scheme will fail to work.

Moreover, in public-key cryptosystems user's public key is a random string unrelated to his identity. When a sender wants to send a message to a receiver, he must obtain the receiver's public key authenticated by the trusted Certificate Authority. So the problems with the PKI-based GE schemes are the high cost in authenticating and managing the public keys, and the difficulty in managing multiple communities.

It seems appealing to use IBE schemes to replace the PKI-based public-key encryption in GE. In this way, the variant of GE will be suited to the closed environment and works more efficiently. Identity-based cryptosystems were introduced by Shamir in 1984 [22]. Its main idea is that the public keys of a user can be easily derived from arbitrary strings corresponding to his identity information such as name, telephone number or email address. A Private Key Generator (PKG) computes private keys from a master secret key and distributes them to the users participating in the scheme. This eliminates the need for certificates that have been in a traditional PKI system. Identity-based systems may be a good alternative for PKI-based systems from the viewpoint of efficiency and convenience.

1.1 Our Contribution

Motivated by the above scenarios, we propose a new cryptographic primitive called identity-based group encryption (IBGE). We first contribute the model and security notions of IBGE. We then construct a concrete identity-based group encryption scheme and prove its related security properties.

IBGE involves five parties, a group manager (GM), a group of legitimate users, a sender, a verifier and a private key generator (PKG). IBGE consists of the six procedures. They are parameter generation procedure, group key generation procedure, user key generation procedure, encryption procedure, decryption procedure and trace procedure.

Besides correctness, we define two security notions in IBGE. The first property, called anonymity and semantic security against chosen-identity and chosen-plaintext attacks, protects the users from a hostile environment where the attacker may want to extract information about the message and extracting information about the receiver's identity. The second property, i.e., traceability, ensures that the tracking is reliable and the prevention of collusion attacks. We formally define the adversary models to capture the realistic attacks.

We design a concrete IBGE scheme in a modular way. In order to get an efficient and practical scheme, we use three primitives, i.e., a public-key encryption scheme which satisfies CCA2 security, an IBE scheme which satisfies anonymity and semantic security, and a zero-knowledge proof which satisfies special properties. Our proposal is the first scheme with anonymity and semantic security under chosen-identity and chosen-plaintext attacks, as well as traceability.

We prove the security of our concrete IBGE scheme according to our security notions. And we give the analysis of probability as well as time complexity. Then we prove that the identity of the real receiver can be traced correctly. Our IBGE is fully functional identity-based group encryption scheme proven secure in standard model. IBGE can also be used for a fundamental component of other cryptosystems.

1.2   Related Work

Kiayias, Tsiounis and Yung provided the conception of Group Encryption [14] and a modular design including zero-knowledge proofs, digital signature schemes, public-key encryption schemes with CCA2 security and key-privacy and commitment schemes. They showed an efficient instantiation by using Paillier's cryptosystem [20], a modification of the Cramer-Shoup public-key cryptosystem [8]. And their GM scheme requires an interaction between the sender and a verifier using a $\sum$-protocol, but using Fiat-Shamir paradigm [11] the interaction can be removed. Cathalo, Libert and Yung [9] proposed a group encryption with non-interactive realization in the standard model. Independently, Qin, Wu, Susilo, and Mu [21] considered a similar primitive called Group Decryption. The Group Decryption has non-interactive proofs and short ciphertexts. Libert, Yung, Joye, and Peters proposed a traceable GE [16] which can trace all the ciphertexts encrypted by a specific user without abolishing the anonymity of the others.

The notion of custodian-hiding verifiable encryption was proposed by Liu, et al. [17–19]. A sender can encrypt a message using a public key chosen from a public key list but the recipient is anonymous. But there is no group manager to manage the potential receivers. Their notion is designed for Ad-Hoc applications.

A ciphertext has to contain the public key list of potential receivers. In the case of dispute, no group manager can reveal the identity of the real receiver.

Identity-based cryptosystems were introduced by Shamir [22]. Boneh, Franklin [3,4] proposed a fully functional IBE scheme. This scheme's security based on computational Diffie-Hellman assumption and it has chosen ciphertext security in the random oracle model. Boneh, Franklin also gave the definition of chosen-ciphertext security and chosen-plaintext security of an IBE scheme as well as a concrete IBE system. Groth presented an IBE scheme [12] that is fully secure in the standard model and provided an efficient solution to the problem of achieving anonymous IBE without random oracles.

2   Preliminaries

2.1   Bilinear Groups

Let p be a large prime. $\mathbb{G}, \hat{\mathbb{G}}, \mathbb{G}_T$ are three cyclic groups of prime order p. $g, \hat{g}$ are generators of $\mathbb{G}, \hat{\mathbb{G}}$ respectively. We say that $\mathbb{G}, \hat{\mathbb{G}}$ are bilinear groups if there is a bilinear map $e : \mathbb{G} \times \hat{\mathbb{G}} \to \mathbb{G}_T$ that satisfies the following properties [1,2]:

- *Bilinear.* We say a map $e : \mathbb{G} \times \hat{\mathbb{G}} \to \mathbb{G}_T$ is bilinear if $e(u^a, \hat{u}^b) = e(u, \hat{u})^{ab}$ for all $u \in \mathbb{G}, \hat{u} \in \hat{\mathbb{G}}, a, b \in \mathbb{Z}_p$.
- *Non-degenerate.* If $g, \hat{g}$ are generators of $\mathbb{G}, \hat{\mathbb{G}}$ respectively, then $e(g, \hat{g})$ is a generator of $\mathbb{G}_T$.
- *Computable.* There is an efficient algorithm to compute $e(u, \hat{u})$ for all $u \in \mathbb{G}, \hat{u} \in \hat{\mathbb{G}}$.

The bilinear group defined above [10] is asymmetric, since $\mathbb{G}$ and $\hat{\mathbb{G}}$ are distinct cyclic groups. An asymmetric bilinear map can be constructed using curves described by Barrrto, Naehring [5]. We use bilinear groups as a black box. If $\mathbb{G} = \hat{\mathbb{G}}$, the group is a symmetrical bilinear group. In this paper, our IBGE scheme relies on the symmetrical bilinear group.

2.2   Complexity Assumptions

Our IBGE scheme's security is based on decisional augmented bilinear Diffie-Hellman exponent (decisional ABDHE) assumption [12].

First, we review the q-BDHE problem: Given a vector of $2q + 1$ elements

$$(g', g, g^\alpha, g^{\alpha^2}, ..., g^{\alpha^q}, g^{\alpha^{q+2}}, ..., g^{\alpha^{2q}}) \in \mathbb{G}^{2q+1}$$

as input, output $e(g, g')^{\alpha^{q+1}} \in \mathbb{G}_T$. Since the term $g^{\alpha^{q+1}}$ is missing in the input, it is intractable to compute $e(g, g')^{\alpha^{q+1}}$.

The definition of the q-ABDHE problem is almost identical: given a vector of $2q + 2$ elements

$$(g', g'^{\alpha^{q+2}}, g, g^\alpha, g^{\alpha^2}, ..., g^{\alpha^q}, g^{\alpha^{q+2}}, ..., g^{\alpha^{2q}}) \in \mathbb{G}^{2q+2}$$

as input, output $e(g, g')^{\alpha^{q+1}} \in \mathbb{G}_T$. Since the term $g^{\alpha^{-1}}$ is missing in the input, it is intractable to compute $e(g, g')^{\alpha^{q+1}}$, even though the term $g'^{\alpha^{q+2}}$ is added.

We will use a truncated version of the q-ABDHE problem, in which the terms $(g^{\alpha^{q+2}}, ..., g^{\alpha^{2q}})$ are omitted from the input, because of this version of q-ABDHE problem is more useful for our concrete IBGE scheme.

The truncated q-ABDHE problem: given a vector of q elements

$$(g', g'^{\alpha^{q+2}}, g, g^{\alpha}, g^{\alpha^2}, ..., g^{\alpha^q}) \in \mathbb{G}^q$$

as input, output $e(g, g')^{\alpha^{q+1}} \in \mathbb{G}_T$. The truncated q-ABDHE problem is hard if the q-ABDHE problem is hard, since the input vector of truncated q-ABDHE is less than q-ABDHE. $\mathcal{A}$ has advantage ϵ in solving truncated q-ABDHE if

$$\Pr[\mathcal{A}(g', g'^{\alpha^{q+2}}, g, g^{\alpha}, g^{\alpha^2}, ..., g^{\alpha^q}) = e(g_{q+1}, g')] \geqslant \epsilon$$

where the probability is over the randomly chosen $g, g' \xleftarrow{R} \mathbb{G}$, the randomly chosen $\alpha \xleftarrow{R} \mathbb{Z}_p$ and the randomly chosen bits by $\mathcal{A}$.

We use g_i and g'_i to denote g^{α^i} and g'^{α^i}. Now, it is easy to define the decisional version of truncated q-ABDHE. An algorithm $\mathcal{B}$ that outputs $b \in \{0,1\}$ has advantage ϵ in solving truncated decision q-ABDHE if

$$\mid \Pr[\mathcal{B}(g', g'_{q+2}, g, g_1, ..., g_q, e(g_{q+1}, g')) = 0] - \Pr[\mathcal{B}(g', g'_{q+2}, g, g_1, ..., g_q, Z) = 0] \mid \geqslant \epsilon$$

where the probability is over the randomly chosen $g, g' \xleftarrow{R} \mathbb{G}$, the randomly chosen $\alpha \xleftarrow{R} \mathbb{Z}_p$, the randomly chosen $Z \xleftarrow{R} \mathbb{G}_T$ and the randomly chosen bits of $\mathcal{B}$. We refer to the distribution on the left as P_{ABDHE} and the distribution on the right as R_{ABDHE}.

Definition 1. *We say that the decisional version of truncated (t, ϵ, q)-ABDHE assumption holds in $\mathbb{G}$ if no t-time algorithm has advantage at least ϵ in solving the decisional version of truncated q-ABDHE problem in $\mathbb{G}$.*

2.3   Proof of Knowledge

Let $R = (x, w)$ be a NP relation, namely we can verify whether $(x, w) \in R$ in polynomial time. We say that x is input and w is the witness of x. $\mathcal{P}$ is a polynomial time prover with the input $(x, w) \in R$. $\mathcal{V}$ is a polynomial time verifier with the input x. We consider a three-step protocol between $\mathcal{P}$ and $\mathcal{V}$. $\mathcal{P}$ selects a random r, then computes $t = Commitment(x, w; r)$ and sends t to $\mathcal{V}$. $\mathcal{V}$ selects a random c from an appropriate domain and sends c to $\mathcal{P}$, we consider this procedure as *Challenge*. Finally, $\mathcal{P}$ responds $\mathcal{V}$ with $s = Response(x, w, c; r)$. $\mathcal{V}$ computes a bit $b = Check(x, t, c, z)$. We require that $Commitment, Challenge, Check$ are polynomial time algorithms. A $\sum$-protocol is made up of $Commitment, Challenge, Response$ and satisfies completeness, correctness, soundness with knowledge extraction and honest-verifier zero-knowledge.

- *Completeness.* Completeness is achieved if $\Pr[(\mathcal{P}, \mathcal{V})(x) = 1 | (x, w) \in R] \geqslant 1 - \mu(k)$, where $\mu(k)$ is a negligible function. This means that if $(x, w) \in R$, $\mathcal{V}$ will accept with probability at least $1 - \mu(k)$. $(\mathcal{P}, \mathcal{V})(x)$ means the output of the system when the input is x.
- *Correctness.* Correctness is achieved if $\Pr[(\tilde{\mathcal{P}}, \mathcal{V})(x) = 1 | (x, w) \notin R] \leqslant \mu(k)$, where $\tilde{P}$ is a dishonest prover. This means that if $(x, w) \notin R$, $\mathcal{V}$ will accept with probability at most $\mu(k)$.
- *Soundness with knowledge extraction.* We consider a polynomial time algorithm, called *Extractor*. *Extractor* plays the role of $\mathcal{V}$ and interacts with $\mathcal{P}$. If the input (z, t, x, z, c', z') satisfies $Check(x, t, c, z) = Check(x, t, c', z') = 1$, then $Extractor(z, t, x, z, c', z')$ will output a witness that satisfies $(x, w) \in R$. This means $\mathcal{P}$ indeed has the knowledge.
- *Honest-verifier zero-knowledge.* We consider a polynomial time algorithm, called *Simulator*. For all $(x, w) \in R$ and c the following two distributions are indistinguishable. The first one is (x, t, c, z) which $\mathcal{V}$ can obtain by interacting with $\mathcal{P}$. The second one is (x, t, c', z') which *Simulator* can obtain by computing. That is to say a proof transcript can be produced by a polynomial time with the same probability distributions.

3 Modelling IBGE

3.1 The IBGE System

IBGE involves five parties, a GM who administers the group and traces the receivers when it is necessary. A group of legitimate users who receive messages from senders anonymously, a sender who might be one of the group members or not and has secret messages to be sent to the legitimate members, and a verifier who can prove the encrypted identity and the identity that forms IBE ciphertext are identical, and a PKG who can issue the private keys to the users. The PKG can quit from an IBGE scheme after the execution of ParaGen and UKGen, but the GM should be always online to manage the group and trace the receiver when disputes occur. IBGE consists of the following procedures.

- $(Params, MSK) \leftarrow$ ParaGen(λ). This is a polynomial time algorithm which takes as input a security parameter λ, outputs the system parameter $Params$ and a master-key MSK. It is operated by PKG.
- $(PK_{GM}, SK_{GM}) \leftarrow$ GKGen($Params$). This is a polynomial time algorithm which takes as input system parameter $Params$, outputs the group public key and private key (PK_{GM}, SK_{GM}). It is operated by GM.
- $(SK_{ID}) \leftarrow$ UKGen($Params, ID, MSK$). This is a polynomial time algorithm which takes as input system parameter $Params$, user's ID and MSK, outputs the user's corresponding private key SK_{ID}. It is operated by PKG. Each user can register his identity as a group member to GM. GM maintains the ID list $I = \{ID_1, ..., ID_i\}$.
- $(C) \leftarrow$ Encryption($M, Params, ID, PK_{GM}$). This is a polynomial time algorithm which takes as input a message M in the structured message space,

system parameter $Params$, the intended group member's ID, and group public key PK_{GM}, outputs a final ciphertext C in the ciphertext space. It is operated by the sender.

- $(M) \leftarrow$ Decryption($Params, C, SK_{ID}$). This is a polynomial time algorithm which takes as input system parameter $Params$, ciphertext C, user's private key SK_{ID}, outputs the message M in the message space. It is operated by the receiver.
- $(ID) \leftarrow$ Trace(C, SK_{GM}). GM first verifies if the verifier $\mathcal{V}$ outputs 1, then verifies the correctness of the encryption of ID. If both of them are correct, GM runs a polynomial time algorithm takes as input ciphertext C and group private key SK_{GM}, outputs the ID of the receiver.

Definition 2. *We say that an IBGE scheme is correct if the following correctness game return 1 with overwhelming probability.*

We use this notation to denote a two-party protocol

$$\langle output_A | output_B \rangle \leftarrow \langle A(input_A), B(input_B) \rangle (common - input).$$

1. Run ParaGen(λ), the algorithm outputs system parameter $Params$ and MSK.
2. Run GKGen($Params$), the algorithm outputs group public key and private key (PK_{GM}, SK_{GM}).
3. Run UKGen(ID, MSK), the algorithm outputs the user's corresponding private key SK_{ID}.
4. Run Encryption(M, ID, PK_{GM}), the algorithm outputs C.
5. Verify if

$$((M \neq \text{Decryption}(SK_{ID}, C)) \vee (\langle done|0\rangle \leftarrow$$
$$\langle P(s, n, ID), \mathcal{V}\rangle (C_{10}, C_{11}, g, g_1, g_2, g_3, k_1, k_2, \psi, l, t, v, w, d)) = 0)$$
$$\vee (ID \neq \text{Trace}(SK_{GM}, C))$$

return 0 else return 1.

3.2 Adversarial Models

In following games, adversary $\mathcal{A}$ can adaptive query a series of oracles. These oracles are maintained by a challenger. In anonymity and semantic security game, the adversary can only adaptive query the Extract oracle. In traceability game the adversary can adaptive query all of the following oracles.

- Extract oracle. The adversary queries the oracle with user's ID, obtains the user's corresponding private key SK_{ID}.
- Corruption oracle. The adversary queries the oracle with a PK_{GM}. The challenger responds with the corresponding secret key SK_{GM}.
- Encryption oracle. The adversary queries the oracle with (PK_{GM}, ID, M). The challenger responds with the corresponding ciphertext C.
- Decrypt oracle. The adversary queries the oracle with a valid ciphertext C for decryption. The challenger responds with the corresponding message M.
- Trace oracle. The adversary queries the oracle with a valid ciphertext C. The challenger responds with the identity ID of the real receiver.

3.3   Security Notions of IBGE

Anonymity and Semantic security. In order to protect the message security and the receiver's identity from attack, we propose the following definition. When the ciphertext can not reveal information of the message, we say that the cryptosystem is semantic secure. When the ciphertext can not reveal information of the identity of the receiver, we say that the cryptosystem is anonymous. Now, we consider the combination of these two notions.

Definition 3. *We say that an IBGE scheme has anonymity and semantic security against chosen-identity attacks and chosen-plaintext attacks (ANO-IND-CIA-CPA) if no polynomially bounded adversary $\mathcal{A}$ has non-negligible advantage in the following game.*

- **Setup.** The challenger builds the system. It takes as input security parameter λ and runs the algorithm $\mathsf{ParaGen}(\lambda)$ which outputs system parameter *Params* and master-key *MSK*. It gives the adversary *Params* but keeps *MSK* to itself.
- **Phase 1.** The adversary can adaptively issue extraction query of $\langle ID_i \rangle$ using Extract oracle, then obtains the user's private key SK_{ID_i}.
- **Challenge.** After Phase 1, adversary chooses two identities ID_0, ID_1 and two equal length plaintexts M_0, M_1. The only restriction is that the two identities did not appear in any private key extraction query in Phase 1. Challenger chooses a random bit $b \in \{0, 1\}$ and a random bit $c \in \{0, 1\}$, and sends the ciphertext $C = \mathsf{Encryption}(Param, ID_b, M_c)$ to adversary.
- **Phase 2.** It is similar to Phase 1. The two constraints are $ID_i \neq ID$ and can not query Trace oracle.
- **Guess.** The adversary outputs $b' \in \{0, 1\}$ and $c' \in \{0, 1\}$. The adversary wins the game if $b = b' \wedge c = c'$.

We define adversary $\mathcal{A}$'s advantage with security parameter λ in ANO-IND-CIA-CPA game as $Adv_{\mathcal{A}}(\lambda) =| \Pr[b = b' \wedge c = c'] - \frac{1}{4} |$.

Traceability. In order to prevent adversary from colluding with others in IBGE, we give the following definition. GM has capacity to trace the real receiver when disputes occur.

Definition 4. *We say that an IBGE scheme is traceable if no polynomially bounded adversary has non-negligible probability to win in the following game.*

- **Setup.** The challenger builds the system. It takes as input the security parameter λ and runs the algorithm $\mathsf{ParaGen}(\lambda)$ which outputs system parameter *Params* and master-key *MSK*. It gives the adversary *Params* but keeps *MSK* to itself.
- **Inspect phase.** The adversary can adaptively query all the oracles defined above and controls the prover $\mathcal{P}$ in the zero-knowledge proof.
- **Output.** The adversary outputs a valid ciphertext C^*. The adversary wins if the group manager outputs a wrong identity of the recipient.

4   The Proposal

4.1   High Level Description of the Scheme

In this section, we provide a bird-view of our IBGE scheme. The scheme involves three building block, i.e., an IBGE scheme with ANO-IND-ID-CPA security, a public-key encryption with CCA2 security, a zero-knowledge proof with specific properties. In a high level our scheme works as follow.

First, a GE scheme should protect identity of the receivers from being leaked since the attacker may extract the receivers' identity then obtain the total constituent of the group. So, our IBGE scheme should achieve the anonymity of the receivers. We employ an identity-based encryption with ANO-IND-ID-CPA security [13] to produce the IBE ciphertext. This IBE ciphertext has anonymity and semantic security against chosen-identity attacks and chosen-plaintext attacks. We use $-s \cdot ID$ to blind the identity to ensure the anonymity of our scheme.

Second, our IBGE scheme needs traceability to identify the real receiver's identity if the need arises. But traditional IBE schemes do not have this property. We employ public-key encryption with CCA2 security to encrypt the identity of the anonymous recipient to achieve traceability. The encrypted identity is a part of the resulting ciphertext. GM can trace the receiver by decrypting this part of ciphertext. We use the Cramer-Shoup public-key cryptosystem [8] to encrypt the identity. Because the public-key cryptosystem satisfies CCA2 security, the encrypted identity can not been tampered.

Third, in order to show that the encrypted identity and the identity that forms IBE ciphertext are identical, we link the identity-based encryption with the public-key encryption using a zero-knowledge proof with correctness, completeness, soundness with knowledge extraction and honest-verifier zero-knowledge. This zero-knowledge proof indicates that the IBE ciphertext has not been tampered as well as the ciphertext is well-formed. That is to say the zero-knowledge proof makes our scheme achieve CCA2 security.

The IBE scheme achieves the anonymity and semantic security of IBGE according to our security definition. The public-key encryption and zero-knowledge proof ensure the traceability. The primitives above meet the requirements of a secure IBGE scheme.

4.2   A Concrete IBGE Scheme

Now we are ready to describe our IBGE scheme. It works as follows.

ParaGen. Let a user's identity be $ID \in \mathbb{Z}_p$. Let $\mathbb{G}, \mathbb{G}_T$ be two groups of order p, and let $e : \mathbb{G} \times \mathbb{G} \to \mathbb{G}_T$ be a bilinear map. Let $\bar{\mathbb{G}}$ be an Abelian group of order p in which the DDH problem [8] is hard. PKG chooses random $g, h \xleftarrow{R} \mathbb{G}$ and random $\alpha \xleftarrow{R} \mathbb{Z}_p$. It sets $g_1 \leftarrow g^\alpha \in \mathbb{G}$. The program chooses random $g_2, g_3, t \xleftarrow{R} \bar{\mathbb{G}}$ and a universal one-way hash function H. The system parameters and private master-key are given by $Pramas = (g, g_1, h, g_2, g_3, t, H)$, $MSK = \alpha$.

GKGen. This procedure chooses random $x_1, x_2, y_1, y_2, z \xleftarrow{R} \mathbb{Z}_p$, then computes $w = g_2^{x_1} g_3^{x_2}, d = g_2^{y_1} g_3^{y_2}, l = g_2^z$. Group public key and secret key are $PK_{GM} = (g_2, g_3, w, d, l, H)$ and $SK_{GM} = (x_1, x_2, y_1, y_2, z)$.

UKGen. Let a user's identity be $ID \in \mathbb{Z}_p$, PKG chooses random $r \xleftarrow{R} \mathbb{Z}_p$, and calculates the user's private key $SK_{ID} = (r, h_{ID})$, where $h_{ID} = (hg^{-r})^{1/(\alpha - ID)}$. The user can register his identity as a group member to GM.

Encryption. This encryption procedure can be divided into two sub-procedures.

1. Message encryption. Given plaintext $M \in \mathbb{G}_T$, the member's identity $ID \in \mathbb{Z}_p$, the procedure chooses random $s \xleftarrow{R} \mathbb{Z}_p$, then it computes the ciphertext $C_1 = (g_1^s g^{-s \cdot ID}, e(g,g)^s, M \cdot e(g,h)^{-s}) = (C_{10}, C_{11}, C_{12})$.
2. Member's identity encryption. Given member's identity $ID \in \mathbb{Z}_p$, the procedure chooses random $n \xleftarrow{R} \mathbb{Z}_p$ then it computes $k_1 = g_2^n, k_2 = g_3^n, \psi = l^n t^{ID}, \epsilon = H(k_1, k_2, \psi), v = w^n d^{n\epsilon}$. The ciphertext is $C_2 = (k_1, k_2, \psi, v)$.

The sender sends the ciphertext $C = (C_1, C_2)$ to the anonymous recipient.

Zero-knowledge proof. We construct a zero-knowledge proof which can prove the encrypted ID and the ID that forms the IBE ciphertext are identical. It proves the IBE ciphertext has not been tampered as well as the ciphertext is well-formed. This is an interactive protocol between the sender (prover) and a verifier. We denote the protocol by

$$ZK \left\{ s, n, ID \; \middle| \; \begin{array}{l} C_{10} = g_1^s g^{-s \cdot ID}, C_{11} = e(g,g)^s, \\ k_1 = g_2^n, k_2 = g_3^n, \psi = l^n t^{ID}, v = w^n d^{n\epsilon} \end{array} \right\}$$

This zero-knowledge proof is difficult to constructed directly. We convert this zero-knowledge proof into an equivalent one as follow.

$$ZK \left\{ s, n, ID \; \middle| \; \begin{array}{l} C_{10} = g_1^s g^{-s \cdot ID}, C_{11} = e(g,g)^s, k_1 = g_2^n, k_2 = g_3^n, \\ \psi = l^n t^{ID}, v = w^n d^{n\epsilon}, A = \psi^s, A = A_1 A_2, \\ A_1 = l^{ns}, A_2^{-1} = t^{-s \cdot ID}, k = k_1^s, k = g_2^{ns} \end{array} \right\}$$

The 3-move protocol is as follows.

1. Prover randomly chooses integers $\bar{s}, \bar{ID}, \bar{n}$ and computes $\bar{C}_{10} = g_1^{\bar{s}} g^{-\bar{s} \cdot ID}, \bar{C}_{11} = e(g,g)^{\bar{s}}, \bar{k}_1 = g_2^{\bar{n}}, \bar{k}_2 = g_3^{\bar{n}}, \bar{\psi} = l^{\bar{n}} t^{\bar{ID}}, \bar{v} = w^{\bar{n}} d^{\bar{n}\epsilon}, \bar{A} = \psi^{\bar{s}}, \bar{A} = \bar{A}_1 \bar{A}_2, \bar{A}_1 = l^{\bar{n}\bar{s}}, \bar{A}_2^{-1} = t^{-\bar{s} \cdot ID}, \bar{k} = \bar{k}_1^{\bar{s}}, \bar{k} = g_2^{\bar{n}\bar{s}}$ then sends these to verifier.
2. The verifier challenges the prover with a random $c \in \mathbb{Z}_p$.
3. The prover responses with $r_1 \equiv \bar{s} + cs \bmod p, r_2 \equiv \bar{n} + cn \bmod p, r_3 \equiv \bar{ID} + c \cdot ID \bmod p, r_4 \equiv -\bar{s}\bar{ID} - c \cdot s \cdot ID \bmod p, r_5 \equiv \bar{n}\bar{s} + c \cdot ns \bmod p$.
4. The verifier checks that $\psi^{r_1} \overset{?}{=} A^c \bar{A}, k_1^{r_1} \overset{?}{=} k^c \bar{k}, e(g,g)^{r_1} \overset{?}{=} C_{11}^c \bar{C}_{11}, g_2^{r_2} \overset{?}{=} k_1^c \bar{k}_1, g_3^{r_2} \overset{?}{=} k_2^c \bar{k}_2, (wd^\epsilon)^{r_2} \overset{?}{=} v^c \bar{v}, l^{r_2} t^{r_3} \overset{?}{=} \psi^c \bar{\psi}, g_1^{r_1} g^{r_4} \overset{?}{=} \bar{C}_{10} C_{10}^c, t^{r_4} \overset{?}{=} A_2^{-1}(A_2^{-1})^c, l^{r_5} \overset{?}{=} A_1^c \bar{A}_1, g_2^{r_5} \overset{?}{=} k^c \bar{k}$. The verifier outputs 1 if all checks hold; otherwise it outputs 0.

This zero-knowledge proof is an interactive protocol. It can be converted into a non-interactive protocol using a hash function $\bar{H}$. Specifically, the sender can compute $\bar{H}(C_1, C_2, \bar{C}_{10}, \bar{C}_{11}, \bar{k}_1, \bar{k}_2, \bar{\psi}, \bar{v}, \bar{A}, \bar{A}_1, \bar{A}_2, A_2^{-1}, \bar{k}) = c$. In this way, the sender no longer needs to interact with the GM during encryption. But the resulting ciphertext is $C = (C_1, C_2, C_3)$, where the $C_3 = (r_1, r_2, r_3, r_4, r_5)$.

Decryption. Input ciphertext $C = (C_1, C_2)$, where $C_1 = (C_{10}, C_{11}, C_{12})$ and user's private key $SK_{ID} = (r, h_{ID})$. Output plaintext $M = C_{12} \cdot e(C_{10}, h_{ID})C_{11}^r$.

Receiver Tracing. Group manager can trace the receiver as follows.

1. If zero-knowledge proof's verifier outputs 1, then the procedure executes step 2, else returns "reject".
2. The procedure outputs $t^{ID} = \psi/k_1^z$. For all $ID_i \in I$, compute t^{ID_i} and test $t^{ID_i} \stackrel{?}{=} t^{ID}$. If $t^{ID_i} = t^{ID}$ GM outputs ID, else returns "reject".

Correctness of Our Scheme. We show that the above scheme is correct. We first verify that the ciphertext can be decrypted correctly.

$$e(C_{10}, h_{ID})C_{11}^r = e(g^{s(\alpha-ID)}, h^{1/(\alpha-ID)}g^{-r/(\alpha-ID)})e(g,g)^{sr} = e(g,h)^s.$$

The receiver can decrypt because it possess an $(\alpha - ID)$-th root of h. When this is paired with an $(\alpha - ID)$-th root of g^s, the receiver obtains $e(g,h)^s$.

We then verify that the receiver can be traced correctly. Since $k_1 = g_2^n, k_2 = g_3^n$, we have $k_1^{x_1}k_2^{x_2} = g_2^{nx_1}g_3^{nx_2} = w^n$. Similarly, we have $k_1^{y_1}k_2^{y_2} = d^n$ and $k_1^z = l^n$. The test $k_1^{x_1+y_1\epsilon}k_2^{x_2+y_2\epsilon} = v$ will pass. The output is $t^{ID} = \psi/l^n$.

Regarding security, the following theorems guarantee that our IBGE scheme satisfies semantic security, anonymity and traceability in the standard model. The proofs are provided in Appendix A.2 and A.3.

Theorem 1. *Our IBGE scheme satisfies* $(t', \varepsilon', q_{ID})$ *ANO-IND-CIA-CPA security assuming the truncated decision* $(t, \epsilon, q) - ABDHE$ *assumption holds for* $(\mathbb{G}, \mathbb{G}_T, e)$, *where* $q = q_{ID} + 1, t' = t - O(t_{exp} \cdot q^2), \epsilon' = \epsilon + 2/q, t_{exp}$ *is the time required to exponentiate in* $\mathbb{G}$.

Theorem 2. *Our IBGE scheme satisfies traceability.*

4.3 Efficiency

In Table 1, we denote τ_m as one multiplication operation time in $\mathbb{G}$ and $\mathbb{G}_T$, τ_e as one exponent operation time in $\mathbb{G}$ and $\mathbb{G}_T$, τ_p as one pairing operation time in $\mathbb{G}$ and $\mathbb{G}_T$, $\bar{\tau}_m$ as one multiplication operation time in $\bar{\mathbb{G}}$, $\bar{\tau}_e$ as one exponent operation time in $\bar{\mathbb{G}}$. $e(g,g), e(g,h)$ can be pre-computed. We note that the ciphertext can be divided into two parts. One is computed in $\mathbb{G}$ with size 3, another one is computed in $\bar{\mathbb{G}}$ with size 4.

The storage complexity and computational complexity of our schemes are constant. Table 1 shows that our scheme is efficient.

Table 1. Efficiency of Our IBGE Scheme

PK_{GM} Size	5	SK_{GM} Size	5
SK_{ID} Size	2	Ciphertext Size	7
ParaGen Time	$3\tau_e + 2\bar{\tau}_e$	GKGen Time	$2\bar{\tau}_m + 5\bar{\tau}_e$
UKGen Time	$\tau_m + 2\tau_e$	Encryption Time	$2(\tau_m + \bar{\tau}_m) + 4\tau_e + 6\bar{\tau}_e$
Decryption Time	$2\tau_m + \tau_e + \tau_p$	Trace Time	$\bar{\tau}_e$

5   Conclusion

We formalized a new cryptographic primitive, referred to as identity-based group encryption which is more efficient and convenient than PKI-based group encryption. It allows a sender to send a ciphertext to any group member and the receiver of the ciphertext remains anonymous. The group manager can trace the identity of the receiver if the need arises. We propose a concrete construction of identity-based group encryption which achieves anonymity, semantic security and traceability. Our scheme has constant complexity in computation and communication.

Acknowledgments. This paper is supported by the National Key Basic Research Program (973 program) through project 2012CB315905, by the National High Technology Research and Development Program of China (863 Program) through project 2015AA017205, by the Natural Science Foundation of China through projects 61370190, 61173154, 61272501, 61402029, 61472429, 61202465, 61532021 and 61521091, by the Beijing Natural Science Foundation through project 4132056, by the Guangxi natural science foundation through project 2013GXNSFBB053005, the Innovation Fund of China Aerospace Science and Technology Corporation, Satellite Application Research Institute through project 2014-CXJJ-TX-10, the Open Project of Key Laboratory of Cryptologic Technology and Information Security, Ministry of Education, Shandong University.

A   Proofs of Security

In this section, we prove the following zero-knowledge properties and two security properties of our scheme.

A.1   Zero-Knowledge Properties

Lemma 1. *The protocol* $ZK\{s, n, ID | C_{10} = g_1^s g^{-s \cdot ID}, C_{11} = e(g,g)^s, k_1 = g_2^n, k_2 = g_3^n, \psi = l^n t^{ID}, v = w^n d^{n\epsilon}\}$ *is a* $\sum$*-protocol.*

Proof. It is straightforward to validate the *Correctness* and *Completeness* of the knowledge proof protocol.

Soundness with knowledge extraction: We construct an extractor who plays the role of the verifier. The extractor interacts with prover two times. Because the responses of the extractor are $c, c'(c \neq c')$, respectively, it obtains two equations $r_1 \equiv \bar{s} + cs \bmod p$ and $r_1' \equiv \bar{s} + c's \bmod p$. It is easy to get that $s = \frac{r_1 - r_1'}{c - c'} \bmod p$. The extractor can obtain $n, ID, s \cdot ID$ and ns in the same way.

Honest-verifier zero-knowledge: We will construct a simulator S as following steps. A simulator will play the role of the prover and interact with verifier.

1. S chooses random $\bar{C}_{10}, \bar{C}_{11}, \bar{k}_1, \bar{k}_2, \bar{\psi}, \bar{v}, \bar{A}, \bar{A}_1, \bar{A}_2, \bar{A}_2^{-1}, \bar{k}$. It sends them to verifier.
2. S receives c from verifier, then chooses random $r_1, r_2, r_3, r_4, r_5 \in \mathbb{Z}_p$ and computes new $\bar{C}_{10}, \bar{C}_{11}, \bar{k}_1, \bar{k}_2, \bar{\psi}, \bar{v}, \bar{A}, \bar{A}_1, \bar{A}_2, \bar{A}_2^{-1}, \bar{k}$.
3. S inter-
   acts with verifier again. It sends new $\bar{C}_{10}, \bar{C}_{11}, \bar{k}_1, \bar{k}_2, \bar{\psi}, \bar{v}, \bar{A}, \bar{A}_1, \bar{A}_2, \bar{A}_2^{-1}, \bar{k}$ to verifier.
4. S receives c from verifier, then sends $r_1, r_2, r_3, r_4, r_5 \in \mathbb{Z}_p$ to verifier.

Let the output of verifier be $\{\bar{C}_{10}, \bar{C}_{11}, \bar{k}_1, \bar{k}_2, \bar{\psi}, \bar{v}, \bar{A}, \bar{A}_1, \bar{A}_2, \bar{A}_2^{-1}, \bar{k}, c, r_1, r_2, r_3, r_4, r_5\}$, and it is uniform random. Let the output of S be $\{\bar{C}_{10}', \bar{C}_{11}', \bar{k}_1', \bar{k}_2', \bar{\psi}', \bar{v}', \bar{A}', \bar{A}_1', \bar{A}_2', \bar{A}_2'^{-1}, \bar{k}', c', r_1', r_2', r_3', r_4', r_5'\}$, and it is also uniform random. We say that this protocol is perfect zero knowledge.

Equality of Identity: Let $C_{10} = g_1^s g^{-s \cdot ID}, A_2^{-1} = t^{-s \cdot ID}, ID \neq ID'$. Prover chooses $-\bar{s} \cdot I\bar{D}_1, -\bar{s} \cdot I\bar{D}_2, I\bar{D}_1 \neq I\bar{D}_2$ (if $I\bar{D}_1 = I\bar{D}_2$, since $g_1^{r_1} g^{r_4} = \bar{C}_{10} C_{10}^c, t^{r_4} = \bar{A}_2^{-1} (A_2^{-1})^c$, we obtain $r_4 \equiv -\bar{s} I\bar{D}_1 + (-s \cdot ID)c \bmod p, r_4 \equiv -\bar{s} I\bar{D}_2 + (-s \cdot ID')c \bmod p, ID = ID'$), then computes $\bar{C}_{10} = g_1^{\bar{s}} g^{-\bar{s} \cdot I\bar{D}_1}, \bar{A}_2^{-1} = t^{-\bar{s} \cdot I\bar{D}_2}$. $g_1^{r_1} g^{r_4} = \bar{C}_{10} C_{10}^c$ and $t^{r_4} = \bar{A}_2^{-1} (A_2^{-1})^c$ both hold, if and only if $-\bar{s} I\bar{D}_1 + (-s \cdot ID)c \equiv -\bar{s} I\bar{D}_2 + (-s \cdot ID')c \bmod p$ holds. This means that $c \equiv \frac{\bar{s}(I\bar{D}_1 - I\bar{D}_2)}{s(ID' - ID)}$. This equation holds if and only if the verifier chooses this c exactly. But the probability is negligible.

A.2 Proof of Theorem 1

Proof. Suppose A is an $(t', \varepsilon', q_{ID})$ ANO-IND-CIA-CPA adversary against our scheme. We construct a simulator B solves the truncated decision q-ABDHE problem. B takes as input $(g', g_{q+2}', g, g_1, ...g_q, Z)$, where $Z = e(g_{q+1}, g')$ or a random element of $\mathbb{G}_T$.

Setup. B generates a random polynomial $f(x) \in \mathbb{Z}_p[x]$ of degree q. It let $h = g^{f(\alpha)}$ and computes h from $(g, g_1, ..., g_q)$. It sends public parameters (g, g_1, h) to A.

Phase 1. A adaptively queries Extract oracle. B responds as follows. If $ID = \alpha$, B can solve the truncated decision q-ABDHE immediately. Other-wise, let $F_{ID}(x) = (f(x) - f(ID))/(x - ID)$ be the $(q - 1)$-degree polynomial. B let $(f(ID), g^{F_{ID}(\alpha)})$ be the user's secret key (r, h_{ID}). Since $g^{F_{ID}(\alpha)} = g^{(f(\alpha) - f(ID)/(\alpha - ID))} = (hg^{-f(ID)})^{1/(\alpha - ID)}$, secret key (r, h_{ID}) is valid of ID.

Challenge. A outputs two identities ID_0, ID_1 and two messages M_0, M_1. The restriction is that the two identities did not appear in any secret key extraction query. Note that if $\alpha \in \{ID_0, ID_1\}$, $\mathcal{B}$ can solve the truncated decision q-ABDHE immediately. Otherwise, $\mathcal{B}$ chooses bits $b, c \in \{0, 1\}$, and computes secret key (r_b, h_{ID_b}) for ID_b same to phase 1.

Let $f_2(x) = x^{q+2}$ and let $F_{2,ID_b(x)} = (f_2(x) - f_2(ID_b))/(x - ID_b)$, which is a polynomial of degree of $q + 1$. $\mathcal{B}$ sets

$$C_{10} = g'^{f_2(\alpha) - f_2(ID_b)}, C_{11} = Z \cdot e(g', \prod_{i=0}^{q} g^{F_{2,ID_b,i}\alpha^i}), C_{12} = M_c/e(C_{10}, h_{ID_b})C_{11}^{r_b}$$

where $F_{2,ID_b,i}$ is the coefficient of x^i in $F_{2,ID_b}(x)$. It sends $C_1 = (C_{10}, C_{11}, C_{12})$ as the ciphertext to be challenged.

Let $s = (\log_g g')F_{2,ID_b}(\alpha)$. If $Z = e(g_{q+1}, g')$, then $C_{10} = g^{s(\alpha - ID_b)}, C_{11} = e(g, g)^s$, and $M_c/C_{12} = e(C_{10}, h_{ID_b})C_{11}^{r_b} = e(g, h)^s$, We let $C_1 = (C_{10}, C_{11}, C_{12})$ be an effective ciphertext of identity ID_b as well as message M_c under random value s.

Phase 2. $\mathcal{A}$ adaptively queries Extract oracle as in phase 1. The restriction is that the two identities did not appear in any private key extraction query. Besides, the adversary $\mathcal{A}$ can not query Trace oracle.

Guess. Finally, adversar $\mathcal{A}$ outputs guesses $b', c' \in \{0, 1\}$ of b, c. If $b' = b \wedge c' = c$ $\mathcal{B}$ outputs 1 else 0.

The analysis of probability and time complexity is as follow.

Analysis of probability. If $Z = e(g_{q+1}, g')$ the simulation is perfect. Adversary $\mathcal{A}$ can guess the bits (b, c) correctly with probability $\frac{1}{4} + \epsilon'$. Otherwise, Z is uniformly random, so (C_{10}, C_{11}) is a uniformly random and independent element of $(\mathbb{G}, \mathbb{G}_T)$. When this happen, the inequalities

$$C_{11} \neq e(C_{10}, g)^{1/(\alpha - ID_0)}, C_{11} \neq e(C_{10}, g)^{1/(\alpha - ID_1)}$$

both hold in the same time with probability $1 - 2/p$. When the two inequalities hold,

$$e(C_{10}, h_{ID_b})C_{11}^{r_b} = e(C_{10}, (hg^{-r_b})^{1/(\alpha - ID_b)})C_{11}^{r_b}$$
$$= e(C_{10}, h)^{\alpha - ID_b}(C_{11}/e(C_{10}, g)^{1/(\alpha - ID_b)})^{r_b}$$

is a uniformly random and independent value from the view of adversar $\mathcal{A}$, because of r_b is a uniformly random and independent value from the view of adversar $\mathcal{A}$. So, C_{12} is uniformly random and independent. C_1 will not reveal any information of the bits (b, c). Assuming that no queried identity equals α, it is easy to see that $| \Pr[\mathcal{B}(g', g'_{q+2}, g, g_1, ..., g_q, Z) = 0] - \frac{1}{4} | \leqslant \frac{2}{p}$ when $(g', g'_{q+2}, g, g_1, ..., g_q, Z)$ is sampled from R_{ABDHE}. To the contrary, we can see that $| \Pr[\mathcal{B}(g', g'_{q+2}, g, g_1, ..., g_q, Z) = 0] - \frac{1}{4} | \geqslant \epsilon'$ when $(g', g'_{q+2}, g, g_1, ..., g_q, Z)$ is sampled from P_{ABDHE}. Thus, we have that

$$| \Pr[\mathcal{B}(g', g'_{q+2}, g, g_1, ..., g_q, e(g_{q+1}, g')) = 0]$$
$$- \Pr[\mathcal{B}(g', g'_{q+2}, g, g_1, ..., g_q, Z) = 0] | \geqslant \epsilon' - \frac{2}{p}.$$

Analysis of Time Complexity. In the simulation procedure, the overhead of $\mathcal{B}$ is computing $g^{F_{ID}(\alpha)}$ in order to response $\mathcal{A}$'s extraction query for the ID, where $F_{ID}(x)$ is polynomial of $q - 1$ degree. Every computation requires $O(q)$ exponentiation in $\mathbb{G}$. $\mathcal{A}$ makes at most $q - 1$ queries, thus $t = t' + O(t_{exp} \cdot q^2)$.

A.3   Proof of Theorem 2

Proof. Setup is same as the above proof. In inspect phase adversary can adaptability query all of the oracles. The challenger will respond adversary. The adversary will choose a group public key $PK'_{GM} = (g_2, g_3, w', d', l', H')$ and obtain secret key are $SK'_{GM} = (x'_1, x'_2, y'_1, y'_2, z')$. Adversary will choose an identity ID and obtain use's private key SK_{ID}, as well as an other ID'. Adversary computes C'_1 using ID and computes C'_2 using ID'. Thus, adversary outputs a valid ciphertext $C' = (C'_1, C'_2)$ which the GM can not trace correctly if and only if $c \equiv \frac{\bar{s}(I\bar{D}_1 - I\bar{D}_2)}{s(ID' - ID)}$ (Part 5.1). But the probability is negligible.

References

1. Boneh, D., Lynn, B., Shacham, H.: Short signatures from the Weil pairing. J. Cryptology **17**(4), 297–319 (2004)
2. Boneh, D., Lynn, B., Shacham, H.: Short signatures from the Weil pairing. In: Boyd, C. (ed.) ASIACRYPT 2001. LNCS, vol. 2248, pp. 514–532. Springer, Heidelberg (2001)
3. Boneh, D., Franklin, M.: Identity-based encryption from the Weil pairing. In: Kilian, J. (ed.) CRYPTO 2001. LNCS, vol. 2139, pp. 213–229. Springer, Heidelberg (2001)
4. Boneh, D., Franklin, M.: Identity-based encryption from the Weil pairing. SIAM J. Comput. **32**(3), 586–615 (2003)
5. Barreto, P.S.L.M., Naehrig, M.: Pairing-friendly elliptic curves of prime order. In: Preneel, B., Tavares, S. (eds.) SAC 2005. LNCS, vol. 3897, pp. 319–331. Springer, Heidelberg (2006)
6. Boyen, X., Waters, B.: Compact group signatures without random oracles. In: Vaudenay, S. (ed.) EUROCRYPT 2006. LNCS, vol. 4004, pp. 427–444. Springer, Heidelberg (2006)
7. Chaum, D., van Heyst, E.: Group signatures. In: Davies, D.W. (ed.) EUROCRYPT 1991. LNCS, vol. 547, pp. 257–265. Springer, Heidelberg (1991)
8. Cramer, R., Shoup, V.: A practical public key cryptosystem provably secure against adaptive chosen ciphertext attack. In: Krawczyk, H. (ed.) CRYPTO 1998. LNCS, vol. 1462, pp. 13–25. Springer, Heidelberg (1998)
9. Cathalo, J., Libert, B., Yung, M.: Group encryption: non-interactive realization in the standard model. In: Matsui, M. (ed.) ASIACRYPT 2009. LNCS, vol. 5912, pp. 179–196. Springer, Heidelberg (2009)
10. Ducas, L.: Anonymity from asymmetry: new constructions for anonymous HIBE. In: Pieprzyk, J. (ed.) CT-RSA 2010. LNCS, vol. 5985, pp. 148–164. Springer, Heidelberg (2010)
11. Fiat, A., Shamir, A.: How to prove yourself: practical solutions to identification and signature problems. In: Odlyzko, A.M. (ed.) CRYPTO 1986. LNCS, vol. 263, pp. 186–194. Springer, Heidelberg (1987)

12. Groth, J.: Simulation-sound NIZK proofs for a practical language and constant size group signatures. In: Lai, X., Chen, K. (eds.) ASIACRYPT 2006. LNCS, vol. 4284, pp. 444–459. Springer, Heidelberg (2006)

13. Gentry, C.: Practical identity-based encryption without random oracles. In: Vaudenay, S. (ed.) EUROCRYPT 2006. LNCS, vol. 4004, pp. 445–464. Springer, Heidelberg (2006)

14. Kiayias, A., Tsiounis, Y., Yung, M.: Group encryption. In: Kurosawa, K. (ed.) ASIACRYPT 2007. LNCS, vol. 4833, pp. 181–199. Springer, Heidelberg (2007)

15. Kiayias, A., Yung, M.: Secure scalable group signature with dynamic joins and separable authorities. Int. J. Secur. Netw. **1**(1/2), 24–45 (2006)

16. Libert, B., Yung, M., Joye, M., Peters, T.: Traceable group encryption. In: Krawczyk, H. (ed.) PKC 2014. LNCS, vol. 8383, pp. 592–610. Springer, Heidelberg (2014)

17. Liu, J.K., Tsang, P.P., Wong, D.S.: Efficient verifiable ring encryption for Ad Hoc groups. In: Molva, R., Tsudik, G., Westhoff, D. (eds.) ESAS 2005. LNCS, vol. 3813, pp. 1–13. Springer, Heidelberg (2005)

18. Liu, J.K., Wei, V.K., Wong, D.S.: Custodian-hiding verifiable encryption. In: Lim, C.H., Yung, M. (eds.) WISA 2004. LNCS, vol. 3325, pp. 51–64. Springer, Heidelberg (2005)

19. Liu, J.K., Tsang, P.P., Wong, D.S., Zhu, R.W.: Universal custodian-hiding verifiable encryption for discrete logarithms. In: Won, D.H., Kim, S. (eds.) ICISC 2005. LNCS, vol. 3935, pp. 389–409. Springer, Heidelberg (2006)

20. Paillier, P.: Public-key cryptosystems based on composite degree residuosity classes. In: Stern, J. (ed.) EUROCRYPT 1999. LNCS, vol. 1592, pp. 223–238. Springer, Heidelberg (1999)

21. Qin, B., Wu, Q., Susilo, W., Mu, Y.: Publicly verifiable privacy-preserving group decryption. In: Yung, M., Liu, P., Lin, D. (eds.) Inscrypt 2008. LNCS, vol. 5487, pp. 72–83. Springer, Heidelberg (2009)

22. Shamir, A.: Identity-based cryptosystems and signature schemes. In: Blakely, G.R., Chaum, D. (eds.) CRYPTO 1984. LNCS, vol. 196, pp. 47–53. Springer, Heidelberg (1985)

Edit Distance Based Encryption
and Its Application

Tran Viet Xuan Phuong[1(✉)], Guomin Yang[1], Willy Susilo[1], and Kaitai Liang[2]

[1] Centre for Computer and Information Security Research,
School of Computing and Information Technology, University of Wollongong,
Wollongong, Australia
tvxp750@uowmail.edu.au, {gyang,wsusilo}@uow.edu.au
[2] Department of Computer Science, Aalto University, Espoo, Finland
kaitai.liang@aalto.fi

Abstract. Edit distance, also known as Levenshtein distance, is a very useful tool to measure the similarity between two strings. It has been widely used in many applications such as natural language processing and bioinformatics. In this paper, we introduce a new type of fuzzy public key encryption called Edit Distance-based Encryption (EDE). In EDE, the encryptor can specify an alphabet string and a threshold when encrypting a message, and a decryptor can obtain a decryption key generated from another alphabet string, and the decryption will be successful if and only if the edit distance between the two strings is within the pre-defined threshold. We provide a formal definition and security model for EDE, and propose an EDE scheme that can securely evaluate the edit distance between two strings embedded in the ciphertext and the secret key. We also show an interesting application of our EDE scheme named Fuzzy Broadcast Encryption which is very useful in a broadcasting network.

Keywords: Edit distance · Fuzzy encryption · Dynamic programming · Viète's Formulas

1 Introduction

Measuring the similarity between two strings is an important task in many applications such as natural language processing, bio-informatics, and data mining. One of the common similarity metrics that has been widely used in the above applications is the Edit Distance (a.k.a. Levenshtein distance), which counts the minimum number of operations (namely, insertion, deletion, and substitution) required to transform one string into the other. In this paper, we investigate a challenging problem of building fuzzy public key encryption schemes based on edit distance.

Our work is motivated by an open problem raised by Sahai and Waters in [21], where the notion of Fuzzy Identity-Based Encryption (IBE) was proposed. The Fuzzy IBE scheme introduced in [21] can be regarded as the first Attribute-Based Encryption (ABE) scheme with a threshold access policy. To be more

© Springer International Publishing Switzerland 2016
J.K. Liu and R. Steinfeld (Eds.): ACISP 2016, Part II, LNCS 9723, pp. 103–119, 2016.
DOI: 10.1007/978-3-319-40367-0_7

precise, it allows to use a private key corresponding to an identity string I' to decrypt a ciphertext encrypted with another identity string I if and only if the "set overlap" between I and I' (i.e., $|I \cap I'|$) is larger than a pre-defined threshold. One of the open problems raised in [21] is to construct fuzzy encryption schemes based on other similarity metrics.

We should note that edit distance is very different from the "set overlap" distance used in Fuzzy IBE. For example, consider the biometric identity application of Fuzzy IBE described in [21], given two strings $I =$ "ATCG" and $I' =$ "GACT", we have $|I \cap I'| = 4$ (i.e., the distance is 0). However, the edit distance between I and I' is 3. It is easy to see that the order of the alphabets in those strings will affect the edit distance, but not the set overlap distance. This simple example shows that to a certain extent edit distance provides better accuracy than the set overlap distance in measuring the similarity of two strings. As another example, given an encryption string $I =$ "admirer" and a threshold distance $d = 1$, for edit distance, we can allow a decryption key associated with $I' =$ "admirers" to decrypt the message; while for set overlap distance, we can have some totally unrelated anagrams of I, such as $I' =$ "married", whose corresponding secret key can also decrypt the message. Due to the difference between the two distances (or similarity metrics), we cannot easily extend the technique used in [21] to construct a fuzzy encryption scheme for edit distance. Also, in order to distinguish our fuzzy encryption scheme based on edit distance from the Fuzzy IBE proposed in [21], we name our new encryption scheme Edit Distance-based Encryption (or EDE, for short).

1.1   This Work

In this paper, we introduce the notion of Edit Distance-based Encryption (EDE), formalize its security, and propose a practical scheme in the standard model.

Edit distance can be measured in polynomial time using different techniques, such as dynamic programming or recursion. However, in an EDE scheme, the two strings I and I' are embedded in the ciphertext CT and the user secret key SK, respectively. Hence, the problem becomes how to measure the distance of I and I' using CT and SK. We observe that the most important operation in the edit distance algorithms is the equality test between two alphabets $I[x]$ and $I'[y]$. Based on this observation, our proposed EDE scheme uses bilinear map [6] to solve this issue. We illustrate our idea using the following example.

Suppose we have two strings $I =$ "ATTGA" and $I' =$ "AGTA". We first encode each alphabet as a group element. Then in the encryption process, we create a randomized vector $\boldsymbol{I} = (A^s, T^s, T^s, G^s, A^s)$ using the same random number s. Similarly, we create another randomized vector $\boldsymbol{I'} = (A^r, G^r, T^r, A^r)$ in the key generation process. Then we apply bilinear map to conduct equality test between I and I' using the two vectors $\boldsymbol{I}$ and $\boldsymbol{I'}$ which are included in the ciphertext and the secret key respectively. The crux of the idea is illustrated in Fig. 1. In order to deal with the threshold problem, we apply the technique of Viète's formulas [22] to solve the problem. In the encryption process, we create a vector $\boldsymbol{d} = (1, 2, \ldots, d, 0, \ldots, 0)$ for the threshold distance d and embed the vector $\boldsymbol{d}$ in the ciphertext. Also, based on the edit distance d' between I and I', we create another vector $\boldsymbol{d'} = (1, 2, \ldots, d', *, \ldots, *)$ where $*$ denotes the wildcard (i.e., don't care) symbol. Then based on $\boldsymbol{d}$ and $\boldsymbol{d'}$, we ensure that the decryption can be successful if and only if $d' \leq d$. Also, we overcome the issue of malleability by using the composite order group in constructing the EDE scheme. We prove that our proposed scheme is selectively secure under the L-composite Decisional Diffie-Hellman (L-cDDH) assumption.

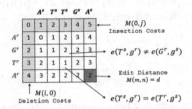

Fig. 1. Edit distance evaluation using bilinear map

We also show an interesting application of our EDE scheme named Fuzzy Broadcast Encryption (FBE), which is very useful in broadcasting networks. An FBE scheme allows the encryptor (i.e., message sender) to specify a set of receiver identities during the encryption process, and a user can decrypt the message if and only if the *minimum* edit distance between his/her identity and all the identities chosen by the encryptor is below a threshold that is also specified by the encryptor during the encryption process.

1.2   Related Work

Since the seminal work of Sahai and Waters [21], many Attribute Based Encryption (ABE) schemes with the threshold access structure have been proposed (e.g., [5,8,9,11]). In [9], Goyal et al. extended the work of Sahai and Waters to construct more expressive Key-Policy (KP) ABE where the access structure is defined via a tree of threshold gates. Bethencourt et al. [5] proposed the first Ciphertext-Policy (CP) ABE using the same access structure. Under the motivation of reducing the ciphertext size, which is linear in the size of the encryption attribute set in most of the existing ABE schemes, Herranz et al. [11] proposed a constant-size ABE scheme for the threshold access structure, which is essentially the same as the set overlap distance metric used in Fuzzy IBE [21]. In [8], Ge et al. proposed another constant-size ABE scheme with the same threshold access structure but under a relatively weaker assumption. As of independent interest, some interesting fuzzy encryption techniques have been proposed in the literature, such as [15–17].

Another type of fuzzy identity-based encryption is the Wildcarded IBE (or WIBE for short) proposed by Abdalla et al. [1–3]. A WIBE allows wildcard symbols to appear in an identity string used in the encryption process, and the wildcard positions will be ignored when measuring the equality of two identity strings. Another notion that is similar to WIBE is the Hidden Vector Encryption (HVE) [12,14,18,19,22], which also allows wildcards to appear in either the encryption string or the key generation string. However, both WIBE and HVE are based on the fuzzy equality test between two strings, which is different from the problem we aim to solve in this paper.

There are also a few works on the privacy-preserving edit distance evaluation between two strings [4,7,13,20,23]. These works mainly focused on finding the edit distance of two (perhaps encrypted) strings in a privacy-preserving manner, and hence is completely different from this work.

2   Preliminaries

2.1   Edit Distance

Consider a finite alphabet set $\mathcal{A}$ whose elements are used to construct strings. Let Z_I , Z_D and Z_S be finite sets of integers. Let the function $I : \mathcal{A} \rightarrow Z_I$ be the insertion cost function, i.e., $I(a)$ is the cost of inserting the element $a \in A$ into a given string. Similarly, define the deletion cost function as $D : \mathcal{A} \rightarrow Z_D$ so that $D(a)$ is the cost of deleting the element $a \in A$ from a given string. Finally, define the substitution cost function $S : \mathcal{A} \times \mathcal{A} \rightarrow Z_S$ so that for $a, b \in \mathcal{A}$, $S(a,b)$ is the cost of replacing the element a by the element b in a given string.

Given two strings of length m and n, denoted by $X \in \mathcal{A}^m$ and $Y \in \mathcal{A}^n$ respectively, consider the sequence of insertion, deletion and substitution operations needed to transform X into Y and the corresponding aggregate cost of the transformation.

Definition 1. *The edit distance between X and Y is defined as the minimum aggregate cost of transforming X into Y.*

The general definition of edit distance given above considers different weights for different operations. In this paper we will consider a simpler definition which is given below.

Definition 2. *For all $a, b \in \mathcal{A}$, let $I(a) = D(a) = 1$, $S(a,b) = 1$ when $a \neq b$, and $S(a,a) = 0$. Then, the edit distance is defined as the minimum number of insertion, deletion and substitution operations required to convert X into Y.*

Dynamic Programming for Edit Distance. Let $X = X_1 X_2 ... X_m \in \mathcal{A}^m$ and $Y = Y_1 Y_2 ... Y_n \in \mathcal{A}^n$ be two strings. We use $M(i,j)$ to denote the edit distance between the two sub strings $X_1 X_2 ... X_i$ and $Y_1 Y_2 ... Y_j$. The problem of finding the edit distance between X and Y can be solved in $O(mn)$ time via dynamic programming [10], which will be used in our scheme.

Let $M(0,0) = 0$. For $1 \leq i \leq m, 1 \leq j \leq n$, define $M(i,0) = \sum_{k=1}^{i} I(x_k)$, and

$$M(0,j) = \sum_{k=1}^{j} D(y_k).$$

Then, the edit distance $M(m,n)$ is defined by the following recurrence relation for $1 \le i \le m, 1 \le j \le n$: $M(i,j) = \min\{M(i-1,j) + D(Y_j), M(i,j-1) + I(X_i), M(i-1,j-1) + S(X_i,Y_j)\}$.

2.2 The Viète's Formulas

Consider two vectors: $\overrightarrow{v} = (v_1, v_2, \ldots, v_L)$, $\overrightarrow{z} = (z_1, z_2, \ldots, z_L)$ where $\overrightarrow{v}$ contains both alphabets and wildcard symbols (*) and $\overrightarrow{z}$ only contains alphabets. Let $J = \{j_1, \ldots, j_n\} \subset \{1, \ldots, L\}$ denote the wildcard positions in $\overrightarrow{v}$. Then according to [22], the statement $(v_i = z_i \lor v_i = *$ for $i = 1 \ldots L)$ can be expressed as:

$$\sum_{i=1, i \notin J}^{L} v_i \prod_{j \in J}(i-j) = \sum_{i=1}^{L} z_i \prod_{j \in J}(i-j). \tag{1}$$

Expand $\prod_{j \in J}(i-j) = \sum_{k=0}^{n} \lambda_k i^k$, where λ_k are the coefficients dependent on J, then (1) becomes:

$$\sum_{i=1, i \notin J}^{L} v_i \prod_{j \in J}(i-j) = \sum_{k=0}^{n} \lambda_k \sum_{i=1}^{L} z_i i^k. \tag{2}$$

To hide the computation, we choose random group element H_i and put v_i, z_i as the exponents of group elements: $H_i^{v_i}, H_i^{z_i}$. Then (2) becomes:

$$\prod_{i=1, i \notin J}^{L} H_i^{v_i \prod_{j \in J}(i-j)} = \prod_{k=0}^{n} (\prod_{i=1}^{L} H_i^{z_i i^k})^{\lambda_k}.$$

Using the Viète's formulas we can construct the coefficient λ_k in (2) by: $\lambda_{n-k} = (-1)^k \sum_{1 \le i_1 < i_2 < \ldots < i_k \le n} j_{i_1} j_{i_2} \cdots j_{i_k}$, $0 \le k \le n$. where $n = |J|$. For example, if we have $J = \{j_1, j_2, j_3\}$, the polynomial is $(x - j_1)(x - j_2)(x - j_3)$, then $\lambda_3 = 1, \lambda_2 = -(j_1 + j_2 + j_3), \lambda_1 = (j_1 j_2 + j_1 j_3 + j_2 j_3), \lambda_0 = -j_1 j_2 j_3$.

2.3 Bilinear Map on Composite Order Groups and Its Assumption

Let p, q be two large prime numbers and $n = pq$. Let $\mathbb{G}, \mathbb{G}_T$ be cyclic groups of order n. We say $e : \mathbb{G} \times \mathbb{G} \to \mathbb{G}_T$ is bilinear map over composite order groups if e satisfies the following properties: (1) Bilinearity : $e(u^a, v^b) = e(u^b, v^a) = e(u,v)^{ab}$ for all $u, v \in \mathbb{G}$ and $a, b \in \mathbb{Z}_p$; (2)Non-degeneracy : $e(g,g) \ne 1$.

Let $\mathbb{G}_p$ and $\mathbb{G}_q$ be two subgroups of $\mathbb{G}$ of order p and q, respectively. Then $\mathbb{G} = \mathbb{G}_p \times \mathbb{G}_q$, $\mathbb{G}_T = \mathbb{G}_{T,p} \times \mathbb{G}_{T,q}$. We use g_p and g_q to denote generators of $\mathbb{G}_p$ and $\mathbb{G}_q$, respectively. It is easy to see that $e(h_p, h_q) = 1$ for all elements $h_p \in \mathbb{G}_p$ and $h_q \in \mathbb{G}_q$ since $e(h_p, h_q) = e(g_p^a, g_q^b) = e(g^{qa}, g^{pb}) = e(g,g)^{pqab} = 1$ for a generator g of $\mathbb{G}$.

The Decisional $L-\text{cBDHE}$ assumption:

Let $g_p, h \xleftarrow{R} \mathbb{G}_p, g_q \xleftarrow{R} \mathbb{G}_q, \alpha \xleftarrow{R} \mathbb{Z}_n, Z = (g_p, g_q, h, g_p^{\alpha}, \ldots, g_p^{\alpha^L}, g_p^{\alpha^{L+2}}, \ldots, g_p^{\alpha^{2L}}),$
$T = e(g_p, h)^{\alpha^{L+1}}$, and $R \leftarrow \mathbb{G}_{T,p}$

We say that the decisional $L-\text{cBDHE}$ assumption holds if for any probabilistic polynomial-time algorithm $A : |\Pr[A(Z, T) = 1] - \Pr[A(Z, R) = 1]| \le \epsilon(k)$, where $\epsilon(k)$ denotes an negligible function of k.

3   Edit Distance Based Encryption

An Edit Distance Based Encryption (EDE) scheme consists of the following four probabilistic polynomial-time algorithms:

- **Setup**$(1^n, \Sigma)$: on input a security parameter 1^n, an alphabet Σ, the algorithm outputs a public key PK and a master secret key MSK.
- **Encrypt**$(PK, \overrightarrow{v}, M, d)$: on input a public key PK, a message M, a vector $\overrightarrow{v} \in \Sigma^n$ and a distance d, the algorithm outputs a ciphertext CT.
- **KeyGen**$(MSK, \overrightarrow{x})$: on input a master secret key MSK, a vector $\overrightarrow{x} \in \Sigma^m$, the algorithm outputs a decryption key SK.
- **Decrypt**(CT, SK): on input a ciphertext CT and a secret key SK, the algorithm outputs either a message M if $EditDistance(\overrightarrow{v}, \overrightarrow{x}) \le d$, or a special symbol $\perp$.

Security Model. The security model for an EDE scheme is defined via the following game between an adversary A and a challenger B.

- **Setup**: The challenger B run **Setup**$(1^n, \Sigma)$ to generate the PK and MSK. PK is then passed to A.
- **Query Phase 1**: The challenger answers all private key queries for a vector $\overrightarrow{\sigma}$ by returning: $sk_{\sigma} \leftarrow KeyGen(MSK, \overrightarrow{\sigma})$.
- **Challenge**: A submits two equal-length messages M_0 and M_1, a target vector $\overrightarrow{v}^* \in \Sigma^n$ and threshold τ such that $EditDistance(\overrightarrow{v}^*, \overrightarrow{\sigma}) > \tau$ for any vector $\overrightarrow{\sigma}$ that has been queried in Phase 1. The challenger then flips a coin $\beta \leftarrow \{0, 1\}$ and computes the challenge ciphertext $C^* \leftarrow Encrypt(PK, \overrightarrow{v}^*, M_\beta, \tau)$, which is given to A.
- **Query Phase 2**: same as Query Phase 1 except that $EditDistance$ $(\overrightarrow{v}^*, \overrightarrow{\sigma}) > \tau$ for any vector σ queried in this phase.
- **Output**: A outputs a bit β' as her guess for β.

Define the advantage of A as $\mathbf{Adv}_A^{\mathsf{EDE}}(k) = |\Pr[\beta' = \beta] - 1/2|$.

Selective Security. In the selective security model, the adversary A is required to submit the target vector $\overrightarrow{v}^* \in \Sigma^n$ and threshold τ before the game setup, and A is only allowed to make private key queries for any vector $\overrightarrow{\sigma}$ that satisfies $EditDistance(\overrightarrow{v}^*, \overrightarrow{\sigma}) > \tau$ throughout the game.

4 Edit Distance Based Encryption Scheme

In this section, we introduce our EDE scheme, which is based on the Dynamic Programming [10] algorithm for calculating edit distance.

- **Setup**($1^n, \Sigma$): The setup algorithm first chooses $L = poly(n)$ as the maximum number of length of a word that would appear in the encryption and key generation. It then picks large primes p, q, generates bilinear groups $\mathbb{G}, \mathbb{G}_T$ of composite order $n = pq$, and selects generators $g_p \in \mathbb{G}_p, g_q \in \mathbb{G}_q$. After that, generate:

$$v_0, v_0', b_0, g, f, \omega, h_1, \ldots, h_L, u_1, \ldots, u_L \in_R \mathbb{G}_p, x_1, \ldots, x_L, x_1', \ldots, x_L' \in_R \mathbb{Z}_n,$$
$$v_1 = v_0^{x_1}, \ldots, v_L = v_0^{x_L}, v_1' = (v_0')^{x_1}, \ldots, v_L' = (v_0')^{x_L}, b_1 = b_0^{x_1}, \ldots, b_L = b_0^{x_L'},$$
$$R_g, R_f, R_{v_0}, \ldots, R_{v_L}, R_{v_0'}, \ldots, R_{v_L'},$$
$$R_{b_0}, \ldots, R_{b_L}, R_{h_1}, \ldots, R_{h_L}, R_{u_1}, \ldots, R_{u_L} \in \mathbb{G}_q,$$
$$G = gR_g, F = fR_f, Y = e(g, \omega),$$
$$V_0 = v_0 R_{v_0}, \ldots, V_L = v_L R_{v_L}, V_0' = v_0' R_{v_0'}, \ldots, V_L' = v_L' R_{v_L'}, B_0 = b_0 R_{b_0}, \ldots,$$
$$B_L = b_L R_{b_L}, H_1 = h_1 R_{h_1}, \ldots, H_L = h_L R_{h_L}, U_1 = u_1 R_{u_1}, \ldots, U_L = u_L R_{u_L},$$

and set the public key and secret key as:

Algorithm 1. Edit distance evaluation via dynamic programming

---

input : CT, SK
output: d', pos

$len_v = n + 1; len_z = m + 1;$
Creat $cost[len_v];$ Creat $newcost[len_v];$ Creat $pos[2][];$
//setup two arrays to store the position matching pos[0][] for vector v, pos[1][] for vector z;
for $i \leftarrow 0$ **to** len_v **do**
  | $cost[i] = i;$
end
$k = 0;$
for $j \leftarrow 1$ **to** len_z **do**
  | $newcost[0] = j;$
  | **for** $i \leftarrow 1$ **to** len_v **do**
  | | *// matching current letters in both strings*
  | | $match = (e(K_2, C_{3,i-1}) == e(C_1, K_{3,j-1}))?0 : 1$ (1);
  | | *// store the i match in array pos[0], j match in array pos[1]*
  | | **if** $i \notin pos[0], j \notin pos[1]$ **then**
  | | | $pos[0][k++] = i, pos[1][k++] = j, ;$
  | | **end**
  | | *// computing cost for each transformation*
  | | $replace = cost[i - 1] + match; insert = cost[i] + 1; delete = newcost[i - 1] + 1;$
  | | *// keep minimum cost*
  | | $newcost[i] = Math.min(Math.min(cost - insert, cost - delete), cost - replace);$
  | **end**
  | *// swap cost-newcost arrays*
  | $swap[] = cost; cost = newcost; newcost = swap;$
end
// return the cost for transforming all letters in both strings and array list pos including pos[0], pos[1]
return $cost[len_v - 1], pos;$

$$PK = \{Y, G, F, (V_0, \ldots, V_L), (V_0', \ldots, V_L'), (B_0, \ldots, B_L), (H_1, \ldots, H_L), (U_1, \ldots, U_L)\},$$
$$MSK = \{g, f, \omega, (v_0, \ldots, v_L), (v_0', \ldots, v_L'), (b_0, \ldots, b_L), (h_1, \ldots, h_L), (u_1, \ldots, u_L)\}.$$

- **Encrypt**($PK, \vec{v} = (v_1, \ldots, v_{n_1}) \in \Sigma^{n_1}, M, d$): On input the public key PK, a vector $\vec{v} = (v_1, \ldots, v_{n_1})$ with $n_1 \leq L$, it first generates for each alphabet v_i a vector $\boldsymbol{x_i} = (v_i, 1, \ldots, 1_L)$, and expands $\vec{v}$ to $\vec{v} = (v_1, v_2, \ldots, v_{n_1}, \ldots, 1_L)$ and sets $\vec{d} = (1, \ldots, d, 0_{d+1}, \ldots, 0_L)$. Then choose $s \in_R \mathbb{Z}_n$, and $Z_1, Z_2, Z_3, Z_4, Z_5 \in_R \mathbb{G}_q$, and compute:

$$C_0 = MY^s, C_1 = G^s Z_1, C_2 = F^s Z_2, C_{3,i} = (V_i \prod_{j=1}^{L} H_i^{x_{ij}})^s Z_3,$$

$$C_4 = (V_0' \prod_{i=1}^{L} H_i^{v_i})^s \cdot Z_4, C_{5,k,t} = (V_t'(B_k \prod_{i=1}^{L} (U_i)^{d_i i^k})(\prod_{j=1}^{L} (H_j)^{v_j j^t}))^s \cdot Z_5.$$

Set the ciphertext as: $CT = (n_1, C_0, C_1, C_2, \{C_{3,i}\}_{i=1}^{n_1}, C_4, \{\{C_{5,k,t}\}_{k=0}^{L}\}_{t=0}^{L})$.

- **KeyGen**($MSK, \vec{z} = (z_1, \ldots, z_m) \in \Sigma^m$): Given a key vector $\vec{z} = (z_1, \ldots, z_m)$, it generates $\boldsymbol{y_i} = (z_i, 1, \ldots, 1_L)$ for each alphabet z_i, and creates $\vec{\sigma} = (1, 2, \ldots, L)$ and expands $\vec{z}$ to $\vec{z} = (z_1, z_2, \ldots, z_m, \ldots, 1_L)$. Then choose $r_1, r_2 \in_R \mathbb{Z}_n$, and compute:

$$K_1 = g^{r_1}, K_2 = g^{r_2}, K_{3,i} = (v_i \prod_{j=1}^{L} h_i^{y_{ij}})^{r_2},$$

$$\begin{pmatrix} K_{4,0,0} = \omega(v_0' \prod_{i=1}^{L} h_i^{z_i})^{r_2} \\ ((b_0 \prod_{i=1}^{L} (u_i^{\sigma_i}))(v_0' \prod_{j=1}^{L} h_j^{z_j}))^{r_1} f^{r_1} \\ K_{4,1,0} = (b_1 \prod_{i=1}^{L} (u_i^{\sigma_i})^i (v_0' \prod_{j=1}^{L} h_j^{z_j}))^{r_1} \\ \ldots, \\ K_{4,L,0} = (b_L \prod_{i=1}^{L} (u_i^{\sigma_i})^{i^L} (v_0' \prod_{j=1}^{L} h_j^{z_j}))^{r_1} \end{pmatrix}, \begin{pmatrix} K_{4,0,t} = (b_0 \prod_{i=1}^{L} (u_i^{\sigma_i})(v_t' \prod_{j=1}^{L} h_j^{z_j})^{j^t})^{r_1} \\ K_{4,1,t} = (b_1 \prod_{i=1}^{L} (u_i^{\sigma_i})^i (v_t' \prod_{j=1}^{L} h_j^{z_j})^{j^t})^{r_1} \\ \ldots, \\ K_{4,L,t} = (b_L \prod_{i=1}^{L} (u_i^{\sigma_i})^{i^L} (v_t' \prod_{j=1}^{L} h_j^{z_j})^{j^t})^{r_1} \end{pmatrix},$$

($t = 1, \ldots, L$). Then set the user secret key as $SK = (m, K_1, K_2, \{K_{3,i}\}_{i=1}^{m}, \{\{K_{4,k,t}\}_{k=0}^{L}\}_{t=0}^{L})$.

- **Decrypt**(CT, SK): The decryption algorithm first executes the dynamic programming algorithm for edit distance by following Algorithm 1 which returns a distance $d' = cost[len_v - 1]$, the matching indices array $pos[0][]$ for $\vec{v}$ and $pos[1][]$ for $\vec{z}$. It sets $\tau = L - d'$, and applies the Viète's formulas to compute
  • for the index set

$$\Omega_v = \{L \backslash \{pos[0][0], \ldots, pos[0][d'-1]\}\} = \{\omega_1, \ldots, \omega_{L-d'}\},$$

then

$$a_{\tau-k} = (-1)^k \sum_{1 \leq i_1 < i_2 < \ldots < i_k \leq \tau} \omega_{i_1} \omega_{i_2} \ldots \omega_{i_k} \quad (0 \leq k \leq \tau), \tag{3}$$

- for the index set

$$\Omega_z = \{L \backslash \{pos[1][0], \ldots, pos[1][d'-1]\}\} = \{\bar{\omega}_1, \ldots, \bar{\omega}_{L-d'}\},$$

then

$$\bar{a}_{\tau-k} = (-1)^k \sum_{1 \leq i_1 < i_2 < \ldots < i_k \leq \tau} \bar{\omega}_{i_1} \bar{\omega}_{i_2} \ldots \bar{\omega}_{i_k} \quad (0 \leq k \leq \tau), \qquad (4)$$

- for the threshold index set

$$J = \{j_1, \ldots, j_\tau\} \text{ with } j_1 = d'+1, \ldots, j_\tau = L,$$

then

$$\hat{a}_{\tau-k} = (-1)^k \sum_{1 \leq i_1 < i_2 < \ldots < i_k \leq \tau} j_{i_1} j_{i_2} \ldots j_{i_k} \quad (0 \leq k \leq \tau). \qquad (5)$$

Then recover M as:

$$M = \frac{e(K_2, C_4) \cdot e(K_1, C_2) \prod\limits_{k=0}^{\tau} e(K_1^{\frac{1}{\bar{a}_0 \hat{a}_0}}, \prod\limits_{t=0}^{\tau} C_{5,k,t}^{a_t})^{\hat{a}_k}}{\prod\limits_{k=0}^{\tau} e(\prod\limits_{t=0}^{\tau} K_{4,k,t}^{\bar{a}_t}, C_1^{\frac{1}{\bar{a}_0 \hat{a}_0}})^{\hat{a}_k}} \cdot C_0.$$

Correctness. In Algorithm 1:

$$e(g^{r_2}, (V_i \prod_{j=1}^{L} H_i^{x_{ij}})^s Z_3) \overset{?}{=} e(G^s Z_1, (v_i \prod_{j=1}^{L} h_i^{y_{ij}})^{r_2}).$$

$$e(g, v_i)^{sr_2} e(g, \prod_{j=1}^{L} h_i^{x_{ij}})^{sr_2} \overset{?}{=} e(g, v_i)^{sr_2} e(g, \prod_{j=1}^{L} h_i^{y_{ij}})^{sr_2}$$

We then illustrate an example:

Input: "AAGTA", "AAAGG"
Output:
- $d' = 2$
- $pos = <pos[0][], pos[1][]>$, with $pos[0][] = \{1, 2\}, pos[1][] = \{1, 2\}$

In message recovery:

$$C_0 = M \cdot e(g, \omega)^s$$

$$e(K_2, C_4) = e(g^{r_2}, (V_0' \prod_{i=1}^{L} H_i^{v_i})^s \cdot Z_4)$$

$$= e(g, v_0')^{sr_2} e(g, \prod_{i=1}^{L} (h_i^{v_i})^{sr_2})$$

$$e(K_1, C_2) = e(g^{r_1}, F^s Z_2) = e(g, f)^{sr_1}$$

$$\prod_{k=0}^{\tau} e(K_1^{\frac{1}{\bar{a}_0 \hat{a}_0}}, \prod_{t=0}^{\tau} C_{5,k,t}^{a_t})^{\hat{a}_k} = \prod_{k=0}^{\tau} e(g^{\frac{r_1}{\bar{a}_0}}, \prod_{t=0}^{\tau} (V_t'(B_k \prod_{i=1}^{L} (U_i)^{d_i i^k})(\prod_{j=1}^{L} (H_j)^{v_j j^t}))^{sa_t})^{\hat{a}_k}$$

$$= e(g, v_0')^{\frac{sr_1 \sum_{t=0}^{\tau} x_t a_t \sum_{k=0}^{\tau} \hat{a}_k}{\bar{a}_0 \hat{a}_0}} e(g, b_0)^{\frac{sr_1 \sum_{t=0}^{\tau} a_t \sum_{k=0}^{\tau} x_k' \hat{a}_k}{\bar{a}_0 \hat{a}_0}} \prod_{i=1}^{L}$$

$$e(g, u_i)^{\frac{sr_1 \sum_{t=0}^{\tau} a_t \prod_{k=1}^{\tau} (i - d_k)}{\bar{a}_0 \hat{a}_0}} \prod_{j=1}^{L} e(g, h_j)^{\frac{v_j sr_1 \prod_{t=1}^{\tau} (i - \omega_t) \sum_{k=0}^{\tau} \hat{a}_k}{\bar{a}_0 \hat{a}_0}}.$$

$$\prod_{k=0}^{\tau} e(\prod_{t=0}^{\tau} K_{4,k,t}^{\bar{a}_t}, C_1^{\frac{1}{\bar{a}_0 \hat{a}_0}})^{\hat{a}_k} = e(\omega^{\bar{a}_0 \hat{a}_0}(v_0' \prod_{i=1}^{L} (h_i^{z_i}))^{r_2 \bar{a}_0 \hat{a}_0} \prod_{k=1}^{\tau} ((\prod_{t=1}^{\tau} (v_t'(b_k \prod_{i=1}^{L} (u_i)^{\sigma_i i^k})$$

$$(\prod_{j=1}^{L} (h_j)^{z_j j^t}))^{r_1 \bar{a}_t})^{\hat{a}_k} f^{r_1 \bar{a}_0 \hat{a}_0}, G^{\frac{s}{\bar{a}_0 \hat{a}_0}} Z_1)$$

$$= e(g, \omega)^s e(g, v_0')^{sr_2} e(g, \prod_{i=1}^{L} (h_i^{z_i})^{sr_2})$$

$$e(g, v_0')^{\frac{r_1 s \sum_{t=0}^{\tau} x_t \bar{a}_t \sum_{k=1}^{\tau} \hat{a}_k}{\bar{a}_0}} e(g, b_0)^{\frac{sr_1 \sum_{t=0}^{\tau} \bar{a}_t \sum_{k=0}^{\tau} x_k' \hat{a}_k}{\bar{a}_0 \hat{a}_0}} \prod_{i=1}^{L}$$

$$e(g, u_i)^{\frac{sr_1 \sum_{t=0}^{\tau} \bar{a}_t \prod_{k=1}^{\tau} (i - \sigma_k)}{\bar{a}_0 \hat{a}_0}}) \prod_{j=1}^{L} e(g, h_j)^{\frac{sr_1 z_j \prod_{t=1}^{\tau} (i - \bar{\omega}_t) \sum_{k=0}^{\tau} \hat{a}_k}{\bar{a}_0 \hat{a}_0}}$$

$$e(g, f)^{sr_1}.$$

5 Security Analysis for the Proposed EDE Scheme

Theorem 1. *Assume that the Decisional $L-cBDHE$ assumption holds, then for any PPT adversary, our EDE scheme is selectively secure.*

Let B denote the algorithm to solve the Decisional $L-cBDHE$ problem. B is given a challenge instance Z, T' of the problem, where $Z = (g_p, g_q, h, g_p^{\alpha}, \ldots, g_p^{\alpha^L}, g_p^{\alpha^{L+2}}, \ldots, g_p^{\alpha^{2L}})$ and T' is either $T = e(g_p, h)^{\alpha^{L+1}}$ or $R \in_R \mathbb{G}_{T,p}$. B simulates the game for A as follows:

- **Init**: A submits a target vector $\overrightarrow{v}^* \in \Sigma^n$, and target threshold τ. Let $\overrightarrow{d} = (1, \ldots, \tau, \tau + 1, \ldots, L)$ denote a vector of length L. We denote $ind(\overrightarrow{d}) = \{1 \le i \le L | d_i = 0\}$ and $\overline{ind}(\overrightarrow{d}) = \{1 \le i \le L | d_i \ne 0\}$, and $ind(\overrightarrow{d})|_j^{\phi}$ as $\{i \in ind(\overrightarrow{d}) | j \le i \le \phi\}$.

- **Setup**: In this phase, $\mathcal{B}$ generates:

$\gamma, \psi, v_0, v_0', b_0, g, f, h_1', \ldots, h_L', u_1', \ldots, u_L' \in_R \mathbb{G}_p, x_1, \ldots, x_L, x_1', \ldots, x_L' \in_R \mathbb{Z}_n,$

$v_1 = v_0^{x_1}, \ldots, v_L = v_0^{x_L}, v_1' = (v_0')^{x_1}, \ldots, v_L' = (v_0')^{x_L}, b_1 = b_0^{x_1'}, \ldots, b_L = b_0^{x_L'},$

$R_y, R_g, R_f, R_{v_0}, \ldots, R_{v_L}, R_{v_0'}, \ldots, R_{v_L'}, R_{b_0}, \ldots, R_{b_L}, R_{h_1'}, \ldots, R_{h_L'}, R_{u_1'}, \ldots,$

$R_{u_L'} \in_R \mathbb{G}_q,$

$G = g_p R_g, F = g_p^\psi R_f, Y = e(g_p^\alpha, g_p^{\alpha^L} g_p^\gamma),$

$V_t = g_p^{v_0 x_t} R_{v_t}, V_t' = g_p^{v_0' x_t} R_{v_t'},$ with $t = 1, \ldots, L,$

$B_k = g_p^{b_0 x_k'} \prod_{k \in ind(\vec{d})} g_p^{\alpha^{L+1-i} d_i \cdot i^k} R_{b_k},$ with $k = 1, \ldots, L,$

$H_i = g_p^{h_i'} R_{h_i}, \{U_i = g_p^{u_i' - \alpha^{L+1-i}} R_{u_i'}\}_{i \in ind(\vec{d})}, \{U_i = g_p^{u_i'} R_{u_i'}\}_{i \in \overline{ind}(\vec{d})}$

The corresponding master secret key components are: $g = g_p, f = g_p^\psi, h_i = g_p^{h_i'}, \{u_i = g_p^{u_i' - \alpha^{L+1-i}}\}_{i \in \overline{ind}(\vec{d})}, \{u_i = g_p^{u_i'}\}_{i \in ind(\vec{d})}, v_t = v_0^{x_t}, v_t' = v_0'^{x_t},$ with $t = 1, \ldots, L, b_k = b_0^{x_t'} \prod_{i \in ind(\vec{d})} g_p^{\alpha^{L+1-i} d_i},$ with $k = 1, \ldots, L.$ Notice that the master key component ω is $g_p^{\alpha^{L+1} + \alpha\gamma}.$ Since B does not have $g_p^{\alpha^{L+1}},$ B cannot compute ω directly.

- **Query Phase 1**: A queries the user secret key for a string $\vec{z} = (z_1, z_2, \ldots, z_m)$ under the constraint that $EditDistance(\vec{v}^*, \vec{z}) > \tau.$ Assume $EditDistance(\vec{v}^*, \vec{z}) = \sigma$ and denote $\vec{\sigma} = (1, 2, \ldots, \sigma, 0, \ldots, 0)$ and $\vec{d} = (1, 2, \ldots, \tau, 0, \ldots, 0).$ Note that since $\sigma > \tau,$ there exists at least one position i such that $d_i = 0$ and $\sigma_i \neq 0.$ Let $\phi \in ind(\vec{d})$ be the smallest integer such that $\sigma_\phi \neq d_\phi.$ B simulates the user key generation process as follows:

$$K_{4,0,0} = \omega(v_0' \prod_{i=1}^L h_i^{\bar{w}_i})^{r_2} (b_0 \prod_{i=1}^L (u_i^{\sigma_i}))^{r_1} (v_0' \prod_{i=1}^L h_i^{\bar{w}_i})^{r_1} f^{r_1}$$

$$= g_p^{\alpha^{L+1} + \alpha\gamma} (v_0' \prod_{i=1}^L h_i^{\bar{w}_i})^{r_2} (g_p^{b_0} \prod_{i \in ind(\vec{d})} g_p^{\alpha^{L+1-i} d_i} \prod_{ind(\vec{\sigma})} (g^{u_i' - \alpha^{L+1-i}})^{\sigma_i}$$

$$\cdot \prod_{ind(\vec{\sigma})} (g^{u_i'})^{\sigma_i})^{r_1} (v_0' \prod_{j=1}^L h_j^{\bar{w}_j})^{r_1} f^{r_1}$$

$$\stackrel{def}{=} g_p^{\alpha^{L+1} + \alpha\gamma} (v_0' \prod_{i=1}^L u_i^{\bar{w}_i})^{r_2} (g_p^X)^{r_1} (v_0' \prod_{i=j}^L h_j^{\bar{w}_j})^{r_1} f^{r_1}$$

where $X = \sum_{ind(\vec{d})} \alpha^{n+1-i} d_i + b_0 + \sum_{ind(\vec{\sigma})} (u_i' - \alpha^{L+1-i}) \sigma_i + \sum_{ind(\vec{\sigma})} u_i' \sigma_i.$ Since $\sum_{ind(\vec{\sigma})} (u_i' - \alpha^{L+1-i}) \sigma_i + \sum_{ind(\vec{\sigma})} u_i' \sigma_i = -\sum_{ind(\vec{\sigma})} \alpha^{L+1-i} \sigma_i + \sum_{i=1}^L u_i' \sigma_i,$ and recall $\sigma_i = d_i$ for $i \in \overline{ind}(\vec{d})|_1^{\phi-1}$ and $\sigma_\phi \neq d_\phi.$ Hence, we have:

$$X = \sum_{ind(\vec{d})|_1^\phi} \alpha^{L+1-i} (d_i - \sigma_i) + \sum_{i=1}^L u_i' \sigma_i + b_0 = \alpha^{L+1-\phi} \Delta_\phi + \sum_{i=1}^L u_i' \sigma_i + y$$

where $\Delta_\phi = (d_\phi - \sigma_\phi).$ Then we choose $\hat{r}, r_2'$ randomly in $\mathbb{Z}_n,$ and set $r_1 = \frac{-\alpha^\phi}{\Delta_\phi} + r_1', r_2 = r_2'.$ Then $K_{4,0,0}$ can be represented as:

$$K_{4,0,0} = g_p^{\alpha^{L+1}+\alpha\gamma}(v_0' \prod_{i=1}^{L} (h_i)^{\bar{w}_i})^{r_2'} \cdot (g_p^{\alpha^{L+1-\phi}\Delta_\phi + \Sigma_{i=1}^{L} u_i'\sigma_i})^{\frac{-\alpha^\phi}{\Delta_\phi}+r_1'}$$

$$(v_0' \prod_{j=1}^{L} h_j^{\bar{w}_j}))^{\frac{-\alpha^\phi}{\Delta_\phi}+r_1'} f^{\frac{-\alpha^\phi}{\Delta_\phi}+r_1'}$$

$$= g_p^{\alpha^{L+1}+\alpha\gamma}(v_0' \prod_{i=1}^{L} h_i^{\bar{w}_i})^{r_2'} \cdot g_p^{-\alpha^{L+1}} (g_p^{\alpha^{L+1-\phi}\Delta_\phi})^{r_1'} (g_p^{\Sigma_{i=1}^{L} u_i'\sigma_i})^{\frac{-\alpha^\phi}{\Delta_\phi}+r_1'}$$

$$(v_0' \prod_{j=1}^{L} h_j^{\bar{w}_j}))^{\frac{-\alpha^\phi}{\Delta_\phi}+r_1'} f^{\frac{-\alpha^\phi}{\Delta_\phi}+r_1'}$$

$$= (v_0' \prod_{i=1}^{L} h_i^{\bar{w}_i})^{r_2'} \cdot (g_p^{\alpha^{L+1-\phi}\Delta_\phi})^{r_1'} (g_p^{\Sigma_{i=1}^{L} u_i'\sigma_i})^{\frac{-\alpha^\phi}{\Delta_\phi}+r_1'} (v_0' \prod_{j=1}^{L} h_j^{\bar{w}_j}))^{\frac{-\alpha^\phi}{\Delta_\phi}+r_1'} f^{\frac{-\alpha^\phi}{\Delta_\phi}+r_1'}$$

Then we simulate $T_{4,k,t}$ with $k, t \neq 0$ as:

$$T_{4,k,t} = ((b_k \prod_{i=1}^{L} (u_i^{i^L \sigma_i})(v_t' \prod_{j=1}^{L} h_i^{\bar{w}_i i^t}))^{r_1}$$

$$= (g_p^{b_k} \prod_{\phi \in ind(\vec{d})|_{\phi+1}^L} g_p^{\alpha^{L+1-\phi} d_\phi} \prod_{\phi \in \overline{ind(\vec{\sigma})}|_{\phi+1}^L} (g^{u_\phi' - \alpha^{L+1-\phi}})^{\sigma_\phi}$$

$$\cdot \prod_{\phi \in ind(\vec{\sigma})} (g^{u_\phi'})^{\sigma_\phi})^{\frac{-\alpha^\phi}{\Delta_\phi}+r_1'} \cdot (v_t' \prod_{j=1}^{L} h_j^{\bar{w}_j i^t}))^{\frac{-\alpha^\phi}{\Delta_\phi}+r_1'}$$

Next, it generates for each alphabet in $\vec{z}$:
$$\begin{cases} y_1 & = (z_1, 1, \ldots, 1_L) \\ \ldots, \\ y_m & = (z_m, 1, \ldots, 1_L) \end{cases}, \text{ then}$$

computes $K_{3,i} = (v_i \prod_{j=1}^{L} h_i^{y_{ij}})^{r_2'}$. Other elements in the key can also be simulated: $K_1 = g^{r_1} = g^{\frac{-\alpha^\phi}{\Delta_\phi}+r_1'}, K_2 = g^{r_2'}$.

- **Challenge**: A sends two message M_0, M_1 to B. The challenger then flips a coin $\beta \leftarrow \{0, 1\}$.

First, $\mathcal{B}$ generates for each alphabet in $\vec{v}^*$:
$$\begin{cases} x_1^* & = (v_1, 1, \ldots, 1_L) \\ \ldots, \\ x_m^* & = (v_m, 1, \ldots, 1_L) \end{cases}, \text{ then}$$

generates $Z_1, Z_2, Z_3, Z_4, Z_5 \xleftarrow{R} \mathbb{G}_q$ and sets:

$$C_0 = M_b \cdot T' \cdot e(g_p^\alpha, h)^\gamma, C_1 = hZ_1, C_2 = h^\psi Z_2, C_{3,i} = h^{v_0 x_i + \sum_{j=1}^{L} h_i' x_{i,j}^*} Z_3,$$

$$C_4 = h^{v_0' + \sum_{i=1}^{L} h_i' v_i^*} Z_4, C_{5,k,t} = h^{b_k x_k' \sum_{i=1}^{L} u_i' d_i i^k + v_t' \sum_{j=1}^{L} v_j' h_j' j^t} Z_5$$

where $h = g_p^c$ for some unknown $c \in \mathbb{Z}_p$. B returns the challenge ciphertext

$$CT^* = (n_1, C_1, C_2, \{C_{3,i}\}_{i=1}^{n_1}, C_4, \{\{C_{5,k,t}\}_{k=0}^{L}\}_{t=0}^{L})$$

to A. If $T' = T = e(g_p, h)^{\alpha^L + 1}$, then:

$$C_0 = M_b \cdot e(g_p, g_p^c)^{\alpha^{L+1}} \cdot e(g_p^\alpha, g_p^c)^\gamma = M_b \cdot e(g_p, g_p^{\alpha^{L+1}})^c \cdot e(g_p^\alpha, g_p^\gamma)^c = M_b \cdot Y^c$$

$$C_1 = (g_p^c) \cdot Z_1 = G^c \cdot Z_1', C_2 = (g_p^c)^\psi \cdot Z_2 = F^c \cdot Z_2',$$

$$C_{3,i} = (g_p^c)^{v_0 x_i + \sum_{j=1}^{L} h_i' x_{i,j}^*} Z_3 = (g_p^{v_0 x_i + \sum_{j=1}^{L} h_i' x_{i,j}^*})^c Z_3 = (V_i \prod_{j=1}^{L} H_i^{x_{ij}^*})^c \cdot Z_3',$$

$$C_4 = (g_p^c)^{v_0' + \sum_{i=1}^{L} h_i' v_i^*} \cdot Z_4 = ((g_p)^{v_0' + \sum_{i=1}^{L} h_i' v_i^*})^c \cdot Z_4 = (V_0' \prod_{i=1}^{L} H_i^{v_i^*})^c \cdot Z_4'.$$

$$C_{5,k,t} = (g_p^c)^{b_k x_k' \sum_{i=1}^{L} u_i' d_i i^k + v_t' \sum_{j=1}^{L} v_j^* h_j' j^t} \cdot Z_5 = ((g_p)^{b_k x_k' \sum_{i=1}^{L} u_i' d_i i^k + v_t' \sum_{j=1}^{L} v_j^* h_j' j^t})^c \cdot Z_5.$$

$$= (V_t'(B_k \prod_{i=1}^{L}(U_i)^{d_i i^k})(\prod_{j=1}^{L}(H_j)^{v_j^* j^t}))^c \cdot Z_5'.$$

the challenge ciphertext is a valid encryption of M_b. On the other hand, when T' is uniformly distributed in $\mathbb{G}_{T,p}$, the challenge ciphertext is independent of b.

- **Query Phase 2**: Same as Phase 1.
- **Guess**: A output $b' \in \{0, 1\}$. If $b' = b$ then B outputs 1; otherwise outputs 0.

If $b' = 0$, then the simulation is the same as in the real game. Hence, A will have the probability $\frac{1}{2} + \epsilon$ to guess b correctly. If $b' = 1$, then T' is random in $\mathbb{G}_{T,p}$, then A will have probability $\frac{1}{2}$ to guess b correctly.

Therefore, B can solve the Decisional $L-cBDHE$ assumption also with advantage ϵ. $\qquad \square$

6 Extension - Fuzzy Broadcast Encryption (FBE)

We demonstrate an extension of the proposed EDE scheme to achieve Fuzzy Broadcast Encryption. To illustrate how the scheme works, let's consider the following example. Suppose we encrypt a message under a keyword vector $W = \{$Labour Party, Defence Unit$\}$ and a threshold distance $d = 2$. Subsequently, people who have the attributes related to the keyword $w =$ Labor Party or $w' =$ Defense Unit can decrypt the message since the minimum edit distance between w (w', respectively) and all the keywords in W is 1, which is less than the threshold $d = 2$.

6.1 Definition

A Fuzzy Broadcast Encryption (FBE) scheme consists of the following four probabilistic polynomial-time algorithms:

- **Setup**$(1^n, \Sigma)$: on input a security parameter 1^n, an alphabet Σ, the algorithm outputs a public key PK and the corresponding master secret key MSK.

- **Encrypt**$(PK, M, W = (w_{1,l_1}, w_{2,l_2}, \ldots, w_{k,l_k}) \in \Sigma^{n_1}, d)$: on input a public key PK, a list of k keywords $W = (w_{1,l_1}, w_{2,l_2}, \ldots, w_{k,l_k})$ in which each keyword w_{i,l_i} has l_i characters, and a threshold distance d, the algorithm outputs a ciphertext CT.
- **Key Gen**$(MSK, w \in \Sigma^m)$: on input the master secret key MSK and a keyword w of length m, the algorithm outputs a secret key SK_w.
- **Decrypt**(CT, SK_w): on input a ciphertext CT with keywords $W = (w_{1,l_1}, w_{2,l_2}, \ldots, w_{k,l_k})$ and a secret key SK_w with keyword w, the algorithm outputs M if $Min\{EditDistance(w_{i,l_i}, w)\}_{i=1}^k \leq d$, or $\perp$ otherwise.

6.2   FBE Scheme

Below we present a FBE scheme based on our EDE scheme.

- **Setup**$(1^n, \Sigma)$: The setup algorithm is generated similar to the original EDE scheme.
- **Encrypt**$(PK, W = (w_{1,l_1}, w_{2,l_2}, \ldots, w_{k',l_{k'}}), M, d)$: On input the public key PK, a list of k keywords $W = (w_{1,l_1}, w_{2,l_2}, \ldots, w_{k',l_{k'}})$ in which each keyword w_{i,l_i} has l_i alphabets, it first generates for each alphabet $w_{i,j}$ in keyword w_{i,l_i} a vector

$$\begin{cases} \boldsymbol{x}_{11} = (w_{11}, 1, \ldots, 1_L), \ldots, \boldsymbol{x}_{1l_1} & = (w_{1l_1}, 1, \ldots, 1_L), \\ \cdots \\ \boldsymbol{x}_{k'1} = (w_{k'1}, 1, \ldots, 1_L), \ldots, \boldsymbol{x}_{k'l'_k} & = (w_{k'l_{k'}}, 1, \ldots, 1_L). \end{cases}$$

Algorithm 2. Multi-keyword Edit Distance Evaluation via Dynamic Programming

---

```
input  : CT, SK
output: distance d′, index pos_w, array pos[2][]
Create Array[len(W)]; Create pos[2][]; Create Array < pos > aPos;
for θ ← 1 to len(W) do
    len_v = n_θ + 1; len_z = m + 1;
    Creat cost[len_v]; Creat newcost[len_v];
    for i ← 0 to len_v do
    |   cost[i] = i;
    end
    k = 0;
    for j ← 1 to len_z do
        newcost[0] = j;
        for i ← 1 to len_v do
            match = (e(K_1, C_{3,θ,i-1}) == e(C_1, K_{3,j-1}))?0 : 1;
            if i ∉ pos[0], j ∉ pos[1] then
            |   pos[0][k + +] = i, pos[1][k + +] = j, ;
            end
            aPos.add(pos);
            cost − replace = cost[i − 1] + match; cost − insert =
            cost[i] + 1; cost − delete = newcost[i − 1] + 1;
            newcost[i] =
            Math.min(Math.min(cost − insert, cost − delete), cost − replace);
        end
        swap[] = cost; cost = newcost; newcost = swap;
    end
    Array[t + +] = cost[len_v − 1]; Refreshpos;
end
return Min(Array[]), pos_w = index[Array[i] == Min(Array[])], pos = aPos[pos_w];
```

Define

$$\begin{cases} \boldsymbol{w_1} &= (w_{11}, w_{1,2}, \ldots, w_{1,l_1}, \ldots, 1_L), \\ \cdots, \\ \boldsymbol{w_{k'}} &= (w_{k'1}, w_{k'2}, \ldots, w_{k',l_{k'}}, \ldots, 1_L), \end{cases}$$

and $\vec{d} = (1, \ldots, d, 0_{d+1}, \ldots, 0_L)$. Then choose $s \in_R \mathbb{Z}_n$, and $Z_1, Z_2, Z_3, Z_4, Z_5 \in_R \mathbb{G}_q$, and compute:

$$C_0 = MY^s, C_1 = G^s Z_1, C_2 = F^s Z_2, C_{3,\delta,i} = (V_i \prod_{j=1}^{L} H_i^{x_{\delta ij}})^s Z_3,$$

$$C_{4,\delta} = (V_0' \prod_{i=1}^{L} H_i^{w_{\delta i}})^s \cdot Z_4, C_{5,k,\delta,t} = (V_t'(B_k \prod_{i=1}^{L} (U_i)^{d_i i^k})(\prod_{j=1}^{L} (H_j)^{v_{\delta j} j^t}))^s \cdot Z_5.$$

Set the ciphertext as: $CT = (\{l_\delta\}_{\delta=1}^{k'}, C_0, C_1, C_2, \{\{C_{3,\delta,i}\}_{\delta=1}^{k'}\}_{i=1}^{l_\delta}, \{C_{4,\delta}\}_{\delta=1}^{k'}, \{\{\{C_{5,k,\delta,t}\}_{k=0}^{L}\}_{\delta=1}^{k'}\}_{t=0}^{L}).$

- **KeyGen**$(MSK, \bar{w} = (\bar{w}_1, \ldots, \bar{w}_m) \in \Sigma^m)$: given a keyword $\bar{w}$ of length m, it generates $\boldsymbol{y}_i = (\bar{w}_i, 1, \ldots, 1_L)$ for each alphabet $\bar{w}_i$, and creates $\vec{\sigma} = (1, 2, \ldots, L)$ and expands $\bar{w}$ to $\bar{w} = (z_1, z_2, \ldots, z_m, \ldots, 1_L)$. Then choose $r_1, r_2 \in_R \mathbb{Z}_n$, and compute:

$$K_1 = g^{r_1}, K_2 = g^{r_2}, K_{3,i} = (v_i \prod_{j=1}^{L} h_j^{y_{ij}})^{r_2},$$

$$\begin{pmatrix} K_{4,0,0} = \omega(v_0' \prod_{i=1}^{L} h_i^{\bar{w}_i})^{r_2} \\ \quad ((b_0 \prod_{i=1}^{L} (u_i^{\sigma_i}))(v_0' \prod_{j=1}^{L} h_j^{\bar{w}_j}))^{r_1} f^{r_1} \\ K_{4,1,0} = (b_1 \prod_{i=1}^{L} (u_i^{\sigma_i})^i (v_0' \prod_{j=1}^{L} h_j^{\bar{w}_j}))^{r_1} \\ \cdots, \\ K_{4,L,0} = (b_L \prod_{i=1}^{L} (u_i^{\sigma_i})^{i^L} (v_0' \prod_{j=1}^{L} h_j^{\bar{w}_j}))^{r_1} \end{pmatrix}, \begin{pmatrix} K_{4,0,t} = (b_0 \prod_{i=1}^{L} (u_i^{\sigma_i})(v_t' \prod_{j=1}^{L} h_j^{\bar{w}_j})^{j^t})^{r_1} \\ K_{4,1,t} = (b_1 \prod_{i=1}^{L} (u_i^{\sigma_i})^i (v_t' \prod_{j=1}^{L} h_j^{\bar{w}_j})^{j^t})^{r_1} \\ \cdots, \\ K_{4,L,t} = (b_L \prod_{i=1}^{L} (u_i^{\sigma_i})^{i^L} (v_t' \prod_{j=1}^{L} h_j^{\bar{w}_j})^{j^t})^{r_1} \end{pmatrix},$$

for $t = 1, \ldots, L$. Then set the secret key as $SK = (m, K_1, K_2, \{K_{3,i}\}_{i=1}^{m}, \{\{K_{4,k,t}\}_{k=0}^{L}\}_{t=0}^{L}).$

- **Decrypt**(CT, SK): The decryption algorithm first executes the dynamic programming algorithm for edit distance by following Algorithm 2 which returns a minimum distance d', the index pos_w of the corresponding keyword w in W, the matching indices array $pos[0][]$ for w and $pos[1][]$ for $\bar{w}$. It sets $\tau = L - d'$, and applies the Viète's formulas to compute
We then set $a_{\tau-k}, \bar{a}_{\tau-k}, \hat{a}_{\tau-k}$ similar to (3), (4), (5).
Then recover M as:

$$M = \frac{e(K_2, C_{4,pos_w}) \cdot e(K_1, C_2) e(K_1^{\frac{1}{a_0}}, \prod_{t=0}^{\tau} C_{5,k,pos_w,t}^{a_t})}{e(\prod_{t=0}^{\tau} K_{4,k,t}^{\bar{a}_t}, C_1^{\frac{1}{\bar{a}_0}})} \cdot C_0.$$

Theorem 2. *Assume that the Decisional $L-cBDHE$ assumption holds, then for any PPT adversary, our FBE scheme is selectively secure.*

We give the security definition in the full version since the limited space. The security proof follows that of Theorem 1 and is omitted here.

7   Conclusions and Future Work

We introduced a new type of fuzzy public key encryption in this paper. Our new encryption scheme, called Edit Distance-based Encryption (EDE), allows a user associated with an identity or attribute string to decrypt a ciphertext encrypted under another string if and only if the edit distance between the two strings are within a threshold specified by the encrypter. We provide the formal definition, security model, and a concrete EDE scheme in the standard model. We also showed an extension of our EDE scheme for fuzzy broadcast encryption. We leave the construction of an anonymous EDE scheme, which implies a Fuzzy Public-key Encryption with Keyword Search scheme to preserve the privacy of the matching keyword by the dynamic programming algorithm.

Acknowledgement. Kaitai Liang is supported by privacy-aware retrieval and modelling of genomic data (PRIGENDA, No. 13283250), the Academy of Finland.

References

1. Abdalla, M., Birkett, J., Catalano, D., Dent, A.W., Malone-Lee, J., Neven, G., Schuldt, J.C.N., Smart, N.P.: Wildcarded identity-based encryption. J. Cryptol. **24**(1), 42–82 (2011)
2. Abdalla, M., Caro, A.D., Phan, D.H.: Generalized key delegation for wildcarded identity-based and inner-product encryption. IEEE Trans. Inf. Forensics Secur. **7**(6), 1695–1706 (2012)
3. Abdalla, M., Catalano, D., Dent, A.W., Malone-Lee, J., Neven, G., Smart, N.P.: Identity-based encryption gone wild. In: Bugliesi, M., Preneel, B., Sassone, V., Wegener, I. (eds.) ICALP 2006. LNCS, vol. 4052, pp. 300–311. Springer, Heidelberg (2006)
4. Atallah, M.J., Kerschbaum, F., Du, W.: Secure and private sequence comparisons. In: ACM Workshop on WPES, pp. 39–44 (2003)
5. Bethencourt, J., Sahai, A., Waters, B.: Ciphertext-policy attribute-based encryption. In: 2007 IEEE Symposium on Security and Privacy (S&P 2007), pp. 321–334 (2007)
6. Boneh, D., Franklin, M.: Identity-based encryption from the weil pairing. In: Kilian, J. (ed.) CRYPTO 2001. LNCS, vol. 2139, pp. 213–229. Springer, Heidelberg (2001)
7. Cheon, J.H., Kim, M., Lauter, K.: Homomorphic computation of edit distance. Cryptology ePrint Archive, Report 2015/132 (2015)
8. Ge, A., Zhang, R., Chen, C., Ma, C., Zhang, Z.: Threshold ciphertext policy attribute-based encryption with constant size ciphertexts. In: Susilo, W., Mu, Y., Seberry, J. (eds.) ACISP 2012. LNCS, vol. 7372, pp. 336–349. Springer, Heidelberg (2012)

9. Goyal, V., Pandey, O., Sahai, A., Waters, B.: Attribute-based encryption for fine-grained access control of encrypted data. In: 13th ACM Conference on Computer and Communications Security, CCS 2006, pp. 89–98 (2006)

10. Gusfield, D.: Algorithms on Strings, Trees and Sequences. Cambridge University Press, New York (1997)

11. Herranz, J., Laguillaumie, F., Ràfols, C.: Constant size ciphertexts in threshold attribute-based encryption. In: 13th International Conference-PKC 2010, pp. 19–34 (2010)

12. Iovino, V., Persiano, G.: Hidden-vector encryption with groups of prime order. In: Galbraith, S.D., Paterson, K.G. (eds.) Pairing 2008. LNCS, vol. 5209, pp. 75–88. Springer, Heidelberg (2008)

13. Jha, S., Kruger, L., Shmatikov, V.: Towards practical privacy for genomic computation. In: 2008 IEEE Symposium on Security and Privacy (S&P 2008), pp. 216–230 (2008)

14. Katz, J., Sahai, A., Waters, B.: Predicate encryption supporting disjunctions, polynomial equations, and inner products. In: Smart, N.P. (ed.) EUROCRYPT 2008. LNCS, vol. 4965, pp. 146–162. Springer, Heidelberg (2008)

15. Liang, K., Liu, J.K., Wong, D.S., Susilo, W.: An efficient cloud-based revocable identity-based proxy re-encryption scheme for public clouds data sharing. In: Kutyłowski, M., Vaidya, J. (eds.) ESORICS 2014, Part I. LNCS, vol. 8712, pp. 257–272. Springer, Heidelberg (2014)

16. Liang, K., Susilo, W.: Searchable attribute-based mechanism with efficient data sharing for secure cloud storage. IEEE Trans. Inf. Forensics Secur. 10(9), 1981–1992 (2015)

17. Liang, K., Susilo, W., Liu, J.K.: Privacy-preserving ciphertext multi-sharing control for big data storage. IEEE Trans. Inf. Forensics Secur. 10(8), 1578–1589 (2015)

18. Park, J.H.: Efficient hidden vector encryption for conjunctive queries on encrypted data. IEEE Trans. Knowl. Data Eng. 23(10), 1483–1497 (2011)

19. Phuong, T.V.X., Yang, G., Susilo, W.: Efficient hidden vector encryption with constant-size ciphertext. In: Kutyłowski, M., Vaidya, J. (eds.) ESORICS 2014, Part I. LNCS, vol. 8712, pp. 472–487. Springer, Heidelberg (2014)

20. Rane, S., Sun, W.: Privacy preserving string comparisons based on levenshtein distance. In: 2010 IEEE WIFS, pp. 1–6 (2010)

21. Sahai, A., Waters, B.: Fuzzy identity-based encryption. In: Cramer, R. (ed.) EUROCRYPT 2005. LNCS, vol. 3494, pp. 457–473. Springer, Heidelberg (2005)

22. Sedghi, S., van Liesdonk, P., Nikova, S., Hartel, P., Jonker, W.: Searching keywords with wildcards on encrypted data. In: Garay, J.A., De Prisco, R. (eds.) SCN 2010. LNCS, vol. 6280, pp. 138–153. Springer, Heidelberg (2010)

23. Wang, X.S., Huang, Y., Zhao, Y., Tang, H., Wang, X., Bu, D.: Efficient genome-wide, privacy-preserving similar patient query based on private edit distance. In: 22nd ACM CCS 2015 (2015)

Proxy Re-encryption with Delegatable Verifiability

Xiaodong Lin[1(✉)] and Rongxing Lu[2]

[1] Faculty of Business and Information Technology,
University of Ontario Institute of Technology, Oshawa, ON L1H 7K4, Canada
xiaodong.lin@uoit.ca
[2] School of Electrical and Electronic Engineering,
Nanyang Technological University, 50 Nanyang Avenue, Singapore, Singapore
rxlu@ntu.edu.sg

Abstract. Proxy re-encryption is a public key encryption technique that allows a proxy to perform re-encryption without exposing the corresponding plaintext. As a result, proxy re-encryption has increased utility, and can be used in a number of fields including cloud computing. In previous proxy re-encryption schemes, a proxy is assumed to follow the protocol explicitly. However, this is far from the norm, and the assumption is not always true, especially in cloud computing where public cloud is considered untrusted. In this paper, we investigate the verifiability of the re-encryption process. Specifically, we first formalize the proxy re-encryption with delegatable verifiability and its corresponding security model. Then, we propose the first proxy re-encryption scheme with delegatable verifiability. Finally, security proofs of the proposal are also formally given in the proposed security models.

Keywords: Proxy re-encryption · Delegatable verifability · Trust level

1 Introduction

Proxy re-encryption [6] is a special type of public key encryption that allows proxies with re-encryption keys to perform transformations on ciphertexts, while proxies are unable to access the corresponding plaintexts. Due to this useful property, proxy re-encryption has been found very useful, and can be applied to various scenarios where dynamic ciphertext format is required, e.g., cloud and fog computing [19,20,22]. In previous proxy re-encryption schemes, a proxy is assumed to be semi-trusted, i.e., the proxy would follow the protocol exactly, and execute the specified re-encryption steps. However, this assumption is not always true in all proxy re-encryption based applications. For instance, in a cloud storage applying proxy re-encryption [19,20,22], the cloud plays the role of the proxy in proxy re-encryption. Cloud servers, in their efforts to perform computations quickly and inexpensively, may skip on re-encryption steps, for example, in order to save computing resources for other transactions. It is therefore quite likely that

© Springer International Publishing Switzerland 2016
J.K. Liu and R. Steinfeld (Eds.): ACISP 2016, Part II, LNCS 9723, pp. 120–133, 2016.
DOI: 10.1007/978-3-319-40367-0_8

best practices are overlooked. Obviously, proxy re-encryption, while secure with a trusted proxy following the protocol explicitly, can fall apart when the proxy is dishonest and cannot be trusted. A natural question arises "how can the users trust that the cloud performs re-encryption correctly?"

To the best of our knowledge, there are no proxy re-encryption schemes explicitly dealing with the verifiability problem. In this paper, we would like to take this for the first step. In particular, we define verifiable proxy re-encryption and its corresponding security models. In layman's terms, we say a re-encryption process is performed correctly if and only if the original ciphertext and re-encrypted ciphertext can pass the verification. Additionally, with any source authentication, the validity of re-encrypted ciphertext can be verified. Similar with the verifiability in outsourced computation [4,10,17], there are three kinds of verifiability which vary by the verifier: public, private, and delegatable. After evaluating the previous proxy re-encryption schemes, we find that some existing proxy re-encryption schemes satisfy public verifiability, others hold private verifiability. However, there are no available delegatable verifiability. As we know, the delegatable verifiability is more powerful than its counterparts, since it can be easily converted into others by revealing the verifiable key or not. Hence, proxy re-encryption schemes with delegatable verifiability have wider spectrums of applications. In this paper, we focus on the design of proxy re-encryption scheme with delegatable verifiability, and propose the first such proxy re-encryption scheme along with security proofs in our proposed security models.

1.1 Related Work

One common way to divide proxy re-encryption schemes is according to the allowed re-encryption directions with one re-encryption key: if the re-encryption can be proceeded in both directions with the same re-encryption key, it is bidirectional; otherwise, it is unidirectional. The schemes proposed by Blaze et al. [6] and Ateniese et al. [3] are the first bidirectional and unidirectional proxy re-encryption scheme, respectively. These two schemes are CPA-secure, but cannot supply the verifiable functionality.

The first CCA-secure bidirectional proxy re-encryption scheme is proposed by Canetti and Hohenberger [8]. Surprisingly, their scheme can provide public verifiability. Given one original ciphertext (A, B, C, D, E) and one re-encrypted ciphertext (A', B', C', D', E') in the CH07 scheme, one can easily decide whether they can yield the same plaintext by checking the validity of the two ciphertexts and the following equalities: $A = A'$, $C = C'$, $D = D'$, $E = E'$, and $e(B, pk_2) = e(pk_1, B')$, where pk_1, pk_2 are the underlying public keys, and $e(\cdot, \cdot)$ is a bilinear map. Similarly, the first RCCA-secure unidirectional proxy re-encryption scheme due to Libert and Vergnaud [16] can also supply the public verifiability by only checking the validity of the two ciphertexts and the same elements in the two ciphertexts.

The first CCA-secure unidirectional proxy re-encryption scheme is proposed by Shao and Cao [18]. However, the SC09 scheme only provides private verifiability. This is because the check factor (exponent r) can be computed if and only if the corresponding plaintext is obtained. Similar with the SC09 scheme, Chow et al. [9] proposed a more efficient CCA-secure unidirectional proxy re-encryption scheme by using the Fujisaki-Okamoto technique [11]. Hence, their scheme also supports private verifiability. Later on, several other CCA-secure unidirectional proxy re-encryption schemes are proposed [13], however, only a few of them support verifiability.

Till now, many other proxy re-encryption schemes with some special properties are proposed, such as conditional proxy re-encryption [21], proxy re-encryption with invisible proxy [14], attribute-based proxy re-encryption [15], identity-based proxy re-encryption [12], and anonymous proxy re-encryption [2]. Nevertheless, only a few of the CCA-secure schemes provide verifiability.

To the best of our knowledge, there is no existing proxy re-encryption scheme supporting delegatable verifiability.

1.2   Paper Organization

The remainder of this paper is organized as follows. In Sect. 2, the definition and security models of proxy re-encryption with delegatable verifiability are introduced. In Sect. 3, we first present a generic construction for proxy re-encryption with delegatable verifiability and give the security proofs. In what follows, we give an extension of delegatable verifiability. At last, we conclude the paper in Sect. 5.

2   Preliminaries

2.1   Definitions for Single-Hop Unidirectional Proxy Re-Encryption with Delegatable Verifiability (PREDV)

Definition 1 (Single-hop Unidirectional PREDV). *A single-hop unidirectional PREDV scheme* PREDV *is a tuple of probabilistic polynomial time (PPT) algorithms (*KeyGen, VKGen, RKGen, Enc, ReEnc, Dec, Ver*):*

- KeyGen(1^λ) → (pk, sk). *When inputting a security parameter* λ, *the key generation algorithm* KeyGen *outputs the public/private key pair* (pk, sk) *of a user. This algorithm is performed by the user who is the corresponding owner of the generated key pair.*
- VKGen(sk) → vk. *When inputting a private key* sk, *the verification key generation algorithm* VKGen *outputs the verification key* vk. *This algorithm is performed by the user who holds the private key* sk.
- RKGen(sk_1, pk_2) → $rk_{1,2}$. *When inputting a private key* sk_1 *and a public key* pk_2, *the re-encryption key generation algorithm* RKGen *outputs a re-encryption key* $rk_{1,2}$. *This algorithm is performed by the user who holds the private key* sk_1.
- Enc(pk, m) → C. *When inputting a public key* pk, *and a message* m *from the message space* $\mathcal{M}$, *the encryption algorithm* Enc *outputs a ciphertext* C *under the public key* pk. *This algorithm is performed by an encryptor.*

- $\text{ReEnc}(rk_{1,2}, C_1) \rightarrow C_2$. *When inputting a re-encryption key $rk_{1,2}$ and a ciphertext C_1, the re-encryption algorithm ReEnc outputs a re-encrypted ciphertext C_2 under the public key pk_2 or a special symbol $\perp$. This algorithm is performed by the proxy holding the re-encryption key $rk_{1,2}$.*
- $\text{Dec}(sk, C) \rightarrow m$. *When inputting a private key sk and a ciphertext C, the decryption algorithm Dec outputs m in the message space or a special symbol $\perp$. This algorithm is performed by the decryptor who holds the private key sk.*
- $\text{Ver}(C_1, C_2, vk) \rightarrow 0$ or 1. *When inputting an original ciphertext C_1, a re-encrypted ciphertext C_2, and a verification key vk, the verify algorithm Ver outputs 1 if C_1 and C_2 are corresponding to the same plaintext; or 0 otherwise.*

Correctness. For any message m in the message space $\mathcal{M}$, $(pk_0, sk_0) \leftarrow \text{KeyGen}(1^\lambda)$, and $(pk_1, sk_1) \leftarrow \text{KeyGen}(1^\lambda)$ the following conditions must hold:

$$\text{Dec}(sk_i, \text{Enc}(pk_i, m)) = m,$$

$$\text{Dec}(sk_2, \text{ReEnc}(\text{RKGen}(sk_1, pk_2), \text{Enc}(pk_1, m))) = m,$$

and

$$\text{Ver}(\text{Enc}(pk_1, m), \text{ReEnc}(\text{RKGen}(sk_1, pk_2), \text{Enc}(pk_1, m')), \text{VKGen}(sk_2)) = \begin{cases} 1, & \text{if } m = m'; \\ 0, & \text{if } m \neq m'. \end{cases}$$

Remark 1. Compared with previous definitions for single-hop unidirectional proxy re-encryption [3, 16], our definition additionally has the content related to verifiability: algorithms VKGen and Ver, and the third requirement of correctness.

2.2 Security Models for Single-Hop Unidirectional PREDV

Replayable Chosen-Ciphertext Security for Single-Hop Unidirectional PREDV. In most of the previous unidirectional proxy re-encryption schemes, there are two formats of ciphertexts. One is for original ciphertexts, and the other is for re-encrypted ciphertexts. Hence, there are two cases in this definition.

The challenge ciphertext is an original ciphertext.

Setup: The challenger $\mathcal{C}$ sets up the system parameters according to the security parameter (1^λ).

Phase 1: $\mathcal{A}$ issues queries $q_1, \cdots, q_{n_1}$ where query q_i is one of:
  - Public key generation oracle $\mathcal{O}_{pk}$: $\mathcal{C}$ runs $\text{KeyGen}(1^\lambda)$ to generate a new key pair (pk, sk), gives pk to $\mathcal{A}$ and records (pk, sk) in Table $\mathbb{T}_{pk}$. For all other oracle queries which involves pk_i, we require that (pk_i, sk_i) can be found in $\mathbb{T}_{pk}$, otherwise the oracle just returns $\perp$.
  - Private key generation oracle $\mathcal{O}_{sk}$: When inputting pk_i, $\mathcal{C}$ returns sk_i, or $\perp$ if it does not exist in $\mathbb{T}_{pk}$.

- Verification key generation oracle $\mathcal{O}_{vk}$: When inputting pk_i, $\mathcal{C}$ returns $vk_i = \mathtt{VKGen}(sk_i)$.
- Re-encryption key generation oracle $\mathcal{O}_{rk}$: When inputting (pk_i, pk_j), where $pk_i \neq pk_j$, $\mathcal{C}$ returns $rk_{i,j} = \mathtt{RKGen}(sk_i, pk_j)$ and records it in Table $\mathbb{T}_{rk}$.
- Re-encryption oracle $\mathcal{O}_{re}$: When inputting (pk_i, pk_j, C_i), where $pk_i \neq pk_j$, $\mathcal{C}$ returns $C_j = \mathtt{ReEnc}(\mathtt{RKGen}(sk_i, pk_j), pk_i, C_i)$. Note that $\mathcal{A}$ can ask the oracle to return the corresponding re-encrypted ciphertext generated by a previous re-encryption key or a new re-encryption key.
- Decryption oracle $\mathcal{O}_{dec}$: When inputting (pk_i, C_i), $\mathcal{C}$ returns $\mathtt{Dec}(sk_i, C_i)$.
- Verify oracle $\mathcal{O}_{ver}$: When inputting (pk_i, C_i, pk_j, C_j), $\mathcal{C}$ returns $\mathtt{Ver}(C_i, C_j, vk_j)$, where vk_j is corresponding verification key of pk_j.

These queries may be asked adaptively, that is, each query q_i may depend on the replies to $q_1, \cdots, q_{i-1}$.

Challenge: Once $\mathcal{A}$ decides that Phase 1 is over, it outputs two equal length plaintexts m_0, m_1 from the message space $\mathcal{M}$, and a public key pk^* on which it wishes to challenge. There are two restrictions on the public key pk^*, (i) pk^* has not appeared in any query to $\mathcal{O}_{sk}$; (ii) if $(pk^*, \star)$ has appeared in any query to $\mathcal{O}_{rk}$, then $\star$ should not appear in any query to $\mathcal{O}_{sk}$. $\mathcal{C}$ picks a random bit $\mathbf{b} \in \{0,1\}$ and sets $C^* = \mathtt{Enc}(pk^*, m_{\mathbf{b}})$. It sends C^* as the challenge to $\mathcal{A}$.

Phase 2: Same as Phase 1 but the challenger will output $\perp$ in the following cases.

- $\mathcal{O}_{sk}$: We have the two natural restrictions inherited from the challenge phase: $pk_i = pk^*$, or (pk^*, pk_i) has been queried to $\mathcal{O}_{rk}$. Additionally, we do not allow query pk_i when (pk^*, pk_i, C^*) has been queried to $\mathcal{O}_{re}$. Similar concerns for $\mathcal{O}_{rk}$ and $\mathcal{O}_{re}$ below.
- $\mathcal{O}_{rk}$: $pk_i = pk^*$ and pk_j has been queried to $\mathcal{O}_{sk}$.
- $\mathcal{O}_{re}$: $(pk_i, C_i) = (pk^*, C^*)$ and pk_j has been queried to $\mathcal{O}_{sk}$.
- $\mathcal{O}_{dec}$: $pk_i = pk^*$ and $\mathtt{Dec}(sk^*, C_i) \in \{m_0, m_1\}$.

Guess: Finally, the adversary $\mathcal{A}$ outputs a guess $\mathbf{b}' \in \{0,1\}$ and wins the game if $\mathbf{b} = \mathbf{b}'$.

The advantage $\mathbf{Adv}_{\mathsf{PREDV}}^{\mathsf{RCCA\text{-}O}}(\lambda)$ is defined as $|\Pr[\mathbf{b} = \mathbf{b}'] - 1/2|$. The scheme PREDV is said to be *RCCA-O* secure if all efficient adversaries $\mathcal{A}$ specified as above, the advantage $\mathbf{Adv}_{\mathsf{PREDV}}^{\mathsf{RCCA\text{-}O}}(\lambda)$ is negligible.

The challenge ciphertext is a re-encrypted ciphertext.

Phase 1: Identical to that in the challenge original ciphertext case.

Challenge: Once $\mathcal{A}$ decides that Phase 1 is over, it outputs two equal-length plaintexts m_0^*, m_1^* from the message space, and two public keys pk, pk^* on which it wishes to be challenged. The public key pk^* has not been queried to $\mathcal{O}_{sk}$. The challenger picks a random bit $\mathbf{b} \in \{0,1\}$ and sets $C'^* = \mathtt{ReEnc}(rk, \mathtt{Enc}(pk, m_{\mathbf{b}}^*))$, where rk is a re-encryption key from pk to pk^*. It sends C'^* as the challenge ciphertext to $\mathcal{A}$.

Phase 2: Almost the same as that in Phase 1 but with the following constraints: if $pk_i = pk^*$ in $\mathcal{O}_{sk}$ or $(pk_i, C_i) = (pk^*, C'^*)$ in $\mathcal{O}_{dec}$, $\mathcal{C}$ returns $\bot$.

Guess: Identical to that in the challenge original ciphertext case.

The advantage $\mathbf{Adv}_{PREDV}^{RCCA-R}(\lambda)$ is defined as $|\Pr[\mathbf{b} = \mathbf{b}'] - 1/2|$. The scheme PREDV is said to be *RCCA-R* secure if all efficient adversaries $\mathcal{A}$ specified as above, the advantage $\mathbf{Adv}_{PREDV}^{RCCA-R}(\lambda)$ is negligible.

Remark 2. Compared with the previous RCCA security model for single-hop unidirectional proxy re-encryption [16], our model additionally allows the adversary to issue queries to $\mathcal{O}_{vk}$ and $\mathcal{O}_{ver}$.

Private Verifiability for Single-Hop Unidirectional PREDV. This security model guarantees that without the corresponding verification key, the verifiability remains private.

Phase 1: Identical to Phase 1 of the RCCA-O game for single-hop unidirectional PREDV.

Guess: Once $\mathcal{A}$ decides that Phase 1 is over, it outputs a public key pk^*, and an original ciphertext C^* under public key pk, on which it wishes to challenge. There are two restrictions on the public key pk^*, i.e., pk^* has not appeared in any query to $\mathcal{O}_{sk}$ or $\mathcal{O}_{vk}$. $\mathcal{C}$ picks a random bit $\mathbf{b} \in \{0,1\}$. If $\mathbf{b} = 1$, $\mathcal{C}$ computes $C'^* = \texttt{ReEnc}(rk, C^*)$, where rk is the re-encryption key corresponding to the delegation from pk to pk^*; otherwise, $\mathcal{C}$ chooses a random value from the space of re-encrypted ciphertexts and sets it as C'^*. At last, $\mathcal{C}$ sends C'^* as the challenge to $\mathcal{A}$.

Phase 2: Almost the same as that in Phase 1 but with the following constraints: if $pk_i = pk^*$ in $\mathcal{O}_{sk}$ or $\mathcal{O}_{vk}$, or $(pk_i, C_i) = (pk^*, C'^*)$ in $\mathcal{O}_{dec}$, $\mathcal{C}$ returns $\bot$.

Guess: Finally, the adversary $\mathcal{A}$ outputs a guess $\mathbf{b}' \in \{0,1\}$ and wins the game if $\mathbf{b} = \mathbf{b}'$.

The advantage $\mathbf{Adv}_{PREDV}^{VK}(\lambda)$ is defined as $|\Pr[\mathbf{b} = \mathbf{b}'] - 1/2|$. The scheme PREDV is said to be *VK* secure if all efficient adversaries $\mathcal{A}$ specified as above, the advantage $\mathbf{Adv}_{PREDV}^{VK}(\lambda)$ is negligible.

3   Our Proposal

As we mentioned above, some of previous proxy re-encryption scheme are publicly verifiable and RCCA-secure, such as the scheme in [16]. In this section, we will make use of this kind of proxy re-encryption (denoted as PREPV) and CCA-secure public key encryption (denoted as PKE) to propose a generic construction of proxy re-encryption with delegatable verifiability. The details of the proposed PREDV are as follows. For clarification, we will use $^-$ and $\hat{\ }$ to denote the output of algorithms of PREPV and PKE, respectively.

- KeyGen: When inputting the security parameter 1^λ, the user runs PREPV.KeyGen(1^λ) $\rightarrow$ $(\overline{pk}, \overline{sk})$ and PKE.KeyGen(1^λ) $\rightarrow$ $(\widehat{pk}, \widehat{sk})$, and sets the public key pk and private key sk as $(\overline{pk}, \widehat{pk})$ and $(\overline{sk}, \widehat{sk})$, respectively.
- VKGen: The verification key of the user is $\overline{sk}$ which will be sent to the verifier. That is, $vk = \widehat{sk}$.
- RKGen: When inputting a private key $sk_1 = (\overline{sk}_1, \widehat{sk}_1)$ and a public key $pk_2 = (\overline{pk}_2, \widehat{pk}_2)$, the user holding the private key sk_1 runs PREPV.RKGen($\overline{sk}_1, \overline{pk}_2$) $\rightarrow$ $\overline{rk}_{1,2}$, and sets the re-encryption key $rk_{1,2}$ as $(\overline{rk}_{1,2}, \widehat{pk}_2)$.
- Enc: When inputting a message m from the message space of PREPV and a public key $pk = (\overline{pk}, \widehat{pk})$, the encryptor runs PREPV.Enc($\overline{pk}, m$) $\rightarrow$ $\overline{C}$, and sets $C = \overline{C}$.
- ReEnc: When inputting an original ciphertext C under public key $pk_1 = (\overline{pk}_1, \widehat{pk}_1)$ and a re-encryption key $rk_{1,2} = (\overline{rk}_{1,2}, \widehat{pk}_2)$, the proxy holding the re-encryption key $rk_{1,2}$ runs PREPV.ReEnc($\overline{rk}_{1,2}, C$) $\rightarrow$ $\overline{C}'$ and PKE.Enc($\widehat{pk}_2, \overline{C}'$) $\rightarrow$ $\widehat{C}$. At last, the proxy sets $C' = \widehat{C}$. Note that in this algorithm, we simply assume that $\overline{C}'$ belongs to the message space of PKE, which can be realized by the hybrid encryption method.
- Dec: Since there are two kinds of ciphertexts, we have two cases in this algorithm.
    - If the ciphertext is an original ciphertext C, the decryptor can get the message m by simply running PREPV.Dec($\overline{sk}, C$).
    - If the ciphertext is a re-encrypted ciphertext C', the decryptor firstly gets $\overline{C}'$ by running PKE.Dec($\widehat{sk}, C'$), and then obtains the message m by running PREPV.Dec($\overline{sk}, \overline{C}'$).
- Ver: When inputting an original ciphertext C, a re-encrypted ciphertext C', and verification key vk, the verifier firstly gets gets $\overline{C}'$ by running PKE.Dec(vk, C'), and then performs PREPV.Ver($C, \overline{C}'$).

Correctness. The correctness of the above PREDV can be easily obtained by the correctness of PREPV and PKE. Hence, we omit it here.

Security Analysis. Now we will show that the above PREDV is secure in the sense of our proposed security definitions.

Theorem 1. *The proposed PREDV is RCCA-O secure only if the underlying PREPV is RCCA-O secure.*

Proof. We show that if there exists an adversary $\mathcal{A}$ that can break the RCCA-O security of the proposed PREDV, we can build an algorithm $\mathcal{B}$ that can break the RCCA-O security of the underlying PREPV by using $\mathcal{A}$. In particular, $\mathcal{B}$ will act as a challenger with A to play the following RCCA-O security game.

Setup: $\mathcal{B}$ sets up the system parameters according to the security parameter (1^λ).

Phase 1: $\mathcal{B}$ responds $\mathcal{A}$'s queries as follows.

- $\mathcal{O}_{pk}$: $\mathcal{B}$ runs PKE.KeyGen(1^{λ}) to generate a new key pair $(\widehat{pk}, \widehat{sk})$, and queries its own public key generation oracle $\mathcal{O}_{pk}$ for PREPV to obtain a public key $\overline{pk}$ in PREPV. After that, $\mathcal{B}$ records $(pk, sk) = ((\overline{pk}, \widehat{pk}), (-, \widehat{sk}))$ in $\mathbb{T}_{pk}$, and returns pk to $\mathcal{A}$.

- $\mathcal{O}_{sk}$: When inputting $pk_i = (\overline{pk}_i, \widehat{pk}_i)$, $\mathcal{B}$ searches the corresponding $\widehat{sk}_i$ in $\mathbb{T}_{pk}$, and queries its own private key generation oracle $\mathcal{O}_{sk}$ for PREPV to obtain a private key $\overline{sk}_i$ corresponding to $\overline{pk}_i$ in PREPV. At last, $\mathcal{B}$ returns $(\overline{sk}_i, \widehat{sk}_i)$ as the private key sk_i to $\mathcal{A}$.

- $\mathcal{O}_{vk}$: When inputting pk_i, $\mathcal{B}$ searches the corresponding $\widehat{sk}_i$ in $\mathbb{T}_{pk}$, and returns it to $\mathcal{A}$.

- $\mathcal{O}_{rk}$: When inputting $(pk_i, pk_j) = ((\overline{pk}_i, \widehat{pk}_i), (\overline{pk}_j, \widehat{pk}_j))$, $\mathcal{B}$ queries its own re-encryption key generation oracle $\mathcal{O}_{rk}$ for PREPV to obtain a re-encryption key $\overline{rk}_{i,j}$ corresponding to the delegation from $\overline{pk}_i$ to $\overline{pk}_j$ in PREPV. At last, $\mathcal{B}$ returns $(\overline{rk}_{i,j}, \widehat{pk}_j)$ as the re-encryption key $rk_{i,j}$ to $\mathcal{A}$.

- $\mathcal{O}_{re}$: When inputting (pk_i, pk_j, C_i), where $(pk_i, pk_j) = ((\overline{pk}_i, \widehat{pk}_i), (\overline{pk}_j, \widehat{pk}_j))$, $\mathcal{B}$ queries its own re-encryption oracle $\mathcal{O}_{re}$ for PREPV to obtain a re-encrypted ciphertext $\overline{C}'$ corresponding to $(\overline{pk}_i, \overline{pk}_j, C_i)$ in PREPV, and then computes the re-encrypted ciphertext C' by running PKE.Enc($\widehat{pk}_j, \overline{C}'$). At last, $\mathcal{B}$ returns C' to $\mathcal{A}$.

- $\mathcal{O}_{dec}$: When inputting (pk_i, C_i), $\mathcal{B}$ finds the tuple in $\mathbb{T}_{pk}$ corresponding to pk_i. If C_i is a re-encrypted ciphertext, $\mathcal{B}$ obtains $\overline{C}'_i$ by running PKE.Dec($\widehat{sk}_i, C_i$), and then queries its own decryption oracle $\mathcal{O}_{dec}$ for PREPV to obtain a message m corresponding to $(\overline{pk}_i, \overline{C}'_i)$ in PREPV. If C_i is an original ciphertext, $\mathcal{B}$ simply queries $\mathcal{O}_{dec}$ for PREPV to obtain a message m corresponding to $(\overline{pk}_i, C_i)$ in PREPV. At last, $\mathcal{B}$ returns m to $\mathcal{A}$.

- $\mathcal{O}_{ver}$: When inputting (pk_i, C_i, pk_j, C_j), $\mathcal{B}$ finds the tuple in $\mathbb{T}_{pk}$ corresponding to pk_j, and obtains $\overline{C}'_j$ by running PKE.Dec($\widehat{sk}_j, C_j$). After that, $\mathcal{B}$ returns the result of PREPV.Ver($C_i, \overline{C}'_j$) to $\mathcal{A}$.

Challenge: Once $\mathcal{A}$ decides that Phase 1 is over, it outputs two equal length plaintexts m_0^*, m_1^* from the message space $\mathcal{M}$, and a public key $pk^* = (\overline{pk}^*, \widehat{pk}^*)$ on which it wishes to challenge. $\mathcal{B}$ queries its own challenge oracle for PREPV with $(m_0^*, m_1^*, \overline{pk}^*)$ to obtain its challenge original ciphertext $\overline{C}^*$. At last, $\mathcal{B}$ returns $\overline{C}^*$ as the challenge ciphertext to $\mathcal{A}$.

Phase 2: Same as Phase 1 but with the restrictions specified in the RCCA-O security game.

Guess: Finally, the adversary $\mathcal{A}$ outputs a guess $\mathbf{b}' \in \{0, 1\}$ that is also the guess for $\mathcal{B}$.

It is easy to see that only if $\mathcal{A}$ outputs the right guess in Guess Phase, so does $\mathcal{B}$. Hence, we obtain this theorem. $\qquad\square$

Theorem 2. *The proposed* PREDV *is RCCA-R secure only if the underlying* PREPV *is RCCA-R secure.*

Proof. Similar with the proof of Theorem 1, we show that if there exists an adversary $\mathcal{A}$ that can break the RCCA-R security of the proposed PREDV, we can build an algorithm $\mathcal{B}$ that can break the RCCA-R security of the underlying PREPV by using $\mathcal{A}$. In particular, $\mathcal{B}$ will act as a challenger with A to play the following RCCA-R security game.

Setup: $\mathcal{B}$ sets up the system parameters according to the security parameter (1^λ).

Phase 1: $\mathcal{B}$ responds $\mathcal{A}$'s queries as that in Phase 1 in the proof of Theorem 1.

Challenge: Once $\mathcal{A}$ decides that Phase 1 is over, it outputs two equal length plaintexts m_0^*, m_1^* from the message space $\mathcal{M}$, and two public keys $(pk, pk^*) = ((\overline{pk}, \widehat{pk}), (\overline{pk}^*, \widehat{pk}^*))$. $\mathcal{B}$ queries its own challenge oracle for PREPV with $(m_0^*, m_1^*, \overline{pk}, \overline{pk}^*)$ to obtain its challenge re-encrypted ciphertext $\overline{C}'^*$. At last, $\mathcal{B}$ runs PKE.Enc$(\widehat{pk}^*, \overline{C}'^*)$ to obtain the final challenge ciphertext C'^*, and sends it to $\mathcal{A}$.

Phase 2: Same as Phase 1 but with the restrictions specified in the RCCA-R security game.

Guess: Finally, the adversary $\mathcal{A}$ outputs a guess $\mathbf{b}' \in \{0, 1\}$ that is also the guess for $\mathcal{B}$.

Like the proof of Theorem 1, only if $\mathcal{A}$ outputs the right guess in Guess Phase, so does $\mathcal{B}$. Hence, we obtain this theorem.   □

Theorem 3. *The proposed* PREDV *is SV secure only if the underlying* PREPV *is SV secure.*

Proof. Similar with the proof of Theorem 1, we show that if there exists an adversary $\mathcal{A}$ that can break the SV security of the proposed PREDV, we can build an algorithm $\mathcal{B}$ that can break the SV security of the underlying PREPV by using $\mathcal{A}$. In particular, $\mathcal{B}$ will act as a challenger with A to play the following SV security game.

Setup: $\mathcal{B}$ sets up the system parameters according to the security parameter (1^λ).

Phase 1: $\mathcal{B}$ responds $\mathcal{A}$'s queries as that in Phase 1 in the proof of Theorem 1.

Challenge: Once $\mathcal{A}$ decides that Phase 1 is over, it outputs one message m^* from the message space, and two public keys $pk_0^* = (\overline{pk}_0^*, \widehat{pk}_0^*), pk_1^* = (\overline{pk}_1^*, \widehat{pk}_1^*)$ on which it wishes to be challenged. $\mathcal{B}$ queries its own challenge oracle for PREPV with $(m^*, \overline{pk}_0^*, \overline{pk}_1^*)$ to obtain its challenge ciphertext $\overline{C}^*$, and sends it to $\mathcal{A}$ as the challenge ciphertext C^*.

Phase 2: Same as Phase 1 but with the restrictions specified in the SV security game.

Output: Finally, the adversary $\mathcal{A}$ outputs a re-encrypted ciphertext C'^* satisfying $\text{Ver}(C^*, C'^*, vk_1^*) = 1$ and $\text{Dec}(sk_1^*, C'^*) \neq m^*$. $\mathcal{B}$ first runs $\text{Dec}(\widehat{sk}_1^*, C'^*)$ to obtain a re-encrypted ciphertext $\overline{C}'$ of PREPV. According to the correctness of PREDV and PREPV, we have that $\text{Ver}(C^*, \overline{C}') = \text{Ver}(\overline{C}^*, \overline{C}') = 1$ and $\text{Dec}(\widehat{sk}_1^*, \overline{C}') \neq m^*$. Hence, $\overline{C}'$ is a valid output for $\mathcal{B}$'s SV security game, and $\mathcal{B}$ wins the game.

Hence, we obtain this theorem. □

Theorem 4. *The proposed* PREDV *is PV secure only if the underlying* PKE *is CCA secure.*

Proof. To prove this theorem, we will show that if there exists an adversary $\mathcal{A}$ that can break the PV security of the proposed PREDV, we can build an algorithm $\mathcal{B}$ that can break the CCA security of the underlying PKE by using $\mathcal{A}$. In particular, $\mathcal{B}$ will act as a challenger with A to play the following PV security game.

Setup: $\mathcal{B}$ sets up the system parameters according to the security parameter (1^λ).

Phase 1: $\mathcal{B}$ responds $\mathcal{A}$'s queries as follows.

- $\mathcal{O}_{pk}$: $\mathcal{B}$ runs PREPV.KeyGen(1^λ) to generate a new key pair $(\overline{pk}, \overline{sk})$, and decides the value of $\theta \in \{0, 1\}$ with the probability $\Pr[\theta = 1] = \delta$. If $\theta = 1$, $\mathcal{B}$ runs PKE.KeyGen(1^λ) to generate a new key pair $(\widehat{pk}, \widehat{sk})$, and records $(pk, sk, \theta) = ((\overline{pk}, \widehat{pk}), (\overline{sk}, \widehat{sk}), 1)$ in $\mathbb{T}_{pk}$. If $\theta = 0$, $\mathcal{B}$ queries its own key generation oracle for PKE to obtain a public key $\widehat{pk}$, and records $(pk, sk, \theta) = ((\overline{pk}, \widehat{pk}), (\overline{sk}, -), 0)$ in $\mathbb{T}_{pk}$. At last, $\mathcal{B}$ returns pk to $\mathcal{A}$.
- $\mathcal{O}_{sk}$: When inputting $pk_i = (\overline{pk}_i, \widehat{pk}_i)$, $\mathcal{B}$ searches the tuple in $\mathbb{T}_{pk}$ corresponding to pk_i. If $\theta = 1$, $\mathcal{B}$ returns the corresponding $(\overline{sk}_i, \widehat{sk}_i)$ to $\mathcal{A}$. If $\theta = 0$, $\mathcal{B}$ outputs `failure` and aborts the simulation.
- $\mathcal{O}_{vk}$: When inputting $pk_i = (\overline{pk}_i, \widehat{pk}_i)$, $\mathcal{B}$ searches the tuple in $\mathbb{T}_{pk}$ corresponding to pk_i. If $\theta = 1$, $\mathcal{B}$ returns the corresponding $\widehat{sk}_i$ to $\mathcal{A}$. If $\theta = 0$, $\mathcal{B}$ outputs `failure` and aborts the simulation.
- $\mathcal{O}_{rk}$: When inputting $(pk_i, pk_j) = ((\overline{pk}_i, \widehat{pk}_i), (\overline{pk}_j, \widehat{pk}_j))$, $\mathcal{B}$ searches the tuple in $\mathbb{T}_{pk}$ corresponding to pk_i, and returns $(\text{PREPV.RKGen}(\overline{sk}_i, \overline{pk}_j), \widehat{pk}_j)$ to $\mathcal{A}$.
- $\mathcal{O}_{re}$: When inputting (pk_i, pk_j, C_i), $\mathcal{B}$ firstly queries $\mathcal{O}_{rk}$ with (pk_i, pk_j) to obtain the corresponding re-encryption key $rk_{i,j}$, and then returns the result of PREDV.ReEnc$(rk_{i,j}, C_i)$ to $\mathcal{A}$.
- $\mathcal{O}_{dec}$: When inputting (pk_i, C_i), $\mathcal{B}$ finds the tuple in $\mathbb{T}_{pk}$ corresponding to pk_i. If C_i is a re-encrypted ciphertext, $\mathcal{B}$ obtains $\overline{C}'_i$ by querying its own decryption oracle with $(\widehat{pk}_i, C_i)$, and returns PREPV.Dec$(\overline{sk}_i, \overline{C}'_i)$ to $\mathcal{A}$. If C_i is an original ciphertext, $\mathcal{B}$ can simply return PREPV.Dec$(\overline{sk}_i, C_i)$ to $\mathcal{A}$.

– $\mathcal{O}_{ver}$: When inputting (pk_i, C_i, pk_j, C_j), $\mathcal{B}$ finds the tuple in $\mathbb{T}_{pk}$ corresponding to pk_j, and obtains $\overline{C}'_j$ by querying its own decryption oracle with $(\widehat{pk}_j, C_j)$ After that, $\mathcal{B}$ returns the result of $\mathtt{PREPV.Ver}(C_i, \overline{C}'_j)$ to $\mathcal{A}$.

Challenge: Once $\mathcal{A}$ decides that Phase 1 is over, it outputs a public key $pk^* = (\widehat{pk}^*, \widehat{pk}^*)$, and an original ciphertext C^* under public key $pk = (\widehat{pk}, \widehat{pk})$. $\mathcal{B}$ finds the tuple in $\mathbb{T}_{pk}$ corresponding to pk_j, if $\theta^* = 1$, then $\mathcal{B}$ outputs **failure** and aborts the simulation; otherwise, $\mathcal{B}$ continues to do the following steps. $\mathcal{B}$ runs $\mathtt{PREPV.ReEnc}(\mathtt{PREPV.RKGen}(\overline{sk}, pk^*), C^*)$ to obtain a re-encrypted ciphertext $\overline{C}'$ for $\mathtt{PREPV}$, and chooses a random value R from the re-encrypted ciphertext space of $\mathtt{PREPV}$. After that, $\mathcal{B}$ queries its own challenge oracle with $(\overline{C}', R, \widehat{pk}^*)$ to obtain a ciphertext $\widehat{C}$. At last, $\mathcal{B}$ sends returns $\widehat{C}$ as the challenge ciphertext C'^* to $\mathcal{A}$.

Phase 2: Same as Phase 1 but with the restrictions specified in the PV security game.

Guess: Finally, the adversary $\mathcal{A}$ outputs a guess $\mathbf{b}' \in \{0,1\}$ that is also the guess for $\mathcal{B}$.

It is easy to see that only if $\mathcal{A}$ outputs the right guess in Guess Phase without abort event, $\mathcal{B}$ also outputs the right guess for its own CCA security game. To complete the proof of Theorem 4, we need to calculate the probability that $\mathcal{B}$ does not abort in the simulation. Assume that $\mathcal{A}$ issues a total of q_{vk} verification key generation queries and q_{sk} private key generation queries. Then the probability that $\mathcal{B}$ does not abort in phases 1 or 2 is $\delta^{q_{vk}+q_{sk}}$. Regarding the probability in Challenge Phase, it is $1 - \delta$. Hence, the probability that $\mathcal{B}$ does not abort in the simulation is $\delta^{q_{vk}+q_{sk}}(1 - \delta)$. Similar with that in [7], this probability is at least $1/e(1 + q_{vk} + q_{sk})$. If $\mathcal{A}$ breaks the PV security of the proposed $\mathtt{PREDV}$ with advantage ϵ, then we have that $\mathcal{B}$ breaks the CCA security of the underlying $\mathtt{PKE}$ with advantage $\epsilon/e(1 + q_{vk} + q_{sk})$. □

4 Proxy Re-encryption with Fine-Grained Delegatable Verifiability

In the proposed $\mathtt{PREDV}$, once the verification key vk is given out, the verifier has the verifiability on all ciphertexts all the time. This situation is not desired in many cases. For example, there is always a possibility that the user wants to revoke the verifying right at some point, or the user wants to delegate the verifiability according to the intending verifier's attributes, or the user wants to delegate the verifiability per ciphertext. All of these demand the fine-grained delegatable verifiability. Fortunately, by modifying the $\mathtt{PREDV}$ scheme proposed in Sect. 3, we can have the proxy re-encryption scheme with fine-grained delegatable verifiability.

To obtain the fine-grained delegatable verifiability, we require attribute-based encryption (denoted as $\mathtt{ABE}$) [1,5] instead of public key encryption. The details are as follows.

- KeyGen: When inputting the security parameter 1^λ, the user runs PREPV.KeyGen$(1^\lambda) \to (\overline{pk}, \overline{sk})$ and ABE.KeyGen$(1^\lambda) \to (\widehat{mpk}, \widehat{msk})$, and sets the public key pk and private key sk as $(\overline{pk}, \widehat{mpk})$ and $(\overline{sk}, \widehat{msk})$, respectively.
- VKGen: The verification key vk is ABE.Ext$(\widehat{mpk}, \widehat{msk}, \mathbb{A})$, where $\mathbb{A}$ is the attribute set of the intending verifier.
- RKGen: When inputting a private key $sk_1 = (\overline{sk}_1, \widehat{msk}_1)$ and a public key $pk_2 = (\overline{pk}_2, \widehat{mpk}_2)$, the user holding the private key sk_1 runs PREPV.RKGen$(\overline{sk}_1, \widehat{mpk}_2) \to \overline{rk}_{1,2}$, and sets the re-encryption key $rk_{1,2}$ as $(\overline{rk}_{1,2}, \widehat{mpk}_2)$.
- Enc: Identical to that in PREDV.
- ReEnc: When inputting an original ciphertext C under public key $pk_1 = (\overline{pk}_1, \widehat{mpk}_1)$ and a re-encryption key $rk_{1,2} = (\overline{rk}_{1,2}, \widehat{mpk}_2)$, the proxy holding the re-encryption key $rk_{1,2}$ runs PREPV.ReEnc$(\overline{rk}_{1,2}, C) \to \overline{C}'$ and ABE.Enc$(\widehat{pk}_2, \overline{C}', \mathcal{P}) \to \widehat{C}$, where $\mathcal{P}$ is the delegation policy of the verifiability. At last, the proxy sets $C' = \widehat{C}$. As in PREDV, we simply assume that $\overline{C}'$ belongs to the message space of ABE, which can be also realized by the hybrid encryption method.
- Dec: Since there are two kinds of ciphertexts, we have two cases in this algorithm.
  - Identical to that in PREDV.
  - If the ciphertext is a re-encrypted ciphertext C', the decryptor firstly gets $\overline{C}'$ by running ABE.Dec(vk, C'), and then obtains the message m by running PREPV.Dec$(\overline{sk}, \overline{C}')$.
- Ver: When inputting an original ciphertext C, a re-encrypted ciphertext C', and verification key vk, the verifier firstly gets $\overline{C}'$ by running ABE.Dec(vk, C'), and then performs PREPV.Ver$(C, \overline{C}')$.

Correctness and Security Analysis. The definitions of proxy re-encryption with fine-grained delegatable verifiability can be proposed as those in Sect. 2, and the analysis of correctness and security of the above proxy re-encryption scheme can be obtained by the same method used in Sect. 3. Hence, we omit them here.

5 Conclusions

In this paper, we explicitly investigated the problem on how to verify the re-encryption process in the proxy re-encryption schemes. We divided the verifiability into three types: public, private, and delegatable. We found that with some slight modification, some of existing proxy re-encryption schemes can support public verifiability, others can support private verifiability. However, none of them provides delegatable verifiability. On the other hand, delegatable verifiability is more powerful than other types of verifiability, since it can be converted into others by publishing the verification key or not. The first proxy re-encryption scheme with delegatable verifiability along with its security proofs are proposed in this paper. At last, we extended the concept of delegatable verifiability, named fine-grained delegatable verifiability, which allows users to delegate the verifiability in a fine-grained way.

The proposal in this paper can only achieve the RCCA security even if the underlying PREPV is CCA secure, since the adversary with the verification key can always modify the re-encrypted ciphertext without changing the corresponding plaintext or losing the validity of the ciphertext. Therefore, in future work, it is interesting to design a new method to obtain the delegatable verifiability without losing the CCA security.

Acknowledgements. This work is partly supported by Nanyang Technological University under Grant MOE Tier 1 (M4011450) and NSERC (Natural Sciences and Engineering Research Council of Canada), Canada.

References

1. Sahai, A., Waters, B.: Fuzzy identity-based encryption. In: Cramer, R. (ed.) EUROCRYPT 2005. LNCS, vol. 3494, pp. 457–473. Springer, Heidelberg (2005)
2. Ateniese, G., Benson, K., Hohenberger, S.: Key-private proxy re-encryption. In: Fischlin, M. (ed.) CT-RSA 2009. LNCS, vol. 5473, pp. 279–294. Springer, Heidelberg (2009)
3. Ateniese, G., Fu, K., Green, M., Hohenberger, S.: Improved proxy re-encryption schemes with applications to secure distributed storage. In: NDSS (2005)
4. Benabbas, S., Gennaro, R., Vahlis, Y.: Verifiable delegation of computation over large datasets. In: Rogaway, P. (ed.) CRYPTO 2011. LNCS, vol. 6841, pp. 111–131. Springer, Heidelberg (2011)
5. Bethencourt, J., Sahai, A., Waters, B.: Ciphertext-policy attribute-based encryption. In: IEEE S&P 2007, pp. 321–334 (2007)
6. Blaze, M., Bleumer, G., Strauss, M.J.: Divertible protocols and atomic proxy cryptography. In: Nyberg, K. (ed.) EUROCRYPT 1998. LNCS, vol. 1403, pp. 127–144. Springer, Heidelberg (1998)
7. Boneh, D., Franklin, M.: Identity-Based Encryption from the Weil Pairing. In: Kilian, J. (ed.) CRYPTO 2001. LNCS, vol. 2139, pp. 213–229. Springer, Heidelberg (2001)
8. Canetti, R., Hohenberger, S.: Chosen-ciphertext secure proxy re-encryption. In: Ning, P., De Capitani di Vimercati, S., Syverson, P.F. (eds.) ACM CCS, pp. 185–194. ACM (2007)
9. Chow, S.S.M., Weng, J., Yang, Y., Deng, R.H.: Efficient unidirectional proxy re-encryption. In: Bernstein, D.J., Lange, T. (eds.) AFRICACRYPT 2010. LNCS, vol. 6055, pp. 316–332. Springer, Heidelberg (2010)
10. Faust, S., Hazay, C., Venturi, D.: Outsourced pattern matching. In: Fomin, F.V., Freivalds, R., Kwiatkowska, M., Peleg, D. (eds.) ICALP 2013, Part II. LNCS, vol. 7966, pp. 545–556. Springer, Heidelberg (2013)
11. Fujisaki, E., Okamoto, T.: Secure integration of asymmetric and symmetric encryption schemes. In: Wiener, M. (ed.) CRYPTO 1999. LNCS, vol. 1666, pp. 537–554. Springer, Heidelberg (1999)

12. Green, M., Ateniese, G.: Identity-based proxy re-encryption. In: Katz, J., Yung, M. (eds.) ACNS 2007. LNCS, vol. 4521, pp. 288–306. Springer, Heidelberg (2007)
13. Hanaoka, G., Kawai, Y., Kunihiro, N., Matsuda, T., Weng, J., Zhang, R., Zhao, Y.: Generic construction of chosen ciphertext secure proxy re-encryption. In: Dunkelman, O. (ed.) CT-RSA 2012. LNCS, vol. 7178, pp. 349–364. Springer, Heidelberg (2012)
14. Jia, X., Shao, J., Jing, J., Liu, P.: CCA-secure type-based proxy re-encryption with invisible proxy. In: CIT, pp. 1299–1305. IEEE Computer Society (2010)
15. Liang, X., Cao, Z., Lin, H., Shao, J.: Attribute based proxy re-encryption with delegating capabilities. In: ACM ASIACCS 2009, pp. 276–286 (2009)
16. Libert, B., Vergnaud, D.: Unidirectional chosen-ciphertext secure proxy re-encryption. In: Cramer, R. (ed.) PKC 2008. LNCS, vol. 4939, pp. 360–379. Springer, Heidelberg (2008)
17. Parno, B., Raykova, M., Vaikuntanathan, V.: How to delegate and verify in public: Verifiable computation from attribute-based encryption. In: Cramer, R. (ed.) TCC 2012. LNCS, vol. 7194, pp. 422–439. Springer, Heidelberg (2012)
18. Shao, J., Cao, Z.: CCA-secure proxy re-encryption without pairings. In: Jarecki, S., Tsudik, G. (eds.) PKC 2009. LNCS, vol. 5443, pp. 357–376. Springer, Heidelberg (2009)
19. Shao, J., Rongxing, L., Xiaodong Lin, F.: A fine-grained privacy-preserving location-based service framework for mobile devices. In: INFOCOM, pp. 244–252. IEEE (2014)
20. Shao, J., Lu, R., Lin, X.: Fine-grained data sharing in cloud computing for mobile devices. In: INFOCOM, pp. 2677–2685. IEEE (2015)
21. Tang, Q.: Type-based proxy re-encryption and its construction. In: Chowdhury, D.R., Rijmen, V., Das, A. (eds.) INDOCRYPT 2008. LNCS, vol. 5365, pp. 130–144. Springer, Heidelberg (2008)
22. Yu, S., Wang, C., Ren, K., Lou, W.: Achieving secure, scalable, and fine-grained data access control in cloud computing. In: INFOCOM, pp. 534–542. IEEE (2010)

Efficient Completely Non-Malleable and RKA Secure Public Key Encryptions

Shi-Feng Sun[1,2], Udaya Parampalli[2], Tsz Hon Yuen[3],
Yu Yu[1], and Dawu Gu[1(✉)]

[1] Shanghai Jiao Tong University, Shanghai 200240, China
{yyuu,dwgu}@sjtu.edu.cn
[2] The University of Melbourne, Parkville, VIC 3010, Australia
{shifeng.sun,udaya}@unimelb.edu.au
[3] Huawei, Singapore
Yuen.Tsz.Hon@huawei.com

Abstract. Motivated by tampering attacks in practice, two different but related security notions, termed *complete non-malleability* and *related-key attack security*, have been proposed recently. In this work, we study their relations and present the first public key encryption scheme that is secure in both notions under standard assumptions. Moreover, by exploiting the technique for achieving complete non-malleability, we give a practical scheme for the related-key attack security. Precisely, the scheme is proven secure against polynomial functions of bounded degree d under a newly introduced hardness assumption called d-modified extended decisional bilinear Diffie-Hellman assumption. Since the schemes are constructed in a direct way instead of relying on the non-interactive zero knowledge proof or signature techniques, they not only achieve the strong security notions but also have better performances.

Keywords: Public key encryption · Complete non-malleability · Related-key attack · Chosen-ciphertext attack

1 Introduction

Public key encryption (PKE) is one of the most basic and widely deployed cryptographic primitives, the security of which has been formalized in terms of various security goals and attack scenarios. The de facto standard security of PKE is the notion of indistinguishability against chosen-ciphertext attacks (IND-CCA), which was proved in [5] to be equivalent to that of non-malleability against chosen ciphertext attacks (NM-CCA) [13]. Roughly speaking, the later notion demands that it is difficult for an adversary, given a challenge public key pk and a ciphertext ct of some message m sampled from a distribution of her choice, to produce a relation R and a ciphertext ct' of message m' that is related to m through R.

Whilst already sufficient for many applications, IND-CCA/NM-CCA security is not strong enough for high-level systems where users may be allowed to

© Springer International Publishing Switzerland 2016
J.K. Liu and R. Steinfeld (Eds.): ACISP 2016, Part II, LNCS 9723, pp. 134–150, 2016.
DOI: 10.1007/978-3-319-40367-0_9

issue keys on-the-fly. Motivated by constructing non-malleable commitments [15] on top of PKE, Fischlin [14] introduced the notion of *complete* non-malleability against chosen ciphertext attacks (CNM-CCA). This is a stronger flavor of NM-CCA security, where the adversary is additionally allowed to tamper with the public key. Accordingly, the current goal of the adversary is to produce a cipher-text under the tampered public key such that the encrypted message is related to the challenge one via a more general relation which also takes the public keys. As shown in [14], CNM-CCA security is powerful, but it also turns out that such PKE is extremely hard to construct in the plain model without random oracles.

With focus on high-level applications, the CNM-CCA security considers such attackers that have the ability to tamper with the *public key*. The recent popular side-channel attacks [3,8,10,17,18] demonstrated that the attackers, given physical access to a cryptographic hardware device, may also be able to tamper with and induce modifications to the *internal secret state* of the device. When an attacker launches a tampering attack on the key stored in a cryptographic device, she can subsequently learn partial secret information by observing the outcome of the cryptographic primitive under this modified key, which is usually referred to as related-key attacks (RKAs).

The theoretical treatment of RKAs was initiated by Bellare et al. [6], where they captured RKAs by a class Φ of efficiently computable functions termed related-key derivation (RKD) functions and formally defined the RKA-security with respect to (w.r.t) Φ. In general, the security against RKAs captured by Φ (Φ-RKA security) requires that the standard security of a cryptographic primitive hold even against such attackers that observe the outcomes of the cryptographic primitive under modified keys $\phi(sk)$ for all $\phi \in \Phi$.

In fact, these two notions are somewhat related to each other, both of which are defined by allowing attackers to tamper with the keys to gain extra attacking advantages. Although they are well-studied separately, there is no work showing the relationship between them. In light of the fact that encryption schemes used in complex scenarios may suffer from both kinds of tampering attacks, we initiate the study of their relations and the design of efficient PKE schemes that are secure against these types of attacks.

1.1   Related Works

CNM-CCA SECURITY. In order to comprehend the notion of CNM-CCA security introduced in [14], Ventre et al. [28] revisited it recently. Following the comparison-based approach [5], they introduced a game-based definition, which is always believed to be much more convenient to work with than the simulation-based version [14]. Moreover, they showed the reachability of their definition in the standard model via two different approaches: the first is based on the non-malleable non-interactive zero knowledge (NM-NIZK) proofs in the common reference string setting and the other is under the assumption that oracle queries are issued sequentially in the interactive setting. However, these solutions are mostly feasibility proofs than practical realizations, and they left the efficient design of CNM-CCA secure schemes open.

Later, under the game-based definition, Libert et al. [23] put forward two efficient constructions of CNM-CCA secure PKE in the common reference string setting. The first built on the selective identity-based encryption (IBE) [9] and a general one-time signature is inspired by the Canetti-Halevi-Katz (CHK) paradigm [11]. Its security is established in the standard model under the standard decisional bilinear Diffie-Hellman (DBDH) assumption. The other is based on the lossy trapdoor functions [25], which is more general but suffers from long ciphertexts compared to the first. Almost concurrently, another concrete CNM-CCA secure PKE scheme [2] was presented by employing the techniques of Waters' IBE [29] and certificateless encryption [1]. This scheme was actually proven secure in the standard model under a stronger security notion called indistinguishability against strong chosen ciphertext attacks (IND-SCCA) [2], which implies CNM-CCA security. Due to Waters' hash, however, it suffers from long public parameters. Most recently, a lattice-based CNM-CCA secure scheme [27] was presented under the similar framework [23]. Another relevant work is [31] where the authors studied related public key attacks by showing a practical attack on the ElGamal-based multi-recipient encryption system and initially introduced the notion of security against such attacks, which in some sense is relevant to CNM-CCA security but with different security goals.

Φ-RKA SECURITY. RKA-security was pioneered by Bellare et al. [6], where they mainly investigated the RKA security of symmetric primitives. Following this work, the notion was also extended to public settings [4, 7, 12, 20, 24, 26, 30, 31] such as PKE, IBE and key-encapsulation mechanisms (KEM). Previously, most of the works could only achieve RKA security against limited RKD functions such as linear functions. To resist a larger class of tampering attacks, a recent research focus has been to construct cryptographic primitives that are secure against a broader class of RKD functions.

In 2012, Bellare et al. [7] studied how to achieve RKA-security beyond the linear barrier and presented a generic framework through IBE. Specifically, by extending Waters' IBE [29] they presented a RKA-secure scheme against polynomial functions of bounded degree d, and reduced its security to the d-extended DBDH (d-EDBDH) assumption. Most recently, Qin et al. [26] and Fujisaki et al. [16] managed to achieve RKA-security against even richer RKD function classes. In addition, there are some other relevant works that can realize RKA-security beyond the linear barrier, e.g., the continuous non-malleable code [19].

For various primitives including IBE, signature and KEM, all recent works [7, 16, 19, 26] can achieve RKA-security against polynomial (of bounded degree) or even richer RKD functions directly. For the basic primitive PKE, however, almost all of them realized its RKA-security via one of the following approaches: the first is by the KEM/DEM framework [7], where a RKA-secure PKE follows directly from RKA-security of KEM and one-time CCA security of DEM, and the other is by the CHK transformation [4,7], where a RKA secure PKE can be derived from any RKA-secure IBE, as shown in [7,16,26]. This approach can realize the RKA-security of PKE against the same RKD function classes as IBE, but also inherits the same shortcomings of the underlying IBE such as long public parameters due to Waters' hash. Moreover, as analyzed in [21] the transformation always brings some unnecessary computation/communication redundancy.

1.2 Motivations and Our Contributions

To resist different kinds of powerful attacks in practice, many strong security notions are well-studied separately. CNM-CCA security captures such attackers in high-level systems that have the ability to tamper with the public keys to obtain extra advantages, while RKA-security captures similar tampering attacks on the internal secret state of cryptographic implementations. Initially motivated by the similarities between them and the fact that cryptosystems in real life may suffer from both kinds of attacks, in this work we try to study their relations and construct efficient encryption schemes that are secure against both types of attacks. Specifically, we first present a practical PKE based on [22] and prove it CNM-CCA and RKA secure in the standard model under the standard assumptions. For the CNM-CCA security, similar to [27] it follows the idea in [23]: conceal some escrow keys in the common reference string and use them to properly decrypt the ciphertexts output by the adversary. Our construction, however, is different from previous works in that it avoids using the generic NIZK or signature techniques. For RKA-security, it is inspired by the observation that the simulator in the proof of CNM-CCA security needs to be capable of decrypting ciphertexts encrypted under arbitrarily adversarial chosen public keys. Thus, we can reduce the process of related-key decryption queries to the strong decryption capability of the simulator if the corresponding public keys can be successfully derived from the queried RKD functions and the public information. Further following this rough idea, we simply extend the key generation algorithm of the previous scheme and present a practical RKA-secure PKE against polynomial functions of bounded degree in a direct way, instead of following the indirect approaches mentioned before. To prove its security, we introduce a new hardness assumption called d-modified extended decisional bilinear Diffie-Hellman assumption, which is simplified from the d-EDBDH assumption in [7], and then reduce the security to this relatively weak assumption.

2 Preliminaries

Notation. We use κ to denote the security parameter. For a finite set S, $s \leftarrow S$ denotes the operation of sampling s from S uniformly at random. For a distribution M, we use $m \leftarrow M$ to denote the action of sampling an element m according to the distribution. For a randomized algorithm $A(\cdot)$, we denote by $a \leftarrow A(\cdot)$ the operation of running the algorithm and obtaining a as its output. PPT and $negl(\kappa)$ denote the abbreviation of probabilistic polynomial time and some negligible function in κ respectively.

2.1 Hardness Assumptions

Definition 1 (CDH Problem). *Let $\mathbb{G}$ be a multiplicative group of prime order p, the computational Diffie-Hellman (CDH) problem is given (g, g^a, g^b) to compute g^{ab}, where the elements $g \in \mathbb{G}$ and $a, b \in \mathbb{Z}_p$ are chosen independently and uniformly at random. Given a random instance (g, g^a, g^b), the advantage for any PPT adversary $\mathcal{B}$ is defined as: $Adv_{\mathcal{B},\mathbb{G}}^{CDH}(\kappa) = |\Pr[\mathcal{B}(g, g^a, g^b) = g^{ab}]|$.*

We say that the CDH assumption holds if for any efficient adversary $\mathcal{B}$, its advantage $Adv_{\mathcal{B},\mathbb{G}}^{CDH}(\kappa)$ is negligible in κ.

Definition 2 (d-mEDBDH Assumption). *Let $\mathbb{G}$ and $\mathbb{G}_T$ be two multiplicative groups of prime order p, and $e : \mathbb{G} \times \mathbb{G} \to \mathbb{G}_T$ be an efficiently computable map such that $e(g^a, h^b) = e(g, h)^{ab}$ for all $g, h \in \mathbb{G}, a, b \in \mathbb{Z}_p^*$ and $e(g, h) \neq 1_{\mathbb{G}_T}$ whenever $g, h \neq 1_{\mathbb{G}}$. For some integer $d \in \mathbb{N}$, the d-modified extended decisional bilinear Diffie-Hellman (d-mEDBDH) problem is to distinguish the ensembles $\{(g, g^a, g^{a^2}, \cdots, g^{a^d}, g^b, g^c, e(g, g)^{abc})\}$ from $\{(g, g^a, g^{a^2}, \cdots, g^{a^d}, g^b, g^c, e(g, g)^z)\}$, where the elements $g \in \mathbb{G}$ and $a, b, c, z \in \mathbb{Z}_p$ are chosen independently and uniformly at random. Formally, the advantage for any PPT distinguisher $\mathcal{D}$ is defined as: $Adv_{\mathcal{D},\mathbb{G},\mathbb{G}_T}^{d\text{-}mEDBDH}(\kappa) = |\Pr[\mathcal{D}(g, g^a, g^{a^2}, \cdots, g^{a^d}, g^b, g^c, e(g, g)^{abc}) = 1] - \Pr[\mathcal{D}(g, g^a, g^{a^2}, \cdots, g^{a^d}, g^b, g^c, e(g, g)^z) = 1]|$.*

We say that the d-mEDBDH assumption holds if for any efficient distinguisher $\mathcal{D}$, its advantage $Adv_{\mathcal{D},\mathbb{G},\mathbb{G}_T}^{d\text{-}mEDBDH}(\kappa)$ is negligible in κ.

We remark that our d-mEDBDH problem is simplified from the d-EDBDH problem [7], which additionally contains the elements $(g^{(a^2)b}, \cdots, g^{(a^d)b})$, so its hardness can be easily reduced to the latter. More precisely, if there exists an efficient algorithm $\mathcal{D}$ that can break our hardness assumption, then it is easy to design an efficient algorithm $\mathcal{D}'$ to break the d-EDBDH assumption: given a random d-EDBDH instance, $\mathcal{D}'$ only needs to discard the extra elements $(g^{(a^2)b}, \cdots, g^{(a^d)b})$ and then invoke $\mathcal{D}$ with the left part. Hence, our construction is based on a weaker assumption compared to [7]. Specially, it is the standard DBDH assumption when $d = 1$.

Definition 3 (Collision-Resistant Hash). *A hash function $H : \mathcal{U} \to \mathcal{V}$ is called collision-resistant if for any PPT algorithm $\mathcal{B}$, it holds that $Adv_{\mathcal{B},H}^{CR}(\kappa) = \Pr[u' \neq u \wedge H(u') = H(u) | u, u' \leftarrow \mathcal{B}(H)] \leq negl(\kappa)$.*

2.2 Security Definitions

In general, a public key encryption scheme consists of a tuple of polynomial time algorithms (Setup, KeyGen, Enc, Dec). As in [30], we think of the cryptographic system as having the following components: algorithms (code), public parameters, public/secret key pairs. Of these, only the public and secret keys are subject to tampering attacks. The public parameters generated in Setup are system-wide and independent of users. In practice, these parameters can be hardwired into a device in implementations.

For the completely non-malleable security, we will use the game-based definition [28]. Before going ahead, we first recall an important ingredient named complete relation, which is considered in both the simulation-based [14] and the game-based definition [28]. A complete relation R is an efficient (probabilistic) algorithm, which takes as input a message m, two public keys pk and pk^*, a vector of ciphertext ct^* encrypted under pk^* and the corresponding plaintext vector m^* (i.e., the decryption of ct^*), and finally outputs a boolean value $0/1$.

Definition 4 [23,28]. *Let PKE=(Setup, KeyGen, Enc, Dec) be a public key encryption scheme. For any $\kappa \in \mathbb{N}$ and adversary $\mathcal{A} = (\mathcal{A}_1, \mathcal{A}_2)$, we define*

$$Adv_{\mathcal{A},PKE}^{CNM\text{-}CCA}(\kappa) = \left| \Pr[\mathbf{Expt}_{\mathcal{A},PKE}^{CNM\text{-}CCA\text{-}0}(\kappa) = 1] - \Pr[\mathbf{Expt}_{\mathcal{A},PKE}^{CNM\text{-}CCA\text{-}1}(\kappa) = 1] \right|.$$

where $\mathbf{Expt}_{\mathcal{A},PKE}^{CNM\text{-}CCA\text{-}0}(\kappa)$ and $\mathbf{Expt}_{\mathcal{A},PKE}^{CNM\text{-}CCA\text{-}1}(\kappa)$ are defined as below.

$\mathbf{Expt}_{\mathcal{A},PKE}^{CNM\text{-}CCA\text{-}0}(\kappa)$:	$\mathbf{Expt}_{\mathcal{A},PKE}^{CNM\text{-}CCA\text{-}1}(\kappa)$:
$pp \leftarrow \mathsf{Setup}(1^\kappa)$, $(pk, sk) \leftarrow \mathsf{KeyGen}(pp)$	$pp \leftarrow \mathsf{Setup}(1^\kappa)$, $(pk, sk) \leftarrow \mathsf{KeyGen}(pp)$
$(M, st) \leftarrow \mathcal{A}_1^{\mathcal{D}_{sk}(\cdot)}(pp, pk)$	$(M, st) \leftarrow \mathcal{A}_1^{\mathcal{D}_{sk}(\cdot)}(pp, pk)$
$m \leftarrow M$, $ct = \mathsf{Enc}(pk, m)$	$m, \tilde{m} \leftarrow M$, $ct = \mathsf{Enc}(pk, m)$
$(R, pk^*, ct^*) \leftarrow \mathcal{A}_2^{\mathcal{D}_{sk}(\cdot)}(st, M, pp, pk, ct)$	$(R, pk^*, ct^*) \leftarrow \mathcal{A}_2^{\mathcal{D}_{sk}(\cdot)}(st, M, pp, pk, ct)$
return 1 iff $\exists\, m^*$ such that	**return** 1 iff $\exists\, m^*$ such that
$(ct^* = \mathsf{Enc}(pk^*, m^*)) \wedge$	$(ct^* = \mathsf{Enc}(pk^*, m^*)) \wedge$
$(ct \notin ct^* \vee pk \neq pk^*) \wedge$	$(ct \notin ct^* \vee pk \neq pk^*) \wedge$
$(m^* \neq \bot) \wedge$	$(m^* \neq \bot) \wedge$
$(R(m, m^*, pk, pk^*, ct^*) = 1)$	$(R(\tilde{m}, m^*, pk, pk^*, ct^*) = 1)$

In the above, $\mathcal{D}_{sk}(\cdot)$ denotes the decryption oracle, which $\mathcal{A}$ is permitted to query even after the challenge phase but except for ct. The message distribution M is deemed valid if $|m| = |m'|$ for any m, m' with non-zero probability in M. The condition $m^* \neq \bot$ means that there exists at least one valid ciphertext in ct^*, i.e., at least one of the messages in m^* is different from $\bot$.

Definition 5 (CNM-CCA Security). *The scheme PKE is said to be CNM-CCA secure if for any PPT adversary $\mathcal{A}$, its advantage $Adv_{\mathcal{A},PKE}^{CNM\text{-}CCA}(\kappa)$ is negligible.*

In the following, let us recall the RKA security of PKE, which is parameterized by a family Φ of RKD functions. Assuming the secret key space is $\mathcal{SK}$, the RKD function is always defined as an efficiently computable map on $\mathcal{SK}$, such as the affine function class $\Phi_{aff} = \{\phi_{a,b}\}_{a,b \in \mathcal{SK}}$ with $\phi_{a,b} = a \cdot sk + b$ and the polynomial function class $\Phi_{poly}(d) = \{\phi_q\}_{q \in \mathcal{SK}_d[x]}$ of bounded degree d, where $\mathcal{SK}$ is a finite field as in [7].

Definition 6 [4,30]. *Let PKE=(Setup, KeyGen, Enc, Dec) be a public key encryption scheme and $\mathcal{A} = (\mathcal{A}_1, \mathcal{A}_2)$ a PPT adversary. For any $\kappa \in \mathbb{N}$ and related-key derivation function family Φ, we define*

$$Adv_{\mathcal{A},\mathsf{PKE}}^{\Phi\text{-RKA}}(\kappa) = \left| \Pr[\mathbf{Expt}_{\mathcal{A},\mathsf{PKE}}^{\Phi\text{-RKA}}(\kappa) = 1] - 1/2 \right|,$$

where the experiment $\mathbf{Expt}_{\mathcal{A},\mathsf{PKE}}^{\Phi\text{-RKA}}(\kappa)$ *is defined as:*

$\mathbf{Expt}_{\mathcal{A},\mathsf{PKE}}^{\Phi\text{-RKA}}(\kappa)$:

$pp \leftarrow \mathsf{Setup}(1^\kappa)$, $(pk, sk) \leftarrow \mathsf{KeyGen}(pp)$
$(m_0, m_1, st) \leftarrow \mathcal{A}_1^{\mathcal{RKD}_{sk}(\cdot,\cdot)}(pp, pk)$
$\beta \leftarrow \{0,1\}, ct^* \leftarrow \mathsf{Enc}(pk, m_\beta)$
$\beta' \leftarrow \mathcal{A}_2^{\mathcal{RKD}_{sk}(\cdot,\cdot)}(st, ct^*)$
return $(\beta' = \beta)$.

In the experiment, the adversary is given access to a related-key decryption oracle, denoted by $\mathcal{RKD}_{sk}(\cdot, \cdot)$. Normally, each query to this oracle consists of a related-key derivation function $\phi \in \Phi$ and a ciphertext ct. In response to such query (ϕ, ct), the oracle returns $\mathsf{Dec}(\phi(sk), ct)$. After the challenge phase, the adversary is still allowed to query the related-key decryption oracle $\mathcal{RKD}_{sk}(\cdot, \cdot)$ even for ct^*, but with the restriction that $(\phi(sk), ct) \neq (sk, ct^*)$.

Definition 7 (Φ-RKA Security). *The encryption scheme PKE is called Φ-RKA secure if for any PPT adversary $\mathcal{A}$, its advantage $Adv_{\mathcal{A},\mathsf{PKE}}^{\Phi\text{-RKA}}(\kappa)$ is negligible.*

3   CNM-CCA and RKA Secure PKE

Our construction is derived from Lai et al.' IND-CCA secure PKE scheme [22]. In order to achieve CNM-CCA security, we first extract from their public key a common reference string, in which we could perfectly hide an escrow key and use it to deal with the ciphertexts encrypted under new public keys. Put differently, the ciphertexts (under the new public key) could be correctly decrypted in the security proof by employing the escrow key together with the new public key, instead of using the corresponding secret key. To this end, we also need to include the public key into the inputs of hash function.

To simultaneously achieve RKA security, our main idea is to exploit the magic decryption capability of the simulator in the CNM-CCA security to answer the related-key decryption queries. To this goal, we should be able to derive the corresponding public keys from the queried RKD functions and the public information, which we could realize by relying on the property of key-malleability. Additionally, to resist such kind of attacks $(\phi(sk) \neq sk, ct^*)$ we have to make the secret key as partial input of the hash function.

So, to achieve the above goals at the same time, we take the public key as partial input of the hash in encryption and uses the secret key to calculate the hash in decryption. More concretely, our construction PKE comprises the following algorithms (Setup, KeyGen, Enc, Dec):

Setup(1^κ): given a security parameter 1^κ, generate cyclic groups $\mathbb{G}, \mathbb{G}_T$ of prime order p, which are endowed with an efficiently computable map $e : \mathbb{G} \times \mathbb{G} \to \mathbb{G}_T$. Next, choose random elements $g, g_1, u, v, w \in \mathbb{G}$ and a collision-resilient hash function $H : \{0, 1\}^* \to \mathbb{Z}_p$. At last, set and output the common reference string crs $= (1^\kappa, \mathbb{G}, \mathbb{G}_T, e, g, g_1, u, v, w, H)$.

KeyGen(crs): given the common reference string crs, choose a random $\alpha \in \mathbb{Z}_p$ and then set the secret key $sk = \alpha$ and the public key $pk = g^\alpha$.

Enc(pk, m): given pk and a message $m \in \mathbb{G}_T$, choose random $r, s \in \mathbb{Z}_p$ and compute the ciphertext components C_1, C_2, C_3 as follows:

$$C_1 = g^r, \quad C_2 = e(pk, g_1)^r \cdot m, \quad C_3 = (u^t v^s w)^r,$$

where $t = H(pk, C_1, C_2)$. At last, return the ciphertext $ct = (C_1, C_2, C_3, s)$.

Dec(sk, ct): given sk and $ct = (C_1, C_2, C_3, s)$, compute $t = H(g^{sk}, C_1, C_2)$ and check if $e(C_1, u^t v^s w) = e(g, C_3)$. If false, return $\bot$; otherwise, output the plaintext $m = C_2/e(C_1, g_1)^{sk}$.

Remark 1. If we only consider the CNM-CCA security, just using public key to compute the hash in both encryption and decryption (i.e., $H(pk, C_1, C_2)$) is actually sufficient. However, it is easy to find that the scheme in this case still suffers from the related-key attacks, which demonstrates the separation of these two notions. To further make it immune to such attacks, we instead calculate the input pk of hash with the secret key in decryption, which also implicitly plays the role of pk for CNM-CCA security in this construction. By this way, we can achieve both the CNM-CCA and RKA securities simultaneously.

4   Security Proofs

In this section, we analyze the CNM-CCA security and the RKA security of our construction successively. First, we give the analysis of CNM-CCA security, which is formulated in Theorem 1. In the security proof, we have to deal with two types of ciphertexts: the ones in the decryption query, which are generated under the challenge public key pk, and those in the adversary's final output, which are generated under the adversarial chosen public key pk^*. In case $pk^* = pk$, the security can be analyzed in a similar way as in [22]. On the other hand, we should be able to properly decrypt the ciphertexts under pk^* without using its corresponding secret key. To achieve this goal, the essential idea is to implicitly conceal in the common reference string an escrow key, by which these ciphere-texts could be correctly opened in the simulation even without any knowledge of the associated secret key. The details are shown in the following.

Theorem 1 (CNM-CCA Security). *The PKE scheme proposed above is CNM-CCA secure under the CDH and DBDH assumptions and the collision-resistance of H. More precisely, for any κ and PPT adversary $\mathcal{A}$, it holds that*
$$Adv_{\mathcal{A}, PKE}^{CNM\text{-}CCA}(\kappa) \le 2Adv_{\mathcal{B}_1, H}^{CR}(\kappa) + Adv_{\mathcal{B}_2, \mathbb{G}}^{CDH}(\kappa) + 2Adv_{\mathcal{B}_3, \mathbb{G}, \mathbb{G}_T}^{DBDH}(\kappa) + 2(q+1)/p,$$
where q denotes the number of ciphertext produced by $\mathcal{A}$ including the decryption queries as well as the elements of his final output ct^*.

Proof. The proof is conducted via a sequence of games. Hereafter, we use $Suc_i(\beta)$ to denote the event that the challenger outputs 1 in the i-th game $\mathbf{Game}_i(\beta)$.

$\mathbf{Game}_0(\beta)$: This is the real game of the definition. Particularly, given the common reference string crs and the public key pk, the adversary $\mathcal{A}$ starts to issue the decryption queries, which could be answered by the challenger using the secret key sk. In the challenge phase, the adversary submits a challenge query for a plaintext distribution M of her choice. Then, the challenger chooses $m_0, m_1 \leftarrow M$, computes $C_1 = g^r$, $C_2 = e(pk, g_1)^r \cdot m_\beta$, $C_3 = (u^t v^s w)^r$, where $r, s \leftarrow \mathbb{Z}_p$ and $t = H(pk, C_1, C_2)$, and returns the ciphertext $ct = (C_1, C_2, C_3, s)$. The adversary continues to query the decryption oracle for any ciphertext but ct. Finally, $\mathcal{A}$ outputs a possibly new public key pk^*, a ciphertext-vector $\boldsymbol{ct}^*$ and the description of a relation R. At this point, the challenger invokes an all powerful oracle that computes α^* such that $pk^* = g^{\alpha^*}$, and exploits the corresponding secret key $sk^* = \alpha^*$ to decrypt $\boldsymbol{ct}^*$, i.e., $\boldsymbol{m}^* = \mathsf{Dec}(sk^*, \boldsymbol{ct}^*)$. After that the challenger uses $\boldsymbol{m}^*$ to evaluate the relation $\mathsf{R}(m_0, \boldsymbol{m}^*, crs, pk, pk^*, \boldsymbol{ct}^*)$ and check if $\boldsymbol{m}^* \neq \perp$. If all these conditions hold, the challenger outputs 1, otherwise 0. Obviously, we have $Adv_{\mathcal{A},\mathsf{PKE}}^{\mathsf{CNM\text{-}CCA}}(\kappa) = |\Pr[Suc_0(0)] - \Pr[Suc_0(1)]|$.

$\mathbf{Game}_1(\beta)$: This is identical to the above game except for the treatment of the ciphertexts (including the decryption queries and the elements of $\boldsymbol{ct}^*$) output by the adversary after the challenge phase. For such a ciphertext ct', it is with respect to a public key pk' which is either pk or a new adversarial chosen public key pk^*. Without loss of generality, we assume that $pk' = g^{\alpha'}$ for some $\alpha' \in \mathbb{Z}_p$ and thus the associated secret key is $sk' = \alpha'$.

In this game, an additional rule is introduced for the process of such ciphertexts. More concretely, the challenger now computes $t' = H(g^{sk'}, C_1', C_2') = H(pk', C_1', C_2')^1$ and checks if $(pk', C_1', C_2') \neq (pk, C_1, C_2)$ but $t' = t$. If so, the challenger aborts. Otherwise, it continues to verify the validity of ct' and decrypts it as before.

Obviously, this game is identical to the above unless that $(pk', C_1', C_2') \neq (pk, C_1, C_2)$ and $t' = t$ happens. However, if this occurs we would find a collision of H. Thus, due to the collision-resistance property we get that $|\Pr[Suc_1(\beta)] - \Pr[Suc_0(\beta)]| \leq Adv_{\mathcal{B}_1,H}^{CR}(\kappa)$.

$\mathbf{Game}_2(\beta)$: This game is the same as the previous, expect for the introduction of a new rejection rule for the process of the ciphertexts generated after the challenge phase. Specifically, the ciphertext $ct' = (C_1', C_2', C_3', s')$ in this game is processed as follows:

- $(C_1', C_2') = (C_1, C_2)$: return $\perp$.
- $(C_1', C_2') \neq (C_1, C_2)$: decrypt it as previous.

---

[1] Note that for any element pk' in public key space $\mathbb{G}$ of our construction, there exists a corresponding private key $sk' \in \mathbb{Z}_p$ satisfying $pk' = g^{sk'}$, so all elements of $\mathbb{G}$ are admissible public keys. Hence, the value $H(g^{sk'}, C_1', C_2')$ can be always computed using pk' even without knowing sk'.

From the above we can see that $\textbf{Game}_2$ is identical to $\textbf{Game}_1$ unless the adversary could generate a valid ciphertext $ct' = (C_1', C_2', C_3', s')$ such that $(C_1', C_2') = (C_1, C_2)$. For simplicity, we denote this event by Valid. Thus we have $|\Pr[Suc_2(\beta)] - \Pr[Suc_1(\beta)]| \leq \Pr[\textsf{Valid}]$.

Lemma 1. *Under the CDH assumption, the adversary cannot generate a valid ciphertext (C_1', C_2', C_3', s') satisfying $(C_1', C_2') = (C_1, C_2)$ except with a negligible probability. More precisely, $\Pr[\textsf{Valid}] \leq Adv_{\mathcal{B}_2,\mathbb{G}}^{CDH}(\kappa) + 1/p$.*

$\textbf{Game}_3(\beta)$: This game is almost the same as the above, except for the way of generating crs. In particular, the challenger at the beginning randomly chooses $x_v, x_w, y_u, y_v, y_w \in \mathbb{Z}_p$ and sets $u = g_1 g^{y_u}, v = g_1^{x_v} g^{y_v}, w = g_1^{x_w} g^{y_w}$, instead of randomly picking u, v, w from $\mathbb{G}$.

Clearly, crs generated in this way is identically distributed to the original from the view of the adversary's point. Thus, we get $\Pr[Suc_3(\beta)] = \Pr[Suc_2(\beta)]$.

$\textbf{Game}_4(\beta)$: The only difference of this game from $\textbf{Game}_3(\beta)$ is that the ciphertext is generated in a different way. Precisely, the ciphertext $ct = (C_1, C_2, C_3, s)$ in this game is generated in the following way:

1. Choose $m_0, m_1 \leftarrow M$ and a random $r \leftarrow \mathbb{Z}_p$.
2. Compute $C_1 = g^r, C_2 = e(pk, g_1)^r \cdot m_\beta$ and $t = H(pk, C_1, C_2)$.
3. Set $s = -(t + x_w)/x_v$ and $C_3 = (g^{t y_u + s y_v + y_w})^r$.

It is easy to verify that the ciphertext ct is well-formed and properly-distributed. Thus we have $\Pr[Suc_4(\beta)] = \Pr[Suc_3(\beta)]$.

$\textbf{Game}_5(\beta)$: This game is identical to the previous except for the treatment of the ciphertexts produced by the adversary, including those submitted to the decryption oracle and the elements of its final output ct^*. Specifically, the ciphertext $ct' = (C_1', C_2', C_3', s')$ is treated as follows.

For the ciphertext ct' queried before $\mathcal{A}$ receiving the challenge ciphertext ct, the challenger first computes $t' = H(g^{sk}, C_1', C_2') = H(pk, C_1', C_2')$ and checks the validity of ct', which ensures that $C_1' = g^{r'}$ and $C_3' = (u^{t'} v^{s'} w)^{r'}$ for some r' by using the pairing. If invalid, it outputs $\bot$. Otherwise, checks if $t' + s' x_v + x_w = 0$. If so, the challenger aborts. Otherwise, it randomly chooses $\gamma \in \mathbb{Z}_p$ and computes

$$d_{ct',1} = pk^{-(t' y_u + s' y_v + y_w)/(t' + s' x_v + x_w)} (u^{t'} v^{s'} w)^\gamma,$$
$$d_{ct',2} = pk^{-1/(t' + s' x_v + x_w)} g^\gamma.$$

Let $\gamma' = \gamma - \frac{\alpha}{t' + s' x_v + x_w}$, then we have $d_{ct',1} = g_1^\alpha (u^{t'} v^{s'} w)^{\gamma'}$ and $d_{ct',2} = g^{\gamma'}$, from which the challenger could in turn get $e(C_1', g_1)^\alpha = e(C_1', d_{ct',1})/e(C_3', d_{ct',2})$ and recover the plaintext by evaluating $C_2'/e(C_1', g_1)^\alpha$.

For the ciphertext ct' appearing after the challenge phase, the challenger first computes $t' = H(pk', C_1', C_2') = H(g^{sk'}, C_1', C_2')$, where pk' is the associated public key with ct' and sk' is the corresponding secret key satisfying $pk' = g^{sk'}$. Then it checks whether $(C_1', C_2') = (C_1, C_2)$ and proceeds as follows:

1. $(C'_1, C'_2) = (C_1, C_2)$: return $\perp$.
2. $(C'_1, C'_2) \neq (C_1, C_2)$: in this case $t' \neq t$. Verify if ct' is valid, if not return $\perp$. Otherwise, check if $s' = s$ and proceed as below:
   - $s' \neq s$: check whether $t' + s'x_v + x_w = 0$. If so, the challenger aborts; otherwise, recover the plaintext as above. More precisely, the challenger first randomly chooses $\gamma \in \mathbb{Z}_p$ and computes

$$d_{ct',1} = pk'^{-(t'y_u+s'y_v+y_w)/(t'+s'x_v+x_w)}(u^{t'}v^{s'}w)^{\gamma},$$
$$d_{ct',2} = pk'^{-1/(t'+s'x_v+x_w)}g^{\gamma}.$$

   Let $\gamma' = \gamma - \frac{sk'}{t'+s'x_v+x_w}$, we have $d_{ct',1} = g_1^{sk'}(u^{t'}v^{s'}w)^{\gamma'}$ and $d_{ct',2} = g^{\gamma'}$. Then the challenger could get $e(C'_1, g_1)^{sk'} = e(C'_1, d_{ct',1})/e(C'_3, d_{ct',2})$ and recover the plaintext by computing $C'_2/e(C'_1, g_1)^{sk'}$.
   - $s' = s$: in this case $t' + s'x_v + x_w \neq 0$ holds, so the ciphertext can be decrypted similarly.

From the above, we know that unless the challenger aborts, the decryption oracle is perfectly simulated and the final output (pk^*, ct^*) is also perfectly treated as if it were directly decrypted using the associated secret key sk^*. In the following, we denote this event by abort.

By the simulation we know that abort happens only when $t' + s'x_v + x_w = 0$ holds. From the setup of crs, it is easily observed that the values x_v and x_w are blinded using y_v and y_w respectively, and so they are initially hidden from the adversary $\mathcal{A}$. When $\mathcal{A}$ queries the decryption oracle for $ct' = (C'_1, C'_2, C'_3, s')$, the challenger returns either $\perp$ if ct' is invalid or the encrypted message. More precisely, it answers in the following way:

1. If $e(C'_1, u^{t'}v^{s'}w) \neq e(g, C'_3)$, where $t' = H(g^{sk}, C'_1, C'_2)$, it returns $\perp$.
2. Otherwise, it computes $d_{ct',1} = g_1^{\alpha}(u^{t'}v^{s'}w)^{\gamma'}$ and $d_{ct',2} = g^{\gamma'}$, and returns $C'_2 \cdot e(C'_3, d_{ct',2})/e(C'_1, d_{ct',1}) = C'_2/e(C'_1, g_1)^{\alpha}$.

Thus, the adversary could not get any information about either x_v or x_w from these queries. After seeing the challenge ciphertext ct, the adversary gets the fact that $t + sx_v + x_w = 0$. However, there are exactly p possible and equally likely pairs (x_v, x_w) satisfying this equation. So, the probability that $t' + s'x_v + x_w = 0$ is at most $1/p$. Considering that the adversary produces at most q ciphertexts including the decryption queries as well as the elements of ct^*, the probability that $t' + s'x_v + x_w = 0$ holds for at least one ciphertext is at most q/p.

Therefore, we have that $|\Pr[Suc_5(\beta)] - \Pr[Suc_4(\beta)]| \leq \Pr[\text{abort}] \leq q/p$.

Game$_6(\beta)$: This game is essentially the same as the above except that both the crs and ct are generated using the DBDH tuple $(g, g^a, g^b, g^c, e(g,g)^{abc})$, where $a, b, c \leftarrow \mathbb{Z}_p$. In particular, the challenger randomly chooses $x_v, x_w, y_u, y_v, y_w \in \mathbb{Z}_p$ and sets $g_1 = g^b, u = g^b g^{y_u}, v = g^{bx_v}g^{y_v}, w = g^{bx_w}g^{y_w}$ and $pk = g^a$.

For the challenge ciphertext $ct = (C_1, C_2, C_3, s)$, it is generated as follows:

1. Choose $m_0, m_1 \leftarrow M$.
2. Let $C_1 = g^c$, $C_2 = e(g, g)^{abc} \cdot m_\beta$ and compute $t = H(pk, C_1, C_2)$.
3. Set $s = -(t + x_w)/x_v$ and $C_3 = (g^c)^{ty_u + sy_v + y_w}$.

Clearly, this game is identical to the above, so we have $\Pr[Suc_6(\beta)] = \Pr[Suc_5(\beta)]$.

Game$_7(\beta)$: In the final game, the message m_β is perfectly hidden by a random element $e(g, g)^z$, where $z \leftarrow \mathbb{Z}_p$.

Lemma 2. *Under the DBDH assumption, **Game$_7(\beta)$** is computationally indistinguishable from **Game$_6(\beta)$**. More concretely,*

$$| \Pr[Suc_7(\beta)] - \Pr[Suc_6(\beta)]| \leq Adv_{\mathcal{B}_3, \mathbb{G}, \mathbb{G}_T}^{DBDH}(\kappa).$$

By assuming the correctness of Lemmas 1 and 2, the proofs of which will be given in the full version, and combining all the probabilities before, we get that

$$\begin{aligned}
Adv_{\mathcal{A}, PKE}^{CNM\text{-}CCA}(\kappa) &= | \Pr[Suc_0(0)] - \Pr[Suc_0(1)]| \\
&\leq | \Pr[Suc_0(0)] - \Pr[Suc_7(0)]| + | \Pr[Suc_7(0)] - \Pr[Suc_7(1)]| \\
&\quad + | \Pr[Suc_7(1)] - \Pr[Suc_0(1)]| \\
&\leq 2Adv_{\mathcal{B}_1, H}^{CR}(\kappa) + 2Adv_{\mathcal{B}_2, \mathbb{G}}^{CDH}(\kappa) + 2Adv_{\mathcal{B}_3, \mathbb{G}, \mathbb{G}_T}^{DBDH}(\kappa) + 2(q + 1)/p.
\end{aligned}$$

Note that $e(g, g)^z$ perfectly hides m_β, so we have $\Pr[Suc_7(0)] = \Pr[Suc_7(1)]$. $\square$

Second, we give the analysis of RKA security, which is formulated in Theorem 2. In the simulation, we need to properly deal with the related-key decryption queries of the form (ϕ, ct). To this end, we should be able to (1) check if $\phi(sk) = sk$ and (2) open the ciphertext ct under $\phi(sk)$ both without knowledge of the secret key sk. For the first task, we accomplish it by relying on the property of key-malleability. As to the second, we decrypt the ciphertext by exploiting the malleability property and the escrow keys concealed in the common reference string, which is inspired by the proof of CNM-CCA security.

Theorem 2 (Φ-RKA Security). *The PKE scheme proposed above is Φ_{aff}-RKA secure under the CDH and DBDH assumptions and the collision-resistance of H. More precisely, for any κ, $\phi \in \Phi_{aff}$ and PPT adversary $\mathcal{A}$, it holds that $Adv_{\mathcal{A}, PKE}^{\Phi_{aff}\text{-}RKA}(\kappa) \leq Adv_{\mathcal{B}_1, H}^{CR}(\kappa) + Adv_{\mathcal{B}_2, \mathbb{G}}^{CDH}(\kappa) + Adv_{\mathcal{B}_3, \mathbb{G}, \mathbb{G}_T}^{DBDH}(\kappa) + (q+1)/p$, where q denotes the number of related-key decryption queries made by $\mathcal{A}$.*

5 $\Phi_{poly}(d)$-RKA Secure PKE

As shown before, we can achieve RKA security by exploiting the key-malleability and the strong decryption capability of the simulator for CNM-CCA security. Following this way, we further give a direct and efficient construction of $\Phi_{poly}(d)$-RKA secure PKE by simply extending the algorithm KeyGen of the previous construction, the details of which are as follows.

Setup(1^κ): given a security parameter 1^κ, generate cyclic groups $\mathbb{G}, \mathbb{G}_T$ of prime order p, endowed with a bilinear map $e : \mathbb{G} \times \mathbb{G} \to \mathbb{G}_T$. Next, choose random elements $g, g_1, u, v, w \in \mathbb{G}$ and a collision-resilient hash function $H : \{0,1\}^* \to \mathbb{Z}_p$. Finally, output the common reference string $\mathrm{crs} = (1^\kappa, \mathbb{G}, \mathbb{G}_T, e, g, g_1, u, v, w, H)$.

KeyGen(crs): given crs, choose a random $\alpha \in \mathbb{Z}_p$ and compute $\pi = g^\alpha$. Finally, set the secret key $sk = \alpha$ and the public key $pk = (\pi, g^{\alpha^2}, g^{\alpha^3}, \cdots, g^{\alpha^d})$ for positive integer d.

Enc(pk, m): given pk and a message $m \in \mathbb{G}_T$, choose random elements $r, s \in \mathbb{Z}_p$ and compute the ciphertext components C_1, C_2 and C_3 as follows:

$$C_1 = g^r, \ C_2 = e(\pi, g_1)^r \cdot m, \ C_3 = (u^t v^s w)^r,$$

where $t = H(\pi, C_1, C_2)$. At last, return the ciphertext $ct = (C_1, C_2, C_3, s)$.

Dec(sk, ct): given sk and $ct = (C_1, C_2, C_3, s)$, first compute $t = H(g^{sk}, C_1, C_2)$, and then check if $e(C_1, u^t v^s w) = e(g, C_3)$. If false, return $\bot$; otherwise, output the plaintext $m = C_2 / e(C_1, g_1)^{sk}$.

Remark 2 Similar to [7], the elements $g^{\alpha^2}, g^{\alpha^3}, \cdots, g^{\alpha^d}$ is mainly to assist in achieving key-malleability for $\Phi_{poly}(d)$. In fact, they are not used in the actual system but for the proof of RKA-security.

Theorem 3 (Φ-RKA Security). *The PKE scheme proposed above is $\Phi_{poly}(d)$-RKA secure under the CDH and d-mEDBDH assumptions and the collision-resistance of H. More precisely, for any κ and PPT adversary $\mathcal{A}$, it holds that* $Adv_{\mathcal{A}, PKE}^{\Phi_{poly}\text{-}RKA}(\kappa) \leq Adv_{\mathcal{B}_1, H}^{CR}(\kappa) + Adv_{\mathcal{B}_2, \mathbb{G}}^{CDH}(\kappa) + Adv_{\mathcal{B}_3, \mathbb{G}, \mathbb{G}_T}^{d\text{-}mEDBDH}(\kappa) + (q+1)/p$, *where q denotes the number of related-key decryption queries made by $\mathcal{A}$.*

We remark that the proof of Theorems 2 (and 3) is inspired by that of Theorem 1. The main difference for the proof is that $g^{\phi(sk)}$ will play the role of pk'. Note that $g^{\phi(sk)}$ can be seen as a transformed public key with the corresponding secret key $\phi(sk)$. For lack of space, we will give the detailed proofs in the full version.

6   Performance Analysis

In this part, we give a detailed performance analysis of our constructions and a brief comparison with the related works. In the comparison, we use $[\cdot]_1$ and $[\cdot]_2$ to denote PKEs derived from the related work $[\cdot]$ by the KEM/DEM approach and CHK transformation respectively. Regarding the KEM/DEM approach, we write SE=$(\mathcal{E}, \mathcal{D})$ to denote an one-time CCA-secure symmetric encryption, where $\mathcal{E}$ and $\mathcal{D}$ denote the encryption and decryption algorithm respectively. In addition, we use Sig=$(\mathcal{G}, \mathcal{S}, \mathcal{V})$ to denote the one-time signature used in the CHK transformation, where $\mathcal{G}$ outputs a signing and verification key pair (sk_{Sig}, vk) and $\mathcal{S}$ generates a signature $\sigma \leftarrow \mathcal{S}(sk_{\mathsf{Sig}}, m)$ for a given message m. For the instantiation of [26], we use the efficient IBE in [9] and denote the continuous non-malleable key derivation function used in the conversion by $\mathsf{KDF} = (\mathsf{K.G}, \mathsf{K.S}, \mathsf{K.E})$, where $\mathsf{K.G}$ outputs public parameters pp, $\mathsf{K.S}$ generates a derivation key and a corresponding public key pair belonging to $\mathcal{S}_1 \times \mathcal{S}_2$, and $\mathsf{K.E}$ calculates a pseudorandom key. The detailed analysis is summarized in Table 1.

Table 1. Performance Analysis and Comparison with Related Works

Scheme	pk^a	ciphertext	KeyGen	Enc	Dec	CNM	Φ-RKA
LY[23]	$|G|+|G_T|$	$2|G|+|G_T|+vk+\sigma$	$\exp_1$	$2\exp_1+\exp_2+S$	$3pr+2\exp_1+\mathcal{V}$	✓	×
BF[2]	$2|G|+|G_T|$	$2|G|+|G_T|$	$2\exp_1$	$2pr+2\exp_1+\exp_2$	$3pr+4\exp_1$	✓	×
Sect. 3	$|G|+|G_T|$	$2|G|+|G_T|+|Z_p|$	$\exp_1$	$2\exp_1+\exp_2$	$3pr+3\exp_1$	✓	Φ_{aff}
Sect. 5	$d|G|+|G_T|$	$2|G|+|G_T|+|Z_p|$	$d\exp_1$	$2\exp_1+\exp_2$	$3pr+3\exp_1$	×	$\Phi_{poly}(d)$
BP+[7]$_1^b$	$|G|$	$2|G|+ct$	$\exp_1$	$2\exp_1+\exp_2+\mathcal{E}$	$3pr+3\exp_1+\mathcal{D}$	–	Φ_{aff}
BP+[7]$_2$	$(2d-1)|G|$	$2|G|+|G_T|+vk+\sigma$	$(2d-1)\exp_1$	$2\exp_1+\exp_2+S$	$2pr+4\exp_1+\mathcal{V}$	–	$\Phi_{poly}(d)$
QL+[26]	$|G|+|S_2|$	$2|G|+|G_T|+vk+\sigma$	$\exp_1+K.S+K.E$	$2\exp_1+\exp_2+S$	$2pr+3\exp_1+K.E+\mathcal{V}$	–	$\Phi^+_{poly}(d)$
FX[16]$_1$	$2|G|$	$4|G|+ct$	$3\exp_1$	$2\exp_1+\exp_2+\mathcal{E}$	$7pr+2\exp_1+\mathcal{D}$	–	$\Phi^+_{poly}(d)$
FX[16]$_2$	$2|G|$	$4|G|+|G_T|+vk+\sigma$	$3\exp_1$	$2\exp_1+\exp_2+S$	$6pr+3\exp_1+\mathcal{V}$	–	$\Phi^+_{poly}(d)$

^{a}: identical to other works, the pairing operation $e(pk, g_1)$ in our scheme could be pre-computed and put into the public key; ^{b}: for comparison, the KEM in [7] is adapted into the symmetric pairing setting; n: the bit-length of a user's "identity"/the output-length of H; ct: the ciphertext of the symmetric encryption SE; $|\cdot|$: the size of an element in a group or a finite set, e.g., $|G|$; "$\exp_1$": an exponentiation operation over G (some of the exponentiations are actually multi-exponentiation); "$\exp_2$": an exponentiation operation over G_T; "pr": a bilinear pairing operation; $\Phi^+_{poly}(d)$: a family of RKD functions beyond polynomials of bounded degree d.

It is easy to observe from the table that our construction in Sect. 3 not only have a comparable performance to the related works in [2,23] and [7]$_1$, but also achieves CNM-CCA security and RKA security simultaneously. As to the RKA security, it is clear that our direct construction in Sect. 5 is more efficient than [7]$_2$, but secure against a less broad function class than [16,26]. We left the direct and efficient constructions of PKE with CNM-CCA security and/or RKA security against larger function classes as future work.

7 Further Discussion

As remarked in Sect. 3, CNM-CCA security cannot imply RKA security. However, it gives a new way to design practical RKA secure PKE schemes, as indicated by our constructions. From the proofs we can see that the magic decryption capability of the simulator for CNM-CCA security plays an important role for realizing RKA security. Thus it is a natural question that under what conditions the CNM-CCA secure PKE can be generically converted into RKA-secure PKE.

On the other hand, our construction in Sect. 5 also demonstrates that RKA security does not imply CNM-CCA security. Actually, given a challenge ciphertext ct for pk, the adversary can output such a public key and ciphertext pair $(pk^*, ct^* = ct)$ where $pk^* \neq pk$ but with the same π. Obviously, ct^* is a valid ciphertext of $m^* = m$ under pk^*. To avoid such trivial attacks, an easy way is to take the whole pk as the input of H in encryption and accordingly use sk to calculate it in decryption. However, it still cannot be proved CNM-CCA secure like Theorem 1, because pk^* chosen by the adversary may be not well-formed and thus the corresponding secret key does not exist. Intuitively, to achieve CNM-CCA security, we have to enforce the adversary to output a valid pk^*.

From the above discussion, we know that these two notions are somewhat related to each other, but they are completely separated. Thus, it remains interesting and meaningful to find general methods to achieve both kinds of securities.

8   Conclusion

In this work, we present the first efficient public key encryption scheme which achieves CNM-CCA security and RKA-security simultaneously. Thus it provides a stronger security guarantee for the complex application scenarios. Relying on the strong decryption capability implied by CNM-CCA security, we further give a practical RKA-secure public key encryption scheme in a direct way. Based on the newly introduced hardness assumption, it can be proven secure against polynomial functions of bounded degree.

Acknowledgements. The authors would like to thank all anonymous reviewers for their valuable comments. The work is supported by the Major State Basic Research Development Program (No. 2013CB338004), the Natural Science Foundation of China (No. 61472250) and the Scientific Research Foundation of Ministry of Education of China and China Mobile (No. MCM20150301).

References

1. Al-Riyami, S.S., Paterson, K.G.: Certificateless public key cryptography. In: Laih, C.-S. (ed.) ASIACRYPT 2003. LNCS, vol. 2894, pp. 452–473. Springer, Heidelberg (2003)
2. Barbosa, M., Farshim, P.: Relations among notions of complete non-malleability: indistinguishability characterisation and efficient construction without random oracles. In: Steinfeld, R., Hawkes, P. (eds.) ACISP 2010. LNCS, vol. 6168, pp. 145–163. Springer, Heidelberg (2010)
3. Barenghi, A., Breveglieri, L., Koren, I., Naccache, D.: Fault injection attacks on cryptographic devices: Theory, practice, and countermeasures. Proc. IEEE **100**(11), 3056–3076 (2012)
4. Bellare, M., Cash, D., Miller, R.: Cryptography secure against related-key attacks and tampering. In: Lee, D.H., Wang, X. (eds.) ASIACRYPT 2011. LNCS, vol. 7073, pp. 486–503. Springer, Heidelberg (2011)
5. Bellare, M., Desai, A., Pointcheval, D., Rogaway, P.: Relations among notions of security for public-key encryption schemes. In: Krawczyk, H. (ed.) CRYPTO 1998. LNCS, vol. 1462, pp. 26–45. Springer, Heidelberg (1998)
6. Bellare, M., Kohno, T.: A theoretical treatment of related-key attacks: RKA-PRPs, RKA-PRFs, and applications. In: Biham, E. (ed.) EUROCRYPT 2003. LNCS, vol. 2656. Springer, Heidelberg (2003)
7. Bellare, M., Paterson, K.G., Thomson, S.: RKA security beyond the linear barrier: IBE, encryption and signatures. In: Wang, X., Sako, K. (eds.) ASIACRYPT 2012. LNCS, vol. 7658, pp. 331–348. Springer, Heidelberg (2012)

8. Biham, E., Shamir, A.: Differential fault analysis of secret key cryptosystems. In: Kaliski Jr., B.S. (ed.) CRYPTO 1997. LNCS, vol. 1294, pp. 513–525. Springer, Heidelberg (1997)

9. Boneh, D., Boyen, X.: Efficient selective-ID secure identity-based encryption without random oracles. In: Cachin, C., Camenisch, J.L. (eds.) EUROCRYPT 2004. LNCS, vol. 3027, pp. 223–238. Springer, Heidelberg (2004)

10. Boneh, D., DeMillo, R.A., Lipton, R.J.: On the importance of checking cryptographic protocols for faults. In: Fumy, W. (ed.) EUROCRYPT 1997. LNCS, vol. 1233, pp. 37–51. Springer, Heidelberg (1997)

11. Canetti, R., Halevi, S., Katz, J.: Chosen-ciphertext security from identity-based encryption. In: Cachin, C., Camenisch, J.L. (eds.) EUROCRYPT 2004. LNCS, vol. 3027, pp. 207–222. Springer, Heidelberg (2004)

12. Cui, H., Mu, Y., Au, M.H.: Public-key encryption resilient to linear related-key attacks. In: Zia, T., Zomaya, A., Varadharajan, V., Mao, M. (eds.) SecureComm 2013. LNICST, vol. 127, pp. 182–196. Springer, Heidelberg (2013)

13. Dolev, D., Dwork, C., Naor, M.: Nonmalleable cryptography. SIAM J. Comput. 30(2), 391–437 (2000)

14. Fischlin, M.: Completely non-malleable schemes. In: Caires, L., Italiano, G.F., Monteiro, L., Palamidessi, C., Yung, M. (eds.) ICALP 2005. LNCS, vol. 3580, pp. 779–790. Springer, Heidelberg (2005)

15. Fischlin, M., Fischlin, R.: Efficient non-malleable commitment schemes. In: Bellare, M. (ed.) CRYPTO 2000. LNCS, vol. 1880, pp. 413–431. Springer, Heidelberg (2000)

16. Fujisaki, E., Xagawa, K.: Efficient RKA-secure KEM and IBE schemes against invertible functions. In: Lauter, K., Rodríguez-Henríquez, F. (eds.) LatinCrypt 2015. LNCS, vol. 9230, pp. 3–20. Springer, Heidelberg (2015)

17. Gandolfi, K., Mourtel, C., Olivier, F.: Electromagnetic analysis: Concrete results. In: Koç, Ç.K., Naccache, D., Paar, C. (eds.) CHES 2001. LNCS, vol. 2162, pp. 251–261. Springer, Heidelberg (2001)

18. Hutter, M., Schmidt, J.-M., Plos, T.: RFID and its vulnerability to faults. In: Oswald, E., Rohatgi, P. (eds.) CHES 2008. LNCS, vol. 5154, pp. 363–379. Springer, Heidelberg (2008)

19. Jafargholi, Z., Wichs, D.: Tamper detection and continuous non-malleable codes. In: Dodis, Y., Nielsen, J.B. (eds.) TCC 2015, Part I. LNCS, vol. 9014, pp. 451–480. Springer, Heidelberg (2015)

20. Jia, D., Li, B., Lu, X., Mei, Q.: Related key secure PKE from hash proof systems. In: Yoshida, M., Mouri, K. (eds.) IWSEC 2014. LNCS, vol. 8639, pp. 250–265. Springer, Heidelberg (2014)

21. Kiltz, E.: Chosen-ciphertext security from tag-based encryption. In: Halevi, S., Rabin, T. (eds.) TCC 2006. LNCS, vol. 3876, pp. 581–600. Springer, Heidelberg (2006)

22. Lai, J., Deng, R.H., Liu, S., Kou, W.: Efficient CCA-secure PKE from identity-based techniques. In: CT-RSA 2010, San Francisco, CA, USA, March 1–5, 2010, pp. 132–147 (2010)

23. Libert, B., Yung, M.: Efficient completely non-malleable public key encryption. In: Abramsky, S., Gavoille, C., Kirchner, C., Meyer auf der Heide, F., Spirakis, P.G. (eds.) ICALP 2010. LNCS, vol. 6198, pp. 127–139. Springer, Heidelberg (2010)

24. Lu, X., Li, B., Jia, D.: Related-key security for hybrid encryption. In: Chow, S.S.M., Camenisch, J., Hui, L.C.K., Yiu, S.M. (eds.) ISC 2014. LNCS, vol. 8783, pp. 19–32. Springer, Heidelberg (2014)

25. Peikert, C., Waters, B.: Lossy trapdoor functions and their applications. In: Proceedings of the 40th Annual ACM Symposium on Theory of Computing, Victoria, British Columbia, Canada, May 17–20, 2008, pp. 187–196 (2008)
26. Qin, B., Liu, S., Yuen, T.H., Deng, R.H., Chen, K.: Continuous non-malleable key derivation and its application to related-key security. In: Proceedings of the PKC 2015, Gaithersburg, MD, USA, March 30 - April 1, 2015, pp. 557–578 (2015)
27. Sepahi, R., Steinfeld, R., Pieprzyk, J.: Lattice-based completely non-malleable public-key encryption in the standard model. Des. Codes Crypt. **71**(2), 293–313 (2014)
28. Ventre, C., Visconti, I.: Completely non-malleable encryption revisited. In: PKC 2008, Barcelona, Spain, March 9–12, 2008, pp. 65–84 (2008)
29. Waters, B.: Efficient identity-based encryption without random oracles. In: Cramer, R. (ed.) EUROCRYPT 2005. LNCS, vol. 3494, pp. 114–127. Springer, Heidelberg (2005)
30. Wee, H.: Public key encryption against related key attacks. In: PKC 2012, Darmstadt, Germany, May 21–23, 2012, pp. 262–279 (2012)
31. Yuen, T.H., Zhang, C., Chow, S.S.M., Yiu, S.: Related randomness attacks for public key cryptosystems. In: ASIACCS 2015, Singapore, April 14–17, 2015, pp. 215–223 (2015)

Searchable Encryption

Verifiable Searchable Encryption with Aggregate Keys for Data Sharing in Outsourcing Storage

Tong Li[1][(✉)], Zheli Liu[1], Ping Li[2], Chunfu Jia[1], Zoe L. Jiang[3], and Jin Li[4]

[1] College of Computer and Control Engineering, Nankai University, Tianjin, China
litongziyi@mail.nankai.edu.cn, {liuzheli,cfjia}@nankai.edu.cn
[2] School of Mathematics and Computational Science, Sun Yat-sen University,
Guangzhou, China
liping26@mail2.sysu.edu.cn
[3] Harbin Institute of Technology Shenzhen Graduate School, Shenzhen, China
zoeljiang@gmail.com
[4] School of Computer Science, Guangzhou University, Guangzhou, China
lijin@gzhu.edu.cn

Abstract. In a secure data sharing system, the keyword search over encrypted files is a basic need of a user with appropriate privileges. Although the traditional searchable encryption technique can provide the privacy protection, two critical issues still should be considered. Firstly, a cloud server may be selfish in order to save its computing resources, and thus returns only a fragment of results to reply a search query. Secondly, since different keys are always used for different document sets, making a search query over massive sets and verifying the search results are both impractical for a user with massive keys. In this paper, we propose a scheme named "verifiable searchable encryption with aggregate keys". In the scheme, a data owner need only distribute a single aggregate key to other users to selectively share both search and verification privileges over his/her document sets. After obtaining such a key, a user can use it not only for generating a single trapdoor as a keyword search query, but for verifying whether the server just conducts a part of computing for the search request. Then, we define the requirements of the scheme and give a valid construction. Finally, our analysis and performance evaluation demonstrate that the scheme are practical and secure.

Keywords: Cloud storage · Data sharing · Verifiable searchable encryption

1 Introduction

With the proliferation of demands for personal data storage conveniently, the outsourced data storage technology becomes widely used in the wake of the arrival of the cloud computing paradigm [1]. A group of file owners always want that their sensitive files could be securely shared with each other via a cloud server. In addition, an owner would like to authorize others several appreciate

© Springer International Publishing Switzerland 2016
J.K. Liu and R. Steinfeld (Eds.): ACISP 2016, Part II, LNCS 9723, pp. 153–169, 2016.
DOI: 10.1007/978-3-319-40367-0_10

privileges like retrieving files over a subset of his/her. Beside the storage, today's commercial outsourcing storage systems, such as Dropbox and Sycany, provide more or less other services to satisfy clients' sharing requirements. For the keyword search mentioned above, the searchable encryption (SE) technology [2,3] is proposed to ensure the privacy and confidentiality while the server performs search operations. Then, the public-key encryption with keyword search (PEKS) schemes [4–6] can be adapted to various scenarios on the cloud.

However, sometimes sharing the search privilege over massive document sets is not easy for their owner. In a traditional PEKS scheme, for confidentiality and efficiency considerations, different keys are always used for different document sets, so that the number of keys the users hold will scale with the number of document sets they can retrieve. Thus, the sharing will naturally involve transmission and key management troubles which are difficult to process for mobile devices. Moreover, for some commercial reasons and hardware restrictions in the peak period, a public cloud server may tend to save its computation or bandwidth. That means, it executes only a fraction of search operations honestly instead of the whole, and then returns the corresponding results. Thus, users probably receive just a part of the search results. It is very essential to add the verification mechanism to PEKS schemes. To ensure the keyword privacy, only the users who hold appropriate verification tokens can verify the results over related document sets. What is worse, the number of tokens used for the verification is also considerable while the user finishes the search over massive document sets.

In this paper, the semi-honest-but-curious server [7], who may execute only a fraction of honest search operations, is set as a computationally bounded adversary. And we propose a verifiable scheme called verifiable searchable encryption with aggregate keys (VSEAK) for data sharing systems to fight against it. In the scheme, the search keys and verification tokens, which is used over a subset of a owner's document sets, are aggregated to one single key. Therefore, in our proposed scheme, to selectively sharing the search privileges of documents, the owner can only send them a single aggregate key instead of massive keys for both the search and verification. Thus, each user only needs to generate a single aggregate trapdoor of a keyword by such a key to perform the keyword search, and then execute the verification by the same key. Somewhat similar to the most existing searchable encryption schemes for the group sharing [8–10], the proposed scheme also set several auxiliary values as public for reducing the repeated calculations and pass some tasks to the server securely. The contribution summarized as follows:

1. We give some requirements of multi-key PEKS scheme in an outsourced data sharing system. Then, we propose a scheme that enables each authorized user to confidentially retrieve encrypted documents selectively shared by a document provider using a single aggregate key, and to verify the results using the same key.

2. We give a concrete construction which can meet the requirements. In the construction, we design an algorithm to generate a single aggregate key for both search and verification.
3. We also conduct related performance evaluation. The evaluation confirms that the scheme is practical for applications.

1.1 Related Work

Multi-user Search Encryption for Data Sharing. Boneh et al. [4] introduced the public key searchable encryption based on the identity-based encryption, and there is a rich literature on both symmetric searchable encryption (SSE) schemes [2,3] and PEKS schemes [5,6,11]. Under the multi-user setting [10,12], data owners always want to share their documents with a group of authorized users, and each user who has the search privilege can provide trapdoors of a keyword to perform the search over the shared documents.

For confidentiality considerations, different keys are always used for different documents in data sharing systems during both searching and decrypting. Thus, in most cases of the access control [13], the main problem is how to control which users can access which documents, whereas how to reduce the number of shared keys and trapdoors is not considered. Zheng et al. [14,15] proposed the attribute-based keyword search scheme, which allows a data owner to control the search privilege according to some access control key- or ciphertext-policy.

Verifiable Searchable Encryption. A threat model was considered by Chai et al. [7], in which there is a computationally bounded adversary called semi-honest-but-curious server. Such an adversary satisfies: (1) the server is a storage provider who neither modifies nor destroys the stored documents; (2) the server tries to learn the underlying plaintext or sensitive information from stored documents; (3) the server may forge a fraction of the search outcome as it may execute only a fraction of search operations honestly.

Some approaches about the verifiable keyword search over plaintext have been conducted in [16,17], which is not suitable for the threat model. In the PEKS setting, the keyword search has some requirements like other verifiable computations [18]. Note that, to ensure the keyword privacy, the access control of the verification [19,20] should be achieved. The Bloom filter is used by Zheng et al. [14] to verify whether a keyword really exists in a document set.

Key-aggregate Method. To reduce the number of distributed data encryption keys in a data sharing system, Chu et al. [8] proposed the key-aggregate encryption (KAE) scheme that allows a set of documents encrypted by different keys to be decrypted with a single aggregate key. In addition, such a method of the aggregation can be also applied in the group keyword search [9]. Aiming at the challenge of reducing keys, a PEKS scheme for sharing privileges conveniently is proposed to generate an aggregate key, by which the user can perform the keyword search over each encrypted document set in the key's scope. Therefore, the key-aggregate method allows the efficiently delegating of both decryption and search privileges in a group. This is the main inspiration of our study that the verification privileges of several document sets can also be aggregated.

1.2   Organization

The rest of the work is organized as follows: In Sect. 2, we state some preliminaries. Section 3 describes the problem statement, the framework of our scheme, and the definition of requirements. In Sect. 4, we give the concrete construction and some analyses. And Sect. 5 reports the performance evaluation. Finally, Sect. 6 concludes the work with a discussion.

2   Preliminary

In this section, we review some basic assumptions and cryptology concepts which will be needed later in this paper.

2.1   Complexity Assumption

Bilinear Map. A bilinear map is a map $e : \mathcal{G} \times \mathcal{G} \to \mathcal{G}_1$ with the following properties:

1. Bilinearity: for all $u, v \in \mathcal{G}$ and $a, b \in \mathcal{Z}_p^*$, we have $e(u^a, v^b) = e(u, v)^{ab}$.
2. Non-degeneracy: $e(g, g) \neq 1$.
3. Computability: there is an efficient algorithm to compute $e(u, v)$ for any $u, v \in \mathcal{G}$.

Bilinear Diffie-Hellman Exponent Assumption. The l-BDHE problem in $\mathcal{G}$ is stated as follows. Given a vector of $2l + 1$ elements $(h, g, g^{\alpha}, g^{(\alpha^2)}, \cdots$ $\cdots, g^{(\alpha^l)}, g^{(\alpha^{l+2})}, \cdots, g^{(\alpha^{2l})}) \in (\mathcal{G}^*)^{2l+1}$ as input, output $e(g, h)^{(\alpha^{l+1})} \in \mathcal{G}_1$. An algorithm $\mathcal{A}$ has advantage ε in solving l-BDHE in $\mathcal{G}$ if $\mathbf{Pr}[\mathcal{A}(h, g, g^{\alpha}, g^{(\alpha^2)}, \cdots$ $\cdots, g^{(\alpha^l)}, g^{(\alpha^{l+2})}, \cdots, g^{(\alpha^{2l})}) = e(g^{(\alpha^{l+1})}, h)] \geq \varepsilon$.

Definition 1. *The $(l, \varepsilon)-BDHE$ assumption holds in $\mathcal{G}$ if no algorithm has advantage more than ε in solving the $l-BDHE$ problem in $\mathcal{G}$.*

2.2   Bloom Filter

A m-bit Bloom filter can be seen as an array of m bits, which are all initialized as 0. In this structure, k independent hash functions $H_1, \cdots, H_k$ with the same range $\{0, \cdots, m - 1\}$ is designed for verification. In the generation step, for each element $s \in S = \{s_1, \cdots, s_n\}$, each $H_j(s)$-bit of the array is set to 1, where $1 \leq j \leq k$. In the verification step, the value of the $H_j(s)$-bit can determine whether an element s belongs to S or not. If the value is 0, it is certain that $s \notin S$; otherwise, $s \in S$ with a high probability. Assume that the hash functions are perfectly random, the false-positive rate is $(1 - (1 - \frac{1}{m})^{kn})^k \approx (1 - e^{-kn/m})^k$. Note that $k = (ln2)m/n$ hash functions will lead to the minimal false-positive rate $(0.6185)m/n$. A m-bit Bloom filter includes two algorithms:

1. **BFGen**($\{H_1, \cdots, H_k\}, \{s_1, \cdots, s_n\}$): This algorithm generates a m-bit Bloom filter BF by hashing a data set $S = \{s_1, \cdots, s_n\}$ with $\{H_1, \cdots, H_k\}$.
2. **BFVerify**($\{H_1, \cdots, H_k\}, BF, s$): This algorithm returns 1 if $s \in S$, and 0 otherwise.

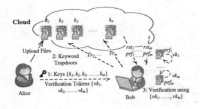 

(a) Traditional Verifiable Approach   (b) Verifiable Searchable Encryption with Aggregate keys

Fig. 1. Keyword Search in a verification scenario

3 Proposed Scheme

3.1 Problem Statement

There is a common scenario that several data owner as a group of a social circle would like to share some confidential private data with each other via a public cloud storage service. With a approach of the traditional PEKS scheme with the verifiable mechanism, a data owner Alice encrypts her document sets and their keywords, and then uploads them. Imagine that Bob is one of the closest member who wants to obtain retrieving and verification privileges on a part of those sets. As shown in Fig. 1(a), Alice is assumed to have massive document sets $\{docs_i\}_{i=1}^n$. Without loss of generality, we suppose that Alice try to selectively share a subset $S(|S| = m)$ of her document sets. In this case, Alice has to send all $\{k_i\}_{i=1}^m$ along with all $\{vk_i\}_{i=1}^m$ to Bob, where the search key k_i and the verification token vk_i are used for the document set $docs_i$. To search over S, for each target document set in S, Bob need generate a target trapdoor of one keyword w. And then, he submits all trapdoors to the cloud server. Also, to verify the results, Bob must using massive verification tokens. When m is sufficient large, the key distribution and storage as well as the trapdoor generation will be too hard for Bob's device, which basically defies the purpose of using the cloud storage and computing.

In this paper, we propose the VSEAK scheme which partly applies the approach of key aggregation to a verifiable scenario as shown in Fig. 1(b). The scheme pass most computation and storage burdens to the cloud server without loss of the privacy. In above scenario with VSEAK, Alice only needs distribute a single aggregate key, instead of $\{k_i\}_{i=1}^m$ and $\{vk_i\}_{i=1}^m$, for both the keyword search and verification. And Bob only needs to generate a single aggregate trapdoor and submit them, instead of $\{Tr_i\}_{i=1}^m$, to the server. Moreover, Bob can using the only one key during verifying. That is to say, in VSEAK, the delegation of appreciate privileges can be achieved by selectively sharing a single aggregate key (Fig. 2).

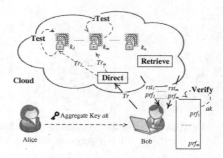

Fig. 2. Framework of verifiable searchable encryption with aggregate keys

3.2   Framework

A verifiable searchable encryption with aggregate keys scheme $\mathcal{VSE} =$ (**ParamGen, KeyGen, Encrypt, Share, Trapdoor, Retrieve, Verify**) is composed of seven algorithms as follow:

1. **ParamGen**(1^λ, n) → *params*: Based on the security parameter λ and the maximum possible number n of document sets which belongs to a data owner, this algorithm is run by the *system* to set up the scheme. It outputs the public system parameter *params* which can be stored in the cloud server.
2. **KeyGen** → (pk, sk): The indeterminate key generation algorithm is run by the data owner to generate a random key pair (pk,sk). The public key pk is used for encrypting keywords, and the secret key sk for sharing is kept private by the owner.
3. **Encrypt**$_{pk}$(i, W_i) → (Δ_i, CW_i): On input of the keyword group W_i of the i-th document set, this algorithm is run by the data owner to encrypt all keywords in W_i. This algorithm will generate and outputs the ciphertext group CW_i of W_i, along with a public auxiliary value Δ_i. Then, Δ_i and CW_i are stored in the cloud server.
4. **Share**$_{sk}$(S) → ak: Using his/her secret key sk, the data owner runs this algorithm to generate and output an aggregate key ak for sharing. The user who holds such a key is allow to perform both the keyword search and verification over each i-th document set where $i \in S$. Thus, the owner can securely distribute ak to others to share corresponding privileges over S.
5. **Trapdoor**$_{ak}$(w) → Tr: this algorithm is run by the user who holds an aggregate key ak to generate and output an aggregate trapdoor Tr. Then, the user should submit Tr and S to the server for a search query with keyword w.
6. **Retrieve**(Tr, S, $\{CW_i\}$, $\{\Delta_i\}$) → (RST, PRF): The cloud server run the retrieve algorithm which consists of two steps **Direct** and **Test**. Through the **Direct** step, the input aggregate trapdoor Tr is transform to several Tr_i for each $i \in S$. Each Tr_i is an actual trapdoor for the keyword search operation over the i-th document set. Using a Tr_i, the server performs **Test** to determine whether the ciphertext of the keyword is cw where $cw \in CW_i$. After finishes all operations, the algorithm first outputs a result set RST which consists

of each rst_i where $i \in S$. A rst_i is a result over the i-th document set, and contains each identity of the set's document where the queried keyword is existed. Note that a rst_i could be empty. The algorithm also outputs a proof set PRF which is for the following verification and consists of each prf_i where $i \in S$.

7. **Verify**$_{ak}(w, S, RST, PRF) \rightarrow ACC$: After receive a result set RST which has any empty member, this algorithm is run by the user who holds an aggregate key ak to verify whether each "empty" is true or caused by a selfish behaviour. If S is out of the scope of the key ak, then the output is $\bot$. Using ak, the algorithm takes the document sets S, the set RST, and a proof set PRF as input, then outputs a set ACC of acc_i where $i \in S$. A bit acc_i is 1 if the verification proofs that the keyword w exists in the i-th document set, and 0 otherwise. Note that the user will reject a rst_i if the corresponding acc_i is 1, and accept otherwise.

3.3 Requirement Definition

The VSEAK scheme introduced in the previous section provides guidance to designing a concrete construction. Further, a valid VSEAK construction must satisfy several functional, security, and efficiency requirements.

The *correctness* enables a user to generate desired trapdoors for any given keyword for searching encrypted document sets, and accepts with large probability if all the three parties are honest. The *query privacy* allows that the user may ask an untrusted cloud server to search for a sensitive word without revealing the word to the server. The *controllability* of the scheme means that the adversary cannot search for an arbitrary word and verify its existence without the data owner's authorization.

Definition 2 (*CORRECTNESS*). *A $\mathcal{VSE}$ is correct if it satisfies that if for any document sets S and keyword w, $(pk, sk) \leftarrow \textbf{KeyGen}$, $(\Delta_i, CW_i) \leftarrow \textbf{Encrypt}_{pk}(i, W_i)$, $ak \leftarrow \textbf{Share}_{sk}(S)$, $Tr \leftarrow \textbf{Trapdoor}_{ak}(w)$, $(RST, PRF) \leftarrow \textbf{Retrieve}(Tr, S, \{CW_i\}, \{\Delta_i\})$, $ACC \leftarrow \textbf{Verify}_{ak}(w, S, RST, PRF)$, and 1) one document doc_j of i-th set in S contains the keyword w, then $j \in rst_i$; or 2) no document of i-th set in S, then acc_i is 1 with large probability.*

Definition 3 (*QUERY PRIVACY*). *A $\mathcal{VSE}$ is query private if it satisfies that if for any keyword w and adversary $\mathcal{A}$ running in PPT, $(pk, sk) \leftarrow \textbf{KeyGen}$, $(\Delta_i, CW_i) \leftarrow \textbf{Encrypt}_{pk}(i, W_i)$, $ak \leftarrow \textbf{Share}_{sk}(S)$, and $Tr \leftarrow \textbf{Trapdoor}_{ak}(w)$, then the $Pr[\mathcal{A}(params, pk, S, Tr, \{CW_i\}, \{\Delta_i\}) = w]$ is negligible.*

Definition 4 (*CONTROLLABILITY*). *A $\mathcal{VSE}$ is controllable if it satisfies that if for any keyword w in any j-th keyword group W_j $(pk, sk) \leftarrow \textbf{KeyGen}$, $(\Delta_i, CW_i) \leftarrow \textbf{Encrypt}_{pk}(i, W_i)$, $ak \leftarrow \textbf{Share}_{sk}(\{1, ..., j-1, j+1, ..., n\})$, $\textbf{Trapdoor}_{ak}(w)$, $(RST, PRF) \leftarrow \textbf{Retrieve}(Tr, \{j\}, \{CW_j\}, \{\Delta_j\})$, and $ACC \leftarrow \textbf{Verify}_{ak}(w, \{j\}, RST, PRF)$, then RST is empty and ACC is $\bot$.*

The *compactness* of the scheme is to ensure the size of the aggregate key to be independent of the number of document sets to be shared. For the *effectiveness*, the time to generate a trapdoor and verify results must be smaller than the time to retrieve over the appreciate document sets.

Definition 5 *(COMPACTNESS). A VSEAK scheme $\mathcal{VSE}$ is compact if for any m where $S = \{docs_i\}_{i=1}^m$, **Share**$_{sk}(S)$ outputs a single aggregate key which is fixed-length.*

Definition 6 *(EFFECTIVENESS). A $\mathcal{VSE}$ is effective if for any keyword w and valid S, the time required for **Trapdoor**$_{ak}(w)$ plus the time require for **Verify**$_{ak}(w, S, RST, PRF)$ is $o(T)$, where T is the time required to retrieve.*

4 Construction

4.1 Overview

In our construction, in order to generate an valid single aggregate key instead of original massive keys, the aggregate key should be created by embedding the owner's secret key and the operation scale. Then, for a user, it is very easy to generate an aggregate trapdoor about keyword w using the key. To meet the effectiveness, we pass most actual trapdoor generating tasks to the cloud server without loss of the privacy, and thus the server can finish retrieving correctly. Moreover, the aggregate key can be also used as a token to verify the search results. In this construction, we choose the Bloom filter as a verification tool.

4.2 Design of the Scheme

Based on the scheme described in Sect. 3.2, we propose a concrete construction as follows.

1. **ParamGen**$(1^\lambda, n) \to params$:
   The *system* will run this algorithm to initialize system parameters as follows:
   - Generate a bilinear map group system $\mathcal{B}=(p, \mathcal{G}, \mathcal{G}_1, e(\cdot, \cdot))$, where p is the order of $\mathcal{G}$ and $2^\lambda \le p \le 2^{\lambda+1}$;
   - Set n as the maximum possible number of documents which belongs to a data owner;
   - Pick a random generator $g \in \mathcal{G}$ and a random $\alpha \in \mathbb{Z}_p$, and computes $g_i = g^{(\alpha^i)} \in \mathcal{G}$ for $i = \{1, 2, \cdots, n, n + 2, \cdots, 2n\}$;
   - Choose a one-way hash function $H_0: \{0, 1\}^* \to \mathcal{G}$;
   - Choose m as the maximum length of Bloom filters;
   - Choose k independent universal hash functions; $H_1', \cdots, H_k'$ which are used to construct a m-bit Bloom filter, and let another one-way hash function $H_1: \mathcal{G}_1 \to \{0, 1\}^m$ be a secure pseudo-random generator.
   The output is the system parameters $params = (\mathcal{B}, (g, g_1, \cdots, g_n, g_{n+2}, \ldots, g_{2n}), H_0, H_1, \{H_1', \cdots, H_k'\})$.

2. **KeyGen** $\rightarrow$ (pk, sk):
Each data owner runs this algorithm to generate his/her key pair. It chooses a random $\gamma \in \mathbb{Z}_p$, and outputs:

$$pk = g^\gamma, sk = \gamma.$$

3. **Encrypt**$_{pk}(i, W_i) \rightarrow (\Delta_i, CW_i)$:
This algorithm takes as input the file index $i \in \{1, ..., n\}$, and:
   - randomly chooses a $t \in \mathbb{Z}_p$ as the actual searchable encryption key k_i of this document set;
   - generates a Bloom filter for this document set's keyword set W_i by computing:
$$BF_i = \textbf{BFGen}(\{H'_1, \cdots, H'_k\}, W_i);$$
   - randomly chooses a $M \in \mathcal{G}_1$ and generates a public auxiliary value Δ_i associated with the owner's himself/herself for k_i and M by computing:

$$c_1 = g^t, c_2 = (v \cdot g_i)^t,$$

$$c_3 = H_1(M) \oplus BF_i, c_4 = M \cdot e(g_1, g_n)^t;$$

   - for each keyword w in this set's keyword set W_i, computes its ciphertext cw as:
$$cw = e(g, H_0(w))^t / e(g_1, g_n)^t.$$

Finally, The algorithm outputs (Δ_i, CW_i).

4. **Share**$_{sk}(S) \rightarrow ak$:
For any subset $S \subseteq \{1, \cdots, n\}$ which contains the indices of document sets, this algorithm takes as input the owner's secret key sk and outputs the aggregate key ak by computing:

$$ak = \Pi_{j \in S} g_{n+1-j}^{sk}.$$

5. **Trapdoor**$_{ak}(w) \rightarrow Tr$:
Using the ak, the user runs this algorithm to generate a trapdoor of keyword w. All document sets which are relevant to the aggregate key ak are also relevant to the trapdoor. The algorithm computes and outputs:

$$Tr = ak \cdot H_0(w).$$

6. **Retrieve**$(Tr, S, \{CW_i\}, \{\Delta_i\}) \rightarrow (RST, PRF)$:
The two steps are designed as follow, and each Δ_i has its (c_1, c_2, c_3, c_4).
Direct$(Tr, i, S) \rightarrow Tr_i$:
This step is to produce a actual trapdoor for the document set with index $i \in S$. The trapdoor Tr_i is generated by computing:

$$Tr_i = Tr \cdot pub_i$$

where $pub_i = \Pi_{j \in S, j \neq i} g_{n+1-j+i}$.
Test$(Tr_i, cw, \Delta_i) \rightarrow \delta$:

This step is to test whether the ciphertext cw is encrypted from the queried keyword w whose the i-th actual trapdoor is Tr_i from the **Direct**. Judge

$$cw \overset{?}{==} e(Tr_i, c_1)/e(pub_0, c_2)$$

where $pub_0 = \Pi_{j \in S} g_{n+1-j}$, to decide whether δ is *true* or *false*.

Taking keyword ciphertext sets $\{CW_i\}$ and auxiliary sets $\{\Delta_i\}$ of S, the **Retrieve** algorithm executes as follow:

- For each $i \in S$, compute $Tr_i \leftarrow$ **Direct**(Tr, i, S);
- For each $i \in S$, compute

$$p_1 = c_4 \cdot e(pub_i, c_1)/e(pub_0, c_2),$$

and set $p_2 = c_1$, $p_3 = c_3$, and $prf_i = (p_1, p_2, p_3)$;
- Reset the set RST, and for each $i \in S$, compute rst_i:

for each keyword ciphertext $cw \in CW_i$, compute $\delta \leftarrow$ **Test**(Tr_i, cw, Δ_i), and add the identity of the corresponding document to rst_i if δ is true.

Finally, the algorithm outputs a pair of set (RST, PRF) indicating the search result and proof over each document set in S. In this scheme, for efficiency consideration, the PRF and series of pub for the set S can be computed only once.

7. **Verify**$_{ak}(w, S, RST, PRF) \rightarrow ACC$:

This algorithm takes as input the set S, the testing keyword w, and the received pair (RST, PRF), and then executes:

- For each $i \in S$, compute acc_i:

compute $M' = p_1 \cdot e(ak, p_2)$;

recover the i-th Bloom filter by computing:

$$BF'_i = H_1(M') \oplus p_3;$$

once there is any BF'_i cannot be recovered, break and output $\bot$; verifies the keyword w's existence:

$$acc_i \leftarrow \neg \mathbf{BFVerify}(\{H'_1, \cdots, H'_k\}, BF'_i, w).$$

The algorithm outputs ACC which is a set of acc_i.

4.3 Analysis

We assume that the public cloud is "semi-honest-but-curious" (described in Sect. 1.1). We also assume that the authorized users may try to access data either within or out of the scopes of their privileges. Moreover, communication channels involving the public cloud are assumed to be insecure naturally.

Theorem 1. *The proposed construction is correct.*

Proof: Theorem 1 is equivalent to the correctness (described 'in Sect. 3.3) of both the keyword search function and the verification function. After receiving the submitted single trapdoor Tr, the cloud server can execute VSEAK.$Retrieve$ algorithm to conduct the test on each keyword group. We can see that:

$$e(Tr_i, c_1)/e(pub_0, c_2) = \frac{e(ak \cdot \Pi_{j \in S, j \neq i} g_{n+1-j+i} \cdot H_0(w), g^t)}{e(\Pi_{j \in s} g_{n+1-j}, (v \cdot g_i)^t)}$$

$$= \frac{e(ak, g^t) \cdot e(\Pi_{j \in S, j \neq i} g_{n+1-j+i} \cdot H_0(w), g^t)}{e(\Pi_{j \in s} g_{n+1-j}, g^{sk^t}) \cdot e(\Pi_{j \in S} g_{n+1-j}, (g_i)^t)}$$

$$= \frac{e(\Pi_{j \in S, j \neq i} g_{n+1-j+i} \cdot H_0(w), g^t)}{e(\Pi_{j \in s} g_{n+1-j}, (g_i)^t)} = \frac{e(\Pi_{j \in S, j \neq i} g_{n+1-j+i}, g^t) \cdot e(H_0(w), g^t)}{e(\Pi_{j \in S} g_{n+1-j+i}, g^t)}$$

$$= \frac{e(H_0(w), g^t) \cdot \frac{e(\Pi_{j \in s} g_{n+1-j+i}, g^t)}{e(g_{n+1}, g^t)}}{e(\Pi_{j \in s} g_{n+1-j+i}, g^t)} = \frac{e(H_0(w), g^t)}{e(g_{n+1}, g^t)} = \frac{e(H_0(w), g)^t}{e(g_1, g_n)^t} = cw \quad (1)$$

So, the user with the aggregate key can perform a successful keyword search.

To get a Bloom filter, the user can decrypt corresponding ciphertext of the i-th document in the S via the aggregate key. For correctness, the M is get by:

$$p_1 \cdot e(ak \cdot p_2) = c_4 \cdot e(ak \cdot pub_i, c_1)/e(pub_0, c_2)$$

$$= \frac{c_4 \cdot e(ak \cdot \Pi_{j \in S, j \neq i} g_{n+1-j+i}, g^t)}{e(\Pi_{j \in S} g_{n+1-j}, (v \cdot g_i)^t)} = \frac{c_4 \cdot e(ak, g^t) \cdot e(\Pi_{j \in S, j \neq i} g_{n+1-j+i}, g^t)}{e(\Pi_{j \in S} g_{n+1-j}, (v \cdot g_i)^t)}$$

$$= \frac{c_4 \cdot e(ak, g^t) \cdot e(\Pi_{j \in S, j \neq i} g_{n+1-j+i}, g^t)}{e(\Pi_{j \in S} g_{n+1-j}, g^{sk^t}) \cdot e(\Pi_{j \in S} g_{n+1-j}, (g_i)^t)} = \frac{c_4 \cdot e(\Pi_{j \in S, j \neq i} g_{n+1-j+i}, g^t)}{e(\Pi_{j \in S} g_{n+1-j}, (g_i)^t)}$$

$$= \frac{c_4 \cdot e(\Pi_{j \in S, j \neq i} g_{n+1-j+i}, g^t)}{e(\Pi_{j \in S} g_{n+1-j+i}, g^t)} = \frac{c_4 \cdot \frac{e(\Pi_{j \in s} g_{n+1-j+i}, g^t)}{e(g_{n+1}, g^t)}}{e(\Pi_{j \in s} g_{n+1-j+i}, g^t)}$$

$$= \frac{M \cdot e(g_1, g_n)^t}{e(g_{n+1}, g^t)} = \frac{M \cdot e(g_1, g_n)^t}{e(g_1, g_n)^t} = M \quad (2)$$

After get M, the user can easily recover the Bloom filter BF_i from the third component of Δ_i by computing: $BF_i = H_1(M) \oplus c_3$.

Finally, the existing of w can be verified via the algorithm **BFVerify**, and thus whether the server just perform a part of search operations is known. So, the user with the aggregate key can perform a successful verification.   □

Theorem 2. *The proposed construction is controllable.*

Proof: The controllability (described in Sect. 3.3) can be derived from the following lemmas: □

Lemma 1. *Even the cloud server colludes with a malicious authorized user, they are unable to perform any keyword search and result verification over any document out of the scope of his/her aggregate key.*

Proof: In the case of collusion, an attacker $\mathcal{A}$ may have the knowledge of both a curious cloud server and a malicious authorized user. This kind of attacker may try to perform keyword search over a document not in the scope of his/her aggregate key. From the Eq. 1, we can see that if pub_0 is generated by a wrong set S', the expression $e(ak, g^t)$ will be equal to the expression $e(pub_0, v^t)$ (that is $e(\Pi_{j \in s} g_{n+1-j}, g^{sk^t})$), and they cannot cancel out of the equation. So, the pub_i must be computed by the same set S of the aggregate key. Based on the above-mentioned fact, after receiving the single trapdoor Tr, the attacker may take a target set S' as the input of VSEAK.**Retrieve.Direct** step to generate the actual trapdoor, but for the reason that pub_0 must be computed by the set S, such that the VSEAK.**Retrieve.Test** step will output *false* for any document set with index $i \notin S$.

The verification controllability is similar. The Eq. 2 shows that if pub_0 is generated by a wrong set S', the expression $e(ak, g^t)$ will be equal to the expression $e(pub_0, v^t)$, and they cannot cancel out of the equation to get M. Thus, the attacker may take the index i' of a document set in the target set S' as the input of VSEAK.**Verify** algorithm to test what keyword exists in such a document, but for the reason that pub_0 must be computed by the set S, such that the VSEAK.**Verify** algorithm will output the wrong result for any document set with index $i \notin S$. □

Lemma 2. *An attacker is unable to produce the new aggregate key for any new set of documents from the known aggregate key.*

Proof: A malicious user $\mathcal{A}$ that owns an aggregate key ak of a set of document sets S from an owner, always tries to generate a new aggregate key for the set S' $(S' \nsubseteq S)$ of the same owner. To achieve the goal, $\mathcal{A}$ should compute the value of g_{n+1-j}^{sk} for any $j \in S'$. Although $\mathcal{A}$ has obtained the $ak = \Pi_{j \in s} g_{n+1-j}^{sk}$, he still cannot get any multiplier from the product, and each multiplier is protected by the owner's secret key sk. According to the assumption in Sect. 2.1, $\mathcal{A}$ is unable to generate the new key. □

Theorem 3. *The proposed construction can achieve the goal of query privacy (described in Sect. 3.3).*

Proof: The cloud server can obtain the stored keyword ciphertexts and auxiliary values $\{\Delta_i\}$. A malicious authorized user, who can have an aggregate key ak with privileges over a set of documents of an owner. Theorem 3 can be deduced from the following lemmas: □

Lemma 3. *An attacker is unable to determine a keyword in a query from the submitted trapdoor nor the VSEAK.**Retrieve.Direct** step.*

Proof: Since an attacker $\mathcal{A}$ wants to determine a keyword in a query after getting the submitted trapdoor $Tr = ak \cdot H_0(w)$, $\mathcal{A}$ must guess the aggregate key ak to succeed. In the view of $\mathcal{A}$, the public information is (1) the system parameters *params* and the set S. However, to obtain the ak, for each $j \in S$, the attacker $\mathcal{A}$ must compute the g_{n+1-j}^{sk}. Because sk is the owner's secret master key, whose leakage is not considered, $\mathcal{A}$ can only have a negligible probability to get it.

Alternatively, the VSEAK.**Retrieve.Direct** step executing in cloud server only involves a product of some public information, i.e., $Tr_i = Tr \cdot \Pi_{j \in s, j \neq i} g_{n+1-j+i}$. Since multipliers are all public, this algorithm provides no help for the attacker to determine a keyword in the trapdoor. Above all, a successful attack cannot be launched in this case. $\qquad\qquad\square$

Lemma 4. *An attacker is unable to determine a keyword in a document from the stored keyword ciphertexts and the related public information.*

Proof: The curious server $\mathcal{A}$ could try to learn something from the stored encrypted data. With the knowledge of $params$, (c_1, c_2, c_3, c_4), and cw, $\mathcal{A}$ may try to launch three kinds of attacks as follows:

1. Retrieve the value of t from the known c_1 or c_2. However, the discrete logarithm problem means $\mathcal{A}$ cannot compute the value of t in this case.
2. Compute the value of $e(g_1, g_n)^t$. Notice that $\mathcal{A}$ can get the value of $e(g, H_0(w))^t$ by computing $e(c_1, H_0(w))$, so when he gets the value of $e(g_1, g_n)^t$, he will determine whether keyword w is in the cw of the target document set. To obtain $e(g_1, g_n)^t$, $\mathcal{A}$ will compute $e(c_1, g_{n+1})$. However, because $params$ is missing the term $g_{n+1} = g^{a^{n+1}}$, the attacker $\mathcal{A}$ cannot finish this computation. In fact, this result is ensured by the assumption of the intractability of BDHE problem.
3. Reveal the content of a document via the verification function. However, such an attack is not feasible. First, retrieving the value of BF_i from the known c_3 is very hard while H_1 is good enough for application. Moreover, the above fact prevents retrieving the value of M from the known c_4.

As a result, $\mathcal{A}$ cannot learn any useful content from the stored information. $\quad\square$

Remark. Our construction clearly achieves constant-size keyword ciphertexts, trapdoors, and aggregate keys.

5 Performance Evaluation

5.1 Overview

Since the performance is highly dependent on the basic cryptographic operations in the pairing computation, we use two cryptographic libraries: (1) *jpbc* library is to implement cryptographic operations running in mobile smartphone; (2) *pbc* library is to implement cryptographic operations running in computer. Since the generation algorithms of the aggregate key and the trapdoor only contain operations on $\mathcal{G}$, we choose the Type-A pairing to speed up them. In addition, we adopt MD5 to implement hash functions in each Bloom filter for the verification. The two different platforms are: one is in Java on *Samsung G3502U* phone with Android OS 5.0, the other is in C++ on Computer of Intel(R) Core(TM)i5-3337U CPU @ 1.80 GHZ with Windows7 OS.

There are some useful experiment results [21,22] about pairing computation. Table 1 lists the average time of pairing computation in each platform. Obviously, in computers, the average times of pairing and *pow* computation are much faster.

Table 1. Execution times of type A pairing computation (ms)

	Pairing	pow(in $\mathcal{G}$)	pow(in $\mathcal{G}_1$)
Mobile Devices	487	244	72
Computer	10.0	12.9	1.6

5.2 Evaluation of VSEAK Algorithms

Considering that the algorithms and their steps including VSEAK.**ParamGen**, VSEAK.**Retrieve.Direct** and VSEAK.**Retrieve.Test** are only run in the cloud server, only the execution times in computer are tested. As shown in Fig. 3, we can see that:

1. The execution time of VSEAK.**ParamGen** is linear in the maximum number of document sets belonging to one owner, and when the maximum number grows up to 30000, it is reasonable that VSEAK.**ParamGen** algorithm only needs 397 s.
2. The execution time of VSEAK.**Encrypt** is linear in the number of keywords in a document set, and when the number grows up to 4000, VSEAK.**Encrypt** algorithm only needs 166 s in computers, but 8018 s in mobile devices.
3. The execution time of VSEAK.**Share** is linear in the number of shared document sets, and when the number grows up to 15000, VSEAK.**Share** algorithm only needs 200 s in computer, but 3610 s in mobile devices. Because the KASE.**Share** always runs along with the VSEAK.**Encrypt**, it is not suggested to be executed in the mobile devices.

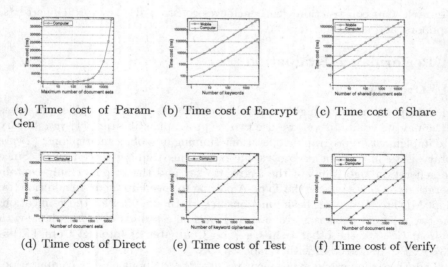

(a) Time cost of Param- (b) Time cost of Encrypt (c) Time cost of Share
Gen

(d) Time cost of Direct   (e) Time cost of Test   (f) Time cost of Verify

Fig. 3. Time cost of VSEAK algorithms

4. The execution time of VSEAK.**Retrieve.Direct** is linear in the number of document sets. In fact, the mathematical operation in VSEAK.**Retrieve. Direct** is the i multiplication in $\mathcal{G}$, where i is the index of a document set in someone subset of a owner's. When the number grows up to 10000, it will take 235 s.
5. The execution time of VSEAK.**Retrieve.Test** is linear in the number of keyword ciphertexts. In fact, the mathematical operation in VSEAK.**Retrieve. Test** is pairing computations. When the number grows up to 30000, it will take 701 s.
6. In order to reduce the error of Bloom filter, we assume that there are about 1000 keywords in each document, and set $k = 30$. The execution time of VSEAK.**Verify** with one keyword w is linear in the number of document sets. In fact, the main repeatedly mathematical operation in VSEAK.**Verify** is running the **BFVerify** algorithm to test whether w is in each keyword group. When the number grows up to 10000, the algorithm only needs 16.4 s in computer, but 316 s in mobile devices.

6   Conclusion

Considering two practical problem of privacy-preserving data sharing system, we propose the scheme of verifiable searchable encryption with aggregate keys (VSEAK) and give a concrete construction. By reducing the number of both keyword search keys and verification tokens, our proposal is remarkably facilitates client-side users. Finally, our evaluation of the performance demonstrates the construction's efficiency. Our future work is to design an algorithm to reduce the number of trapdoors and auxiliary values under the multi-owners setting.

Acknowledgement. This work was supported by the National Key Basic Research Program of China (No. 2013CB834204), National Natural Science Foundation of China (Nos. 61272423, 61300241, and 61472091), Natural Science Foundation of Guangdong Province for Distinguished Young Scholars (2014A030306020), and Distinguished Young Scholars Fund of Department of Education(No. Yq2013126), Guangdong Province.

References

1. Kamara, S., Lauter, K.: Cryptographic cloud storage. In: Sion, R., Curtmola, R., Dietrich, S., Kiayias, A., Miret, J.M., Sako, K., Sebé, F. (eds.) RLCPS, WECSR, and WLC 2010. LNCS, vol. 6054, pp. 136–149. Springer, Heidelberg (2010)
2. Bellare, M., Boldyreva, A., O'Neill, A.: Deterministic and efficiently searchable encryption. In: Menezes, A. (ed.) CRYPTO 2007. LNCS, vol. 4622, pp. 535–552. Springer, Heidelberg (2007)
3. Kamara, S., Papamanthou, C., Roeder, T.: Dynamic searchable symmetric encryption. In: Proceedings of the 2012 ACM Conference on Computer and Communications Security, pp. 965–976 (2012)

4. Boneh, D., Di Crescenzo, G., Ostrovsky, R., Persiano, G.: Public key encryption with keyword search. In: Cachin, C., Camenisch, J.L. (eds.) EUROCRYPT 2004. LNCS, vol. 3027, pp. 506–522. Springer, Heidelberg (2004)

5. Hwang, Y.-H., Lee, P.J.: Public key encryption with conjunctive keyword search and its extension to a multi-user system. In: Takagi, T., Okamoto, T., Okamoto, E., Okamoto, T. (eds.) Pairing 2007. LNCS, vol. 4575, pp. 2–22. Springer, Heidelberg (2007)

6. Li, J., Wang, Q., Wang, C., Cao, N., Ren, K., Lou, W.: Fuzzy keyword search over encrypted data in cloud computing. In: 2010 Proceedings IEEE INFOCOM, pp. 1–5 (2010)

7. Chai, Q., Gong, G.: Verifiable symmetric searchable encryption for semi-honest-but-curious cloud servers. In: 2012 IEEE International Conference on Communications (ICC), pp. 917–922 (2012)

8. Chu, C.-K., Chow, S.S.M., Tzeng, W.-G., Zhou, J., Deng, R.H.: Key-aggregate cryptosystem for scalable data sharing in cloud storage. IEEE Trans. Parallel Distrib. Syst. **25**(2), 468–477 (2014)

9. Cui, B., Liu, Z., Wang, L.: Key-aggregate searchable encryption for group data sharing via cloud storage. IEEE Trans. Comput. **PP**(99), 1 (2015)

10. Zhao, F., Nishide, T., Sakurai, K.: Multi-user keyword search scheme for secure data sharing with fine-grained access control. In: Kim, H. (ed.) ICISC 2011. LNCS, vol. 7259, pp. 406–418. Springer, Heidelberg (2012)

11. Dong, C., Russello, G., Dulay, N.: Shared and searchable encrypted data for untrusted servers. In: Atluri, V. (ed.) DAS 2008. LNCS, vol. 5094, pp. 127–143. Springer, Heidelberg (2008)

12. Liu, X., Zhang, Y., Wang, B., Yan, J.: Mona: secure multi-owner data sharing for dynamic groups in the cloud. IEEE Trans. Parallel Distrib. Syst. **24**(6), 1182–1191 (2013)

13. Shucheng, Y., Wang, C., Ren, K., Lou, W.: Achieving secure, scalable, and fine-grained data access control in cloud computing. In: 2010 Proceedings IEEE INFOCOM, pp. 1–9 (2010)

14. Zheng, Q., Shouhuai, X., Ateniese, G.: Vabks: Verifiable attribute-based keyword search over outsourced encrypted data. In: 2014 Proceedings IEEE, INFOCOM, pp. 522–530 (2014)

15. Sun, W., Yu, S., Lou, W., Hou, T., Li, H.: Protecting your right: Verifiable attribute-based keyword search with fine-grainedowner-enforced search authorization in the cloud. IEEE Trans. Parallel Distrib. Syst. **PP**(99), 1 (2014)

16. Benabbas, S., Gennaro, R., Vahlis, Y.: Verifiable delegation of computation over large datasets. In: Rogaway, P. (ed.) CRYPTO 2011. LNCS, vol. 6841, pp. 111–131. Springer, Heidelberg (2011)

17. Fiore, D., Gennaro, R.: Publicly verifiable delegation of large polynomials and matrix computations, with applications. In: Proceedings of the 2012 ACM Conference on Computer and Communications Security, pp. 501–512 (2012)

18. Fiore, D., Gennaro, R., Pastro, V.: Efficiently verifiable computation on encrypted data. In: Proceedings of the 2014 ACM SIGSAC Conference on Computer and Communications Security, pp. 844–855 (2014)

19. Lewko, A., Waters, B.: New proof methods for attribute-based encryption: achieving full security through selective techniques. In: Safavi-Naini, R., Canetti, R. (eds.) CRYPTO 2012. LNCS, vol. 7417, pp. 180–198. Springer, Heidelberg (2012)

20. Sun, W., Wang, B., Cao, N., Li, M., Lou, W., Hou, Y.T., Li, H.: Verifiable privacy-preserving multi-keyword text search in the cloud supporting similarity-based ranking. IEEE Trans. Parallel Distrib. Syst. **25**(11), 3025–3035 (2014)
21. Oliveira, L.B., Aranha, D.F., Morais, E., Daguano, F., Lopez, J., Dahab, R.: Tinytate: computing the tate pairing in resource-constrained sensor nodes. In: Sixth IEEE International Symposium on Network Computing and Applications, pp. 318–323 (2007)
22. Li, M., Lou, W., Ren, K.: Data security and privacy in wireless body area networks. IEEE Wirel. Commun. **17**(1), 51–58 (2010)

Public Key Encryption with Authorized Keyword Search

Peng Jiang[1,2(✉)], Yi Mu[2], Fuchun Guo[2], and Qiaoyan Wen[1]

[1] State Key Laboratory of Networking and Switching Technology,
Beijing University of Posts and Telecommunications, Beijing 100876, China
wqy@bupt.edu.cn
[2] Centre for Computer and Information Security Research,
School of Computing and Information Technology, University of Wollongong,
Wollongong, NSW 2522, Australia
{pj688,ymu,fuchun}@uow.edu.au

Abstract. Public key encryption with keyword search (PEKS) provides an elegant mechanism for a user to identify the specific encrypted data. PEKS protects data against disclosure while making it searchable. In this paper, we propose a new cryptographic primitive called public key encryption with authorized keyword search (PEAKS). In PEAKS, keywords are encrypted with one public key and users without corresponding secret key need authorization from the authority to search keywords. We present a concrete PEAKS construction which allows the authority to authorize users to search different keyword sets. The proposed scheme features with the constant-size authorized token, independent of the size of keyword set size, which cuts down bandwidth consumption considerably. This property makes our PEAKS quite useful when the authorized token needs to be frequently updated with time for security purpose. The semantical security against chosen keyword attack and trapdoor unforgeability are formally proved.

Keywords: Encrypted keyword search · Public key encryption · Low bandwidth

1 Introduction

Efficient data retrieval and data mining become more difficult with coming of big data era. One of the instructive methods is that the user downloads and decrypts all the encrypted data to search for his interested one. This method could consume considerable communication bandwidth and computational resources. Another way is that the user employs a server to execute the decryption operation with the secret key and return target data. However, this method could compromise data privacy.

Boneh et al. [5] introduced the notion of public key encryption with keyword search (PEKS) to search encrypted data. PEKS solves the above problems and avoids complicated key management of symmetric searchable encryption [22].

© Springer International Publishing Switzerland 2016
J.K. Liu and R. Steinfeld (Eds.): ACISP 2016, Part II, LNCS 9723, pp. 170–186, 2016.
DOI: 10.1007/978-3-319-40367-0_11

In PEKS, a sender uploads the encrypted data with the searchable ciphertext. The user produces the trapdoor associated with some keyword to the server for searching. Then the server returns corresponding encrypted data to the receiver when the keyword in trapdoor is identical to that in searchable ciphertext.

The searchable ciphertext of PEKS is generated using a specific user's public key and only one entity (secret key owner) can search. In the scenario of an enterprise, many employees are required holding the search right over the encrypted keyword based on the enterprise's public key. By PEKS, each employee has to be given the enterprise's secret key to create trapdoors. This trivial solution suffers from key abuse and also has limitations. For example, each employee might be at a different access level and can only search some keywords. The possible solution is that the authority (i.e. manager) keeps the enterprise's secret key and authorizes the certain search right to each employee. The authority sets an authorized keyword set to each employee, who can search the keywords given in the authorized keyword set. A potential solution is to allow the authority to generate the authorized token for each authorized keyword. For security purpose, each authorized token only works for a short time interval and the authority needs to re-authorize a token for an online employee when the time expires. The process needs to be repeated for each online employee at a new time interval. Unfortunately, this approach could consume significant bandwidth. How to effectively authorize the keyword search becomes an important problem needed to be addressed.

Contribution. The contributions of this paper are twofold. First, we propose a new notion named public key encryption with authorized keyword search (PEAKS). In PEAKS, keywords are encrypted with one public key and users without corresponding secret key need authorization from the authority in order to search keywords. Each authorization process is conducted by the authority by issuing an authorized token to the user and updates with time. The authorized user can then search authorized keywords. Second, we construct a provably secure PEAKS scheme which allows the authority to authorize users to search different keyword sets. Authorization process features with the constant-size authorized token independent of the authorized keyword set size. The user can generate the trapdoors for the keyword in this authorized keyword set. The success of a test process relies on: trapdoor freshness, trapdoor authorization and keyword consistency. We formally prove the semantic security against chosen keyword attacks and trapdoor unforgeability.

1.1 Related Work

Song et al. [22] initiated the research on symmetric searchable encryption (SSE), which fails to provide encrypted data sharing to/from other entities. When sharing data, SSE needs to distribute the secret key to users, which is subjected to complicated key distribution/management. SSE have many improvement in performance [9, 10, 16].

Boneh et al. [5] introduced the notion of PEKS to address above weaknesses and presented a concrete scheme. In their scheme, the sender creates the searchable ciphertext using a keyword and user's public key. The user creates a trapdoor using his secret key and keyword and provides the trapdoor to the server for searching. The server returns the corresponding encrypted data to the user only when the keyword in the trapdoor matches the keyword in the ciphertext.

Many PEKS variants have been proposed to improve PEKS since its introduction. Public-key encryption with conjunctive keyword search (PECKS) schemes [2,3,7,17–19] were proposed to improve the query expressiveness. Combinable multi-keyword search using PECKS were achieved in [2,17,18]. Bethencourt et al. [3] presented a public-key encryption scheme with conjunctive keyword range search. Boneh and Waters [7] applied a novel technique named hidden vector encryption (HVE) to achieve conjunctive, range and subset keyword search. Sedghi et al. [19] utilized wildcards to develop the scalability and expression of searching query. PEKS schemes with extensional keywords [1,8] were presented to enhance the database system usability. Abdalla et al. [1] constructed a public key encryption with temporary keyword search (PETKS) scheme based on the universal transformation from anonymous identity-based encryption (AIBE) to PEKS to guarantee consistency. Camenisch et al. [8] proposed the public key encryption with oblivious keyword search (PEOKS) and constructed an authorized private information retrieval (PIR) scheme based on PEOKS. However, PEOKS employed computationally expensive commitment and zero-knowledge proof (ZKP), and their proposed scheme needed the user to download the entire database, which are inefficient and impractical. Data search schemes based on attribute-based encryption (ABE) [21,23,25] were proposed to benefit data search control. Sun et al. [23] designed the attribute-based keyword search scheme with user revocation for multi-user and multi-contributor scenario. Zheng et al. [25] constructed a verifiable attribute-based keyword search (VABKS) scheme to solve the server's faithful searching verification. Shi et al. [21] also presented an ABE-based searchable encryption to support fine-grained search and access control. These schemes focused user identity/attributes control but not keyword control, and keyword privacy would be compromised if directly replacing attribute with keyword. Proxy re-encryption with keyword search (PRES) [12,20,24] was proposed to allow a proxy server to execute the test function and the delegation decryption, which combined the primitives proxy re-encryption (PRE) and PEKS. The authorization based on the keyword was not considered in these PRES schemes.

The generation of short keys have been investigated in some public key encryption schemes [6,11,13–15]. These methods cannot be directly applied to the authorized key for searching due to keyword privacy and trapdoor generation. Therefore, how to achieve constant size authorized token and reduce the bandwidth consumption is a challenging problem during authorization.

Organization. The remainder of the paper is organized as follows. In Sect. 2, we describe the authorized keyword search system with relevant definitions. A PEAKS construction with constant size authorized key is given in Sect. 3 and its security is formally proved in Sect. 4. Finally, we conclude the paper in Sect. 5.

2   Problem Formulation

2.1   System Model

A PEAKS system involves *Sender, Server, Authority* and *User* as illustrated in
Fig. 1. There is only one public/secret key pair (pk, sk) in the system and pk is
published.

- *Sender.* It uploads the encrypted data and encrypted keyword to the server
  for storage and index, where the stored data is possibly available for all system
  users.
- *Authority.* It acts as a manager in the system and keeps sk secret. It re-
  authorizes the online user at a new time by issuing a new authorized token.
- *User.* It generates the trapdoor for some authorized keyword and submits it
  to the server for searching, where only authorized user can generate a valid
  trapdoor.
- *Server.* It executes verification for authorization and keyword matching operation, and decides whether to return the corresponding data to the user. It is
  honest-but-curious, executing the searching operation honestly but inferring
  the keyword from encrypted keyword curiously.

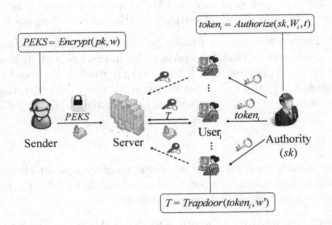

Fig. 1. PEAKS system.

Workflow. A PEAKS system generally provides data indexing service for registered users, where no collusion among users is considered. The uploaded data
from the sender includes encrypted data for sharing and encrypted keyword
$PEKS$ for indexing. The sender generates the searchable ciphertext $PEKS$
with pk and a specific keyword w. To obtain searching right, the user needs the
authorization from the authority. The authority authorizes different keyword set
to different users, where some online user $User_i$ is authorized the keyword set
W_i. For authorized time t, the authority produces the authorized token $token_i$

using sk, W_i, t. Then the authorized user generates the trapdoor with $token$ and w', where $w' \in W$, and submits the trapdoor T to the server. When the received T is verified to be freshly authorized and matches $PEKS$, the server returns the corresponding encrypted data to the user.

2.2 Algorithm Definitions

Definition 1. *A PEAKS scheme consists of the following algorithms.*

Setup(1^k). Taking as input the security parameter 1^k, it outputs the system public key and secret key (pk, sk).

Authorize(sk, W, t). Taking as input the secret key sk, an authorized keyword set W and the authorized time t, it outputs the authorized key ak with its signature σ. Then the authorized token is denoted as $token = (ak, \sigma, t)$.

Encrypt(pk, w_i). Taking as input the public key pk and the keyword w_i, it outputs a searchable ciphertext $PEKS$.

Trapdoor($pk, token, w_i'$). Taking as input the public key pk, the authorized token $token$ and the keyword $w_i' \in W$, it outputs a trapdoor T. Then the trapdoor tuple is denoted as $TT = (T, \sigma, t)$.

Test($pk, PEKS, TT, t'$). Taking as input the public key pk, the searchable ciphertext $PEKS$, the trapdoor tuple TT and the trapdoor-received time t', if $t' \leq t$, σ can be accepted and $w_i = w_i'$, it outputs 1; otherwise, it outputs 0.

Correctness. The correctness of public key encryption with authorized keyword search must satisfy that for system paramters (pk, sk), token $token \leftarrow$ Authorize(sk, W, t), ciphertext $PEKS \leftarrow$ Encrypt(pk, w_i), trapdoor $TT \leftarrow$ Trapdoor($pk, token, w_i'$) and the trapdoor-received time t', if $t' \leq t$, the signature in TT can be verified and $w_i = w_i'$, we can have Test($pk, PEKS, TT, t'$) = 1.

2.3 Security Models

We define two games from terms of semantic security against chosen keyword attacks (SS-CKA) and trapdoor existential unforgeability (T-EUF), respectively. The universal keyword space is assumed to be U.

Semantic Security against Chosen Keyword Attacks. The SS-CKA game follows Boneh et al.'s model [5] and allows the adversary $\mathcal{A}$ to launch the chosen keyword attacks. $\mathcal{A}$ is given some private keys and trapdoors with some restrictions and attempts to distinguish a searchable ciphertext for the keyword w_0 from a ciphertext for the keyword w_1, where he is not allowed to obtain the associated trapdoor. $\mathcal{A}$ plays with the challenger $\mathcal{C}$ as follows.

Init. The adversary $\mathcal{A}$ declares the challenge keyword set $W^* \subseteq U$.

Setup. $\mathcal{C}$ runs Setup algorithm and sends the public key pk to $\mathcal{A}$.

Phase 1. $\mathcal{A}$ performs a polynomially bounded number of queries.

- Authorization Query. $\mathcal{A}$ issues the keyword set $W = U - W^*$ and the authorized time t to $\mathcal{C}$ for authorization query. $\mathcal{C}$ responds the authorized token *token* to $\mathcal{A}$ by running Authorize algorithm.
- Trapdoor Query. $\mathcal{A}$ issues a keyword w_i and the time t to $\mathcal{C}$. $\mathcal{C}$ responds the trapdoor tuple TT to $\mathcal{A}$ by running the Trapdoor algorithm.

Challenge. $\mathcal{A}$ generates two equal length keywords $w_0, w_1 \in W^*$ on which it wants to be challenged. $\mathcal{A}$ did not previously query the authorized token for W^*, or trapdoor for w_0, w_1. $\mathcal{C}$ takes a random bit $b \in \{0, 1\}$ and responds the challenge ciphertext $PEKS_b^*$ to $\mathcal{A}$.

Phase 2. $\mathcal{A}$ continues to ask for the authorization query and the trapdoor query for any keyword for $w_i \neq w_0, w_1$. $\mathcal{C}$ responds as Phase1.

Guess. $\mathcal{A}$ outputs a bit $b' \in \{0, 1\}$ and wins the game if $b' = b$.

Definition 2. *A PEAKS scheme provides semantic security against the chosen keyword attacks if there is no probabilistic polynomial time (PPT) adversary $\mathcal{A}$ who wins the above game with a non-negligible advantage ϵ.*

Trapdoor Existential Unforgeability. This T-EUF game allows an adversary $\mathcal{A}$ to launch the impersonation attack. Clearly, it is hard to prevent the impersonation attack if the adversary is authorized. $\mathcal{A}$ is allowed to query the authorization and the trapdoor with some restrictions and $\mathcal{A}$ attempts to forge a valid trapdoor. $\mathcal{A}$ interacts with the challenger as follows.

Init. The adversary $\mathcal{A}$ declares the challenge keyword set W^*.

Setup. The challenger $\mathcal{C}$ runs the Setup algorithm and sends the public key pk to $\mathcal{A}$.

Query. $\mathcal{A}$ performs a polynomially bounded number of queries.

- Authorization Query. $\mathcal{A}$ issues a keyword set and the authorized time t to $\mathcal{C}$. $\mathcal{C}$ responds the authorized token *token* to $\mathcal{A}$ by running the Authorize algorithm.
- Trapdoor Query. $\mathcal{A}$ issues keyword w_i and t to $\mathcal{C}$. $\mathcal{C}$ responds the trapdoor tuple TT to $\mathcal{A}$ by running the Trapdoor algorithm.

Forgery. $\mathcal{A}$ outputs a trapdoor tuple for keyword set W^* which had not been queried.

Definition 3. *A PEAKS scheme provides the trapdoor unforgeability if there is no PPT adversary $\mathcal{A}$ who can forge a valid trapdoor with a correct signature and time with a non-negligible advantage ϵ.*

2.4   Hard Problems

We present two Multi-Sequence of Exponents Diffie-Hellman (MSE-DH) problems, which are two special cases of the general Diffie-Hellman exponent problems in [4]. The intractability analysis is given in full version.

(n, l)-**MSE-DDH Problem.** Let n be integers and $(p, \mathbb{G}, \mathbb{G}_T, e(\cdot, \cdot))$ be a bilinear map group system. Let g_0, h_0 be the generators of $\mathbb{G}$. Given random coprime polynomials q_1, q_2, q in α with pairwise distinct roots, of respective orders $\deg q_1 = l - 1, \deg q_2 = n - l$ and $\deg q = 1$, as well as several sequences of group elements,

$$
S_1 = \begin{cases}
g_0, & \cdots, & g_0^{\alpha^{n-1}}, & g_0^{\beta_1}, & g_0^{\beta_2}, g_0^{r\beta_1}, \\
g_0^x, & h_0^{\beta_1\beta_2q_2}, h_0^{s\beta_1\beta_2q_1q}, & h_0^{\beta_1q_1q_2q}, & \cdots, h_0^{\beta_1\alpha^{n-1}q_1q_2q}, \\
h_0^{\beta_2q_1q_2q}, & \cdots, & h_0^{\beta_2\alpha^{n-1}q_1q_2q}, & h_0^{s\beta_1q_1q_2q^2}, & \cdots, h_0^{s\beta_1\alpha^{l-2}q_1q_2q^2}, \\
h_0^{s\beta_2q_1q_2q^2}, & \cdots, & h_0^{s\beta_2\alpha^{l-2}q_1q_2q^2},
\end{cases}
$$

and $Z \in \mathbb{G}$, distinguish whether Z is equal to $g_0^{rq_1q_2}$ or a random element of $\mathbb{G}$.

(n, l)-**MSE-CDH Problem.** Let n be integers and g_0 be the generator of group $\mathbb{G}$. Given random coprime polynomials q_1, q_2 in α with pairwise distinct roots, of respective orders $\deg q_1 = l, \deg q_2 = n - l$, as well as several sequences of group elements,

$$
S_2 = \begin{cases}
g_0, & \cdots, g_0^{\alpha^{n-1}}, & g_0^{\beta_1}, & g_0^{\beta_2}, h_0^{\beta_1\beta_2q_1}, & h_0^{\beta_1\beta_2q_2}, \\
g_0^a, & g_0^b, g_0^c, & g_0^{ab}, & g_0^{bc}, g_0^{ac}, \\
h_0^{\beta_1q_1q_2}, & \cdots, h_0^{\beta_1\alpha^{n-1}q_1q_2}, h_0^{\beta_2q_1q_2}, & \cdots, h_0^{\beta_2\alpha^{n-1}q_1q_2},
\end{cases}
$$

where $a, b, c \in \mathbb{Z}_p$, compute $g_0^{abc} \in \mathbb{G}$.

3 Public Key Encryption with Authorized Keyword Search

In this section, we give a concrete PEAKS scheme with its efficiency analysis. Borrowing the property of complementary set, the token in our PEAKS construction achieves constant size, independent of the size of the authorized keyword set. Since focusing on the authorization of negotiated keywords, user revocation is not in our scope and the token from the authority will be only issued to the user with time.

3.1 Bilinear Pairing

Let $\mathbb{G}, \mathbb{G}_T$ be two cyclic groups of the same prime p and a map $e : \mathbb{G} \times \mathbb{G} \to \mathbb{G}_T$ be a bilinear pairing [5].

- Bilinearity: $e(g^a, h^b) = e(g, h)^{ab}$ for all $g, h \in \mathbb{G}$ and $a, b \in \mathbb{Z}_p$.
- Non-degenerate: if $g \in \mathbb{G}$, $e(g, g)$ is a generator of $\mathbb{G}_T$.
- Computability: there exists an efficient algorithm to compute $e(g, h)$ for $g, h \in \mathbb{G}$.

3.2   Construction

Setup(1^k). The system generates the bilinear pairing group $(p, \mathbb{G}, \mathbb{G}_T, e)$ at the security level k. Group generators $g, h \in \mathbb{G}$ and secret values $\alpha, x, \beta_1, \beta_2 \in_R \mathbb{Z}_p$ are selected, and $u_1 = g^{\beta_1}, u_2 = g^{\beta_2}, v_1 = h^{\beta_1}, v_2 = h^{\beta_2}$ are set. Choose two cryptographic one-way hash functions $H_1 : \{0,1\}^* \to \mathbb{Z}_p$ and $H_2 : \{0,1\}^* \to \mathbb{G}$. The universal keyword space is denoted as U with size n. The public/secret key is published/kept by the authority as

$$pk = \left(g, g^\alpha, \cdots, g^{\alpha^{n-1}}, g^x, \{u_i, v_i, v_i^\alpha, \cdots, v_i^{\alpha^{n-1}}\}_{i=1,2}\right),$$

$$sk = (\alpha, x, \beta_1, \beta_2, h).$$

Authorize(sk, W, t). For some online user, we assume that the authority would authorize the keyword set $W(W \subseteq U)$ to it, where the size of W is $l, l \leq n$. For better readability, it first sets polynomials

$$f_1(\alpha) = \prod_{w_j \in U} (\alpha + H_1(w_j)),$$

$$f_2(\alpha) = \prod_{w_j \in W} (\alpha + H_1(w_j)),$$

$$F(\alpha) = \frac{f_1(\alpha)}{f_2(\alpha)} = \prod_{w_j \in U-W} (\alpha + H_1(w_j)).$$

With a time update, the authority will re-authorize the user with a new authorized token. The authority chooses $s \in_R \mathbb{Z}_p$ and generates the authorized key with its signature as

$$ak = h^{\frac{\beta_1 \beta_2}{F(\alpha)}}, \quad \sigma = H_2(ak^s, t)^x,$$

where t is the authorized time. It distributes the authorized token $token = (ak, \sigma, s, t)$ to the user by a secure channel.

Encrypt(pk, w_i). The sender chooses $r, r_1 \in_R \mathbb{Z}_p$ and computes

$$PEKS = \left(C_1 = g^{rf_{1i}(\alpha)}, \quad C_2 = u_1^{r-r_1}, \quad C_3 = u_2^{r_1}\right)$$

as the searchable ciphertext, where $f_{1i}(\alpha) = \frac{f_1(\alpha)}{\alpha+H_1(w_i)}$ for $w_i \in U$, $g^{f_{1i}(\alpha)}$ can be computed from $g, g^\alpha, \cdots, g^{\alpha^{n-1}}$. Then it uploads $PEKS$ to the server.

Trapdoor($pk, token, w_i$). The authorized user computes the trapdoor with the received authorization tuple

$$T = \left(T_1 = ak^s, \quad T_2 = v_1^{sf_{2i}(\alpha)}, \quad T_3 = v_2^{sf_{2i}(\alpha)}\right),$$

where $f_{2i}(\alpha) = \frac{f_2(\alpha)}{\alpha + H_1(w_i)}$ for $w_i \in W$ and $v_1^{f_{2i}(\alpha)}, v_2^{f_{2i}(\alpha)}$ can be computed from $v_1, v_1^\alpha, \cdots, v_1^{\alpha^{n-1}}, v_2, v_2^\alpha, \cdots, v_2^{\alpha^{n-1}}$. Then it sends the trapdoor tuple $TT = (T, \sigma, t)$ to the server for search.

Test$(pk, PEKS, TT, t')$. Upon receiving the tuple (T, σ, t) at the time t', the server first checks whether $t' \leq t$. If so, the trapdoor is in the authorized time. The server verifies the signature by checking

$$e(\sigma, g) \stackrel{?}{=} e(H_2(T_1, t), g^x).$$

If the equation holds, the trapdoor is from an authorized user. Then the server checks

$$e(C_1, T_1) \stackrel{?}{=} e(C_2, T_3) \cdot e(C_3, T_2).$$

If the equation holds, it outputs 1 and the server returns corresponding encrypted data to the authorized user, otherwise, outputs 0.

Correctness. We show that our construction meets the requirements of correctness as we claimed in Sect. 2.2. If the signature in trapdoor is correctly issued by authority, we can verify it by

$$e(\sigma, g) = e(H_2(ak^s, t)^x, g) = e(H_2(ak^s, t), g^x) = e(H_2(T_1, t), g^x).$$

Then if the keywords in the searchable ciphertext $PEKS$ and the trapdoor T are the same, i.e. w_i, we have

$$e(C_1, T_1) = e\left(g^{r \prod_{w_j \in U, j \neq i}(\alpha + H_1(w_j))}, h^{\frac{s\beta_1\beta_2}{\prod_{w_j \in U - W}(\alpha + H_1(w_j))}}\right)$$

$$= e(g, h)^{rs\beta_1\beta_2 \prod_{w_j \in W, j \neq i}(\alpha + H_1(w_j))}$$

$$= e\left(u_1^{r-r_1}, v_2^{s \prod_{w_j \in W, j \neq i}(\alpha + H_1(w_j))}\right) \cdot e\left(u_2^{r_1}, v_1^{s \prod_{w_j \in W, j \neq i}(\alpha + H_1(w_j))}\right)$$

$$= e(C_2, T_3) \cdot e(C_3, T_2).$$

3.3 Efficiency

We analyze the communication cost in different phases, where $|\mathbb{G}|, |\mathbb{G}_T|, |t|$ represent the size of a group element in group $\mathbb{G}, \mathbb{G}_T$ and timestamp t, respectively. The sender runs Encrypt algorithm to upload data. The size of the searchable ciphertext represents the communication cost between the sender and the server. It takes 3 group elements in group $\mathbb{G}$. With a time update, the authority needs to re-authorize an online user with a new authorized token. In each authorization process, the authority issues a constant-size authorized token for a keyword set W. The bandwidth consumption in Authorize phase is mainly dominated by the size of authorized token *token*, which costs 2 group elements in $\mathbb{G}$ and a timestamp, independent of the size of the authorized keyword set W. To retrieve data, user needs to run the Trapdoor algorithm and submit the trapdoor tuple to the server. The bandwidth consumption is mainly due to the size of trapdoor tuple TT, which costs 4 group elements in group $\mathbb{G}$ and a timestamp.

The computational cost is also given in corresponding phases, where exp, mul, h represent the time to compute the modular exponentiation, modular multiplication and the hash function, respectively. In Encrypt phase, it takes the sender $(n + 2)exp + (n - 1)mul$ to generate the ciphertext. With a time update in Authorize phase, the authority computes a token to the user, which costs $3exp + 1h$, independent of the size of the keyword set W. The user needs to pay $(2n + 1)exp + (2n + 2)mul$ in Trapdoor phase to generate the trapdoor for a keyword. The analysis result is listed in Table 1. Due to frequent update of the token with time, the computational cost and communication cost in Authorize phase should get a priority in our PEAKS. Through the above analysis, PEAKS can achieve fast token generation and constant size bandwidth between the authority and the user. The short token is at the expense of $O(n)$ to generate ciphertext and trapdoor, which is a trade-off in this PEAKS and will be considered in future work.

Table 1. Communication Cost.

Phase	Authorize	Encrypt	Trapdoor
Communication Cost	$2|\mathbb{G}| + |t|$	$3|\mathbb{G}|$	$4|\mathbb{G}| + |t|$
Computational Cost	$3exp + 1h$	$(n + 1)exp + (n - 1)mul$	$(2n + 1)exp + (2n - 2)mul$

4   Security Proof

4.1   SS-CKA

Theorem 1. *The proposed PEAKS scheme is semantically secure against chosen keyword attacks in the random oracle if (n, l)-MSE-DDH Problem is hard to solve in probabilistic polynomial time.*

Proof. Suppose there exists a PPT adversary $\mathcal{A}$ in the SS-CKA game, who can attack our scheme with advantage ϵ, we build a simulator $\mathcal{B}$ with advantage ϵ/eq_T against (n, l)-*MSE-DDH Problem*. $\mathcal{B}$'s running time is approximately the same as $\mathcal{A}$'s. The universal keyword space is assume to be U with size n.

Init. The adversary $\mathcal{A}$ declares the challenge keyword set W^* with size l.

Setup. The simulator $\mathcal{B}$ is given a group system $(p, \mathbb{G}, \mathbb{G}_T, e(\cdot, \cdot))$ as input, and the (n, l)-*MSE-DDH* instance $\mathcal{S}_1$. We also have coprime polynomials q_1, q_2, q of respective orders $l - 1, n - l, 1$, with their pairwise distinct roots. $\mathcal{B}$ is further given $Z \in \mathbb{G}$, where Z is either equal to $g_0^{rq_1q_2}$ or to some random element of $\mathbb{G}$. We denote the challenge keyword set as $W^* = \{w_1, \cdots, w_l\}$. $\mathcal{B}$ specifies a keyword $w_\theta \in W^*$. It implicitly sets the polynomials

$$q_1(\alpha) = \prod_{i=1, i \neq \theta}^{l} (\alpha + a_i), \quad q_2(\alpha) = \prod_{i=l+1}^{n} (\alpha + a_i), \quad q(\alpha) = \alpha + a_\theta.$$

For $i \in [1, l], i \neq \theta$, we set $q_{1i}(\alpha) = \dfrac{q_1(\alpha)}{\alpha + a_i}$.

The simulator $\mathcal{B}$ formally sets $g = g_0$, $h = h_0^{q_1 q_2 q}$, and we have

$$\begin{aligned}
u_1 &= g_0^{\beta_1}, & u_2 &= g_0^{\beta_2}, g^x = g_0^x, \\
v_1 &= h_0^{\beta_1 q_1 q_2 q}, \cdots, & v_1^{\alpha^{n-1}} &= h_0^{\beta_1 \alpha^{n-1} q_1 q_2 q}, \\
v_2 &= h_0^{\beta_2 q_1 q_2 q}, \cdots, & v_2^{\alpha^{n-1}} &= h_0^{\beta_2 \alpha^{n-1} q_1 q_2 q}.
\end{aligned}$$

$\mathcal{B}$ sends $\mathcal{A}$ public key

$$pk = \left(g_0, \cdots, g_0^{\alpha^{n-1}}, g_0^x, \{u_i, v_i, \cdots, v_i^{\alpha^{n-1}}\}_{i=1,2} \right).$$

H_1 Query. $\mathcal{B}$ maintains the hash list $L(w_i, h_i)$, which is initially empty. Upon receiving an H_1 query for w_i, if w_i is in the list L, $\mathcal{B}$ returns the corresponding h_i to $\mathcal{A}$. Otherwise, $\mathcal{B}$ sets the hash value h_i as follows.

$$h_i = H_1(w_i) = \begin{cases} a_\theta, & \text{if } w_i = w_\theta, \\ a_i, & \text{if } w_i \neq w_\theta. \end{cases}$$

Then $\mathcal{B}$ adds (w_i, h_i) to the list and returns h_i to $\mathcal{A}$.

H_2 Query. $\mathcal{B}$ maintains the hash list $L'(ak^{s_i}, t_i, r_i, h_i')$, which is initially empty. Upon receiving an H query for (ak^{s_i}, t_i), if it is in the list L', $\mathcal{B}$ returns the corresponding h_i' to $\mathcal{A}$. Otherwise, $\mathcal{B}$ chooses $r_i \in_R \mathbb{Z}_p$ and sets the hash value $h_i' = H_2(ak^{s_i}, t_i) = g_0^{r_i}$. Then $\mathcal{B}$ adds $(ak^{s_i}, t_i, r_i, h_i')$ to the list and returns h_i to $\mathcal{A}$.

Phase 1.

- Authorization Query. $\mathcal{A}$ queries the authorized token for the keyword set $U - W^*$ for the time t_i. To each keyword $w_i \in U - W^*$, let (w_i, h_i) be the corresponding tuples on the L list and we have $h_i = H_1(w_i) = a_i$, where $i \in [l+1, n]$. $\mathcal{B}$ obtains $ak = h_0^{\beta_1 \beta_2 q_2}$, where

$$ak = h^{\frac{\beta_1 \beta_2}{\prod_{w_j \in U - (U - W^*)} (\alpha + H_1(w_j))}} = h_0^{\frac{\beta_1 \beta_2 q_1 q_2 q}{q_1 q}} = h_0^{\beta_1 \beta_2 q_2}.$$

$\mathcal{B}$ chooses $s_i \in_R \mathbb{Z}_p$, let $(ak^{s_i}, t_i, r_i, h_i')$ be the corresponding tuple on the list L', we have $h_i' = H_2(ak^{s_i}, t_i) = g_0^{r_i}$, and the signature is $\sigma = g_0^{x r_i}$. $\mathcal{B}$ responds $token = (ak, \sigma, s_i, t_i)$ to $\mathcal{A}$.

- Trapdoor Query. When $\mathcal{A}$ asks the trapdoor query for the keyword w_i for time t_i. $\mathcal{B}$ performs Trapdoor algorithm and responds to $\mathcal{A}$ with simulated results.

- If $w_i \in U - W^*$, $\mathcal{A}$ can obtain the authorized token with the above Authorization Query and generate the trapdoor by himself.
- If $w_i \in W^*$, $\mathcal{B}$ responds the following trapdoor.
  * If $w_i = w_\theta$, it outputs abort.
  * If $w_i \neq w_\theta$, let (w_i, h_i) be the corresponding tuple on the L list and we have $h_i = H(w_i) = a_i$, where $i \in [1, l], i \neq \theta$. $\mathcal{B}$ chooses $s'' \in_R \mathbb{Z}_p^*$ and computes the trapdoor T as

$$T_1 = \left(h_0^{s\beta_1\beta_2 q_1 q}\right)^{s''}, T_2 = \left(h_0^{s\beta_1 q_1 q_2 q^2 q_{1i}}\right)^{s''}, T_3 = \left(h_0^{s\beta_2 q_1 q_2 q^2 q_{1i}}\right)^{s''},$$

where T_1 is directly from $h_0^{s\beta_1\beta_2 q_1 q}$ and T_2, T_3 can be computed from elements $h_0^{s\beta_1 q_1 q_2 q^2}, \cdots, h_0^{s\beta_1 \alpha^{l-2} q_1 q_2 q^2}, h_0^{s\beta_2 q_1 q_2 q^2}, \cdots, h_0^{s\beta_2 \alpha^{l-2} q_1 q_2 q^2}$ in the (n, l)-*MSE-DDH Problem* instance.

One can verify the trapdoor by implicitly setting $s' = s'' s$, and then

$$T_1 = ak^{s'} = \left(h_0^{\frac{\beta_1\beta_2 q_1 q_2 q}{q_2}}\right)^{s'} = \left(h_0^{s\beta_1\beta_2 q_1 q}\right)^{s''},$$

$$T_2 = v_1^{s'\prod_{w_j \in W, j \neq i}(\alpha + H_1(w_j))} = \left(h_0^{\beta_1 q_1 q_2 q}\right)^{s' q_{1i} q} = \left(h_0^{s\beta_1 q_1 q_2 q^2 q_{1i}}\right)^{s''},$$

$$T_3 = v_2^{s'\prod_{w_j \in W, j \neq i}(\alpha + H_1(w_j))} = \left(h_0^{\beta_2 q_1 q_2 q}\right)^{s' q_{1i} q} = \left(h_0^{s\beta_2 q_1 q_2 q^2 q_{1i}}\right)^{s''}.$$

Let $(ak^{s'}, t_i, r_i, h'_i)$ be the corresponding tuple on the list L', we have $h'_i = H_2(T_1, t_i) = g_0^{r_i}$. The signature is implicitly set $\sigma = g_0^{xr_i}$. $\mathcal{B}$ responds $TT = (T, \sigma, t_i)$ to $\mathcal{A}$.

Challenge. $\mathcal{A}$ produces a pair of keywords $w_0, w_1 \in W^*$ that it wishes to be challenged on and sends (w_0, w_1) to $\mathcal{B}$. $\mathcal{A}$ did not previously query the authorized token for W^*, or the trapdoor for w_0, w_1. $\mathcal{B}$ responds as follows.

- If $w_\theta \notin \{w_0, w_1\}$, $\mathcal{B}$ outputs failure and terminates.
- Otherwise, we have $w_\theta \in \{w_0, w_1\}$. Let (w_θ, h_θ) be the corresponding tuple on the L list and we have $h_\theta = H_1(w_\theta) = a_\theta$. $\mathcal{B}$ chooses $r_1 \in_R \mathbb{Z}_p$ and responds $\mathcal{A}$ with the challenge ciphertext

$$PEKS^* = \left(C_1 = Z, C_2 = g_0^{r\beta_1} u_1^{-r_1}, C_3 = u_2^{r_1}\right).$$

These items can be obtained from the elements in (n, l)-*MSE-DDH* instances. Note that if $Z = g_0^{rq_1 q_2}$, by setting $r' = r$, one can verify that

$$C_1 = g^{r'\prod_{w_j \in U, j \neq \theta}(\alpha + H_1(w_j))} = g_0^{rq_1 q_2} = Z,$$

$$C_2 = u_1^{r'-r_1} = g_0^{\beta_1(r-r_1)} = g_0^{r\beta_1} u_1^{-r_1}, \quad C_3 = u_2^{r_1}.$$

Phase 2. $\mathcal{A}$ continues to ask for the authorization query and the trapdoor query for any keyword for $w_i \neq w_0, w_1$. $\mathcal{C}$ responds as **Phase 1**.

Guess. $\mathcal{A}$ outputs its guess θ' and wins the game if $\theta' = \theta$.

This completes the description of our simulation. If $\mathcal{B}$ does not abort then $|\Pr[\theta' = \theta] - \frac{1}{2}| \geqslant \epsilon$. The probability is over the random bits used by $\mathcal{A}$ and $\mathcal{B}$ as follows, where $\mathcal{B}$'s running time is approximately the same as $\mathcal{A}$'s. According to the above process, a trapdoor query causes $\mathcal{B}$ to abort is $1/(q_T + 1)$ and the authorization query does not cause $\mathcal{B}$'s aborting. Suppose $\mathcal{A}$ makes a total of q_A authorization queries and q_T trapdoor queries, the probability that $\mathcal{B}$ does not abort as a result of all queries is at least $(1 - 1/(q_T + 1))^{q_T} \geqslant 1/e$ in Phase 1 or 2. In Challenge phase, $\mathcal{B}$ will abort if $\mathcal{A}$ can produce w_0, w_1 with $w_\theta \notin \{w_0, w_1\}$. Therefore, $\Pr[w_\theta = w_i] = 1/(q_T + 1)$ for $i = 0, 1$, and the two values are independent of one another, we have $\Pr[w_\theta \neq w_0, w_1] = (1 - 1/(q_T + 1))^2 \leqslant 1 - 1/q_T$. Hence, the probability that $\mathcal{B}$ does not abort is at least $1/q_T$. Observe that since $\mathcal{A}$ can never query for the challenge keywords w_0, w_1, we have $\mathcal{B}$'s advantage is at least ϵ/eq_T.

4.2   T-EUF

Theorem 2. *The PEAKS scheme is trapdoor existentially unforgeable in the random oralce model if (n, l)-MSE-CDH Problem is hard in polynomial time.*

Proof. Suppose there exists a PPT adversary $\mathcal{A}$ in T-EUF game, who can attack our scheme with advantage ϵ, we build a simulator $\mathcal{B}$, who has advantage $\epsilon/((1 + q_A)e)$ against (n, l)-*MSE-CDH Problem*. $\mathcal{B}$'s running time is approximately the same as $\mathcal{A}$'s. The universal keyword space is assumed to be U with size n.

Init. The adversary $\mathcal{A}$ declares the challenge keyword set W^* with size l.

Setup. The simulator $\mathcal{B}$ is given the (n, l)-*MSE-CDH* instance $\mathcal{S}_2$. We also have coprime polynomials q_1, q_2, of respective orders $l, n - l$, with their pairwise distinct roots. $\mathcal{B}$'s goal is to output $g_0^{abc} \in \mathbb{G}$. We denote $W^* = \{w_1, \cdots, w_l\}$. It sets

$$q_1(\alpha) = \prod_{i=1}^{l}(\alpha + a_i), \quad q_2(\alpha) = \prod_{i=l+1}^{n}(\alpha + a_i).$$

The simulator $\mathcal{B}$ implicitly sets $g = g_0, h = h_0^{q_1 q_2}$ and $x = a$, and we have

$$\begin{aligned}
u_1 &= g_0^{\beta_1}, & u_2 &= g_0^{\beta_2}, g^x = g_0^a, \\
v_1 &= h_0^{\beta_1 q_1 q_2}, \cdots, & v_1^{\alpha^{n-1}} &= h_0^{\beta_1 \alpha^{n-1} q_1 q_2}, \\
v_2 &= h_0^{\beta_2 q_1 q_2}, \cdots, & v_2^{\alpha^{n-1}} &= h_0^{\beta_2 \alpha^{n-1} q_1 q_2}.
\end{aligned}$$

Then $\mathcal{B}$ sends $\mathcal{A}$ the public key

$$pk = \left(g_0, \cdots, g_0^{\alpha^{n-1}}, g_0^a, \{u_i, v_i, \cdots, v_i^{\alpha^{n-1}}\}_{i=1,2} \right).$$

H_1 **Query.** $\mathcal{B}$ maintains the hash list $L(w_i, h_i)$, which is initially empty. Upon receiving a query for w_i, if w_i is in the list L, $\mathcal{B}$ returns the corresponding h_i to $\mathcal{A}$. Otherwise, $\mathcal{B}$ chooses $a_i \in \mathbb{Z}_p$ and sets $h_i = H_1(w_i) = a_i$. Then $\mathcal{B}$ adds (w_i, h_i) to the list L and returns h_i to $\mathcal{A}$.

H_2 **Query.** $\mathcal{B}$ maintains two lists L^1 and L^2.

- $\mathcal{B}$ maintains a list $L^1(ak_{W*}^{s_i^1}, t_i^1, c_i^1, r_i^1, h_i^1)$, which is initially empty. Upon receiving a query for $(ak_{W*}^{s_i^1}, t_i^1)$, $\mathcal{B}$ looks up L^1 to find h_i^1 and returns it to $\mathcal{A}$.

  If $(ak_{W*}^{s_i^1}, t_i^1)$ is not on the list, $\mathcal{B}$ checks whether $ak_{W*}^{s_i^1}$ is on the list or not.

  If no, $\mathcal{B}$ creates a tuple $(ak_{W*}^{s_i^1}, t_i^1, c_i^1, r_i^1, h_i^1)$ with randomly choosing $c_i^1, r_i^1 \in_R \mathbb{Z}_p$ andcomputing the hash value

$$h_i^1 = H_2\left(ak_{W*}^{s_i^1}, t_i^1\right) = \begin{cases} g_0^{r_i^1} g_0^c, & \text{if } c_i^1 = t_i^1, \\ g_0^{r_i^1} g_0^{bc}, & \text{if } c_i^1 \neq t_i^1. \end{cases}$$

  Then $\mathcal{B}$ adds $(ak_{W*}^{s_i^1}, t_i^1, c_i^1, r_i^1, h_i^1)$ to L^1 and returns corresponding h_i^1 to $\mathcal{A}$.

  If yes, it indicates that $ak_{W*}^{s_i^1}$ has been asked before, that is to say that $\mathcal{A}$ asked the hash query for different t_i^1. $\mathcal{B}$ looks up the list to get the c_i^1, randomly chooses another r_i^1 to compute the corresponding hash value according to the above function and adds the result to the list and sends the result to $\mathcal{A}$.

- $\mathcal{B}$ maintains a list $L^2(ak_{U-W*}^{s_i^2}, t_i^2, c_i^2, r_i^2, h_i^2)$, which is initially empty. Upon receiving a query for $(ak_{U-W*}^{s_i^2}, t_i^2)$, $\mathcal{B}$ looks up L^2 to find h_i^2 and returns it to $\mathcal{A}$.

  If $(ak_{U-W*}^{s_i^2}, t_i^2)$ is not on the list, $\mathcal{B}$ checks whether $ak_{U-W*}^{s_i^2}$ is on the list or not.

  If no, $\mathcal{B}$ creates a tuple $(ak_{U-W*}^{s_i^2}, t_i^2, c_i^2, r_i^2, h_i^2)$ with randomly choosing $c_i^2, r_i^2 \in_R \mathbb{Z}_p$ and computing the hash value below

$$h_i^2 = H_2\left(ak_{U-W*}^{s_i^2}, t_i^2\right) = \begin{cases} g_0^{r_i^2}, & \text{if } c_i^2 = t_i^2, \\ g_0^{r_i^2} g_0^b, & \text{if } c_i^2 \neq t_i^2. \end{cases}$$

  $\mathcal{B}$ adds $(ak_{U-W*}^{s_i^2}, t_i^2, c_i^2, r_i^2, h_i^2)$ to the list L^2 and returns corresponding h_i^2 to $\mathcal{A}$.

  If yes, it indicates that $ak_{U-W*}^{s_i^2}$ has been asked before, that is to say that $\mathcal{A}$ asked the hash query for different t_i^2. $\mathcal{B}$ looks up the list to get the c_i^2, randomly chooses another r_i^2 to compute the corresponding hash value according to the above function. Then $\mathcal{B}$ adds the tuple to the list and sends the result to $\mathcal{A}$.

Query.

- Authorization Query. $\mathcal{A}$ can ask for the authorized token as follows.
  - If the keyword set is W^*, to each keyword $w_i \in W^*$, let (w_i, h_i) be the corresponding tuples on the L list and we have $h_i = H_1(w_i) = a_i$, where $i \in [1, l]$. $\mathcal{B}$ computes $ak = h_0^{\beta_1 \beta_2 q_1}$. Then $\mathcal{B}$ chooses $s_i^1 \in \mathbb{Z}_p$ and looks up the list L^1 to find the corresponding c_i^1. If $t_i^1 \neq c_i^1$, outputs abort.

Otherwise, $\mathcal{B}$ sets $t_i^1 = c_i^1$ and obtains r_i^1 from L^1. $\mathcal{B}$ computes $\sigma = g_0^{ac} g_0^{ar_i^1}$ and responds $token = (ak, \sigma, s_i^1, t_i^1)$ to $\mathcal{A}$. One can verify the validity

$$ak = h^{\dfrac{\beta_1 \beta_2}{\prod\limits_{w_j \in U - W^*}(\alpha + H_1(w_j))}} = h_0^{\frac{\beta_1 \beta_2 q_1 q_2}{q_2}} = h_0^{\beta_1 \beta_2 q_1},$$

$$\sigma = H_2\left(ak^{s_i^1}, t_i^1\right)^x = \left(g_0^c g_0^{r_i^1}\right)^a = g_0^{ac} g_0^{ar_i^1}.$$

- If the keyword set is $U - W^*$, to each keyword $w_i \in U - W^*$, let (w_i, h_i) be the corresponding tuples on the L list and we have $h_i = H_1(w_i) = a_i$, where $i \in [l+1, n]$. $\mathcal{B}$ computes $ak = h_0^{\beta_1 \beta_2 q_2}$. One can verify it by

$$ak = h^{\dfrac{\beta_1 \beta_2}{\prod\limits_{w_j \in U - (U - W^*)}(\alpha + H_1(w_j))}} = h_0^{\frac{\beta_1 \beta_2 q_1 q_2}{q_1}} = h_0^{\beta_1 \beta_2 q_2}.$$

Then $\mathcal{B}$ chooses $s_i^2 \in \mathbb{Z}_p$ and looks up the list L^2 to find the corresponding c_i^2.
  * If $t_i^2 = c_i^2$, obtains r_i^2 from L^2. $\mathcal{B}$ responds $token = (ak, \sigma, s_i^2, t_i^2)$ to $\mathcal{A}$, where $\sigma = H_2\left(ak^{s_i^2}, t_i^2\right)^x = \left(g_0^{r_i^2}\right)^a = g_0^{ar_i^2}$.
  * If $t_i^2 \neq c_i^2$, obtains r_i^2 from L^2, $\mathcal{B}$ responds $token = (ak, \sigma, s_i^2, t_i^2)$ to $\mathcal{A}$, where $\sigma = H_2\left(ak^{s_i^2}, t_i^2\right)^x = \left(g_0^b g_0^{r_i^2}\right)^a = g_0^{ab} g_0^{ar_i^2}$.

- Trapdoor Query. $\mathcal{A}$ can ask for the trapdoor for the keyword w_i. $\mathcal{A}$ can obtain the authorized token $token$ by Authorization Query and generate the trapdoor by himself.

Forgery. $\mathcal{A}$ outputs a trapdoor $TT = (T^*, \sigma^*, t^{1*})$ for $w_i \in W^*$ for time t^{1*}, where $T^* = (T_1^*, T_2^*, T_3^*)$ and (T_1^*, t^{1*}) had not been queried before. Since $TT = (T^*, \sigma^*, t^{1*})$ is a valid trapdoor tuple, σ^* is a valid signature and it implicitly means $\left(ak_{W^*}^{s^{1*}}, t^{1*}, c^{1*}, r^{1*}, h^{1*}\right)$ is on the list L^1.

- If $t^* = c^{1*}$, outputs abort.
- If $t^* \neq c^{1*}$, outputs $\dfrac{\sigma^*}{g_0^{ar^{1*}}}$ as the solution to (n, l)-*MSE-CDH Problem*. Since

$$H_2\left(ak_{W^*}^{s^{1*}}, t^{1*}\right) = g_0^{bc} g_0^{r^{1*}},$$

$$\sigma^* = H_2\left(T_1^*, t^{1*}\right)^x = H_2\left(ak_{W^*}^{s^{1*}}, t^{1*}\right)^x = \left(g_0^{bc} g_0^{r^{1*}}\right)^a = g_0^{abc} g_0^{ar^{1*}},$$

we can extract g_0^{abc} by $g_0^{abc} = \dfrac{\sigma^*}{g_0^{ar^{1*}}}$.

This completes the description of our simulation. As the method in Theorem 1, and we have $\mathcal{B}$'s advantage as $\epsilon/((1 + q_A)e)$.

5   Conclusion

We proposed a new notion of public key encryption with authorized keyword search, which extends the PEKS primitive. In PEAKS, the keyword is encrypted with one public key and each authorized user, without secret key, obtains search right from the authority. The authority distributes the authorized token to the user with time and the user generates the trapdoor for any authorized keyword. We constructed a provably secure PEAKS scheme, where the size of the authorized token is independent of the size of the keyword set. The proposed scheme reduces the bandwidth between the authority and the user significantly and allows only the freshly authorized trapdoor with the correct keyword to pass the test conducted by the server. We proved that our scheme possesses the semantical security against chosen keyword attacks and trapdoor unforgeability.

Acknowledgments. This work is supported by BUPT Excellent Ph.D. Students Foundation (Grant No. CX2015312), NSFC (Grant Nos. 61300181, 61502044, 61572390), the Fundamental Research Funds for the Central Universities (Grant No. 2015RC23).

References

1. Abdalla, M., Bellare, M., Catalano, D., Kiltz, E., Kohno, T., Lange, T., Malone-Lee, J., Neven, G., Paillier, P., Shi, H.: Searchable encryption revisited: consistency properties, relation to anonymous IBE, and extensions. In: Shoup, V. (ed.) CRYPTO 2005. LNCS, vol. 3621, pp. 205–222. Springer, Heidelberg (2005)
2. Ballard, L., Kamara, S., Monrose, F.: Achieving efficient conjunctive keyword searches over encrypted data. In: Qing, S., Mao, W., López, J., Wang, G. (eds.) ICICS 2005. LNCS, vol. 3783, pp. 414–426. Springer, Heidelberg (2005)
3. Bethencourt, J., Song, D.X., Waters, B.: New constructions and practical applications for private stream searching (extended abstract). In: 2006 IEEE Symposium on Security and Privacy (S&P 2006), pp. 132–139 (2006)
4. Boneh, D., Boyen, X., Goh, E.-J.: Hierarchical identity based encryption with constant size ciphertext. In: Cramer, R. (ed.) EUROCRYPT 2005. LNCS, vol. 3494, pp. 440–456. Springer, Heidelberg (2005)
5. Boneh, D., Di Crescenzo, G., Ostrovsky, R., Persiano, G.: Public key encryption with keyword search. In: Cachin, C., Camenisch, J.L. (eds.) EUROCRYPT 2004. LNCS, vol. 3027, pp. 506–522. Springer, Heidelberg (2004)
6. Boneh, D., Gentry, C., Waters, B.: Collusion resistant broadcast encryption with short ciphertexts and private keys. In: Shoup, V. (ed.) CRYPTO 2005. LNCS, vol. 3621, pp. 258–275. Springer, Heidelberg (2005)
7. Boneh, D., Waters, B.: Conjunctive, subset, and range queries on encrypted data. In: Vadhan, S.P. (ed.) TCC 2007. LNCS, vol. 4392, pp. 535–554. Springer, Heidelberg (2007)
8. Camenisch, J., Kohlweiss, M., Rial, A., Sheedy, C.: Blind and anonymous identity-based encryption and authorised private searches on public key encrypted data. In: Jarecki, S., Tsudik, G. (eds.) PKC 2009. LNCS, vol. 5443, pp. 196–214. Springer, Heidelberg (2009)
9. Cash, D., Jarecki, S., Jutla, C., Krawczyk, H., Roşu, M.-C., Steiner, M.: Highly-scalable searchable symmetric encryption with support for boolean queries. In: Canetti, R., Garay, J.A. (eds.) CRYPTO 2013, Part I. LNCS, vol. 8042, pp. 353–373. Springer, Heidelberg (2013)

10. Curtmola, R., Garay, J.A., Kamara, S., Ostrovsky, R.: Searchable symmetric encryption: improved definitions and efficient constructions. In: Proceedings of the 13th ACM Conference on Computer and Communications Security, CCS 2006, pp. 79–88 (2006)
11. Delerablée, C.: Identity-based broadcast encryption with constant size ciphertexts and private keys. In: Kurosawa, K. (ed.) ASIACRYPT 2007. LNCS, vol. 4833, pp. 200–215. Springer, Heidelberg (2007)
12. Fang, L., Susilo, W., Ge, C., Wang, J.: Chosen-ciphertext secure anonymous conditional proxy re-encryption with keyword search. Theor. Comput. Sci. **462**, 39–58 (2012)
13. Guo, F., Mu, Y., Chen, Z.: Identity-based encryption: how to decrypt multiple ciphertexts using a single decryption key. In: Takagi, T., Okamoto, T., Okamoto, E., Okamoto, T. (eds.) Pairing 2007. LNCS, vol. 4575, pp. 392–406. Springer, Heidelberg (2007)
14. Guo, F., Mu, Y., Chen, Z., Xu, L.: Multi-identity single-key decryption without random oracles. In: Pei, D., Yung, M., Lin, D., Wu, C. (eds.) Inscrypt 2007. LNCS, vol. 4990, pp. 384–398. Springer, Heidelberg (2008)
15. Guo, F., Mu, Y., Susilo, W., Wong, D.S., Varadharajan, V.: CP-ABE with constant-size keys for lightweight devices. IEEE Trans. Inf. Forensics Secur. **9**(5), 763–771 (2014)
16. Kamara, S., Papamanthou, C., Roeder, T.: Dynamic searchable symmetric encryption. In: The ACM Conference on Computer and Communications Security, CCS 2012, pp. 965–976 (2012)
17. Park, D.J., Kim, K., Lee, P.J.: Public key encryption with conjunctive field keyword search. In: Lim, C.H., Yung, M. (eds.) WISA 2004. LNCS, vol. 3325, pp. 73–86. Springer, Heidelberg (2005)
18. Ryu, E., Takagi, T.: Efficient conjunctive keyword-searchable encryption. In: 21st International Conference on Advanced Information Networking and Applications (AINA 2007), vol. 1, pp. 409–414 (2007)
19. Sedghi, S., van Liesdonk, P., Nikova, S., Hartel, P., Jonker, W.: Searching keywords with wildcards on encrypted data. In: Garay, J.A., De Prisco, R. (eds.) SCN 2010. LNCS, vol. 6280, pp. 138–153. Springer, Heidelberg (2010)
20. Shao, J., Cao, Z., Liang, X., Lin, H.: Proxy re-encryption with keyword search. Inf. Sci. **180**(13), 2576–2587 (2010)
21. Shi, J., Lai, J., Li, Y., Deng, R.H., Weng, J.: Authorized keyword search on encrypted data. In: Kutyłowski, M., Vaidya, J. (eds.) ICAIS 2014, Part I. LNCS, vol. 8712, pp. 419–435. Springer, Heidelberg (2014)
22. Song, D.X., Wagner, D., Perrig, A.: Practical techniques for searches on encrypted data. In: 2000 IEEE Symposium on Security and Privacy (S&P 2000), pp. 44–55 (2000)
23. Sun, W., Yu, S., Lou, W., Hou, Y.T., Li, H.: Protecting your right: Attribute-based keyword search with fine-grained owner-enforced search authorization in the cloud. In: 2014 IEEE Conference on Computer Communications, INFOCOM 2014, pp. 226–234 (2014)
24. Wang, X.A., Huang, X., Yang, X., Liu, L., Wu, X.: Further observation on proxy re-encryption with keyword search. J. Syst. Softw. **85**(3), 643–654 (2012)
25. Zheng, Q., Xu, S., Ateniese, G.: VABKS: verifiable attribute-based keyword search over outsourced encrypted data. In: 2014 IEEE Conference on Computer Communications, INFOCOM 2014, pp. 522–530 (2014)

Linear Encryption with Keyword Search

Shiwei Zhang$^{(\boxtimes)}$, Guomin Yang, and Yi Mu

Centre for Computer and Information Security Research,
School of Computing and Information Technology, University of Wollongong,
Wollongong, Australia
{sz653,gyang,ymu}@uow.edu.au

Abstract. Nowadays an increasing amount of data stored in the public cloud need to be searched remotely for fast accessing. For the sake of privacy, the remote files are usually encrypted, which makes them difficult to be searched by remote servers. It is also harder to efficiently share encrypted data in the cloud than those in plaintext. In this paper, we develop a searchable encryption framework called *Linear Encryption with Keyword Search* (LEKS) that can semi-generically convert some existing encryption schemes meeting our *Linear Encryption Template* (LET) to be searchable without re-encrypting all the data. For allowing easy data sharing, we convert a Key-Policy Attributed-Based Encryption (KP-ABE) scheme to a Key-Policy Attributed-Based Keyword Search (KP-ABKS) scheme as a concrete instance of our LEKS framework, making both the encrypted data and the search functionality under fine-grained access control. Notably, the resulting KP-ABKS is the first proven secure ABKS scheme with IND-sCKA security in the random oracle model, assuming the hardness of the ℓ-DCBDH problem derived from the (P, f)-DBDH problem family.

Keywords: Searchable encryption · Keyword search · Cloud security

1 Introduction

Cloud computing [14] provides on-demand computing resources that are accessible via the Internet, including computing power and data storage. With the convenient cloud services, users can outsource their computing resources to the cloud, and access them through terminals with low computing capabilities, such as mobile devices. Usually, those terminals also have low network connectivity due to the transmission technology, access cost, and other factors.

In terms of data storage, one important function is data search. Since all the user data are stored on the cloud server, users have to send search queries to the server to search for the data containing certain keywords. However, the normal search operation for plaintext is no longer working when data privacy is considered, since all the data are encrypted and cannot be read by the server.

To perform search on encrypted data, it is impractical for the user to do the search locally with all the data downloaded from the server, due to the high

© Springer International Publishing Switzerland 2016
J.K. Liu and R. Steinfeld (Eds.): ACISP 2016, Part II, LNCS 9723, pp. 187–203, 2016.
DOI: 10.1007/978-3-319-40367-0_12

demand on the bandwidth. It is also impractical to give the server the user secret key due to privacy concerns. Thus searchable encryption has been introduced such that the search operation is performed by the server, but the server cannot get any meaningful information from the search query or the encrypted data. In searchable encryption, all the data files and their associated keywords are encrypted. To search for the data with certain keyword, the user generates a trapdoor for the keyword and enquires the server with the trapdoor. The server searches the whole database to locate the data where the encrypted keyword matches the keyword embedded in the trapdoor. During the searching process, the server only knows whether an encrypted keyword matches the user trapdoor or not, and nothing else. After that, the server returns the search result to the user who can download the ciphertexts and decrypt the data.

In Public-key Encryption with Keyword Search (PEKS) [8], the data and the keywords are encrypted for only one user (i.e., the intended receiver of the data). In contrast, data can be encrypted with certain attributes in Attribute-Based Encryption (ABE) [16]. For instance, Alice can encrypt some data with attributes "full-time" and "student". Later, any user can decrypt the resulting ciphertext if the attributes in the ciphertext match the policy associated with the user. Thus Bob associated with a policy "(full time AND student) OR staff" can decrypt the above ciphertext. The corresponding searchable encryption for ABE is named Attribute-Based Keyword Search (ABKS) [19,21]. As in ABE, Alice can encrypt the data and its associated keywords using certain attributes. After uploading the ciphertexts to the server, Bob can do the search and decryption since the attributes used by Alice in the encryption matches Bob's policy. This feature is very important in the cloud environment where a user can share data with multiple users by encrypting the data only once. However, to the best of our knowledge, no ABKS scheme proposed in the literature is proven secure. Hence, one of our goals is to construct ABKS schemes with provable security.

In addition, keyword search functionality is usually associated with an encryption scheme where both the data and the keywords are encrypted for the same receiver(s). This paper also aims to provide a universal construction of searchable encryption schemes from some existing encryption schemes. This enables us to add a compatible keyword search functionality to an existing cryptosystem without re-encrypting all the data.

1.1 Related Work

Diffie and Hellman introduced the notion of Public-Key Encryption (PKE) [11] where Alice encrypts a message with Bob's public key, and Bob decrypts the ciphertext with his secret key. Based on the idea of using the user identity as the public key [17], Boneh and Franklin proposed a practical Identity-Based Encryption (IBE) scheme [9] where Alice encrypts the message with Bob's identity. In 2005, Sahai and Waters introduced Fuzzy Identity-Based Encryption which can be treated as the first Attribute-Based Encryption (ABE) [16], an instance of Function Encryption [20]. In ABE, the decryption keys of the users and the ciphertexts are associated with access policies and attributes, respectively. If and only if the attributes match the policy, the ciphertext can be successfully decrypted. Depending on how the identity and the ciphertext are associated, Attribute-Based Encryption schemes are classified into Key-Policy ABE (KP-ABE) [3,12,15,16] and Ciphertext-Policy ABE (CP-ABE) [4]. In KP-ABE, Bob's secret key is associated with a policy. After receiving the ciphertext encrypted with some attributes from Alice, Bob can decrypt it if and only if the attributes match his policy. In CP-ABE, the ciphertexts are associated with policies, and the secret keys are associated with attributes.

To enable the search functionality for encrypted data, various searchable encryption schemes [1,8,10,13,19,21] have been proposed under different settings. Boneh et al. [8] introduced PEKS, which is used with a conventional public key encryption scheme. Later, Identity-Based Keyword Search (IBKS) schemes were also proposed [1,10]. Recently, due to the popularity of ABE, there have been some research works on ABKS [19,21]. In addition, there are also keyword search schemes for other encryption variants, such as Broadcast Encryption [2].

To the best of our knowledge, [19,21] are the only ABKS schemes proposed in the literature. However, neither of those schemes is proven secure. In particular, after analysing the ABKS scheme in [19], we found the scheme is flawed where an adversary can always distinguish keywords from a ciphertext by testing $e(\hat{D}, T_{i'}^{\frac{1}{H(w_{\mu'})}}) \stackrel{?}{=} e(g, D_{i'})$. For the KP-ABKS scheme in [21], the security proof is invalid (see Sect. 4.3) and thus the security of this scheme remains unknown. For the CP-ABKS scheme in [21], no formal security proof has been provided.

In terms of provable security, it depends on the hardness of some computational problems (e.g. Discrete Logarithm Problem (DLP), Diffie-Hellman Problem (DHP) [11], etc.). Shoup [18] introduced the generic group model which was used to obtain the complexity lower bound regarding the hardness of DLP and DHP. Later, dealing with bilinear maps, Boneh et al. [6] introduced the generic bilinear group model and the general Diffie-Hellman Exponent Problem. Besides, the generic bilinear group model is also used in [5,7] for analysing the Decisional Linear (DLIN) Problem and q-Strong Diffie-Hellman (q-SDH) Problem.

1.2 Our Contribution

In this paper, we introduce a new problem family named *Decisional Bilinear (P, f)-Diffie-Hellman problem* $((P, f)$-DBDH problem, for short). We prove the (P, f)-DBDH problem is computationally hard in generic bilinear group model if the polynomial f is not dependent on the polynomial set P. Based on the (P, f)-DBDH problem, we derive a hard computational problem named *Decisional ℓ-Combined Bilinear Diffie-Hellman problem* (ℓ-DCBDH problem).

As the main contribution of this work, we introduce two new notions named *Linear Encryption Template* (LET) and *Linear Encryption with Keyword Search* (LEKS), and provide their formal definitions. LET can model different asymmetric encryption schemes, including but not limited to PKE, IBE and ABE schemes, which have the property of linearity. The linearity property requires a sub-algorithm $e(g,g)^{\alpha s} \leftarrow \mathcal{D}(SK, C_1, \dots)$ in the decryption algorithm where SK is the secret key involved, $(C_1, \dots)$ are the ciphertext components and for all $t \in \mathbb{Z}_p$, $\mathcal{D}(SK^t, C_1, \dots) = \mathcal{D}(SK, C_1, \dots)^t$. Given an encryption fitting LET, we provide a semi-generic conversion to a LEKS scheme where the construction is generic but we require security proofs for individual conversions. We also define two security models for LEKS schemes: Indistinguishability under Adaptive Chosen Keyword Attack (IND-CKA) and its weaker Selective-ID version (IND-sCKA). With LET and our conversion from LET to LEKS, we can construct PEKS from PKE, IBKS from IBE, ABKS from ABE, and so on.

To illustrate the feasibility of our semi-generic framework, we give an instance of LET and then apply our conversion to procude a LEKS scheme. We first show that a variant [15] of Goyal et al.'s ABE scheme [12] fits LET by proving it has the property of linearity. Then we apply our LEKS conversion to convert the KP-ABE scheme into a KP-ABKS scheme. After that, we prove the resulting KP-ABKS scheme is IND-sCKA secure in the random oracle model under ℓ-DCBDH assumption. It is worth noting that to the best of our knowledge, our converted KP-ABKS scheme is the first proven secure KP-ABKS scheme.

1.3 Paper Organisation

The rest of this paper is organised as follows. Beginning with Sect. 2, we define (P, f)-DBDH problem family and ℓ-DCBDH problem, and prove the hardness of those problems. In Sect. 3, we define LEKS and its security model, followed by the definition of LET and the LEKS conversion from LET. After that, an instance of LEKS conversion is given in Sect. 4, converting a KP-ABE scheme to a KP-ABKS scheme. The resulted KP-ABKS scheme is proven secure in Sect. 4.3 under the security model defined in Sect. 3.2. Finally, the conclusion is addressed in Sect. 5.

2   Decisional Diffie-Hellman Problem Family

In this paper, we use the same bilinear map $e : \mathbb{G}_1 \times \mathbb{G}_1 \to \mathbb{G}_2$ as in [9] for simplicity where $\mathbb{G}_1$, $\mathbb{G}_2$ are multiplicative cyclic groups of prime order p and g is a generator of $\mathbb{G}_1$.

Definition 1. *Let* $P = (p_1, \dots, p_s) \in \mathbb{F}_p[X_1, \dots, X_n]^s$ *be a s-tuples of n-variate polynomial over* $\mathbb{F}_p$. *We define that a polynomial* $f \in \mathbb{F}_p[X_1, \dots, X_n]^s$ *is dependent on* P *if exists* $s^2 + 2s$ *constants* $a_{i,j}$, b_k *and* c_l *such that*

$$f = \frac{\sum_{i=1}^{s}\sum_{j=1}^{s} a_{i,j} p_i p_j}{\sum_{k=1}^{s} b_k p_k} + \sum_{l=1}^{s} c_l p_l \quad or \quad f = \sum_{l=1}^{s} c_l p_l \pm \sqrt{\sum_{i=1}^{s}\sum_{j=1}^{s} a_{i,j} p_i p_j}$$

Equivalently, f is dependent on P if exists $s^2 + s + 1$ constants $a_{i,j}$, b_k and c

$$cf^2 + \sum_{k=1}^{s} b_k p_k f + \sum_{i=1}^{s} \sum_{j=1}^{s} a_{i,j} p_i p_j = 0$$

where at least one of b_k or c is non-zero.

Let $g^{P(x_1,\ldots,x_n)} = (g^{p_1(x_1,\ldots,x_n)}, \ldots, g^{p_s(x_1,\ldots,x_n)})$, d_f denote the total degree of $f \in \mathbb{F}_p[X_1, \ldots, X_n]$, and $d_P = \max\{d_f \mid f \in P \in \mathbb{F}_p[X_1, \ldots, X_n]^s\}$. We present the family of Diffie-Hellman problems as follows.

Definition 2 (Decisional Bilinear (P, f)-Diffie-Hellman problem). *Let $P = (p_1, \ldots, p_s) \in \mathbb{F}_p[X_1, \ldots, X_n]^s$ be a s-tuples of n-variate polynomial over $\mathbb{F}_p$, $f \in \mathbb{F}_p[X_1, \ldots, X_n]$ be a n-variate polynomial over $\mathbb{F}_p$. Let $(x_1, \ldots, x_n) \in_R \mathbb{Z}_p^n$, and $Z \in_R \mathbb{G}_1$. Giving two probability distributions $\mathcal{D}_\tau = (g^{P(x_1,\ldots,x_n)}, g^{f(x_1,\ldots,x_n)})$ and $\mathcal{D}_\rho = (g^{P(x_1,\ldots,x_n)}, Z)$, there is an algorithm $\mathcal{A}$ can distinguish $\mathcal{D}_\tau$ and $\mathcal{D}_\rho$ with advantage:*

$$Adv_{\mathcal{A}}^{(P,f)-DBDH} = \frac{1}{2} \left| \Pr[1 \leftarrow \mathcal{A}(D \in_R \mathcal{D}_\tau)] - \Pr[1 \leftarrow \mathcal{A}(D \in_R \mathcal{D}_\rho)] \right|$$

where $D \in_R \mathcal{D}$ represents that D is uniformly and independently chosen from $\mathcal{D}$. Alternatively, the problem can be represented as

$$b \in_R \{0, 1\}, \quad Z_b = g^{f(x_1,\ldots,x_n)}, \quad Z_{1-b} \in_R \mathbb{G}_1,$$

$$Adv_{\mathcal{A}}^{(P,f)-DBDH} = \left| \Pr\left[b = b' \leftarrow \mathcal{A}(g^{P(x_1,\ldots,x_n)}, Z_0, Z_1)\right] - \frac{1}{2} \right|$$

As from the definition above, Decisional Bilinear (P, f)-Diffie-Hellman $((P, f)$-DBDH in short) problem family is an enhanced DDH problem on the group $\mathbb{G}_1$ where the adversary $\mathcal{A}$ is now able to do bilinear pairing operations on $\mathbb{G}_1$. The (P, f)-DBDH problem family is computational hard if and only if the advantage $Adv_{\mathcal{A}}^{(P,f)-DBDH}$ is negligible. Since there is no known proof of the hardness of this problem family, we show the complexity lower bound in the generic bilinear group model [6]. As in [6], we emphasise that a lower bound in generic groups does not imply a lower bound in any specific group.

Theorem 1. *Let $\varepsilon_1, \varepsilon_2 : \mathbb{Z}_p^+ \to \{0, 1\}^m$ be two random encodings (injective maps) where $\mathbb{G}_1 = \{\varepsilon_1(x) \mid x \in \mathbb{Z}_p^+\}$, $\mathbb{G}_2 = \{\varepsilon_2(x) \mid x \in \mathbb{Z}_p^+\}$. Let $d = 2 \cdot \max(d_P, d_f)$. If f is not dependent on P, the lower bound of the advantage $Adv^{(P,f)-DBDH}$ of solving the (P, f)-DBDH problem (Definition 2) for the adversary $\mathcal{A}$ is stated as follows with at most $q_{1,\times}$, $q_{2,\times}$ queries to the group operation oracles $\mathcal{O}_\times^1$, $\mathcal{O}_\times^2$ and q_e queries to the bilinear pairing oracle $\mathcal{O}_e : \varepsilon_1 \times \varepsilon_1 \to \varepsilon_2$.*

$$Adv_{\mathcal{A}}^{(P,f)-DBDH} \leq \frac{(q_{1,\times} + q_{2,\times} + q_e + s + 2)^2 d}{2p}$$

Our schemes are based on a dynamic version of the above (P, f)-DBDH problem. To describe and show the hardness of the problem, we begin with the following lemma.

Lemma 1.   *Let $P = (p_1, \ldots, p_s), Q = (q_1, \ldots, q_s) \in \mathbb{F}_p[X_1, \ldots, X_n]^s$ be two s-tuple of n-variate polynomials over $\mathbb{F}_p$, $f \in \mathbb{F}_p[X_1, \ldots, X_n]$, $O = (P, Q) = (p_1, \ldots, p_s, q_1, \ldots, q_s)$ be a 2s-tuple of n-variate polynomial. Let T be a variate, $R = (P, QT) = (p_1, \ldots, p_s, q_1 T, \ldots, q_s T) = (r_1, \ldots, r_{2s})$ be a 2s-tuple of $(n+1)$-variate polynomial. If f is not dependent on O, f is not dependent on R.*

Lemma 2.   *Let $P = (p_1, \ldots, p_s), Q = (q_1, \ldots, q_s) \in \mathbb{F}_p[X_1, \ldots, X_n]^s$ be two s-tuple of n-variate polynomials over $\mathbb{F}_p$, $f \in \mathbb{F}_p[X_1, \ldots, X_n]$, $O = (P, Q) = (p_1, \ldots, p_s, q_1, \ldots, q_s)$ be a 2s-tuple of n-variate polynomial. Let $T_1, \ldots, T_\ell$ be ℓ variates, $R = (P, QT_1, \ldots, QT_\ell) = (p_1, \ldots, p_s, q_1 T_1, \ldots, q_s T_1, \ldots, q_1 T_\ell, \ldots, q_s T_\ell)$ be an $(\ell+1)s$-tuple of $(n+\ell)$-variate polynomial. If f is not dependent on O, f is not dependent on R.*

Definition 3 (Decisional ℓ-Combined Bilinear Diffie-Hellman problem).
Let $a, b, c, d, e, f_1, \ldots, f_\ell \in_R \mathbb{Z}_p$, $h = \dot{g}^e$, and $Z \in_R \mathbb{G}_1$. Giving two probability distributions $\mathcal{D}_{DCBDH} = (g, g^a, g^b, h, h^c, h^d, \{(g^{f_i}, g^{af_i}, h^{f_i}, h^{af_i})\}_{i=1\ldots\ell}, g^{ab}h^{cd})$ and $\mathcal{D}_\rho = (g, g^a, g^b, h, h^c, h^d, \{(g^{f_i}, g^{af_i}, h^{f_i}, h^{af_i})\}_{i=1\ldots\ell}, Z)$, there is an algorithm $\mathcal{A}$ can distinguish $\mathcal{D}_{DCBDH}$ and $\mathcal{D}_\rho$ with advantage:

$$Adv_{\mathcal{A}}^{\ell\text{-}DCBDH} = \frac{1}{2} \left| \Pr\left[1 \leftarrow \mathcal{A}(D \in_R \mathcal{D}_{DCBDH})\right] - \Pr\left[1 \leftarrow \mathcal{A}(D \in_R \mathcal{D}_\rho)\right] \right|$$

Alternatively, the problem can be represented as

$$b \in_R \{0, 1\}, \quad Z_b = g^{ab} h^{cd}, \quad Z_{1-b} \in_R \mathbb{G}_1, \quad Adv_{\mathcal{A}}^{\ell\text{-}DCBDH} =$$

$$\left| \Pr\left[b = b' \leftarrow \mathcal{A}(g, g^a, g^b, h, h^c, h^d, \{(g^{f_i}, g^{af_i}, h^{f_i}, h^{af_i})\}_{i=1\ldots\ell}, Z_0, Z_1)\right] - \frac{1}{2} \right|$$

The Decisional ℓ-Combined Bilinear Diffie-Hellman (ℓ-DCBDH) problem belongs to the (P, f)-DBDH problem family. We prove that the ℓ-DCBDH problem is hard by showing the advantage $Adv_{\mathcal{A}}^{\ell\text{-}DCBDH}$ is negligible.

Theorem 2.   *The lower bound of the advantage $Adv_{\mathcal{A}}^{\ell\text{-}DCBDH}$ of solving the ℓ-DCBDH problem (Definition 3) for the adversary $\mathcal{A}$ is stated as follows with at most q queries to group operations and bilinear pairing operations.*

$$Adv_{\mathcal{A}}^{\ell\text{-}DCBDH} \leq \frac{3 \cdot (q + 4\ell + 8)^2}{p}$$

Due to the space limitation, the proofs of the above Theorems and Lemmas will be provided in the full version of the paper.

3 Linear Encryption with Keyword Search

3.1 Definition

In general, a searchable encryption scheme involves three roles and consists of two encryption parts. In detail, the roles are **contributor**, **server** and **user**, and the encryption parts are the message encryption part and the keyword encryption part. A general purpose searchable encryption scheme works as follows. Alice, as a **contributor**, encrypts a file using the message encryption scheme and the related keywords using the keyword encryption part for the target **users**, including Bob. Let **header** denote the keyword ciphertext, and **payload** denote the file ciphertext. Since a file may be associated with multiple keywords, Alice may generate multiple headers for the payload. After that, Alice assembles the headers and the payload as a single ciphertext, and sends the ciphertext to the **server**. Bob, as one of the target **user**, can ask the **server** to search the ciphertext with certain keywords. To do secured search, Bob generates a **trapdoor** for each keyword to be searched, and then uploads the trapdoors to the server via a secure communication channel. Once the server receives the query with the trapdoors from Bob, the server begins to test whether the keywords in the headers match those in the trapdoors. Note that the keywords are not visible to the server, and the headers and trapdoors match only when the corresponding keywords are the same and Bob is one of the intended users that the headers are encrypted for. After searching for all related ciphertexts, the server allows Bob to download the matching payloads. Finally, Bob can download the payloads with matching headers. In addition, a **trusted authority** is required in the identity or attribute-based setting.

Formally, we define *Linear Encryption with Keyword Search* as follows, focusing on the keyword encryption part in a general searchable encryption scheme.

Definition 4 (Linear Encryption with Keyword Search). *A linear encryption with keyword search (LEKS) scheme, involving the contributors, the servers, the users and the trusted authority, consists of the following five (probabilistic) polynomial time algorithms:*

- *$(MSK, PK) \leftarrow Setup(1^\lambda)$: The system setup algorithm run by the trusted authority takes a security parameter 1^λ, and outputs a pair of master secret key MSK and public key PK for the trusted authority.*
- *$SK \leftarrow KeyGen(MSK, I_S)$: The user key generation algorithm run by the trusted authority takes a master secret key MSK and a user identity I_S, and generates a user secret key SK for the user associated with that identity.*
- *$C \leftarrow LEKS(PK, I_C, W)$: The keyword encryption algorithm run by the contributor takes a public key PK, a target identity I_C and a keyword W, and outputs a ciphertext C of the keyword W. To maximum the generality, I_C is viewed as a set that the user I_S can access the ciphertext only if $I_S \in I_C$. It is equivalent to $F(I_S, I_C) = 1$ with a predicate function F.*
- *$T \leftarrow Trapdoor(SK, W)$: The trapdoor generation algorithm run by the user takes a secret key SK and a keyword W, and generates a trapdoor T of the keyword W.*

- $1/0 \leftarrow Test(C,T)$: *The deterministic test algorithm run by the server takes a ciphertext* $C \leftarrow LEKS(PK, I_C, W)$ *and a trapdoor* $T \leftarrow Trapdoor(SK, W)$ *where* $SK \leftarrow KeyGen(MSK, I_S)$, *and outputs*

$$\begin{cases} 1 & if \, W = W' \wedge I_S \in I_C, \\ 0 & otherwise. \end{cases}$$

In the public key scenario where users are identified using public keys generated by themselves, the trusted authority is not required and the algorithm *KeyGen* is not used. Instead, the *Setup* algorithm is run by individual users, and outputs a pair of secret key *SK* and public key *PK* for that user. In addition, the scheme is required to be correct.

Definition 5 (Correctness). *A LEKS scheme is correct if the following statement is always true:*

$$\forall (MSK, PK) \leftarrow Setup(1^\lambda), \, \forall I_c, \, \forall W \in \{0,1\}^*, \, \forall C \leftarrow LEKS(PK, I_c, W),$$
$$\forall I_s \in I_c, \forall SK \leftarrow KeyGen(MSK, I_s), \forall T \leftarrow Trapdoor(SK, W), Test(C, T) = 1.$$

3.2   Security Model

In LEKS, we consider that the server is *honest but curious*. In addition, we do not consider the keyword guessing attack (KGA), since the server can always generate ciphertexts with certain keywords to test with the trapdoor legitimately. However, we can prevent anyone from extracting the keyword directly from the trapdoor by applying an one-way function such as a preimage-resistant hash function.

We present two security games: *Indistinguishability under Adaptive Chosen Keyword Attack* (IND-CKA) and its weaker *Selective-ID* version (IND-sCKA). We first define the IND-sCKA game (Game 1) where an adaptive adversary $\mathcal{A}$ tries to distinguish a ciphertext generated from either keywords W_0 or W_1:

1. $\mathcal{A}$ selects a target identity set I_T and submits it to the challenger $\mathcal{S}$.
2. $\mathcal{S}$ runs $Setup(1^\lambda)$ to generate a key pair (MSK, PK) and passes PK to $\mathcal{A}$.
3. $\mathcal{A}$ can adaptively ask $\mathcal{S}$ for the secret key SK of the user with identity I by querying the key generation oracle $\mathcal{O}_{KeyGen}$. At the same point, $\mathcal{S}$ records I in the identity list $\mathcal{I}$. The restriction is that I must not be in I_T.
4. $\mathcal{A}$ can adaptively ask $\mathcal{S}$ for the trapdoor T of the user identity I with the keyword W by querying the trapdoor generation oracle $\mathcal{O}_{Trapdoor}$. If I is not in I_T, it can be resolved that $\mathcal{A}$ queries the oracle $\mathcal{O}_{KeyGen}$ to obtain the secret key SK of I and further obtains the trapdoor $T \leftarrow Trapdoor(SK, W)$. Otherwise, $\mathcal{S}$ runs the algorithm $KeyGen$ and then the algorithm $Trapdoor$ to get the trapdoor, and passes it to $\mathcal{A}$. At the same point, $\mathcal{S}$ records the queried keyword W in the keyword list $\mathcal{W}$.
5. At some point, $\mathcal{A}$ outputs two keywords W_0 and W_1 to be challenged where those two keywords must not be in the keyword list $\mathcal{W}$.

6. S randomly selects b to be either 0 or 1 uniformly. Then S generates a ciphertext $C \leftarrow LEKS(PK, I_T, W_b)$ and passes it to $\mathcal{A}$.
7. $\mathcal{A}$ can continue to query all oracles with the same restriction. In addition, $\mathcal{A}$ cannot query the target keywords W_0 and W_1 to the oracle $\mathcal{O}_{Trapdoor}$.
8. Eventually, $\mathcal{A}$ outputs a bit b'. $\mathcal{A}$ wins the game if $b = b'$.

We define the advantage of winning Game 1 as follows

$$Adv_{\mathcal{A}}^{\text{IND-sCKA}} = \left| \Pr\left[b = b' \wedge \mathcal{I} \cap I_T = \emptyset \wedge W_0, W_1 \notin \mathcal{W} \right] - \frac{1}{2} \right|$$

Definition 6 (IND-sCKA Security). *A LEKS scheme is Indistinguishable under Selective-ID Adaptive Chosen Keyword Attack if $Adv_{\mathcal{A}}^{IND\text{-}sCKA}$ is a negligible function for all adversary $\mathcal{A}$ winning the Game 1 in polynomial time.*

Next, we define the IND-CKA game (Game 2), which is similar as the IND-sCKA game. The difference is that $\mathcal{A}$ is given the public key PK in IND-CKA before submitting the target identity set I_T.

Definition 7 (IND-CKA Security). *A LEKS scheme is Indistinguishable under Adaptive Chosen Keyword Attack if $Adv_{\mathcal{A}}^{IND\text{-}CKA}$ is a negligible function for all adversary $\mathcal{A}$ winning the Game 2 in polynomial time.*

$Game_{\text{IND-sCKA}}^{\lambda}$:
$$\mathcal{I}, \mathcal{W} \leftarrow \emptyset, \quad I_T \leftarrow \mathcal{A}, \quad (MSK, PK) \leftarrow Setup(1^{\lambda}),$$
$$(W_0, W_1) \leftarrow \mathcal{A}^{\mathcal{O}_{KeyGen}, \mathcal{O}_{Trapdoor}}(PK), \quad b \in_R \{0, 1\},$$
$$C \leftarrow LEKS(PK, I_T, W_b), \quad b' \leftarrow \mathcal{A}^{\mathcal{O}_{KeyGen}, \mathcal{O}_{Trapdoor}}(C)$$
$\mathcal{O}_{KeyGen}$: $\quad \mathcal{I} \leftarrow \mathcal{I} \cup \{I\}, \quad$ return $SK \leftarrow KeyGen(MSK, I)$
$\mathcal{O}_{Trapdoor}$: $\quad \mathcal{W} \leftarrow \mathcal{W} \cup \{W\}, \quad$ return $T \leftarrow Trapdoor(SK, W)$
$$Adv_{\mathcal{A}}^{\text{IND-sCKA}} = \left| \Pr\left[b = b' \wedge \mathcal{I} \cap I_T = \emptyset \wedge W_0, W_1 \notin \mathcal{W} \right] - \frac{1}{2} \right|$$

Game 1: IND-sCKA

$Game_{\text{IND-CKA}}^{\lambda}$:
$$\mathcal{I}, \mathcal{W} \leftarrow \emptyset, \quad (MSK, PK) \leftarrow Setup(1^{\lambda}),$$
$$(I_T, W_0, W_1) \leftarrow \mathcal{A}^{\mathcal{O}_{KeyGen}, \mathcal{O}_{Trapdoor}}(PK), \quad b \in_R \{0, 1\},$$
$$C \leftarrow LEKS(PK, I_T, W_b), \quad b' \leftarrow \mathcal{A}^{\mathcal{O}_{KeyGen}, \mathcal{O}_{Trapdoor}}(C)$$
$$Adv_{\mathcal{A}}^{\text{IND-CKA}} = \left| \Pr\left[b = b' \wedge \mathcal{I} \cap I_T = \emptyset \wedge W_0, W_1 \notin \mathcal{W} \right] - \frac{1}{2} \right|$$

Game 2: IND-CKA

3.3 Linear Encryption Template

In this subsection, we define the *Linear Encryption Template* (LET). Informally, a LET models an asymmetric encryption scheme, consisting of the **senders**, the **recipients** and the **trusted authority**. Alice, as the **recipient**, gets her secret key from the **trusted authority** using her identity where her public key is her identity. If LET is modelling a PKE scheme, Alice's secret/public key pair is generated by herself, and the **trusted authority** is not required. To securely send a message to a set of recipients, including Alice, the **sender** Bob encrypts the message into a ciphertext, and sends it to Alice. Once Alice receives the ciphertext, she can decrypts and obtains the original message if and only if she is one of the target recipients. Furthermore, if an encryption scheme fits LET, we can use it to construct the corresponding LEKS scheme in Sect. 3.4. Formally, we describe the definition of *Linear Encryption Template* as follows.

Definition 8 (Linear Encryption Template). *A linear encryption template, involving the senders, the recipients, and the trusted authority, consists of the following four (probabilistic) polynomial algorithms:*

- *$(MSK, PK) \leftarrow Setup(params, \alpha)$: The system setup algorithm run by the trusted authority takes a set of system parameters, such as the description of groups, security parameters and randomnesses, and it reuses these parameters. The algorithm also takes a component α, which is used to create the ciphertext. The output of this algorithm is a pair of master secret key MSK and public key PK of the trusted authority.*
- *$SK \leftarrow KeyGen(MSK, I_S)$: The user key generation algorithm run by the trusted authority takes a master secret key MSK and a user identity I_S, and generates a user secret key SK for the user associated with that identity.*
- *$C \leftarrow Encrypt(PK, I_C, M, s)$: The encryption algorithm run by the sender takes a public key PK, a target identity set I_C, a message M and a randomness s, and outputs a ciphertext C of the message M. The randomness s is used to bind the ciphertext parts in C and further to bind other ciphertext parts when constructing LEKS schemes. It is required that the ciphertext must be in the form of $C = (C_0, C_1, \dots)$ where $C_0 = M \cdot e(g, g)^{\alpha s}$.*
- *$M \leftarrow Decrypt(SK, C)$: The deterministic decryption algorithm run by the recipient takes a secret key SK and a ciphertext C, and outputs the original message M. The decryption process is required to be two steps. The first step is to run the sub-decryption algorithm $\mathcal{D}$ to get $e(g, g)^{\alpha s} \leftarrow \mathcal{D}(SK, C_1, \dots)$. Then the second step is to extract the message $M = \frac{C_0}{e(g,g)^{\alpha s}}$. Importantly, the sub algorithm $\mathcal{D}$ is required to have **linearity**:*

$$\forall t \in \mathbb{Z}_p, \quad \mathcal{D}(SK^t, C_1, \dots) = D(SK, C_1, \dots)^t$$

If SK consists multiple elements that $SK = (SK_1, SK_2, \dots)$, the term SK^t denotes $(SK_1^t, SK_2^t, \dots)$.

If there is no trusted authority that users generate their key pairs by themselves, the algorithm $KeyGen$ is not used and the algorithm $Setup$ is run by the user, outputing a pair of user secret key SK and public key SK. In addition, the scheme is required to be correct.

Definition 9 (Correctness). *A LET scheme is correct if the following statement is always true:*

$$\forall (MSK, PK) \leftarrow Setup(params, \alpha), \forall I_c, \forall I_s \in I_c, \forall SK \leftarrow KeyGen(MSK, I_s),$$
$$\forall M \in \mathbb{G}_2, \quad \forall s \in \mathbb{Z}_p, \quad \forall C \leftarrow Encrypt(PK, I_c, M, s), \quad Decrypt(SK, C) = M.$$

3.4 Keyword Search from Linear Encryption Template

In this subsection, we build our LEKS scheme with from a LET scheme as the keyword encryption part. To construct a fully searchable encryption scheme, we can reuse the LET scheme as the message encryption part, and combine with the LEKS scheme. Alternatively, we also can use other encryption schemes as the message encryption part. The main idea of the construction is to use the LET part for authentication and combine it with a keyword equality test with the same randomness. Let $\Pi = (Setup, KeyGen, Encrypt, Decrypt)$ be a LET modelled encryption scheme. Our LEKS scheme works as follows.

- $(MSK, PK) \leftarrow Setup(1^\lambda)$: Given a security parameter 1^λ, the algorithm generates two groups $\mathbb{G}_1, \mathbb{G}_2$ of prime order p, and specifies a bilinear map $e : \mathbb{G}_1 \times \mathbb{G}_1 \rightarrow \mathbb{G}_2$. The algorithm also selects a random generator g of $\mathbb{G}_1$, and a preimage resistant hash function $H : \{0,1\}^* \rightarrow \mathbb{G}_1$, which may be modelled as an random oracle. After that, the algorithm chooses two randomness $x_1, x_2 \in_R \mathbb{Z}_p^+$, and calculates $g_1 = g^{x_1}$ and $g_2 = g^{x_2}$. Then the algorithm packs all above elements into $params$, sets $\alpha = x_1 x_2$, and passes to the algorithm $\Pi.Setup$ to obtain the key pair $\Pi.MSK$ and $\Pi.PK$. Finally, the algorithm keeps the master secret key $MSK = \Pi.MSK$, and publishes the public key $PK = (\mathbb{G}_1, \mathbb{G}_2, e, g, g_1, g_2, \Pi.PK)$.

$$\mathbb{G}_1 = \langle g \rangle, \quad e : \mathbb{G}_1 \times \mathbb{G}_1 \rightarrow \mathbb{G}_2, \quad H : \{0,1\}^* \rightarrow \mathbb{G}_1, \quad x_1, x_2 \in_R \mathbb{Z}_p^+,$$
$$g_1 = g^{x_1}, \quad g_2 = g^{x_2}, \quad params = (\mathbb{G}_1, \mathbb{G}_2, e, g, H, x_1, x_2),$$
$$(\Pi.MSK, \Pi.PK) \leftarrow \Pi.Setup(params, x_1 x_1)$$

  return $(MSK, PK) = (\Pi.MSK, (\mathbb{G}_1, \mathbb{G}_2, e, g, g_1, g_2, H, \Pi.PK))$.
- $SK \leftarrow KeyGen(MSK, I_S)$: For key generation, the algorithm $\Pi.KeyGen$ is directly invoked. return $SK \leftarrow \Pi.KeyGen(MSK, I_S)$.
- $C \leftarrow LEKS(PK, I_C, W)$: To encrypt a keyword W for a target identity set I_C, the algorithm chooses two randomness $r_1, r_2 \in_R \mathbb{Z}_p^+$. Then it computes $C_1' = g_2^{r_2} H(W)^{r_1}$ and $C_2' = g_1^{r_1}$ to encrypt the keyword W. After that, the algorithm invokes $\Pi.Encrypt$ with r_2 to get the ciphertext $(C_0, C_1, \dots)$ to assure the target identity set I_C. Finally, the algorithm assembles two parts together $C = (C_1', C_2', C_1, \dots)$ as the full ciphertext bound using r_2 where

$C_0 = M \cdot e(g,g)^{x_1 x_2 r_2}$ is dropped. Since C_0 is not used in C, we can safely setting the message M to 0 when invoking $\Pi.Encrypt$.

$$r_1, r_2 \in_R \mathbb{Z}_p^+, \quad C_1' = g_2^{r_2} H(W)^{r_1}, \quad C_2' = g_1^{r_1}$$
$$(C_0, C_1, \dots) \leftarrow \Pi.Encrypt(PK, I_C, 0, r_2)$$

return $C = (C_1', C_2', C_1, \dots)$.
- $T \leftarrow Trapdoor(SK, W)$: To generate a trapdoor of the keyword W, the algorithm selects a randomness $s \in_R \mathbb{Z}_p^+$. Then it calculates $T = (T_1, T_2, T_3)$ where $T_1 = g_1^s$, $T_2 = H(W)^s$ and $T_3 = SK^s$. For SK^s, the operation works the same as in Definition 8.

$$s \in_R \mathbb{Z}_p^+, \quad T_1 = g_1^s, \quad T_2 = H(W)^s, \quad T_3 = SK^s$$

return $T = (T_1, T_2, T_3)$.
- $1/0 \leftarrow Test(C, T)$: For equality tests of both the keyword and the identity, the algorithm tests the equality of the following return statement.

return $e(C_1', T_1)/e(C_2', T_2) \stackrel{?}{=} \Pi.\mathcal{D}(T_3, C_1, \dots)$.

Theorem 3. *The proposed conversion from the LET scheme to the LEKS scheme is correct if the corresponding encryption scheme modelled by LET is correct.*

Proof. To verify, we calculate the left hand side of the test equation first.

$$E_1 = \frac{e(C_1', T_1)}{e(C_2', T_2)} = \frac{e(g_2^{r_2} H(W)^{r_1}, g_1^s)}{e(g_1^{r_1}, H(W)^s)} = \frac{e(g_2^{r_2}, g_1^s) \cdot e(H(W)^{r_1}, g_1^s)}{e(g_1^{r_1}, H(W)^s)} = e(g_1, g_2)^{r_2 s}$$

Then we calculate the right hand side of the test equation.

$$E_2 = \Pi.\mathcal{D}(T_3, C_1, \dots) = \Pi.\mathcal{D}(SK^s, C_1, \dots) = \Pi.\mathcal{D}(SK, C_1, \dots)^s$$
$$= e(g,g)^{x_1 x_2 r_2 s} = e(g_1, g_2)^{r_2 s}$$

As $E_1 = E_2$, the correctness is proved.

However, we are uncertain about the security of the above construction, since some components are shared outside the encryption Π that may break the security of Π in its original model. Therefore, we require individual security proof for each conversion to ensure the security.

4 Key-Policy Attribute-Based Keyword Search

In this section, we show a useful instance of our LEKS conversion by converting a KP-ABE into a KP-ABKS scheme. We starts with an ABE scheme [15] which is a variant of Goyal et al.'s scheme [12] while the function T defined in [12] is replaced with a random oracle. Then we convert it into a LEKS scheme by the method in Sect. 3.4. Finally, we prove the resulted LEKS scheme is IND-sCKA secure in random oracle model.

4.1   Base Scheme

The ABE scheme [15] modelled by LET works as follows.

- $(MSK, PK) \leftarrow Setup(params, \alpha)$: The system setup algorithm reuses the parameters $params$, $g_1 = g^{x_1}$, and $g_2 = g^{x_2}$. The master secret key is $y = x_1$. Since the function T is replaced with a random oracle, the algorithm is required to choose a cryptographic hash function $H : \{0,1\}^* \rightarrow \mathbb{G}_1$. Return $(MSK, PK) = (x_1, (g_1, g_2, H))$.
- $SK \leftarrow KeyGen(MSK, I_S)$: In KP-ABE, the user identity set I_S is the policy modelled as an access tree T (details in [12]). The algorithm chooses a random polynomial q_x for each non-leaf node $x \in T$ in a top-down manner. For each non-leaf node x, the degree d_x of the polynomial q_x is $d_x = k_x - 1$ where k_x is the threshold value of that node. For the root node, the algorithm sets $q_{root}(0) = x_1$. For other nodes, the algorithm sets $q_x(0) = q_{parent(x)}(index(x))$. With polynomials for the access tree T is decided, the algorithm generates the secret key components for the user. For each leaf node x, the algorithm chooses a random number $r_x \in_R \mathbb{Z}_p^+$, and calculates $D_x = g_2^{q_x(0)} H(attr(x))^{r_x}$, $R_x = g^{r_x}$. Return $SK = (T, \{(D_x, R_x)\}_{x \in leaves(T)})$.
- $C \leftarrow Encrypt(PK, I_C, M, t)$: In KP-ABE, the target identity set I_C is the attributes γ. To encrypt, the algorithm calculates $C_0 = M \cdot e(g_1, g_2)^t$, $C_1 = g^t$, $C_2 = \gamma$. For each attribute $attr_i \in \gamma$, the algorithm computes $C_i = H(attr_i)^t$. As required by LET, we note that $C_0 = M \cdot e(g_1, g_2)^t = e(g^{x_1}, g^{x_2})^t = e(g, g)^{x_1 x_2 t} = e(g, g)^{\alpha t}$. Return $C = (C_0, C_1, C_2, \{C_i\}_{attr_i \in \gamma})$.
- $M \leftarrow Decrypt(SK, C)$: At first, the algorithm checks whether $T(\gamma) = 1$ or not. If the attributes do not match the policy that $T(\gamma) = 0$, the algorithm returns $\perp$. Otherwise, the algorithm proceeds the sub-algorithm $\mathcal{D}$ as follows. For those matching attributes $attr_i = attr(x)$, where $attr_i \in \gamma$ and leaf node $x \in T$, the algorithm can decrypt that node by calculating

$$F_x = \frac{e(D_x, C_1)}{e(R_x, C_i)} = \frac{e(g_2^{q_x(0)} H(attr(x))^{r_x}, g^t)}{e(g^{r_x}, H(attr_i)^t)} = e(g, g_2)^{t \cdot q_x(0)}$$

Then the algorithm can decrypt the non-leaf node $x \in T$ by using polynomial interpolation. Let S_x be the child set of the node x.

$$F_x = \prod_{z \in S_x} F_z^{\Delta_{i, S_x}(0)} = \prod_{z \in S_x} \left(e(g, g_2)^{t \cdot q_z(0)} \right)^{\Delta_{i, S_x}(0)}$$
$$= e(g, g_2)^{t \cdot \sum_{z \in S_x} q_z(0) \cdot \Delta_{i, S_x}(0)} = e(g, g_2)^{t \cdot q_x(0)}$$

Since $T(\gamma) = 1$, the algorithm can decrypt the root node that

$$F_{root} = e(g, g_2)^{t \cdot q_{root}(0)} = e(g, g_2)^{x_1 t} = e(g, g_2)^{x_1 x_2 t} = e(g, g)^{\alpha t}$$

The algorithm sets F_{root} as the output of sub-algorithm $\mathcal{D}$. Finally, the algorithm computes the message $M = C_0 / F_{root}$ and returns M.

The correctness has been shown in the description of the decryption algorithm. We also show that the above scheme has the linearity property required by LET.

Theorem 4 (Correctness). *The above KP-ABE scheme is correct.*

Theorem 5 (Linearity). *The sub-algorithm $\mathcal{D}$ has linearity that*

$$\forall s \in \mathbb{Z}_p, \mathcal{D}(SK^s, C_1, C_2, \{C_i\}_{attr_i \in \gamma}) = \mathcal{D}(SK, C_1, C_2, \{C_i\}_{attr_i \in \gamma})^s$$

Proof. For the decryption of leaf nodes, the computation becomes

$$F'_x = \frac{e(D^s_x, C_1)}{e(R^s_x, C_i)} = \left(\frac{e(D_x, C_1)}{e(R_x, C_i)}\right)^s = F^s_x.$$

For the decryption of non-leaf nodes, the computation becomes

$$F'_x = \prod_{z \in S_x} F'^{\Delta_{i,S_x}(0)}_z = \prod_{z \in S_x} F^{s\Delta_{i,S_x}(0)}_z = \left(\prod_{z \in S_x} F^{\Delta_{i,S_x}(0)}_z\right)^s = F^s_x$$

Thus $F'_{root} = F^s_{root}$.

4.2 Construction from the Base Scheme

In this section, we apply the LEKS conversion as follows with some key notes.

- $(MSK, PK) \leftarrow Setup(1^\lambda)$: Although the hash functions in the LEKS and the KP-ABE schemes have the same domain and codomain, they cannot be merged since they will be programmed into two different random oracles.

$$\mathbb{G}_1 = \langle g \rangle, \quad e : \mathbb{G}_1 \times \mathbb{G}_1 \to \mathbb{G}_2, \quad H_1 : \{0,1\}^* \to \mathbb{G}_1, \quad H_2 : \{0,1\}^* \to \mathbb{G}_1,$$
$$x_1, x_2 \in_R \mathbb{Z}_p^+, \quad g_1 = g^{x_1}, \quad g_2 = g^{x_2}$$

return $(MSK, PK) = (x_1, (\mathbb{G}_1, \mathbb{G}_2, e, g, g_1, g_2, H_1, H_2))$.
- $SK \leftarrow KeyGen(MSK, I_S)$:

$$\forall x \in \text{leaves}(\mathcal{T}), \quad r_x \in_R \mathbb{Z}_p^+, \quad D_x = g_2^{q_x(0)} H_2(attr(x))^{r_x}, \quad R_x = g^{r_x}$$

return $SK = (\mathcal{T}, \{(D_x, R_x)\}_{x \in \text{leaves}(\mathcal{T})})$.
- $C \leftarrow LEKS(PK, I_C, W)$:

$$r_1, r_2 \in_R \mathbb{Z}_p^+, \quad C_1 = g_2^{r_2} H_1(W)^{r_1}, \quad C_2 = g_1^{r_1}, \quad C_3 = g^{r_2}$$

return $C = (C_1, C_2, C_3, \gamma, \{C_i = H_2(attr_i)^{r_2}\}_{attr_i \in \gamma})$.
- $T \leftarrow Trapdoor(SK, W)$:

$$s \in_R \mathbb{Z}_p^+, \quad T_1 = g_1^s, \quad T_2 = H_1(W)^s, \quad \{T_{x,1} = D^s_x, T_{x,2} = R^s_x\}_{\forall x \in \text{leaves}(\mathcal{T})}$$

return $T = (T_1, T_2, \mathcal{T}, \{(T_{x,1}, T_{x,2})\}_{x \in \text{leaves}(\mathcal{T})})$.
- $1/0 \leftarrow Test(C, T)$: The algorithm follows the decryption algorithm in the KP-ABE scheme. If $\mathcal{T}(\gamma) = 0$, the algorithm returns $\bot$. Otherwise, for leaf node $x \in \mathcal{T}$, it computes $F_x = e(T_{x,1}, C_1)/e(T_{x,2}, C_i)$. For non-leaf node, it computes exactly the same as in the decryption algorithm using polynomial interpolation. Eventually, the algorithm computes F_{root} and returns $e(C_1, T_1) \overset{?}{=} e(C_2, T_2) \cdot F_{root}$.

4.3 Security Proof

The above converted KP-ABKS scheme is similar to Zheng et al.'s KP-ABKS scheme [21]. The only difference between two schemes is that they use $g_2 g^{b \cdot H(W)}$ as the hash function for the attributes while we use $H_2 : \{0, 1\}^* \to \mathbb{G}_1$.

However, there are some issues in the security proof given in [21]. Before the simulation provided by the challenger, the adversary selects a target set of attributes $Attr^*$. In the simulation, the adversary is allowed to query the token generation oracle $\mathcal{O}_{\text{TokenGen}}(T, W)$ with any keyword W other than the target keywords w_0, w_1 and any policy T that $F(Attr^*, T) = 1$. Stepping into the oracle $\mathcal{O}_{\text{TokenGen}}(T, W)$, the challenger always runs the key generation oracle $\mathcal{O}_{\text{KeyGen}}(T)$ to get the secret key sk, and then uses it to generate the requested trapdoor. Since the oracle $\mathcal{O}_{\text{KeyGen}}(T)$ always aborts when $F(Attr^*, T) = 1$, the oracle $\mathcal{O}_{\text{TokenGen}}(T, W)$ always aborts when the adversary does the queries mentioned above. This renders the proof invalid and hence the security of Zheng et al.'s KP-ABKS scheme is unknown.

We prove our KP-ABKS is secure under the ℓ-DCBDH assumption instead of the standard Decisional Linear Assumption (DLIN).

Theorem 6. *The proposed KP-ABKS is IND-sCKA (Definition 6) secure. If an adversary $\mathcal{A}$ can win Game 1 with the advantage ε, an algorithm $\mathcal{S}$ can be constructed to solve ℓ-DCBDH problem (Definition 3) in polynomial time with the advantage $\varepsilon' \geq \frac{\varepsilon}{2e(q+2)}$, querying $\mathcal{O}_{Trapdoor}$ for at most q times where $q \leq \ell$.*

Due to the space limit, the proof will be provided to the full version of the paper.

5 Conclusion

In this paper, we introduced a (P, f)-DBDH problem family and demonstrated its hardness under the generic bilinear group model. We also derived a hard computational ℓ-DCBDH problem from the (P, f)-DBDH problem family. As the main contribution of this paper, we proposed LEKS and its security model, and defined LET which can be used to convert encryption schemes into the corresponding LEKS schemes. To show a concrete instance of our LEKS conversion framework, we converted a KP-ABE scheme into a KP-ABKS scheme and proved its security in the random oracle model under the ℓ-DCBDH assumption. Our future work will be finding more LET-compatible encryption schemes, converting them into searchable schemes and proving their security.

References

1. Abdalla, M., Bellare, M., Catalano, D., Kiltz, E., Kohno, T., Lange, T., Malone-Lee, J., Neven, G., Paillier, P., Shi, H.: Searchable encryption revisited: consistency properties, relation to anonymous IBE, and extensions. J. Cryptology **21**(3), 350–391 (2008)

2. Attrapadung, N., Furukawa, J., Imai, H.: Forward-secure and searchable broadcast encryption with short ciphertexts and private keys. In: Lai, X., Chen, K. (eds.) ASIACRYPT 2006. LNCS, vol. 4284, pp. 161–177. Springer, Heidelberg (2006)
3. Attrapadung, N., Libert, B., de Panafieu, E.: Expressive key-policy attribute-based encryption with constant-size ciphertexts. In: Catalano, D., Fazio, N., Gennaro, R., Nicolosi, A. (eds.) PKC 2011. LNCS, vol. 6571, pp. 90–108. Springer, Heidelberg (2011)
4. Bethencourt, J., Sahai, A., Waters, B.: Ciphertext-policy attribute-based encryption. In: IEEE Symposium on Security and Privacy, SP 2007, pp. 321–334, May 2007
5. Boneh, D., Boyen, X.: Short signatures without random oracles and the SDH assumption in bilinear groups. J. Cryptology $21(2)$, 149–177 (2007). http://dx.org/10.1007/s00145-007-9005-7
6. Boneh, D., Boyen, X., Goh, E.-J.: Hierarchical identity based encryption with constant size ciphertext. In: Cramer, R. (ed.) EUROCRYPT 2005. LNCS, vol. 3494, pp. 440–456. Springer, Heidelberg (2005). doi:10.1007/11426639_26
7. Boneh, D., Boyen, X., Shacham, H.: Short group signatures. In: Franklin, M. (ed.) CRYPTO 2004. LNCS, vol. 3152, pp. 41–55. Springer, Heidelberg (2004). doi:10. 1007/978-3-540-28628-8_3
8. Boneh, D., Di Crescenzo, G., Ostrovsky, R., Persiano, G.: Public key encryption with keyword search. In: Cachin, C., Camenisch, J.L. (eds.) EUROCRYPT 2004. LNCS, vol. 3027, pp. 506–522. Springer, Heidelberg (2004)
9. Boneh, D., Franklin, M.: Identity-based encryption from the weil pairing. In: Kilian, J. (ed.) CRYPTO 2001. LNCS, vol. 2139, pp. 213–229. Springer, Heidelberg (2001)
10. Boyen, X., Waters, B.: Anonymous hierarchical identity-based encryption (Without Random Oracles). In: Dwork, C. (ed.) CRYPTO 2006. LNCS, vol. 4117, pp. 290–307. Springer, Heidelberg (2006). doi:10.1007/11818175_17
11. Diffie, W., Hellman, M.: New directions in cryptography. IEEE Trans. Inf. Theory $22(6)$, 644–654 (1976)
12. Goyal, V., Pandey, O., Sahai, A., Waters, B.: Attribute-based encryption for fine-grained access control of encrypted data. In: Proceedings of the 13th ACM Conference on Computer and Communications Security, CCS 2006, NY, USA, pp. 89–98. (2006). http://doi.acm.org/10.1145/1180405.1180418
13. Hwang, Y.-H., Lee, P.J.: Public key encryption with conjunctive keyword search and its extension to a multi-user system. In: Takagi, T., Okamoto, E., Okamoto, T., Okamoto, T. (eds.) Pairing 2007. LNCS, vol. 4575, pp. 2–22. Springer, Heidelberg (2007)
14. Mell, P., Grance, T.: The nist definition of cloud computiing. Technical report, National Institue of Standards and Technology (2011)
15. Pirretti, M., Traynor, P., McDaniel, P., Waters, B.: Secure attribute-based systems. In: Proceedings of the 13th ACM Conference on Computer and Communications Security, CCS 2006, NY, USA, pp. 99–112 (2006). http://doi.acm.org/10.1145/1180405.1180419
16. Sahai, A., Waters, B.: Fuzzy identity-based encryption. In: Cramer, R. (ed.) EUROCRYPT 2005. LNCS, vol. 3494, pp. 457–473. Springer, Heidelberg (2005)
17. Shamir, A.: Identity-based cryptosystems and signature schemes. In: Blakely, G.R., Chaum, D. (eds.) CRYPTO 1984. LNCS, vol. 196, pp. 47–53. Springer, Heidelberg (1985)
18. Shoup, V.: Lower bounds for discrete logarithms and related problems. In: Fumy, W. (ed.) EUROCRYPT 1997. LNCS, vol. 1233, pp. 256–266. Springer, Heidelberg (1997). doi:10.1007/3-540-69053-0_18

19. Sun, W., Yu, S., Lou, W., Hou, T., Li, H.: Protecting your right: verifiable attribute-based keyword search with fine-grainedowner-enforced search authorization in the cloud. IEEE Trans. Parallel Distrib. Syst. **PP**(99), 1 (2014)
20. Waters, B.: Functional encryption: origins and recent developments. In: Kurosawa, K., Hanaoka, G. (eds.) PKC 2013. LNCS, vol. 7778, pp. 51–54. Springer, Heidelberg (2013)
21. Zheng, Q., Xu, S., Ateniese, G.: Vabks: verifiable attribute-based keyword search over outsourced encrypted data. In: 2014 Proceedings IEEE INFOCOM, pp. 522–530, April 2014

Broadcast Encryption

Generic Anonymous Identity-Based Broadcast Encryption with Chosen-Ciphertext Security

Kai He[1,2], Jian Weng[1]($\boxtimes$), Man Ho Au[3], Yijun Mao[4,5], and Robert H. Deng[6]

[1] Department of Computer Science, Jinan University, Guangzhou, China
hekai1214@yahoo.com, cryptjweng@gmail.com
[2] Faculty of Information Technology, Monash University, Melbourne, Australia
[3] Department of Computing, Hong Kong Polytechnic University,
Hong Kong, Hong Kong
[4] School of Mathematics and Informatics, South China University of Agriculture,
Guangzhou, China
[5] School of Information Science and Technology, Sun Yat-Sen University,
Guangzhou, China
[6] School of Information Systems, Singapore Management University,
Singapore, Singapore

Abstract. In a broadcast encryption system, a broadcaster can encrypt a message to a group of authorized receivers S and each authorized receiver can use his/her own private key to correctly decrypt the broadcast ciphertext, while the users outside S cannot. Identity-based broadcast encryption (IBBE) system is a variant of broadcast encryption system where any string representing the user's identity (e.g., email address) can be used as his/her public key. IBBE has found many applications in real life, such as pay-TV systems, distribution of copyrighted materials, satellite radio communications. When employing an IBBE system, it is very important to protect the message's confidentiality and the users' anonymity. However, existing IBBE systems cannot satisfy confidentiality and anonymity simultaneously. In this paper, using an anonymous identity-based encryption (IBE) primitive with robust property as a building block, we propose a generic IBBE construction, which can simultaneously ensure the confidentiality and anonymity under chosen-ciphertext attacks. Our generic IBBE construction has a desirable property that the public parameters size, the private key size and the decryption cost are constant and independent of the number of receivers.

Keywords: Identity-based broadcast encryption · Anonymity · Robustness · Chosen-ciphertext security · Random oracle model

1 Introduction

Broadcast encryption (BE), introduced by Fiat and Naor [16], is one kind of one-to-many encryption that allows a broadcaster to encrypt one message to a group of users who are listening to a broadcast channel, and only the authorized users

© Springer International Publishing Switzerland 2016
J.K. Liu and R. Steinfeld (Eds.): ACISP 2016, Part II, LNCS 9723, pp. 207–222, 2016.
DOI: 10.1007/978-3-319-40367-0_13

can get the message. At present, BE causes a wide spread attention in theory and practice. As BE can save most computational cost and communication load relatively to repeatedly utilize point-to-point traditional encryption.

Identity-based broadcast encryption (IBBE) [12,28] is a special kind of public-key BE, in which the public key of each user can be any string just representing the user's identity (e.g., email address) and the private keys of users are generated by a private key generator (PKG) according to their identities. It is the same as in the identity-based encryption [8]. There exists a desired property is that IBBE can support exponentially many users as potential receivers.

While an encryption scheme aims to protect the message's confidentiality, another security requirement, namely, anonymity, which aims to hide the receiver's identity and it is a desirable security property in many application scenarios. Anonymity comes from the key privacy concept, which was first introduced by Bellare et al. [6]. It captures the property that an eavesdropper cannot tell which public key the ciphertext is created under. However, the receiver set S in the traditional IBBE scheme is transmitted as a part of the ciphertext. Obviously, it cannot hide the receivers' identities. Therefore, traditional IBBE schemes are unable to obtain the anonymity requirement.

1.1 Our Contributions

In this paper, we propose a generic identity-based broadcast encryption (IBBE) scheme from a generic anonymous IBE construction, which is the first IBBE scheme simultaneously provide confidentiality and anonymity against chosen-ciphertext attacks under Decisional Bilinear Diffie-Hellman (DBDH) assumption. In addition, the public parameters size, the private key size and the decryption cost are constant and independent of the number of receivers is more efficient than the existing IBBE schemes.

1.2 Related Work

Since broadcast encryption (BE) was introduced by Fiat and Naor [16], many BE schemes have been proposed, e.g., [9,12,13,17,28]. However, these schemes cannot ensure the anonymity of receivers. To address this problem, in 2006, Barth et al. [5] presented two anonymous BE constructions in the public key setting with chosen-ciphertext security. Their first construction is a generic BE construction in the standard model, where the decryption cost is linear with the number of receivers. As it need try to find an appropriate ciphertext component for decryption. Their second construction is an improved construction in which only a constant number of cryptographic operations is required for decryption, whereas the security proof relies on the random oracle model [7]. In PKC 2012, Fazio et al. [15] proposed two outsider-anonymous broadcast encryption constructions with sub-linear ciphertexts, which are adaptive CPA and CCA secure in the standard model, respectively. In the same year, Libert et al. [23] presented several anonymous broadcast encryption constructions with adaptive CCA security in the standard model and gave an united security definition for anonymous BE scheme. However, all of these constructions are in the public key setting.

In 2007, the first IBBE scheme with fix-size ciphertext and private key was proposed by Delerablee [12]. Specially, their scheme supports a flexible number of possible users. That is, the number of users are not determined in the system setup phase. Since then, lots of IBBE schemes with different properties have been proposed, e.g., [19, 21, 24, 25, 28, 30, 31, 33, 34, 37, 40]. When identity-based encryption is incorporated to the multi-receiver setting, many multi-receiver identity-based encryption schemes [3, 4, 10] have been proposed. However, among all of these IBBE and multi-receiver identity-based encryption schemes, the receivers' identities are transmitted as a part of the ciphertext. Obviously, these schemes cannot provide anonymity.

Therefore, many anonymous identity-based broadcast encryption schemes, e.g., [20, 26, 38] and anonymous multi-receiver identity-based encryption schemes, e.g., [11, 14, 22, 29, 35, 36, 39] have been successively proposed. However, none of these schemes can achieve confidentiality and anonymity simultaneously against chosen-ciphertext attacks. In this paper, we have solved this problem.

1.3   Bilinear Groups

We briefly review the concept of bilinear groups which is the underlying algebraic structure of many IBBE including ours.

We assume there is a probabilistic algorithm $\mathcal{G}$ which takes as input a security parameter λ and outputs a tuple $(p, \mathbb{G}, \mathbb{G}_T, e)$, where $\mathbb{G}$ and $\mathbb{G}_T$ are multiplicative cyclic groups of prime order p (of bit-length λ), and $e : \mathbb{G} \times \mathbb{G} \to \mathbb{G}_T$ is a map, which has the following properties: **Bilinearity:** $e(u^a, v^b) = e(u, v)^{ab}$ for all $u, v \in \mathbb{G}$ and $\forall a, b \in \mathbb{Z}_p$. **Non-degeneracy:** $e(g, g) \neq 1_{\mathbb{G}}$, where g is a generator of $\mathbb{G}$. **Computability:** There exists an efficient algorithm to compute $e(u, v)$ for $\forall u, v \in \mathbb{G}$.

1.4   Decisional Bilinear Diffie-Hellman Assumption

The decisional BDH (DBDH) problem in a bilinear group $(p, \mathbb{G}, \mathbb{G}_T, e)$ is as follows: Given a tuple (g, g^a, g^b, g^c, Z) for $a, b, c \leftarrow_R \mathbb{Z}_p$ as input, output 1 if $Z = e(g, g)^{abc}$ and 0 otherwise. For a probabilistic algorithm $\mathcal{A}$, we define its advantage in solving the DBDH problem as $Adv_{\mathcal{A}}^{DBDH} = |\Pr[\mathcal{A}(g, g^a, g^b, g^c, e(g, g)^{abc}) = 1] - \Pr[\mathcal{A}(g, g^a, g^b, g^c, Z) = 1]|$, where g is a random generator in $\mathbb{G}$ and $Z \leftarrow_R \mathbb{G}_T$. We say that the DBDH assumption holds if all probabilistic polynomial-time (PPT) algorithms have a negligible advantage in solving the DBDH problem.

2   Identity-Based Broadcast Encryption

We shall review the definition and security notions for identity-based broadcast encryption [18] as follows.

An identity-based broadcast encryption scheme, associated with message space $\mathcal{M}$, consists of a tuple of four algorithms (Setup, Extract, Enc, Dec):

Setup(1^λ): On input of a security parameter λ, it outputs the public parameters *params* and a master secret key *msk*.

Extract(msk, ID): On input of a master secret key *msk* and an identity ID, it outputs a private key sk_{ID} for the identity ID.

Enc(*params*, S, M): On input of the public parameters *params*, a receiver set S and a message $M \in \mathcal{M}$, it outputs a ciphertext CT.

Dec(sk_{ID}, CT): On input of a private key sk_{ID} and a ciphertext CT, it outputs either a message M or an error symbol $\perp$.

The correctness property requires that, for all $ID \in S$, if $(params, msk) \leftarrow$ Setup (1^λ), $sk_{ID} \leftarrow$ Extract (msk, ID) and $CT \leftarrow$ Enc $(params, S, M)$, then Dec $(sk_{ID}, CT) = M$ with overwhelming probability.

Remark. Identity-based encryption is a special case of identity-based broadcast encryption, when the size of the receiver set is only one.

Next, we shall review the security notions for an IBBE scheme. First, we review the model of indistinguishability under chosen-ciphertext attacks (IND-CCA), which means that the ciphertext does not leak any information of the message. Then, we review the model of anonymity under chosen-ciphertext attacks (ANO-CCA), which means that the ciphertext does not leak any identity in the receiver set. Last, we review the model of weakly robust against chosen-ciphertext attacks (WROB-CCA), which guarantees that the decryption attempts to fail with high probability when the "wrong" private key is used. Respectively, these security models are defined by the following games between a PPT adversary $\mathcal{A}$ and a challenger $\mathcal{C}$.

The IND-CCA Game:

Setup: Challenger $\mathcal{C}$ runs $(params, msk) \leftarrow$ Setup(1^λ), and then sends the public parameters *params* to adversary $\mathcal{A}$ and keeps the master secret key *msk* itself.

Phase 1: Adversary $\mathcal{A}$ adaptively issues the following queries:

- *Extraction Query:* On input of an identity ID, challenger $\mathcal{C}$ returns $sk_{ID} \leftarrow$ Extract(msk, ID) to adversary $\mathcal{A}$.
- *Decryption Query:* On input of an identity ID and a ciphertext CT, challenger $\mathcal{C}$ returns $m \leftarrow$ Dec(sk_{ID}, CT) to adversary $\mathcal{A}$, where $sk_{ID} \leftarrow$ Extract(msk, ID).

Challenge: Adversary $\mathcal{A}$ submits two distinct equal-length messages M_0, M_1 $\in \mathcal{M}$ and a receiver set S^* to challenger $\mathcal{C}$. It is required that $\mathcal{A}$ has not issued *Extraction Query* on $ID \in S^*$. Then challenger $\mathcal{C}$ flips a random coin $\beta \in \{0, 1\}$ and returns the challenge ciphertext $CT^* \leftarrow$ Encrypt $(params, S^*, M_\beta)$ to adversary $\mathcal{A}$.

Phase 2: Adversary $\mathcal{A}$ continues to adaptively issue queries as in Phase 1 subject to the following restrictions: (i) $\mathcal{A}$ cannot issue *Extraction Query* on ID, where $ID \in S^*$; (ii) $\mathcal{A}$ cannot issue *Decryption Query* on (ID, C^*), where $ID \in S^*$.

Guess: Adversary $\mathcal{A}$ outputs a guess $\beta' \in \{0, 1\}$.

Definition 1. *We define adversary $\mathcal{A}$'s advantage in the* IND-CCA *Game as* $Adv_{\mathcal{A},\text{IBBE}}^{\text{IND-CCA}} = |\Pr[\beta' = \beta] - 1/2|$. *We say that an* IBBE *scheme is* IND-CCA *secure, if for any* PPT *adversary $\mathcal{A}$, the advantage $Adv_{\mathcal{A},\text{IBBE}}^{\text{IND-CCA}}$ is negligible in* IND-CCA *Game.*

The ANO-CCA Game:

Setup: It is the same as in the IND-CCA Game.

Phase 1: It is the same as in the IND-CCA Game.

Challenge: Adversary $\mathcal{A}$ submits a message M^* and two distinct sets S_0, S_1 to challenger $\mathcal{C}$. It is required that $|S_0| = |S_1|$ and adversary $\mathcal{A}$ has not issued *Extraction Query* on $ID \in S_0 \triangle S_1$, where $S_0 \triangle S_1$ denotes $S_0 \cup S_1 - S_0 \cap S_1$. Then challenger $\mathcal{C}$ flips a random coin $\beta \in \{0, 1\}$ and returns the challenge ciphertext $CT^* \leftarrow \text{Encrypt}(params, S_\beta, M^*)$ to $\mathcal{A}$.

Phase 2: Adversary $\mathcal{A}$ continues to adaptively issue queries as in Phase 1 with the restrictions as follows: (i) Adversary $\mathcal{A}$ cannot issue *Extraction Query* on ID, where $ID \in S_0 \triangle S_1$; (ii) Adversary $\mathcal{A}$ cannot issue *Decryption Query* on (ID, C^*), where $ID \in S_0 \triangle S_1$.

Guess: Adversary $\mathcal{A}$ outputs a guess $\beta' \in \{0, 1\}$.

Definition 2. *We define adversary $\mathcal{A}$'s advantage in the above* ANO-CCA *Game as $Adv_{\mathcal{A},\text{IBBE}}^{\text{ANO-CCA}} = |\Pr[\beta' = \beta] - 1/2|$. We say that an* IBBE *scheme is* ANO-CCA *secure, if for any* PPT *adversary $\mathcal{A}$, the advantage $Adv_{\mathcal{A},\text{IBBE}}^{\text{ANO-CCA}}$ is negligible in the above* ANO-CCA *Game.*

Remark. Note that the definition captures not only outsider attacks but also insider attacks. In other words, even when an identity $ID \in S_0 \cap S_1$ is corrupted, the anonymity of any non-corrupted $ID \in S_0 \triangle S_1$ is still preserved.

The WROB-CCA Game:

Setup: It is the same as in the IND-CCA Game.

Query Phase: It is the same as Phase 1 in the IND-CCA Game.

Output: Adversary $\mathcal{A}$ outputs a message M, a receiver set $S^* = \{ID_1, ID_2, \cdots, ID_t\}$, where $|S^*| = t$. Challenger $\mathcal{C}$ outputs the challenge ciphertext $CT^* \leftarrow \text{Encrypt}(params, S^*, M)$.

We say that $\mathcal{A}$ wins the WROB-CCA Game if $\text{Dec}(sk_{ID^*}, CT^*) \neq \bot$, where $ID^* \notin S^*$ and $sk_{ID^*} = \text{Extract}(msk, ID^*)$. It is required that $\mathcal{A}$ has not issued *Extraction Query* on ID^* in Query Phase.

We define adversary $\mathcal{A}$'s advantage as the probability of that $\mathcal{A}$ wins.

Definition 3. *We say that an* IBBE *scheme is* WROB-CCA *secure, if for all* PPT *adversaries* $\mathcal{A}$, *the advantage of winning the above* WROB-CCA *Game is negligible.*

Remark. The above security notions of IND-CCA, ANO-CCA and WROB-CCA can be naturally defined for an identity-based encryption (IBE) scheme by limiting the size of the receiver set to be only one.

3   Generic Anonymous IBBE from IBE

In this section, we present a generic IBBE construction which builds on a IND-CCA secure, ANO-CCA secure and WROB-CCA secure IBE primitive. The generic IBBE construction has a desirable property that the public parameters size, the private key size and the decryption cost are all constant and independent of the number of receivers, while the ciphertext size is linear with the size of the receivers.

3.1   Construction

Given an IND-CCA, ANO-CCA and WROB-CCA secure IBE scheme IBE= (IBE.Setup, IBE.Extract, IBE.Enc, IBE.Dec) and a strong one-time signature scheme $\Sigma = (\mathsf{Gen}, \mathsf{Sig}, \mathsf{Ver})$, we construct an IND-CCA and ANO-CCA secure IBBE construction IBBE = (IBBE.Setup, IBBE.Extract, IBBE. Enc, IBBE.Dec).

IBBE.Setup(1^λ): On input of a security parameter λ, it generates a bilinear map $(p, \mathbb{G}, \mathbb{G}_T, e)$, where $\mathbb{G}$ and $\mathbb{G}_T$ are two cyclic groups with prime order p and e is a bilinear map $e : \mathbb{G} \times \mathbb{G} \to \mathbb{G}_T$. Then, it chooses $g \leftarrow_R \mathbb{G}$, $\alpha \leftarrow_R \mathbb{Z}_p$ and computes $g_1 = g^\alpha$. Next, it runs $\langle \widehat{params}, \widehat{msk} \rangle \leftarrow$ IBE.Setup(1^λ). Besides, it chooses three hash functions H_1, H_2, H_3, such that $H_1 : \{0,1\}^* \to \mathbb{G}$, $H_2 : \mathbb{G}_T \to \{0,1\}^\lambda$ and $H_3 : \{0,1\}^* \to \mathbb{Z}_p$. The public parameters are $params = (\mathbb{G}, \mathbb{G}_T, \mathbb{Z}_p, e, p, g, g_1, \widehat{params}, H_1, H_2, H_3)$ and the master secret key is $msk = (\alpha, \widehat{msk})$.

IBBE.Extract(msk, ID): On input of a master secret key msk and an identity ID, it computes $sk_{ID}^0 = H_1(ID)^\alpha$ and $sk_{ID}^1 \leftarrow$ IBE.Extract$(\widehat{msk}, ID)$. It outputs the private key $sk_{ID} = (sk_{ID}^0, sk_{ID}^1)$ for the identity ID.

IBBE.Enc$(params, S, M)$: On input of the public parameters $params$, a receiver set $S = \{ID_1, ID_2, \cdots, ID_t\}$ and a message M, it first generates a signature key pair $(svk, ssk) \leftarrow$ Gen (1^λ). Then it chooses $\delta \leftarrow_R \mathbb{Z}_p$, lets $r = H_3(\delta, M)$ and computes the common part of the ciphertext $T = g^r$. Next, for each $ID \in S$, it computes $c_{ID}^0 = H_2(e(g_1, H_1(ID))^r)$ and $c_{ID}^1 \leftarrow$ IBE.Enc$(\widehat{params}, ID, svk \,\|\, \delta \,\|\, M)$. Let $C_1 = (c_{ID_1}^0, c_{ID_1}^1) \,\|\, \cdots \,\|\, (c_{ID_t}^0, c_{ID_t}^1)$. The ciphertext is $CT = (svk, T, C_1, \sigma)$, where $\sigma = $ Sig $(ssk, T \,\|\, C_1)$.

IBBE.Dec(sk_{ID}, CT): On input of a private key $sk_{ID} = (sk_{ID}^0, sk_{ID}^1)$ and a ciphertext $CT = (svk, T, C_1, \sigma)$, where $C_1 = (c_{ID_1}^0, c_{ID_1}^1) \,\|\, \cdots \,\|\, (c_{ID_t}^0, c_{ID_t}^1)$. It checks whether $\mathsf{Ver}(svk, T\|C_1, \sigma) = 1$ holds. If not, it returns $\bot$. Otherwise, it computes $c_{ID}^0 = H_2(e(T, sk_{ID}^0))$. If $c_{ID}^0 \neq c_{ID_j}^0$ for all $j \in \{1, \cdots, t\}$, returns $\perp$; else considers the smallest index j such that $c_{ID}^0 = c_{ID_j}^0$, then computes $L \leftarrow$ IBE.Dec$(sk_{ID}^1, c_{ID_j}^1)$. If $L = \perp$, returns $\perp$; else parses L as $svk'||\delta'||M$. If $svk' \neq svk$ or $T \neq g^{H_3(\delta', M)}$, returns $\perp$; else returns M.

The correctness of IBBE construction follows directly from the correctness and weak robustness of IBE scheme.

3.2 Security Analysis

In this subsection, we analyze that the above IBBE construction is ANO-CCA secure. Regarding the IND-CCA security, we have the following Theorem 1, whose proof can be found in the full paper.

Theorem 1. *Suppose that H_3 is a random oracle, the IBE scheme is IND-CCA secure and the signature Σ scheme is a strong one-time signature, then the generic IBBE construction in Sect. 3 is IND-CCA secure.*

Next, we shall prove the following Theorem 2, which states that our IBBE construction is ANO-CCA secure.

Theorem 2. *Suppose that H_1, H_2, H_3 are random oracles, the IBE scheme are WROB-CCA and ANO-CCA secure, the signature Σ scheme is a strong one-time signature scheme and the DBDH assumption holds, then the above IBBE construction is ANO-CCA secure.*

Proof. We proceed by a sequence of hybrid games starting with $Game_0$ where adversary $\mathcal{A}$ is given an encryption of M^* on S_0. At the last game, adversary $\mathcal{A}$ is given an encryption of M^* on S_1. Without loss of generality, we suppose S_0 and S_1 are different by only one receiver and $|S_0| = |S_1| = t$. (The general case can be proved through a hybrid argument, which is the adversary $\mathcal{A}$ selects the receiver sets differing by only one receiver each time.) Let ID_v be the unique element of $S_0 \backslash S_1$, ID_w be the unique element of $S_1 \backslash S_0$. (Note that $S_i \backslash S_j = \{ID | ID \in S_i \cap ID \notin S_j\}$)

Game$_0$: The challenge ciphertext CT^* is a correctly encrypted M^* on receiver set S_0, where $CT^* = (svk^*, T^*, C_1^*, \sigma^*)$ and $C_1^* = (c_{ID_1}^{0*}, c_{ID_1}^{1*}) || \cdots || (c_{ID_t}^{0*}, c_{ID_t}^{1*})$. Let $c = (c_{ID_v}^{0*}, c_{ID_v}^{1*}) = (H_2(e(g_1, H_1(ID_v))^r), \text{IBE.Enc}(\widehat{params}, ID_v, svk^*||\delta^*||M^*))$ be the challenge ciphertext component which is related to the identity ID_v.

Game$_1$: It is the same as $Game_0$, but the challenger rejects all post challenge *Decryption Query* $\langle ID, CT \rangle$, where CT contains the same verification key svk^*.

Game$_2$: c is replaced with $(R, \text{IBE.Enc}(\widehat{params}, ID_v, svk^*||\delta^*||M^*))$, where $R \leftarrow_R \{0, 1\}^\lambda$.

Game$_3$: c is replaced with $(R, \text{IBE.Enc}(\widehat{params}, ID_w, svk^*||\delta^*||M^*))$.

Game$_4$: c is replaced with $(H_2(e(g_1, H_1(ID_w))^r), \text{IBE.Enc}(\widehat{params}, ID_w, svk^*||\delta^*||M^*))$. Notice that the component is now encrypted on ID_w instead of ID_v.

Game$_5$: It is the same as $Game_4$, but the challenger does not reject all post challenge *Decryption Query* $\langle ID, CT \rangle$, where CT contains the same verification key svk^*. Notice that the challenge ciphertext CT^* is correctly encrypted M^* under the receiver set S_1 now.

The above games differ slightly from each other. In the following lemmas, we shall show that every two adjacent games are computationally indistinguishable. Transitivity shows that $Game_0$ and $Game_5$ are computationally indistinguishable. The challenge ciphertext CT^* in $Game_0$ is encrypted M^* on receiver set S_0 and the challenge ciphertext CT^* in $Game_5$ is encrypted M^* on receiver set S_1. According to the ANO-CCA Game, we can achieve that the above IBBE construction is ANO-CCA secure.

Lemma 1. *Suppose that the signature scheme Σ is a strong one-time signature scheme, then $Game_0$ and $Game_1$ are computationally indistinguishable.*

Proof. We define event F that adversary $\mathcal{A}$ makes a legal *Decryption Query* on $(ID, CT = (svk, T, C_1, \sigma))$, where $\mathsf{Ver}(svk, T\|C_1, \sigma) = 1$ and $svk = svk^*$ and $\langle (T\|C_1), \sigma \rangle \neq \langle (T^*\|C_1^*), \sigma^* \rangle$. Suppose event F happens, then it is easy to construct a PPT algorithm $\mathcal{C}$, which makes use of adversary $\mathcal{A}$ to break the underlying one-time signature scheme Σ.

Setup: $\mathcal{C}$ is given a verification key svk^*. Then $\mathcal{C}$ runs $(params, msk) \leftarrow$ IBBE.Setup(1^λ). Next, it returns $params$ to $\mathcal{A}$ and keeps msk itself.

Phase 1: $\mathcal{A}$ can adaptively issue *Extraction Query* and *Decryption Query*. $\mathcal{C}$ can answer any *Extraction Query* and *Decryption Query* since it has the master secret key msk.

Challenge: $\mathcal{A}$ submits a message M^* and two distinct sets S_0, S_1 to $\mathcal{C}$. It is required that $\mathcal{A}$ has not issued *Extraction Query* on ID in **Phase 1**, where $ID \in \{ID_v, ID_w\}$. $\mathcal{C}$ first runs IBBE.Enc($params, S_0, M^*$) to obtain a part of ciphertext $\langle T^*, C_1^* \rangle$, and then obtains (from its signing oracle) a signature σ^* on the "message" $\langle T^*\|C_1^* \rangle$. Finally, $\mathcal{C}$ sends challenge ciphertext $CT^* = (svk^*, T^*, C_1^*, \sigma^*)$ to $\mathcal{A}$.

Phase 2: $\mathcal{A}$ continues to adaptively issue queries as follows:

- *Extraction Query:* $\mathcal{A}$ issues *Extraction Query* on ID, such that $ID \notin \{ID_v, ID_w\}$, $\mathcal{C}$ handles them as in **Phase 1**.
- *Decryption Query:* $\mathcal{A}$ issues *Decryption Query* on $\langle ID, CT \rangle$, $\mathcal{C}$ parses CT as (svk, σ, T, C_1), if $\mathsf{Ver}(svk, T\|C_1, \sigma) = 1$, $svk = svk^*$ and $\langle (T\|C_1), \sigma \rangle \neq \langle (T^*\|C_1^*), \sigma^* \rangle$, then $\mathcal{C}$ presents $\langle (T\|C_1), \sigma \rangle$ as a forgery and aborts. Otherwise, $\mathcal{C}$ answers these queries with the master secret key msk as in **Phase 1**.

Guess: $\mathcal{A}$ outputs a bit $b' \in \{0, 1\}$.

Observe that $Game_0$ and $Game_1$ are identical as long as event F does not happen. If event F happens with a non-negligible probability, then $\mathcal{C}$ can forge a valid signature with a non-negligible advantage. However, since the signature scheme Σ is a strong one-time signature scheme, then event F happens with negligible probability.

Hence, $Game_0$ and $Game_1$ are computationally indistinguishable.

Lemma 2. *Suppose that DBDH assumption holds, then $Game_1$ and $Game_2$ are computationally indistinguishable.*

Proof. Suppose there exists an adversary $\mathcal{A}$ who can distinguish $Game_1$ from $Game_2$. It is easy to construct a PPT algorithm $\mathcal{C}$ that makes use of $\mathcal{A}$ to solve the DBDH problem. Suppose $\mathcal{C}$ is given a DBDH challenge (g, g^a, g^b, g^c, Z) with unknown $a, b, c \in \mathbb{Z}_p$, $\mathcal{C}$'s goal is to output 1 if $Z = e(g, g)^{abc}$ and 0 otherwise. $\mathcal{C}$ acts as a challenger with adversary $\mathcal{A}$ as follows.

Setup: $\mathcal{C}$ runs $(\widehat{params}, \widehat{msk}) \leftarrow \mathsf{IBE.Setup}(1^\lambda)$, sets $g_1 = g^a$, and chooses H_1, H_2, H_3 as random oracles. $\mathcal{C}$ gives the public parameters $params = (\widehat{params}, g, g_1, H_1, H_2, H_3)$ to $\mathcal{A}$ and keeps $\widehat{msk}$ itself.

Phase 1: $\mathcal{A}$ adaptively issues queries as follows:

Hash₁ Query: On input of an identity ID, $\mathcal{C}$ does as follows: if there exists a record $\langle ID, Q, q, \varpi \rangle$ in the H_1-list, which the list is initially empty, returns Q; else chooses $\varpi \leftarrow_R \{0, 1\}$ and $q \leftarrow_R \mathbb{Z}_p$. If $\varpi = 0$, computes $Q = g^q$; else computes $Q = g^{bq}$ and adds $\langle ID, Q, q, \varpi \rangle$ into the H_1-list. $\mathcal{C}$ returns Q to $\mathcal{A}$.

Hash₂ Query: On input of X, $\mathcal{C}$ does the following: if there exists a record $\langle X, v \rangle$ in the H_2-list, which the list is initially empty, returns v; else selects $v \leftarrow_R \mathbb{Z}_p$, and adds $\langle X, v \rangle$ into the H_2-list. $\mathcal{C}$ returns v to $\mathcal{A}$.

Hash₃ Query: On input of (δ, M), $\mathcal{C}$ does the following: if there exists a record $\langle \delta, M, r, g^r \rangle$ in the H_3-list, which the list is initially empty, returns r; else selects $r \leftarrow_R \mathbb{Z}_p$, adds $\langle \delta, M, r, g^r \rangle$ into the H_3-list. Returns r to adversary $\mathcal{A}$.

Extraction Query: On input of an identity ID, $\mathcal{C}$ first issues $Hash_1$ Query on the identity ID and gets the tuple $\langle ID, Q, q, \varpi \rangle$. If $\varpi = 1$, $\mathcal{C}$ outputs $\perp$ and aborts; else $\mathcal{C}$ computes $sk_{ID}^0 = g_1^q$. Then runs $\mathsf{IBE.Extract}(\widehat{msk}, ID)$ to obtain sk_{ID}^1. $\mathcal{C}$ returns $sk_{ID} = (sk_{ID}^0, sk_{ID}^1)$ to adversary $\mathcal{A}$.

Decryption Query: On input of $\langle ID, CT \rangle$, $\mathcal{C}$ parses CT as (svk, σ, T, C_1), where $C_1 = (c_{ID_1}^0, c_{ID_1}^1) || \cdots || (c_{ID_t}^0, c_{ID_t}^1)$. If $\mathsf{Ver}(svk, T || C_1, \sigma) = 0$, $\mathcal{C}$ outputs $\perp$; else $\mathcal{C}$ issues $Hash_1$ Query on ID to obtain the tuple $\langle ID, Q, q, \varpi \rangle$. When $\varpi = 0$, $\mathcal{C}$ computes $sk_{ID}^0 = g_1^q$, and then uses sk_{ID}^0 and the master secret key $\widehat{msk}$ to respond this *Decryption Query*. When $\varpi = 1$, $\mathcal{C}$ computes $sk_{ID}^1 \leftarrow \mathsf{IBE.Extract}(\widehat{msk}, ID)$, computes $L = \mathsf{IBE.Dec}(sk_{ID}^1, c_{ID_j}^1)$ in turn for $j \in \{1, 2, \cdots, t\}$. If L is $\perp$, continues to the next j until L as $svk' || \delta' || M'$. Then checks if $svk = svk'$, if not, output $\perp$; else queries $Hash_3$ Query on (δ', M') to gets $(\delta', M', r', g^{r'})$, and then checks if $T = g^{r'}$, if not, outputs $\perp$; else returns M'.

Challenge: Adversary $\mathcal{A}$ submits a message M^* and two distinct sets S_0, S_1 to $\mathcal{C}$. It is required that $\mathcal{A}$ has not issued *Extraction Query* on ID in Phase 1, where $ID \in \{ID_v, ID_w\}$. $\mathcal{C}$ first runs $(svk^*, ssk^*) \leftarrow \mathsf{Gen}(1^\lambda)$ and sets $T^* = g^c$. Then, $\mathcal{C}$ issues $Hash_1$ Query on ID_v to obtain the tuple $\langle ID_v, Q_v, q_v, \varpi_v \rangle$. If $\varpi_v = 0$, $\mathcal{C}$ outputs $\perp$ and aborts; else $\mathcal{C}$ computes $X_v^* = Z^{q_v}$. $\mathcal{C}$ issues $Hash_1$ Query on all ID_j, where $ID_j \in S_0/ID_v$, to obtain the corresponding tuple $\langle ID_j, Q_j, q_j, \varpi_j \rangle$. If there exists some $\varpi_j = 1$, outputs $\perp$ and aborts; else computes $X_j^* = e(g^a, g^c)^{q_j}$. Meanwhile, for all $ID_j \in S_0$, $\mathcal{C}$ queries $Hash_2$ Query on X_j^* to obtain $c_{ID_j}^{0*}$, where $c_{ID_j}^{0*} = H_2(X_j^*)$. Next, $\mathcal{C}$ chooses a random δ^* and runs $c_{ID_j}^{1*} \leftarrow \mathsf{IBE.Enc}(\widehat{params}, ID_j, svk^* || \delta^* || M^*)$ for $ID_j \in S_0$. Let $C_1^* = (c_{ID_1}^{0*}, c_{ID_1}^{1*}) || \cdots || (c_{ID_t}^{0*}, c_{ID_t}^{1*})$. Last, $\mathcal{C}$ runs $\sigma^* \leftarrow \mathsf{Sig}(ssk^*, T^* || C_1^*)$ and returns $CT^* = (svk^*, T^*, C_1^*, \sigma^*)$ to adversary $\mathcal{A}$.

Phase 2: $\mathcal{A}$ continues to adaptively issue queries as follows:

Extraction Query: Adversary $\mathcal{A}$ issues *Extraction Query* on ID, where $ID \notin \{ID_v, ID_w\}$, $\mathcal{C}$ handles them as in Phase 1.

Decryption Query: Adversary $\mathcal{A}$ issues *Decryption Query* on $\langle ID, CT \rangle$. $\mathcal{C}$ parses $CT = (svk, T, C_1, \sigma)$, where $C_1 = (c_{ID_1}^0, c_{ID_1}^1) || \cdots || (c_{ID_t}^0, c_{ID_t}^1)$. If $svk = svk^*$ or $\mathsf{Ver}(svk, T || C_1, \sigma) = 0$, $\mathcal{C}$ outputs $\perp$. Otherwise, $\mathcal{C}$ does as follows:

- When $CT = CT^*$ and $ID \in \{ID_v, ID_w\}$, $\mathcal{C}$ outputs $\perp$;
- When $CT = CT^*$ and $ID \in S_0 \cap S_1$, $\mathcal{C}$ outputs M^*;
- When $(CT = CT^*$ and $ID \notin S_0 \cup S_1)$ or $(CT \neq CT^*$ and $ID \notin \{ID_v, ID_w\})$, $\mathcal{C}$ answers as in Phase 1;
- When $CT \neq CT^*$ and $ID \in \{ID_v, ID_w\}$, $\mathcal{C}$ computes $sk_{ID}^1 \leftarrow \mathsf{IBE.Extract}(\widehat{msk}, ID)$. If there does not exist $j \in \{1, 2, \cdots, t\}$, such that $c_{ID_j}^1 = c_{ID_v}^{1*}$, $\mathcal{C}$ answers as in Phase 1; Otherwise, if there exists some $j \in \{1, 2, \cdots, t\}$, such that $c_{ID_j}^1 = c_{ID_v}^{1*}$, where $c_{ID_v}^{1*} \leftarrow \mathsf{IBE.Enc}(\widehat{params}, ID_v, svk^* || \delta^* || M^*)$. When $ID = ID_v$, $\mathcal{C}$ outputs $\perp$, as the corresponding message is $svk^* || \delta^* || M^*$, as $svk = svk^*$ has been rejected. When $ID = ID_w$, $\mathcal{C}$ answers as in Phase 1.

Guess: $\mathcal{A}$ outputs a bit $b' \in \{0, 1\}$.

It is easy to observe that, if $Z = e(g, g)^{abc}$, then $\mathcal{C}$ has properly simulated $Game_1$. If Z is uniform and independent in G_T then $\mathcal{C}$ has properly simulated $Game_2$. Therefore, if $\mathcal{A}$ can distinguish $Game_1$ and $Game_2$ with a non-negligible advantage, then $\mathcal{C}$ also has a non-negligible advantage to resolve the DBDH problem. However, the DBDH assumption is hard to resolve. Hence, $Game_1$ and $Game_2$ are computationally indistinguishable.

Lemma 3. *Suppose that the IBE scheme are ANO-CCA secure and WROB-CCA secure, then $Game_2$ and $Game_3$ are computationally indistinguishable.*

Proof. Suppose there exists an adversary $\mathcal{A}$ who can distinguish $Game_2$ from $Game_3$, it is easy to construct a PPT algorithm $\mathcal{C}$ who makes use of $\mathcal{A}$ to break the IBE scheme's ANO-CCA security or the IBE scheme's WROB-CCA security. $\mathcal{C}$ acts as a challenger and plays with adversary $\mathcal{A}$ as follows.

Setup: $\mathcal{C}$ first receives the master public key $\widehat{params}$ from the IBE challenger. Then $\mathcal{C}$ picks generator $g \in_R \mathbb{G}$, $\alpha \in_R \mathbb{Z}_p$, computes $g_1 = g^\alpha$ and chooses hash functions H_1, H_2, H_3. Next, $\mathcal{C}$ gives public parameters $params = (\widehat{params}, g, g_1, H_1, H_2, H_3)$ to $\mathcal{A}$ and keeps α itself.

Phase 1: $\mathcal{A}$ adaptively issues queries as follows:

- *Extraction Query:* On input of an identity ID, $\mathcal{C}$ first issues *Extraction Query* on ID to the IBE challenger to obtain sk_{ID}^1, and then $\mathcal{C}$ computes $sk_{ID}^0 = H_1(ID)^\alpha$. Finally, $\mathcal{C}$ returns $sk_{ID} = (\ sk_{ID}^0, sk_{ID}^1)$ to adversary $\mathcal{A}$.

- *Decryption Query:* On input of $\langle ID, CT \rangle$, $\mathcal{C}$ first parses CT as (svk, σ, T, C_1), where $C_1 = (c_{ID_1}^0, c_{ID_1}^1)\ ||\cdots|| (\ c_{ID_t}^0, c_{ID_t}^1)$. If $\mathsf{Ver}(svk, T||C_1, \sigma) = 0$, $\mathcal{C}$ outputs $\perp$; else $\mathcal{C}$ computes $sk_{ID}^0 = H_1(ID)^\alpha$ and $c_{ID}^0 = H_2(\ e(T, sk_{ID}^0))$. If there is no $c_{ID_j}^0 = c_{ID}^0$ for $j \in \{1, \cdots, t\}$, $\mathcal{C}$ returns $\perp$; else $\mathcal{C}$ considers the smallest index j such that $c_{ID_j}^0 = c_{ID}^0$, and then $\mathcal{C}$ issues *Decryption Query* on (ID, c_{ID}^1) to the IBE challenger and obtains a result L. If $L = \perp$, $\mathcal{C}$ outputs $\perp$; else parses L as $svk'||\delta'||M'$, checks if $svk = svk'$, if not, outputs $\perp$; else issues $Hash_3$ Query on (δ', M') and obtains $(\delta', M', r', g^{r'})$, checks whether $T = g^{r'}$ holds, if not, outputs $\perp$; else returns M'.

Challenge: $\mathcal{A}$ submits a message M^* and two distinct sets S_0, S_1 to $\mathcal{C}$. It is required that $\mathcal{A}$ has not issued *Extraction Query* on $ID \in \{ID_v, ID_w\}$ in **Phase 1**. First, $\mathcal{C}$ picks $\delta^* \leftarrow_R \mathbb{Z}_p$, computes $r = H_3(\delta^*, M^*)$ and sets $T^* = g^r$. Second, $\mathcal{C}$ runs $(svk^*, ssk^*) \leftarrow \mathsf{Gen}(1^\lambda)$, sets $m^* = svk^*||\delta^*||M^*$ and sends m^* and (ID_v, ID_w) to the IBE challenger and receives a ciphertext $c_{ID_\beta}^{1*} \leftarrow \mathsf{IBE.Enc}(\widehat{params}, ID_\beta, m^*)$ from IBE challenger. Third, $\mathcal{C}$ chooses a random $R \in \{0,1\}^\lambda$ and sets $c_{ID_\beta}^{0*} = R$. For $ID_j \in S_0 \cap S_1$, $\mathcal{C}$ computes $c_{ID_j}^0 = H_2(e(g_1, H_1(ID_j))^r)$ and $c_{ID_j}^1 \leftarrow \mathsf{IBE.Enc}(\widehat{params}, ID_j, svk^*||\delta^*||M^*)$. Let C_1^* be the concatenation of $(c_{ID_j}^0, c_{ID_j}^1)$ for all $ID_j \in S_\beta$. Fianlly, $\mathcal{C}$ runs $\sigma^* \leftarrow \mathsf{Sig}(ssk^*, T^*||C_1^*)$ and returns the challenge ciphertext $CT^* = (svk^*, T^*, C_1^*, \sigma^*)$ to adversary $\mathcal{A}$.

Phase 2: $\mathcal{A}$ continues to adaptively issue queries as follows:

Extraction Query: $\mathcal{A}$ issues *Extraction Query* on ID, where $ID \notin \{ID_v, ID_w\}$, $\mathcal{C}$ handles them as in **Phase 1**.

Decryption Query: $\mathcal{A}$ issues *Decryption Query* on $\langle ID, CT \rangle$, $\mathcal{C}$ parses CT as (svk, σ, T, C_1), where $C_1 = (c_{ID_1}^0, c_{ID_1}^1)||\cdots|| (\ c_{ID_t}^0, c_{ID_t}^1)$. If $svk = svk^*$ or $\mathsf{Ver}(svk, T||C_1, \sigma) = 0$, then $\mathcal{C}$ outputs $\perp$. Otherwise, $\mathcal{C}$ does as follows:

- When $CT = CT^*$ and $ID \in \{ID_v, ID_w\}$, $\mathcal{C}$ outputs $\perp$;
- When $CT = CT^*$ and $ID \in S_0 \cap S_1$, $\mathcal{C}$ outputs M^*;
- When $(CT = CT^*$ and $ID \notin S_0 \cup S_1)$ or $(CT \neq CT^*$ and $ID \notin \{ID_v, ID_w\})$, $\mathcal{C}$ answers as in **Phase 1**;
- When $CT \neq CT^*$ and $ID \in \{ID_v, ID_w\}$, $\mathcal{C}$ first computes $sk_{ID}^0 = H_1(ID)^\alpha$ and $c_{ID}^0 = H_2(e(T, sk_{ID}^0))$. For each $j \in \{1, \cdots, t\}$, if $c_{ID_j}^0 \neq c_{ID}^0$, $\mathcal{C}$ returns $\perp$; else $\mathcal{C}$ considers the smallest index j such that $c_{ID_j}^0 = c_{ID}^0$. If $c_{ID}^1 = c_{ID_\beta}^{1*}$, $\mathcal{C}$ outputs $\perp$. Since $c_{ID_\beta}^{1*} \leftarrow \mathsf{IBE.Enc}(ID_\beta, svk^*||\delta^*||M^*)$, when $ID = ID_\beta$,

IBE.Dec$(sk_{ID_\beta}, c^{1*}_{ID_\beta})$ and the corresponding message is $svk^*||\delta^*||M^*$, as $svk = svk^*$ has been rejected; When $ID \in \{ID_v, ID_w\}/\{ID_\beta\}$. As the IBE scheme is WROB-CCA secure, then IBE.Dec$(sk_{ID}, c^{1*}_{ID_\beta}) \neq \perp$ with negligible probability. Otherwise, $\mathcal{C}$ issues *Decryption Query* on (ID, c^1_{ID}) to IBE challenger as in **Phase 1**.

Guess: $\mathcal{A}$ outputs a bit $b' \in \{0, 1\}$.

If the IBE challenger encrypts $svk^*||\delta^*||M^*$ under ID_v, then $\mathcal{C}$ is simulating $Game_2$; else the IBE challenger encrypts $svk^*||\delta^*||M^*$ under ID_w, that is $\mathcal{C}$ is simulating $Game_3$. Therefore, if adversary $\mathcal{A}$ can distinguish $Game_2$ from $Game_3$ with a non-negligible advantage, then $\mathcal{C}$ also have a non-negligible advantage to break the ANO-CCA security or WROB-CCA security of the IBE scheme. However, the IBE scheme is ANO-CCA secure and WROB-CCA secure. Hence, $Game_2$ and $Game_3$ are computationally indistinguishable.

Lemma 4. *Suppose that* DBDH *assumption holds, then $Game_3$ and $Game_4$ are computationally indistinguishable.*

Proof. The case for distinguishing $Game_3$ from $Game_4$ is symmetric with the case for distinguishing $Game_1$ from $Game_2$.

Lemma 5. *Suppose that the signature scheme Σ is a strong one-time signature scheme, then $Game_4$ and $Game_5$ are computationally indistinguishable.*

Proof. The case for distinguishing $Game_4$ from $Game_5$ is symmetric with the case for distinguishing $Game_0$ from $Game_1$.

4   Comparisons

In this section, we compare the security and performance among the existing anonymous IBBE schemes and our concrete instantiation from our generic IBBE construction which is presented in Appendix A. The results of comparisons are presented in Table 1.

In Table 1, it shows that the constructions [14, 29] and the first construction [39] have some security flaws in their security proofs. As constructions [11, 29] both pointed out construction [14] does not achieve anonymity. Constructions [22, 35] both pointed out construction [29] does not achieve anonymity. Construction [36] gave an insider attack about anonymity for the first scheme of [39]. Construction [11] and the second construction [39] do not have security proofs. Construction [32] is only an outsider-anonymous IBBE with adaptive CPA security in standard model. Constructions [20, 26, 38] are all CPA, while our construction can simultaneously ensure the confidentiality and anonymity under chosen-ciphertext attacks. In particular, our scheme is not less efficient than these existing IBBE schemes, although all of them cannot obtain the same security as ours. Thus, the comparison results indicate that our concrete IBBE scheme has a better overall security and performance. The symbol "×" means there exists some security flaws or problems in their security proofs and "−" means there is no security proof in the scheme.

Table 1. Security and Performance Comparisons

	[14]	[11]	[29]	[39]-1	[39]-2	[20]	[26]	[38]	[32]	Ours
Confidentiality	CCA	-	CCA	CCA	-	CPA	CPA	CPA	CPA	CCA
Outsider Anonymity	×	-	CCA	CCA	-	CPA	CPA	CPA	CPA	CCA
Insider Anonymity	×	-	×	×	-	CPA	CPA	CPA	–	CCA
Security Model	ROM	-	ROM	ROM	-	ROM	STD	STD	STD	ROM
Pk Size	$\mathcal{O}(1)$	$\mathcal{O}(1)$	$\mathcal{O}(1)$	$\mathcal{O}(1)$	$\mathcal{O}(1)$	$\mathcal{O}(1)$	$\mathcal{O}(n)$	$\mathcal{O}(\ell)$	$\mathcal{O}(\ell)$	$\mathcal{O}(1)$
Sk Size	$\mathcal{O}(1)$	$\mathcal{O}(1)$	$\mathcal{O}(1)$	$\mathcal{O}(1)$	$\mathcal{O}(1)$	$\mathcal{O}(1)$	$\mathcal{O}(1)$	$\mathcal{O}(k)$	$\mathcal{O}(k)$	$\mathcal{O}(1)$
CT Size	$\mathcal{O}(k)$	$\mathcal{O}(k)$	$\mathcal{O}(k)$	$\mathcal{O}(k)$	$\mathcal{O}(k)$	$\mathcal{O}(k)$	$\mathcal{O}(k)$	$\mathcal{O}(1)$	$\mathcal{O}(1)$	$\mathcal{O}(k)$
Decryption time	$\mathcal{O}(1)$	$\mathcal{O}(k)$	$\mathcal{O}(1)$	$\mathcal{O}(k)$	$\mathcal{O}(k)$	$\mathcal{O}(1)$	$\mathcal{O}(1)$	$\mathcal{O}(1)$	$\mathcal{O}(1)$	$\mathcal{O}(1)$

5   Conclusion

In this paper, we propose a generic IBBE scheme from a generic anonymous IBE construction. The generic IBBE scheme obtains the confidentiality and anonymity against chosen-ciphertext attacks simultaneously. In addition, the scheme has a desirable property, that is the public parameters size, the private key size and the decryption cost are constant and independent of the number of receivers. However, our construction is proved in the random oracle model. So our future work is to construct a generic anonymous IBBE construction with chosen-ciphertext security in the standard model.

Acknowledgments. This work was supported by National Science Foundation of China (Grant Nos. 61272413, 61133014, 61272415 and 61472165), Program for New Century Excellent Talents in University (Grant No. NCET-12-0680), Research Fund for the Doctoral Program of Higher Education of China (Grant No. 20134401110011), Foundation for Distinguished Young Talents in Higher Education of Guangdong (Grant No. 2012LYM 0027), the Fundamental Research Funds for the Central Universities (Grant No. 11613106), and this work is also supported by China Scholarship Council.

A   A Concrete Instantiation

We shall present a concrete instantiation based on the generic IBBE construction, employing Boneh-Franklin IBE scheme [8], which is IND-CCA secure and ANO-CCA secure as noticed in [1] and WROB-CCA secure as noticed in [2] and a concrete signature scheme, e.g. [27] which is a strong one-time signature scheme $\Sigma = (\mathsf{Gen}, \mathsf{Sig}, \mathsf{Ver})$.

Setup(1^λ): On input of a security parameter λ, it first chooses a bilinear group $\mathbb{G}, \mathbb{G}_T$ of prime order p with bilinear map $e : \mathbb{G} \times \mathbb{G} \to \mathbb{G}_T$ and a generator $g \leftarrow_R \mathbb{G}$, and then picks $\alpha, \beta \leftarrow_R \mathbb{Z}_p$, computes $g_1 = g^\alpha$ and $g_2 = g^\beta$, chooses hash functions $H_1 : \{0,1\}^* \to \mathbb{G}$, $H_2 : \{0,1\}^\ell \times \{0,1\}^n \to \mathbb{Z}_p$, $H_3 : \mathbb{G}_T \to \{0,1\}^\ell$, $H_4 : \{0,1\}^\ell \to \{0,1\}^{(\lambda+\ell+n)}$, $H_5 : \{0,1\}^\ell \times \{0,1\}^{\lambda+\ell+n} \to \mathbb{Z}_p$ which are modeled as random oracles. The public parameters are $params = (\mathbb{G}, \mathbb{G}_T, \mathbb{Z}_p, p, e, g, g_1, g_2, H_1, H_2, H_3, H_4, H_5)$ and the master secret key is $msk = (\alpha, \beta)$.

Extract(msk, ID): On input of the master secret key msk and an identity ID, it computes $sk_{ID}^0 = H_1(ID)^\alpha$ and $sk_{ID}^1 = H_1(ID)^\beta$. The private key is $sk_{ID} = (sk_{ID}^0, sk_{ID}^1)$.

Enc$(params, S, M)$: On input of the public parameters $params$, a receiver set $S = \{ID_1, ID_2, \cdots, ID_t\}$ and a message $M \in \{0,1\}^n$, it first runs $(svk, ssk) \leftarrow \mathsf{Gen}(1^\lambda)$, chooses $\delta_1, \delta_2 \leftarrow_R \{0,1\}^\ell$, lets $r_1 = H_2(\delta_1 \| M)$ and $r_2 = H_5(\delta_2 \| svk \| \delta_1 \| M)$, and then computes $T_1 = g^{r_1}$ and $T_2 = g^{r_2}$. For each $ID \in S$, it computes $c_{ID}^0 = H_3(e(g_1, H_1(ID))^{r_1})$ and $c_{ID}^1 = (c_{ID}^{10}, c_{ID}^{11}) = (H_3(e(g_2, H_1(ID))^r) \oplus \delta_2, H_4(\delta_2) \oplus (svk \| \delta_1 \| M))$. Let $C_1 = (c_{ID_1}^0, c_{ID_1}^1) \| \cdots \| (c_{ID_t}^0, c_{ID_t}^1)$. The ciphertext is $CT = (svk, T_1, T_2, C_1, \sigma)$, where $\sigma = \mathsf{Sig}(ssk, T_1 \| T_2 \| C_1)$.

Dec(sk_{ID}, CT): On input of a private key sk_{ID} and a ciphertext CT, it parses CT as (svk, σ, T, C_1), where $C_1 = (c_{ID_1}^0, c_{ID_1}^1) \| \cdots \| (c_{ID_t}^0, c_{ID_t}^1)$. If $\mathsf{Ver}(svk, T_1 \| T_2 \| C_1, \sigma) = 0$, returns $\bot$; else computes $c_{ID}^0 = H_3(e(T_1, sk_{ID}^0))$ and determines which ciphertext should be decrypted among $(c_{ID_1}^0, c_{ID_1}^1) \| \cdots \| (c_{ID_t}^0, c_{ID_t}^1)$. For each $ID_j \in S$, if $c_{ID}^0 \neq c_{ID_j}^0$, returns $\bot$; else chooses the smallest index j such that $c_{ID}^0 = c_{ID_j}^0$ and $c_{ID}^1 = c_{ID_j}^1$. It computes $\delta_2' = H_3(e(T_2, sk_{ID}^1)) \oplus c_{ID}^{10}$, $svk \| \delta_1 \| M = H_4(\delta_2') \oplus c_{ID}^{11}$. If $T_1 \neq g^{H_2(\delta_1 \| M)}$ or $T_2 \neq g^{H_5(\delta_2 \| svk \| \delta_1 \| M)}$, returns $\bot$; else returns M.

References

1. Abdalla, M., Bellare, M., Catalano, D., Kiltz, E., Kohno, T., Lange, T., Malone-Lee, J., Neven, G., Paillier, P., Shi, H.: Searchable encryption revisited: consistency properties, relation to anonymous IBE, and extensions. In: Shoup, V. (ed.) CRYPTO 2005. LNCS, vol. 3621, pp. 205–222. Springer, Heidelberg (2005)
2. Abdalla, M., Bellare, M., Neven, G.: Robust encryption. In: IACR Cryptology ePrint Archive, 2008/440 (2008)
3. Baek, J., Safavi-Naini, R., Susilo, W.: Efficient multi-receiver identity-based encryption and its application to broadcast encryption. In: Vaudenay, S. (ed.) PKC 2005. LNCS, vol. 3386, pp. 380–397. Springer, Heidelberg (2005)
4. Barbosa, M., Farshim, P.: Efficient identity-based key encapsulation to multiple parties. In: IACR Cryptology ePrint Archive, 2005/217 (2005)
5. Barth, A., Boneh, D., Waters, B.: Privacy in encrypted content distribution using private broadcast encryption. In: Di Crescenzo, G., Rubin, A. (eds.) FC 2006. LNCS, vol. 4107, pp. 52–64. Springer, Heidelberg (2006)
6. Bellare, M., Boldyreva, A., Desai, A., Pointcheval, D.: Key-privacy in public-key encryption. In: Boyd, C. (ed.) ASIACRYPT 2001. LNCS, vol. 2248, pp. 566–582. Springer, Heidelberg (2001)
7. Bellare, M., Rogaway, P.: Random oracles are practical: A paradigm for designing efficient protocols (1995)

8. Boneh, D., Franklin, M.: Identity-based encryption from the weil pairing. In: Kilian, J. (ed.) CRYPTO 2001. LNCS, vol. 2139, pp. 213–229. Springer, Heidelberg (2001)
9. Boneh, D., Gentry, C., Waters, B.: Collusion resistant broadcast encryption with short ciphertexts and private keys. In: Shoup, V. (ed.) CRYPTO 2005. LNCS, vol. 3621, pp. 258–275. Springer, Heidelberg (2005)
10. Chatterjee, S., Sarkar, P.: Multi-receiver identity-based key encapsulation with shortened ciphertext. In: Barua, R., Lange, T. (eds.) INDOCRYPT 2006. LNCS, vol. 4329, pp. 394–408. Springer, Heidelberg (2006)
11. Chien, H.-Y.: Improved anonymous multi-receiver identity-based encryption. Comput. J. 55(4), 439–446 (2012)
12. Delerablée, C.: Identity-based broadcast encryption with constant size ciphertexts and private keys. In: Kurosawa, K. (ed.) ASIACRYPT 2007. LNCS, vol. 4833, pp. 200–215. Springer, Heidelberg (2007)
13. Dodis, Y., Fazio, N.: Public key broadcast encryption for stateless receivers. In: Security and Privacy in Digital Rights Management, ACM CCS-9 Workshop, DRM 2002, Washington, DC, USA, November 18, 2002, pp. 61–80 (2002)
14. Fan, C.-I., Huang, L.-Y., Ho, P.-H.: Anonymous multireceiver identity-based encryption. IEEE Trans. Comput. 59(9), 1239–1249 (2010)
15. Fazio, N., Perera, I.M.: Outsider-anonymous broadcast encryption with sublinear ciphertexts. In: Proceedings of the Public Key Cryptography - PKC 2012–15th International Conference on Practice and Theory in Public Key Cryptography, Darmstadt, May 21–23, 2012, pp. 225–242 (2012)
16. Fiat, A., Naor, M.: Broadcast encryption. In: Stinson, D.R. (ed.) CRYPTO 1993. LNCS, vol. 773, pp. 480–491. Springer, Heidelberg (1994)
17. Gentry, C., Waters, B.: Adaptive security in broadcast encryption systems (with short ciphertexts). In: Joux, A. (ed.) EUROCRYPT 2009. LNCS, vol. 5479, pp. 171–188. Springer, Heidelberg (2009)
18. He, K., Weng, J., Liu, J.-N., Liu, J.K., Liu, W., Deng, R.H.: Anonymous identity-based broadcast encryption with chosen-ciphertext security. In: Accepted for publication in ASIACCS 2016, January 2016
19. Liang, H., Liu, Z., Cheng, X.: Efficient identity-based broadcast encryption without random oracles. JCP 5(3), 331–336 (2010)
20. Hur, J., Park, C., Hwang, S.: Privacy-preserving identity-based broadcast encryption. Inf. Fusion 13(4), 296–303 (2012)
21. Kim, I., Hwang, S.O.: An optimal identity-based broadcast encryption scheme for wireless sensor networks. IEICE Trans. 96–B(3), 891–895 (2013)
22. Li, H., Pang, L.: Cryptanalysis of wang et al'.s improved anonymous multi-receiver identity-based encryption scheme. IET Inf. Secur. 8(1), 8–11 (2014)
23. Libert, B., Paterson, K.G., Quaglia, E.A.: Anonymous broadcast encryption: Adaptive security and efficient constructions in the standard model. In: Proceedings of Public Key Cryptography - PKC 2012 - 15th InternationalConference on Practice and Theory in Public Key Cryptography, Darmstadt, May 21-23, 2012, pp. 206–224 (2012)
24. Liu, W., Liu, J., Wu, Q., Qin, B.: Hierarchical identity-based broadcast encryption. In: Susilo, W., Mu, Y. (eds.) ACISP 2014. LNCS, vol. 8544, pp. 242–257. Springer, Heidelberg (2014)
25. Ren, Y., Dawu, G.: Fully CCA2 secure identity based broadcast encryption without random oracles. Inf. Process. Lett. 109(11), 527–533 (2009)
26. Ren, Y., Niu, Z., Zhang, X.: Fully anonymous identity-based broadcast encryption without random oracles. I. J. Netw. Sec. 16(4), 256–264 (2014)

27. Rompel, J.: One-way functions are necessary and sufficient for secure signatures. In: Proceedings of the 22nd Annual ACM Symposium on Theory of Computing, May 13–17, 1990, Baltimore pp. 387–394 (1990)
28. Sakai, R., Furukawa, J.: Identity-based broadcast encryption. Cryptology ePrint Archive, Report 2007/217 (2007)
29. Wang, H., Yi-Chun Zhang, H., Xiong, H., Qin, B.: Cryptanalysis and improvements of an anonymous multi-receiver identity-based encryption scheme. IET Inf, Sec. **6**(1), 20–27 (2012)
30. Wang, J., Bi, J.: Lattice-based identity-based broadcast encryption scheme. IACR Cryptology ePrint Archive, 2010/288 (2010)
31. Qing, W., Wang, W.: New identity-based broadcast encryption with constant ciphertexts in the standard model. JSW **6**(10), 1929–1936 (2011)
32. Xie, L., Ren, Y.: Efficient anonymous identity-based broadcast encryption without random oracles. IJDCF **6**(2), 40–51 (2014)
33. Yang, C., Zheng, S., Wang, L., Xiuhua, L., Yang, Y.: Hierarchical identity-based broadcast encryption scheme from LWE. J. Commun. Netw. **16**(3), 258–263 (2014)
34. Zhang, B., Xu, Q.: Identity-based broadcast group-oriented encryption from pairings. In: The Second International Conference on Future Generation Communication and Networking, FGCN 2008, vol. 1, Main Conference, Hainan Island, China, December 13–15, 2008, pp. 407–410 (2008)
35. Zhang, J.H., Cui, Y.B.: Comment an anonymous multi-receiver identity-based encryption scheme. IACR Cryptology ePrint Archive, 2012/201 (2012)
36. Zhang, J., Mao, J.: An improved anonymous multi-receiver identity-based encryption scheme. Int. J. Commun. Syst. **28**(4), 645–658 (2015)
37. Zhang, L., Hu, Y., Mu, N.: An identity-based broadcast encryption protocol for ad hoc networks. In: Proceedings of the 9th International Conference for Young Computer Scientists, ICYCS 2008, Zhang Jia Jie, Hunan, China, November 18–21, 2008, pp. 1619–1623 (2008)
38. Zhang, L., Wu, Q., Mu, Y.: Anonymous identity-based broadcast encryption with adaptive security. In: Wang, G., Ray, I., Feng, D., Rajarajan, M. (eds.) CSS 2013. LNCS, vol. 8300, pp. 258–271. Springer, Heidelberg (2013)
39. Zhang, M., Takagi, T.: Efficient constructions of anonymous multireceiver encryption protocol and their deployment in group e-mail systems with privacy preservation. IEEE Syst. J. **7**(3), 410–419 (2013)
40. Zhao, X., Zhang, F.: Fully CCA2 secure identity-based broadcast encryption with black-box accountable authority. J. Syst. Softw. **85**(3), 708–716 (2012)

Anonymous Identity-Based Broadcast Encryption with Revocation for File Sharing

Jianchang Lai(✉), Yi Mu, Fuchun Guo, Willy Susilo, and Rongmao Chen

Centre for Computer and Information Security Research,
School of Computing and Information Technology, University of Wollongong,
Wollongong, Australia
{jl1967,ymu,fuchun,wsusilo,rc517}@uow.edu.au

Abstract. Traditionally, a ciphertext from an identity-based broadcast encryption can be distributed to a group of receivers whose identities are included in the ciphertext. Once the ciphertext has been created, it is not possible to remove any intended receivers from it without conducting decryption. In this paper, we consider an interesting question: *how to remove target designated receivers from a ciphertext generated by an anonymous identity-based broadcast encryption?* The solution to this question is found applicable to file sharing with revocation. In this work, we found an affirmative answer to this question. We construct an anonymous identity-based broadcast encryption, which offers the user revocation of ciphertext and the revocation process does not reveal any information of the plaintext and receiver identity. In our proposed scheme, the group of receiver identities are anonymous and only known by the encryptor. We prove that our scheme is semantically secure in the random oracle model.

Keywords: Identity-based encryption · Revocation · Anonymity

1 Introduction

In a broadcast encryption system, a file can be encrypted for a group of receivers such that any receiver in the group can decrypt the ciphertext using its respective private key. The users outside the group learn nothing about the encrypted file even if they collude. Broadcast encryption is a useful way for data sharing, where receivers can obtain the broadcast (or shared) data with their private keys. However, directly applying a broadcast encryption for data sharing in database systems or cloud computing might suffer from some drawbacks. For example, it cannot preserve the receiver privacy, since all receiver identities must be attached with the ciphertext. Therefore, if applying an identity-based broadcast encryption scheme to file sharing, an anonymous broadcast encryption would be more desirable.

We consider an application scenario using an anonymous identity-based broadcast encryption, where the file sharing system for a company is supplied by

© Springer International Publishing Switzerland 2016
J.K. Liu and R. Steinfeld (Eds.): ACISP 2016, Part II, LNCS 9723, pp. 223–239, 2016.
DOI: 10.1007/978-3-319-40367-0_14

a cloud service. Without losing generality, let's assume that the system involves a cloud server, file owner, and a group of users. The file owner first encrypts a file for a selected group S, and then stores the encrypted file in the cloud for sharing. When some users R leave the company, the server must revoke them from accessing all files. If the revoked users are in S, they cannot decrypt the ciphertext after the server conducts revocation. Mostly important, it requires the cloud server to be able to revoke users from a ciphertext without knowing the encrypted file and the identities of receivers.

A trivial solution to the scenario is to adopt the "decrypt then re-encrypt" approach. It requires the server to have the ability to decrypt the ciphertext. When some identities should be revoked, the server first decrypts the ciphertext and removes them from the original authorized user set. It then re-encrypts the file using the new authorized user set. However, in this trivial solution, the cloud server is able to learn the content and the identity of authorized users who can access the file. Alternatively, the cloud server without decryption right can encrypt the ciphertext by using the broadcast encryption scheme (e.g. [21]) where anyone can decrypt the ciphertext except the revoked users. This method guarantees that the cloud server cannot get any useful information about the content and the authorized users' identities from the original ciphertext. The limitation is that this method could cause a collusion attack. For example, let ID_i be the identity of User i; if $ID_1 \notin S \cup R$, $ID_2 \in S \cap R$, ID_1 can use its private key to help ID_2 recover the original ciphertext, then ID_2 uses its private key to decrypt the original ciphertext.

Our Contributions. We notice that there is *no* ideal trivial solution to the aforementioned problem. In this work, we provide a solution to the stated problem earlier and show how to revoke users' identities from the ciphertext without the knowledge of the plaintext and the knowledge of the receivers. We propose a new cryptographic notion called *anonymous identity-based broadcast encryption with revocation* (AIBBER) to realize this. Our novel solution allows the cloud server to revoke users' identities without decryption and achieves full anonymity where only the sender knows the receivers' identities. We present two security models to meet the requirements of the proposed notion and show that our construction is secure under the attacks in the proposed model. In our setting, both the system public key and user private key are constant. The computation in revocation phase is small, more precisely $O(t)$, where t is the number of revoked identities.

1.1   Related Work

Anonymous Broadcast Encryption. Since Fiat and Naor [15] formally introduced broadcast encryption, subsequent works [3,6,8–10,16,25] have proposed broadcast encryption systems with different properties. They mainly focused on reducing public key sizes, private key sizes, ciphertext sizes and computational costs for encryption and decryption. The notion of identity-based broadcast encryption was introduced by Sakai and Furukawa [26], and Delerablée's work [8] achieves constant size ciphertext and private keys. In these schemes, the receiver identities must be attached with the ciphertext, which exposes the privacy of the receivers.

The first work addressing the anonymity in broadcast encryption appeared in [1]. The authors presented the notion of private broadcast encryption to protect the identities of the receivers and gave a generic construction from any key indistinguishable CCA scheme, which achieves receiver anonymity and CCA security. The security in [1] depends on a strongly secure one-time signature. Boneh, Sahai and Waters [4] extended this notion to construct private linear broadcast encryption and proposed a fully collusion resistant tracing traitors scheme with sublinear size ciphertexts and constant size private keys. However, the receivers cannot be arbitrary sets of users. Subsequently, many anonymous ID-based broadcast encryption schemes were proposed [12,14,18,22,28].

Libert, Paterson and Quaglia [22] examined the security of the number-theoretic construction in [1] and suggested the proof techniques without the random oracle. The authors proposed an anonymous broadcast encryption scheme that achieves adaptive security without random oracles. The ciphertext in their schemes are linear of the number of receivers and the security depends on a one-time signature. Later, Fazio and Perera [14] formalized the notion of outsider-anonymous broadcast encryption, which lies between the complete lack of protection that characterizes traditional broadcast encryption scheme [15] and the full anonymity in [1]. Their constructions achieve sublinear ciphertext length but fail to obtain anonymity among the receiver.

The work of Kiayias and Samari [19] aimed to study the lower bounds for the ciphertext size of private broadcast encryption. They showed that an atomic private broadcast encryption scheme with fully anonymous must have a ciphertext size of $\Omega(n \cdot k)$, where n is the number of broadcast set and k is the security parameter. Recently, Fazio, Nicolosi and Perera [13] studied the broadcast steganography and introduced a new construction called outsider-anonymous broadcast encryption with pseudorandom ciphertexts, which achieves sublinear ciphertext size and is secure without random oracles.

Revocation. The revocation schemes in the literature only guarantee the revoked users cannot decrypt the ciphertext. While the revocation in our paper focuses on how to revoke the identities from a group of users S. Only the users who are in S but not in the revocation set can retrieve the plaintext. Revocation system is a variant of the broadcast encryption system, where it takes a set of revoked users as input to the encryption function. Several elegant revocation constructions [5,11,17,20,21,23,24] have been proposed. Naor, Naor and Lotspiech [23] presented a technique called subset-cover framework, and based on this framework they proposed the first stateless tree-based revocation scheme which was secure against a collision of any number of users. Boneh and Waters [5] introduced a primitive called augmented broadcast encryption which was claimed to be sufficient for constructing trace and revoke schemes. The authors proposed a revocation scheme with sublinear size ciphertexts and private keys. The scheme was proved to be secure against adaptive adversaries.

Lewko, Sahai and Waters [21] proposed a revocation system with very small private keys using the "two equation" technique. The primary challenge is to achieve full collusion resilience. Anyone can decrypt the ciphertext and get the broadcast message except the revoked users even if they collude. In Lewko et al.'s scheme, the ciphertext size is $O(t)$ and the size of the public key is constant, where t is the number of revoked users. Recently, to narrow the scope of decrypter in [21], a single revocation encryption (SRE) scheme was presented by Lee et al. [20], which allows a sender to broadcast a message to a group of selected users and one group user is revoked. Any group member can decrypt the ciphertext except the revoked user. The authors then proposed a public key trace and revoke scheme by combining the layered subset difference scheme and their SRE scheme.

Broadcast Proxy Re-Encryption. The concept of proxy re-encryption (PRE) was introduced by Blaze, Bleumer and Strauss [2], which provides a flexible and secure way to share data. PRE allows an honest-but-curious proxy to turn a ciphertext intended for a receiver into another ciphertext intended for another receiver. While, the proxy cannot learn any useful information about the plaintext during the transformation. Chu et al. [7] extended this notion to construct the proxy broadcast re-encryption (PBRE). Compared with PRE, PBRE allows the proxy to transform a ciphertext intended for a receiver set to another ciphertext intended for another receiver set. Recently, motivated by the cloud email system, Xu et al. [27] presented a conditional identity-based broadcast proxy re-encryption scheme with constant ciphertext based on [8]. In both the PRE and PBRE system, the data owner has to delegate a re-encryption key to the proxy and the proxy knows the new receivers' identities.

Organization. The rest of the paper is organized as follows. In Sect. 2, we give some preliminaries including complexity assumption, the formal definition of anonymous identity-based broadcast encryption with revocation and the corresponding security models. The concrete construction is presented in Sect. 3. In Sect. 4, we show the security proofs of our scheme. Finally, we conclude the paper in Sect. 5.

2 Preliminaries

2.1 Complexity Assumption

Let $\mathbb{G}$ and $\mathbb{G}_T$ be two cyclic groups of the same prime order p. A bilinear map is a map $e : \mathbb{G} \times \mathbb{G} \to \mathbb{G}_T$ which satisfies the following properties:

1. Bilinear: For all $P, Q \in \mathbb{G}$ and $a, b \in \mathbb{Z}_p^*$, we have $e(aP, bQ) = e(P, Q)^{ab}$.
2. Non-degeneracy: There exists $P, Q \in \mathbb{G}$ such that $e(P, Q) \neq 1$.
3. Computability: It is efficient to compute $e(P, Q)$ for all $P, Q \in \mathbb{G}$.

A bilinear group $\mathbb{BG} = (\mathbb{G}, \mathbb{G}_T, e, p)$ is composed of objects as described above.

Bilinear Diffie-Hellman Problem (BDH). Let $\mathbb{BG} = (\mathbb{G}, \mathbb{G}_T, e, p)$ be a bilinear group with a generator $P \in \mathbb{G}$. The BDH problem in $(\mathbb{G}, \mathbb{G}_T, e)$ is as follows: Given a tuple (P, aP, bP, cP) for some unknown $a, b, c \in \mathbb{Z}_p^*$ as input, output $e(P, P)^{abc} \in \mathbb{G}_T$. An algorithm $\mathcal{A}$ has advantage ε in solving BDH in $(\mathbb{G}, \mathbb{G}_T, e)$ if

$$\Pr\left[\mathcal{A}\left(P, aP, bP, cP\right) = e(P, P)^{abc}\right] \geq \varepsilon,$$

where the probability is over the random choice of a, b, c in $\mathbb{Z}_p^*$ and $P \in \mathbb{G}$.

Definition 1. *We say that the BDH assumption holds in $\mathbb{G}$ if no PPT adversary has advantage at least ε in solving the BDH problem in $\mathbb{G}$.*

2.2 Anonymous ID-Based Broadcast Encryption with Revocation

The AIBBER system is derived from Identity-Based Broadcast Encryption (IBBE) [8] with more functions. Formally, an AIBBER scheme consists of the algorithms $\mathcal{AIBBER} = $ (Setup, KeyGen, Encrypt, Revoke, Decrypt) defined as follows.

Setup (1^λ): Taking a security parameter 1^λ as input, it outputs a master public key mpk and a master secrete key msk. The mpk is publicly known while the msk is kept secretly.

KeyGen (mpk, msk, ID): Taking the master key pair (msk, mpk) and a user identity ID as input, it outputs a private key d_{ID} for ID.

Encrypt (mpk, M, S): Taking the master public key mpk, a message M and a set of identities $S = (ID_1, ID_2, ..., ID_n)$ as input, it outputs a ciphertext CT.

Revoke (mpk, R, CT): Taking the master public key mpk, a ciphertext CT and a revocation identity set $R = (ID_1, ID_2, \cdots, ID_t)$ as input, it outputs a new ciphertext CT' with R.

Decrypt (mpk, CT', ID, d_{ID}): Taking the master public key mpk, a ciphertext CT', an identity ID and the private key d_{ID} as input. It outputs the message M if $ID \in S$ and $ID \notin R$.

Correctness. Note that if $t = 0$, the AIBBER scheme is AIBBE scheme. Thus, it requires that for any $ID \in S$ and $ID \notin R$, if (mpk, msk) $\leftarrow$ Setup(1^λ), $d_{ID} \leftarrow$ KeyGen(mpk, msk, ID), $CT \leftarrow$ Encrypt(mpk, M, S), $CT' \leftarrow$ Revoke(mpk, R, CT), we have Decrypt$(CT, ID, d_{ID}) = M$ and Decrypt$(CT', ID, d_{ID}) = M$.

2.3 Security Models

The security of AIBBER scheme requires that without a valid private key, both the encrypted message and the intended receivers are unknown to the adversary. Let CT be the original ciphertext for receivers S, R be the revoke users and CT' be the ciphertext after revocation. The security requires:

1. The message in the ciphertext CT cannot be distinguished without a valid private key associated with an identity $ID \in S$. The message in CT' cannot be distinguished without a valid private key associated with an identity $ID' \in S$ and $ID' \notin R$.
2. The identity set in the ciphertext CT cannot be distinguished without a valid private key associated with an identity $ID \in S$. The identity set in CT' cannot be distinguished without a valid private key associated with an identity $ID' \in S$ and $ID' \notin R$.

We define the IND-ID-CPA security and ANON-ID-CPA security for the AIBBER system in a similar way as anonymous IBBE system.

IND-ID-CPA Security. IND-ID-CPA security in AIBBER allows the adversary to issue the private key query to obtain the private key associated with any identity ID of her choice. The adversary is challenged on an identity set S^*, two messages M_0, M_1 of its choice and a revocation identity set R^*. Adversary's goal is to distinguish whether the challenge ciphertext is encrypted under M_0 or M_1 for S^* with some restrictions. We say that adversary breaks the scheme if it guesses the message correctly. Specifically, the notion of IND-ID-CPA is defined under the following game between the challenger $\mathcal{C}$ and the PPT adversary $\mathcal{A}$.

Setup: $\mathcal{C}$ runs the **Setup** algorithm to generate the master public key mpk and master secret key msk. Then it sends the mpk to $\mathcal{A}$ and keeps the msk secretly.

Phase 1: $\mathcal{A}$ issues private key queries. Upon receiving a private key query for ID_i. $\mathcal{C}$ runs the **KeyGen** algorithm to generate the private key d_{ID_i} and sends the result back to $\mathcal{A}$.

Challenge: When $\mathcal{A}$ decides that **Phase 1** is over, it outputs two distinct messages M_0, M_1 from the same message space, a challenge identity set $S^* = (ID_1, ID_2, \cdots, ID_n)$ and a revocation identity set $R^* = (ID'_1, ID'_2, \cdots, ID'_t)$ with the restriction that $\mathcal{A}$ has not queried the private key on ID_i in **Phase 1**, where $ID_i \in S^*$ and $ID_i \notin R^*$. $\mathcal{C}$ randomly picks a bit $b \in \{0, 1\}$ and generates the challenge ciphertext CT^* as follows:

$$CT = \mathsf{Encrypt}(\mathsf{mpk}, M_b, S^*), \quad CT' = \mathsf{Revoke}(\mathsf{mpk}, M_b, CT).$$

If $R^* \neq \emptyset$, set $CT^* = CT'$ as the challenge ciphertext, otherwise set $CT^* = CT$ as the challenge ciphertext, then send CT^* to $\mathcal{A}$.

Phase 2: $\mathcal{A}$ issues more private key queries as in **Phase 1**, but it cannot query the private key on ID_i where $ID_i \in S^*$ and $ID_i \notin R^*$.

Guess: Finally, $\mathcal{A}$ outputs its guess $b' \in \{0, 1\}$ and wins the game if $b' = b$.

We refer to such an adversary $\mathcal{A}$ as an IND-ID-CPA adversary and define adversary $\mathcal{A}$'s advantage in attacking the scheme as $\mathsf{Adv}^{\mathsf{IND\text{-}ID\text{-}CPA}}_{\mathcal{AIBER}}(\mathcal{A}) = |\Pr[b = b'] - 1/2|$. The probability is over the random bits used by the challenger and the adversary.

Definition 2. *We say that an AIBBER scheme is IND-ID-CPA secure if there is no IND-ID-CPA adversary $\mathcal{A}$ has a non-negligible advantage in this game.*

ANON-ID-CPA Security. ANON-ID-CPA security in AIBBER allows the adversary to issue the private key query to obtain the private key of any identity ID of its choice. Similarly, the adversary is challenged on a message M^*, two identity sets S_0, S_1 and a revocation identity set R^* of its choice. Adversary's goal is to distinguish whether the challenge ciphertext is generated under S_0 or S_1 with some restrictions. We say that adversary breaks the scheme if it guesses the identity set correctly. Specifically, the notion of ANON-ID-CPA is defined under the following game between the challenger $\mathcal{C}$ and the PPT adversary $\mathcal{A}$.

Setup: $\mathcal{C}$ runs the **Setup** algorithm to generate the master public key mpk and master secret key msk. Then it sends the mpk to $\mathcal{A}$ and keeps the msk secretly.

Phase 1: $\mathcal{A}$ issues private key queries. Upon receiving a private key query for ID_i. $\mathcal{C}$ runs the **KeyGen** algorithm to generate the private key d_{ID_i} and sends the result back to $\mathcal{A}$.

Challenge: When $\mathcal{A}$ decides that **Phase 1** is over, it outputs a message M^*, two distinct identity sets $S_0 = (ID_{0,1}, ID_{0,2}, ..., ID_{0,n})$, $S_1 = (ID_{1,1}, ID_{1,2}, ..., ID_{1,n})$ and a revocation set $R^* = (ID_1', ID_2', \cdots, ID_t')$. We require that $\mathcal{A}$ has not issued the private key queries on ID_i in **Phase 1**, where $ID_i \in (S_0 \cup S_1) \backslash (S_0 \cap S_1)$. $\mathcal{C}$ randomly picks a bit $b \in \{0,1\}$ and generates the challenge ciphertext CT^* as follows:

$$CT = \mathsf{Encrypt}(\mathsf{mpk}, M^*, S_b), \quad CT' = \mathsf{Revoke}(\mathsf{mpk}, M^*, CT).$$

If $R^* \neq \emptyset$, set $CT^* = CT'$ as the challenge ciphertext, otherwise set $CT^* = CT$ as the challenge ciphertext, then send CT^* to $\mathcal{A}$.

Phase 2: $\mathcal{A}$ issues more private key queries as in **Phase 1**, but it cannot query the private key on any ID_i, where $ID_i \in (S_0 \cup S_1) \backslash (S_0 \cap S_1)$.

Guess: Finally, $\mathcal{A}$ outputs its guess $b' \in \{0,1\}$ and wins the game if $b' = b$.

We refer to such an adversary $\mathcal{A}$ as an ANON-ID-CPA adversary and define adversary $\mathcal{A}$'s advantage in attacking the scheme as $\mathsf{Adv}_{\mathcal{AIBBER}}^{\mathsf{ANON\text{-}ID\text{-}CPA}}(\mathcal{A}) = |\Pr[b = b'] - 1/2|$. The probability is over the random bits used by the challenger and the adversary.

Definition 3. *We say that an AIBBER scheme is ANON-ID-CPA secure if there is for any PPT adversary $\mathcal{A}$, $\mathsf{Adv}_{\mathcal{AIBBER}}^{\mathsf{ANON\text{-}ID\text{-}CPA}}(\mathcal{A})$ is negligible.*

3   The Proposed Scheme

3.1   Construction

Setup: Given a security parameter 1^λ, the setup algorithm randomly chooses a bilinear group $\mathbb{BG} = (\mathbb{G}, \mathbb{G}_T, e, p)$ with a generator $P \in \mathbb{G}$, $s \in \mathbb{Z}_p^*$ and computes $P_{pub} = sP$. It then picks four cryptographic hash functions $H : \{0,1\}^* \to \mathbb{Z}_p^*$, $H_1 : \{0,1\}^* \to \mathbb{G}$, $H_2 : \mathbb{G}_T \times \{0,1\}^* \to \mathbb{G}$, $H_3 : \mathbb{G}_T \times \{0,1\}^* \to \mathbb{G}$. The master public key and master secret key are

$$mpk = \{\mathbb{BG}, P, P_{pub}, H, H_1, H_2, H_3\}, \quad msk = s.$$

KeyGen: Given the master key pair (mpk, msk) and an identity $ID \in \{0,1\}^*$, this algorithm outputs the private key

$$d_{ID} = sH_1(ID).$$

Encrypt: Given the master public key mpk, a set of identity $S = (ID_1, ID_2, \ldots, ID_n)$ and a message $M \in \mathbb{G}$, this algorithm randomly chooses $r_1, r_2 \in \mathbb{Z}_p^*$ and $v \in \mathbb{G}$. For $i = 1, 2, \cdots, n$, it computes $x_i = H(ID_i)$,

$$f_i(x) = \prod_{j=1, j \neq i}^{n} \frac{x - x_j}{x_i - x_j} = \sum_{j=0}^{n-1} a_{i,j} x^j \mod p,$$

$$A_i = H_2\left(e\left(H_1(ID_i), P_{pub}\right)^{r_1}, ID_i\right), \quad B_i = v \cdot H_3\left(e\left(H_1(ID_i), P_{pub}\right)^{r_2}, ID_i\right).$$

We have $f_i(x_i) = 1$ and $f_i(x_j) = 0$ for $i \neq j$. Then it creates the ciphertext CT as $C_0 = v \cdot M, C_1 = r_1 P, C_2 = r_2 P$, together with, for each $i = 1, 2, \cdots, n$:

$$Q_i = \prod_{j=1}^{n} A_j^{a_{j,i-1}}, \quad U_i = \prod_{j=1}^{n} B_j^{a_{j,i-1}}.$$

Revoke: Given a ciphertext $CT = (C_0, C_1, C_2, Q_i, U_i, i \in [1, n])$, the master public key mpk and a revocation identity set R, where $|R| = t$. It requires $t < n$. If $R = \emptyset$, this algorithm sets $CT' = CT$. Otherwise, it randomly chooses $u \in \mathbb{G}$ and computes $C_0' = u \cdot C_0$, $x_i = H(ID_i)$ for $ID_i \in R$,

$$g(x) = \prod_{i=1}^{t} (x - x_i) = \sum_{i=0}^{t} b_i x^i \mod p.$$

Then it sets $b_i = 0$ for $i = t+1, t+2, \cdots, n-1$ and for each $i = 1, 2, \cdots, n$ computes

$$Q_i' = Q_i \cdot u^{b_{i-1}}.$$

Then it sets $CT' = (R, C_0', C_1, C_2, Q_i', U_i, i \in [1, n])$.

Decrypt: Given a ciphertext $CT' = (R, C_0', C_1, C_2, Q_i', U_i, i \in [1, n])$, an identity ID_i, a private key d_{ID_i} and the master public key mpk, this algorithm computes $x_i = H(ID_i)$ and

$$U = U_1 \cdot U_2^{x_i} \cdot U_3^{x_i^2} \cdots U_n^{x_i^{n-1}}, \quad Q = Q_1' \cdot Q_2'^{x_i} \cdot Q_3'^{x_i^2} \cdots Q_n'^{x_i^{n-1}}.$$

Then it computes $x_j = H(ID_j)$ for each $ID_j \in R$ to reconstruct $g(x)$ as:

$$g(x) = \prod_{j=1}^{t} (x - x_j) = \sum_{j=0}^{t} b_j x^j \mod p.$$

Finally, it uses the private key d_{ID_i} to compute

$$v' = H_3\big(e(C_2, d_{ID_i}), ID_i\big)^{-1}U, \quad u' = \Big(Q \cdot H_2\big(e(C_1, d_{ID_i}), ID_i\big)^{-1}\Big)^{\frac{1}{g(x_i)}}.$$

and recovers the message $M = C_0' \cdot (u'v')^{-1}$. If the identity $ID_i \in S$ and $ID_i \notin R$, we have $u' = u$, $v' = v$, then it obtains the correct M after decryption.

Note: For simplicity, we omit the modulo operation and assume that the coefficients of all polynomials are from $\mathbb{Z}_p^*$ in the rest of paper.

3.2   Discussion and Correctness

One may think that after revocation, the revocation set may be updated multiple times. Our scheme allows the server to update the revocation set. For each update, the server uses the original ciphertext and the new revocation set to perform the **Revoke** algorithm. Thus, the server needs to store the original ciphertext CT in our scheme. In our setting, there is no requirement of $R \subset S$. The revocation set R can be arbitrary users.

From our setting, only the users in S can decryption the ciphertext CT. After revocation, the revoked users cannot decrypt the ciphertext CT'. We note that if $ID \in R$, $g(H(ID)) = 0$ and $u^{g(H(ID))} = 1$. The user with identity ID cannot retrieve one of the decryption keys u, even all users in R conclude. To obtain the decryption keys u and v, the user must belong to S and not belong to R. Thus our scheme ensures that even if all the revoked users collude, they still cannot access the file and learn the identities of receivers.

Next we show that our construction meets the requirements of correctness as we claimed in the Sect. 2.3. If $x_i = H(ID_i)$ is computed correctly, for any $ID_i \in S$ and $ID_i \notin R$, we have $g(x_i) \neq 0$ and

$$
\begin{aligned}
Q &= Q_1' \cdot Q_2'^{x_i} \cdot Q_3'^{x_i^2} \cdots Q_n'^{x_i^{n-1}} \\
&= \Big(Q_1 \cdot (Q_2)^{x_i} \cdot (Q_3)^{x_i^2} \cdots (Q_n)^{x_i^{n-1}}\Big) \cdot \Big(u^{b_0 + b_1 x_i + b_2 x_i^2 + \cdots + b_{n-1} x_i^{n-1}}\Big) \\
&= \Big((A_1^{a_{1,0}} A_2^{a_{2,0}} \cdots A_n^{a_{n,0}}) \cdots (A_1^{a_{1,n-1}} A_2^{a_{2,n-1}} \cdots A_n^{a_{n,n-1}})^{x_i^{n-1}}\Big) \cdot \Big(u^{g(x_i)}\Big) \\
&= \Big(A_1^{a_{1,0} + a_{1,1} x_i + a_{1,2} x_i^2 + \cdots + a_{1,n-1} x_i^{n-1}}\Big) \cdot \Big(A_2^{a_{2,0} + a_{2,1} x_i + a_{2,2} x_i^2 + \cdots + a_{2,n-1} x_i^{n-1}}\Big) \cdots \\
&\quad \Big(A_n^{a_{n,0} + a_{n,1} x_i + a_{n,2} x_i^2 + \cdots + a_{n,n-1} x_i^{n-1}}\Big) \cdot u^{g(x_i)} \\
&= A_1^{f_1(x_i)} \cdot A_2^{f_2(x_i)} \cdots A_n^{f_n(x_i)} \cdot u^{g(x_i)} \\
&= A_i \cdot u^{g(x_i)} \\
u' &= \Big(Q \cdot H_2\big(e(C_1, d_{ID_i}), ID_i\big)^{-1}\Big)^{\frac{1}{g(x_i)}} \\
&= \Big(A_i \cdot u^{g(x_i)} \cdot H_2\big(e(C_1, d_{ID_i}), ID_i\big)^{-1}\Big)^{\frac{1}{g(x_i)}} \\
&= \Big(H_2\big(e(H_1(ID_i), P_{pub})^{r_1}, ID_i\big) \cdot H_2\big(e(r_1 P, sH_1(ID_i)), ID_i\big)^{-1} \cdot u^{g(x_i)}\Big)^{\frac{1}{g(x_i)}} \\
&= \Big(u^{g(x_i)}\Big)^{\frac{1}{g(x_i)}} \\
&= u.
\end{aligned}
$$

The user ID_i uses its private key d_{ID_i} to remove A_i from Q_i via above computation. As $g(x_i) \neq 0$, the user can obtain u.

$$
\begin{aligned}
U &= U_1 \cdot U_2^{x_i} \cdot U_3^{x_i^2} \cdots U_n^{x_i^{n-1}} \\
&= \left((B_1^{a_{1,0}} B_2^{a_{2,0}} \cdots B_n^{a_{n,0}}) \cdots (B_1^{a_{1,n-1}} B_2^{a_{2,n-1}} \cdots B_n^{a_{n,n-1}})^{x_i^{n-1}} \right) \\
&= \left(B_1^{a_{1,0}+a_{1,1}x_i+a_{1,2}x_i^2+\cdots+a_{1,n-1}x_i^{n-1}} \right) \cdot \left(B_2^{a_{2,0}+a_{2,1}x_i+a_{2,2}x_i^2+\cdots+a_{2,n-1}x_i^{n-1}} \right) \cdots \\
&\quad \left(B_n^{a_{n,0}+a_{n,1}x_i+a_{n,2}x_i^2+\cdots+a_{n,n-1}x_i^{n-1}} \right) \\
&= B_1^{f_1(x_i)} \cdot B_2^{f_2(x_i)} \cdots B_n^{f_n(x_i)} \\
&= B_i \\
v' &= H_3\big(e(C_2, d_{ID_i}), ID_i\big)^{-1} U \\
&= H_3\Big(e\big(r_2 P, s H_1(ID_i)\big), ID_i\Big)^{-1} \cdot B_i \\
&= H_3\Big(e\big(P, H_1(ID_i)\big)^{sr_2}, ID_i\Big)^{-1} \cdot H_3\Big(e\big(H_1(ID_i), P_{pub}\big)^{r_2}, ID_i\Big) \cdot v \\
&= v.
\end{aligned}
$$

After recovering u and v, we get the message as $C_0' \cdot (u'v')^{-1} = Mvuu^{-1}v^{-1} = M$.

4   Security Analysis

Theorem 1. *Suppose the hash functions H_1, H_2, H_3 are random oracles. If the BDH problem is hard, the proposed scheme is IND-ID-CPA secure. Specifically, suppose there is an IND-ID-CPA adversary $\mathcal{A}$ that has advantage ϵ against our proposed scheme. $\mathcal{A}$ makes at most q_E private key queries and q_{H_1}, q_{H_2}, q_{H_3} queries to the functions H_1, H_2 and H_3 respectively. Then there is an algorithm $\mathcal{S}$ to solve the BDH problem with advantage $\epsilon' \geq \dfrac{\epsilon}{n \cdot e \cdot (q_{H_2} + q_{H_3})}$, where n is the number of the broadcast identities.*

Proof. Suppose there exists an adversary $\mathcal{A}$ who can break our scheme with advantage ϵ. We build a simulator $\mathcal{S}$ that can solve the BDH problem with advantage ϵ' by running $\mathcal{A}$. Let (P, aP, bP, cP) be a random instance of BDH problem taken as input by $\mathcal{S}$ and its goal is to compute $e(P, P)^{abc}$. In order to use $\mathcal{A}$ to solve the problem, $\mathcal{S}$ needs to simulate a challenger and respond all the queries for $\mathcal{A}$. For simplicity, we assume that the H_2 and H_3 query is after the H_1 query for the same identity. $\mathcal{S}$ works by interacting with $\mathcal{A}$ in an IND-ID-CPA game as follows:

Setup: $\mathcal{S}$ sets $P_{pub} = aP$ and creates $mpk = (p, P, P_{pub}, e, H)$.

H_1-queries: $\mathcal{A}$ makes H_1 queries. $\mathcal{S}$ responds to a query on ID_i as follow. $\mathcal{S}$ maintains a list L_1 of a tuple (ID_i, c_i, r_i, h_i). This list is initially empty. $\mathcal{S}$ first checks the L_1. If the query ID_i already appears on the L_1 in a tuple (ID_i, c_i, r_i, h_i), it returns the corresponding h_i as the value of $H_1(ID_i)$. Otherwise, do the following:

1. Select $c_i \in_R \{0,1\}$ with $Pr[c_i = 0] = \delta$ for some δ (determine later).
2. Pick $r_i \in_R \mathbb{Z}_p^*$, if $c_i = 0$, compute $h_i = r_i bP$. If $c_i = 1$, compute $h_i = r_i P$.
3. Add the tuple (ID_i, c_i, r_i, h_i) to the L_1 and respond with h_i to $\mathcal{A}$.

H_2-queries: $\mathcal{A}$ makes H_2 queries. $\mathcal{S}$ responds to a query on (X_i, ID_i) as follow. $\mathcal{S}$ maintains a list L_2 of a tuple (X_i, ID_i, λ_i). This list is initially empty. $\mathcal{S}$ first checks the L_2. If the query (X_i, ID_i) already appears on the L_2 in a tuple (X_i, ID_i, λ_i), it returns the corresponding λ_i as the value of $H_2(X_i, ID_i)$. Otherwise, $\mathcal{S}$ randomly picks a $\lambda_i \in \mathbb{G}$ as the value of $H_2(X_i, ID_i)$, then adds the tuple (X_i, ID_i, λ_i) to the L_2 and responds to $\mathcal{A}$ with λ_i.

H_3-queries: $\mathcal{A}$ makes H_3 queries. $\mathcal{S}$ responds to a query on (Y_i, ID_i) as follow. $\mathcal{S}$ maintains a list L_3 of a tuple (Y_i, ID_i, γ_i). This list is initially empty. $\mathcal{S}$ first checks the L_3. If the query (Y_i, ID_i) already appears on the L_3 in a tuple (Y_i, ID_i, γ_i), it returns the corresponding γ_i as the value of $H_3(Y_i, ID_i)$. Otherwise, $\mathcal{S}$ randomly picks a $\gamma_i \in \mathbb{G}$ as the value of $H_3(Y_i, ID_i)$, then adds the tuple (Y_i, ID_i, γ_i) to the L_3 and responds to $\mathcal{A}$ with γ_i.

Phase 1: $\mathcal{A}$ issues the private key queries on ID_i for several times as needed. For each time, $\mathcal{S}$ first runs the H_1 query to get the corresponding c_i and r_i. If $c_i = 0$, $\mathcal{S}$ aborts. If $c_i = 1$, $\mathcal{S}$ computes $d_{ID_i} = sH_1(ID_i) = ar_iP = r_iP_{pub}$.

Challenge: When $\mathcal{A}$ decides Phase 1 is over, it outputs two distinct messages M_0, M_1, a challenge identity set $S^* = (ID_1, ID_2, \cdots, ID_n)$ and a revocation identity set $R^* = (ID_1', ID_2', \cdots, ID_t')$ under the restriction that $\mathcal{A}$ has not queried the private key on ID_i in Phase 1, where $ID_i \in S^*$ and $ID_i \notin R^*$. $\mathcal{S}$ randomly picks a random bit $b \in \{0,1\}$ and does the follows:

Case 1: $R^* = \emptyset$. In this case, $\mathcal{S}$ randomly picks $r^* \in \mathbb{Z}_p^*$, $C_0^* \in \mathbb{G}$, for each $ID_i \in S^*$, $i = 1, 2 \cdots, n$, randomly chooses $A_i, B_i^* \in \mathbb{G}$ and computes $x_i^* = H(ID_i)$,

$$f_i(x) = \prod_{j=1, j \neq i}^{n} \frac{x - x_j^*}{x_i^* - x_j^*} = \sum_{j=0}^{n-1} a_{i,j} x^j,$$

Then $\mathcal{S}$ generates the challenge ciphertext CT^* as $C_0, C_1^* = r^* cP, C_2^* = cP$, together with, for each $i = 1, 2, \cdots, n$:

$$Q_i^* = \prod_{j=1}^{n} A_j^{* a_{j,i-1}}, \quad U_i^* = \prod_{j=1}^{n} B_j^{* a_{j,i-1}}.$$

Case 2: $R^* \neq \emptyset$. In this case, $\mathcal{S}$ does the follows:

1. Pick $r^* \in_R \mathbb{Z}_p^*$, $v^*, u^* \in_R \mathbb{G}$, compute $C_0'^* = v^* \cdot u^* \cdot M_b$, $C_1^* = r^* cP$, $C_2^* = cP$.
2. For each $(ID_i \in S^*) \wedge (ID_i \notin R^*)$, $\mathcal{S}$ randomly chooses $A_i, B_i^* \in \mathbb{G}$. For each $(ID_i \in S^*) \wedge (ID_i \in R^*)$, $\mathcal{S}$ gets r_i from the L_1 (If ID_i is not in the L_1, do H_1 queries to get r_i). Then it computes $X_i = e(aP, cP)^{r^* r_i}$ and checks whether the tuple (X_i, ID_i) in the L_2. If yes, it obtains the corresponding λ_i and sets $A_i^* = \lambda_i$. Otherwise, it randomly choose $A_i^* \in \mathbb{G}$ and adds the new tuple (X_i, ID_i, A_i^*) to the L_2. Then $\mathcal{S}$ computes $Y_i = e(aP, cP)^{r_i}$ and checks

whether the tuple (Y_i, ID_i) in the L_3. If yes, it obtains the corresponding γ_i and sets $w_i^* = \gamma_i$. Otherwise, it randomly chooses $w_i^* \in \mathbb{G}$ and adds the new tuple (Y_i, ID_i, w_i^*) to the L_3, and computes $B_i^* = w_i^* \cdot v^*$.

3. For each $ID_i \in S^*$, $i = 1, 2 \cdots, n$, compute $x_i^* = H(ID_i)$,

$$f_i(x) = \prod_{j=1, j \neq i}^{n} \frac{x - x_j^*}{x_i^* - x_j^*} = \sum_{j=0}^{n-1} a_{i,j} x^j,$$

$$Q_i^* = \prod_{j=1}^{n} A_j^{* a_{j,i-1}}, \quad U_i^* = \prod_{j=1}^{n} B_j^{* a_{j,i-1}}.$$

4. Compute $x_i'^* = H(ID_i)$ for $ID_i \in R^*$ and

$$g(x) = \prod_{i=1}^{t} (x - x_i'^*) = \sum_{i=0}^{t} b_i x^i.$$

Then set $b_i = 0$ for $i = t+1, t+2, \cdots, n-1$. For $1 \leq i \leq n$, compute

$$Q_i'^* = Q_i^* \cdot u^{* b_{i-1}},$$

and set $CT^* = (R^*, C_0'^*, C_1^*, C_2^*, Q_i'^*, U_i^*, i \in [1, n])$.

Phase 2: $\mathcal{A}$ issues private key queries as needed, but it cannot query the private key on ID_i, where $ID_i \in S^*$ and $ID_i \notin R^*$. $\mathcal{S}$ responds as in **Phase 1**.

Guess: Finally, $\mathcal{A}$ outputs its guess $b' \in \{0, 1\}$.

Probability Analysis. Note that in the case $R^* = \emptyset$, we can view v^* as the encryption key to encrypt the challenge message. Let $W = (e(H_1(ID_i), P_{pub})^c, ID_i)$ where $ID_i \in S^*$. In the real scheme, $B_i^* = v^* \cdot H_3(W)$, thus we also can regard $H_3(W)$ as the encryption key to encrypt v^*. Before querying the H_3 value of W, the result of $H_3(W)$ is unknown and random. From the view of adversary, v^* is encrypted with a random number key independent of W. Therefore, B_i^* is a one-time pad. In other words, the challenge ciphertext is a one-time pad. According to the assumption($\mathcal{A}$ can break our scheme with advantage ϵ), the adversary will query H_3 on W. In this case, simulator decides the corresponding hard problem's solution is in the L_3 and can solve it with probability $\frac{\delta}{n}$.

When $R^* \neq \emptyset$, we can view v^* and u^* as the encryption key to encrypt the challenge message. However, in this case, the adversary can retrieve v^* by querying the private key of $(ID_i \in S^*) \wedge (ID_i \in R^*)$. That is, the message encryption key is only u^*. Let $\Omega = (e(H_1(ID_i), P_{pub})^{r^* c}, ID_i)$, where $(ID_i \in S^*) \wedge (ID_i \notin R^*)$. Similarly, in real scheme $Q^* = A_i^* \cdot (u^*)^{g(x_i^*)} = H_2(\Omega) \cdot (u^*)^{g(x_i^*)}$, we can regard Ω as the encryption key to encrypt u^*. Before querying the H_2 value of Ω, the result of $H_2(\Omega)$ is unknown and random. From the view of adversary, u^* is encrypted with a random number key independent of Ω. Therefore, Q^* is a one-time pad, that is, the challenge ciphertext is a one-time pad. According to the assumption($\mathcal{A}$ can break our scheme with advantage ϵ), the adversary will query H_2 on Ω. In this case, simulator can decides the solution of the corresponding hard problem is in the L_3 and solve it with probability $\frac{\delta}{n-l}$ where $l = |S^* \cap R^*|$. Here, we define the query which can solve the hard problem as *useful query*.

If *useful query* happens, it means $c_j = 0$, $H_1(ID_j) = r_j bP$ and $d_{ID_j} = r_j abP$. From the decryption algorithm, we have $e(C_1^*, d_{ID_j}) = e(P,P)^{r^* r_j abc}$ and $e(C_2^*, d_{ID_j}) = e(P,P)^{r_j abc}$. Here S ign ores the guess of $\mathcal{A}$ and picks a random tuple from the L_2 or L_3. It first obtains the corresponding r_j from the L_1. If S picks the tuple (X_j, ID_j, λ_j) from the L_2, it computes $X_j^{(r^* r_j)^{-1}}$ as the solution to the given instance of BDH problem. If S picks the tuple (Y_j, ID_j, γ_j) from the L_3, it computes $X_j^{r_j^{-1}}$ as the solution to the given instance of BDH problem.

The above completes the description of simulation algorithm S. To complete the security proof, it remains to show that S correctly outputs $e(P,P)^{abc}$ with advantage at least ϵ'. According to our above analysis, we first define the following events:

E_1: Simulation dose not abort in private key query.
E_2: At least one of the H_1 values of challenge identities contains hard problem.
E_3: Adversary chooses an identity where $c_i = 0$ to distinguish challenge message.
E_4: Simulator correctly chooses the solution from the L_2 or L_3 list.

The simulator can successfully solve the hard problem if and only if all events happen simultaneously. Next, we analyze the probability of all events. From the private key query, we know when each $c_i = 1$, simulation will not abort, thus

$$\Pr[E_1] = \Pr[c_i = 1, i = 1, 2, \cdots, q_E] = (1 - \delta)^{q_E}.$$

All c_i are chosen by simulator where $c_i = 0$ with probability δ, $c_i = 1$ with probability $1 - \delta$. When $c_i = 0$, the value of H_1 contains the hard problem, thus $\Pr[E_2] = \delta$. Since all c_i are chosen by simulator and they are secretly to adversary, adversary does not know which identity's c_i is equal to 0 or 1. That is, from adversary's point of view, it does not know the probabilities of $c_i = 0$ and $c_i = 1$. Therefore, under event E_2, we have

$$\Pr[E_3] = \Pr[E_3|c_i = 0] \Pr[c_i = 0] + \Pr[E_3|c_i = 1] \Pr[c_i = 1]$$
$$= \tfrac{1}{n-l} \Pr[c_i = 0] + \tfrac{1}{n-l} \Pr[c_i = 1]$$
$$= \tfrac{1}{n-l} \geq \tfrac{1}{n}.$$

Note that the identity $ID_i \in S^* \cap R^*$ allows to query the corresponding private key. In our setting, these identities cannot be used to distinguish the challenge messages. Since $|S^* \cap R^*| = l$, the potential useful identity is $n - l$. Thus we have above result $\Pr[E_3] = \frac{1}{n-l} \geq \frac{1}{n}$.

Finally, from the simulator's point of view, if adversary can guess the correct b' and with the conditions that E_1, E_2, E_3 happen, it only knows that the solution of the hard problem is in the L_2 or L_3, but it dose not know which one is, thus $\Pr[E_4] \geq \frac{1}{q_{H_2}+q_{H_3}}$. It is clear that these four events are independent, therefore, we have

$$
\begin{aligned}
\epsilon' &\geq \Pr[E_1 \wedge E_2 \wedge E_3 \wedge E_4] \cdot \epsilon \\
&= \Pr[E_1] \cdot \Pr[E_2] \cdot \Pr[E_3] \cdot \Pr[E_4] \cdot \epsilon \\
&\geq (1-\delta)^{q_E} \cdot \delta \cdot \frac{1}{n} \cdot \frac{1}{q_{H_2}+q_{H_3}} \cdot \epsilon \\
&= (1-\delta)^{q_E} \cdot \delta \cdot \frac{\epsilon}{n(q_{H_2}+q_{H_3})}.
\end{aligned}
$$

The function $(1-\delta)^{q_E} \cdot \delta$ is maximized at $\delta = \frac{1}{q_E+1}$, we have

$$
(1-\delta)^{q_E} \cdot \delta = \frac{1}{q_E+1} \cdot \left(1 - \frac{1}{q_E+1}\right)^{q_E} = \frac{1}{q_E} \cdot \left(1 - \frac{1}{q_E+1}\right)^{q_E+1}.
$$

For a large q_E, $\left(1 - \frac{1}{q_E+1}\right)^{q_E+1} \approx \frac{1}{e}$, thus we have

$$
\epsilon' \geq (1-\delta)^{q_E} \cdot \delta \cdot \frac{\epsilon}{n(q_{H_2}+q_{H_3})} \approx \frac{\epsilon}{n \cdot e \cdot (q_{H_2}+q_{H_3})}.
$$

This completes the proof. $\qquad\qquad\qquad\qquad\qquad\qquad\qquad\qquad\qquad$ $\square$

Discussion. When $R^* = \emptyset$, the challenge message is encrypted by v^*. If the adversary can distinguish the message, the simulator can decide it must have queried the H_3 value with the input embedding the hard problem, but simulator does not know which input embeds the hard problem. In this case, $\Pr[E_4] = \frac{1}{q_{H_3}} \geq \frac{1}{q_{H_2}+q_{H_3}}$. When $R^* \neq \emptyset$, even the inputs of H_3 contain the hard problem, the adversary can retrieve v^* by the identity $ID_i \in S^*$ and $ID_i \in R^*$. Thus the *useful queries* are from H_2 and $\Pr[E_4] = \frac{1}{q_{H_2}} \geq \frac{1}{q_{H_2}+q_{H_3}}$.

Theorem 2. *Suppose the hash functions H_1, H_2, H_3 are random oracles. The proposed scheme is ANON-ID-CPA secure under the BDH assumption. Specifically, suppose there is an ANON-ID-CPA adversary $\mathcal{A}$ that has advantage ϵ against our proposed scheme. $\mathcal{A}$ makes at most q_E private key queries and q_{H_1}, q_{H_2}, q_{H_3} queries to the functions H_1, H_2 and H_3 respectively. Then there is an algorithm $\mathcal{S}$ to solve the BDH problem with advantage $\epsilon' \geq \frac{\epsilon}{n \cdot e \cdot (q_{H_2}+q_{H_3})}$, where n is the number of broadcast identities.*

Proof. The proof of Theorem 2 is similar to the proof of Theorem 1. Given a random instance of BDH problem (P, aP, bP, cP), $\mathcal{S}$ works by interacting with $\mathcal{A}$ in an ANON-ID-CPA game. The **Setup**, H_1-**query**, H_2-**query**, H_3-**query** and **Phase 1** query are the same as in Theorem 1.

Challenge: When $\mathcal{A}$ decides **Phase 1** is over, it outputs a challenge message M^*, two distinct identity sets $S_0 = (ID_{0,1}, ID_{0,2}, \cdots, ID_{0,n})$, $S_1 = (ID_{1,1}, ID_{1,2}, \cdots, ID_{1,n})$ and a revocation identity set $R^* = (ID_1', ID_2', \cdots, ID_t')$. We require that any identity $ID_i \in (S_0 \cup S_1) \backslash (S_0 \cap S_1)$ has not been queried the private key in **Phase 1**. $\mathcal{S}$ picks a random bit $b \in \{0,1\}$ and dose the follows:

1. Pick $r^* \in_R \mathbb{Z}_p^*$, $v^* \in \mathbb{G}$, compute $C_0^* = v^* \cdot M$, $C_1^* = r^* cP$, $C_2^* = cP$.
2. For each $ID_i \in S_b \backslash (S_0 \cap S_1)$, randomly choose $A_i^*, B_i^* \in \mathbb{G}$. For each $ID_i \in S_0 \cap S_1$, $\mathcal{S}$ first gets r_i from the L_1 (If ID_i is not in the L_1, do H_1 queries to get r_i). Then it computes $X_i = e(aP, cP)^{r^* r_i}$ and checks whether the tuple (X_i, ID_i) is in the L_2. If yes, it obtains the corresponding λ_i and sets $A_i^* = \lambda_i$. Otherwise, it randomly chooses $A_i^* \in \mathbb{G}$ and adds the new tuple (X_i, ID_i, A_i^*) to the L_2. Then $\mathcal{S}$ computes $Y_i = e(aP, cP)^{r_i}$ and checks whether the tuple (Y_i, ID_i) in the L_3. If yes, it obtains the corresponding γ_i and sets $w_i^* = \gamma_i$. Otherwise, it randomly chooses $w_i^* \in \mathbb{G}$ and adds the new tuple (Y_i, ID_i, w_i^*) to the L_3, and computes $B_i^* = w_i^* \cdot v^*$.
3. For each $i = 1, 2 \cdots, n$, compute $x_i^* = H(ID_i)$,

$$ f_i(x) = \prod_{j=1, j \neq i}^{n} \frac{x - x_j^*}{x_i^* - x_j^*} = \sum_{j=0}^{n-1} a_{i,j} x^j, $$

$$ Q_i^* = \prod_{j=1}^{n} A_j^{* a_{j,i-1}}, \quad U_i^* = \prod_{j=1}^{n} B_j^{* a_{j,i-1}} $$

and set $CT = (R^*, C_0^*, C_1^*, C_2^*, Q_i^*, U_i^*, i \in [1, n])$.

Case 1: $R^* = \emptyset$. $\mathcal{S}$ sets the challenge ciphertext $CT^* = CT$.

Case 2: $R^* \neq \emptyset$. $\mathcal{S}$ randomly chooses $u^* \in \mathbb{G}$ and computes $C_0'^* = u^* \cdot C_0^*$. For each $ID_i \in R^*$, $\mathcal{S}$ computes $x_i'^* = H(ID_i)$,

$$ g(x) = \prod_{i=1}^{t} (x - x_i'^*) = \sum_{i=0}^{t} b_i x^i, $$

and sets $b_i = 0$ for $i = t+1, t+2, \cdots, n-1$. Finally, for each $i = 1, 2, \cdots, n$, $\mathcal{S}$ computes

$$ Q_i'^* = Q_i^* \cdot u^{* b_{i-1}}, $$

and sets $CT^* = (R^*, C_0'^*, C_1^*, C_2^*, Q_i'^*, U_i^*, i \in [1, n])$.

Phase 2: $\mathcal{A}$ issues more private key queries, but it cannot query the private key on ID_i, where $ID_i \in (S_0 \cup S_1) \backslash (S_0 \cap S_1)$. $\mathcal{S}$ responds as in **Phase 1**.

Guess: Finally, $\mathcal{A}$ outputs its guess $b' \in \{0, 1\}$.

The probability analysis is almost similar to the one of Theorem 1. Due to space constraints, we omit it here.

5   Conclusion

We presented an anonymous identity-based broadcast encryption with revocation scheme for file sharing. The file owner can encrypt a file for sharing with a group of users and stores the encrypted file in the cloud server (or any other third party). The server can revoke target users without knowing the file and the receiver identities. Our scheme ensures that even if all the revoked users collude, they still cannot access the file and learn the identities of receivers. The cloud server also learns nothing about the file and the receiver identities. Finally, we proved that the proposed scheme is IND-ID-CPA secure and ANON-ID-CPA secure under the BDH assumption in the random oracle model.

References

1. Barth, A., Boneh, D., Waters, B.: Privacy in encrypted content distribution using private broadcast encryption. In: Di Crescenzo, G., Rubin, A. (eds.) FC 2006. LNCS, vol. 4107, pp. 52–64. Springer, Heidelberg (2006)
2. Blaze, M., Bleumer, G., Strauss, M.J.: Divertible protocols and atomic proxy cryptography. In: Nyberg, K. (ed.) EUROCRYPT 1998. LNCS, vol. 1403, pp. 127–144. Springer, Heidelberg (1998)
3. Boneh, D., Gentry, C., Waters, B.: Collusion resistant broadcast encryption with short ciphertexts and private keys. In: Shoup, V. (ed.) CRYPTO 2005. LNCS, vol. 3621, pp. 258–275. Springer, Heidelberg (2005)
4. Boneh, D., Sahai, A., Waters, B.: Fully collusion resistant traitor tracing with short ciphertexts and private keys. In: Vaudenay, S. (ed.) EUROCRYPT 2006. LNCS, vol. 4004, pp. 573–592. Springer, Heidelberg (2006)
5. Boneh, D., Waters, B.: A fully collusion resistant broadcast, trace, and revoke system. In: CCS 2006 Proceedings of the 13th ACM Conference on Computer and Communications Security. pp. 211–220 (2006)
6. Boneh, D., Waters, B., Zhandry, M.: Low overhead broadcast encryption from multilinear maps. In: Garay, J.A., Gennaro, R. (eds.) CRYPTO 2014, Part I. LNCS, vol. 8616, pp. 206–223. Springer, Heidelberg (2014)
7. Chu, C.-K., Weng, J., Chow, S.S.M., Zhou, J., Deng, R.H.: Conditional proxy broadcast re-encryption. In: Boyd, C., González Nieto, J. (eds.) ACISP 2009. LNCS, vol. 5594, pp. 327–342. Springer, Heidelberg (2009)
8. Delerablée, C.: Identity-based broadcast encryption with constant size ciphertexts and private keys. In: Kurosawa, K. (ed.) ASIACRYPT 2007. LNCS, vol. 4833, pp. 200–215. Springer, Heidelberg (2007)
9. Delerablée, C., Paillier, P., Pointcheval, D.: Fully collusion secure dynamic broadcast encryption with constant-size ciphertexts or decryption keys. In: Takagi, T., Okamoto, T., Okamoto, E., Okamoto, T. (eds.) Pairing 2007. LNCS, vol. 4575, pp. 39–59. Springer, Heidelberg (2007)
10. Dodis, Y., Fazio, N.: Public key broadcast encryption for stateless receivers. In: Feigenbaum, J. (ed.) DRM 2002. LNCS, vol. 2696, pp. 61–80. Springer, Heidelberg (2003)
11. Dodis, Y., Fazio, N.: Public key trace and revoke scheme secure against adaptive chosen ciphertext. In: Desmedt, Y.G. (ed.) PKC 2003. LNCS, vol. 2567. Springer, Heidelberg (2002)
12. Fan, C., Huang, L., Ho, P.: Anonymous multireceiver identity-based encryption. IEEE Trans. Comput. 59(9), 1239–1249 (2010)
13. Fazio, N., Nicolosi, A.R., Perera, I.M.: Broadcast steganography. In: Benaloh, J. (ed.) CT-RSA 2014. LNCS, vol. 8366, pp. 64–84. Springer, Heidelberg (2014)
14. Fazio, N., Perera, I.M.: Outsider-anonymous broadcast encryption with sublinear ciphertexts. In: Fischlin, M., Buchmann, J., Manulis, M. (eds.) PKC 2012. LNCS, vol. 7293, pp. 225–242. Springer, Heidelberg (2012)

15. Fiat, A., Naor, M.: Broadcast encryption. In: Stinson, D.R. (ed.) CRYPTO 1993. LNCS, vol. 773, pp. 480–491. Springer, Heidelberg (1994)

16. Gentry, C., Waters, B.: Adaptive security in broadcast encryption systems (with short ciphertexts). In: Joux, A. (ed.) EUROCRYPT 2009. LNCS, vol. 5479, pp. 171–188. Springer, Heidelberg (2009)

17. Goodrich, M.T., Sun, J.Z., Tamassia, R.: Efficient tree-based revocation in groups of low-state devices. In: Franklin, M. (ed.) CRYPTO 2004. LNCS, vol. 3152, pp. 511–527. Springer, Heidelberg (2004)

18. Hur, J., Park, C., Hwang, S.: Privacy-preserving identity-based broadcast encryption. Inf. Fusion 13(4), 296–303 (2012)

19. Kiayias, A., Samari, K.: Lower bounds for private broadcast encryption. In: Kirchner, M., Ghosal, D. (eds.) IH 2012. LNCS, vol. 7692, pp. 176–190. Springer, Heidelberg (2013)

20. Lee, K., Koo, W.K., Lee, D.H., Park, J.H.: Public-key revocation and tracing schemes with subset difference methods revisited. In: Kutyłowski, M., Vaidya, J. (eds.) ICAIS 2014, Part II. LNCS, vol. 8713, pp. 1–18. Springer, Heidelberg (2014)

21. Lewko, A., Sahai, A., Waters, B.: Revocation systems with very small private keys. In: 2010 IEEE Symposium on Security and Privacy, pp. 273–285 (2010)

22. Libert, B., Paterson, K.G., Quaglia, E.A.: Anonymous broadcast encryption: adaptive security and efficient constructions in the standard model. In: Fischlin, M., Buchmann, J., Manulis, M. (eds.) PKC 2012. LNCS, vol. 7293, pp. 206–224. Springer, Heidelberg (2012)

23. Naor, D., Naor, M., Lotspiech, J.: Revocation and tracing schemes for stateless receivers. In: Kilian, J. (ed.) CRYPTO 2001. LNCS, vol. 2139, pp. 41–62. Springer, Heidelberg (2001)

24. Naor, M., Pinkas, B.: Efficient trace and revoke schemes. In: Frankel, Y. (ed.) FC 2000. LNCS, vol. 1962, pp. 1–20. Springer, Heidelberg (2001)

25. Phan, D.-H., Pointcheval, D., Shahandashti, S.F., Strefler, M.: Adaptive CCA Broadcast encryption with constant-size secret keys and ciphertexts. In: Susilo, W., Mu, Y., Seberry, J. (eds.) ACISP 2012. LNCS, vol. 7372, pp. 308–321. Springer, Heidelberg (2012)

26. Sakai, R., Furukawa, J.: Identity-based broadcast encryption. IACR Cryptology ePrint Archive 2007, 217 (2007)

27. Xu, P., Jiao, T., Wu, Q., Wang, W., Jin, H.: Conditional identity-based broadcast proxy re-encryption and its application to cloud email. IEEE Trans. Comput. 65(1), 66–79 (2016)

28. Zhang, L., Wu, Q., Mu, Y.: Anonymous identity-based broadcast encryption with adaptive security. In: Wang, G., Ray, I., Feng, D., Rajarajan, M. (eds.) CSS 2013. LNCS, vol. 8300, pp. 258–271. Springer, Heidelberg (2013)

Mathematical Primitives

Partial Key Exposure Attacks on RSA with Multiple Exponent Pairs

Atsushi Takayasu$^{(\boxtimes)}$ and Noboru Kunihiro

The University of Tokyo, Tokyo, Japan
a-takayasu@it.k.u-tokyo.ac.jp, kunihiro@k.u-tokyo.ac.jp

Abstract. So far, several papers have analyzed attacks on RSA when attackers know the least significant bits of a secret exponent d as well as a public modulus N and a public exponent e, the so-called partial key exposure attacks. Aono (ACISP 2013), and Takayasu and Kunihiro (ACISP 2014) generalized the attacks when there are multiple pairs of a public/secret exponent $(e_1, d_1), \ldots, (e_n, d_n)$ for the same public modulus N. The standard RSA is a special case of the generalization, i.e., $n = 1$. They revealed that RSA becomes more vulnerable when there are more exponent pairs. However, their results have *two obvious drawbacks*. First, partial key exposure situations which they considered are restrictive. They have proposed the attacks only for small secret exponents, although attacks for large secret exponents have also been analyzed for the standard RSA. Second, they could not generalize the attacks perfectly. More concretely, their attacks for $n = 1$ do not correspond to the currently known best attacks on the standard RSA.

In this paper, we propose improved partial key exposure attacks on RSA with multiple exponent pairs. Our results completely solve the above drawbacks. Our attacks are the first results for large exponents, and our attacks for $n = 1$ correspond to the currently known best attacks on the standard RSA. Our results for small secret exponents are superior to previous results when $n = 1$ and 2, and when $n \geq 3$ and $d_1, \ldots, d_n > N^{3(n-1)/(3n+1)}$.

1 Introduction

1.1 Background

Partial Key Exposure Attacks on RSA. RSA is one of the most widely used cryptosystems. For a public modulus $N = pq$ where p and q are distinct primes with the same bit size, there are an encryption/verifying exponent e and a decryption/signing exponent d that satisfy $ed = 1 \mod \phi(N)$ where $\phi(N) = (p-1)(q-1)$. To encrypt a plaintext m (resp. verify a signature σ), $m^e \mod N$ (resp. $\sigma^e \mod N$) should be computed. Similarly, to decrypt a ciphertext c (resp. sign a message m), $c^d \mod N$ (resp. $m^d \mod N$) should be computed. To reduce the complexity of the heavy modular exponentiation, we can use a small public exponent $e \approx N^\alpha$ or a small decryption exponent $d \approx N^\beta$. However, Wiener [28] showed that too small d makes RSA insecure. Their attack factors

© Springer International Publishing Switzerland 2016
J.K. Liu and R. Steinfeld (Eds.): ACISP 2016, Part II, LNCS 9723, pp. 243–257, 2016.
DOI: 10.1007/978-3-319-40367-0_15

public modulus N in polynomial time when $\alpha = 1$ and $\beta < 1/4$. Later, Boneh and Durfee [4] further improved the bound to $\beta < 1 - 1/\sqrt{2} = 0.292\cdots$.

Boneh, Durfee, and Frankel [5] analyzed the security of RSA when attackers know some portions of d, that is, the so-called *partial key exposure attacks*. In this paper, we focus on the situation when attackers know $\tilde{d} > N^{\beta-\delta}$ which is the least significant bits of d. In this situation, the attack of Boneh et al. works only for extremely small $e = \text{poly}(\log N)$.

Thus far, several generalizations and improvements of partial key exposure attacks have been proposed. In this paper, we focus on three situations[1];

(a) $\alpha \leq 1$ and $\beta = 1$,
(b) $\alpha \leq 1$ and $\beta > 1$,
(c) $\alpha = 1$ and $\beta \leq 1$.

Blömer and May [3] analyzed the situation (a), and their attack works when $\alpha < 7/8 = 0.875$. Joye and Lepoint [15] analyzed the situation (b), and their attack works when $\beta < 15/8$ for extremely small α. Ernst et al. [11] analyzed the situation (c), and their attack works when $\beta < 7/8$. In the last situation, Aono [1] proposed an improved attack. When $1 - 1/\sqrt{2} < \beta < (9 - \sqrt{21})/12 = 0.368\cdots$, Aono's attack works with less partial information than that of Ernst et al. Later, in the same range of β, Takayasu and Kunihiro [27] further improved the attack.

RSA with Multiple Exponent Pairs. As opposed to the standard RSA setting, the security of RSA with multiple exponent pairs has also been studied in several papers [2, 14, 21, 23, 24, 26]. In this setting, there are multiple public/secret exponent pairs $(e_1, d_1), \ldots, (e_n, d_n)$ for the same public modulus N such that $e_j d_j = 1 \mod \phi(N)$ for all $j = 1, 2, \ldots, n$. In this context, the standard RSA can be regarded as the special case, i.e., $n = 1$. We denote sizes of public exponents as $e_1, \ldots, e_n \approx N^\alpha$ and sizes of secret exponents as $d_1, \ldots, d_n \approx N^\beta$. These works showed that RSA becomes more vulnerable when there are more exponent pairs. Takayasu and Kunihiro [26] proposed a generalization of Boneh and Durfee's attack [4] that works when $\beta < 1 - \sqrt{2/(3n+1)}$ only with public information N and $e_1, \ldots, e_n$. When there are more exponent pairs, i.e., larger n, larger secret exponents can be recovered. Especially, full size secret exponents, i.e., $\beta = 1$, can be recovered with infinitely many exponent pairs.

Partial key exposure attacks on RSA with multiple exponent pairs have also been analyzed. For the attacks, attackers know $\tilde{d}_1, \ldots, \tilde{d}_n > N^{\beta-\delta}$ which are the least significant bits of $d_1, \ldots, d_n$. Aono [2] analyzed a partial key exposure attack[2] in the situation (c). Although the attack on the standard

---

[1] At a glance, a situation (b) seems useless, since d is defined as $d \in \mathbb{Z}^*_{\phi(N)}$ in many cases, and $\beta \leq 1$ always holds. However, some implementations use an exponent which is larger than N. To decrypt/sign, one may use $d + k\phi(N)$ in turn for some integer $k > 0$. This implementation offers better resistance against side-channel attacks [9] or faster calculation by setting the exponent as low Hamming weight.

[2] In [2, 26], they use δ, not $\beta-\delta$ as ours, to represent portions of exposed bits. However, we follow the notation from [11, 27].

RSA [2,11,26], i.e., $n = 1$, cannot be applied to full size secret exponent[3] , i.e., $\beta = 1$, Aono's attack can be applied to the case when $n \geq 3$. Takayasu and Kunihiro [26] further improved the attack when $n \geq 3$ and $\beta < 3(n-1)/(3n+1)$. These results are theoretically interesting to ensure the security of RSA.

In this paper, we focus on partial key exposure attacks on RSA with multiple exponent pairs since previous results [2,26] have *two obvious drawbacks*. First, the results focus only on the situation (c). Therefore, there have been no results which analyzed the situations (a) and (b) with multiple exponent pairs. Second, the previous attacks [2,26] cannot be the best even in the situation (c), since the attacks for $n = 1$ do not correspond to the currently known best attacks with a single exponent pair [11,27]. As a result, although the generalization of Boneh and Durfee's small secret exponent attack suggests that partial key exposure attacks should always work when $\beta < 1 - \sqrt{2/(3n+1)}$ in the situation (c) even with no partial information, when $n = 1$ and 2, previous attacks [2,26] does not work in the range with small amounts of partial information.

1.2 Our Contributions

In this paper, we propose improved partial key exposure attacks on RSA with multiple exponent pairs and completely solve the above drawbacks of previous works [2,26]. Unlike previous works, we analyze not only the situation (c), but also the situations (a) and (b). Therefore, we offer the first result for the attack with multiple exponent pairs in (a) and (b). Moreover, our attack in the situation (c) is superior to previous attacks [2,26] when $n = 1$ and 2, and when $n \geq 3$ and $\beta > 3(n-1)/(3n+1)$. Our attack always works when $\beta < 1 - \sqrt{2/(3n+1)}$ for $n = 1$ and 2. When $\beta = 1$, although previous attacks work when $n \geq 3$, our attack works when $n \geq 2$. For all the situations (a), (b), and (c), our proposed attacks for $n = 1$ correspond to the currently known best attacks with a single exponent pair.

1.3 Technical Overview

Almost all the above attacks [2,3,26,27] used the Coppersmith method to solve modular equations that have small solutions [6,13]. In the method, we construct a lattice whose basis vectors are coefficients of polynomials that have the same solutions as the original modular equations. To improve partial key exposure attacks, we should construct algorithms which can find larger solutions. For the improvement, we should select appropriate lattice bases for the resulting lattice to have shorter vectors. We call polynomials which shorten lattice vectors *helpful polynomials*. The exact criteria that decide if polynomials are helpful or not have already been analyzed in [18,25]. To maximize solvable bounds of

---

[3] From May [17] and Coron and May's [10] results, given whole bits of d then the factorization of N is a trivial. However, it does not immediately suggest that partial key exposure attacks always work when whole bits of d are given. Indeed, Ernst et al. [11] claimed to find such improved attacks is an interesting open problem.

solutions, we should select as many helpful polynomials as possible and as few unhelpful polynomials as possible in lattice bases. For example, first, Boneh and Durfee [4] constructed lattices to obtain Wiener's bound $\beta < 1/4$ [28]. Afterward, they added extra polynomials, which are helpful, in lattice basis and improved the bound to $\beta < 1 - 1/\sqrt{2}$.

As noted in [26], Aono's lattice can be viewed as a generalization of the lattice to obtain Wiener's bound for the small secret exponent attack. The selection of lattice bases is too simple, since it does not depend on any values of n, β and δ. Therefore, the lattice can be applied to attacks in situations (a) and (b), although Aono did not analyze them. However, that means the lattice cannot provide the best bounds when the values of n, α, β, and δ change. In [26], Takayasu and Kunihiro work out new lattice constructions that depend on the values of n, α, β, and δ. They revealed that Aono's lattice contains unhelpful polynomials when n is large and β is small, and they constructed lattices by eliminating as many unhelpful polynomials as possible. The lattice provides an improved results when $n \geq 3$ and $\beta < 3(n-1)/(3n+1)$.

Conversely, the above observation suggests that Aono's lattice does not contain all helpful polynomials when $n = 1$ and 2, and $n \geq 3$ and $\beta > 3(n-1)/(3n+1)$. Therefore, all we have to do is to add as many helpful polynomials as possible. However, Takayasu and Kunihiro [26] could not do the task since adding helpful polynomials is rather difficult compared with eliminating unhelpful polynomials. We work out the analyses required to understand the essence of the lattice constructions for the standard RSA [3,11,15,27]. Although we analyze the three situations, i.e., (a), (b), and (c), there are only two types of lattices in these previous works. We call them the Blömer-May lattice and the Takayasu-Kunihiro lattice. Ernst et al.'s result [11], and Joye and Lepoint's result [15] can be obtained via the Blömer-May lattice. The classification offers better understanding for the lattice constructions and we generalize the two types of lattices in subsequent sections. As a result, this paper completes the analysis of partial key exposure attacks on RSA with multiple exponent pairs.

1.4 Organization

In Sect. 2, we define a scenario of partial key exposure attacks and formulate them as simultaneous modular equations. Afterward, we briefly summarize previous results [2,3,11,26,27]. In Sect. 3, we introduce the Coppersmith method to solve modular equations [6,13]. In Sect. 4, we propose generalized lattice constructions of the Blömer-May. In Sect. 5, we propose generalized lattice constructions of the Takayasu-Kunihiro.

2   Definitions of the Attack and Previous Results

For multiple exponent pairs setting, RSA key generations can be written as $e_j d_j = 1 + \ell_j (N - (p+q) + 1)$ for $j = 1, 2, \ldots, n$ with some integers $\ell_j \approx N^{\alpha+\beta-1}$. We assume that all public exponents $e_1, \ldots, e_n$ are pairwise co-prime as previous works [2,26]. Let $\tilde{d}_j \approx N^{\beta-\delta}$ (resp. $d'_j \approx N^\delta$) denote the least (resp. the most) significant bits of d_j. We can rewrite $d_j = d'_j M + \tilde{d}_j$ with some integers $M \approx N^{\beta-\delta}$. We consider partial key exposure attacks when attackers know $\tilde{d}_1, \ldots, \tilde{d}_n$. Rewrite RSA key generations

$$e_j \left(d'_j M + \tilde{d}_j \right) = 1 + \ell_j(N - (p+q) + 1),$$

and consider the following modular polynomials

$$f_j(x_j, y) = 1 - e_j \tilde{d}_j + x_j(N + y) \pmod{e_j M} \text{ and}$$
$$g_j(x_j, y) = 1 + x_j(N + y) \pmod{e_j}$$

for $j = 1, 2, \ldots, n$. The polynomials have the roots

$$(x_1, \ldots, x_n, y) = (\ell_1, \ldots, \ell_n, -(p+q) + 1).$$

The absolute values of the roots are bounded above by $X_j := N^{\alpha+\beta-1}$ for $j = 1, 2, \ldots, n$ and $Y := 3N^{1/2}$. If we can find the roots, we can easily factor RSA modulus N.

In the rest of this section, we summarize previous attacks. First, we show the previous results for the standard RSA. All conditions when Blömer and May's attack [3], Ernst et al.'s attack [11], and Joye and Lepoint's attack [15] work can be written as

$$\delta < \frac{5}{6} - \frac{\sqrt{-5 + 6(\alpha+\beta)}}{3}. \tag{1}$$

All the attacks are based on the Blömer-May lattice and the lattices are constructed to solve a modular equation $f_1(x_1, y) = 0$. Takayasu and Kunihiro's attack [27] works when

$$\delta < \frac{1 + \beta - \sqrt{2 - 3(1-\beta)^2}}{2} \text{ and } \beta < \frac{9 - \sqrt{21}}{12}. \tag{2}$$

The Takayasu-Kunihiro lattices are constructed to solve simultaneous modular equations $f_1(x_1, y) = 0$ and $g_1(x_1, y) = 0$.

Next, we show the previous results with multiple exponent pairs. The following attacks work in time polynomial in $\log N$ and exponential in n. Although Aono [2] only considered the situation (c), their lattice can also be applied to the situations (a) and (b). The attack works when

$$\delta < \frac{3}{2} - \frac{4}{3n+1}\alpha - \beta. \tag{3}$$

Aono's lattice is constructed to solve simultaneous modular equations $f_1(x_1, y) = 0, \ldots, f_n(x_n, y) = 0$. In the situation (c) for $n \geq 3$, Takayasu and Kunihiro [26] solved the same modular equations as Aono and improved the bound to

$$\delta < -\frac{1}{2} + \beta + \frac{(3n+1)(1-\beta)^2}{4} \text{ and } \beta < \frac{3(n-1)}{3n+1}. \tag{4}$$

3   Preliminaries

Consider the modular equations $h(x_1, \ldots, x_n) = 0 \pmod{W}$. All absolute values of the solutions $(\tilde{x}_1, \ldots, \tilde{x}_n)$ are bounded above by $X_1, \ldots, X_n$. When $\prod_{j=1}^{n} X_j$ is reasonably smaller than W, the Coppersmith method can find all the solutions in polynomial time. We write the norm of a polynomial as $\|h(x_1, \ldots, x_n)\|$, which represents the Euclidean norm of the coefficient vector. The following Howgrave-Graham's Lemma reduces the modular equations into integer equations.

Lemma 1 (Howgrave-Graham's   Lemma [13]**).** *Let* $\tilde{h}(x_1, \ldots, x_n) \in \mathbb{Z}[x_1, \ldots, x_n]$ *be a polynomial with at most* w *monomials. Let* $m, W, X_1, \ldots, X_n$ *be positive integers. Suppose that:*

1. $\tilde{h}(\tilde{x}_1, \ldots, \tilde{x}_n) = 0 \pmod{W^m}$, *where* $|\tilde{x}_1| < X_1, \ldots, |\tilde{x}_n| < X_n$,
2. $\|\tilde{h}(x_1 X_1, \ldots, x_n X_n)\| < W^m / \sqrt{w}$.

Then $\tilde{h}(\tilde{x}_1, \ldots, \tilde{x}_n) = 0$ *holds over the integers.*

To solve n-variate modular equations $h(x_1, \ldots, x_n) = 0 \pmod{W}$, it suffices to find n new polynomials $\tilde{h}_1(x_1, \ldots, x_n), \ldots, \tilde{h}_n(x_1, \ldots, x_n)$ whose roots are the same as the original solutions $(\tilde{x}_1, \ldots, \tilde{x}_n)$ and whose norms are small enough to satisfy Howgrave-Graham's Lemma.

To find such polynomials from the original polynomial $h(x_1, \ldots, x_n)$, lattices and the LLL algorithm are often used. Lattices represent the integer linear combinations of the basis vectors. All vectors are row representation. For the basis vectors $\boldsymbol{b}_1, \ldots, \boldsymbol{b}_w$, which are all k dimensional linearly independent vectors in $\mathbb{Z}^k$, the lattice spanned by these vectors is defined as $L(\boldsymbol{b}_1, \ldots, \boldsymbol{b}_w) := \{\sum_{j=1}^{w} c_j \boldsymbol{b}_j : c_j \in \mathbb{Z} \text{ for all } j = 1, 2, \ldots, w\}$. We also use the matrix representation for the basis. We define the basis matrix $\boldsymbol{B}$ as $w \times k$ matrix which has the basis vectors $\boldsymbol{b}_1, \ldots, \boldsymbol{b}_w$ in each row. In the same way, the lattice can be rewritten as $L(\boldsymbol{B})$. We call the lattice full-rank when $w = k$. The volume of the lattice $\mathrm{vol}(L(\boldsymbol{B}))$ is defined as the w-dimensional volume of the parallelepiped $\mathcal{P}(\boldsymbol{B}) := \{\boldsymbol{c}\boldsymbol{B} : \boldsymbol{c} \in \mathbb{R}^w, 0 \le c_j < 1, \text{for all } j = 1, 2, \ldots, w\}$. The volume can be computed as $\mathrm{vol}(L(\boldsymbol{B})) = \sqrt{\det(\boldsymbol{B}\boldsymbol{B}^T)}$ in general, and the volume of a full-rank lattice can be computed as $\mathrm{vol}(L(\boldsymbol{B})) = |\det(\boldsymbol{B})|$.

Lattice has been used in many places in cryptographic research. See [7,8, 19,20] for detailed information. In cryptanalysis, to find non-zero short lattice vectors is essential. In this paper, we introduce the LLL algorithm [16] which outputs short lattice vectors in polynomial time.

Proposition 1 (LLL algorithm [16]**).** *Given basis vectors* $\boldsymbol{b}_1, \ldots, \boldsymbol{b}_w$ *in* $\mathbb{Z}^k$, *the LLL algorithm finds LLL-reduced bases* $\tilde{\boldsymbol{b}}_1, \ldots, \tilde{\boldsymbol{b}}_w$ *that satisfy*

$$\|\tilde{\boldsymbol{b}}_j\| \le 2^{w(w-1)/4(w-j+1)} (\mathrm{vol}(L(\boldsymbol{B})))^{1/(w-j+1)} \quad \text{for } 1 \le j \le w,$$

in time polynomial in w, k, *and the maximum input length.*

Again, we consider how to solve the modular equation $h(x_1, \ldots, x_n) = 0$ (mod W). First, we construct w polynomials $h_1(x_1, \ldots, x_n), \ldots, h_w(x_1, \ldots, x_n)$ that have the roots $(\tilde{x}_1, \ldots, \tilde{x}_n)$ modulo W^m with some positive integer m. We construct w basis vectors $\boldsymbol{b}_1, \ldots, \boldsymbol{b}_w$ each whose elements are coefficients of $h_j(x_1 X_1, \ldots, x_n X_n)$ for $j = 1, 2, \ldots, w$, and construct a basis matrix $\boldsymbol{B}$. We span a lattice $L(\boldsymbol{B})$. Since all lattice vectors are integer linear combinations of the basis vectors, all polynomials whose coefficients are derived from lattice vectors have the roots $(\tilde{x}_1, \ldots, \tilde{x}_n)$ modulo W^m. We apply the LLL algorithm to the lattice bases, and obtain n LLL-reduced vectors $\tilde{\boldsymbol{b}}_1, \ldots, \tilde{\boldsymbol{b}}_n$. The new polynomials $\tilde{h}_1(x_1, \ldots, x_n), \ldots, \tilde{h}_n(x_1, \ldots, x_n)$ which are derived from the above n LLL-reduced vectors satisfy Howgrave-Graham's Lemma provided that $(\text{vol}(L(\boldsymbol{B})))^{1/w} < W^m$. Here, we omit small terms. When we obtain the polynomials $\tilde{h}_1(x_1, \ldots, x_n), \ldots, \tilde{h}_n(x_1, \ldots, x_n)$, it is easy to solve the modular equation $h(x_1, \ldots, x_n) = 0$ (mod W). What we should do is to find the roots of the polynomials over the integers by computing resultant or Gröbner bases. We should note that the method needs heuristic argument if we consider multivariate problems, since the polynomials $\tilde{h}_1(x_1, \ldots, x_n), \ldots, \tilde{h}_n(x_1, \ldots, x_n)$ have no assurance of algebraic independency. In this paper, we assume that the polynomials derived from outputs of the LLL algorithm are algebraic independent as previous works [2–4,15,26,27]. Indeed, there are few papers that contradict the assumption.

Although we introduce a lattice construction to solve a single multivariate modular equation, the method can be easily applied to simultaneous modular equations in the same way. To attack RSA with multiple exponent pairs, we use *Minkowski sum based lattices* introduced by Aono [2]. To solve n simultaneous modular equations, the technique combine n lattices each of which is a lattice to solve a single equation.

4   Generalizations of the Blömer-May Lattice

4.1   Our Algorithm

In this section, we solve simultaneous modular equations

$$f_j(x_j, y) = 1 - e_j \tilde{d}_j + x_j(N + y) \pmod{e_j M}$$

for $j = 1, 2, \ldots, n$ by generalizing the Blömer-May lattice [3], and obtain the following result.

Theorem 1. *Let $N = pq$ be an RSA modulus. Let (e_j, d_j) be pubic/secret exponents where $e_j \approx N^\alpha, d_j \approx N^\beta$, and $e_j d_j = 1 \pmod{(p-1)(q-1)}$ for $j = 1, 2, \ldots, n$. Given public elements $N, e_1, \ldots, e_n$, and $\tilde{d}_1, \ldots, \tilde{d}_n > N^{\beta-\delta}$ that are the least significant bits of $d_1, \ldots, d_n$, respectively. Assume $e_1, \ldots, e_n$ are pairwise co-prime and the LLL algorithm outputs algebraically independent polynomials. If*

$$\delta < \frac{9n + 1 - \sqrt{(3n+1)^2 + 96n\alpha - 24n(3n+1)(1-\beta)}}{12n},$$

then public modulus N can be factored in time polynomial in $\log N$ and exponential in n.

Proof. At first, we show the Blömer-May lattice to solve each single modular equation $f_j(x_j, y) = 0$ for $j = 1, 2, \ldots, n$ that yields the bound (1). To solve the single equation, we use shift-polynomials

$$x_j^{i_j} \cdot f_j(x_j, y)^{u_j} \cdot (e_j M)^{m-u_j} \text{ with } i_j = 0, 1, \ldots, m; u_j = 0, 1, \ldots, m - i_j,$$

$$y^{k_j} \cdot f_j(x_j, y)^{i_j} \cdot (e_j M)^{m-i_j} \text{ with } i_j = 0, 1, \ldots, m; k_j = 1, 2, \ldots, \lfloor \tau m \rfloor,$$

in lattice bases with some positive integer m. The parameter $\tau \geq 0$ should be optimized later. All these shift-polynomials modulo $(e_j M)^m$ have the same roots as the original solutions, e.g., $(x_j, y) = (\ell_j, -(p+q)+1)$ for $j = 1, 2, \ldots, n$. These polynomials generate a triangular basis matrix with diagonals

$$X_j^{i'_j} Y^{u'_j} (e_j M)^{m-\min\{i'_j, u'_j\}} \text{ with } i'_j = 0, 1, \ldots, m; u'_j = 0, 1, \ldots, i'_j,$$

$$X_j^{i'_j} Y^{i'_j + k'_j} (e_j M)^{m-i'_j} \qquad \text{with } i'_j = 0, 1, \ldots, m; k'_j = 1, 2, \ldots, \lfloor \tau m \rfloor.$$

We set the parameter $\tau = (1 - 2\delta)/2$, and the lattice yields the bound (1).

Next, we combine these n lattices based on Minkowski sum. Since we combine triangular basis matrices, the combined basis matrix also becomes triangular with diagonals

$$X_j^{i'_j} Y^{u'_j} (e_j M)^{m-\min\{i'_j, u'_j\}} \text{ with } i'_j = 0, 1, \ldots, m; u'_j = 0, 1, \ldots, i'_j,$$

$$X_1^{i'_1} \cdots X_n^{i'_n} Y^{\sum_{j=1}^n i'_j + k'} e_1^{m-i'_1} \cdots e_n^{m-i'_n} M^{nm - \sum_{j=1}^n i'_j}$$

$$\text{with } i'_j = 0, 1, \ldots, m \text{ for } j = 1, 2, \ldots, n; k' = 1, 2, \ldots, \lfloor \tau m \rfloor.$$

All polynomials which are derived from resulting lattice vectors modulo $(e_1 \cdots e_n)^m M^{nm}$ have the same roots as the original solutions.

We show that the above lattice offers the bound of Theorem 1. Ignoring low order terms of m, we can compute the dimension

$$w = \sum_{i'_1=0}^m \cdots \sum_{i'_n=0}^m \sum_{u'=0}^{\sum_{j=1}^n i'_j} 1 + \sum_{i'_1=0}^m \cdots \sum_{i'_n=0}^m \sum_{k'=1}^{\lfloor \tau m \rfloor} 1 = \left(\frac{n}{2} + \tau \right) m^{n+1},$$

and the volume of the lattice $\mathrm{vol}(L(\boldsymbol{B})) = X_1^{s_{X_1}} \cdots X_n^{s_{X_n}} Y^{s_Y} e_1^{s_{e_1}} \cdots e_n^{s_{e_n}} M^{s_M}$, where

$$s_{X_j} = \sum_{i'_1=0}^m \cdots \sum_{i'_n=0}^m \sum_{u'=0}^{\sum_{j=1}^n i'_j} i'_j + \sum_{i'_1=0}^m \cdots \sum_{i'_n=0}^m \sum_{k'=1}^{\lfloor \tau m \rfloor} i'_j = \left(\frac{3n+1}{12} + \frac{\tau}{2} \right) m^{n+2},$$

$$s_{e_j} = \sum_{i'_1=0}^m \cdots \sum_{i'_n=0}^m \sum_{u'=0}^{\sum_{j=1}^n i'_j} (m - \min\{i'_j, u'\}) + \sum_{i'_1=0}^m \cdots \sum_{i'_n=0}^m \sum_{k'=1}^{\lfloor \tau m \rfloor} (m - i'_j)$$

$$= \left(\frac{3n+1}{12} + \frac{\tau}{2} \right) m^{n+2}$$

for $j = 1, 2, \ldots, n$,

$$s_Y = \sum_{i'_1=0}^{m} \cdots \sum_{i'_n=0}^{m} \sum_{u'=0}^{\sum_{j=1}^{n} i'_j} u' + \sum_{i'_1=0}^{m} \cdots \sum_{i'_n=0}^{m} \sum_{k'=1}^{\lfloor \tau m \rfloor} \left(\sum_{j=1}^{n} i'_j + k' \right)$$

$$= \left(\frac{n(3n+1)}{24} + \frac{n\tau}{2} + \frac{\tau^2}{2} \right) m^{n+2},$$

$$s_M = \sum_{i'_1=0}^{m} \cdots \sum_{i'_n=0}^{m} \sum_{u'=0}^{\sum_{j=1}^{n} i'_j} (nm - u') + \sum_{i'_1=0}^{m} \cdots \sum_{i'_n=0}^{m} \sum_{k'=1}^{\lfloor \tau m \rfloor} \left(nm - \sum_{j=1}^{n} i'_j \right)$$

$$= \left(\frac{n(9n-1)}{24} + \frac{n}{2}\tau \right) m^{n+2}.$$

We can solve the simultaneous modular equations $f_j(x_j, y) = 0$ for $j = 1, 2, \ldots, n$, when $(\text{vol}(L(\boldsymbol{B})))^{1/w} < (e_1 \cdots e_n)^m M^{nm}$, that is,

$$-12\tau^2 + 24n(1-\delta)\tau + 3n(3n+1) - 8n\alpha - 2n(3n+1)(\beta+\delta) > 0.$$

To maximize the left-hand side of the above inequality, we set the parameter $\tau = n(1-2\delta)/2$, and the condition becomes

$$12n\delta^2 - 2(9n+1)\delta + 12n + 3 - 8\alpha - 2(3n+1)\beta > 0.$$

The inequality results in the bound of Theorem 1,

$$\delta < \frac{9n + 1 - \sqrt{(3n+1)^2 + 96n\alpha - 24n(3n+1)(1-\beta)}}{12n}$$

as required. $\square$

4.2   Observation

Compared with Aono's lattice, we select extra shift-polynomials, e.g., $y^{k_j} \cdot f_j(x_j, y)^{i_j} \cdot (e_j M)^{m-i_j}$. As the case of the standard RSA, these extra shift-polynomials reduce the output length of the LLL algorithm and improve partial key exposure attacks.

The bound of Theorem 1 becomes the same as the bound (1) of the Blömer-May lattice when $n = 1$. In situation (a) and (b), the bound is always superior to the bound (3) which is derived from Aono's lattices. In the situation (c), the bound is superior to the bound (3) when $n = 1, 2$, and when $n \geq 3$ and $\beta > 3(n-1)/(3n+1)$. When there are infinitely many exponent pairs n for extremely small α, Aono's attack (3), and Takayasu and Kunihiro's attack (4) work when $\beta < 3/2$ and $\beta < 1$, respectively, although Joye and Lepoint's attack (1), which uses only one exponent pair, works when $\beta < 15/8$. Our attack works when $\beta < 2$ with infinitely many exponent pairs.

5 Generalizations of the Takayasu-Kunihiro Lattice

5.1 Our Algorithm

In this section, we solve simultaneous modular equations

$$f_j(x_j, y) = 1 - e_j \tilde{d}_j + x_j(N + y) \pmod{e_j M} \quad \text{and}$$
$$g_j(x_j, y) = 1 + \dot{x}_j(N + y) \pmod{e_j},$$

for $j = 1, 2, \ldots, n$ by generalizing the Takayasu-Kunihiro lattice [27], and obtain the following result.

Theorem 2. *Let $N = pq$ be an RSA modulus. Let (e_j, d_j) be pubic/secret exponents where $e_j \approx N, d_j \approx N^\beta$, and $e_j d_j = 1 \pmod{(p-1)(q-1)}$ for $j = 1, 2, \ldots, n$. Given public elements $N, e_1, \ldots, e_n$, and $\tilde{d}_1, \ldots, \tilde{d}_n > N^{\beta - \delta}$ that are the least significant bits of $d_1, \ldots, d_n$, respectively. Assume $e_1, \ldots, e_n$ are pairwise co-prime and the LLL algorithm outputs algebraically independent polynomials. If*

$$\delta < \frac{3n + 1 + (9n - 5)\beta - \sqrt{16(3n - 1) - 3(3n + 1)(7n - 3)(1 - \beta)^2}}{4(3n - 1)} \quad and$$

$$\beta < \frac{3(11n + 1) - \sqrt{-3(21n^2 - 130n - 3)}}{48n}$$

for $n = 1$ and 2, then public modulus N can be factored in time polynomial in $\log N$ and exponential in n.

Proof. At first, we show the Takayasu-Kunihiro lattice to solve each single modular equation $f_j(x_j, y) = 0$ and $g_j(x_j, y) = 0$ for $j = 1, 2, \ldots, n$ that yields the bound (2). To solve the single equation, when $1 + 2\delta - 4\beta > 0$, we define a function

$$l_1(k) = \max\left\{0, \frac{k - 2(\beta - \delta)m}{1 + 2\delta - 4\beta}\right\},$$

and use shift-polynomials

$$x_j^{i_j} \cdot f_j(x_j, y)^{u_j} \cdot (e_j M)^{m - u_j} \text{ with } i_j = 0, 1, \ldots, m; u_j = 0, 1, \ldots, m - i_j,$$
$$y^{k_j} \cdot f(x, y)^{i_j - \lceil l_1(k_j) \rceil} \cdot g(x, y)^{\lceil l_1(k_j) \rceil} \cdot e^{m - i_j} M^{m - (i_j - \lceil l_1(k_j) \rceil)}$$
$$\text{with } i_j = 0, 1, \ldots, m; k_j = 1, 2, \ldots, \lfloor 2(\beta - \delta)m + (1 + 2\delta - 4\beta)i_j \rfloor$$

in lattice bases with some positive integer m. All these shift-polynomials modulo $(e_j M)^m$ have the same roots as the original solutions, $(x_j, y) = (\ell_j, -(p+q)+1)$ for $j = 1, 2, \ldots, n$. Although these polynomials do not directly generate a triangular basis matrix, we can transform it into triangular by using unravelled linearization [12]. See [27] for the detailed analysis of the proof. After the transformation, sizes of diagonals are

$$X_j^{i'_j} Y^{u'_j} (e_j M)^{m - \min\{i'_j, u'_j\}} \qquad \text{with } i'_j = 0, 1, \ldots, m; u'_j = 0, 1, \ldots, i'_j,$$

$$X_j^{i'_j} Y^{i'_j + k'_j} e_1^{m - i'_j} M^{m - (i'_j - l_1(k'_j))} \text{ with } i'_j = 0, 1, \ldots, m;$$

$$k'_j = 1, 2, \ldots, \lfloor 2(\beta - \delta)m + (1 + 2\delta - 4\beta)i'_j \rfloor.$$

When $1 + 2\delta - 4\beta > 0$, the lattice yields the bound (2).

Next, we combine these n lattices based on Minkowski sum. When $1 + 2\delta - 4\beta > 0$, we define a function

$$l_n(k) = \max\left\{0, \frac{k - 2(\beta - \delta)nm}{1 + 2\delta - 4\beta}\right\}$$

where the validities of the definition will be discussed later. Since we combine triangular basis matrices, the combined basis matrix becomes triangular with diagonals

$$X_j^{i'_j} Y^{u'_j} (e_j M)^{m - \min\{i'_j, u'_j\}} \text{ with } i'_j = 0, 1, \ldots, m; u'_j = 0, 1, \ldots, i'_j,$$

$$X_1^{i'_1} \cdots X_n^{i'_n} Y^{\sum_{j=1}^n i'_j + k'} e_1^{m - i'_1} \cdots e_n^{m - i'_n} M^{nm - (\sum_{j=1}^n i'_j - l_n(k'))}$$

$$\text{with } i'_j = 0, 1, \ldots, m \text{ for } j = 1, 2, \ldots, n;$$

$$k' = 1, 2, \ldots, \lfloor 2(\beta - \delta)nm + (1 + 2\delta - 4\beta) \sum_{j=1}^n i'_j \rfloor.$$

All polynomials which are derived from resulting lattice vectors modulo $(e_1 \cdots e_n)^m M^{nm}$ have the same roots as the original solutions.

We show that the above lattice offers the bound of Theorem 2. Ignoring low order terms of m, we can compute the dimension

$$w = \sum_{i'_1=0}^m \cdots \sum_{i'_n=0}^m \sum_{u'=0}^{\sum_{j=1}^n i'_j} 1 + \sum_{i'_1=0}^m \cdots \sum_{i'_n=0}^m \sum_{k'=1}^{\lfloor 2(\beta-\delta)nm + (1+2\delta-4\beta) \sum_{j=1}^n i'_j \rfloor} 1$$

$$= n(1 - \delta)m^{n+1},$$

and the volume of the lattice $\mathrm{vol}(L(\boldsymbol{B})) = X_1^{s_{X_1}} \cdots X_n^{s_{X_n}} Y^{s_Y} e_1^{s_{e_1}} \cdots e_n^{s_{e_n}} M^{s_M}$, where

$$s_{X_j} = \sum_{i'_1=0}^m \cdots \sum_{i'_n=0}^m \sum_{u'=0}^{\sum_{j=1}^n i'_j} i'_j + \sum_{i'_1=0}^m \cdots \sum_{i'_n=0}^m \sum_{k'=1}^{\lfloor 2(\beta-\delta)nm + (1+2\delta-4\beta) \sum_{j=1}^n i'_j \rfloor} i'_j$$

$$= \left(\frac{3n+1}{12} + (\beta - \delta)n + \frac{3n+1}{12}(1 + 2\delta - 4\beta)\right) m^{n+2},$$

$$s_{e_j} = \sum_{i_1'=0}^{m} \cdots \sum_{i_n'=0}^{m} \sum_{u'=0}^{\sum_{j=1}^{n} i_j'} (m - \min\{i_j', u'\})$$

$$+ \sum_{i_1'=0}^{m} \cdots \sum_{i_n'=0}^{m} \sum_{k'=1}^{\lfloor 2(\beta-\delta)nm+(1+2\delta-4\beta)\sum_{j=1}^{n} i_j' \rfloor} (m - i_j')$$

$$= \left(\frac{3n+1}{12} + n(\beta - \delta) + \frac{3n-1}{12}(1 + 2\delta - 4\beta) \right) m^{n+2}$$

for $j = 1, 2, \ldots, n$,

$$s_Y = \sum_{i_1=0}^{m} \cdots \sum_{i_n=0}^{m} \sum_{u=0}^{\sum_{j=1}^{n} i_j} u$$

$$+ \sum_{i_1'=0}^{m} \cdots \sum_{i_n'=0}^{m} \sum_{k'=1}^{\lfloor 2(\beta-\delta)nm+(1+2\delta-4\beta)\sum_{j=1}^{n} i_j' \rfloor} \left(\sum_{j=1}^{n} i_j' + k' \right)$$

$$= \left(\frac{n(3n+1)}{24} + n^2(\beta - \delta) + 2n^2(\beta - \delta)^2 + n^2(\beta - \delta)(1 + 2\delta - 4\beta) \right) m^{n+2}$$

$$+ \left(\frac{n(3n+1)}{12}(1 + 2\delta - 4\beta) + \frac{n(3n+1)}{24}(1 + 2\delta - 4\beta)^2 \right) m^{n+2},$$

$$s_M = \sum_{i_1'=0}^{m} \cdots \sum_{i_n'=0}^{m} \sum_{u'=0}^{\sum_{j=1}^{n} i_j'} (nm - u')$$

$$+ \sum_{i_1'=0}^{m} \cdots \sum_{i_n'=0}^{m} \sum_{k'=1}^{\lfloor 2(\beta-\delta)nm+(1+2\delta-4\beta)\sum_{j=1}^{n} i_j' \rfloor} \left(nm - \left(\sum_{j=1}^{n} i_j' - l_n(k') \right) \right)$$

$$= \left(\frac{n(9n-1)}{24} + n^2(\beta - \delta) + \frac{n(9n-1)}{24}(1 + 2\delta - 4\beta) \right) m^{n+2}.$$

We can solve the simultaneous modular equations $f_j(x_j, y) = 0$ and $g_j(x_j, y) = 0$ for $j = 1, 2, \ldots, n$, when $(\mathrm{vol}(L(\boldsymbol{B})))^{1/w} < (e_1 \cdots e_n)^m M^{nm}$, that is,

$$4(3n-1)(\beta - \delta)^2 + 2(3n+1)(1 - \beta)(\beta - \delta)$$
$$+6n - 2 - (12n+4)\beta + (6n+2)\beta^2 > 0.$$

The inequality results in the bound of Theorem 2,

$$\delta < \frac{3n + 1 + (9n - 5)\beta - \sqrt{16(3n - 1) - 3(3n + 1)(7n - 3)(1 - \beta)^2}}{4(3n - 1)}$$

as required. The bound is valid only when $1 + 2\delta - 4\beta > 0$ that is equivalent to

$$24n\beta^2 - 3(11n + 1)\beta + 2(6n - 1) > 0,$$

that is,

$$\beta < \frac{3(11n+1) - \sqrt{-3(21n^2 - 130n - 3)}}{48n}.$$

$\square$

5.2 Observation

As with the lattice in the previous section, compared with Aono's lattice, we select extra shift-polynomials, e.g., $y^{k_j} \cdot f_j(x_j, y)^{i_j} \cdot (e_j M)^{m-i_j}$. As the case of the standard RSA, these extra shift-polynomials reduce the output length of the LLL algorithm and improve partial key exposure attacks. Moreover, we eliminate some shift-polynomials from lattices in the previous section. This appropriate elimination enables us to obtain better bounds with some parameters. In particular, to generalize the attack [27], we define a function $l_n(k)$ to satisfy the following property.

Proposition 2. *When* $1 + 2\delta - 4\beta > 0$, *polynomials whose diagonals are* $X_1^{i_1'} \cdots X_n^{i_n'} Y^{\sum_{j=1}^n i_j' + k'}$ *are helpful when* $k' \leq 2(\beta-\delta)nm + (1+2\delta-4\beta)\sum_{j=1}^n i_j'$. *In addition, the polynomials are unhelpful when* $k' > 2(\beta - \delta)nm + (1 + 2\delta - 4\beta)\sum_{j=1}^n i_j'$.

The bound of Theorem 2 becomes the same as the bound (2) when $n = 1$. The bound of Theorem 2 is superior to that of Theorem 1 when

$$\beta < \frac{3(11n+1) - \sqrt{-3(21n^2 - 130n - 3)}}{48n}$$

for $n = 1$ and 2, $\beta < \left(9 - \sqrt{21}\right)/12 = 0.368\cdots$ for $n = 1$ and $\beta < \left(69 - \sqrt{537}\right)/96 = 0.477\cdots$ for $n = 2$. Using the attack, partial key exposure attack always works when $\beta < 1 - \sqrt{2/(3n+1)}$.

6   Concluding Remarks

In this paper, we study partial key exposure attacks on RSA with multiple exponent pairs when attackers know the least significant bits of secret exponents. The attacks have been analyzed for a single exponent pair case and we propose generalizations of the attacks. Our proposed attacks cover every situation that is worth studying and provide significant improvements.

Although we think our work completes the attack in this direction, there still remains an open problem. In this paper, we only analyze the case when attackers know the least significant bits of secret exponents. However, for a single exponent pair, partial key exposure attacks on RSA when attackers know the most significant bits of secret exponents have also been analyzed [11, 22, 27]. To generalize the attack with multiple exponent pairs remains as future work.

Acknowledgements. The author is supported by a JSPS Fellowship for Young Scientists. This research was supported by CREST, JST, and supported by JSPS Grant-in-Aid for JSPS Fellows 14J08237 and KAKENHI Grant Number 25280001.

References

1. Aono, Y.: A new lattice construction for partial key exposure attack for RSA. In: Jarecki, S., Tsudik, G. (eds.) PKC 2009. LNCS, vol. 5443, pp. 34–53. Springer, Heidelberg (2009)
2. Aono, Y.: Minkowski sum based lattice construction for multivariate simultaneous coppersmith's technique and applications to RSA. In: Boyd, C., Simpson, L. (eds.) ACISP. LNCS, vol. 7959, pp. 88–103. Springer, Heidelberg (2013)
3. Blömer, J., May, A.: New partial key exposure attacks on RSA. In: Boneh, D. (ed.) CRYPTO 2003. LNCS, vol. 2729, pp. 27–43. Springer, Heidelberg (2003)
4. Boneh, D., Durfee, G.: Cryptanalysis of RSA with private key d less than $N^{0.292}$. IEEE Trans. Inf. Theory 46(4), 1339–1349 (2000)
5. Boneh, D., Durfee, G., Frankel, Y.: An attack on RSA given a small fraction of the private key bits. In: Ohta, K., Pei, D. (eds.) ASIACRYPT 1998. LNCS, vol. 1514, pp. 25–34. Springer, Heidelberg (1998)
6. Coppersmith, D.: Finding a small root of a univariate modular equation. In: Maurer, U.M. (ed.) EUROCRYPT 1996. LNCS, vol. 1070, pp. 155–165. Springer, Heidelberg (1996)
7. Coppersmith, D.: Small solutions to polynomial equations, and low exponent RSA vulnerabilities. J. Cryptol. 10(4), 233–260 (1997)
8. Coppersmith, D.: Finding small solutions to small degree polynomials. In: Silverman, J.H. (ed.) CaLC 2001. LNCS, vol. 2146, pp. 20–31. Springer, Heidelberg (2001)
9. Coron, J.-S.: Resistance against differential power analysis for elliptic curve cryptosystems. In: Koç, Ç.K., Paar, C. (eds.) CHES 1999. LNCS, vol. 1717, pp. 292–302. Springer, Heidelberg (1999)
10. Coron, J.-S., May, A.: Deterministic polynomial-time equivalence of computing the RSA secret key and factoring. J. Cryptol. 20(1), 39–50 (2007)
11. Ernst, M., Jochemsz, E., May, A., de Weger, B.: Partial key exposure attacks on RSA up to full size exponents. In: Cramer, R. (ed.) EUROCRYPT 2005. LNCS, vol. 3494, pp. 371–386. Springer, Heidelberg (2005)
12. Herrmann, M., May, A.: Attacking power generators using unravelled linearization: when do we output too much? In: Matsui, M. (ed.) ASIACRYPT 2009. LNCS, vol. 5912, pp. 487–504. Springer, Heidelberg (2009)
13. Howgrave-Graham, N.: Finding small roots of univariate modular equations revisited. In: Darnell, M.J. (ed.) Cryptography and Coding 1997. LNCS, vol. 1355, pp. 131–142. Springer, Heidelberg (1997)
14. Howgrave-Graham, N., Seifert, J.-P.: Extending wiener's attack in the presence of many decrypting exponents. In: Baumgart, R. (ed.) CQRE 1999. LNCS, vol. 1740, pp. 153–166. Springer, Heidelberg (1999)
15. Joye, M., Lepoint, T.: Partial key exposure on RSA with private exponents larger than N. In: Ryan, M.D., Smyth, B., Wang, G. (eds.) ISPEC 2012. LNCS, vol. 7232, pp. 369–380. Springer, Heidelberg (2012)
16. Lenstra, A.K., Lenstra Jr., H.W., Lovász, L.: Factoring polynomials with rational coefficients. Math. Ann. 261, 515–534 (1982)
17. May, A.: Computing the RSA secret key is deterministic polynomial time equivalent to factoring. In: Franklin, M. (ed.) CRYPTO 2004. LNCS, vol. 3152, pp. 213–219. Springer, Heidelberg (2004)
18. May, A.: Using LLL-reduction for solving RSA and factorization problems: A survey. In: [21] (2010). http://www.cits.rub.de/permonen/may.html

19. Nguyên, P.Q., Stern, J.: The two faces of lattices in cryptology. In: Silverman, J.H. (ed.) CaLC 2001. LNCS, vol. 2146, pp. 146–180. Springer, Heidelberg (2001)
20. Nguyen, P.Q., Vallée, B. (eds.): The LLL Algorithm: Survey and Applications. Information Security and Cryptography. Springer, Heidelberg (2010)
21. Peng, L., Hu, L., Lu, Y., Sarkar, S., Xu, J., Huang, Z.: Cryptanalysis of Variants of RSA with Multiple Small Secret Exponents. In: Biryukov, A., Goyal, V. (eds.) INDOCRYPT 2015. LNCS, vol. 9462, pp. 105–123. Springer, Heidelberg (2015)
22. Sarkar, S., Sen Gupta, S., Maitra, S.: Partial key exposure attack on RSA – improvements for limited lattice dimensions. In: Gong, G., Gupta, K.C. (eds.) INDOCRYPT 2010. LNCS, vol. 6498, pp. 2–16. Springer, Heidelberg (2010)
23. Sarkar, S., Maitra, S.: Cryptanalysis of RSA with two decryption exponents. Inf. Process. Lett. **110**, 178–181 (2010)
24. Sarkar, S., Maitra, S.: Cryptanalysis of RSA with more than one decryption exponents. Inf. Process. Lett. **110**, 336–340 (2010)
25. Takayasu, A., Kunihiro, N.: Better lattice constructions for solving multivariate linear equations modulo unknown divisors. In: Boyd, C., Simpson, L. (eds.) ACISP. LNCS, vol. 7959, pp. 118–135. Springer, Heidelberg (2013)
26. Takayasu, A., Kunihiro, N.: Cryptanalysis of RSA with multiple small secret exponents. In: Susilo, W., Mu, Y. (eds.) ACISP 2014. LNCS, vol. 8544, pp. 176–191. Springer, Heidelberg (2014)
27. Takayasu, A., Kunihiro, N.: Partial key exposure attacks on RSA: achieving the boneh-durfee bound. In: Joux, A., Youssef, A. (eds.) SAC 2014. LNCS, vol. 8781, pp. 345–362. Springer, Heidelberg (2014)
28. Wiener, M.J.: Cryptanalysis of short RSA secret exponents. IEEE Trans. Inf. Theory **36**(3), 553–558 (1990)

A New Attack on Three Variants of the RSA Cryptosystem

Martin Bunder[1], Abderrahmane Nitaj[2], Willy Susilo[3], and Joseph Tonien[3(✉)]

[1] School of Mathematics and Applied Statistics, University of Wollongong,
Wollongong, Australia
mbunder@uow.edu.au
[2] Département de Mathématiques, Université de Caen, Caen, France
abderrahmane.nitaj@unicaen.fr
[3] School of Computing and Information Technology,
Centre for Computer and Information Security Research, University of Wollongong,
Wollongong, Australia
{wsusilo,joseph_tonien}@uow.edu.au

Abstract. In 1995, Kuwakado, Koyama and Tsuruoka presented a new RSA-type scheme based on singular cubic curves $y^2 \equiv x^3 + bx^2$ (mod N) where $N = pq$ is an RSA modulus. Then, in 2002, Elkamchouchi, Elshenawy and Shaban introduced an extension of the RSA scheme to the field of Gaussian integers using a modulus $N = PQ$ where P and Q are Gaussian primes such that $p = |P|$ and $q = |Q|$ are ordinary primes. Later, in 2007, Castagnos proposed a scheme over quadratic field quotients with an RSA modulus $N = pq$. In the three schemes, the public exponent e is an integer satisfying the key equation $ed - k\left(p^2 - 1\right)\left(q^2 - 1\right) = 1$. In this paper, we apply the continued fraction method to launch an attack on the three schemes when the private exponent d is sufficiently small. Our attack can be considered as an extension of the famous Wiener attack on the RSA.

Keywords: RSA · Elliptic curves · Continued fractions

1 Introduction

The public key cryptosystem RSA was introduced by Rivest, Shamir and Adleman [10] in 1978. It is the most popular and widely used public-key cryptosystem. The RSA operations system are based on modular arithmetic. Let p and q be two large primes. The product $N = pq$ is called the RSA modulus and the product $\phi(N) = (p-1)(q-1)$ is the Euler totient function. In RSA, the public exponent e and the private exponent d are integers satisfying $ed \equiv 1$ (mod $\phi(N)$). A message m is encrypted as $c \equiv m^e$ (mod N) and decrypted using $m \equiv c^d$ (mod N).

Since its introduction, the RSA cryptosystem has been generalized in various ways, including extensions to singular elliptic curves and Gaussian integers.

© Springer International Publishing Switzerland 2016
J.K. Liu and R. Steinfeld (Eds.): ACISP 2016, Part II, LNCS 9723, pp. 258–268, 2016.
DOI: 10.1007/978-3-319-40367-0_16

In 1995, Kuwakado, Koyama and Tsuruoka [8] presented a new RSA-type scheme based on singular cubic curves with equation $y^2 \equiv x^3 + bx^2 \pmod{N}$ where $N = pq$ is an RSA modulus and $b \in \mathbb{Z}/N\mathbb{Z}$. The public exponent is an integer e such that $\gcd\left(e, (p^2-1)(q^2-1)\right) = 1$ and the decryption exponent is the integer $d \equiv e^{-1} \pmod{(p^2-1)(q^2-1)}$. From this, we deduce that e and d satisfy a key equation of the form $ed - k(p^2-1)(q^2-1) = 1$ where k is a positive integer.

In 2002, Elkamchouchi, Elshenawy and Shaban [5] introduced an extension of RSA to the ring of Gaussian integers. A Gaussian integer is a complex number of the form $a + ib$ where both a and b are integers and $i^2 = -1$. The set of all Gaussian integers is denoted $\mathbb{Z}[i]$. A Gaussian prime number is a Gaussian integer that cannot be represented as a product of non-unit Gaussian integers. The only unit Gaussian integers are ± 1, $\pm i$. Let $P = a + ib$ and $Q = a' + ib'$ be two Gaussian primes. Consider the Gaussian integer $N = PQ$ and the Euler totient function $\phi(N) = (|P| - 1)(|Q| - 1) = (a^2 + b^2 - 1)(a'^2 + b'^2 - 1)$. Let e be an integer such that $d \equiv e^{-1} \pmod{\phi(N)}$ exists. Then, in the RSA scheme over the domain of Gaussian integers, a message $m \in \mathbb{Z}[i]$ is encrypted using $c \equiv m^e$ $\pmod{N}$ and decrypted using $m \equiv c^d \pmod{N}$. We note that, in this RSA variant, the key equation is $ed - k(|P| - 1)(|Q| - 1) = 1$ for $N = PQ \in \mathbb{Z}[i]$. In the situation that $N = pq$ is an ordinary RSA modulus, the key equation becomes $ed - k(p^2-1)(q^2-1) = 1$, which is the same than in the Kuwakado-Koyama-Tsuruoka elliptic curve variant of RSA.

In 2007, Castagnos [3] proposed a probabilistic scheme based on an RSA modulus $N = pq$ and using arithmetical operations in quadratic field quotients. Let e be a integer such that $\gcd\left(e, (p^2-1)(q^2-1)\right) = 1$. For any integer r, let $V_e(r)$ be the eth term of the Lucas sequence defined by $V_0(r) = 2$, $V_1(r) = r$ and $V_{k+2} = rV_{k+1}(r) - V_k(r)$ for $k \geq 0$. In this scheme, a message $m \in \mathbb{Z}/N\mathbb{Z}$ is encrypted using $c \equiv (1 + mN)V_e(r) \pmod{N^2}$ where r is a random integer with $2 \leq r \leq N - 2$. Then some arithmetical properties, one can decrypt c to get the original message m. Similarly to the Kuwakado-Koyama-Tsuruoka elliptic curve variant of RSA and RSA with Gaussian integers, Castagnos scheme leads to the key equation $ed - k(p^2-1)(q^2-1) = 1$.

The security of the RSA cryptosystem and its variants are based on the difficulty of factoring large integers of the shape $N = pq$. Nevertheless, in some cases, the modulus N can be factored by algebraic methods that are not based on factoring algorithms. For example, in 1990, Wiener [11] showed how to break the RSA when the decryption exponent d satisfies $d < \frac{1}{3}N^{0.25}$. Wiener's method is based on solving the key equation $ed - k(p-1)(q-1) = 1$ by applying the continued fraction algorithm to the public rational fraction $\frac{e}{N}$. When d is small enough, $\frac{k}{d}$ is one of the convergents of the continued fraction expansion of $\frac{e}{N}$. Later, Boneh and Durfee [1] applied lattice reduction and Coppersmith's technique [4] and extended the bound to $d < N^{0.292}$. Recently, using the convergents of the continued fraction expansion of $\frac{e}{N'}$ where N' is a number depending on N, Bunder and Tonien [2] could break the RSA if $d^2 e < 8N^{1.5}$.

The complexity of the encryption and decryption algorithms are based on the size of the encryption key e and the size of decryption key d, respectively. In a cryptosystem with a limited resource such as a credit card, it is desirable to have a smaller value of d. In some scenario, for convenience, e is set to a small constant, such as $e = 3$.

In this paper, we consider one of the following scenarios where $N = pq$ is the product of two large primes and the public exponent e satisfies an equation $ed - k\left(p^2 - 1\right)\left(q^2 - 1\right) = 1$ with a suitably small secret exponent d:

- an instance of the Kuwakado-Koyama-Tsuruoka cryptosystem [8],
- an instance of the RSA over Gaussian integers [5],
- an instance of Castagnos scheme [3].

Our method is inspired by Bunder and Tonien's technique [2]. We show that when $d^2 e < 2N^3 - 18N^2$ then one can find p and q and then factor the modulus N. Our method is based on the continued fraction algorithm as in Bunder and Tonien's attack. Under the condition $d < \sqrt{\frac{2N^3 - 18N^2}{e}}$, we show that one can find $\frac{k}{d}$ among the convergents of the continued fraction expansion of the public rational number $\frac{e}{N^2 - \frac{9}{4}N + 1}$.

The paper is organized as follows. In Sect. 2, we present the Kuwakado-Koyama-Tsuruoka RSA-type scheme, the RSA scheme over Gaussian integers and the Castagnos scheme. In Sect. 3, we review some facts and lemmas used in our attack. In Sect. 4, we present our new attack with a numerical example. We conclude the paper in Sect. 5.

2 Preliminaries

In this section, we present the three variants of the RSA cryptosystem for which our attack works, namely the Kuwakado-Koyama-Tsuruoka RSA-type scheme, the RSA scheme over Gaussian integers and the Castagnos scheme.

2.1 The Kuwakado-Koyama-Tsuruoka RSA-type Scheme

The Kuwakado-Koyama-Tsuruoka RSA-type scheme is based on the use of an RSA modulus $N = pq$ as the modulus of a singular elliptic curve. Let $\mathbb{Z}_N = \mathbb{Z}/N\mathbb{Z}$ be the ring of integers modulo N and $\mathbb{F}_p$ be the finite field. Let a and b be integers with $\gcd(ab, N) = 1$ and $\gcd(4a^3 + 27b^2, N) = 1$. A singular elliptic curve $E_N(a, b)$ over the ring $\mathbb{Z}_N$ is the concatenation of a point $\mathcal{O}_N$, called the point at infinity, and the set of points $(x, y) \in \mathbb{Z}_N^2$ satisfying the Weierstrass equation

$$y^2 + axy \equiv x^3 + bx^2 \pmod{N}.$$

If we consider this form modulo p, we get an elliptic curve $E_p(a, b)$ over $\mathbb{F}_p$

$$E_p(a, b) : y^2 + axy \equiv x^3 + bx^2 \pmod{p},$$

with the point at infinity $\mathcal{O}_p$. It is well known that the chord-and-tangent method defines an addition law on singular elliptic curves, as for all elliptic curves on $\mathbb{F}_p$. The addition law can be summarized as follows.

- For any point $P \in E_p(a, b)$, $P + \mathcal{O}_p = \mathcal{O}_p + P = P$.
- If $P = (x, y) \in E_p(a, b)$, then $-P = (x, -ax - y)$.
- If $P = (x, y)$, then $2P = P_3 = (x_3, y_3)$ with

$$x_3 = \left(\frac{3x^2 + 2bx - ay}{2ay + ax} \right)^2 + a \left(\frac{3x^2 + 2bx - ay}{2ay + ax} \right) - b - 2x,$$

$$y_3 = - \left(\frac{3x^2 + 2bx - ay}{2ay + ax} + a \right) x_3 - \frac{-x^3}{2ay + ax}.$$

- If $P_1 = (x_1, y_1)$ and $P_2 = (x_2, y_2)$ with $P_1 \neq \pm P_2$, then $P_1 + P_2 = P_3 = (x_3, y_3)$ with

$$x_3 = \left(\frac{y_2 - y_1}{x_2 - x_1} \right)^2 + a \left(\frac{y_2 - y_1}{x_2 - x_1} \right) - b - x_1 - x_2,$$

$$y_3 = - \left(\frac{y_2 - y_1}{x_2 - x_1} + a \right) x_3 - \frac{y_1 x_2 - y_2 x_1}{x_2 - x_1}.$$

The addition law can be extended to the elliptic curve $E_N(a, b)$ in the same way as the addition in $E_p(a, b)$ by replacing computations modulo p by computations modulo N. In $E_N(a, b)$, a specific problem can occur. Sometimes, the inverse modulo N does not exist. In this case, this could lead to finding a prime factor of N, which is unlikely to happen when p and q are large. Note that this is one of the principles of Elliptic Curve Method of factorization [9].

In 1995, Kuwakado, Koyama and Tsuruoka [8] proposed a system based on singular elliptic curves modulo an RSA modulus, which can be summarized as follows.

1. **Key Generation:**
   - Choose two distinct prime numbers p and q of similar bit-length.
   - Compute $N = pq$.
   - Choose e such that $\gcd \left(e, (p^2 - 1)(q^2 - 1) \right) = 1$.
   - Compute $d = e^{-1} \pmod{(p^2 - 1)(q^2 - 1)}$.
   - Keep p, q, d secret and publish N, e.
2. **Encryption:**
   - Transform the message as $m = (m_x, m_y) \in \mathbb{Z}_N \times \mathbb{Z}_N$.
   - Compute $b = \frac{m_y^2 - m_x^3}{m_x^2} \pmod{N}$.
   - Compute the ciphertext point $(c_x, c_y) = e(m_x, m_y)$ on the elliptic curve $y^2 = x^3 + bx^2 \pmod{N}$.
3. **Decryption:**
   - Compute $b = \frac{c_y^2 - c_x^3}{c_x^2} \pmod{N}$.
   - Compute the plaintext point $(m_x, m_y) = d(c_x, c_y)$ on the elliptic curve $y^2 = x^3 + bx^2 \pmod{N}$.

Observe the modular inverse $d = e^{-1}$ (mod $(p^2 - 1)(q^2 - 1)$) can be transformed as a key equation

$$ed - k(p^2 - 1)(q^2 - 1) = 1,$$

which will be the starting equation of our new attack.

2.2 RSA Over the Domain of Gaussian Integers

We now focus on how to extend the RSA cryptosystem to the ring of Gaussian integers. We begin by reviewing the main properties of Gaussian integers.

A Gaussian integer is a complex number of the form $a + bi$ where $a, b \in \mathbb{Z}$ and $i^2 = -1$. The set of all Gaussian integers is the ring $\mathbb{Z}[i]$. Let α and $\beta \neq 0$ be two Gaussian integers. We say that β divides α if there exists a Gaussian integer γ such that $\alpha = \beta\gamma$. The norm of a Gaussian integer $a + bi$ is $|a + bi| = a^2 + b^2$. A Gaussian prime is a Gaussian integer which is divisible only by a unit. The units in $\mathbb{Z}[i]$ are ± 1 and $\pm i$ and have norm 1. As a consequence, if $a^2 + b^2$ is a prime number in $\mathbb{Z}$, then $a + ib$ is a Gaussian prime. Conversely, if $p \in Z$ is an ordinary prime number, then Gaussian integers p and pi are Gaussian primes if and only if $p \equiv 3 \pmod 4$. The existence of prime factorization in $\mathbb{Z}[i]$ allows us to consider Gaussian integers of the form $N = PQ$ where P and Q are Gaussian primes with large norm. Similarly, the existence of Euclidean division and Euclidean algorithm in $\mathbb{Z}[i]$ allow us to consider arithmetic operations modulo N. On the other hand, if P is a Gaussian prime, then $\alpha^{|P|-1} \equiv 1 \pmod P$ whenever $\alpha \not\equiv 0 \pmod P$. Similarly, if $N = PQ$ is the product of two Gaussian primes, then $\alpha^{(|P|-1)(|Q|-1)} \equiv 1 \pmod N$ whenever $\alpha \not\equiv 0 \pmod N$. In particular, if $N = pq \in \mathbb{Z}$ is the product of two ordinary primes, then $\alpha^{(p^2-1)(q^2-1)} \equiv 1 \pmod N$ whenever $\alpha \not\equiv 0 \pmod N$.

Using the arithmetical operations on the ring $\mathbb{Z}[i]$, Elkamchouchi, Elshenawy and Shaban [5] proposed an extension of the RSA cryptosystem to Gaussian integers. The scheme can be summarized as follows.

1. **Key Generation:**
   - Choose two distinct Gaussian primes P and Q of similar norm.
   - Compute $N = PQ$.
   - Choose e such that $\gcd(e, (|P| - 1)(|Q| - 1)) = 1$.
   - Determine $d = e^{-1} \pmod{(|P| - 1)(|Q| - 1)}$.
   - Keep P, Q, d secret, publish N, e.
2. **Encryption:**
   - Transform the message as a Gaussian integer $M \in \mathbb{Z}[i]$.
   - Compute $C \equiv M^e \pmod N$.
3. **Decryption:**
   - Compute $M \equiv C^d \pmod N$.

When $N = pq \in \mathbb{Z}$ where p and q are ordinary prime numbers of the form $4m+3$, the modular inverse of e becomes $d = e^{-1} \pmod{(p^2 - 1)(q^2 - 1)}$ and can be rewritten as

$$ed - k(p^2 - 1)(q^2 - 1) = 1.$$

This is the same key equation that comes up in the Kuwakado-Koyama-Tsuruoka RSA-type scheme.

2.3 Castagnos Scheme

Castagnos scheme [3] was proposed in 2007 and uses an RSA modulus $N = pq$ and a public exponent e such that $\gcd\left(e, (p^2 - 1)(q^2 - 1)\right) = 1$. The encryption and the decryption algorithms make use of the Lucas series. Let r be an integer. Define $V_0(r) = 2$ and $V_1(r) = r$. For $k \geq 0$, the $k + 2$th term of the Lucas sequence is defined by $V_{k+2} = rV_{k+1}(r) - V_k(r)$. The Lucas series can be computed efficiently by the square and multiply algorithm. The Castagnos scheme can be summarized as follows, where $\left(\frac{x}{p}\right)$ is the Jacobi symbol.

1. **Key Generation:**
   - Choose two distinct prime numbers p and q of similar bit-length.
   - Compute $N = pq$.
   - Choose e such that $\gcd\left(e, (p^2 - 1)(q^2 - 1)\right) = 1$.
   - Keep p, q secret and publish N, e.
2. **Encryption:**
   - Transform the message as an integer $m \in \mathbb{Z}/N\mathbb{Z}$.
   - Choose a random integer $r \in [2, n - 2]$.
   - Compute the ciphertext $c \equiv (1 + mN)V_e(r) \pmod{N^2}$.
3. **Decryption:**
   - Compute $i_p = \left(\frac{c^2 - 4}{p}\right)$ and $d(p, i_p) \equiv e^{-1} \pmod{p - i_p}$.
   - Compute $i_q = \left(\frac{c^2 - 4}{q}\right)$ and $d(q, i_q) \equiv e^{-1} \pmod{q - i_q}$.
   - Compute $r_p \equiv V_{d(p,i_p)} \pmod p$ and $r_q \equiv V_{d(q,i_q)} \pmod q$.
   - Compute $p' \equiv p^{-1} \pmod q$ and $r = r_p + p(r_p - r_q)p' \pmod N$.
   - Compute $t_p \equiv \frac{c}{V_e(r)} \pmod{p^2}$ and $m_p \equiv \frac{t_p - 1}{p} \cdot q^{-1} \pmod p$.
   - Compute $t_q \equiv \frac{c}{V_e(r)} \pmod{q^2}$ and $m_q \equiv \frac{t_q - 1}{q} \cdot p^{-1} \pmod q$.
   - Compute the plaintext $m \equiv m_p + p(m_q - m_p)p' \pmod N$.

Despite the inverse $d \equiv e^{-1} \pmod{(p^2 - 1)(q^2 - 1)}$ is not being used directly in the scheme, we use the key equation $ed - k(p^2 - 1)(q^2 - 1) = 1$ to launch an attack on Castagnos scheme when d is suitably small.

3 Useful Lemmas

In this section, we review the main properties of the continued fractions and state a useful lemma that will be used in the attack.

A **continued fraction** is an expression of the form

$$a_0 + \cfrac{1}{a_1 + \cfrac{1}{a_2 + \cfrac{1}{\ddots}}}$$

The continued fraction expansion of a number is formed by subtracting away the integer part of it and inverting the remainder and then repeating this process again and again. The coefficients a_i of the continued fraction of a number x are constructed as follows:

$$x_0 = x, \ a_n = [x_n], \ x_{n+1} = \cfrac{1}{x_n - a_n}$$

We use the following notation to denote the continued fraction

$$x = [a_0, a_1, \ldots, a_n] = a_0 + \cfrac{1}{a_1 + \cfrac{1}{\ddots + \cfrac{1}{a_n}}}$$

If $k \leq n$, the continued fraction $[a_0, a_1, \ldots, a_k]$ is called the kth *convergent* of x. The following theorem gives us the *fundamental recursive formulas* to calculate the convergents.

Theorem 1 [6]. *The kth convergent can be determined as*

$$[a_0, \ldots, a_k] = \frac{p_k}{q_k}$$

where the sequences $\{p_n\}$ and $\{q_n\}$ are specified as follows:

$$p_{-2} = 0, \quad p_{-1} = 1, \quad p_n = a_n p_{n-1} + p_{n-2}, \quad \forall n \geq 0,$$
$$q_{-2} = 1, \quad q_{-1} = 0, \quad q_n = a_n q_{n-1} + q_{n-2}, \quad \forall n \geq 0.$$

Theorem 2 [6]. *Let p, q be positive integers such that*

$$0 < \left| x - \frac{p}{q} \right| < \frac{1}{2q^2}$$

then $\frac{p}{q}$ is a convergent of the continued fraction of x.

Now, we present a useful result that will be used throughout the paper.

Lemma 1. *Let $N = pq$ be an RSA modulus with $q < p < 2q$. Let $\phi_1 = N^2 + 1 - \frac{5}{2}N$ and $\phi_2 = N^2 + 1 - 2N$. Then*

$$\phi_1 < (p^2 - 1)(q^2 - 1) < \phi_2.$$

Proof. Suppose that $q < p < 2q$. Then $1 < \frac{p}{q} < 2$, so since the function $f(x) = x + \frac{1}{x}$ is increasing on $[1, +\infty)$, we get $f(1) < f\left(\frac{p}{q}\right) < f(2)$, that is

$$2 < \frac{p}{q} + \frac{q}{p} < \frac{5}{2}.$$

Multiplying by N, we get

$$2N < p^2 + q^2 < \frac{5}{2}N.$$

Since $(p^2 - 1)(q^2 - 1) = N^2 + 1 - (p^2 + q^2)$, we get

$$N^2 + 1 - \frac{5}{2}N < (p^2 - 1)(q^2 - 1) < N^2 + 1 - 2N,$$

that is $\phi_1 < (p^2 - 1)(q^2 - 1) < \phi_2$. This terminates the proof.

4 A New Attack on RSA Variants Based on Continued Fractions

In this section, we propose a new attack on the Kuwakado-Koyama-Tsuruoka cryptosystem as well as RSA over the Gaussian integer domain and the Castagnos scheme in the situation that the key equation $ed - k(p^2 - 1)(q^2 - 1) = 1$ is satisfied with a suitably small secret exponent d.

Theorem 3. *Let (N, e) be a public key in the Kuwakado-Koyama-Tsuruoka cryptosystem or in the RSA cryptosystem with Gaussian integers or in the Castagnos scheme with $N = pq$ and $q < p < 2q$. If $e < (p^2 - 1)(q^2 - 1)$ satisfies an equation $ed - k(p^2 - 1)(q^2 - 1) = 1$ with*

$$d < \sqrt{\frac{2N^3 - 18N^2}{e}},$$

then one can factor N in polynomial time.

Proof. Let $\phi_1 = N^2 + 1 - \frac{5}{2}N$ and $\phi_2 = N^2 + 1 - 2N$. Then $N' = N^2 - \frac{9}{4}N + 1$ is the midpoint of the interval $[\phi_1, \phi_2]$. Since $(p^2 - 1)(q^2 - 1) \in [\phi_1, \phi_2]$, then

$$\left|(p^2 - 1)(q^2 - 1) - N'\right| < \frac{1}{2}(\phi_2 - \phi_1) = \frac{1}{4}N. \tag{1}$$

Using the equation $ed - k(p^2 - 1)(q^2 - 1) = 1$, we get

$$\left|\frac{e}{N'} - \frac{k}{d}\right| \leq e\left|\frac{1}{N'} - \frac{1}{(p^2 - 1)(q^2 - 1)}\right| + \left|\frac{e}{(p^2 - 1)(q^2 - 1)} - \frac{k}{d}\right|$$

$$= e\frac{\left|(p^2 - 1)(q^2 - 1) - N'\right|}{N'(p^2 - 1)(q^2 - 1)} + \frac{1}{(p^2 - 1)(q^2 - 1)d}$$

Then, using $d = \frac{k(p^2-1)(q^2-1)+1}{e}$ and (1), we get

$$\left|\frac{e}{N'} - \frac{k}{d}\right| < \frac{eN}{4N'(p^2-1)(q^2-1)} + \frac{e}{(p^2-1)(q^2-1)(k(p^2-1)(q^2-1)+1)}.$$

Now, using Lemma 1, we get

$$\left|\frac{e}{N'} - \frac{k}{d}\right| < \frac{eN}{4\phi_1^2} + \frac{e}{\phi_1^2} < \frac{e(N+4)}{4(\phi_1-1)^2} = \frac{e(N+4)}{4\left(N^2 - \frac{5}{2}N\right)^2}. \tag{2}$$

A straightforward calculation shows that

$$\frac{N+4}{4\left(N^2 - \frac{5}{2}N\right)^2} < \frac{1}{4N^3 - 36N^2}.$$

Combining this with (2), we get

$$\left|\frac{e}{N'} - \frac{k}{d}\right| < \frac{e}{4N^3 - 36N^2}.$$

If $d < \sqrt{\frac{2N^3 - 18N^2}{e}}$, then $\left|\frac{e}{N'} - \frac{k}{d}\right| < \frac{1}{2d^2}$ and by Theorem 2, $\frac{k}{d}$ is a convergent of the continued fraction expansion of $\frac{e}{N'}$. Using k and d, we get

$$(p^2-1)(q^2-1) = \frac{ed-1}{k}.$$

Combining with $N = pq$, we get the values of p and q which leads to the factorization of N. Observe that every step in the proof can be done in polynomial time. This terminates the proof.

4.1   A Numerical Example

In connection with Theorem 3, we present an experimental result. We consider the RSA modulus N and the public exponent e as follows.

$$N = 261793922055331530274546209l,$$

$$e = 56560393323059524365594244618317839555728723511570041 85.$$

The first partial quotients of $\frac{e}{N^2 - \frac{9}{4}N + 1}$ are

$$0, 1, 4, 1, 2, 1, 1, 1, 1, 3, 1, 1, 1, 46, 3, 5, 1, 1, 2, 26, 2, 2, 39, 1, 3, 2, 3, 1, 23104, 1, 9,$$
$$1, 1, 2, 1, 3, 2, 2, \dots.$$

We found $\frac{k}{d}$ at the 28th convergent

$$\frac{k}{d} = \frac{981582747476}{1189415557289}$$

and obtain

$$\left(p^2 - 1\right)\left(q^2 - 1\right) = \frac{ed - 1}{k}$$

$$= 6853605762511300064473195588212095096351361928469816064.$$

Combining with the equation $N = pq$, we get

$$p = 68410308889243,$$

$$q = 38268197630737.$$

which completes the factorization of N. In this example, we can check that the condition $d < \sqrt{\frac{2N^3 - 18N^2}{e}}$ is satisfied as required in Theorem 3.

5   Conclusion

We have proposed an attack on three variants of the RSA cryptosystem, namely the Kuwakado-Koyama-Tsuruoka extension for singular elliptic curves, Elkamchouchi et al.'s extension of RSA to the Gaussian integer ring and Castagnos scheme. For the three extensions, we showed that the RSA modulus $N = pq$ can be factored in polynomial time if the public exponent e is related to a suitably small secret exponent d. The attack is based on the theory of continued fractions and can be seen as an extension of Wiener's [11] and Bunder-Tonien's [2] attacks on the RSA.

References

1. Boneh, D., Durfee, G.: Cryptanalysis of RSA with private key d less than $N^{0.292}$. In: Stern, J. (ed.) EUROCRYPT 1999. LNCS, vol. 1592, pp. 1–11. Springer, Heidelberg (1999)
2. Bunder, M., Tonien, J.: A new improved attack on RSA. In: Proceedings of the 5th International Cryptology and Information Security Conference (2016)
3. Castagnos, G.: An efficient probabilistic public-key cryptosystem over quadratic field quotients. Finite Fields Appl. 13, 563–576 (2007)
4. Coppersmith, D.: Small solutions to polynomial equations, and low exponent RSA vulnerabilities. J. Cryptol. 10, 233–260 (1997)
5. Elkamchouchi, H., Elshenawy, K., Shaban, H.: Extended RSA cryptosystem and digital signature schemes in the domain of Gaussian integers. In: Proceedings of the 8th International Conference on Communication Systems, pp. 91–95 (2002)
6. Hardy, G.H., Wright, E.M.: An Introduction to the Theory of Numbers. Oxford University Press, London (1965)

7. Koyama, K., Maurer, U.M., Okamoto, T., Vanstone, S.A.: New public-key schemes based on elliptic curves over the ring Z_n. In: Feigenbaum, J. (ed.) CRYPTO 1991. LNCS, vol. 576, pp. 252–266. Springer, Heidelberg (1992)
8. Kuwakado, H., Koyama, K., Tsuruoka, Y.: A new RSA-type scheme based on singular cubic curves $y^2 = x^3 + bx^2$ (mod n). IEICE Trans. Fundam. **E78–A**, 27–33 (1995)
9. Lenstra, H.: Factoring integers with elliptic curves. Ann. Math. **126**, 649–673 (1987)
10. Rivest, R., Shamir, A., Adleman, L.: A Method for obtaining digital signatures and public-key cryptosystems. Commun. ACM **21**, 120–126 (1978)
11. Wiener, M.: Cryptanalysis of short RSA secret exponents. IEEE Trans. Inf. Theory **36**, 553–558 (1990)

Generalized Hardness Assumption
for Self-bilinear Map with Auxiliary Information

Takashi Yamakawa[1,2]([✉]), Goichiro Hanaoka[2], and Noboru Kunihiro[1]

[1] The University of Tokyo, Tokyo, Japan
yamakawa@it.k.u-tokyo.ac.jp, kunihiro@k.u-tokyo.ac.jp
[2] National Institute of Advanced Industrial Science and Technology (AIST),
Tokyo, Japan
hanaoka-goichiro@aist.go.jp

Abstract. A self-bilinear map (SBM) is a bilinear map where source and target groups are identical. An SBM naturally yields a multilinear map, which has numerous applications in cryptography. In spite of its usefulness, there is known a strong negative result on the existence of an ideal SBM. On the other hand, Yamakawa et al. (CRYPTO'14) introduced the notion of a self-bilinear map with auxiliary information (AI-SBM), which is a weaker variant of SBM and constructed it based on the factoring assumption and an indistinguishability obfuscation ($i\mathcal{O}$). In their work, they proved that their AI-SBM satisfies the Auxiliary Information Multilinear Computational Diffie-Hellman (AI-MCDH) assumption, which is a natural analogue of the Multilinear Computational Diffie-Hellman (MCDH) assumption w.r.t. multilinear maps. Then they show that they can replace multilinear maps with AI-SBMs in some multilinear-map-based primitives that is proven secure under the MCDH assumption.

In this work, we further investigate what hardness assumptions hold w.r.t. their AI-SBM. Specifically, we introduce a new hardness assumption called the Auxiliary Information Generalized Multilinear Diffie-Hellman (AI-GMDH) assumption. The AI-GMDH is parameterized by some parameters and thus can be seen as a family of hardness assumptions. We give a sufficient condition of parameters for which the AI-GMDH assumption holds under the same assumption as in the previous work. Based on this result, we can easily prove the AI-SBM satisfies certain hardness assumptions including not only the AI-GMDH assumption but also more complicated assumptions. This enable us to convert a multilinear-map-based primitive that is proven secure under a complicated hardness assumption to AI-SBP-based (and thus the factoring and $i\mathcal{O}$-based) one. As an example, we convert Catalano et al.'s multilinear-map-based homomorphic signatures (CRYPTO'14) to AI-SBP-based ones.

1 Introduction

Bilinear maps are fundamental tools in cryptography and they enable us to construct various cryptographic primitives including (but not limited to)

The first author is supported by a JSPS Fellowship for Young Scientists.

© Springer International Publishing Switzerland 2016
J.K. Liu and R. Steinfeld (Eds.): ACISP 2016, Part II, LNCS 9723, pp. 269–284, 2016.
DOI: 10.1007/978-3-319-40367-0_17

identity-based encryption [3,4], attribute-based encryption [27], and non-interactive zero-knowledge proof system [20,21]. In these works, bilinear maps on elliptic curves are considered where source and target groups are different. On the other hand, Cheon et al. [12] considered the notion of self-bilinear map (SBM) where source and target groups are identical and observed that such a map implies multilinear map [7], which is a very powerful tool that enables us to construct non-interactive multiparty key exchange [7], broadcast encryption [7,8], attribute-based encryption [6,17], obfuscation [16] etc. Therefore if we can construct an SBM, then we immediately obtain a multilinear map and thus we may obtain various multilinear-map based cryptographic primitives as stated above. However, Cheon et al. [12] also proved a strong negative result on the existence of an efficiently computable SBM, which implies constructing ideal SBMs is implausible.

On the other hand, Yamakawa et al. [29] weakened the definition of SBM to define a self-bilinear map with auxiliary information (AI-SBM), where certain "auxiliary information" is needed to efficiently compute the map. They constructed it by combining techniques of factoring-based cryptography and indistinguishability obfuscation ($i\mathcal{O}$). Though AI-SBMs is a weaker notion than ideal SBMs, it still yields a useful version of multilinear maps, which can replace multilinear maps in some multilinear-map-based cryptographic primitives. Specifically, the authors of [29] proved that their AI-SBM satisfies the auxiliary information multilinear computational Diffie-Hellman (AI-MCDH) assumption[1], which is a natural analogue of the multilinear computational Diffie-Hellman (MCDH) assumption [15] originally defined for multilinear maps. Thus they showed that they can replace multilinear maps with AI-SBMs in the MCDH-based schemes such as multiparty key exchange [7], broadcast encryption [7] and attribute based encryption [17].

On the other hand, there exist some other multilinear-map-based primitives whose security rely on different, stronger and more complicated assumptions than the MCDH assumption. For example, Boneh et al. [6] constructed attribute based encryption for circuit with compact ciphertext based on the Multilinear Diffie-Hellman Exponent (MDHE) assumption, Boneh et al. [8] constructed a broadcast encryption with compact parameters based on the Hybrid Diffie-Hellman Exponent (HDHE) assumption, and Catalano et al. [9] constructed a homomorphic signature scheme based on the Augmented Power Multilinear Diffie-Hellman (APMDH) assumption, all of which are rather complicated and parametrized (e.g., q-type) assumptions for multilinear maps. Our motivation is to investigate whether we can replace multilinear maps with AI-SBMs in these schemes. To do so, we investigate what types of assumptions hold w.r.t. Yamakawa et al.'s AI-SBMs.

---

[1] Actually in [29], this assumption is called Multilinear Computational Diffie-Hellman with Auxiliary Information (MCDHAI) assumption. We rename the assumption for the consistency with other assumptions in this paper.

1.1   Our Result

We define a generalized assumption that we call Auxiliary Information Generalized Multilinear Diffie-Hellman (AI-GMDH) assumption for AI-SBMs. Then we give a sufficient condition that the AI-GMDH assumption holds w.r.t. Yamakawa et al.'s AI-SBM. Since the condition is very easy to check, this can be seen as a useful tool that enables us to easily prove that certain hardness assumptions hold w.r.t. their AI-SBM. Specifically, we show that the AI-MCDH assumption holds w.r.t. their AI-SBM as an immediate corollary of our result. Thus our result generalizes the result in [29]. Moreover, we show that the Auxiliary Information Augmented Power Multilinear Diffie-Hellman (AI-APMDH) assumption, which is a natural analogue of the APMDH assumption also holds. Thus we can construct homomorphic signatures in the similar way as in [9] by replacing multilinear maps with AI-SBMs.

Main theorem. First we review the definition of AI-SBMs. For AI-SBMs on a group G, a set T_X of auxiliary information is defined for each element of $X \in G$. We require that a self-bilinear map $e(X, Y)$ can be computed efficiently if auxiliary information $\tau_X \in T_X$ or $\tau_Y \in T_Y$ is given. The AI-GMDH assumption is parametrized by polynomials $f_1, \ldots, f_m$ and f^* on variables $x_1, \ldots, x_n$ and a natural number $\ell^* \geq 2$ and we denote it by $(\{f_j\}_{j \in [m]}, f^*, \ell^*)$-AI-GMDH assumption[2]. Intuitively, the $(\{f_j\}_{j \in [m]}, f^*, \ell^*)$-AI-GMDH assumption claims the following. For any PPT adversary $\mathcal{A}$ that is given g, $g^{f_j(x_1, \ldots, x_n)}$ for $j \in [m]$ and auxiliary information corresponding to these elements cannot compute $e_{\ell^*}(g, \ldots, g)^{f^*(x_1, \ldots, x_n)}$ with non-negligible probability, where e_{ℓ^*} denote the ℓ^*-multilinear map induced by the underlying AI-SBM e. In this paper, we only consider the case where $f_1, \ldots, f_m$ and f^* are monic monomials, i.e., written as $\prod_{i=1}^n x_i^{t_i}$ where t_i is a natural number for $i \in [n]$. For a monic monomial $f(x_1, \ldots, x_n) = \prod_{i=1}^n x_i^{t_i}$, we define $\bar{f}(x_1, \ldots, x_n) := \sum_{i=1}^n t_i x_i$. Then our main theorem can be stated as follows. (See Theorem 1 for the full statement of our theorem.)

Theorem 1 *(informal). If there exist integers $a_1, \ldots, a_n$ such that $\bar{f}_i(a_1, \ldots, a_n) \leq -1$ and $\ell^* + \bar{f}^*(a_1, \ldots, a_n) \geq -1$ hold, then the $(\{f_j\}_{j \in [m]}, f^*, \ell)$-AI-GMDH holds w.r.t. Yamakawa et al.'s AI-SBM if iO is secure and the factoring assumption holds.*

Though the condition in the above theorem may seem a bit strange, it is actually not difficult to check the condition holds in many cases. For example, we explain the case of the AI-MCDH assumption. The AI-MCDH assumption claims that any PPT adversary that is given g, g^{x_1}, $\ldots$, g^{x_n} and corresponding auxiliary information for these elements cannot compute $e_{n-1}(g, \ldots, g)^{\prod_{i=1}^n x_i}$ with non-negligible probability. It is easy to see that the AI-MCDH assumption is equivalent to the AI-GMDH assumption if we set $m := n$, $\ell^* := n - 1$,

---

[2] Actually, the AI-GMDH assumption is also parametrized by an additional natural number M. We omit it here for making the intuition simpler. For more details, see Definition 3 followed by Remark 2.

$f_i(x_1, \ldots, x_n) := x_i$ for $i \in [n]$ and $f^*(x_1, \ldots, x_n) := \prod_{i=1}^n x_i$. Then if we set $a_i := -1$ for all $i \in [n]$, we have $\bar{f}_i(a_1, \ldots a_n) = -1$ and $\ell^* + \bar{f}^*(a_1, \ldots, a_n) = (n-1) + n \cdot (-1) = -1$ and thus the condition is satisfied and the AI-MCDH assumption holds w.r.t. the AI-SBM if iO is secure and the factoring assumption holds. As shown above, our main theorem enables us to validate certain hardness assumptions w.r.t. the AI-SBM in an easy manner.

Interpretation of our result. In this work, we prove that a wide range of hardness assumptions w.r.t. AI-SBM including some complicated and parameterized assumptions can be reduced to simple and well-studied assumptions (the factoring assumption and the existence of iO). Formerly, the only way to validate counterparts of these assumptions for multilinear maps was relying on the generic multilinear map group model, which is an ideal model and rather problematic. Our technique can be used to convert a multilinear-map-based primitive based on such a complicated assumption to an AI-SBM-based (and thus factoring and iO-based) one. One may wonder if this is meaningful since candidate constructions of iO depend on multilinear maps. However, to construct a iO, what is required is a "symmetric version" of multilinear maps, where group elements are generated only privately rather than usual "public" multilinear maps. Thus it seems that breaking iO is rather more difficult than breaking the underlying multilinear map. Thus converting a multilinear-map-based primitive to iO-based one is still meaningful. Indeed, there are some existing work in the similar spirit [1, 26].

Applications. As an application of our result, we convert multilinear-map-based homomorphic signatures for polynomial-degree polynomials proposed by Catalano et al. [9] to AI-SBM-based one. The security of their scheme relies on the APMDH assumption, which is complicated and validated only in the generic multilinear group model. We prove that the counterpart of the APMDH assumption for the AI-SBM (which we call the AI-APMDH assumption) hold by using our main theorem. Then we can simply replace multilinear maps with AI-SBMs in the Catalano's construction. Since our purpose here is to demonstrate how we can replace multilinear maps with AI-SBMs in an easy-to-follow manner, we focus on the simplest definition of homomorphic signatures (e.g., selective security for single dataset). Note that we do not claim that we construct a homomorphic signature scheme with a useful property existing works never have. Indeed, there already exists a fully homomorphic signature scheme based on iO [28], which can handle any (bounded) polynomial-size circuit rather than polynomial-degree polynomials.

Though we find only one application of our technique in this paper, we believe that there will be further applications in the future.

1.2   Related Work

Indistinguihshability obfuscation. The concept of indistinguishability obfuscation (iO) is first proposed by Barak et al. [2] and the first candidate construction was proposed by Garg et al. [16]. Their construction of iO depends on multilinear maps, whose first candidate was proposed by Garg et al. [15] followed by some others [13, 14, 18]. Until now, many cryptanalyses are done against the above multilinear maps and some of them appear not to be secure [10, 11, 23]. Almost all of the above cryptanalysis relies on that "low level encodings of zero" are published, which is not needed for constructing $i\mathcal{O}$ and thus these attacks are not applicable to attacking $i\mathcal{O}$ based on these multilinear maps. Very recently, some works [24, 25] attacks the GGH multilinear map [15] without using low level encodings of zero. Thus $i\mathcal{O}$ based on the GGH multilinear map is no longer secure. However, their works are limited to the GGH multilinear map and it is not clear whether their attacks can be extended to attack other candidate multilinear maps. Therefore, for example, we can use $i\mathcal{O}$ based on the CLT multilinear map [14] as an instantiation of our scheme.

Multilinar map from $i\mathcal{O}$. There are some works that shows the relation between multilinear maps and $i\mathcal{O}$. Paneth and Sahai [26] constructed a polynomial jigsaw puzzle, which is a variant of a multilinear map, solely based on $i\mathcal{O}$. However, they does not provide any application of polynomial jigsaw puzzles and thus it is unclear how that is useful in constructions of cryptographic primitives. Albrecht et al. [1] constructed a multilinear map based on $i\mathcal{O}$, non-interactive zero-knowledge proof system, and additive homomorphic encryption. Since the assumptions they rely on is incomparable to ours, their result is incomparable to ours. Moreover, their multilinear map does not provide a graded encoding system [15] and thus some applications of multilinear maps such as attribute based encryption [17] and homomorphic signatures [9] cannot be instantiated.

Homomorphic signature. Boneh and Freeman [5] were the first to propose homomorphic signatures that can handle a wider class of functions than linear functions. Their scheme can handle arbitrary polynomial and security is proven in the random oracle based on the hardness of the short integer solution (SIS) problem. Catalano et al. [9] proposed such a scheme in the standard model based on a multilinear map. Gorbunov et al. [19] constructed a (leveled) fully homomorphic signature, which can handle any polynomial size function based on the learning with errors (LWE) assumption. Xie et al. [28] proposed (bounded) fully homomorphic signatures based on $i\mathcal{O}$.

1.3 Notations

We use $\mathbb{N}$ to denote the set of all natural numbers, and $[n]$ to denote the set $\{1, \ldots n\}$ for $n \in \mathbb{N}$. If S is a finite set, then we use $x \xleftarrow{\$} S$ to denote that x is chosen uniformly at random from S. If $\mathcal{A}$ is an (randomized) algorithm, we use $x \leftarrow \mathcal{A}(y)$ to mean that x is output by $\mathcal{A}$ whose input is y. We say that a function $f(\cdot) : \mathbb{N} \to [0, 1]$ is negligible if for all positive polynomials $p(\cdot)$ and all sufficiently large $\lambda \in \mathbb{N}$, we have $f(\lambda) < 1/p(\lambda)$. We say that an algorithm $\mathcal{A}$ is probabilistic polynomial time (PPT) if there exists a polynomial p such that the running time of $\mathcal{A}$ with input length λ is less than $p(\lambda)$. For two integers $x \neq 0$ and y, we say that x and y are negligibly close if $|x - y|/x$ is negligible. For a set

S and a random variable x over S, we say that x is almost uniform on S if the statistical distance between the distribution of x and the uniform distribution on S is negligible. poly denotes an unspecified polynomial.

2   Preliminaries

Definition 1 (*Indistinguishability Obfuscator*). *Let C_λ be the class of circuits of size at most λ. An efficient randomized algorithm $i\mathcal{O}$ is called an indistinguishability obfuscator for P/poly if the following conditions are satisfied:*

- *For all security parameters $\lambda \in \mathbb{N}$, for all $C \in C_\lambda$, we have that*

$$\Pr[\forall x \; C'(x) = C(x) : C' \leftarrow i\mathcal{O}(\lambda, C)] = 1.$$

- *For any (not necessarily uniform) efficient algorithm $\mathcal{A} = (\mathcal{A}_1, \mathcal{A}_2)$, there exists a negligible function α such that the following holds: if $\mathcal{A}_1(1^\lambda)$ always outputs (C_0, C_1, σ) such that we have $C_0, C_1 \in C_\lambda$ and $\forall x \; C_0(x) = C_1(x)$, then we have*

$$| \Pr[\mathcal{A}_2(\sigma, i\mathcal{O}(\lambda, C_0)) = 1 : (C_0, C_1, \sigma) \leftarrow \mathcal{A}_1(1^\lambda)]$$
$$- \Pr[\mathcal{A}_2(\sigma, i\mathcal{O}(\lambda, C_1)) = 1 : (C_0, C_1, \sigma) \leftarrow \mathcal{A}_1(1^\lambda)]| \leq \alpha(\lambda)$$

Note that a candidate construction of $i\mathcal{O}$ that satisfies the above definition is given in [16].

2.1   Group of Signed Quadratic Residues

Here, we recall the definition and some properties of a group of signed quadratic residues [22] that we mainly work with in this paper. An integer $N = PQ$ is called a Blum integer if P and Q are distinct primes with the same length and $P \equiv Q \equiv 3 \bmod 4$ and $\gcd(P - 1, Q - 1) = 2$ hold. Let $\mathsf{RSAGen}(1^\lambda)$ be an efficient algorithm which outputs a random ℓ_N-bit Blum integer $N = PQ$ and its factorization (P, Q). We say that the factoring assumption holds with respect to RSAGen if for any efficient adversary $\mathcal{A}$, $\Pr[x \in \{P, Q\} : (N, P, Q) \leftarrow \mathsf{RSAGen}(1^\lambda), x \leftarrow \mathcal{A}(1^\lambda, N)]$ is negligible. We define the group of signed quadratic residues as $\mathbb{QR}_N^+ := \{|u^2| : u \in \mathbb{Z}_N^*\}$ where $|u^2|$ denotes the absolute value of u^2 when it is represented as an element of $\{-(N - 1)/2, \ldots, (N - 1)/2\}$. For simplicity, we assume that a random element of $\mathbb{QR}_N^+$ is a generator of the group with overwhelming probability for every N generated by RSAGen^3. A remarkable property of $\mathbb{QR}_N^+$ is that it is efficiently recognizable. That is, there exists an efficient algorithm that determines whether a given string is an element of $\mathbb{QR}_N^+$ or not [22]. It is easy to prove that if there exists an efficient algorithm that computes the square root of a random element $h \in \mathbb{QR}_N$, then N is factorized efficiently [22].

---

[3] This holds for example, if we assume the existence of a constant δ such that all prime factors of $(P - 1)(Q - 1)/4$ is no less than $\delta \ell_N$-bit as in [22,29]. Especially, strong RSA moduli (e.g., $N = PQ = (2p + 1)(2q + 1)$ such that P, Q, p and q are distinct primes) suffice.

2.2 Self-bilinear Map

Here, we recall the definition of a self-bilinear map. A self-bilinear map is a bilinear map where the domain and target groups are identical. The formal definition is as follows.

Definition 2 *(Self-bilinear Map [12]). For a cyclic group G, a self-bilinear map $e : G \times G \to G$ has the following properties.*

- *For all $g_1, g_2 \in G$ and $\alpha \in \mathbb{Z}$, it holds that*

$$e(g_1^\alpha, g_2) = e(g_1, g_2^\alpha) = e(g_1, g_2)^\alpha.$$

- *The map e is non-degenerate, i.e., if $g_1, g_2 \in G$ are generators of G, then $e(g_1, g_2)$ is a generator of G.*

We can construct an n-multilinear map for any integer $n \geq 2$ from a self-bilinear map e. We denote this n-multilinear map by e_n. This can be seen by easy induction: suppose that an n-multilinear map e_n can be constructed from a self-bilinear map e, then we can construct an $(n + 1)$-multilinear map e_{n+1} by defining

$$e_{n+1}(g_1, \ldots, g_n, g_{n+1}) := e(e_n(g_1, \ldots, g_n), g_{n+1}).$$

3 Self-bilinear Map with Auxiliary Information

In this section, we give the definition and construction of self-bilinear maps with auxiliary information (AI-SBMs). Though they are almost the similar to that in [29], we made some modifications so that they become more useful.

Definition. Here, we recall the definition of AI-SBM introduced by Yamakawa et al. [29]. We slightly modify the definition from the original one so that it is more useful in applications. The differences between our definition and theirs are summarized right below the definition.

InstGen$(1^\lambda) \to$ params $= (G, e, g)$: InstGen takes the security parameter 1^λ as input and outputs the public parameters params which consists of descriptions of an efficiently recognizable cyclic group G on which the group operation is efficiently computable, a self-bilinear map e on G and an element g of G. We require that g is a generator of G with overwhelming probability and that an approximation Approx(G) of ord(G) can be computed efficiently from params, which is negligibly close to ord(G). By using g and Approx(G), we can generate an almost uniform element h of G by taking $x \xleftarrow{\$} [\text{Approx}(G)]$ and outputting $h := g^x$. With a slight abuse of notation, we often simply write $h \xleftarrow{\$} G$ to mean the above procedure. Additionally, params specifies sets T_X of auxiliary information for all $X \in G$. Since params is input for all algorithms below, we omit it for simplicity.

AIGen$(x) \to \tau_{g^x}$: AIGen takes an integer x as input, and outputs an auxiliary information $\tau_{g^x} \in T_{g^x}$ that corresponds to g^x.

$\mathsf{Map}(X, \tau_Y) \rightarrow e(X, Y)$: Map takes $X \in G$ and $\tau_Y \in T_Y$ as input and outputs $e(X, Y)$. By using this algorithm iteratively, we can compute $e_n(X_1, X_2, \ldots, X_n)$ if we are given $X_1, \ldots, X_n$ and $\tau_{X_1}, \ldots, \tau_{X_n}$[4].

$\mathsf{AIMult}(\tau_X, \tau_Y) \rightarrow \tau_{XY}$: AIMult takes $\tau_X \in T_X$, τ_Y as input and outputs $\tau_{XY} \in T_{XY}$. We require that $|\tau_{XY}| \le |\tau_X| + |\tau_Y| + \mathsf{poly}(\lambda)$ holds. With a slight abuse of notation, we often write $\tau_X \cdot \tau_Y$ to mean applying this algorithm.

$\mathsf{AIMap}(\tau_X, \tau_Y) \rightarrow \tau_{e(X,Y)}$: AIMap takes $\tau_X \in T_X$, τ_Y as input and outputs $\tau_{e(X,Y)} \in T_{e(X,Y)}$. We require that $|\tau_{e(X,Y)}| \le |\tau_X| + |\tau_Y| + \mathsf{poly}(\lambda)$ holds. With a slight abuse of notation, we often write $e(\tau_X \cdot \tau_Y)$ to mean applying this algorithm.

$\mathsf{AIExp}(\tau_X, \alpha) \rightarrow \tau_{X^\alpha}$: AIMap takes $\tau_X \in T_X$ and a integer α as input and outputs $\tau_{X^\alpha} \in T_{X^\alpha}$. We require that $|\tau_{X^\alpha}| \le |\tau_X| + \mathsf{poly}(\lambda, \log \alpha)$ holds. With a slight abuse of notation, we often write τ_X^α to mean applying this algorithm.

$\mathsf{AIRand}(S, \tau_X) \rightarrow \tau'_X$: AIRand takes a natural number S and $\tau_X \in T_X$ such that $|\tau_X| \le S$ as input and outputs $\tau'_X \in T_X$ such that $|\tau'_X| \le \mathsf{poly}(S, \lambda)$.

We require for AIRand to satisfy the following property.

– **Indistinguishability of Auxiliary Information.** Intuitively, two auxiliary information corresponding to the same group element output by AIRand are computationally indistinguishable. More formally, for any $\mathsf{params} \leftarrow \mathsf{InstGen}(1^\lambda)$, $X \in G$, if $\tau_{X,i} \in T_X$ and $|\tau_{X,i}| \le S$ hold and we set $\tau'_{X,i} \leftarrow \mathsf{AIRand}(S, \tau_{X,i})$ $(i = 0, 1)$, then $\tau'_{X,0}$ and $\tau'_{X,1}$ are computationally indistinguishable.

Differences between our Definition and that in [29]. Our definition of AI-SBM differs from the original definition in [29] in the following four aspects. First, we write auxiliary information of $X = g^x$ by τ_X rather than τ_x as in [29]. This is because in some situations, discrete logarithm value x is complicated to write and simply writing a group element X is rather simple. We note that this is only a notational convention and does not cause any significant difference. Second, we abandon the concept of the level of auxiliary information defined in [29]. In [29], the level of auxiliary information actually means the size of the auxiliary information in their real construction. Thus we treat the sizes of auxiliary information directly rather than abstracting them as levels. Third, we divide the algorithm AIMult in [29] into two algorithms AIMult and AIRand. In the original definition of AIMult, this algorithm, given auxiliary information for X and Y, computes auxiliary information for XY and then "randomize" it. This randomizing process is done by applying obfuscation in the real construction and this makes the size of auxiliary information polynomially larger. We separate these two processes since randomization is not always required right after a multiplication. Finally, we added two algorithms AIMap and AIExp. They are useful in applications and these algorithms can be naturally derived from their construction of AI-SBM.

---

[4] Note that actually not all of these elements are needed to evaluate the map e_n.

Remark 1. *As pointed out in [1], AI-SBMs have a significant drawback compared with ideal self-bilinear maps that the size of auxiliary information grows almost double in each computation of* AIMult *and* AIMap. *Thus if we apply these computations recursively, then the size grows exponentially in the number of computations. Thus we cannot compute polynomial depth circuit on auxiliary information. We remark, however, that we can compute logarithmic depth circuits on auxiliary information.*

Construction. Here, we review the construction of an AI-SBM given by Yamakawa et. al. [29]. We note that we define a selfbilinear map e as $e(g^x, g^y) := g^{2^k xy}$ for some integer k wheres they defined as $e(g^x, g^y) := g^{2xy}$ in [29]. This is due to a technical reason and cause minor changes. First we prepare some notations for circuits on $\mathbb{QR}_N^+$.

Notation for Circuits on $\mathbb{QR}_N^+$. In the following, for an ℓ_N-bit RSA modulus N and an integer $x \in \mathbb{Z}$, $\mathcal{C}_{N,x}$ denotes a set of circuits $C_{N,x}$ that computes x-th power on the group $\mathbb{QR}_N^+$. If an input is not an element of $\mathbb{QR}_N^+$, $C_{N,x}$ outputs 0^{ℓ_N} (that is interpreted as $\bot$). We define the canonical circuit $\tilde{C}_{N,x}$ in $\mathcal{C}_{N,x}$ in a natural way[5]. For circuits C_1, C_2 whose output can be interpreted as elements of $\mathbb{QR}_N^+$, $\mathsf{Mult}(C_1, C_2)$ denotes a circuit that takes a as input and outputs $C_1(a) \cdot C_2(a)$ where $\cdot$ denotes the multiplication on $\mathbb{QR}_N^+$. $C_1 \circ C_2$ denotes a circuit that takes a as input and outputs $C_1(C_2(a))$. The sizes of $\mathsf{Mult}(C_1, C_2)$ and $C_1 \circ C_2$ can be bounded by $|C_1| + |C_2| + \mathsf{poly}(\log N)$.

Now we are ready to describe the construction. Let k be an arbitrary natural number. The construction is as follows.

$\mathsf{InstGen}(1^\lambda) \to \mathsf{params} = (N, g)$: Run $\mathsf{RSAGen}(1^\lambda)$ to obtain (N, P, Q), chooses $g \xleftarrow{\$} \mathbb{QR}_N^+$ and outputs $\mathsf{params} = (N, g)$. params defines the underlying group $G := \mathbb{QR}_N^+$, the self bilinear map $e(g^x, g^y) := g^{2^k xy}$ and $\mathsf{Approx}(G) := (N-1)/4$. For any element $X = g^x \in G$, the set T_X is defined as the set of all circuits that computes $2^k x$-th power on $\mathbb{QR}_N^+$ (and outputs $\bot$ for input out of $\mathbb{QR}_N^+$).

$\mathsf{AIGen}(x) \to \tau_{g^x}$: Take the canonical circuit $\tilde{C}_{N,2^k x} \in \mathcal{C}_{N,2^k x}$, set $\tau_{g^x} := \tilde{C}_{N,2^k x}$ and output τ_{g^x}.

$\mathsf{Map}(X, \tau_Y) \to e(X, Y)$: Compute $\tau_Y(X)$ and output it. (Recall that τ_Y is a circuit that computes the $2^k y$-th power for an element of $\mathbb{QR}_N^+$ where $Y = g^y$.)

$\mathsf{AIMult}(\tau_X, \tau_Y) \to \tau_{XY}$: Compute $\tau_{XY} \leftarrow \mathsf{Mult}(\tau_X, \tau_Y)$ and output it.

$\mathsf{AIMap}(\tau_X, \tau_Y) \to \tau_{e(X,Y)}$: Compute $\tau_{e(X,Y)} \leftarrow \tau_X \circ \tau_Y$ and output it.

$\mathsf{AIExp}(\tau_X, \alpha) \to \tau_{X^\alpha}$: Take the canonical circuit $\tilde{C}_{N,\alpha} \in \mathcal{C}_{N,\alpha}$, compute $\tau_X \circ \tilde{C}_{N,\alpha}$ and output it.

$\mathsf{AIRand}(S, \tau_X') $: Compute $\tau_X' \leftarrow i\mathcal{O}(S, \tau_X)$ and output it.

---

[5] There is flexibility for the definition of the canonical circuit. However, any definition works if the size of $\tilde{C}_{N,x}$ is polynomially bounded in λ and $|x|$.

The indistinguishability of auxiliary information easily follows from the definition of indistinguishability obfuscation.

4   Hardness Assumptions for AI-SBM

In this section, we first define the Auxiliary Information Generalized Multilinear Diffie-Hellman (AI-GMDH) assumption. Then we prove our main theorem that gives a sufficient condition for that the AI-GMDH assumption holds. Finally, we give some applications of our main theorem.

4.1   Our Main Theorem

First, we define the AI-GMDH assumption.

Definition 3 $((\{f_i\}_{i\in[m]}, f^*, \ell^*, M)$-AI-GMDH assumption$)$. *Let $f_1, \ldots, f_m, f^*$ be n-variable polynomials and ℓ^* and M be natural numbers. Then we say that the Auxiliary Information Generalized Multilinear Diffie-Hellman (AI-GMDH) assumption holds if the following holds. There exists a polynomial $S(\lambda)$ such that for any PPT adversary $\mathcal{A}$,*

$$\Pr[(c^*, F^{*c^*}) \leftarrow \mathcal{A}(\mathsf{params}, \{F_i\}_{i\in[m]}, \{\tau_{F_i}\}_{i\in[m]}), c^* \neq 0, |c^*| \leq M]$$

is negligible, where $\mathsf{params} \xleftarrow{\$} \mathsf{InstGen}(1^\lambda)$, $x_1, \ldots, x_m \xleftarrow{\$} [\mathsf{Approx}(G)]$, $F_i := g^{f_i(x_1,\ldots,x_n)}$, $\tau_{F_i} \leftarrow \mathsf{AIRand}(S, \mathsf{AIGen}(f_i(x_1,\ldots,x_n)))$ (for $i \in [m]$), and $F^* := e_{\ell^*}(g,\ldots,g)^{f^*(x_1,\ldots,x_n)}$.

Remark 2. *If G is a group of known prime order, then it is the same if we only consider the case of $c^* = 1$. However, since we consider a group of unknown order, we formulate the assumption as the above. Indeed, it is crucial to consider the case of $c^* \neq 1$ in the application in Sect. 5.*

In the following, we give a sufficient condition for that $(\{f_i\}_{i\in[M]}, f^*, \ell^*, M)$-AI-GMDH assumption holds when $\{f_i\}_{i\in[M]}$ and f^* are monic polynomials, i.e., written as $\prod_{i=1}^n x_i^{t_i}$ where t_i is a natural number. First, we define a notation.

Definition 4. *For a monic monomial f defined by $f(x_1,\ldots,x_n) = \prod_{i=1}^n x_i^{t_i}$, we define its corresponding polynomial $\bar{f}$ by $\bar{f}(x_1,\ldots,x_n) := \sum_{i=1}^n t_i x_i$.*

Our main theorem is as follows.

Theorem 1. *Let $f_1, \ldots, f_m$ and f^* be functions of the form as in Definition 4. If there exists $(a_1, \ldots, a_n) \in \mathbb{Z}^n$ such that $\bar{f}_i(a_1,\ldots,a_n) \geq -1$ for all $i \in [m]$ and $\ell^* + \bar{f}^*(a_1,\ldots,a_n) \leq -1$ hold. Then if $i\mathcal{O}$ is an indistinguishability obfuscation and the factoring assumption holds w.r.t. RSAGen, then $(\{f_i\}_{i\in[m]}, f^*, \ell^*, 2^{k-1})$-AI-GMDH assumption holds w.r.t. the AI-SBM constructed in Sect. 3.*

Proof. Assume that there exists a PPT adversary $\mathcal{A}$ that breaks the $(\{f_i\}_{i\in[m]}, f^*, \ell^*, 2^{k-1})$-AI-GMDH assumption. We construct a PPT algorithm $\mathcal{B}$ that computes the square root of a random element of $\mathbb{QR}_N^+$ with non-negligible probability. (As remarked in Sect. 2.1, such an algorithm yields a PPT algorithm that breaks the factoring assumption.) The description of $\mathcal{B}$ is as follows.

$\mathcal{B}(N, h)$: Let $g := h^{2^k}$ and params $:= (N, g)$. Pick $x_i' \xleftarrow{\$} [(N-1)/4]$ and implicitly define $x_i := 2^{ka_i}(2x_i'+1) \bmod \mathrm{ord}(\mathbb{QR}_N^+)$. (Since $\mathcal{B}$ do not know $\mathrm{ord}(\mathbb{QR}_N^+)$, it cannot compute x_i. It defines as above only in mind.) Then for all $i \in [m]$, we have

$$f_i(x_1, \ldots, x_n) \equiv 2^{k\bar{f}_i(a_1,\ldots,a_n)}\mathrm{odd}_i \bmod \mathrm{ord}(\mathbb{QR}_N^+), \text{ and}$$

$$f^*(x_1, \ldots, x_n) \equiv 2^{k\bar{f}^*(a_1,\ldots,a_n)}\mathrm{odd}^* \bmod \mathrm{ord}(\mathbb{QR}_N^+)$$

where odd_i and odd^* are odd numbers efficiently computable from $\{x_i'\}_{i\in[n]}$. Here, we let $A_i := 2^{k(\bar{f}_i(a_1,\ldots,a_n)+1)}\mathrm{odd}_i$, $F_i := h^{A_i}$, and $\tau_{F_i} := i\mathcal{O}(S, \tilde{C}_{N,A_i})$ where $\tilde{C}_{N,A_i}$ is the canonical circuit that computes A_i-th power on $\mathbb{QR}_N^+$. Then $\mathcal{B}$ runs $(c^*, T) \leftarrow \mathcal{A}(\mathrm{params}, \{F_i\}_{i\in[m]}, \{\tau_{F_i}\}_{i\in[m]})$. We can express c^* as $c^* = 2^v\mathrm{odd}_{c^*}$ where odd_{c^*} is the odd part of c^*. Then we have $v \leq k-1$ since we have $|c^*| \leq M \leq 2^{k-1}$. If $\mathcal{A}$ succeeds, then we have

$$T = e_{\ell^*}(g, \ldots, g)^{c^* f^*(x_1,\ldots,x_n)}$$
$$= g^{2^{k(\ell^*-1)}c^* f^*(x_1,\ldots,x_n)}$$
$$= h^{2^{k\ell^*}c^* 2^{k\bar{f}^*(a_1,\ldots,a_n)}\mathrm{odd}^*}$$
$$= h^{2^{k(\ell^*+\bar{f}^*(a_1,\ldots,a_n))+v}\mathrm{odd}'}$$

where we define $\mathrm{odd}' := \mathrm{odd}^* \cdot \mathrm{odd}_{c^*}$. Here, since we have $\ell^* + \bar{f}^*(a_1, \ldots, a_n) \leq -1$ by the assumption and $v \leq k-1$, we have $k(\ell^* + \bar{f}^*(a_1, \ldots, a_n)) + v \leq -1$. Then if we define a natural number α by $\alpha := -(k(\ell^* + \bar{f}^*(a_1, \ldots, a_n)) + v)$, then we have $T = h^{2^{-\alpha}\mathrm{odd}'}$. Therefore we have $T^{\alpha-1} = h^{2^{-1}\mathrm{odd}'}$. Then if we let $\mathrm{odd}' := 2\mathrm{even}' + 1$, then we have $T^{\alpha-1} = h^{\mathrm{even}'+1/2}$. Therefore $\mathcal{B}$ can compute $h^{1/2}$ by computing $T^{\alpha-1}h^{-\mathrm{even}'}$.

This completes the description of $\mathcal{B}$. In the above description, we already show that if $\mathcal{A}$ succeeds, then $\mathcal{B}$ also succeeds. What is left is to prove the distribution of $\mathcal{A}$'s input in the above algorithm is computationally indistinguishable from that in the AI-GMDH assumption. N is generated in the same way as in the AI-GMDH assumption (it is generated as $N \leftarrow \mathsf{RSAGen}(1^\lambda)$). g is uniformly distributed on $\mathbb{QR}_N^+$ as in the AI-GMDH assumption since h is uniformly distributed on $\mathbb{QR}_N^+$ and 2^k is coprime to $\mathrm{ord}(\mathbb{QR}_N^+)$. Since $\{x_i'\}_{i\in[n]}$ are almost uniformly distributed on $[\mathrm{ord}(\mathbb{QR}_N^+)]$ and 2 is coprime to $\mathrm{ord}(\mathbb{QR}_N^+)$, $\{x_i\}_{i\in[n]}$ are also almost uniformly distributed on $[\mathrm{ord}(\mathbb{QR}_N^+)]$. Since we have $F_i = h^{A_i}$ and $A_i \equiv 2^k f_i(x_1, \ldots, x_n) \bmod \mathrm{ord}(\mathbb{QR}_N^+)$, we have $h^{A_i} = h^{2^k f_i(x_1,\ldots,x_n)} = g^{f_i(x_1,\ldots,x_n)}$ for $i \in [m]$. Thus we can see that $g^{f_i(x_1,\ldots,x_n)}$ is simulated correctly. What is left is to prove that the distribution of τ_{F_i} ($i \in [m]$) simulated by $\mathcal{B}$ is computationally indistinguishable from the real distribution in the AI-GMDH assumption conditioned on any fixed params, $\{F_i\}_{i\in[m]}$. τ_{F_i} is generated as $\tau_{F_i} := i\mathcal{O}(S, \tilde{C}_{N,A_i})$ in the simulation by $\mathcal{B}$, and $\tau_{F_i} := i\mathcal{O}(S, \tilde{C}_{N,2^k f_i(x_1,\dots,x_n)})$ in the AI-GMDH assumption. Here, since we have $A_i \equiv 2^k f_i(x_1,\dots,x_n)$ mod $\mathrm{ord}(\mathbb{QR}_N^+)$, $\tilde{C}_{N,2^k f_i(x_1,\dots,x_n)}$ and $\tilde{C}_{N,A_i}$ have the completely the same functionality. Therefore if S is larger than the sizes od these circuits, then the above two are computationally indistinguishable by the property of the indistinguishability obfuscation.

4.2   Implications of Our Main Theorem

Here, we give some implications of Theorem 1. We define two assumptions w.r.t. AI-SBMs. The first is the Auxiliary Information Multilinear Computational Diffie-Hellman (AI-MCDH) assumption that was introduced in [29][6].

Definition 5 *(n-AI-MCDH assumption). We say that the Auxiliary Information Multilinear Computational Diffie-Hellman (AI-MCDH) assumption if there exists a polynomial $S(\lambda)$ such that for any PPT adversary $\mathcal{A}$,*

$$\Pr[e_{n-1}(g,\dots,g)^{\prod_{i=1}^{n} x_i} \leftarrow \mathcal{A}(\mathsf{params}, \{g^{x_i}\}_{i\in[n]}, \{\tau_{g^{x_i}}\}_{i\in[n]})]$$

is negligible, where $\mathsf{params} \xleftarrow{\$} \mathsf{InstGen}(1^\lambda)$, $x_1,\dots,x_n \xleftarrow{\$} [\mathsf{Approx}(G)]$ *and* $\tau_{g^{x_i}} \leftarrow \mathsf{AIRand}(S, \mathsf{AIGen}(x_i))$ *(for $i \in [n]$).*

Corollary 1. *If $i\mathcal{O}$ is a secure indistinguishability obfuscation and the factoring assumption holds, then for any (polynomially bounded) n, the n-AI-MCDH assumption holds w.r.t. our AI-SBM.*

Proof. We define $f_i(x_1,\dots,x_n) := x_i$ for $i \in [n]$, and $f^*(x_1,\dots,x_n) := \prod_{i=1}^{n} x_i$. Then the n-AI-MCDH assumption is equivalent to $(\{f_i\}_{i\in[n]}, f^*, n-1, 1)$-AI-GMDH assumption. If we let $a_i := -1$ for $i \in [n]$, then we have $\bar{f}_i(a_1,\dots,a_n) = -1$ for $i \in [n]$, $\ell + \bar{f}^*(a_1,\dots,a_n) = n-1+n\cdot(-1) = -1$, and thus the condition of Theorem 1 is satisfied. Therefore this corollary follows from Theorem 1.

Definition 6 *((ℓ, M)-AI-APMDH assumption). We say that the (ℓ, M)-auxiliary information augmented power multilinear Diffie-Hellman((ℓ, M)-AI-APMDH) holds if there exists a polynomial $S(\lambda)$ such that for any PPT adversary $\mathcal{A}$,*

$$\Pr[(c^*, F^{*c^*}) \leftarrow \mathcal{A}(\mathsf{params}, \{F_i\}_{i\in[4]}, \{\tau_{F_i}\}_{i\in[4]}), c^* \neq 0, |c^*| \leq M]$$

is negligible where $\mathsf{params} \xleftarrow{\$} \mathsf{InstGen}(1^\lambda)$, $x_1, x_2, x_3 \xleftarrow{\$} [\mathsf{Approx}(G)]$, $F_1 := g^{x_2}$, $F_2 := g^{x_3}$, $F_3 := g^{x_1 x_2}$, $F_4 := g^{x_1 x_2 x_3}$, $F^* := e_\ell(g,\dots,g)^{x_1^{\ell-1}(x_2 x_3)^\ell}$, $\tau_{F_1} \leftarrow \mathsf{AIRand}(S, \mathsf{AIGen}(x_2))$, $\tau_{F_2} \leftarrow \mathsf{AIRand}(S, \mathsf{AIGen}(x_3))$, $\tau_{F_3} \leftarrow \mathsf{AIRand}(S, \mathsf{AIGen}(x_1 x_2))$, *and* $\tau_{F_4} \leftarrow \mathsf{AIRand}(S, \mathsf{AIGen}(x_1 x_2 x_3))$

---

[6] The actual presentation is slightly modified due to the modification of the definition.

Remark 3. *In the original definition of the APMDH assumption, an adversary is also given g^{x_1} and $g^{x_1 x_3}$ additionally. In our application in Sect. 5, they are not needed and thus we omit them.*

Corollary 2. *If $i\mathcal{O}$ is a secure indistinguishability obfuscation and the factoring assumption holds, then for any (polynomially bounded) ℓ, the $(\ell, 2^{k-1})$-AI-APMDH assumption holds w.r.t. our AI-SBM.*

Proof. We define $f_1(x_1, x_2, x_3) := x_2$, $f_2(x_1, x_2, x_3) := x_3$, $f_3(x_1, x_2, x_3) := x_1 x_2$, $f_4(x_1, x_2, x_3) := x_1 x_2 x_3$, and $f^*(x_1, x_2, x_3) := x_1^{\ell-1}(x_2 x_3)^{\ell}$ Then the $(\ell, 2^{k-1})$-AI-APMDH assumption is equivalent to $(\{f_i\}_{i \in [4]}, f^*, \ell, 2^{k-1})$-AI-GMDH assumption. If we let $(a_1, a_2, a_3) := (1, -1, -1)$, then we have $\bar{f}_1(a_1, a_2, a_3) = -1$, $\bar{f}_2(a_1, a_2, a_3) = -1$, $\bar{f}_3(a_1, a_2, a_3) = 1 - 1 = 0$, $\bar{f}_4(a_1, a_2, a_3) = 1 - 1 - 1 = -1$, and $\ell + \bar{f}^*(a_1, a_2, a_3) = \ell + (\ell - 1) - \ell - \ell = -1$, and thus the condition of Theorem 1 is satisfied. Therefore this corollary follows from Theorem 1.

5   Homomorphic Signature

In this section, we construct homomorphic signatures based on AI-SBMs. We define homomorphic signatures similarly as in [19]. The full definition is given in the full version of this paper.

5.1   Construction

Here, we construct a selectively secure single data homomorphic signature scheme for the class of all polynomials. Our scheme is based on the idea of [9]. Namely, our scheme is almost automatically obtained by replacing multilinear maps by AI-SBP in the scheme of [9]. We let $[M]$ be the message space.

KeyGen$(1^{\lambda}, 1^n) \to (vk, sk)$: Generate $(G, e, g) = $ params $\leftarrow$ ParamGen(1^{λ}), choose $r_i \xleftarrow{\$} [\mathsf{Approx}(G)]$ $(i = 1, \ldots, n)$ and $x_1, x_2, x_3 \xleftarrow{\$} [\mathsf{Approx}(G)]$, and set $R_i := g^{r_i}$ $(i = 1, \ldots, n)$, $A := g^{x_2}$, $B := g^{x_3}$, $C := g^{x_1 x_2}$, $U := g^{x_1 x_2 x_3}$, $\tau_{R_i} := \mathsf{AIRand}(S', \mathsf{AIGen}(r_i))$ $(i = 1, \ldots, n)$, $\tau_A := \mathsf{AIRand}(S, \mathsf{AIGen}(x_2))$, $\tau_B := \mathsf{AIRand}(S, \mathsf{AIGen}(x_3))$, $\tau_C := \mathsf{AIRand}(S, \mathsf{AIGen}(x_1 x_2))$, $\tau_U := \mathsf{AIRand}(S, \mathsf{AIGen}(x_1 x_2 x_3))$, where S' can be set as an arbitrary integer larger than the maximal size of auxiliary information that is used as a second input of AIRand when generating R_i through the real scheme and the security proof. Then set
$vk := ($params$, \{R_i\}_{i \in [N]}, A, B, C, U, \{\tau_{R_i}\}_{i \in [N]}, \tau_A, \tau_B, \tau_C, \tau_U)$, $sk := (x_1, x_2, vk)$
and output $(vk.sk)$.

Sign$(sk, i, m) \to \sigma$:
Compute $\Lambda := (R_i B^{-m})^{x_2}$, $\Gamma := \Lambda^{x_1}$, $\tau_{\Lambda} := \mathsf{AIRand}(S'', (\tau_{R_i} \tau_B^{-m})^{x_2})$, $\tau_{\Gamma} := \mathsf{AIRand}(S'', (\tau_{R_i} \tau_B^{-m})^{x_1 x_2})$
and output $\sigma := (\Lambda, \Gamma, \tau_{\Lambda}, \tau_{\Gamma})$, where S' can be set as an arbitrary integer

larger than the maximal size of auxiliary information that is used as a second input of AIRand when generating τ_Γ through the real scheme and the security proof.

$\mathsf{Eval}(f, (m_1, \sigma_1), \ldots, (m_n, \sigma_n)) \to \sigma^*$: Let f be a polynomial of degree d. Then f can be seen as an arithmetic circuit of depth $O(\log(d))$. We let $\sigma_i = (\Lambda_i, \Gamma_i, \tau_{\Lambda_i}, \tau_{\Gamma_i})$. We label the i-th input wire of f by $(1, m_i, \sigma_i)$. For all $i \in [d]$, compute $U_i := e_i(U, \ldots, U)$, $\tau_{U_i} := e_i(\tau_U, \ldots, \tau_U)$.

For each gate of f, compute the following.

Addition: Assume that the input wires for this gate is labeled by
$(i, m^{(1)}, (\Lambda^{(1)}, \Gamma^{(1)}, \tau_{\Lambda^{(1)}}, \tau_{\Gamma^{(1)}}))$, $(j, m^{(2)}, (\Lambda^{(2)}, \Gamma^{(2)}, \tau_{\Lambda^{(2)}}, \tau_{\Gamma^{(2)}}))$.

Without loss of generality, we assume that $i \geq j$. First, adjust the "degree" of each value. That is, set
$\Lambda'^{(2)} := e_{i-j+1}(\Lambda^{(2)}, g, \ldots, g)$, $\Gamma'^{(2)} := e_{i-j+1}(\Gamma^{(2)}, g, \ldots, g)$,
$\tau_{\Lambda'^{(2)}} := e_{i-j+1}(\tau_{\Lambda^{(2)}}, \tau_g, \ldots, \tau_g)$, $\tau_{\Gamma'^{(2)}} := e_{i-j+1}(\tau_{\Gamma^{(2)}}, \tau_g, \ldots, \tau_g)$.

Then set
$m^* := m_1 + m_2$, $\Lambda^* := \Lambda^{(1)} \cdot \Lambda'^{(2)}$, $\Gamma^* := \Gamma^{(1)} \cdot \Gamma'^{(2)}$, $\tau_{\Lambda^*} := \tau_{\Lambda^{(1)}} \cdot \tau_{\Lambda'^{(2)}}$,
$\tau_{\Gamma^*} := \tau_{\Gamma^{(1)}} \cdot \tau_{\Gamma'^{(2)}}$,

and assign $(i, m^*, (\Lambda^*, \Gamma^*, \tau_{\Lambda^*}, \tau_{\Gamma^*}))$ to the output wire of this gate.

Multiplication by constant c: Let $(i, m, (\Lambda, \Gamma, \tau_\Lambda, \tau_\Gamma))$ be the value labeled to the input wire of this gate. Then compute
$m^* := c \cdot m$ $\Lambda^* := \Lambda^c$ $\Gamma^* := \Gamma^c$ $\tau_\Lambda := \tau_\Lambda^c$ $\tau_\Gamma := \tau_\Gamma^c$

and assign $(i, m^*, (\Lambda^*, \Gamma^*, \tau_{\Lambda^*}, \tau_{\Gamma^*}))$ to the output wire of this gate.

Multiplication: Assume that the input wires for this gate is labeled by
$(i, m^{(1)}, (\Lambda^{(1)}, \Gamma^{(1)}, \tau_{\Lambda^{(1)}}, \tau_{\Gamma^{(1)}}))$,
$(j, m^{(2)}, (\Lambda^{(2)}, \Gamma^{(2)}, \tau_{\Lambda^{(2)}}, \tau_{\Gamma^{(2)}}))$.

Then compute
$m^* := m_A \cdot m_B$,
$\Lambda^* := e(\Lambda^{(1)}, \Gamma^{(2)}) \cdot e(\Lambda^{(1)}, U_j^{m_2}) \cdot e(U_i^{m_i}, \Lambda^{(2)})$, $\Gamma^* := e(\Gamma^{(1)}, \Gamma^{(2)}) \cdot$
$e(\Gamma^{(1)}, U_j^{m_2}) \cdot e(U_i^{m_i}, \Gamma^{(2)})$ $\tau_{\Lambda^*} := e(\tau_{\Lambda^{(1)}}, \tau_{\Gamma^{(2)}}) \cdot e(\tau_{\Lambda^{(1)}}, \tau_{U_j}^{m_2}) \cdot$
$e(\tau_{U_i}^{m_1}, \tau_{\Lambda^{(2)}})$, $\tau_{\Gamma^*} := e(\tau_{\Gamma^{(1)}}, \tau_{\Gamma^{(2)}}) \cdot e(\tau_{\Gamma^{(1)}}, \tau_{U_j}^{m_2}) \cdot e(\tau_{U_i}^{m_1}, \tau_{\Gamma^{(2)}})$, and assign
$(i + j, m^*, (\Lambda^*, \Gamma^*, \tau_{\Lambda^*}, \tau_{\Gamma^*}))$ to the output wire of this gate.

We can see that the output wire of f is labeled by $(d, f(m_1, \ldots, m_n), (\Lambda_{\text{out}}, \Gamma_{\text{out}}, \tau_{\Lambda_{\text{out}}}, \tau_{\Gamma_{\text{out}}}))$ for some $(\Lambda_{\text{out}}, \Gamma_{\text{out}}, \tau_{\Lambda_{\text{out}}}, \tau_{\Gamma_{\text{out}}})$. Then Eval outputs Λ_{out}.

$\mathsf{Verify}(vk, f, m, \sigma = \Lambda) \to 1/0$: Set $g_d := e_d(g, \ldots, g)$ and compute $R = g_d^{f(r_1, \ldots, r_N)}$ and its corresponding auxiliary information τ_R. This can be computed by evaluating f on the values $R_1, \ldots, R_n$. Namely, replace an addition in f by a multiplication in G and a multiplication by an evaluation of e. Let $B_d := e_d(B, \ldots, B)$ and verify $e(R \cdot B_d^{-m}, g_d^{x_1^{d-1} x_2^d}) = e(\Lambda_d, g_d)$. If this equation holds, then output 1, and otherwise output 0. Here, required values for the verification can be computed as $\tau_{R \cdot B_d^{-m}} := \tau_R \cdot e(\tau_B, \ldots, \tau_B)^{-m}$, $g_d^{x_1^{d-1} x_2^d} := e_d(A, C, \ldots, C)$, and $\tau_{g_d} := e_d(\tau_g, \ldots, \tau_g)$.

5.2 Security

Theorem 2 *If $(\ell, M) - AI - APMDH$ assumption hold for all polynomially bounded ℓ then the above scheme is selectively secure.*

Combining with Corollary 2, we obtain the following corollary.

Corollary 3 *If iO is an indistinguishability obfuscation and the factoring assumption holds, then the above homomorphic signature scheme instantiated by the AI-SBM given in Sect. 3 is selectively secure as long as we have $2^{k-1} \geq M$.*

The proof of Theorem 2 can be found in the full version.

Acknowledgment. We would like to thank the anonymous reviewers of ACISP 2016 and members of the study group "Shin-Akarui-Angou-Benkyou-Kai" for their helpful comments. This work was supported by CREST, JST and JSPS KAKENHI Grant Number 14J03467.

References

1. Albrecht, M.R., Farshim, P., Hofheinz, D., Larraia, E., Paterson, K.G.: Multilinear maps from obfuscation. In: Kushilevitz, E., et al. (eds.) TCC 2016-A. LNCS, vol. 9562, pp. 446–473. Springer, Heidelberg (2016). doi:10.1007/978-3-662-49096-9_19
2. Barak, B., Goldreich, O., Impagliazzo, R., Rudich, S., Sahai, A., Vadhan, S.P., Yang, K.: On the (im)possibility of obfuscating programs. In: Kilian, J. (ed.) CRYPTO 2001. LNCS, vol. 2139, pp. 1–18. Springer, Heidelberg (2001)
3. Boneh, D., Boyen, X.: Efficient selective-ID secure identity-based encryption without random oracles. In: Cachin, C., Camenisch, J.L. (eds.) EUROCRYPT 2004. LNCS, vol. 3027, pp. 223–238. Springer, Heidelberg (2004)
4. Boneh, D., Franklin, M.: Identity-based encryption from the weil pairing. In: Kilian, J. (ed.) CRYPTO 2001. LNCS, vol. 2139, pp. 213–229. Springer, Heidelberg (2001)
5. Boneh, D., Freeman, D.M.: Homomorphic signatures for polynomial functions. In: Paterson, K.G. (ed.) EUROCRYPT 2011. LNCS, vol. 6632, pp. 149–168. Springer, Heidelberg (2011)
6. Boneh, D., Gentry, C., Gorbunov, S., Halevi, S., Nikolaenko, V., Segev, G., Vaikuntanathan, V., Vinayagamurthy, D.: Fully key-homomorphic encryption, arithmetic circuit ABE and compact garbled circuits. In: Nguyen, P.Q., Oswald, E. (eds.) EUROCRYPT 2014. LNCS, vol. 8441, pp. 533–556. Springer, Heidelberg (2014)
7. Boneh, D., Silverberg, A.: Applications of multilinear forms to cryptography. Contemporary Mathematics **324**, 71–90 (2002)
8. Boneh, D., Waters, B., Zhandry, M.: Low overhead broadcast encryption from multilinear maps. In: Garay, J.A., Gennaro, R. (eds.) CRYPTO 2014, Part I. LNCS, vol. 8616, pp. 206–223. Springer, Heidelberg (2014)
9. Catalano, D., Fiore, D., Warinschi, B.: Homomorphic signatures with efficient verification for polynomial functions. In: Garay, J.A., Gennaro, R. (eds.) CRYPTO 2014, Part I. LNCS, vol. 8616, pp. 371–389. Springer, Heidelberg (2014)
10. Cheon, J.H., Fouque, P.-A., Lee, C., Minaud, B., Ryu, H.: Cryptanalysis of the new CLT multilinear map over the integers. In: Fischlin, M., Coron, J.-S. (eds.) EUROCRYPT 2016. LNCS, vol. 9665, pp. 509–536. Springer, Heidelberg (2016). doi:10.1007/978-3-662-49890-3_20

11. Cheon, J.H., Han, K., Lee, C., Ryu, H., Stehlé, D.: Cryptanalysis of the multilinear map over the integers. In: Oswald, E., Fischlin, M. (eds.) EUROCRYPT 2015. LNCS, vol. 9056, pp. 3–12. Springer, Heidelberg (2015)

12. Cheon, J.H., Lee, D.H.: A note on self-bilinear maps. Bull. Korean Math. Soc. **46**(2), 303–309 (2009)

13. Coron, J.-S., Lepoint, T., Tibouchi, M.: Practical multilinear maps over the integers. In: Canetti, R., Garay, J.A. (eds.) CRYPTO 2013, Part I. LNCS, vol. 8042, pp. 476–493. Springer, Heidelberg (2013)

14. Coron, J.-S., Lepoint, T., Tibouchi, M.: New multilinear maps over the integers. CRYPTO **1**, 267–286 (2015)

15. Garg, S., Gentry, C., Halevi, S.: Candidate multilinear maps from ideal lattices. In: Johansson, T., Nguyen, P.Q. (eds.) EUROCRYPT 2013. LNCS, vol. 7881, pp. 1–17. Springer, Heidelberg (2013)

16. Garg, S., Gentry, C., Halevi, S., Raykova, M., Sahai, A., Waters, B.: Candidate indistinguishability obfuscation and functional encryption for all circuits. In: FOCS, pp. 40–49 (2013)

17. Garg, S., Gentry, C., Halevi, S., Sahai, A., Waters, B.: Attribute-based encryption for circuits from multilinear maps. In: Canetti, R., Garay, J.A. (eds.) CRYPTO 2013, Part II. LNCS, vol. 8043, pp. 479–499. Springer, Heidelberg (2013)

18. Gentry, C., Gorbunov, S., Halevi, S.: Graph-induced multilinear maps from lattices. In: Dodis, Y., Nielsen, J.B. (eds.) TCC 2015, Part II. LNCS, vol. 9015, pp. 498–527. Springer, Heidelberg (2015)

19. Gorbunov, S., Vaikuntanathan, V., Wichs, D.: Leveled fully homomorphic signatures from standard lattices. In: STOC 2015, 469–477 (2015)

20. Groth, J., Ostrovsky, R., Sahai, A.: Perfect non-interactive zero knowledge for NP. In: Vaudenay, S. (ed.) EUROCRYPT 2006. LNCS, vol. 4004, pp. 339–358. Springer, Heidelberg (2006)

21. Groth, J., Sahai, A.: Efficient non-interactive proof systems for bilinear groups. In: Smart, N.P. (ed.) EUROCRYPT 2008. LNCS, vol. 4965, pp. 415–432. Springer, Heidelberg (2008)

22. Hofheinz, D., Kiltz, E.: The group of signed quadratic residues and applications. In: Halevi, S. (ed.) CRYPTO 2009. LNCS, vol. 5677, pp. 637–653. Springer, Heidelberg (2009)

23. Hu, Y., Jia, H.: Cryptanalysis of GGH map. In: Fischlin, M., Coron, J.-S. (eds.) EUROCRYPT 2016. LNCS, vol. 9665, pp. 537–565. Springer, Heidelberg (2016). doi:10.1007/978-3-662-49890-3_21

24. Lee, C., Cheon, J.H., Jeong, J.: An algorithm for ntru problems and cryptanalysis of the ggh multilinear map without an encoding of zero. Cryptology ePrint Archive, Report 2016/139 (2016). http://eprint.iacr.org/

25. Miles, E., Sahai, A., Zhandry, M.: Annihilation attacks for multilinear maps: Cryptanalysis of indistinguishability obfuscation over ggh13. Cryptology ePrint Archive, Report 2016/147 (2016). http://eprint.iacr.org/

26. Paneth, O., Sahai, A.: On the equivalence of obfuscation and multilinear maps. Cryptology ePrint Archive, Report 2015/791 (2015). http://eprint.iacr.org/

27. Sahai, A., Waters, B.: Fuzzy identity-based encryption. In: Cramer, R. (ed.) EUROCRYPT 2005. LNCS, vol. 3494, pp. 457–473. Springer, Heidelberg (2005)

28. Xie, X., Xue, R.: Bounded fully homomorphic signature schemes. Cryptology ePrint Archive, Report 2014/420 (2014). http://eprint.iacr.org/

29. Yamakawa, T., Yamada, S., Hanaoka, G., Kunihiro, N.: Self-bilinear map on unknown order groups from indistinguishability obfuscation and its applications. In: Garay, J.A., Gennaro, R. (eds.) CRYPTO 2014, Part II. LNCS, vol. 8617, pp. 90–107. Springer, Heidelberg (2014)

Deterministic Encoding into Twisted Edwards Curves

Wei Yu[1,2(✉)], Kunpeng Wang[1], Bao Li[1], Xiaoyang He[1,3], and Song Tian[1]

[1] State Key Laboratory of Information Security,
Institute of Information Engineering, Chinese Academy of Sciences,
Beijing 100093, China
{yuwei,wangkunpeng,libao,hexiaoyang,tiansong}@iie.ac.cn
[2] Data Assurance and Communication Security Research Center,
Chinese Academy of Sciences, Beijing 100093, China
yuwei_1_yw@163.com
[3] University of Chinese Academy of Sciences, Beijing, China

Abstract. This paper describes a deterministic encoding f from a finite field $\mathbb{F}_q$ to a twisted Edwards curve E when $q \equiv 2 \pmod 3$. This encoding f satisfies all 3 properties of deterministic encoding in Boneh-Franklin's identity-based scheme. We show that the construction $f(h(m))$ is a hash function if $h(m)$ is a classical hash function. We present that for any nontrivial character χ of $E(\mathbb{F}_q)$, the character sum $S_f(\chi)$ satisfies $S_f(\chi) \leqslant 20\sqrt{q} + 2$. It follows that $f(h_1(m)) + f(h_2(m))$ is indifferentiable from a random oracle in the random oracle model for h_1 and h_2 by Farashahi, Fouque, Shparlinski, Tibouchi, and Voloch's framework. This encoding saves 3 field inversions and 3 field multiplications compared with birational equivalence composed with Icart's encoding; saves 2 field inversions and 2 field multiplications compared with Yu and Wang's encoding at the cost of 2 field squarings; and saves 2 field inversions, 3 field multiplications and 3 field squarings compared with Alasha's encoding. Practical implementations show that f is 46.1 %,35.7 %, and 38.9 % faster than the above encodings respectively.

Keywords: Twisted Edwards curve · Deterministic encoding · Elliptic curve · Hashing · Random oracle model

1 Introduction

The deterministic encodings into elliptic curves can be traced back to Schoof in [1] where he asked for an approach to deterministically construct points on an elliptic curve. Identity-based schemes [2–4] and Lindell's universally composable commitment scheme [5] require messages to be hashed into elliptic curves where

This research is supported in part by National Research Foundation of China under Grant Nos. 61502487, 61272040, and in part by National Basic Research Program of China (973) under Grant No. 2013CB338001.

J.K. Liu and R. Steinfeld (Eds.): ACISP 2016, Part II, LNCS 9723, pp. 285–297, 2016.
DOI: 10.1007/978-3-319-40367-0_18

the hash function is a deterministic encoding composed with a classical hash function. Also, indifferentiable hashing into ordinary elliptic curves [6,7] needs deterministic encodings.

There exist various encodings mapping elements of $\mathbb{F}_q$ to an elliptic curve in deterministic polynomial time. Shallue and Woestijne's encoding [8] is based on Skalba's equality [9] and uses a modification of Tonelli–Shanks algorithm for computing square roots efficiently. Icart [10] in Crypto 2009 proposed an encoding based on finding cube roots efficiently as $x^{1/3} = x^{(2q-1)/3}$ when $q \equiv 2$ (mod 3). Both encodings map an element of a finite field into Weierstrass-form elliptic curves. These two methods of constructing encodings also applied to other algebraic curves such as hyperelliptic curves [11,12], Hessian curves [13], Montgomery curves [14], and Jacobi quartic curves [15].

Unlike the more well known Weierstrass form elliptic curves, the Edwards form elliptic curve, first proposed by Edwards [16], admits a unified addition formula which is very useful in providing resistance to timing attacks [17]. The group law on Edwards curves was improved using projective coordinates [18] and using inverted coordinates [19] by Bernstein and Lange. The twisted form of Edwards curves was investigated [20,21], which also has efficient group law and is against timing attacks. The pairing on twisted Edwards curves [23–25] has attracted many interests for the pairing was used to construct the first practical identity-based encryption scheme [2]. Hence, Yu and Wang [26] introduced an deterministic encoding into twisted Edwards curves in 2010. In 2012, Alasha [27] proposed a new deterministic encoding into twisted Edwards curves based on calculating a cube root. Moreover, birational equivalence from Montgomery curve to twisted Edwards curve composed with birational equivalence from Weierstrass curve to Montgomery curve composed with Icart's encoding [10] is also a deterministic encoding into twisted Edwards curves.

These encodings all satisfy the three properties of the deterministic encoding $\psi : S \to R$ in Boneh-Franklin's identity-based scheme [2]: (1) computable: ψ is computable in deterministic polynomial time; (2) l-to-1: for any $r \in R$, $\#\psi^{-1}(r) = l$; (3) samplable: there exists a probabilistic polynomial time algorithm that for any $r \in R$ returns a random element in $\psi^{-1}(r)$. For the second property, the smaller l is, the better the encoding is.

This paper presents a deterministic encoding from a finite field $\mathbb{F}_q$ to twisted Edwards curves over $\mathbb{F}_q$ when $q \equiv 2$ (mod 3) which satisfies all 3 properties of the deterministic encoding in Boneh-Franklin's identity-based scheme. This encoding is based on computing a cube root and mainly constructed by symmetrical characteristic of twisted Edwards curves.

Our encoding is efficiently computable. Without precomputations, this encoding costs 3 field inversions and 3 field multiplications less than Icart's algorithm; 2 field inversions and 2 field multiplications less than Yu and Wang's encoding at the cost of 2 field squarings; and 2 field inversions, 3 field multiplications and 3 field squarings less than Alasha's deterministic encoding. Experimental results show that with precomputations this encoding f is 20.2 %, 22.2 % 36.5 % faster than the above algorithms respectively and without precomputations f is $46.1\%, 35.7\%$ 38.9% faster than the above algorithms respectively. In a word, f is fastest among these existing encodings not only with precomputations but also without precomputations.

For the second property, f is 4-to-1 whereas the deterministic encodings in [10] is 4-to-1; in [26] is 8-to-1, in [27] is 9-to-1. From these facts, our encoding is superior. Additionally, the image of f satisfies $|\#Im(f) - \frac{5}{8}\#E(\mathbb{F}_q)| \leqslant \frac{5}{4}(31q^{1/2} + 72q^{1/4} + 67)$.

Moreover, we show that the construction $f(h(m))$ is a hash function if $h(m)$ is a hash function. We prove that for any nontrivial character χ of $E(\mathbb{F}_q)$, the character sum $S_f(\chi)$ is less than or equal to $20\sqrt{q} + 2$. This property follows that $f(h_1(m)) + f(h_2(m))$ is indifferentiable from a random oracle in the random oracle model for h_1 and h_2 by Farashahi, Fouque, Shparlinski, Tibouchi, and Voloch's framework.

The paper is organized as follows. In Sect. 2, we recall some basic facts about twisted Edwards curves and introduce existing deterministic encodings into twisted Edwards curves. In Sect. 3, we introduce our encoding from $\mathbb{F}_q$ into twisted Edwards curves. In Sect. 4, we give the properties of f. In Sect. 5, we compare our encoding f with other existing deterministic encodings. Finally, we conclude the paper.

2   Existing Deterministic Encodings into Twisted Edwards Curves

In 2007, Edwards [16] noticed an addition law on a special case of the elliptic curve $x^2 + y^2 + x^2y^2 = 1$ hinted by Euler and explicitly stated by Gauss, and followed an addition law for the curves defined by

$$x^2 + y^2 = c^2(1 + x^2y^2) \tag{1}$$

over a non-binary field K. He showed that if K is algebraically closed, every elliptic curve over K can be expressed in the form (1). However, over finite fields, only a small fraction of elliptic curves can be expressed in this form. All eliptic curves defined by Eq. (1) are isomorphic to curves of the form

$$x^2 + y^2 = 1 + dx^2y^2,$$

with $d \neq 1, d \in K$.

In [20], Bernstein et al. generalized the equation of Edwards curves in [16] to the equation

$$E : ax^2 + y^2 = 1 + dx^2y^2, \tag{2}$$

where $ad \neq 0, a \neq d$, which are twisted Edwards curves. The neutral element is $(0, 1)$, and the negative of (x_1, y_1) is $(-x_1, y_1)$.

Edwards curves are a variant of twisted Edwards curves with $a = 1$. The addition law for points on twisted Edwards curves is given by

$$(x_1, y_1) + (x_2, y_2) = \left(\frac{x_1 y_2 + x_2 y_1}{1 + dx_1 x_2 y_1 y_2}, \frac{y_1 y_2 - ax_1 x_2}{1 - dx_1 x_2 y_1 y_2} \right).$$

If a is a square and d is not a square in K, then the addition law is valid for all points, with no exceptions, which leads to the resistance of timing attacks.

In the following, three deterministic encodings from a finite field $\mathbb{F}_q$ to twisted Edwards curves in the literature are listed when $q \equiv 2 \pmod 3$. Let $q = p^n \equiv 2 \pmod 3$ where p is an odd prime. The function $x \mapsto x^3$ is a bijection with its inverse function $x \mapsto x^{\frac{1}{3}} = x^{\frac{2p^n - 1}{3}} = x^{\frac{2q-1}{3}}$, which enables the following three encodings from $\mathbb{F}_q$ to a subset of elliptic curve $E_{a,d}$ to be calculated efficiently.

2.1   Icart's Encoding [10]

For convenience, let M denote field multiplication, S field squaring, I field inversion, C the cube root. For purposes of simplification, we disregard field additions/subtractions and discard multiplications/divisions by small constants.

Icart proposed a deterministic encoding from a finite field $\mathbb{F}_q$ to Weierstrass curves when $q \equiv 2 \pmod 3$. Birational equivalence from Montgomery curve to twisted Edwards curve composed with birational equivalence from Weierstrass curve to Montgomery curve composed with Icart's function [10] is a deterministic encoding from a finite field to twisted Edwards curves shown as follows.

One can first precompute $A = \frac{2(a+d)}{a-d}, B = \frac{4}{a-d}, \alpha = \frac{A}{3B}, F = \frac{1}{B^2} - 3\alpha^2, G = -\alpha^3 - F\alpha$ at the cost of $2I + 3M + 2S$, which also can be computed in the process. Next, compute as

$$v = \frac{3F - u^4}{6u},$$

$$m = \left(v^2 - G - \frac{u^6}{27} \right)^{1/3} + \frac{u^2}{3},$$

$$n = um + v,$$

$$s = B(m - \alpha), \quad t = Bn,$$

$$x = \frac{s}{t}, \quad y = \frac{s-1}{s+1}.$$

This deterministic encoding $u \mapsto (x, y)$ is denoted by f_{Icart} where $u \neq 0$. The cost of v, m, n, s together with t, and x together with y are $I + 2S + M, C + M + S, M, 2M$, and $I + 5M$ respectively. The total cost of this encoding is $C + 2I + 10M + 3S$ with precomputations and $C + 4I + 13M + 5S$ without precomputations.

2.2   Yu and Wang's Encoding [26]

Yu and Wang [26] proposed a deterministic encoding directly into twisted Edwards curves when $q \equiv 2 \pmod 3$. One can precompute $A = 2(a + d)/(a - d), B = 4/(a - d)$ at the cost of $I + M$. Next, compute as

$$v = \frac{1}{2Bu} \left(1 - \frac{(A - Bu^2)^2}{3} \right),$$

$$s = -\frac{A - Bu^2}{3} + \left(\left(\frac{A - Bu^2}{3} \right)^3 + Bv^2 \right)^{1/3},$$

$$t = us + v,$$

$$x = s/t, \quad y = (s - 1)/(s + 1).$$

This deterministic encoding $u \mapsto (x, y)$ is denoted by f_{YuWang} where $u \neq 0$. The cost of v, s together with t, and x together with y are $I + 3M + 2S$, $C + 3M + S$, and $I + 5M$ respectively. The total cost is $C + 2I + 11M + 3S$ with precomputations and $C + 3I + 12M + 3S$ without precomputations.

2.3   Alasha's Encoding [27]

Alasha also proposed an efficiently deterministic encoding directly into twisted Edwards curves when $q \equiv 2 \pmod 3$. One can precompute $a^2, ad, d^2, ad(a + d)$ at the cost of $2M + 2S$. Next, compute as

$$v = -\frac{a^2 + 14ad + d^2 + 2u^2(a + d) + u^4}{12u},$$

$$m = \frac{a + d + u^2}{6},$$

$$s = \left(-2m^3 + \frac{ad(a + d) - v^2}{2} - (ad + uv)m \right)^{1/3} + m,$$

$$x = \frac{us + v}{s^2 - ad},$$

$$\delta = \frac{(s - d)(s - a)}{s^2 - ad},$$

$$y = \frac{\delta}{dx^2 - 1}.$$

This deterministic encoding $u \mapsto (x, y)$ is denoted by f_{Alasha} where $u \neq 0$. The cost of v together with m, s, x, δ, and y are $I + 2M + 2S$, $C + 3M + 2S$, $I + 2M + S$, $2M$, and $I + 2M + S$ respectively. The total cost of this encoding is $C + 3I + 11M + 6S$ with precomputations and $C + 3I + 13M + 8S$ without precomputations.

In the next section, we present our encoding from $\mathbb{F}_q$ to twisted Edwards curves.

3   Our Encoding

Our construction $f : u \mapsto (x, y)$ is also based on computing a cube root where (x, y) satisfies $ax^2 + y^2 = 1 + dx^2y^2$. We first precompute $(a - d)^2$ at the cost of S. Then, compute as

$$x = \frac{t(t + 24(a - d)u)}{(ut + s)(t + 24(a - d)u)},$$

$$y = \frac{(ut + s)(t - 24(a - d)u)}{(ut + s)(t + 24(a - d)u)}, \tag{3}$$

where

$$s = 3(a - d)^2 - 4(a + d - 2u^2)^2,$$

$$t = -16u(a + d - 2u^2) + \left((16u(a + d - 2u^2))^3 + 24 \cdot 4us^2\right)^{1/3}.$$

The expressions of x and y are constructed mainly by symmetrical property of twisted Edwards curves. The cost of x, y, s, and t are $I + 5M$, $2M$, $2S$, and $C + 3M + 2S$ respectively. The total cost of f is $C + I + 10M + 4S$ with precomputations and $C + I + 10M + 5S$ without precomputations. In the following, we will prove that the point (x, y) is on E.

Lemma 1. *Let $\mathbb{F}_q$ be a finite field where $q \equiv 2 \pmod 3$. For any $u \in \mathbb{F}_q$, $f(u)$ is a point of twisted Edwards curve $E_{a,d}(\mathbb{F}_q)$: $ax^2 + y^2 = 1 + dx^2y^2$, $a \neq d$, $ad \neq 0$.*

Proof. Let $M = 24(a - d)u$, $N = a + d - 2u^2$.

Since $t = -16uN + \left((16uN)^3 + 24 \cdot 4us^2\right)^{1/3}$, then

$$(t + 16uN)^3 = \left((16uN)^3 + 24 \cdot 4us^2\right).$$

Combing like terms, it follows $(a - d)t^3 + 2M[a + d - 2u^2]t^2 + M[(a - d)M - 8us]t - 4Ms^2 = 0$. Rearrange it and we obtain

$$at(t + M)^2 - 4M(ut + s)^2 = dt(t - M)^2.$$

Multiply by $\frac{t}{(ut+s)^2(t+M)^2}$ on each side of equation, then we gain $a(\frac{t}{ut+s})^2 - 2\frac{2M}{t+M} + (\frac{2M}{t+M})^2 = d(\frac{t}{ut+s})^2(\frac{t-M}{t+M})^2$. By rearranging, we obtain

$$a\left(\frac{t}{ut + s}\right)^2 + \left(1 - \frac{2M}{t + M}\right)^2 = 1 + d\left(\frac{t}{ut + s}\right)^2\left(\frac{t - M}{t + M}\right)^2,$$

which is $ax^2 + y^2 = 1 + dx^2y^2$. ∎

We show that the encoding f ia valid for any input u. The only three special cases are $u = 0$, $ut + s = 0$, and $t + 24(a - d)u = 0$. When $u = 0$, $f(u) = (0, 1)$; when $ut + s = 0$, $x = \infty$, then $a = d$, which is impossible; when $t + 24(a - d)u = 0$, $y = \infty$, then $a = d$, which is impossible. Thus, f is valid for any input u. For $f_{Icart}, f_{YuWang}, f_{Alasha}$ all have invalid input $u = 0$ whose image need to be given separately, thus our encoding is well.

Next, we will discuss the properties of f.

4 Properties of f

Lemma 2 is convenient for calculating $\#f^{-1}$ and the character sum of f.

Lemma 2. *Let P be a point on an Edwards curve E. The solutions of $f(u) = P$ are in the solutions of polynomial equation:*

$$H_{a,d}(u) = 16x(y-1)u^4 + [24(a-d)(y+1) - 16(y-1)(a+d)]xu^2$$
$$- 24(a-d)(y+1)u + x(y-1)(a^2 + d^2 + 14ad) = 0.$$

Proof. Let s and t be defined as in Eq. (3).

$$
\begin{cases}
ax^2 + y^2 = 1 + dx^2y^2 \\
16x(y-1)u^4 + [24(a-d)(y+1) - 16(y-1)(a+d)]xu^2 \\
\quad -24(a-d)(y+1)u + x(y-1)(a^2 + d^2 + 14ad) = 0
\end{cases}
$$

$$
\Leftrightarrow
\begin{cases}
ax^2 + y^2 = 1 + dx^2y^2 \\
x(1-y)\left[3(a-d)^2 - 4(a+d-2u^2)^2\right] \\
\quad = 24(a-d)u(1-xu)(y+1)
\end{cases}
$$

$$
\Leftrightarrow
\begin{cases}
ax^2 + y^2 = 1 + dx^2y^2 \\
xs(1-y) = 24(a-d)u(1-xu)(y+1)
\end{cases}
$$

$$
\Leftrightarrow
\begin{cases}
x = \frac{t}{ut+s} \\
xs(1-y) = 48(a-d)u(1-xu)
\end{cases}
\Leftrightarrow
\begin{cases}
x = \frac{t}{ut+s} \\
y = \frac{t-24(a-d)u}{t+24(a-d)u}.
\end{cases}
$$

∎

Lemma 2 leads to the following result.

Lemma 3. $f^{-1}(P)$ *is computable in polynomial time and* $\#f^{-1}(P) \leqslant 4$, *for all* $P \in E(\mathbb{F}_q)$.

Proof. Lemma 2 ensures that to compute f^{-1}, it is sufficient to solve a degree 4 equation over $\mathbb{F}_q$. Because solving polynomial equations of degree m over a finite field can be solved in $\mathcal{O}(m^2 \log^3 q)$ binary operations using the Berlekamp algorithm [29]. Thus, f^{-1} can be solved in polynomial time. Since the pre-images are solution of a degree 4 equation about u over $\mathbb{F}_q$, then there are at most 4 solutions for any point P. ∎

It is easy to check that this encoding f satisfies the 3 properties of Boneh-Franklin's identity-based scheme. Particularly, our encoding is 4-to-1 while f_{Icart}, f_{YuWang}, and f_{Alasha} are 4-to-1, 8-to-1, and 9-to-1 respectively.

Lemma 4. *The function $f_{a,d}$ can be implemented in deterministic polynomial time, with $\mathcal{O}(\log^3 q)$ running time and in a constant number of operations over $\mathbb{F}_q$.*

Proof. When $q \equiv 2 \pmod 3$, computing $x \mapsto x^{1/3}$ is an exponentiation with exponent $(2q - 1)/3$. This can be implemented in a constant number of operations over $\mathbb{F}_q$. We calculate f from $\mathbb{F}_q$ to twisted Edwards curves which mainly compute a cube root, about $\log q$ times multiplications. Thus the function f can be implemented in deterministic polynomial time, with $\mathcal{O}(\log^3 q)$ running time. The computation of $f(u)$ for any u needs the same operations over $\mathbb{F}_q$, then the function f can be implemented in a constant number of operations over $\mathbb{F}_q$. ∎

This map f satisfies the condition in [10] which requires that $\max_{P \in E} (\#f^{-1}(P))$ is a constant when constructing hash function into elliptic curves. Then $f(h(m))$ is a hash function if $h(m)$ is a classical hash function. Next, we prove that $f(h_1(m)) + f(h_2(m))$ is indifferentiable from a random oracle in the random oracle model for h_1 and h_2 by character sum.

4.1 Character Sum of f

Consider the graph of f:

$$C = \{(x, y, u) \in E \times \mathbb{P}^1(\overline{\mathbb{F}}_q) | f(u) = (x, y)\}$$
$$= \{(x, y, u) \in E \times \mathbb{P}^1(\overline{\mathbb{F}}_q) | H_{a,d}(u) = 0\}.$$

Now we calculate the genus of C. The projection $g : C \to E$ is a morphism of degree 4, hence the fiber at each point of E contains 4 points. The branch points are points (x, y) on E where $H_{a,d}$ has multiple roots, which means that its discriminant D vanishes at (x, y). By substituting $x^2 = -\frac{y^2-1}{a-dy^2}$ into D, it can be represented as

$$D = 2^{20} \cdot 3^2 \frac{(y^2 - 1)(P(y)x + Q(y))}{(dy^2 - a)^3},$$

where $P(y)$ is a polynomial of degree 8, $Q(y)$ is a sextic polynomial. By calculation, there are at most 20 different branch points on E, with ramification index 2. By Riemann-Hurwitz formula $2g_C - 2 \leqslant 4 \cdot (2 \cdot 1 - 2) + 20$, we get $g_C \leqslant 11$.

Definition 1 [7]. *Suppose f is an encoding from $\mathbb{F}_q$ into an elliptic curve E, χ is a character of $E(\mathbb{F}_q)$. We define the character sum*

$$S_f(\chi) = \sum_{s \in \mathbb{F}_q} \chi(f(s)).$$

And we say f is B-well-distributed if for any nontrivial character χ of $E(\mathbb{F}_q)$, the inequality $|S_f(\chi)| \leqslant B\sqrt{q}$ holds.

Lemma 5. *(See Corollary 2, Sect. 3, [7]). If $f : \mathbb{F}_q \to E(\mathbb{F}_q)$ is a B-well-distributed encoding into a curve E, then the statistical distance between the distribution defined by $f^{\otimes s}$ on $E(\mathbb{F}_q)$ and the uniform distribution is bounded as:*

$$\sum_{D \in E(\mathbb{F}_q)} |\frac{N_s(D)}{q^s} - \frac{1}{\#E(\mathbb{F}_q)}| \leqslant \frac{B^s}{q^{s/2}} \sqrt{\#E(\mathbb{F}_q)},$$

where

$$f^{\otimes s}(u_1, \ldots, u_s) = f(u_1) + \ldots + f(u_s),$$

$$N_s(D) = \#\{(u_1, \ldots, u_s) \in (\mathbb{F}_q)^s | D = f(u_1) + \ldots + f(u_s)\},$$

i.e., $N_s(D)$ is the size of preimage of D under $f^{\otimes s}$. In particular, when s is greater than the genus of E, the distribution defined by $f^{\otimes s}$ on $E(\mathbb{F}_q)$ is statistically indistinguishable from the uniform distribution. Especially, the hash function construction

$$m \mapsto f^{\otimes s}(h_1(m), \ldots, h_s(m)) \qquad (s = g_E + 1)$$

is indifferentiable from a random oracle if $h_1, \ldots, h_s$ are seen as independent random oracles into $\mathbb{F}_q$.

Next, we focus on the character sums of f.

Definition 2 (Artin Character). *Let X be an elliptic curve, $E(\mathbb{F}_q)$ is the Jacobian group of X. Let χ be a character of $E(\mathbb{F}_q)$. Extend χ to a multiplicative map $\overline{\chi} : Div_{\mathbb{F}_q}(X) \to \mathbb{C}$:*

$$\overline{\chi}(n(P)) = \begin{cases} \chi(P)^n, & P \in S \\ 0, & P \notin S, \end{cases}$$

S is a finite point set on $E(\mathbb{F}_q)$, usually denotes the ramification locus of a morphism $Y \to X$. Then we call $\overline{\chi}$ an Artin character of X.

Theorem 1. *Let $h : \tilde{X} \to X$ be a nonconstant morphism of projective curves, and χ an Artin character of X. Suppose that $h^*\chi$ is unramified and nontrivial, then*

$$|\sum_{P \in \tilde{X}(\mathbb{F}_q)} \chi(h(P))| \leqslant (2\tilde{g} - 2)\sqrt{q}.$$

Proof. See Theorem 3, [7]. ∎

Theorem 2. *Let f be the deterministic encoding from $\mathbb{F}_q$ to E. For any nontrivial character χ of $E(\mathbb{F}_q)$, the character sum $S_f(\chi)$ satisfies:*

$$S_f(\chi) \leqslant 20\sqrt{q} + 2.$$

Proof. Since the genus of the curve C is at most 11, by Theorem 1, we have

$$|S_f(\chi) + \sum_{P \in C(\mathbb{F}_q), u(P) = \infty} \chi \circ h(P)| = |\sum_{P \in C(\mathbb{F}_q)} \chi \circ h(P)|$$

$$\leqslant (2 \cdot 11 - 2)\sqrt{q} = 20\sqrt{q}.$$

It is easy to show that u has 2 poles, then $S_f(\chi) \leqslant 20\sqrt{q} + 2$. ∎

By Lemma 5, $S_f(\chi) \leqslant 20\sqrt{q} + 2$, then $f(h_1(m)) + f(h_2(m))$ is indifferentiable from a random oracle in the random oracle model for h_1 and h_2.

4.2   Calculating the Sizes of Images of f

Apply Chebotarev density theorem onto twisted Edwards curves, we give the sizes of the images of f.

Lemma 6 (Chebotarev [28]). *Let K be an extension of $\mathbb{F}_q(x)$ of degree $n < \infty$ and L be a Galois extension of K of degree $m < \infty$. Assume that $\mathbb{F}_q$ is algebraically closed in L, and fix some subset φ of $Gal(L/K)$ stable under conjugation. Let $s = \#\varphi$ and $N(\varphi)$ be the number of places v of K of degree 1, unramified in L, such that the Artin symbol $\left(\dfrac{L/K}{v}\right)$ (defined up to conjugation) is in φ. Then*

$$|N(\varphi) - \frac{s}{m}q| \leqslant \frac{2s}{m}((m + g_L) \cdot q^{1/2} + m(2g_K + 1) \cdot q^{1/4} + g_L + nm)$$

where g_K and g_L are genera of the function fields of K and L respectively.

Theorem 3. *Let E be the twisted Edwards curve over $\mathbb{F}_q$ defined by equation $ax^2 + y^2 = 1 + dx^2y^2, ad \neq 0, a \neq d$. Then*

$$|\#Im(f) - \frac{5}{8}\#E(\mathbb{F}_q)| \leqslant \frac{5}{4}(31q^{1/2} + 72q^{1/4} + 67).$$

Proof. K is the function field of E which is a quadratic extension of $\mathbb{F}_q(x)$, hence $n = 2$, and by the property of elliptic curves, $g_K = 1$.

In the case that $Gal(L/K) = S_4, m = \#S_4 = 24$. φ is the subset of $Gal(L/K)$ consisting at least one point, which are conjugates of $(1)(2)(3)(4), (12)(3)(4)$ and $(123)(4)$, then $s = 1 + 6 + 8 = 15$. Since the places v of K of degree 1 correspond to the projective unramified points on $E(\mathbb{F}_q)$, hence $|\#Im(f) - \#E(\mathbb{F}_q)| \leqslant 12 + 2 = 14$, where 2 represents the number of infinite points on E, 12 represents the number of branch points. Then we have

$$|\#Im(f) - \frac{5}{8}q| \leqslant |\#Im(f) - N(\varphi)| + |N(\varphi) - \frac{5}{8}q|$$

$$\leqslant 14 + \frac{5}{4}(31q^{1/2} + 72q^{1/4} + 55)$$

$$< \frac{5}{4}(31q^{1/2} + 72q^{1/4} + 67).$$

∎

5   Comparisons

Now, we compare f with f_{Icart}, f_{YuWang}, and f_{Alasha}. Miracl lib [30] is used to implement big number arithmetic. The experiments are tested on an Intel Core 2, 2.66 GHz processor where $S = M$, $I = 18.5M$, and $C = 33M$.

Table 1. Time cost of different deterministic encodings with precomputations

Encoding	Cost	Time(μs)
f_{Icart}	$C + 2I + 10M + 3S = 83M$	174.6
f_{YuWang}	$C + 2I + 11M + 3S = 84M$	179.2
f_{Alasha}	$C + 3I + 11M + 6S = 105.5M$	219.5
f	$C + I + 10M + 4S = 65.5M$	139.4

The cost of different deterministic encodings into twisted Edward curves with precomputations are summarized in Table 1. With precomputations, our encoding f saves $17.5M$ compared with f_{Icart}; $18.5M$ compared with f_{YuWang}; and $40M$ compared with f_{Alasha} which means that f is 21.1 % faster than f_{Icart}, 22.0 % faster than f_{YuWang}, 37.9 % faster than f_{Alasha}. We ran every deterministic encoding 10,000 times using different inputs over different 256 bit prime fields and gained the average value shown in Table 1. Practical implementations show that, with precomputations, f is 20.2 % faster than f_{Icart}, 22.2 % faster than f_{YuWang}, 36.5 % faster than f_{Alasha}.

Table 2. Time cost of different deterministic encodings without precomputation

Encoding	Cost	Time(μs)
f_{Icart}	$C + 4I + 13M + 5S = 125M$	262.3
f_{YuWang}	$C + 3I + 12M + 3S = 103.5M$	219.8
f_{Alasha}	$C + 3I + 13M + 8S = 109.5M$	231.2
f	$C + I + 10M + 5S = 66.5M$	141.3

The cost of different deterministic encodings into twisted Edward curves without precomputations are summarized in Table 2. From Table 2, our deterministic encoding costs 58.5 field multiplications less than f_{Icart}; costs 37 field multiplications less than f_{YuWang}; 43 field multiplications less than f_{Alasha} which mean that f is 46.8 % faster than f_{Icart}, 35.7 % faster than f_{YuWang}, 39.3 % faster than f_{Alasha}. We ran every deterministic encoding 10,000 times using different inputs over different 256 bit prime fields and gained the average value shown in Table 2. Practical implementations show that f is 46.1 % faster than f_{Icart}, 35.7 % faster than f_{YuWang}, 38.9 % faster than f_{Alasha}.

The results of practical implementations have some mistakes with theoretical analyses for that we disregard field additions/subtractions and discard multiplications/divisions by small constants in theoretical analyses. Within the bounds of the errors, the practical implementations is consistent with these analyses. The theoretical analyses and practical implementations both show that f is fastest among existing encodings from finite fields into twisted Edward curves.

6   Conclusion

We have provided an encoding f that encodes an element of a finite field $\mathbb{F}_q$ into twisted Edwards curves in a constant number of field operation when $q \equiv 2$ (mod 3). For any nontrivial character χ of $E(\mathbb{F}_q)$, the character sum $S_f(\chi)$ satisfies: $S_f(\chi) \leqslant 20\sqrt{q} + 2$. As an application, $f(h_1(m)) + f(h_2(m))$ is indifferentiable from a random oracle in the random oracle model for h_1 and h_2. f is fastest among existing deterministic encodings into twisted Edwards curves including f, f_{Icart}, f_{YuWang}, and f_{Alasha} not only in theoretical analyses but also in practice.

References

1. Schoof, R.: Elliptic curves over finite fields and the computation of square roots mod p. Math. Comp. **44**(170), 483–494 (1985)
2. Boneh, D., Franklin, M.: Identity-based encryption from the weil pairing. In: Kilian, J. (ed.) CRYPTO 2001. LNCS, vol. 2139, pp. 213–229. Springer, Heidelberg (2001)
3. Boneh, D., Gentry, C., Lynn, B., Shacham, H.: Aggregate and verifiably encrypted signatures from bilinear maps. In: Biham, E. (ed.) EUROCRYPT 2003. LNCS, vol. 2656, pp. 416–432. Springer, Heidelberg (2003)
4. Boyen, X.: Multipurpose identity-based signcryption. In: Boneh, D. (ed.) CRYPTO 2003. LNCS, vol. 2729, pp. 383–399. Springer, Heidelberg (2003)
5. Lindell, Y.: Highly-efficient universally-composable commitments based on the DDH assumption. In: Paterson, K.G. (ed.) EUROCRYPT 2011. LNCS, vol. 6632, pp. 446–466. Springer, Heidelberg (2011)
6. Brier, E., Coron, J.-S., Icart, T., Madore, D., Randriam, H., Tibouchi, M.: Efficient indifferentiable hashing into ordinary elliptic curves. In: Rabin, T. (ed.) CRYPTO 2010. LNCS, vol. 6223, pp. 237–254. Springer, Heidelberg (2010)
7. Farashahi, R.R., Fouque, P.-A., Shparlinski, I.E., Tibouchi, M., Voloch, J.F.: Indifferentiable deterministic hashing to elliptic and hyperelliptic curves. Math. Comp. **82**, 491–512 (2013)
8. Shallue, A., van de Woestijne, C.E.: Construction of rational points on elliptic curves over finite fields. In: Hess, F., Pauli, S., Pohst, M. (eds.) ANTS 2006. LNCS, vol. 4076, pp. 510–524. Springer, Heidelberg (2006)
9. Skalba, M.: Points on elliptic curves over finite fields. Acta Arith. **117**, 293–301 (2005)
10. Icart, T.: How to hash into elliptic curves. In: Halevi, S. (ed.) CRYPTO 2009. LNCS, vol. 5677, pp. 303–316. Springer, Heidelberg (2009)
11. M, U.: Rational points on certain hyperelliptic curves over finite fields. Bull. Polish Acad. Sci. Math. **55**, 97–104 (2007)

12. Fouque, P.-A., Tibouchi, M.: Deterministic encoding and hashing to odd hyperelliptic curves. In: Joye, M., Miyaji, A., Otsuka, A. (eds.) Pairing 2010. LNCS, vol. 6487, pp. 265–277. Springer, Heidelberg (2010)

13. Farashahi, R.R.: Hashing into hessian curves. In: Nitaj, A., Pointcheval, D. (eds.) AFRICACRYPT 2011. LNCS, vol. 6737, pp. 278–289. Springer, Heidelberg (2011)

14. Yu, W., Wang, K., Li, B., Tian, S.: About hash into montgomery form elliptic curves. In: Deng, R.H., Feng, T. (eds.) ISPEC 2013. LNCS, vol. 7863, pp. 147–159. Springer, Heidelberg (2013)

15. Yu, W., Wang, K., Li, B., He, X., Tian, S.: Hashing into jacobi quartic curves. In: López, J., Mitchell, C.J. (eds.) ISC 2015. LNCS, vol. 9290, pp. 355–375. Springer, Heidelberg (2015)

16. Edwards, H.M.: A normal form for elliptic curves. Bull. Am. Math. Soc. **44**, 393–422 (2007)

17. Kocher, P.C.: Timing attacks on implementations of diffie-hellman, RSA, DSS, and other systems. In: Koblitz, N. (ed.) CRYPTO 1996. LNCS, vol. 1109, pp. 104–113. Springer, Heidelberg (1996)

18. Bernstein, D.J., Lange, T.: Faster addition and doubling on elliptic curves. In: Kurosawa, K. (ed.) ASIACRYPT 2007. LNCS, vol. 4833, pp. 29–50. Springer, Heidelberg (2007)

19. Bernstein, D.J., Lange, T.: Inverted edwards coordinates. In: Boztaş, S., Lu, H.-F.F. (eds.) AAECC 2007. LNCS, vol. 4851, pp. 20–27. Springer, Heidelberg (2007)

20. Bernstein, D.J., Birkner, P., Joye, M., Lange, T., Peters, C.: Twisted edwards curves. In: Vaudenay, S. (ed.) AFRICACRYPT 2008. LNCS, vol. 5023, pp. 389–405. Springer, Heidelberg (2008)

21. Hisil, H., Wong, K.K.-H., Carter, G., Dawson, E.: Twisted edwards curves revisited. In: Pieprzyk, J. (ed.) ASIACRYPT 2008. LNCS, vol. 5350, pp. 326–343. Springer, Heidelberg (2008)

22. Blake, I.F., Murty, V.K., Xu, G.: Refinements of miller's algorithm for computing the weil/tate pairing. J. Algorithms **58**(2), 134–149 (2006)

23. Ionica, S., Joux, A.: Another approach to pairing computation in edwards coordinates. In: Chowdhury, D.R., Rijmen, V., Das, A. (eds.) INDOCRYPT 2008. LNCS, vol. 5365, pp. 400–413. Springer, Heidelberg (2008)

24. Arne, C., Lange, T., Naehrig, M., Ritzenthaler, C.: Faster computation of the tate pairing. J. Number Theor. **131**(5), 842–857 (2011)

25. Le, D., Tan, C.: Improved miller's algorithm for computing pairings on edwards curves. IEEE Trans. Comput. **63**(10), 2626–2632 (2014)

26. Yu, W., Wang, K.: How to hash into twisted edwards form elliptic curves. In: Information Security and Cryptology, Inscrypt 2010, pp. 35–43. Science press (2011)

27. Alasha, T.: Constant-time encoding points on elliptic curve of diffierent forms over finite fields (2012). http://iml.univ-mrs.fr/editions/preprint2012/files/tammam_alasha-IML_paper_2012.pdf

28. Fouque, P.-A., Tibouchi, M.: Estimating the size of the image of deterministic hash functions to elliptic curves. In: Abdalla, M., Barreto, P.S.L.M. (eds.) LATINCRYPT 2010. LNCS, vol. 6212, pp. 81–91. Springer, Heidelberg (2010)

29. Shoup, V.: A new polynomial factorization algorithm and its implementation. J. Symb. Comput. **20**(4), 363–397 (1995)

30. miracl: Multiprecision Integer and Rational Arithmetic Cryptographic Library. http://www.shamus.ie

Symmetric Cipher

Improved Rebound Attacks on AESQ: Core Permutation of CAESAR Candidate PAEQ

Nasour Bagheri[1], Florian Mendel[2], and Yu Sasaki[3(✉)]

[1] IPM, SRTTU, Tehran, Iran
nbagheri@srttu.edu
[2] Graz University of Technology, Graz, Austria
florian.mendel@iaik.tugraz.at
[3] NTT Secure Platform Laboratories, Tokyo, Japan
sasaki.yu@lab.ntt.co.jp

Abstract. In this paper, we present improved rebound attacks against AESQ permutation that is an underlying permutation of PAEQ authenticated encryption scheme currently discussed in the second round of the CAESAR competition. AESQ is an AES-based permutation. Designers claim that no attack should be found with complexity up to 2^{256} and they have shown a rebound attack against 12 (out of 20) rounds with 2^{256} computational cost and 2^{256} memory. In this paper, we present the first third-party cryptanalysis on AESQ. First, we reduce the complexity of the 12-round attack to 2^{128} computational cost and negligible memory. We then extend the number of rounds and present a 16-round attack with 2^{192} computational cost and 2^{128} memory. Moreover, we discuss time-memory tradeoffs and multiple limited birthday distinguishers. In particular, the time-memory tradeoff is useful for the 12-round attack, which allows us to balance the time and memory complexities to $2^{102.4}$.

Keywords: CAESAR · PAEQ · AESQ · Permutation · Authenticated encryption · Rebound attack

1 Introduction

Motivation. Authenticated encryption (AE) describes an important class of cryptographic algorithms with many applications in information security. It provides both confidentiality and authentication of data to two parties communicating via an insecure channel. This is essential for many applications such as SSL/TLS, IPSEC, SSH or hard disk encryption.

However, the security and performance of many of these current approaches is often not satisfying. This situation has inspired new efforts in the design and analysis of authenticated ciphers in the last years. This is also reflected by the ongoing CAESAR competition [1] that aims to select a portfolio of authenticated ciphers with many advantages over current solutions. During the ongoing security evaluation in CAESAR, not only the classical security requirements are

© Springer International Publishing Switzerland 2016
J.K. Liu and R. Steinfeld (Eds.): ACISP 2016, Part II, LNCS 9723, pp. 301–316, 2016.
DOI: 10.1007/978-3-319-40367-0_19

considered. Researchers look at the building block and reduced variants of ciphers to get a good view on the security margins of the authenticated encryptions.

In this paper, we analyse the second-round CAESAR candidate PAEQ [2]. PAEQ is fully parallelizable and uses a 512-bit wide AES based permutation as its core, called AESQ. The only operations that are used in AESQ are AES-round function and some word shuffling. Hence, it can benefit from the Intel Advanced Encryption Standard New Instructions (AES-NI) and it is expected to provide good performance in such platforms.

Security of PAEQ was proven in a random permutation model, thus identifying non-random behaviors of the underlying AESQ permutation has non-negligible impact. In fact, the designers explicitly make a security claim for AESQ; no attack against AESQ exists with complexity below 2^{256}. Besides, the designers' security claim for PAEQ (with the primary choice of the design parameter; 128-bit key and 128-bit tag) is up to 128 bits. Thus discussing attacks with complexity below 2^{128} is of independent interest.

In this work, we present the first third-party security analysis of AESQ. We investigate the security of AESQ against rebound attack [16]. Although the designers also have analysed the security of this permutation against rebound attack, we present attacks that cover more rounds with less computational cost and less memory requirement compared to their results.

Related Work. Although PAEQ is a second-round candidate of CAESAR, no third-party security analysis has been published so far. On the other hand, rebound attack [16] has been widely used to analyse several AES based schemes, e.g. Grøstl [16,17], Whirlpool [12,13] and Kupyna [4]. Moreover, the rebound attack has also been applied to AES-based permutation combining multiple AES states, e.g. LANE [14], 3D [5] and ECHO [8,11,15,18,19,21]. This motivated us to investigate the security of AESQ against rebound attack.

Designers of PAEQ have applied rebound attack to AESQ. AESQ has 20 rounds and they showed that the complexity of the rebound attack on 12 rounds (starting from Round 2) of AESQ almost matches its security claim, i.e. the complexity of their rebound attack has time and memory complexity of 2^{256}. One drawback of their attack is that the complexity to satisfy the same property against a random permutation is 2^{257}, thus the gain is very small.

Our Contribution. In this paper we provide several improvement over the designers' analysis of AESQ. First, we reduce the complexity of the previous 12-round rebound attack, starting from Round 2, to the time complexity of 2^{128} and negligible memory, this should be compared to the designers' attack with time complexity of 2^{256} and memory complexity of 2^{256}. Due to this improvement, the gain of the attack compared to the complexity against a random permutation, 2^{257}, becomes huge. Moreover, we employ time-memory tradeoff of this attack in order to reduce min{Time, Memory} to below 2^{128}, which is the claimed security of PAEQ authenticated encryption. With the tradeoff, we can balance the time and memory complexities to improve min{Time, Memory} to $2^{102.4}$.

Second, 16-round rebound attack, starting from Round 2, with time complexity of 2^{192} and memory complexity of 2^{128} is presented, while the complexity against a random permutation is 2^{257}. We then apply multiple limited birthday distinguishers [10] to reduce its time complexity from 2^{192} to 2^{188}.

The 12-round attack provided by the designers and our 16-round attack need to start from Round 2. We point our that we can start from Round 1 by cutting the first round of those attacks, which leads to a 15-round attack with the same complexity as the 16-round attack.

A summary of our results and the designers' analysis are presented in Table 1. Our attacks cannot be applied to full rounds of AESQ. Thus the security of AESQ is not threatened with our attacks.

Table 1. Summary of attacks. All attacks in the list start from Round 2. 15-round attacks (Round 1–15) can be achieved by removing the first round of 16-round attacks.

Rounds	Time	Memory	Remarks	Reference
12	2^{256}	2^{256}	standard attack	[2]
	2^{128}	negligible	standard attack	Sect. 4.1
	$2^{102.4}$	$2^{102.4}$	time-memory tradeoff	Sect. 5.1
	$2^{128-x/4}$	2^{x}	time-memory tradeoff	Sect. 5.1
16	2^{192}	2^{128}	standard attack	Sect. 4.2
	2^{188}	2^{128}	multi limited-birthday dist	Sect. 4.4
	2^{192+x}	2^{128-x}	time-memory tradeoff	Sect. 5.2

Outline. The rest of the paper is organized as follows. In Sect. 2, we describe PAEQ and AESQ as much as necessary for our analysis and explain basic concept of rebound attacks. In Sect. 3, we describe the only known rebound attack on 12-round AESQ in detail. Our improved rebound attacks are described in Sect. 4. In Sect. 5, we present time-memory tradeoff for rebound attacks. Finally, we provide the closing remarks in Sect. 6.

2 Preliminaries

2.1 Description of AESQ

The AESQ permutation was designed by Biryukov and Khovratovich as an underlying primitive of an authenticated encryption scheme PAEQ [2], which is currently evaluated as one of the second round candidates of CAESAR.

The encryption of PAEQ looks like a counter mode with a big permutation. Let ctr_i, N and K be a counter value for block i, nonce and key, respectively. Those are processed by AESQ and 128 bits are extracted as a keystream, ks. Namely $ks \leftarrow trunc128(\mathrm{AESQ}(ctr_i\|N\|K))$, where $trunc128(\cdot)$ is a 128-bit truncation. Ciphertext C_i for message M_i is computed by $C_i \leftarrow M_i \oplus ks$. Owing to this computation structure, non-random behaviors of AESQ may directly appear in the ciphertext. Moreover, the designers of PAEQ proved its security by assuming that the underlying permutation is a random permutation. Thus AESQ takes an important role to ensure the security of PAEQ.

AESQ Round Function. AESQ is a 512-bit permutation based on AES [3]. Its computation consists of the following three operations.

- four parallel computations of AES round function
- constant addition
- a operation called "Shuffle" to mix data from four different AES states.

The AES round function will be explained later in this section. Constant addition XORs a predefined 8-bit constant to four bytes in each of 128-bit AES states. Because constant addition is irrelevant to rebound attack discussed in this paper, we omit its details. The Shuffle operation exchanges each column of four AES states. Let A, B, C, D be four AES states and $A[j], B[j], C[j], D[j], j = 0, 1, 2, 3$ be four columns of each state. Then, column positions are exchanged with Shuffle as follows.

from	$A[0]$ $A[1]$ $A[2]$ $A[3]$	$B[0]$ $B[1]$ $B[2]$ $B[3]$	$C[0]$ $C[1]$ $C[2]$ $C[3]$	$D[0]$ $D[1]$ $D[2]$ $D[3]$
to	$A[3]$ $D[3]$ $C[2]$ $B[2]$	$A[1]$ $D[1]$ $C[0]$ $B[0]$	$A[2]$ $D[2]$ $C[3]$ $B[3]$	$A[0]$ $D[0]$ $C[1]$ $B[1]$

AESQ consists of 20 rounds.[1] In short, four AES states are independently updated by iterating the AES round function and constant addition twice (this operation corresponds to two rounds), and then columns of four AES states are exchanged with the Shuffle operation. This is iterated 10 times, which makes the entire computation 20 rounds. The constant for the $(2i + j)$-th round and the k-th AES state, $i \in \{1, 2, \ldots, 10\}, j \in \{1, 2\}, k \in \{1, 2, 3, 4\}$ is denoted by $Q_{i,j,k}$. Illustration for two rounds of AESQ is given in Fig. 1 and algorithmic representation of the entire AESQ is given in Algorithm 1.

AES Round Function. AESQ uses AES round function without key to mix a 128-bit data. Firstly, 128-bit input is loaded to the state represented as a 4×4 byte-array.

Let S_i^I be an input state to the AES round function in round i. Then, the state is updated by the following three operations.

SubBytes $S_i^{SB} \leftarrow \text{SB}(S_i^I)$: Apply an 8-bit S-box to each byte of the state.
ShifttRows $S_i^{SR} \leftarrow \text{SR}(S_i^{SB})$: Rotate byte positions in row j to left by j bytes.
MixColumns $S_i^{MC} \leftarrow \text{MC}(S_i^{SR})$: Apply a multiplication with an MDS matrix to each column.

Here, we omit the exact specification of the S-box and the MDS matrix, which can be found in [3]. S_i^{MC} is the output of the AES round function in Round i.

---

[1] The designers starts the round index from 0, while we start from 1 in this paper.

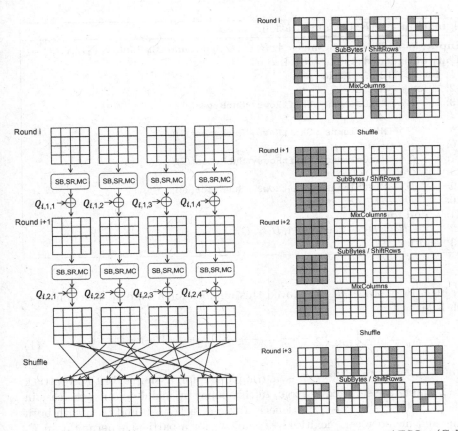

Fig. 1. Two rounds of AESQ.

Fig. 2. MegaSBox in AESQ. (Color figure online)

Security Claim of AESQ. In [2, Sect. 3.2.2], the designers explicitly claim 256-bit security of AESQ against all attacks. Namely, any attack with complexity below 2^{256} should not exist.

2.2 Limited Birthday Problem and Rebound Attack

Limited birthday problem [6] on an n-bit permutation $P(\cdot)$ first defines a subspace of the input difference, $\mathcal{I} \subset \{0,1\}^n$, and a subspace of the output difference, $\mathcal{O} \subset \{0,1\}^n$. The attacker's goal is finding a pair of input values i_1, i_2 such that $i_1 \oplus i_2 \in \mathcal{I}$ and $P(i_1) \oplus P(i_2) \in \mathcal{O}$ more efficiently than finding such i_1, i_2 for a random permutation. More precisely, for a given $|\mathcal{I}|$ and $|\mathcal{O}|$, the number of queries N_q that the attacker needs to make to find the above i_1, i_2 for random permutation is determined. Here, we mean by random permutation the one chosen uniformly at random from a set of all permutations having the same domain

---

Algorithm 1. AESQ Computation.

1 **Input**: four 128-bit state values A, B, C, D and round constant $Q_{i,j,1}, \ldots, Q_{i,j,4}$
2 **Output**: updated state values A, B, C, D
  1: **for** $i = 1, 2, \ldots, 10$ **do**
  2:    **for** $j = 1, 2$ **do**
  3:       $A \leftarrow \texttt{MixColumns} \circ \texttt{ShiftRows} \circ \texttt{SubBytes}(A)$;
  4:       $A \leftarrow A \oplus Q_{i,j,1}$;
  5:       $B \leftarrow \texttt{MixColumns} \circ \texttt{ShiftRows} \circ \texttt{SubBytes}(B)$;
  6:       $B \leftarrow B \oplus Q_{i,j,2}$;
  7:       $C \leftarrow \texttt{MixColumns} \circ \texttt{ShiftRows} \circ \texttt{SubBytes}(C)$;
  8:       $C \leftarrow C \oplus Q_{i,j,3}$;
  9:       $D \leftarrow \texttt{MixColumns} \circ \texttt{ShiftRows} \circ \texttt{SubBytes}(D)$;
 10:      $D \leftarrow D \oplus Q_{i,j,4}$;
 11:   **end for**
 12:   $(A, B, C, D) \leftarrow \texttt{Shuffle}(A, B, C, D)$;
 13: **end for**

---

and range. Iwamoto *et al.* [7] proved this number for a random function case, which is given by

$$N_q = \max\left\{\min\left\{2^{\frac{n-\log|\mathcal{I}|}{2}}, 2^{\frac{n-\log|\mathcal{O}|}{2}}\right\}, 2^{n-\log|\mathcal{I}|-\log|\mathcal{O}|+1}\right\}. \tag{1}$$

$\min\{2^{(n-\log|\mathcal{I}|)/2}, 2^{(n-\log|\mathcal{O}|)/2}\}$ is a complexity for a simple birthday attack where $\mathcal{I}$ and $\mathcal{O}$ are sufficiently large. In this paper we mainly discuss the case in which $2^{n-\log|\mathcal{I}|-\log|\mathcal{O}|+1}$ is a bottleneck. If the attacker can find i_1, i_2 with both of time and memory complexities less than N_q for a particular permutation P, then P is regarded to have a non-random property. Note that the generic complexity of limited-birthday distinguishers against a random permutation is an open problem, while the current best attack complexity matches (1).

Rebound attack [16] is the attacker's approach to efficiently satisfy a type of truncated differential of the target algorithm P. The rebound attack divides P into three parts, $P_{pre}, P_{mid}, P_{post}$, such that

$$P = P_{post} \circ P_{mid} \circ P_{pre}. \tag{2}$$

Then, the attacker searches for the paired values satisfying the differential with a two-stage procedure called *inbound phase* and *outbound phase*.

Inbound Phase. The attacker first determines the differential propagation from the beginning of P_{mid} to the end of P_{mid}. In general, the differential propagation through P_{mid} is dense, i.e. most of internal state bytes are active. This is because the differences at the beginning and the end of P_{mid} are chosen in order to optimize the differential propagation in the outbound phase.

Then, the attacker searches for paired values satisfying the differential propagation through P_{mid}. At this stage, the internal state value is not fixed, thus the attacker can control the differential propagation by choosing the value, in other words, by utilizing the freedom degrees of the internal state value.

Outbound Phase. After the inbound phase, no freedom degrees remain in the internal state value, thus the attacker simply propagates each pair generated in the inbound phase through P_{pre} and P_{post} and expects that the differential propagation is probabilistically satisfied. In general, the differential propagation in the outbound phase is built so that $|\mathcal{I}|$ and $|\mathcal{O}|$ can be small. In the end, if the cost of the inbound and outbound phases are smaller than N_q given by Eq. (1), the attack succeeds.

3 Previous rebound attack on AESQ

So far the only cryptanalytic result against AESQ is the rebound attack shown by the designers [2], which can identify a non-random differential behavior of AESQ reduced to 12 rounds (starting from Round 2 and end with Round 13) with a complexity of 2^{256} computational cost and memory to store 2^{256} AESQ state values. The analysis uses the fact that the middle 3.5 rounds of AESQ can be separated into four 128-bit independent computations. Each of four independent computations is called MegaSBox.

3.1 MegaSBox

MegaSBox is a 128-bit computation through 3.5 rounds that is independent from other 384 bits of the state. More precisely, a MegaSBox covers 3.5 rounds starting from middle of two consecutive AES-round applications, i.e., it covers AES round function, Shuffle, AES round function, AES round function, Shuffle and AES round function without MixColumns. MegaSBox is illustrated in Fig. 2. In Fig. 2, colored bytes show the 16 bytes involved in a MegaSBox. We show the result of applying ShiftRows and MixColumns in different states. Constant addition is removed from the figure for the sake of simplicity.

Set up: We first focus on 16 bytes at the input to Round i, in which 4 bytes in each of 4 AES states are located in a diagonal position.

Round i: Those diagonal 4 bytes in each AES state can be processed by the AES round function independently from the other 12 bytes due to a well-known property of AES. After 1 round, the focused 4 bytes moved to one column.

Shuffle: The subsequent Shuffle operation collects 4 columns in different AES states into the same AES state. The diagonal positions in the set up phase must be chosen so that all 16 bytes can gather in one AES state here.

Round $i + 1$ and $i + 2$: During those rounds, all focused bytes are in the same AES state, thus the AES round function can be computed independently from the other AES states.

Shuffle and Round $i + 3$: 4 columns in an AES state are separated into 4 different AES states with Shuffle. The 4 bytes in each AES state are further separated into different columns with ShiftRows in Round $i + 3$, then no more independent computation can be performed.

In the end, 3.5-round computation on the 512-bit state can be separated into four independent 128-bit MegaSBox. This property is heavily exploited in the rebound attack on AESQ.

3.2   Previous 12-Round Rebound Attack on AESQ

The previous 12-round rebound attack covers from Round 2 to Round 13. The inbound phase P_{mid} covers from Round 6 to Round 8.5, which is composed of a single MegaSBox layer. The outbound phase P_{pre} covers backward computation from Round 5 to Round 2 (4 rounds) and P_{post} covers forward computation from Round 8.5 to Round 12 (4.5 rounds).

Truncated Differential. The rebound attack starts from choosing a truncated differential so that the outbound phase can be optimized. The truncated differential is depicted in Fig. 3, which will be explained below.

P_{pre} and P_{post} are chosen so that all active bytes are located in a single AES state in the middle 2 rounds of P_{pre} and P_{post}. This fixes the truncated differential at the state after applying ShiftRows and before applying MixColumns in Round 5 (S_5^{SR}) so that 4 bytes in the inverse diagonal of each AES state are active. Because MixColumns is linear, this also fixes the truncated differential at the beginning of P_{mid}, i.e. $\Delta S_6^{I} = \text{MixColumns}(\Delta S_5^{SR})$. Therefore, though S_6^{I} are active in all bytes, the number of differences at S_6^{I} is up to 2^{128}.

The same is applied for P_{post} and the end of P_{mid}. S_{10}^{I} has active bytes in the diagonal of each AES state and this is propagated with MC^{-1}, which makes S_9^{SR} all active but the number of differences is up to 2^{128}.

Inbound Phase. The inbound phase P_{mid} covers from Round 6 to Round 8.5 consisting of 4 parallel computations of MegaSBox. In the previous attack [2], the difference at the beginning (ΔS_6^{I}) and the end (ΔS_9^{SR}) are chosen. Then, the goal of the inbound phase is finding paired values satisfying those two differences. In order to find such values, the attacker first constructs differential distribution table (DDT) of each MegaSBox. Once DDT is constructed, the attacker knows which pair of input and output differences can have solutions along with exact paired values. Therefore, the attacker first chooses difference ΔS_6^{I} and ΔS_9^{SR} so that they can have solutions. Then, paired values satisfying the differences can be obtained with a single table look-up.

Constructing a DDT for an n-bit S-box requires 2^{2n} computations and 2^{2n} memory. Therefore, constructing DDTs for 128-bit MegaSBox requires 2^{256} computations and 2^{256} memory. Note that four MegaSBox are different due to the different constant addition. Thus, four different DDTs need to be constructed.

Also note that 1 `MegaSBox` is a quoter of the whole state, thus making 4 DDTs is not evaluated to require the cost of $4 \cdot 2^{256}$ AESQ computations.

Outbound Phase and Comparison with Random Permutation. Outbound phase is a simple differential propagation with probability 1. Thus as soon as a pair of values satisfying the inbound phase is obtained, they also satisfy the outbound phase. As a result of outbound phase, the input difference has 16 active bytes and the subspace of the output difference is limited to 16 bytes.

From Eq. (1), satisfying those input and output differences against a random permutation requires $2^{512-128-128+1} = 2^{257}$ queries. Meanwhile, for AESQ, this property can be detected with complexity 2^{256} which is a cost for generating DDTs in the inbound phase. Because the cost for AESQ is smaller than the random permutation case, the attack is valid (but a gain is very small; 1-bit).

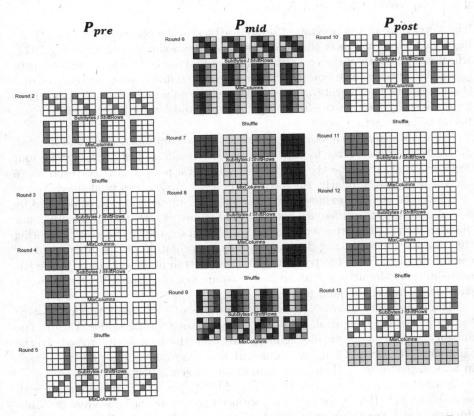

Fig. 3. Previous 12-round rebound attack on AESQ [2]. Colored bytes are active. Four colors correspond to four `MegaSBox`, which can be computed independently. The last state is fully active, but the number of differences, $\mathcal{O}$, is limited to 2^{128}. (Color figure online)

Note that the number of claimed security bits for AESQ by the designers is 256, thus it is unclear if the attack with complexity 2^{256} reveals undesired property of 12-round AESQ.

4   Improved Rebound Attacks on AESQ

First, we significantly reduce the complexity of the previous 12-round attack by improving the inbound phase. Then we extend the attack to 16 rounds by identifying best differential propagation for the outbound phase. We then discuss the application of multiple limited birthday distinguishers on 16-round attack, to make the attack complexity lower. Finally, we give some remarks on the choice of differential propagation in our 16-round attack.

4.1   Improved 12-Round Attack

The bottleneck of the previous 12-round attack is the construction of DDT for MegaSBox. Here, we show that the attack can be mounted without using DDT, which reduces both of the computational cost and memory amount significantly.

In the attack we use exactly the same truncated differential, and only change the procedure to generate a pair to satisfy the inbound part. The idea is to generate such a pair on-the-fly for a given input and output differences for P_{mid}. It can be summarized as follows.

First, the attacker chooses the difference at the beginning, ΔS_6^{I}, and the end, ΔS_9^{SR}. Next, the attacker focuses on a single MegaSBox. Let α, β, γ, δ be four MegaSBox and $\Delta S_6^{\mathrm{I}}|_\alpha$ be the 128-bit difference of a part of ΔS_6^{I} corresponds to the 128 bits of α. Similarly, the output difference $\Delta S_9^{\mathrm{SR}}|_\alpha$ can be defined.

Then, the attacker exhaustively examines 2^{128} input values to α, denoted by x, and computes the difference between $\alpha(x)$ and $\alpha(x \oplus \Delta S_6^{\mathrm{I}}|_\alpha)$. If this difference matches $\Delta S_9^{\mathrm{SR}}|_\alpha$, the attacker obtains the solution for 128 bits of α. By repeating this also for the MegaSBox β, γ and δ, a 512-bit solution of the inbound phase can be obtained. Since the truncated differential trail in the outbound phase has probability 1, the attacker immediately completes the attack by generating 1 pair satisfying the inbound phase.

The complexity of this attack is 4 iterations of 2^{128} computations of each MegaSBox, which is equivalent to 2^{128} computations of 3.5-round AESQ. The memory requirements are negligible. Note that the complexity to satisfy the same property against random permutation is the same as the previous attack in Sect. 3, that is 2^{257}. Hence, the gain of our attack is 2^{129} bits.

Note that for a fixed pair of $\Delta S_6^{\mathrm{I}}|_\alpha$, $\Delta S_9^{\mathrm{SR}}|_\alpha$, we will find a solution with probability 2^{-1}. Hence, for $\alpha, \beta, \gamma, \delta$, we need to iterate the procedure 2^4. Considering that 1 MegaSBox only covers 3.5 rounds and very detailed optimization techniques can be applied, we keep the complexity of 2^{128}.

4.2 16-Round Attack

The attack on 12-round AESQ can be further extended by adding 2 rounds in both the forward and backward direction of the outbound part in the attack, while the inbound part P_{mid} is the same as in the 12-round attack. The result is an attack on 16 rounds (Round 2 – Round 17) of AESQ (see Fig. 4).

First, note that in the attack on 16 rounds of AESQ we use a probabilistic truncated differential in the outbound phase. As can bee seen in Fig. 4 we require that the truncated differential in the outbound phase propagate from 16 to 4 active bytes through the MixColumns transformation of AES, both in Rounds 5 and in Round 13 in the backward and forward direction, respectively. Since each 16 to 4 transition has a probability of 2^{-96}, the probability of the outbound phase of the attack is 2^{-192}.

In other words, we need to generate about 2^{192} solutions for the inbound part P_{mid} of the attack to find one pair following the truncated differential in the outbound part (P_{pre} and P_{post}) of the attack.

In the following, we will show how to find a solution for P_{mid} with amortized cost 1. To be more precise, we can find 2^{128} solutions for the inbound phase of the attack with a complexity of 2^{128} in time and memory. Note that similar methods have been discussed for AES and AES-based hash functions in [6,12]. It can be summarized as follows.

1. Fix a 512-bit input difference to P_{mid}, which is ΔS_8^{I} in the 16-round attack.
2. Compute all 2^{128} 512-bit output differences of P_{mid}, $\Delta S_{11}^{\mathrm{SR}}$, and store them in a table M.
3. Connect the single 512-bit input difference of P_{mid} with the 2^{128} 512-bit output differences of P_{mid} stored in the table M using independent MegaSBox matches. For each MegaSBox α, β, γ, δ we proceed as follows:
   (a) Take all the 2^{128} values for the MegaSBox at the input of P_{mid} and compute both values and differences forward to the output of P_{mid}.
   (b) Check for a matching 128-bit differences in the table M. Since we compute 2^{128} differences forward and have 2^{128} entries in M, we get 2^{128} solutions (differences and values) for the match. We update M to contain these 2^{128} solutions.
4. For each MegaSBox and thus, for the whole inbound phase the number of resulting solutions is 2^{128}.

Since we have generated in total 2^{512} pairs (2^{128} pairs for each MegaSBox) at state S_8^{I} and all those pairs are filtered with the truncated differential of state S_{11}^{SR} (96×4 bits), we expect to find $2^{512-96\times4} = 2^{128}$ valid solutions for the inbound part of the attack. Moreover, the computational cost to find these 2^{128} solutions is 2^{128} in time and memory. Hence, the amortized cost of finding one solution in the inbound phase is 1. Since the inbound phase can be repeated up to 2^{128} times with other differences in state S_8^{I}, leading to a maximum of 2^{256} solutions in the inbound phase of the attack, we can find a pair following the truncated differential trail in the outbound phase of the attack on 16 rounds with a complexity of about 2^{192} and memory requirements of 2^{128}.

The complexity for a random permutation is the same as previous attacks i.e. 2^{257}. Thus, the gain of our attack is 65 bits.

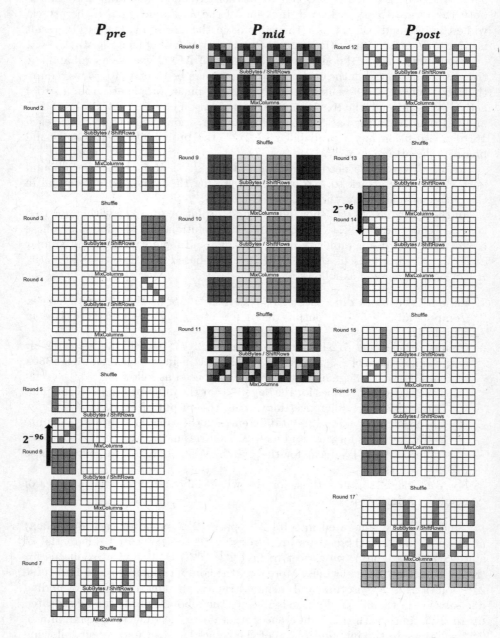

Fig. 4. 16-round rebound attack on AESQ. (Color figure online)

4.3   15-Round Attack Starting from the First Round

Because of the property that `MegaSBox` starts from an even round, optimized attacks need to start from an even round as in the 12-round and 16-round attacks. In order to start from the first round, we can remove one round at the very beginning of those attacks. Thus a 15-round attack starting from the first round is obtained by using round 3 to round 17 of the 16-round attack with the same complexity i.e. 2^{192} computational complexity and memory requirements of 2^{128}.

4.4   16-Round Attack with Multiple Limited Birthday Distinguishers

The complexity of the 16-round attack can be slightly reduced from 2^{192} to 2^{188} by considering multiple limited birthday distinguisher [10].

4.5   Remarks on Choice of Differential

Main difficulty of this research lies in identifying good truncated differentials. In particular, mixing four AES states with light column-shuffling makes the analysis more complicated than simple AES-based permutations. Previous work on this type of permutation, e.g. LANE, 3D and ECHO, shows that identifying the best differential is non-trivial even though attack procedure with a given differential is simple. In fact, this might be a reason why the designers of AESQ only could show the 12-round attack with very high complexity. Hence, we need to search for truncated differentials carefully towards obtaining the optimal attack.

Although we cannot prove that our truncated differential is optimal, we considered various choices of the differential propagation. Regarding the outbound, we considered the following differential propagation for `MC` or `MC`$^{-1}$.

- full active state can be full active with probability 1 or a single (inverse) diagonal with probability 2^{-96}.
- state with a single active column can be a single active column with probability 1 or a single active byte with probability 2^{-24}.

As a result, the best differential propagation is the one shown in Fig. 4. Interestingly, forcing only a single active byte in the 512-bit state does not lead to the best attack. For example in Fig. 4, we can make the number of active byte 1 at state S_{14}^{MC} by paying 2^{24} cost. However, this eventually leads to 1 full active state at S_{16}^{MC}. Then making a state with a single active byte only wastes the computational cost. For 15-round attack, we found other types of differential with the same complexity, but the complexity could not be less than 2^{192}.

Regarding the inbound, we also considered several patterns. The current choice, a single `MegaSBox` layer, corresponds to a single `SuperSBox` layer for simple AES-based permutations, which is one of the most effective choices for them. Improved rebound attack [9] covers three `SubBytes` layers in the inbound phase. However the `MegaSBox` has already covered four `SubBytes` layers. Moreover, the technique cannot be applied when the state consists of only four `MegaSBox`/`SuperSBox`. Regarding Whirlpool, two iterations of "1-column, full active, 1 diagonal" can be included in the inbound [12]. However, this attack essentially requires additional freedom degrees of block-cipher's key, thus cannot be applied to permutation like AESQ.

5   Time-Memory Tradeoff for Rebound Attacks

5.1   Tradeoff for Inbound Part: Application to 12-Round Attack

In Sect. 4.1, we showed that the previous 12-round attack can be improved to 2^{128} computational cost (T) and negligible memory (M). Here, the natural question is: if it is possible to further reduce T by increasing M. Namely, if the attack complexity is measured by $\min\{T, M\}$, what is the best complexity?

This question naturally fits in discussing the security of PAEQ authenticated encryption. The designers claim the security of PAEQ (with the primary choice of the design parameter; 128-bit key and 128-bit tag) up to 128 bits, though 256-bit security is claimed on AESQ. It is not allowed to make 2^{128} queries against PAEQ, thus identifying non-random behavior without reaching 2^{128} complexity is of interest.

Considering that the outbound phase of the 12-round attack has probability 1, the above issue is equivalent to identify time-memory tradeoff to find one solution of the inbound phase consisting of a single MegaSBox layer. The similar tradeoff has been discussed on AES [20], and we apply it to MegaSBox of AESQ. Note that the attacks in Sect. 4.2 use the fact that the amortized computational cost of the inbound phase can be 1 if many solutions are needed. To be more precise, if 2^{128} computational cost can be spent, 2^{128} solutions of the inbound phase can be obtained. Thus, reducing the computation cost from 2^{128} if only one solution is needed is non-trivial.

Let us recall the procedure to achieve the amortized cost 1 for P_{mid}.

1. Fix a 512-bit input difference to P_{mid}, which is ΔS_6^{I} in the 12-round attack.
2. Store 2^{128} 512-bit output differences of P_{mid}, ΔS_9^{SR}, in a table M of size 2^{128}.
3. For each MegaSBox, process 2^{128} input values to find corresponding output difference in M.

Step 2 determines the memory amount M and Step 3 determines the computational cost T. We now consider reducing the number of processed values in Step 3 from 2^{128} to $2^{128}/X$. Then, after each MegaSBox is analyzed, only a fraction of $1/X$ output differences can be reached. Namely, by starting from 2^{128} differences in M, the number of differences that can be reached is $2^{128}/X$ after the first MegaSBox α, $2^{128}/X^2$ after the second MegaSBox β, $2^{128}/X^3$ after the third MegaSBox γ and $2^{128}/X^4$ after the fourth MegaSBox δ. If we start by storing M differences in a memory, M/X^4 output differences can be reached after the analysis, thus the number of solutions of the inbound phase is M/X^4.

Considering that $T = 2^{128}/X$ and finding 1 solution is sufficient for 12-round attack, the time-memory tradeoff of the 12-round attack can be represented by

$$MT^4 = 2^{512}. \tag{3}$$

In general, with memory amount of $M = 2^x$, the computational cost of the 12-round attack is $T = 2^{128-x/4}$. By setting $M = T$, we achieve $M = T = 2^{102.4}$.

5.2   Tradeoff for Outbound Part: Applications to 16-Round Attack

In the tradeoff in Eq. (3), M can take up to 2^{128}. Therefore, if the memory amount of the attack has already reached 2^{128}, it is impossible to reduce the computational cost by increasing the memory amount.

Then, the only direction of time-memory tradeoff for the 16-round attack is a very straightforward one, which reduces the memory amount by increasing the computational cost as discussed for AES and AES-based hash functions in [6,12]. In Step 2 of the procedure in Sect. 5.1, M is set to be smaller than 2^{128}. Then, after processing 2^{128} input values for each MegaSBox in Step 3, M solutions of the inbound phase can be obtained. Thus, the amortized cost, ac, for generating solutions of the inbound phase is $2^{128}/M$.

Let p_{out} be the probability of the outbound phase. Then, the computational cost of the rebound attack is represented by $p_{out}^{-1} \times ac$. By setting $M = 2^{128-x}$, the computational cost of the 16-round and 15-round attacks becomes $2^{192} \times 2^{128}/2^{128-x} = 2^{192+x}$. Note that by setting $x = 0$, this complexity matches the one in Sect. 4.2.

6   Concluding Remarks

In this paper, we investigated the security of AESQ, the core permutation on PAEQ, against rebound attack. We have shown that the designers' attack on 12-round AESQ can be improved significantly, both regarding the computational cost and the amount of memory. In addition, we have extended the attack to 15 and 16 rounds of AESQ, and have discussed time-memory tradeoff and multiple limited birthday distinguishers.

Our results on reduced-round AESQ cannot be applied to full (20) rounds of AESQ. Thus the security of AESQ is not threatened by our attacks. Moreover, the results are not applicable to PAEQ mode of operation. However, the analysis gives some new insights in the security margin of PAEQ against rebound attacks, which will contribute to CAESAR for future selection of good candidates.

Acknowledgements. The authors would like to thank the organizers and the participants of ASK 2015 that initiated this work. Part of this work was done while Florian Mendel was visiting NTU and has been supported in part by the Austrian Science Fund (project P26494-N15).

References

1. CAESAR: Competition for Authenticated Encryption: Security, Applicability, and Robustness (2013). http://competitions.cr.yp.to/caesar.html
2. Biryukov, A., Khovratovich, D.: PAEQ v1. Submitted to CAESAR (2014). http://competitions.cr.yp.to/round1/paeqv1.pdf
3. Daemen, J., Rijmen, V.: The Design of Rijndeal: AES - The Advnced Encryption Standard (AES). Springer, New York (2002)
4. Dobraunig, C., Eichlseder, M., Mendel, F.: Analysis of the kupyna-256 hash function. In: Peyrin, T. (ed.) Fast Software Encryption. Springer, LNCS (2016)
5. Dong, L., Wu, W., Wu, S., Zou, J.: Known-key distinguisher on round-reduced 3D block cipher. In: Jung, S., Yung, M. (eds.) WISA 2011. LNCS, vol. 7115, pp. 55–69. Springer, Heidelberg (2012)

6. Gilbert, H., Peyrin, T.: Super-sbox cryptanalysis: improved attacks for AES-like permutations. In: Hong, S., Iwata, T. (eds.) FSE 2010. LNCS, vol. 6147, pp. 365–383. Springer, Heidelberg (2010)

7. Iwamoto, M., Peyrin, T., Sasaki, Y.: Limited-birthday distinguishers for hash functions. In: Sako, K., Sarkar, P. (eds.) ASIACRYPT 2013, Part II. LNCS, vol. 8270, pp. 504–523. Springer, Heidelberg (2013)

8. Jean, J., Fouque, P.: Practical near-collisions and collisions on round-reduced ECHO-256 Compression Function. In: Joux, A. (ed.) FSE 2012. LNCS, vol. 6733, pp. 107–127. Springer, Heidelberg (2011)

9. Jean, J., Naya-Plasencia, M., Peyrin, T.: Improved rebound attack on the finalist grøstl. In: Canteaut, A. (ed.) FSE 2012. LNCS, vol. 7549, pp. 110–126. Springer, Heidelberg (2012)

10. Jean, J., Naya-Plasencia, M., Peyrin, T.: Multiple limited-birthday distinguishers and applications. In: Lange, T., Lauter, K., Lisoněk, P. (eds.) SAC 2013. LNCS, vol. 8282, pp. 533–550. Springer, Heidelberg (2014)

11. Jean, J., Naya-Plasencia, M., Schläffer, M.: Improved analysis of ECHO-256. In: Miri, A., Vaudenay, S. (eds.) SAC 2011. LNCS, vol. 7118, pp. 19–36. Springer, Heidelberg (2012)

12. Lamberger, M., Mendel, F., Rechberger, C., Rijmen, V., Schläffer, M.: Rebound distinguishers: results on the full whirlpool compression function. In: Matsui, M. (ed.) ASIACRYPT 2009. LNCS, vol. 5912, pp. 126–143. Springer, Heidelberg (2009)

13. Lamberger, M., Mendel, F., Schläffer, M., Rechberger, C., Rijmen, V.: The rebound attack and subspace distinguishers: application to whirlpool. J. Cryptol. 28(2), 257–296 (2015)

14. Matusiewicz, K., Naya-Plasencia, M., Nikolić, I., Sasaki, Y., Schläffer, M.: Rebound attack on the full LANE compression function. In: Matsui, M. (ed.) ASIACRYPT 2009. LNCS, vol. 5912, pp. 106–125. Springer, Heidelberg (2009)

15. Mendel, F., Peyrin, T., Rechberger, C., Schläffer, M.: Improved cryptanalysis of the reduced Grøstl compression function, ECHO permutation and AES block cipher. In: Jacobson Jr., M.J., Rijmen, V., Safavi-Naini, R. (eds.) SAC 2009. LNCS, vol. 5867, pp. 16–35. Springer, Heidelberg (2009)

16. Mendel, F., Rechberger, C., Schläffer, M., Thomsen, S.S.: The rebound attack: cryptanalysis of reduced whirlpool and grøstl. In: Dunkelman, O. (ed.) FSE 2009. LNCS, vol. 5665, pp. 260–276. Springer, Heidelberg (2009)

17. Mendel, F., Rechberger, C., Schläffer, M., Thomsen, S.S.: Rebound attacks on the reduced grøstl hash function. In: Pieprzyk, J. (ed.) CT-RSA 2010. LNCS, vol. 5985, pp. 350–365. Springer, Heidelberg (2010)

18. Peyrin, T.: Improved differential attacks for ECHO and grøstl. In: Rabin, T. (ed.) CRYPTO 2010. LNCS, vol. 6223, pp. 370–392. Springer, Heidelberg (2010)

19. Sasaki, Y., Li, Y., Wang, L., Sakiyama, K., Ohta, K.: Non-full-active super-sbox analysis: applications to ECHO and grøstl. In: Abe, M. (ed.) ASIACRYPT 2010. LNCS, vol. 6477, pp. 38–55. Springer, Heidelberg (2010)

20. Sasaki, Y., Takayanagi, N., Sakiyama, K., Ohta, K.: Experimental verification of super-sbox analysis — confirmation of detailed attack complexity. In: Iwata, T., Nishigaki, M. (eds.) IWSEC 2011. LNCS, vol. 7038, pp. 178–192. Springer, Heidelberg (2011)

21. Schläffer, M.: Subspace distinguisher for 5/8 rounds of the ECHO-256 hash function. In: Biryukov, A., Gong, G., Stinson, D.R. (eds.) SAC 2010. LNCS, vol. 6544, pp. 369–387. Springer, Heidelberg (2011)

Efficient Beyond-Birthday-Bound-Secure Deterministic Authenticated Encryption with Minimal Stretch

Christian Forler[1], Eik List[2(✉)], Stefan Lucks[2], and Jakob Wenzel[2]

[1] Hochschule Schmalkalden, Schmalkalden, Germany
cforler@hs-schmalkalden.de
[2] Bauhaus-Universität Weimar, Weimar, Germany
{eik.list,stefan.lucks,jakob.wenzel}@uni-weimar.de

Abstract. Block-cipher-based authenticated encryption has obtained considerable attention from the ongoing CAESAR competition. While the focus of CAESAR resides primarily on nonce-based authenticated encryption, Deterministic Authenticated Encryption (DAE) is used in domains such as key wrap, where the available message entropy motivates to omit the overhead for nonces. Since the highest possible security is desirable when protecting keys, beyond-birthday-bound (BBB) security is a valuable goal for DAE. In the past, significant efforts had to be invested into designing BBB-secure AE schemes from conventional block ciphers, with the consequences of losing efficiency and sophisticating security proofs.

This work proposes Deterministic Counter in Tweak (DCT), a BBB-secure DAE scheme inspired by the Counter-in-Tweak encryption scheme by Peyrin and Seurin. Our design combines a fast ϵ-almost-XOR-universal family of hash functions, for ϵ close to 2^{-2n}, with a single call to a $2n$-bit SPRP, and a BBB-secure encryption scheme. First, we describe our construction generically with three independent keys, one for each component. Next, we present an efficient instantiation which (1) requires only a single key, (2) provides software efficiency by encrypting at less than two cycles per byte on current x64 processors, and (3) produces only the minimal τ-bit stretch for τ bit authenticity. We leave open two minor aspects for future work: our current generic construction is defined for messages of at least $2n - \tau$ bits, and the verification algorithm requires the inverse of the used $2n$-bit SPRP and the encryption scheme.

Keywords: Deterministic authenticated encryption · Symmetric cryptography · Cryptographic schemes · Provable security · Tweakable block cipher · Universal hash function

1 Introduction

Deterministic Authenticated Encryption. A secure authenticated encryption (AE, hereafter) scheme is nowadays widely understood as a construction

© Springer International Publishing Switzerland 2016
J.K. Liu and R. Steinfeld (Eds.): ACISP 2016, Part II, LNCS 9723, pp. 317–332, 2016.
DOI: 10.1007/978-3-319-40367-0_20

which produces ciphertexts that are indistinguishable from random bitstrings and infeasible to forge. Modern AE schemes are mostly nonce-based [33], i.e., the user is responsible to supply an additional nonce that must be unique for every encryption. In contrast, Deterministic Authenticated Encryption (DAE) [34] is employed for settings where it is more senseful to exploit existing entropy or redundancy in the inputs to avoid the overhead of nonces, e.g., for wrapping cryptographic keys.

Existing Designs. A variety of DAE schemes has been proposed since, e.g., HADDOC [6], BCTR [9], DAEAD [10], MRO/MRS/MROS [14], GCM-SIV [15], BTM [21], HBS [22], DEOXYS [24], JOLTIK [25], HS1-SIV [26], MINICTR [28], MR-OMD [32], and SIV [34]. The naturally raising question is: Which unsolved problem requires the proposal of a novel mode?

Block-cipher-based DAE schemes are inherently efficient. While a myriad of block ciphers is available, the dominating standard state size is still 128 bits, which renders the privacy guarantees of existing DAE schemes built upon them void already after encrypting about 2^{64} blocks under the same key. However, since the highest attainable security is desirable for the protection of cryptographic keys, beyond-birthday-bound (BBB) security is a highly valuable goal for DAE schemes.

At least two straight-forward approaches for achieving BBB security exist in this context: first, by increasing the block size of the underlying cipher [21,22] or second, by using a wide-block permutation or compression function instead [6,14,32]. Though, previous wide-block constructions possessed significant disadvantages in terms of memory and performance, among which the latter aspect was attempted to be compensated by optimistic reduction of the underlying primitive [6,14], which implies the need for further cryptanalysis. The present work shows that neither the number of rounds nor the state size of the underlying cipher need to be modified to achieve our goal in a performant manner with the help of recent advances in the domain of tweakable block ciphers.

Relations to Wide-Block Ciphers. The birthday-bound limit is also relevant for wide-block ciphers and Tweakable Enciphering Schemes (TES). TES are closely related to DAE: Hoang et al. [19] showed that the Encode-then-Encipher [4] approach can be used to transform an STPRP-secure (Strong Tweakable Pseudo-Random Permutation) TES into a provably robust AE scheme using (a hash of) the associated data as tweak. Such designs could offer even more security than necessary for DAE, i.e., *best achievable* AE security [2,19]. Thus, one could theoretically adapt any existing BBB-secure TES scheme for DAE [27,29,39]. Though, for the popular approaches Hash-Encrypt-Hash [37], Hash-Counter-Hash [40], and Protected IV [39], this strategy would also imply more operations than necessary for DAE, i.e., three passes over the plaintext. While Encrypt-Mix-Encrypt-based [18] designs employ only two passes, a BBB-secure variant of Encrypt-Mix-Encrypt with a $2n$-bit primitive would be considerably less efficient than our proposal. Therefore, a motivating observation of this work is the following: one can encode τ bits of redundancy into the message, encrypt it with the Hash-Counter-Hash approach reduced from three to two passes, and can obtain a BBB-secure DAE scheme.

A recent proposal is SIMPIRA [16,17], a family of $128b$-bit cryptographic permutations based on the AES round function. In contrast to the "modes" above, SIMPIRA is a primitive on its own. The initial version [16] based on a flawed general Feistel structure for $b = 4$, which was fixed in SIMPIRAV2 [17]. Though, the prior attacks [12,36] indicated that SIMPIRA may require more intensive studies to become fully mature. While our example instantiation employs its fixed version with $b = 2$ blocks for which no attacks are known, it can be seemlessly replaced by another secure $2n$-bit SPRP.

Contribution. This work proposes Deterministic Counter in Tweak (DCT), a BBB-secure DAE scheme that combines an ϵ-almost-XOR-universal (AXU) family of hash functions, for $\epsilon \approx \mathcal{O}(2^{-2n})$, with a single call to a $2n$-bit SPRP, and a 2^n-block-secure encryption scheme. First, we propose our construction generically with three independent keys, one for each component. Next, we introduce an efficient instantiation which (1) provides software efficiency by encrypting at less than two cycles per byte on current x64 processors, (2) requires only a single key, and (3) produces only the minimal τ-bit stretch. We leave open two minor aspects for future work: our current generic construction is defined for messages of $\geq 2n - \tau$ bits, and the verification algorithm requires the inverse of the SPRP and the encryption scheme. Though, since our instantiation uses a Feistel-based two-block construction as $2n$-bit SPRP and counter mode as encryption scheme, its decryption can fully reuse the components for encryption.

Remark 1. We stress that the HBS [22] and BTM [21] constructions by Iwata and Yasuda are similar to our work, and that Iwata and Yasuda already discussed BBB-secure adaptions. Both their BBB variants suggested the use of a $2n$-bit block cipher for encryption. Their earlier concept employed a (clearly pointed out by the authors to be inefficient) six-round Feistel network [22]; their later construction [21] used a $2n$-bit tweakable block cipher by Minematsu [27]. Both designs still required several keys, lacked software efficiency, and produced a $2n$-bit stretch. This work addresses their open questions.

The rest of this paper is structured as follows: after briefly reviewing preliminaries, Sect. 3 describes the generic DCT framework. Section 4 recalls relevant security notions. Section 5 summarizes our security analysis, Sect. 6 details our instantiation, and Sect. 7 discusses our proposal and concludes.

2   Preliminaries

We use lowercase letters x, y for indices and integers, uppercase letters X, Y for binary strings and functions, and calligraphic uppercase letters $\mathcal{X}, \mathcal{Y}$ for sets. ε denotes the empty string. We denote the concatenation of binary strings X and Y by $X \parallel Y$ and the result of their bitwise XOR by $X \oplus Y$. We indicate the length of X in bits by $|X|$, and write X_i for the i-th block, $X[i]$ for the

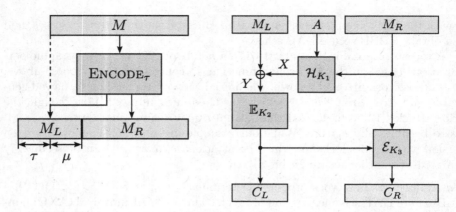

Fig. 1. The encrpytion process of DCT (**right**). The encoding (**left**) encodes τ bits of redundancy into the message M and splits it into a $2n$-bit part M_L and a variable-length part M_R such that the redundancy is fully contained in M_L.

i-th most significant bit of X, and $X[i..j]$ for the bit sequence $X[i], \ldots, X[j]$. $X \leftarrow \mathcal{X}$ denotes that X is chosen uniformly at random from the set $\mathcal{X}$. We define three sets of particular interest: $\mathsf{Perm}(\mathcal{X})$ be the set of all permutations on $\mathcal{X}$, $\widetilde{\mathsf{Perm}}(\mathcal{T}, \mathcal{X})$ the set of all tweaked permutations over $\mathcal{X}$ with associated non-empty tweak space $\mathcal{T}$, and $\mathsf{Func}(\mathcal{X}, \mathcal{Y})$ the set of all functions $F : \mathcal{X} \to \mathcal{Y}$. We define by $X_1, \ldots, X_j \xleftarrow{x} X$ the injective splitting of the string X into x-bit blocks such that $X = X_1 \| \cdots \| X_j$, with $|X_i| = x$ for $1 \le i \le j - 1$, and $|X_j| \le x$. For an event E, we denote by $\Pr[E]$ the probability of E. We write $\langle x \rangle_n$ for the binary representation of an integer x as an n-bit string, or short $\langle x \rangle$ if n is clear from the context, in big-endian manner, i.e., the decimal $\langle 135 \rangle$ is encoded to $(00..00100000111)_2$.

3 Generic Definition of DCT

This section defines the generic DCT construction. Fix integers $n, \tau \ge 1$ with $\tau \le 2n$, and derive $\mu = 2n - \tau$. Let $\mathcal{K}_1$, $\mathcal{K}_2$, and $\mathcal{K}_3$ be non-empty key spaces and $\mathcal{K} = \mathcal{K}_1 \times \mathcal{K}_2 \times \mathcal{K}_3$. Let $\mathcal{A} \subseteq \{0,1\}^*$ denote the associated-data space, $\mathcal{M} \subseteq \{0,1\}^{\ge \mu}$ the message space, and $\mathcal{C} \subseteq \{0,1\}^{\ge 2n}$ denote the ciphertext space, respectively. Let $\mathcal{H} = \left\{ H | H : \mathcal{A} \times \{0,1\}^* \to \{0,1\}^{2n} \right\}$ be a family of ϵ-AXU hash functions, indexed by elements from $\mathcal{K}_1$. Let $\mathbb{E} : \mathcal{K}_2 \times \{0,1\}^{2n} \to \{0,1\}^{2n}$ denote a keyed permutation, and let $\Pi = (\mathcal{E}, \mathcal{D})$ be an IV-based encryption scheme (covered in the next section) with a non-empty key space $\mathcal{K}_3$ and an IV space $\mathcal{IV} = \{0,1\}^{2n}$.

Encoding. Let $\mathrm{ENCODE} : \mathbb{N}_0 \times \mathcal{M} \to \{0,1\}^{2n} \times \{0,1\}^*$ be an injective function that takes an integer $\tau \in \mathbb{N}_0$ and a bit string M as inputs and produces two outputs (M_L, M_R) such that $|M_L| = 2n$ and $|M_R| = |M| - \mu$. Since $\mathrm{ENCODE}_\tau(\cdot)$ is injective, there exists a corresponding unique decoding function $\mathrm{DECODE} :$

Algorithm 1. Encryption and decryption of the generic DCT construction.

1: **function** $\widetilde{\mathcal{E}}_{K_1,K_2,K_3}(A,M)$	11: **function** $\widetilde{\mathcal{D}}_{K_1,K_2,K_3}(A,C)$
2: $(M_L, M_R) \leftarrow \text{ENCODE}_\tau(M)$	12: $(C_L, C_R) \leftarrow C$
3: $X \leftarrow \mathcal{H}_{K_1}(A, M_R)$	13: $M_R \leftarrow \mathcal{D}_{K_3}(C_L, C_R)$
4: $Y \leftarrow M_L \oplus X$	14: $X \leftarrow \mathcal{H}_{K_1}(A, M_R)$
5: $C_L \leftarrow \mathbb{E}_{K_2}(Y)$	15: $Y \leftarrow \mathbb{E}_{K_2}^{-1}(C_L)$
6: $C_R \leftarrow \mathcal{E}_{K_3}(C_L, M_R)$	16: $M_L \leftarrow X \oplus Y$
7: **return** $(C_L \parallel C_R)$	17: **return** $\text{DECODE}_\tau(M_L, M_R)$

$\mathbb{N}_0 \times \{0,1\}^{2n} \times \{0,1\}^{\geq \mu} \to \{0,1\}^* \cup \{\bot\}$ such that, for a fixed $\tau \in \mathbb{N}_0$ and all $X, Y \in \{0,1\}^{2n} \times \{0,1\}^*$, $\text{DECODE}_\tau(X, Y)$ returns the unique $M \in \mathcal{M}$ such that $\text{ENCODE}_\tau(M) = (X, Y)$ if such an M exists, and $\bot$ otherwise.

Encryption. For encryption, $\text{ENCODE}_\tau(M)$ encodes τ bits redundancy into an input message M and splits the result into a $2n$-bit part M_L, and a variable-length part M_R, such that the redundancy is *fully contained in M_L*.[1] The latter part, M_R, is hashed together with the associated data A to a $2n$-bit hash value: $X \leftarrow \mathcal{H}_{K_1}(A, M_R)$. Next, X is XORed to M_L, producing $Y \leftarrow X \oplus M_L$, and the result Y is encrypted by $\mathbb{E}$ to the fixed-length part of the ciphertext: $C_L \leftarrow \mathbb{E}_{K_2}(Y)$. This composition of a hash function and a final call to a PRF is a well-known method for constructing an efficient PRF [8]. Next, the PRF output C_L is used as IV for an encryption scheme $\Pi = (\mathcal{E}, \mathcal{D})$ which enciphers the variable-length part of the message: $C_R \leftarrow \mathcal{E}_{K_3}(C_L, M_R)$. Finally, $(C_L \parallel C_R)$ is returned as the ciphertext. Figure 1 illustrates the encryption process schematically.

Decryption. For decryption, the ciphertext C is split into $(C_L, C_R) \leftarrow C$, such that $|C_L| = 2n$. The variable-length part C_R is decrypted to $M_R \leftarrow \mathcal{D}_{K_3}(C_L, C_R)$. Next, the scheme evaluates $X \leftarrow \mathcal{H}_{K_1}(A, M_R)$ and $Y \leftarrow \mathbb{E}_{K_2}^{-1}(C_L)$, and XORs both results: $M_L \leftarrow X \oplus Y$. $\text{DECODE}_\tau(M_L, M_R)$ can either efficiently remove the redundancy from M_L and determine M with $\text{ENCODE}_\tau(M) = (M_L, M_R)$ if such an M exists; otherwise, it can efficiently detect the invalid redundancy. The decryption returns M in the former case, and $\bot$ in the latter.

Limitations. We define DCT for messages of length at least μ bits, and ciphertexts of at least $2n$ bits length. For simplicity, we assume that, whenever smaller plain- or ciphertexts are passed to the encryption or decryption algorithms, respectively, the response will be $\bot$. We are aware of this current limitation of our proposal, and work actively to overcome it.

Definition 1 (Generic DCT). *Given the definitions above, we define the DAE scheme* $\text{DCT}_{\mathcal{H},\mathbb{E},\Pi} = (\widetilde{\mathcal{E}}, \widetilde{\mathcal{D}})$ *with deterministic encryption algorithm* $\widetilde{\mathcal{E}} : \mathcal{K} \times \mathcal{A} \times \mathcal{M} \to \mathcal{C}$, *and deterministic decryption algorithm* $\widetilde{\mathcal{D}} : \mathcal{K} \times \mathcal{A} \times \mathcal{C} \to \mathcal{M} \cup \{\bot\}$, *as given in Algorithm 1.*

---

[1] Note that encoding redundancy into M_R would require a chosen-ciphertext-secure encryption scheme Π.

For all $K \in \mathcal{K}$, $A \in \mathcal{A}$, $M \in \mathcal{M}$, and $C \in \mathcal{C}$ holds: if $\widetilde{\mathcal{E}}_K^A(M) = C$, then $\widetilde{\mathcal{D}}_K^A(C) = M$, and if $\widetilde{\mathcal{D}}_K^A(C) = M \neq \perp$, then $\widetilde{\mathcal{E}}_K^A(M) = C$.

4 Security Notions

4.1 Adversaries and Advantages

An adversary **A** is an efficient Turing machine that interacts with a given set of oracles that appear as black boxes to **A**. We denote by $\mathbf{A}^{\mathcal{O}}$ the output of **A** after interacting with some oracle $\mathcal{O}$. We write $\Delta_{\mathbf{A}}(\mathcal{O}^L; \mathcal{O}^R)$ for the advantage of **A** to distinguish between oracles $\mathcal{O}^L$ and $\mathcal{O}^R$. All probabilities are defined over the random coins of the oracles and those of the adversary, if any. We write $\mathbf{Adv}_F^X(q, \ell, t) := \max_{\mathbf{A}} \left\{ \mathbf{Adv}_F^X(\mathbf{A}) \right\}$ for the maximal advantage over all X-adversaries **A** on F that run in time at most t and pose at most q queries of at most ℓ blocks in total to its oracles. Wlog., we assume that **A** never asks queries to which it already knows the answer.

If the oracles $\mathcal{O}_i$, $\mathcal{O}_j$ represent a family of algorithms indexed by inputs, the indices must match. For example, when $\widetilde{\mathcal{E}}_K^A(M)$ and $\widetilde{\mathcal{D}}_K^A(C)$ represent encryption and decryption algorithms with a fixed key K and indexed by A, then $\widetilde{\mathcal{E}}_K \hookrightarrow \widetilde{\mathcal{D}}_K$ says that **A** queries first $\widetilde{\mathcal{E}}_K^A(M)$ and later $\widetilde{\mathcal{D}}_K^A(C)$. We often write $\widetilde{\mathcal{E}}_K^A(M)$ and $\widetilde{\mathcal{D}}_K^A(C)$ as short forms for $\widetilde{\mathcal{E}}(K, A, M)$ and $\widetilde{\mathcal{D}}(K, A, C)$.

We define $\perp$, when in place of an oracle, to always return the invalid symbol $\perp$. We define $\$^{\mathcal{O}}$ for an oracle that, given an input X, chooses uniformly at random a value Y equal in length of the expected output, $|Y| = |\mathcal{O}(X)|$, and returns Y. We assume that $\$^{\mathcal{O}}$ performs lazy sampling, i.e., $\$^{\mathcal{O}}(X)$ returns the same value Y when queried with the same input X. We often omit the key for brevity, e.g., $\$^{\widetilde{\mathcal{E}}}(X)$ will be short for $\$^{\widetilde{\mathcal{E}}_K}(X)$.

4.2 Security Definitions for Universal Hashing

Definition 2 (ϵ-Almost-(XOR-)Universal Hash Functions). *Let $\mathcal{X}, \mathcal{Y} \subseteq \{0,1\}^*$. Let $\mathcal{H} = \{H \mid H : \mathcal{X} \to \mathcal{Y}\}$ denote a family of hash functions. $\mathcal{H}$ is called ϵ-almost-universal (ϵ-AU) iff for all distinct elements $X, X' \in \mathcal{X}$, it holds that $\mathrm{Pr}_{H \leftarrow \mathcal{H}}[H(X) = H(X')] \leq \epsilon$.*
$\mathcal{H}$ is called ϵ-almost-XOR-universal (ϵ-AXU) iff for all distinct elements $X, X' \in \mathcal{X}$ and $Y \in \mathcal{Y}$, it holds that $\mathrm{Pr}_{H \leftarrow \mathcal{H}}[H(X) \oplus H(X') = Y] \leq \epsilon$.

In [7], Boesgaard et al. showed the following theorem.

Theorem 1 (Theorem 3 from [7]). *Let $\mathcal{X}, \mathcal{Y} \subseteq \{0,1\}^*$. Further, let $\mathcal{H} = \{H \mid H : \mathcal{X} \to \mathcal{Y}\}$ be a family of ϵ-AXU hash functions. Then, the family $\mathcal{H}' = \{H' \mid H' : \mathcal{X} \times \mathcal{Y} \to \mathcal{Y}\}$ with $H'(X, Y) := H(X) \oplus Y$, is ϵ-AU.*

4.3 Security Definitions for Functions and Ciphers

Definition 3 ((Strong) PRP Advantage). *Fix integers* $n, k \geq 1$. *Let* $E :$ $\{0,1\}^k \times \{0,1\}^n \to \{0,1\}^n$ *be a block cipher and* $\mathbf{A}$ ($\mathbf{A}'$) *be a computationally bounded adversary with access to an oracle (two oracles). Let* $K \twoheadleftarrow \{0,1\}^k$ *and* $\pi \twoheadleftarrow \mathsf{Perm}(\{0,1\}^n)$. *Then, the* PRP *and* SPRP *advantages of* $\mathbf{A}$ *and* $\mathbf{A}'$ *with respect to* E *are defined as* $\mathbf{Adv}_E^{\mathrm{PRP}}(\mathbf{A}) := \Delta_{\mathbf{A}}(E_K; \pi)$ *and* $\mathbf{Adv}_{E,E^{-1}}^{\mathrm{SPRP}}(\mathbf{A}') :=$ $\Delta_{\mathbf{A}'}(E_K, E_K^{-1}; \pi, \pi^{-1})$, *respectively.*

Definition 4 ((Strong) Tweakable PRP Advantage). *Fix two integers* $n, k \geq 1$. *Let* $\mathcal{T}$ *denote a non-empty set. Let* $\widetilde{E} : \{0,1\}^k \times \mathcal{T} \times \{0,1\}^n \to$ $\{0,1\}^n$ *be a tweakable block cipher and* $\mathbf{A}$ ($\mathbf{A}'$) *a computationally bounded adversary with access to an oracle (two oracles). Let* $K \twoheadleftarrow \{0,1\}^k$ *and* $\widetilde{\pi} \twoheadleftarrow$ $\widetilde{\mathsf{Perm}}(\mathcal{T}, \{0,1\}^n)$. *Then, the* TPRP *and* STPRP *advantages of* $\mathbf{A}$ *and* $\mathbf{A}'$ *with respect to* $\widetilde{E}$ *are defined as* $\mathbf{Adv}_{\widetilde{E}}^{\mathrm{TPRP}}(\mathbf{A}) := \Delta_{\mathbf{A}}(\widetilde{E}_K; \widetilde{\pi})$ *and* $\mathbf{Adv}_{\widetilde{E}, \widetilde{E}^{-1}}^{\mathrm{STPRP}}(\mathbf{A}') :=$ $\Delta_{\mathbf{A}'}(\widetilde{E}_K, \widetilde{E}_K^{-1}; \widetilde{\pi}, \widetilde{\pi}^{-1})$, *respectively.*

4.4 Security Definitions for IV-Based Encryption Schemes

An *IV-based encryption scheme* [3] is a tuple $\Pi = (\mathcal{E}, \mathcal{D})$ of encryption and decryption algorithms $\mathcal{E} : \mathcal{K} \times \mathcal{IV} \times \mathcal{M} \to \mathcal{C}$ and $\mathcal{D} : \mathcal{K} \times \mathcal{IV} \times \mathcal{C} \to \mathcal{M}$, with associated non-empty key space $\mathcal{K}$, non-empty IV space $\mathcal{IV}$, and where $\mathcal{M}, \mathcal{C} \subseteq \{0,1\}^*$ denote message and ciphertext space, respectively. We assume *correctness* for all $K \in \mathcal{K}$, $IV \in \mathcal{IV}$, and $M \in \mathcal{M}$, i.e., if $\mathcal{E}_K^{IV}(M) = C$, then $\mathcal{D}_K^{IV}(C) = M$. Moreover, we assume *tidiness*, i.e., if $\mathcal{D}_K^{IV}(C) = M$, then $\mathcal{E}_K^{IV}(M) = C$. The security of IV-based encryption schemes is defined as the distinguishing advantage from random bits. For every query M, the encryption oracle samples uniformly at random $IV \twoheadleftarrow \mathcal{IV}$ and computes $C \leftarrow \mathcal{E}_K^{IV}(M)$. The real oracle outputs (IV, C), whereas $\$^{\mathcal{E}}$ outputs $|(IV \parallel C)|$ random bits.

Definition 5 (IVE Advantage). *Let* $\Pi = (\mathcal{E}, \mathcal{D})$ *be an IV-based encryption scheme and* $K \twoheadleftarrow \mathcal{K}$. *Let* $\mathbf{A}$ *be a computationally bounded adversary with access to an oracle. Then, the* IVE *advantage of* $\mathbf{A}$ *with respect to* Π *is defined as* $\mathbf{Adv}_\Pi^{\mathrm{IVE}}(\mathbf{A}) := \Delta_{\mathbf{A}}(\mathcal{E}_K; \$^{\mathcal{E}})$.

4.5 Security Definitions for DAE Schemes

A deterministic AE scheme [34] is a tuple $\widetilde{\Pi} = (\widetilde{\mathcal{E}}, \widetilde{\mathcal{D}})$ of deterministic algorithms $\widetilde{\mathcal{E}} : \mathcal{K} \times \mathcal{A} \times \mathcal{M} \to \mathcal{C}$ and $\widetilde{\mathcal{D}} : \mathcal{K} \times \mathcal{A} \times \mathcal{C} \to \mathcal{M} \cup \{\bot\}$ with associated non-empty key space $\mathcal{K}$, associated-data space $\mathcal{A}$, and message/ciphertext space $\mathcal{M}, \mathcal{C} \subseteq \{0,1\}^*$. For each $K \in \mathcal{K}$, $A \in \mathcal{A}$, $M \in \mathcal{M}$, $\widetilde{\mathcal{E}}_K^A(M)$ maps (A, M) to an output C such that $|C| = |M| + \tau$ for fixed stretch τ. $\widetilde{\mathcal{D}}_K^A(C)$ outputs the corresponding message M iff C is valid, and $\bot$ otherwise. We assume correctness, i.e., for all $K, A, M \in \mathcal{K} \times \mathcal{A} \times \mathcal{M}$, it holds that $\widetilde{\mathcal{D}}_K^A(\widetilde{\mathcal{E}}_K^A(M)) = M$. Moreover, we assume tidiness, i.e., if there exists an M such that $\widetilde{\mathcal{D}}_K^A(C) = M$, then it holds that $\widetilde{\mathcal{E}}_K^A(\widetilde{\mathcal{D}}_K^A(C)) = C$.

Definition 6 (DETPRIV, DETAUTH, and DAE Advantages [34]). *Let* $\widetilde{\Pi} = (\widetilde{\mathcal{E}}, \widetilde{\mathcal{D}})$ *be a DAE scheme and* $K \leftarrow \mathcal{K}$. *Let* $\mathbf{A}_1$, $\mathbf{A}_2$, $\mathbf{A}_3$ *denote computationally bounded adversaries;* $\mathbf{A}_1$ *has access to one oracle;* $\mathbf{A}_2$ *and* $\mathbf{A}_3$ *have access to two oracles* $\mathcal{O}_1$ *and* $\mathcal{O}_2$ *each.* $\mathbf{A}_2$ *and* $\mathbf{A}_3$ *never submit queries* $\mathcal{O}_1 \hookrightarrow \mathcal{O}_2$. *Then, the* DETPRIV, DETAUTH, *and DAE advantages of* $\mathbf{A}_1$, $\mathbf{A}_2$, *and* $\mathbf{A}_3$ *with respect to* $\widetilde{\Pi}$, *are defined as*

$$\mathbf{Adv}_{\widetilde{\Pi}}^{\mathrm{DETPRIV}}(\mathbf{A}_1) := \underset{\mathbf{A}_1}{\Delta}(\widetilde{\mathcal{E}}_K; \$^{\widetilde{\mathcal{E}}}),$$

$$\mathbf{Adv}_{\widetilde{\Pi}}^{\mathrm{DETAUTH}}(\mathbf{A}_2) := \Pr\left[\mathbf{A}_2^{\widetilde{\mathcal{E}}_K, \widetilde{\mathcal{D}}_K} \text{ forges}\right], \text{ and}$$

$$\mathbf{Adv}_{\widetilde{\Pi}}^{\mathrm{DAE}}(\mathbf{A}_3) := \underset{\mathbf{A}_3}{\Delta}(\widetilde{\mathcal{E}}_K, \widetilde{\mathcal{D}}_K; \$^{\widetilde{\mathcal{E}}}, \bot),$$

where "forges" means that $\widetilde{\mathcal{D}}_K$ *returns anything other than* $\bot$ *for a query.*

Theorem 2 (Proposition 8 in [35]). *Let* $\widetilde{\Pi} = (\widetilde{\mathcal{E}}, \widetilde{\mathcal{D}})$ *be a DAE scheme and* $K \leftarrow \mathcal{K}$. *Let* $\mathbf{A}$ *be a computationally bounded DAE adversary on* $\widetilde{\Pi}$ *with access to two oracles* $\mathcal{O}_1$ *and* $\mathcal{O}_2$ *such that* $\mathbf{A}$ *never queries* $\mathcal{O}_1 \hookrightarrow \mathcal{O}_2$, *and* $\mathbf{A}$ *runs in time at most* t *and submits at most* q *queries of at most* ℓ *blocks in total. Then, there exist a computationally bounded* DETPRIV *adversary* $\mathbf{A}_1$ *and a computationally bounded* DETAUTH *adversary* $\mathbf{A}_2$ *both on* $\widetilde{\Pi}$, *such that*

$$\mathbf{Adv}_{\widetilde{\Pi}}^{\mathrm{DAE}}(\mathbf{A}) \leq \mathbf{Adv}_{\widetilde{\Pi}}^{\mathrm{DETPRIV}}(\mathbf{A}_1) + \mathbf{Adv}_{\widetilde{\Pi}}^{\mathrm{DETAUTH}}(\mathbf{A}_2),$$

where $\mathbf{A}_1$ *and* $\mathbf{A}_2$ *make at most* q *queries of at most* ℓ *blocks and run in time* $O(t)$ *each.*

5   Security Results for the Generic DCT Construction

This section summarizes the security bounds for the generic DCT construction.

Theorem 3 (DAE Security of Generic DCT). *Let* $\widetilde{\Pi} = \mathrm{DCT}_{\mathcal{H}, \mathrm{E}, \Pi}$ *be as defined in Definition 1. Let* $\mathbf{A}$ *be a computationally bounded DAE adversary on* $\widetilde{\Pi}$ *that asks at most* q *queries of at most* ℓ *blocks in total, and runs in time at most* t. *Then,* $\mathbf{Adv}_{\widetilde{\Pi}}^{\mathrm{DAE}}(\mathbf{A})$ *is upper bounded by*

$$\frac{3q^2\epsilon}{2} + \frac{2q^2}{2^{2n}} + \frac{3q\epsilon \cdot 2^{2n}}{2^\tau} + 3 \cdot \mathbf{Adv}_{\mathrm{E}, \mathrm{E}^{-1}}^{\mathrm{SPRP}}(q, O(t)) + 2 \cdot \mathbf{Adv}_{\Pi}^{\mathrm{IVE}}(q, \ell, O(t)).$$

The proof of Theorem 3 follows from Theorem 2 and the individual bounds for the DETPRIV and DETAUTH security in Lemmata 1 and 2. Due to space limitations, the proofs of both lemmas are deferred to the full version of this work [13].

Lemma 1 (DETPRIV Security of Generic DCT). *Let* $\widetilde{\Pi} = \mathrm{DCT}_{\mathcal{H}, \mathrm{E}, \Pi}$ *be as defined in Definition 1. Let* $\mathbf{A}$ *be a computationally bounded* DETPRIV *adversary* on $\widetilde{\Pi}$ that submits at most q queries of at most ℓ blocks in total and runs in time at most t. Then

$$\mathbf{Adv}_{\widetilde{\Pi}}^{\mathrm{DETPRIV}}(\mathbf{A}) \le q^2 \left(\epsilon + \frac{2}{2^{2n}} \right) + 2 \left(\mathbf{Adv}_{\mathrm{E}}^{\mathrm{PRP}}(q, O(t)) + \mathbf{Adv}_{\Pi}^{\mathrm{IVE}}(q, \ell, O(t)) \right).$$

Lemma 2 (DETAUTH Security of Generic DCT). Let $\widetilde{\Pi} = \mathrm{DCT}_{\mathcal{H},\mathrm{E},\Pi}$ be as defined in Definition 1. Let $\mathbf{A}$ be a computationally bounded DETAUTH adversary on $\widetilde{\Pi}$ that submits at most q queries of at most ℓ blocks in total, and runs in time at most t. Then

$$\mathbf{Adv}_{\widetilde{\Pi}}^{\mathrm{DETAUTH}}(\mathbf{A}) \le \epsilon \cdot \left(\frac{q^2}{2} + \frac{3q \cdot 2^{2n}}{2^{\tau}} \right) + \mathbf{Adv}_{\mathrm{E},\mathrm{E}^{-1}}^{\mathrm{SPRP}}(q, O(t)).$$

6   Instantiation

Our proposed instantiation of DCT requires (1) an efficient $2n$-bit SPRP, (2) a beyond-birthday-bound-secure IV-based encryption scheme, and (3) an ϵ-AXU family of hash functions. This section describes the components in detail.

6.1   Components

Efficient Tweakable Block Ciphers. The TWEAKEY framework by Jean et al. [23] provides a set of software-efficient tweakable block ciphers based on the AES. Therefore, they allow to exploit AES native instructions on current x64 processor architectures. Among the three available TWEAKEY ciphers KIASU-BC, JOLTIK-BC, and DEOXYS-BC, we concentrate on DEOXYS-BC-128-128 [24] for its support of 128-bit tweaks. In the remainder, we denote it as $\widetilde{E} : \mathcal{K} \times \mathcal{T} \times \{0,1\}^n \rightarrow \{0,1\}^n$, with a state size of $n = 128$ bits, and with $\mathcal{K} = \mathcal{T} = \{0,1\}^n$.

$2n$-**bit SPRP.** SIMPIRA [16] is a recently proposed family of $128b$-bit cryptographic permutations based on the AES round function by Gueron and Mouha. We employ SIMPIRA with two-block inputs ($b = 2$), which is similar to a Feistel network with 15 rounds (the output halves are swapped). The round function F consists of two AES rounds (an AES round is also denoted by aesenc in the pseudocode); the first AES round in F uses a round counter c and $b = 2$ as key; the second round an all-zeroes key. The construction is used in an Even-Mansour design, so that a 256-bit ciphertext is computed by $C_L \leftarrow \mathrm{SIMPIRA}(Y \oplus (K \parallel 0^{128})) \oplus (K \parallel 0^{128})$, with a 128-bit secret key K, and where $Y \leftarrow M_L \oplus X$.

Since it is hard to prove the security of SIMPIRA, a possible provably secure $2n$-bit SPRP would be the Ψ_3 construction by Coron et al. [11], which consists of three invocations of a tweakable block cipher; though, this construction is a little less performant than our current choice and requires the inverse for decryption.

Encryption Scheme. The recently proposed CTRT mode by Peyrin and Seurin [30] is an IV-based encryption scheme that can provide security for

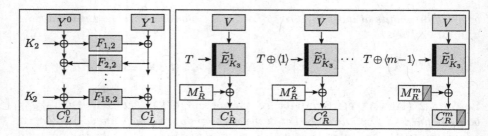

Fig. 2. The components of our instantiation of DCT: the two-block SIMPIRA construction [16] for $\mathbb{E}$ (**left**) and the $\mathrm{CTRT}[\widetilde{E}]$ mode [30] (**right**) for $\mathcal{E}$. F denotes two AES rounds used in the SIMPIRA construction.

close to 2^n blocks encrypted under the same key. Originally, the authors proposed it as a *nonce-IV*-based mode that requires an n-bit nonce V as input to the block cipher $\widetilde{E}$ and an n-bit IV as tweak that is converted by a regular function[2] CONV : $\{0,1\}^n \rightarrow \mathcal{T}$ to an $(n-d)$-bit tweak for a fixed $d \leq n$. Basically, CTRT represents a counter mode built upon a tweakable block cipher, where only the tweak is incremented for each block. We denote encryption and decryption algorithms, instantiated with a tweakable block cipher $\widetilde{E}$, by $\mathrm{CTRT}[\widetilde{E}] = (\mathrm{CTRT}.\mathcal{E}[\widetilde{E}], \mathrm{CTRT}.\mathcal{D}[\widetilde{E}])$. The i-th message block M_i is encrypted to a ciphertext block C_i by $C_i \leftarrow \widetilde{E}_K^{D\,\|\,T+i}(V) \oplus M_i$, where $D \in \{0,1\}^d$ denotes the domain. For our instantiation of DCT, we adopt the purely IV-based variant of CTRT from [30, Appendix C], with a minor modification: to eliminate carry-bit concerns, we XOR the counter to the tweak instead of adding it modulo 2^n. Clearly, since the IV is expected to be random, this modification does not change the probability distribution of tweaks to occur. Thus, the bounds from [30] apply to our adapted mode in a straight-forward manner. Our variant is defined in Algorithm 2; the encryption process is depicted in Fig. 2.

Similar to [24, 30], we encode a domain into the tweak to simplify our security analysis and to avoid multiple keys for the instances of $\widetilde{E}$ inside $\mathrm{CTRT}[\widetilde{E}]$ and for key generation. For the calls to $\widetilde{E}$ inside $\mathrm{CTRT}[\widetilde{E}]$, we set the most significant bit to 1 as domain and truncate the most significant bit of the IV U to derive the tweak: $T \leftarrow U[2..n]$.

Universal Hash Function. We considered several approaches for efficient hashing. Recent works pointed out weak-key issues [1, 31] of Horner-based polynomials (e.g. GHASH or Poly1305) that modern AE schemes should avoid, which motivated our choice of BRW polynomials [5]. If it will turn out that similar attacks apply also to Bernstein-Rabin-Winograd (BRW) polynomials, one can easily switch to a different family of hash functions with similar security guarantees as our construction.

BRW polynomials require only a single n-bit key, half the number of multiplications compared to Horner-based polynomials, and a negligible number of

---

[2] $F : \mathcal{X} \rightarrow \mathcal{Y}$ is called regular iff all outputs $Y \in \mathcal{Y}$ are produced by an equal number of preimages $X \in \mathcal{X}$.

Algorithm 2. Definition of our instantiation of DCT, with $n = 128$ and $\tau \leq 2n$.

101: **function** $\widetilde{\mathcal{E}}_{SK}(A, M)$
102:     $(K_1^1, K_1^2, K_2, K_3) \leftarrow \text{KeyGen}(SK)$
103:     $(M_L, M_R) \leftarrow \text{Encode}_\tau(M)$
104:     $X \leftarrow \mathcal{H}_{K_1^1 \| K_1^2}(A, M_R)$
105:     $Y \leftarrow M_L \oplus X$
106:     $C_L \leftarrow \text{Simpira}_{K_2}(Y)$
107:     $C_R \leftarrow \text{CTRT}.\mathcal{E}[\widetilde{E}]_{K_3}(C_L, M_R)$
108:     **return** $(C_L \| C_R)$

111: **function** $\text{Encode}_\tau(M)$
112:     $\mu \leftarrow 2n - \tau$
113:     $M_L \leftarrow 0^\tau \| M[1..\mu]$
114:     $M_R \leftarrow M[(\mu + 1)..|M|]$
115:     **return** (M_L, M_R)

121: **function** $\text{Simpira}_K(Y)$
122:     $(Y^0, Y^1) \xleftarrow{n} Y$
123:     $Y^1 \leftarrow Y^1 \oplus K$
124:     **for** $c \leftarrow 1$ **to** 15 **do**
125:         $l \leftarrow (c - 1) \bmod 2$
126:         $r \leftarrow c \bmod 2$
127:         $Y^r \leftarrow Y^r \oplus \text{Simpira}.F_{c,2}(Y^l)$
128:     $C_L^0 \leftarrow Y^0 \oplus K$
129:     $C_L^1 \leftarrow Y^1$
130:     **return** $(C_L^0 \| C_L^1)$

131: **function** $\text{Simpira}.F_{c,b}(X)$
132:     $L \leftarrow (c, b, 0, 0)$
133:     **return** $\text{aesenc}(\text{aesenc}(X, L), 0)$

141: **function** $\text{CTRT}.\mathcal{E}[\widetilde{E}]_K(IV, M_R)$
142:     $(U, V) \xleftarrow{n} IV$
143:     $T \leftarrow U[2..n]$
144:     $m \leftarrow \lceil M_R/n \rceil$
145:     $(M_R^1, \ldots, M_R^m) \xleftarrow{n} M_R$
146:     **for** $i \leftarrow 1$ **to** $m - 1$ **do**
147:         $C_R^i \leftarrow \widetilde{E}_K^{1, T \oplus \langle i-1 \rangle}(V) \oplus M_R^i$
148:     $\kappa_m \leftarrow \widetilde{E}_K^{1, T \oplus \langle m-1 \rangle}(V)$
149:     $C_R^m \leftarrow \kappa_m[1..|M_R^m|] \oplus M_R^m$
150:     **return** $(C_R^1 \| \cdots \| C_R^m)$

161: **function** $\text{CTRT}.\mathcal{D}[\widetilde{E}]_K(IV, C_R)$
162:     **return** $\text{CTRT}.\mathcal{E}[\widetilde{E}]_K(IV, C_R)$

171: **function** $\widetilde{E}_K^{D, T}(X)$
172:     **return** $\text{Deoxys-BC-}n\text{-}n_K^{D \| T}(X)$

201: **function** $\widetilde{\mathcal{D}}_{SK}(A, C)$
202:     $(K_1^1, K_1^2, K_2, K_3) \leftarrow \text{KeyGen}(SK)$
203:     $(C_L, C_R) \leftarrow C$
204:     $M_R \leftarrow \text{CTRT}.\mathcal{D}[\widetilde{E}]_{K_3}(C_L, C_R)$
205:     $X \leftarrow \mathcal{H}_{K_1^1 \| K_1^2}(A, M_R)$
206:     $Y \leftarrow \text{Simpira}_{K_2}^{-1}(C_L)$
207:     $M_L \leftarrow X \oplus Y$
208:     **return** $\text{Decode}_\tau(M_L, M_R)$

211: **function** $\text{Decode}_\tau(M_L, M_R)$
212:     $R \leftarrow M_L[1..\tau]$
213:     $M \leftarrow M_L[(\tau + 1)..2n] \| M_R$
214:     **if** $R = 0^\tau$ **then return** M
215:     **return** $\perp$

221: **function** $\text{Simpira}_K^{-1}(C_L)$
222:     $(C_L^0, C_L^1) \xleftarrow{n} C_L$
223:     $Y^0 \leftarrow C_L^0 \oplus K$
224:     $Y^1 \leftarrow C_L^1$
225:     **for** $c \leftarrow 15$ **downto** 1 **do**
226:         $l \leftarrow (c - 1) \bmod 2$
227:         $r \leftarrow c \bmod 2$
228:         $Y^r \leftarrow Y^r \oplus \text{Simpira}.F_{c,2}(Y^l)$
229:     $Y^0 \leftarrow Y^0 \oplus K$
230:     **return** $(Y^0 \| Y^1)$

231: **function** $\text{KeyGen}(SK)$
232:     **for** $i \leftarrow 1$ **to** 4 **do**
233:         $K_i \leftarrow \widetilde{E}_{SK}^{0, \langle i \rangle}(\langle i \rangle)$
234:     **return** (K_1, K_2, K_3, K_4)

241: **function** $\mathcal{H}_K(A, M_R)$
242:     $W \leftarrow \text{Encode}'(A, M_R)$
243:     $(K_1^1, K_1^2) \xleftarrow{n} K$
244:     $H_1 \leftarrow K_1^1 \cdot \text{BRW}_{K_1^1}(W)$
245:     $H_2 \leftarrow K_1^2 \cdot \text{BRW}_{K_1^2}(W)$
246:     **return** $(H_1 \| H_2)$

251: **function** $\text{Encode}'(A, M)$
252:     $\overline{A} \leftarrow \text{PAD}_n(A)$
253:     $\overline{M} \leftarrow \text{PAD}_n(M)$
254:     $L \leftarrow \langle |A| \rangle_{64} \| \langle |M| \rangle_{64}$
255:     **return** $(\overline{A} \| \overline{M} \| L)$

261: **function** $\text{PAD}_n(X)$
262:     **if** $|X| \bmod n = 0$ **then return** X
263:     **return** $(X \| 0^{n - (|X| \bmod n)})$

$\lceil \log_2(m) \rceil$ additional squarings. Hereafter, we denote by $\mathbb{GF}(2^n)$ the Galois Field with a given irreducible polynomial $p(x)$ of degree n. We represent the elements in the field by n-bit strings. In this context, we use big-endian encoding where the most significant bit is on the left, e.g., $M = (10000111)_2$ represents the polynomial $\mathbf{x}^7 + \mathbf{x}^2 + \mathbf{x} + 1$. For $n = 128$, we fix $p(x) = \mathbf{x}^{128} + \mathbf{x}^7 + \mathbf{x}^2 + \mathbf{x} + 1$. Given an m-word message $M = (M_1, \ldots, M_m)$ and a key $K \in \{0, 1\}^n$, the hash function $\text{BRW}_K(M)$ is defined recursively by

- $\text{BRW}_K(\varepsilon) := 0^n$ if $m = 0$,
- $\text{BRW}_K(M_1) := M_1$ if $m = 1$,

- $\mathrm{BRW}_K(M_1, M_2) := (M_1 \cdot K) \oplus M_2$ if $m = 2$,
- $\mathrm{BRW}_K(M_1, M_2, M_3) := (M_1 \oplus K) \cdot (M_2 \oplus K^2) \oplus M_3$ if $m = 3$,
- $\mathrm{BRW}_K(M_1, \ldots, M_m) := \mathrm{BRW}_K(M_1, \ldots, M_{t-1}) \cdot (M_t \oplus K^t) \oplus \mathrm{BRW}_K$
  $(M_{t+1}, \ldots, M_m)$ if $t \leq m < 2t$ for $t \in \{4, 8, 16, 32, \ldots\}$,

where all multiplications are in $\mathbb{GF}(2^n)$. Since BRW hashing XORs the final block M_m when m is *not* a multiple of four, we perform an additional multiplication, $K \cdot BRW_K(M)$, to prevent predictable output differences.

Our family of hash functions – $\mathcal{H}$ or BRW-256 hereafter – takes as inputs the associated data A and the variable-length part of the message M_R. Therefore, we define an injective encoding function $\mathrm{ENCODE}' : \{0,1\}^* \times \{0,1\}^* \to \{0,1\}^*$ for merging both inputs to a single bit string before hashing. First, ENCODE' pads $\overline{A} \leftarrow \mathrm{PAD}_n(A)$ and $\overline{M_R} \leftarrow \mathrm{PAD}_n(M_R)$ with the minimal number of trailing zeroes such that their lengths after padding are multiples of n. Next, their original lengths in bits are encoded as two 64-bit big-endian-encoded integers: $L \leftarrow \langle |A| \rangle_{64} \parallel \langle |M_R| \rangle_{64}$. Finally, ENCODE' returns $(\overline{A} \parallel \overline{M_R} \parallel L)$, which is used as input to $\mathcal{H}$. The procedure is given in Algorithm 2. Applications that have to process messages of more than 2^{64} bits can alternatively encode $|A|$ and $|M|$ as two 128-bit values, with slightly reduced security.

Key Schedule and Change of Key. Our instantiation requires a 128-bit user-supplied secret key SK. In total, our instantiation of DCT uses four independent 128-bit key words: a 256-bit key $K_1^2 \parallel K_1^2$ for $\mathcal{H}$, a 128-bit key K_3 for $\mathbb{E}$, and a 128-bit key K_3 for $\widetilde{E}$ used in the CTRT mode. We borrow the idea from [20] of deriving the keys for the individual components with $\widetilde{E}$ under the secret SK in counter mode with distinct tweaks; neither those tweaks nor SK are used any further in our mode. So, the derived keys are pairwise independent. We recommend a default stretch of $\tau = 128$ bits, at most 2^{64} bits be encrypted under the same key, and the maximum query length be limited to 2^{40} blocks.

6.2   Concrete Security Bounds

We derive the following conjecture from the existing analysis of SIMPIRA [17].

Conjecture 1 (Security of two-block SIMPIRA). Let $n = 128$ and $b = 2$. Let $\mathbb{E}$ denote SIMPIRA for $2n$-bit inputs. Let **A** be a computationally bounded SPRP adversary on $\mathbb{E}$ with access to two oracles, where **A** asks at most q queries and runs in time at most t. Then, there exists an absolute constant c such that

$$\mathbf{Adv}_{\mathbb{E}, \mathbb{E}^{-1}}^{\mathrm{SPRP}}(\mathbf{A}) \leq \frac{c \cdot q}{2^n}.$$

Theorem 1 and Appendix C in [30] provide the following theorem.

Theorem 4 (IVE Advantage of CTRT [30]). *Fix $n \geq 1$. Let $\mathcal{T}$ be a non-empty set and $\widetilde{\pi} \leftarrow \widetilde{\mathrm{Perm}}(\mathcal{T}, \{0,1\}^n)$. Let **A** be an IVE adversary with access to* an oracle, where **A** runs in time at most t and poses at most q queries to its oracles with at most $8 \le \ell \le |\mathcal{T}|$ blocks in total. Then

$$\mathbf{Adv}_{\mathrm{CTRT}[\tilde{\pi}]}^{\mathrm{IVE}}(\mathbf{A}) \le \frac{1}{2^n} + \frac{1}{|\mathcal{T}|} + \frac{4\ell \log_2(q)}{|\mathcal{T}|} + \frac{\ell \log_2(\ell)}{2^n}.$$

Theorem 5.4 in [5] and Theorem 1 in [38] show that $\mathrm{BRW}_K(M_1, \ldots, M_m)$ is a monic polynomial of degree $2^{\lfloor \log_2 m \rfloor + 1} - 1 \le 2m - 1$. The additional multiplications for the length-encoding block and the final multiplication with $K \cdot \mathrm{BRW}_K(M)$ lead to a monic polynomial of degree $2(m+1)$. For our proposed instantiation for $\mathcal{H}$, we can derive the following statement:

Theorem 5 (BRW Hashing). Let $n, m \ge 1$, and let $\mathcal{X} = \bigcup_{i=0}^{m} \mathrm{GF}(2^n)^i$. Then, the family of hash functions $\mathcal{G} = \{\mathrm{BRW} \mid \mathrm{BRW} : \mathcal{X} \to \mathrm{GF}(2^n)\}$ is ϵ-AXU for $\epsilon \le 2(m+1)/2^n$. Moreover, the family of hash functions $\mathcal{H} = \{\mathrm{BRW}_1, \mathrm{BRW}_2 \twoheadleftarrow \mathcal{G} \times \mathcal{G} \mid H(M) := \mathrm{BRW}_1(M) \| \mathrm{BRW}_2(M)\}$ with independent BRW_1 and BRW_2 is ϵ'-AXU for $\epsilon' \le 4(m+1)^2/2^{2n}$.

Inserting the bounds from Conjecture 1 and Theorems 4 and 5 into those from Lemmata 1 and 2, we can derive the following statements for our proposed instantiation $\mathrm{DCT}_{\mathrm{BRW\text{-}256},\mathrm{SIMPIRA},\mathrm{CTRT}[\tilde{E}]}$. The full version of this work discusses also how to reduce the quadratic dependency on m' to a linear one for $\tau \le n$.

Theorem 6. Let $K \twoheadleftarrow \mathcal{K}$ and let $\tilde{\Pi}$ denote $\mathrm{DCT}_{\mathrm{BRW\text{-}256},\mathrm{SIMPIRA},\mathrm{CTRT}[\tilde{E}]}$ as defined in Algorithm 2. Let $n = 128$, $\tau \le 2n$, $|\mathcal{T}| = 2^{n-1}$, m be the sum of the maximal number blocks of message and associated data for each query, and c be an absolute constant. Define $m' = m + 1$. Then, for $8 \le \ell \le |\mathcal{T}|$, it holds that

$$\mathbf{Adv}_{\tilde{\Pi}}^{\mathrm{DETPRIV}}(q, \ell, t) \le 2 \left(\frac{q^2(2m'^2 + 1)}{2^{2n}} + \frac{3 + cq + 8\ell \log_2(q) + \ell \log_2(\ell)}{2^n} + \delta_{\tilde{E}}^{\mathrm{TPRP}} \right)$$

$$\mathbf{Adv}_{\tilde{\Pi}}^{\mathrm{DETAUTH}}(q, \ell, t) \le \frac{2q^2 m'^2}{2^{2n}} + \frac{12qm'^2}{2^\tau} + \frac{cq}{2^n} + \delta_{\tilde{E}, \tilde{E}^{-1}}^{\mathrm{STPRP}},$$

where $\delta_{\tilde{E}}^{\mathrm{TPRP}}$ and $\delta_{\tilde{E}, \tilde{E}^{-1}}^{\mathrm{STPRP}}$ denote $\mathbf{Adv}_{\tilde{E}}^{\mathrm{TPRP}}(q, O(t))$ and $\mathbf{Adv}_{\tilde{E}, \tilde{E}^{-1}}^{\mathrm{STPRP}}(q, O(t))$.

6.3 Software Performance on x64 Processors

We implemented an optimized version of our proposed instance in C. https:// github.com/medsec/dct. Table 1 summarizes the results of our benchmarks. Our code was compiled using gcc v5.2.1 with options -O3 -maes -mavx2 -mpclmul -march=native, and run (1) on an Intel Core i5-4200M (Haswell) at 2.50 GHz, and (2) on an Intel Core i5-5200U (Broadwell), both with TurboBoost, Speed-Step, and HyperThreading options *disabled*. For measuring, we used the mean from 100 medians of 10000 encryptions each in the single-message setting, where we omitted the cost for key setup, and used the rdtsc instruction. Starting from 512 bytes, the values in Table 1 have a standard deviation of less than 0.02

Table 1. Performance results in cycles per byte for optimized implementations of $DCT_{\mathrm{BRW\text{-}256,SIMPIRA,CTRT[}\tilde{E}]}$ on Haswell and Broadwell, respectively. Details of our benchmarking setup are given in the text.

Construction	Message length (bytes)							
	128	256	512	1024	2048	4096	8192	16384
Haswell	6.17	4.48	3.28	2.65	2.28	2.09	2.00	1.96
Broadwell	6.15	4.45	3.16	2.51	2.14	1.98	1.86	1.81

cycles per byte (cpb). The results show that our proposed instance approaches a performance of less than two cpb on current x64 processors for messages of eight KiB and longer. The difference results majorly from the improved inverse throughput of the `pclmulqdq` instruction (2 cycles per instruction on Haswell, 1 on Broadwell).

7 Discussion and Conclusion

This work proposed Deterministic Counter in Tweak (DCT), a beyond-birthday-bound-secure DAE scheme that combines an almost-XOR-universal family of hash functions with a single call to a double-block-length SPRP, and a beyond-birthday-bound-secure encryption scheme. DCT produces the minimal stretch, e.g., $\tau = 128$ bit for 128-bit security. Our generic construction comes with a straight-forward security proof. We proposed a software-efficient instantiation that profits greatly from the recent progress in the domain of tweakable block ciphers and encryption schemes; in particular, from the TWEAKEY framework, the tweaked counter mode as encryption scheme, and the SIMPIRA construction as $2n$-bit SPRP – both of which allow to exploit AES-NI instructions. As a result, our instantiation can encrypt at speeds of less than two cycles per byte on current x64 processors in the single-message setting. While our generic design employs three independent keys, our instantiation requires only a single 128-bit key and provides security close to that of our generic proposal. Moreover, the use of tweaked counter mode and the Feistel-based SIMPIRA as SPRP yields an inverse-free decryption. DCT is currently defined for messages of $\geq 2n - \tau$ bits; one solution to also allow smaller messages could be to use a padding and two additional distinct tweaks T for long and small messages, respectively. For example, Gueron and Mouha proposed to use $K \cdot T$ instead of K as key for SIMPIRA, using a multiplication in $\mathbb{GF}(2^{128})$. Yet, the detailed security and efficiency implications of this approach are interesting aspects for future work.

References

1. Abdelraheem, M.A., Beelen, P., Bogdanov, A., Tischhauser, E.: Twisted polynomials and forgery attacks on GCM. In: Oswald, E., Fischlin, M. (eds.) EUROCRYPT 2015. LNCS, vol. 9056, pp. 762–786. Springer, Heidelberg (2015)

2. Badertscher, C., Matt, C., Maurer, U., Rogaway, P., Tackmann, B.: Robust authenticated encryption and the limits of symmetric cryptography. In: Groth, J., et al. (eds.) IMACC 2015. LNCS, vol. 9496, pp. 112–129. Springer, Heidelberg (2015). doi:10.1007/978-3-319-27239-9_7

3. Bellare, M., Anand Desai, E., Jokipii, P.R.: A Concrete Security Treatment of Symmetric Encryption. In: FOCS, pp. 394–403. Springer, 1997

4. Bellare, M., Rogaway, P.: Encode-Then-encipher encryption: how to exploit nonces or redundancy in plaintexts for efficient cryptography. In: Okamoto, T. (ed.) ASIACRYPT 2000. LNCS, vol. 1976, pp. 317–330. Springer, Heidelberg (2000)

5. Bernstein, D.J.: Polynomial evaluation and message authentication (2007). http://cr.yp.to/papers, *permanent ID:b1ef3f2d385a926123e1517392e20f8c*, 2

6. Bertoni, G., Daemen, J., Peeters, M., Van Assche, G., Van Keer, R.: Using Keccak technology for AE: Ketje, Keyak and more. In: SHA-3 2014 Workshop, UC Santa Barbara, 22 August 2014

7. Boesgaard, M., Christensen, T., Zenner, E.: Badger – a fast and provably secure MAC. In: Ioannidis, J., Keromytis, A.D., Yung, M. (eds.) ACNS 2005. LNCS, vol. 3531, pp. 176–191. Springer, Heidelberg (2005)

8. Carter, L., Wegman, N.: Universal classes of hash functions. J. Comput. Syst. Sci. **18**(2), 143–154 (1979)

9. Chakraborty, Debrup, Mancillas-López, Cuauhtemoc, Sarkar, Palash: Disk Encryption: Do We Need to Preserve Length? IACR Cryptology ePrint Archive 2015:594 (2015)

10. Chakraborty, D., Sarkar, P.: On modes of operations of a block cipher for authentication and authenticated encryption. Cryptography and Communications, pp. 1–57 (2015)

11. Coron, J.-S., Dodis, Y., Mandal, A., Seurin, Y.: A domain extender for the ideal cipher. In: Micciancio, D. (ed.) TCC 2010. LNCS, vol. 5978, pp. 273–289. Springer, Heidelberg (2010)

12. Dobraunig, Christoph, Eichlseder, Maria, Mendel, Florian: Cryptanalysis of Simpira. IACR Cryptology ePrint Archive 2016:244 (2016)

13. Forler, Christian, List, Eik, Lucks, Stefan, Wenzel, Jakob: Efficient Beyond-Birthday-Bound-Secure Deterministic Authenticated Encryption with Minimal Stretch. IACR Cryptology ePrint Archive 2016:395 (2016)

14. Granger, R., Jovanovic, P., Mennink, B., Neves, S.: Improved masking for tweakable blockciphers with applications to authenticated encryption. In: Fischlin, M., Coron, J.-S. (eds.) EUROCRYPT 2016. LNCS, vol. 9665, pp. 263–293. Springer, Heidelberg (2016). doi:10.1007/978-3-662-49890-3_11

15. Gueron, S., Lindell, Y.: GCM-SIV: Full nonce misuse-resistant authenticated encryption at under one cycle per byte. In: Ray, I., Li, N., Kruegel, C. (eds.) ACM Conference on Computer and Communications Security, pp. 109–119. ACM (2015)

16. Gueron, S., Mouha, N.: Simpira: A Family of Efficient Permutations Using the AES Round Function. IACR Cryptology ePrint Archive, 2016: 122 version 20160214:005409 (2016)

17. Gueron, S., Mouha, N.: Simpira v2: A Family of Efficient Permutations Using the AES Round Function. IACR Cryptology ePrint Archive 2016:122 (2016)

18. Halevi, S., Rogaway, P.: A parallelizable enciphering mode. In: Okamoto, T. (ed.) CT-RSA 2004. LNCS, vol. 2964, pp. 292–304. Springer, Heidelberg (2004)

19. Hoang, V.T., Krovetz, T., Rogaway, P.: Robust authenticated-encryption AEZ and the problem that it solves. In: Oswald, E., Fischlin, M. (eds.) EUROCRYPT 2015. LNCS, vol. 9056, pp. 15–44. Springer, Heidelberg (2015)

20. Iwata, T., Kurosawa, K.: OMAC: one-key CBC MAC. In: Johansson, T. (ed.) FSE 2003. LNCS, vol. 2887, pp. 129–153. Springer, Heidelberg (2003)
21. Iwata, T., Yasuda, K.: BTM: a single-key, inverse-cipher-free mode for deterministic authenticated encryption. In: Jacobson Jr., M.J., Rijmen, V., Safavi-Naini, R. (eds.) SAC 2009. LNCS, vol. 5867, pp. 313–330. Springer, Heidelberg (2009)
22. Iwata, T., Yasuda, K.: HBS: a single-key mode of operation for deterministic authenticated encryption. In: Dunkelman, O. (ed.) FSE 2009. LNCS, vol. 5665, pp. 394–415. Springer, Heidelberg (2009)
23. Jean, J., Nikolic, I., Peyrin, T.: Tweaks and keys for block ciphers: the TWEAKEY framework. In: Sarkar, P., Iwata, T. (eds.) ASIACRYPT 2014. LNCS, vol. 8874, pp. 274–288. Springer, Heidelberg (2014)
24. Jean, J., Nikolić, I., Peyrin, T.: Deoxys v1.3, 2015. Second-round submission to the CAESAR competition, http://competitions.cr.yp.to/caesar-submissions.html
25. Jean, J., Nikolić, I., Peyrin, T.: Joltik v1.3 (2015). Second-round submission to the CAESAR competition, http://competitions.cr.yp.to/caesar-submissions.html
26. Ted Krovetz.:HS1-SIV (2014). http://competitions.cr.yp.to/caesar-submissions.html
27. Minematsu, K.: Beyond-birthday-bound security based on tweakable block cipher. In: Dunkelman, O. (ed.) FSE 2009. LNCS, vol. 5665, pp. 308–326. Springer, Heidelberg (2009)
28. Minematsu, K.: Authenticated Encryption without Tag Expansion (or, How to Accelerate AERO). IACR Cryptology ePrint Archive, 2015:738 (2015)
29. Minematsu, K.: Building blockcipher from small-block tweakable blockcipher. Des. Code Crypt. **74**(3), 645–663 (2015)
30. Peyrin, T., Seurin, Y.: Counter-in-Tweak: Authenticated Encryption Modes for Tweakable Block Ciphers. Cryptology ePrint Archive, Report 2015/1049 (2015)
31. Procter, G., Cid, C.: On weak keys and forgery attacks against polynomial-based mac schemes. In: Moriai, S. (ed.) FSE 2013. LNCS, vol. 8424, pp. 287–304. Springer, Heidelberg (2014)
32. Reyhanitabar, R., Vaudenay, S., Vizár, D.: Misuse-resistant variants of the OMD authenticated encryption mode. In: Chow, S.S.M., Liu, J.K., Hui, L.C.K., Yiu, S.M. (eds.) ProvSec 2014. LNCS, vol. 8782, pp. 55–70. Springer, Heidelberg (2014)
33. Rogaway, P.: Nonce-based symmetric encryption. In: Roy, B., Meier, W. (eds.) FSE 2004. LNCS, vol. 3017, pp. 348–359. Springer, Heidelberg (2004)
34. Rogaway, P., Shrimpton, T.: A provable-security treatment of the key-wrap problem. In: Vaudenay, S. (ed.) EUROCRYPT 2006. LNCS, vol. 4004, pp. 373–390. Springer, Heidelberg (2006)
35. Rogaway, P., Shrimpton, T.: Deterministic authenticated-encryption: a provable-security treatment of the key-wrap problem. Cryptology ePrint Archive, Report 2006/221. (Full Version) (2006)
36. Rønjom, S.: Invariant subspaces in Simpira. IACR Cryptology ePrint Archive, 2016:248 (2016)
37. Sarkar, P.: Improving upon the TET mode of operation. In: Nam, K.-H., Rhee, G. (eds.) ICISC 2007. LNCS, vol. 4817, pp. 180–192. Springer, Heidelberg (2007)
38. Sarkar, P.: Efficient tweakable enciphering schemes from (Block-Wise) universal hash functions. IEEE Trans. Inf. Theory **55**(10), 4749–4760 (2009)
39. Shrimpton, T., Terashima, R.S.: A modular framework for building variable-input-length tweakable ciphers. In: Sako, K., Sarkar, P. (eds.) ASIACRYPT 2013, Part I. LNCS, vol. 8269, pp. 405–423. Springer, Heidelberg (2013)
40. Wang, P., Feng, D., Wu, W.: HCTR: a variable-input-length enciphering mode. In: Feng, D., Lin, D., Yung, M. (eds.) CISC 2005. LNCS, vol. 3822, pp. 175–188. Springer, Heidelberg (2005)

Improved (related-key) Attacks on Round-Reduced KATAN-32/48/64 Based on the Extended Boomerang Framework

Jiageng Chen[1]([⊠]), Je Sen Teh[2]([⊠]), Chunhua Su[3], Azman Samsudin[2], and Junbin Fang[4]

[1] Computer School, Central China Normal University, Wuhan 430079, China
jiageng.chen@mail.ccnu.edu.cn
[2] School of Computer Sciences, Universiti Sains Malaysia, George Town, Malaysia
jesen_teh@hotmail.com, Azman.samsudin@usm.my
[3] School of Information Science,
Japan Advanced Institute of Science and Technology,
1-1 Asahidai, Nomi, Ishikawa 923-1292, Japan
chsu@jaist.ac.jp
[4] Department of Optoelectronic Engineering,
Jinan University, Guangzhou 510632, China
junbinfang@gmail.com

Abstract. The boomerang attack is one of the many extensions of the original differential attack. It has been widely applied to successfully attack many existing ciphers. In this paper, we investigate an extended version of the boomerang attack and show that it is still a very powerful tool especially in the related-key setting. A new branch-and-bound searching strategy which involves the extended boomerang framework is then introduced. We provide an improved cryptanalysis on the KATAN family (a family of hardware-oriented block ciphers proposed in CHES 2009) based on the boomerang attack. In the related-key setting, we were able to greatly improve upon the previous results to achieve the best results, namely 150 and 133 rounds by far for KATAN48/64 respectively. For KATAN32 in the related-key setting and all KATAN variants in the single-key setting, our results are the best ones in the differential setting although inferior to the meet-in-the-middle attack.

Keywords: KATAN32/48/64 · Related-key attack · Boomerang attack · Differential attack

1 Introduction

The statistical attack is one of the most effective attacks against symmetric key cryptography. It includes many popular cryptanalysis techniques such as the linear attack, differential attack and so on. Among these methods, the differential attack is one of the most popular approaches due to its wide range of

© Springer International Publishing Switzerland 2016
J.K. Liu and R. Steinfeld (Eds.): ACISP 2016, Part II, LNCS 9723, pp. 333–346, 2016.
DOI: 10.1007/978-3-319-40367-0_21

applications to many ciphers including DES and AES. More importantly, it has many variations such as the impossible differential attack [5], multi-differential attack [7] and others which make differential attacks more flexible compared to linear attacks. Among these variations, the boomerang attack [22] proposed by Wagner back in 1999 provides an interesting approach to differential cryptanalysis. By considering quartets of differences instead of pairs, the attack separates traditional cipher distinguishers into two parts. This way, the burden of finding good differential characteristics can be greatly eased, leading to better distinguishers. The amplified boomerang attack [14] and rectangle attack [3] were later proposed to improve the efficiency of the boomerang attack. Unlike the original version which requires adaptive chosen plaintext and ciphertext queries, the modified boomerang attacks only require chosen plaintext queries which is a more practical attack assumption. The power of this attack has been demonstrated when it was used to break the full-round AES-192/256 [6] in the related-key setting. Since the boomerang attack falls under the differential attack framework, one natural question is which of these two methods will lead to better results. Although there are a lot of recent research work focusing on exploiting the relationship between statistical attacks such as the differential and linear attacks [8] as well as the zero correlation linear and integral attacks [21], the relationship between the boomerang and differential attack has not been fully investigated. However, the boomerang attack often outperforms the differential attack which suggests that under the condition of limited computing resources, the boomerang attack is a feasible option.

The design of lightweight block ciphers and cryptanalysis of these ciphers have recently attracted a lot of research attention. The KATAN family proposed in CHES 2009 [9] is one example. Although the cipher KTANTAN [9] proposed by the same authors was broken with a meet-in-the-middle attack [23], the KATAN family still remains secure after many years of cryptanalysis. There have been several attacks on the KATAN family in both single-key and related-key settings. In the single-key setting, a conditional differential attack [15] was able to break 78, 70 and 68 rounds of KATAN32/48/64 respectively. In [2], the authors took advantage of the full differential distribution to improve the attack on KATAN32, breaking 115 rounds. However, this approach cannot be applied on KATAN48/64 since the full differential distribution cannot be easily computed. Later on, more research work put focus on meet-in-the-middle attacks (MITM) [10,12,13,24]. In particular, [20] was recently published on e-print claiming to break 206 rounds of KATAN32 using MITM. The cube attack was also applied to KATAN32 in the single key model [1] with better results than the differential attack.

In the related-key setting, [16] introduced 120, 103 and 90-round attacks on KATAN32/48/64 respectively. By taking advantage of the key scheduling, [11] further improved the result to 174, 145 and 130 rounds respectively using the boomerang attack. In this paper, we investigate the extended boomerang technique to improve upon the previously found boomerang differential characteristics. As a result, we can achieve the best records in attacking KATAN48/64 in the related-key setting. In all the other cases, while the results are inferior to the MITM attacks, we are able to deliver the best differential attack results so far. Particularly in the single key setting, our approach is able to outperform the attack on KATAN32 [2] which uses the full differential distribution. Although their distinguisher is better than ours, we point out that using the full distribution will result in an inefficient key recovery attack. Their methods are also not applicable to larger block sizes. From this point of view, our approach is more realistic in practice. We summarize our results along with previous related results in Table 1.

We organize the paper as follows: In Sect. 2, the boomerang attack and its extended version are described. In Sect. 3, we demonstrate the boomerang distinguisher search and key recovery attack on the KATAN family in both single-key and related-key settings. Finally, we conclude our paper with a summary of findings in Sect. 4.

2   The Framework of the Boomerang Cryptanalysis

Ever since its proposal, differential cryptanalysis [5] quickly became one of the main cryptanalytic methods used today. Based on its original form, researchers have later derived many extended variants such as truncated differential cryptanalysis, multi-differential cryptanalysis and so on. The boomerang attack can also be viewed as an extension of differential attack, but it is more unique because it modifies the original attack in a structural manner. Let m be the block size of a block cipher E, and we assume E to be a cascade cipher consisting of three concatenated parts $E_K = E_2 \circ E_1 \circ E_0$ influenced by a secret key K. Here E is a n-bit to n-bit keyed permutation $E : \{0,1\}^n \times \{0,1\}^k \to \{0,1\}^n$. E_2 is the final rounds where the subkey bits are the primary target whereas $E_1 \circ E_0$ is the distinguisher.

Boomerang Attack. The motivation behind the boomerang attack is that finding two short efficient differential distinguishers is easier than finding a long one. The original version of the boomerang attack is a combination of a chosen plaintext and ciphertext attack, which is a cryptanalysis model that makes very strong assumptions with regard to the capabilities of an attacker. Furthermore, the original boomerang attack is not efficient when performing the last round attack due to its "boomerang" property. Later, the amplified boomerang attack was proposed to solve these problems. Given that the rectangle attack is an extension of the original boomerang attack, we will refer to the amplified or rectangle attack as a boomerang throughout the paper.

In the chosen plaintext setting, an attacker chooses plaintext pairs with differences (α, α), and expect the differences between C_1, C_3 and C_2, C_4 to be (δ, δ). Randomly, $P_R((\alpha, \alpha) \to (\delta, \delta)) = 2^{-2m}$, thus the boomerang distinguisher should have probability greater than 2^{-2m}. For E_0, the attacker searches for high probability differential paths $\alpha \to \beta_i$, where $0 \le i \le 2^m - 1$. For any differential path

Table 1. Comparison of attacks against KATAN family

Cipher	Attacking Technique	# Attacking Rounds	Time Complexity	Data Complexity	Memory Complexity	Reference
KATAN32	Differential (Single Key)	78	2^{76}	2^{16} CP	Not given	[15]
	MitM (Single Key)	110	2^{77}	138 KP	$2^{75.1}$	[12]
	Differential (Single Key)	115	2^{79}	138 KP	$2^{75.1}$	[2]
	Boomerang (Single Key)	**117**	$\mathbf{2^{79.3}}$	$\mathbf{2^{27.3}}$ **CP**	$\mathbf{2^{29.9}}$	**Ours**
	MitM (Single Key)	119	$2^{79.1}$	144 CP	$2^{79.1}$	[13]
	MitM (Single Key)	153	$2^{78.5}$	2^5 CP	2^{76}	[10]
	Cube (Single Key)	155	$2^{78.3}$	2^{32} CP	$2^{33.5}$	[1]
	MitM (Single Key)	175	$2^{79.3}$	3 KP	$2^{79.58}$	[24]
	MitM (Single Key)	206	2^{79}	3 KP	$2^{78.1}$	[20]
	Differential (Related Key)	120	2^{31}	Practical (CP)	Practical	[16]
	Boomerang (Related Key)	174	$2^{78.8}$	$2^{27.6}$ CP	$2^{26.6}$	[11]
	Boomerang (Related Key)	**187**	$\mathbf{2^{78.4}}$	$\mathbf{2^{31.8}}$ **CP**	$\mathbf{2^{33.9}}$	**Ours**
KATAN48	Differential (Single Key)	70	2^{78}	2^{31} CP	Not given	[15]
	Boomerang (Single Key)	**87**	$\mathbf{2^{78}}$	$\mathbf{2^{36.7}}$ **CP**	$\mathbf{2^{39.3}}$	**Ours**
	MitM (Single Key)	100	2^{78}	128 KP	2^{78}	[12]
	MitM (Single Key)	105	$2^{79.1}$	144 KP	$2^{79.1}$	[13]
	MitM (Single Key)	129	$2^{78.5}$	2^5 CP	2^{76}	[10]
	MitM (Single Key)	130	$2^{79.45}$	2 KP	2^{79}	[24]
	MitM (Single Key)	148	2^{79}	2 KP	2^{77}	[20]
	Differential (Related Key)	103	2^{25}	Practical (CP)	Practical	[16]
	Boomerang (Related Key)	145	$2^{78.5}$	$2^{38.4}$ CP	$2^{37.4}$	[11]
	Boomerang (Related Key)	**150**	$\mathbf{2^{77.6}}$	$\mathbf{2^{47.2}}$ **CP**	$\mathbf{2^{49.8}}$	**Ours**
KATAN64	Differential (Single Key)	68	2^{78}	2^{32} CP	Not given	[15]
	Boomerang (Single Key)	**72**	$\mathbf{2^{78}}$	$\mathbf{2^{55.1}}$ **CP**	$\mathbf{2^{58.1}}$	**Ours**
	MitM (Single Key)	94	$2^{77.68}$	116 KP	$2^{77.68}$	[12]
	MitM (Single Key)	99	$2^{79.1}$	142 KP	$2^{79.1}$	[13]
	MitM (Single Key)	112	$2^{79.45}$	2 KP	2^{79}	[24]
	MitM (Single Key)	119	$2^{78.5}$	2^5 CP	2^{74}	[10]
	MitM (Single Key)	129	2^{79}	2 KP	2^{77}	[20]
	Differential (Related Key)	90	2^{27}	Practical (CP)	Practical	[16]
	Boomerang (Related Key)	130	$2^{78.1}$	$2^{53.1}$ CP	$2^{52.1}$	[11]
	Boomerang (Related Key)	**133**	$\mathbf{2^{78.5}}$	$\mathbf{2^{58.4}}$ **CP**	$\mathbf{2^{61.4}}$	**Ours**

KP: Known Plaintext, CP: Chosen Plaintext

$\alpha \rightarrow \beta_i$ starting from a message pair P_1, P_2, the attacker expects that the differential path starting from the message pair P_3, P_4 should have the same form. Thus after E_0, the probability cost is $\sum_{i=0}^{r-1} p_i^2$ where $r < 2^m$ and $p_i = P(\alpha \rightarrow \beta_i)$.

Two edges in the middle quartet have the difference value β_i. Therefore if we assume the third edge to have a difference γ_j with a random probability of 2^{-m}, then the last edge will have difference value γ_j with probability 1 since the XOR sum of the quartet edges should be 0. Here again we can choose as many γ_j as possible where j is also bounded by the block size 2^m. For E_1 due to the middle quartet shift, we start from two γ_j differences and hope to reach the output difference δ. Denote $q_j = P(\gamma_j \rightarrow \delta)$, then the probability can be similarly computed as $\sum_{j=0}^{t-1} q_j^2, t < 2^m$. The total probability can be computed as:

$$P_{bmg}((\alpha, \alpha) \rightarrow (\delta, \delta)) = \sum_{i=0}^{r-1} p_i^2 \cdot \sum_{j=0}^{t-1} q_j^2 \cdot 2^{-m}$$

Since $P_{bmg}((\alpha, \alpha) \rightarrow (\delta, \delta)) > 2^{-2m}$, thus we need:

$$P_{bmg-dist} = \sum_{i=0}^{r-1} p_i^2 \cdot \sum_{j=0}^{t-1} q_j^2 > 2^{-m} \tag{1}$$

Here $P_{bmg-dist}$ denotes the distinguisher probability, which is consistent with previous work such as in [11]. Please refer to Fig. 1 for the boomerang model.

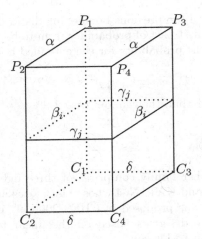

Fig. 1. The model of Boomerang attack

The framework of the boomerang can be further improved by considering various differential quartets in the middle. The idea was first introduced in [22] and was later mentioned in [4]. We refer to the concept as an extended boomerang in this paper. In the boomerang setting, we are assuming that E_0 has two differential paths $\alpha \rightarrow \beta_i$ that has to appear at the same time so that the middle quartet has the format such as $(\beta_i, \beta_i, \gamma_j, \gamma_j)$. However, the two differential paths in E_0 need not be the same, thus we actually missed a lot of combinations in the middle. For example, let us consider the following scenario:

$$E_0 : p_i = P(\alpha \rightarrow \beta_i), p_j = P(\alpha \rightarrow \beta_j)$$

$$E_1 : q_s = P(\gamma_s \rightarrow \delta), q_t = P(\gamma_t \rightarrow \delta)$$

$$Quartet : (\beta_i, \beta_j, \gamma_s, \gamma_t) \text{ satisfying } \beta_i \oplus \beta_j \oplus \gamma_s \oplus \gamma_t = 0$$

Now we have all combinations in the middle quartet that can still lead to the output difference δ. This will potentially increase the total probability when all these cases are taken into consideration. Let u and v be the size of the differential set for $\alpha \rightarrow \beta_i$ and $\gamma_s \rightarrow \delta$ respectively. This leads us to the new calculation formula:

$$P_{exBmg} = \sum_{j=0}^{u-1}\sum_{i=0}^{u-1} p_{\beta_i} \cdot p_{\beta_j} \times \sum_s \sum_t q_{\gamma_s} \cdot q_{\gamma_t} \times 2^{-m}$$

Once $\beta_i, \beta_j, \gamma_s$ is decided in the middle quartet, γ_t is determined with probability one, namely, $\gamma_t = \beta_i \oplus \beta_j \oplus \gamma_s$, thus we have:

$$P_{exBmg} = \sum_{j=0}^{u-1}\sum_{i=0}^{u-1} p_{\beta_i} \cdot p_{\beta_j} \times \sum_{i=0}^{u-1}\sum_{j=0}^{u-1}\sum_{s=0}^{v-1} q_{\gamma_s} \cdot q_{\beta_i \oplus \beta_j \oplus \gamma_s} \times 2^{-m} \tag{2}$$

To be consistent with the previous boomerang distinguisher for ease of comparison, we denote the first part of probability term to be $\hat{p}^2$, and second part to be $\hat{q}^2$. We then define the probability for the extended boomerang distinguisher to be:

$$P_{exBmg-dist} = \hat{p}^2 \times \hat{q}^2 > 2^{-m}$$

which should be greater than the random case 2^{-m}.

3   KATAN Family

The KATAN block cipher family comprises of three lightweight block ciphers KATAN32, KATAN48 and KATAN64 whose block sizes are 32 bits, 48 bits and 64 bits respectively. It was proposed in CHES 2009 [9] and it is a well known cipher in the area. The design is based on the linear feedback shift register (LFSR) and supports an 80-bit key.

The key scheduling function expands an 80-bit user-provided key k_i ($0 \leq i < 80$) into a 508-bit subkey sk_i ($0 \leq i < 508$) by the following linear operations,

$$sk_i = \begin{cases} k_i \ (0 \leq i < 80), \\ k_{i-80} \oplus k_{i-61} \oplus k_{i-50} \oplus k_{i-13} \ (80 \leq i < 508). \end{cases}$$

These operations are expressed as an 80-bit LFSR whose polynomial is $x_{80} + x_{61} + x_{50} + x_{13} + 1$ as shown in Fig. 2.

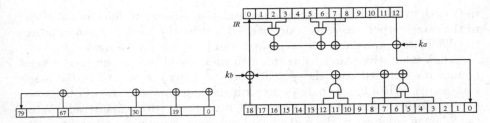

Fig. 2. Key scheduling function of   **Fig. 3.** Round function of KATAN32
KATAN32/48/64

In the round function, each bit of a plaintext is loaded into registers L_1 and L_2. Then, these are updated as follows:

$$f_a(L_1) = L_1[x_1] \oplus L_1[x_2] \oplus (L_1[x_3] \cdot L_1[x_4]) \oplus (L_1[x_5] \cdot IR) \oplus k_a,$$
$$f_b(L_2) = L_2[y_1] \oplus L_2[y_2] \oplus (L_2[y_3] \cdot L_2[y_4]) \oplus (L_2[y_5] \cdot L_2[y_6]) \oplus k_b,$$
$$L_1[i] = L_1[i-1]\ (1 \leq i < |L_1|),\quad L_1[0] = f_b(L_2),$$
$$L_2[i] = L_2[i-1]\ (1 \leq i < |L_2|),\quad L_2[0] = f_a(L_1),$$

where $\oplus$ and $\cdot$ are bitwise XOR and AND operations, respectively, and $L[x]$ denotes the x-th bit of L, IR is the round constant value defined in the specification, and k_a and k_b are two subkey bits. Table 2 shows the detailed parameters of KATAN32/48/64. For round i, k_a and k_b correspond to $sk_{2(i-1)}$ and $sk_{2(i-1)+1}$, respectively. After 254 rounds (1-254 round), values of registers are output as a ciphertext. Fig. 3 illustrates the round function of KATAN32.

Table 2. Parameters of KATAN family

Algorithm	$|L_1|$	$|L_2|$	x_1	x_2	x_3	x_4	x_5	y_1	y_2	y_3	y_4	y_5	y_6
KATAN32	13	19	12	7	8	5	3	18	7	12	10	8	3
KATAN48	19	29	18	12	15	7	6	28	19	21	13	15	6
KATAN64	25	39	24	15	20	11	9	38	25	33	21	14	9

4   Improved Attack on KATAN Family

4.1   Novel Searching Strategy

The basic searching strategy used to find differentials is a branch-and-bound algorithm divided into two parts. The first part (*single trail search*) is based on the branch-and-bound algorithm proposed by Matsui [19]. It performs a search for individual differential paths that have the best probabilities. These paths are then used in the second part of the algorithm (*cluster search*) which expands the search to find other paths that start from the same input difference and lead to the same output difference. Any paths found by the *cluster search* improves the differential probability of the paths found by *single trail search*.

As an exhaustive search using this algorithm would take a long time, several bounds are imposed onto the search. The first bound, θ is used in the *single trail search*. When $\theta = 1$, only paths with the best probabilities will be stored for the *cluster search* whereas $\theta = 0$ will store every path exhaustively. When the θ bound is loosened, the paths found can range from high probability paths to extremely low probability paths. To filter out paths with low probability, a second bound λ is used. As an example, if $\lambda = 2^{-16}$, only paths with probabilities larger than 2^{-16} will be stored for the *cluster search*. The *cluster search* itself has a bound μ which ranges from [0,1] (similar to θ).

For ciphers with block size less than 32-bit, it is possible to derive all the differential paths, so that the size of the differential set u or v could reach $2^m - 1$. However, for larger size greater than say 48 bits, we are still bounded to searching a subset of all differential paths with relatively high probabilities. Based on the extended boomerang framework, we derive the following advanced algorithm which can be used to improve the cryptanalytic capability of the boomerang attack:

Extended Boomerang Characteristic Searching Algorithm.

1. For E_0 precompute the good differential paths $(\alpha \rightarrow \beta_i)$ using branch-and-bound algorithm where $i \leq u$. Store all the β_i in a set Φ.
2. Proceed similarly for E_1 to find paths $(\gamma_j \rightarrow \delta)$, $j \leq v$, and save the output differences in a set Ω.
3. For all the $\beta_i, \beta_j \in \Phi$ and $\gamma_s \in \Omega$, compute $\gamma_t = \beta_i \oplus \beta_j \oplus \gamma_s$. If $\gamma_t \in \Omega$, then $(\beta_i, \beta_j, \gamma_s, \gamma_t)$ is a valid quartet, and we can add the corresponding paths' probability to the total boomerang probability.

4.2   Related Key Boomerang Distinguisher Search

To perform a basic boomerang search, the *single trail search* and *cluster search* algorithms are performed separately for E_0 and E_1. As the clustering effect for E_1 starts from one output difference δ to multiple intermediary differences γ, the branch-and-bound algorithm has to be applied in reverse (decryption) starting from δ to find multiple γ. The search is performed for various combinations of E_0 and E_1 rounds to find the optimal middle point for the boomerang attack. In the related key setting, the search algorithm also involves key differences. As a starting point, we build upon the findings of Isobe et al. [11] who found a 140-round distinguisher with a probability of $2^{-27.2}$. In their paper, they identified sets of plaintext/key differences that lead to *blank steps* that have no differences in registers and subkeys. We use these sets as the inputs of our E_0 search and also use them to find ciphertext/key sets for the reverse E_1 search.

To find starting points for the E_1 search (ciphertext and key differences), we first perform the E_0 search starting from a designated intermediate round.

E.g. if the number of rounds for E_0 is 70, we start our search from round 71 onwards. By using the same sets from [11] as a guide, we obtain the output and key differences which are used as inputs to the E_1 search. The best results for the basic related key boomerang search is shown in Table 3 with the following settings: $(\theta = 0, \mu = 0.5, \lambda = 2^{-20})$. It can be seen that the branch-and-bound algorithm is able to improve Isobe's 140-round distinguisher probability $(2^{-27.2} \rightarrow 2^{-26.58214})$. We are also able to push a valid distinguisher for 2 more rounds to obtain a 142-round distinguisher with probability of $2^{-30.58214}$.

Next, the extended search algorithm is applied where β_i and γ_s from the basic boomerang search are stored in sets Φ and Ω respectively. We found that for certain values of α and δ, the extended search is unable to find additional quartets, therefore did not improve the existing distinguisher probability. However, there also exist other α and δ values that lead to a large amount of additional quartets. The following settings were used for the branch-and-bound search: $(\theta = 0, \mu = 0.5)$ whereas the λ bound varies based on input. We provide only the best result found in Table 4 where large improvements to the overall distinguisher probability are obtained. We are able to improve upon the previously found 142-round distinguisher by 12 rounds, obtaining a 154-round distinguisher with a probability of $2^{-29.7209}$ after applying the extended boomerang search.

The conditional difference is another technique which has been used in previous research work such as [11,16]. For KATAN, the only non-linear part is the AND logic gate. According to the AND table, if we fix one of the two inputs to the AND gate to be 0, then any difference in the other input will be canceled out and the final output difference will be 0. Based on this observation, we can improve the probability of E_0 by fixing some of the plaintext bits. The downside of using this technique is that the message space will be reduced, thus we have to determine if the probability gain will surpass the decrease of the message space. Fortunately, the extended boomerang technique can potentially amplify the effect of the conditional difference approach due to the extra quartets we can collect in the middle. For KATAN32, we set $L_2[1] = L_2[4] = L_2[8] = 0$ for the input difference $\alpha = 10020040$ and key differences located at k_6, k_{25}. As a result, we can improve the distinguisher probability to $2^{-23.7209}$. The results of the distinguisher for KATAN32/48/64 are located in Table 4. The application of the extended boomerang in the single key setting follows the same steps, but with the exclusion of key differences. Please refer to the appendix for the distinguishers in the single-key setting. The overall related key extended boomerang search algorithm is summarized below:

1. Identify an input set that leads to *blank rounds* for the E_0 search. For this input, determine the fixed bits for the conditional difference technique.
2. Perform *single trail search* and *cluster search* for $\#E_0$ rounds. Store all intermediary differences, β_i in a set Φ along with their probabilities (which have been improved using the sufficient condition technique).
3. Identify an input set that leads to *blank rounds* for the E_1 search. Using this input set, start from $(\#E_0 + 1)$ rounds and perform the *single trail search* for $\#E_1$ rounds to obtain the corresponding output difference, δ and output key difference.

4. Using δ and output key difference as a starting point, the *single trail search* and *cluster search* is performed in reverse (decryption) starting from round-$(\#E_0+\#E_1)$ for $\#E_1$ rounds. Store all intermediary differences, γ_i in a set Ω along with their probabilities.
5. For all the $\beta_i, \beta_j \in \Phi$ and $\gamma_s \in \Omega$, compute $\gamma_t = \beta_i \oplus \beta_j \oplus \gamma_s$. If $\gamma_t \in \Omega$, then $(\beta_i, \beta_j, \gamma_s, \gamma_t)$ is a valid quartet, and we can add the corresponding paths' probability to the total boomerang probability.

Table 3. Related Key Boomerang Distinguisher on KATAN32 (before extended search)

α	$\#E_0$	Prob p (log_2)	δ	$\#E_1$	Prob q (log_2)	Total Rounds	Final Prob (log_2)
10020040	70	-6.79	280184	70	-6.5	140	-26.58
10020040	70	-6.79	280184	71	-7.5	141	-28.58
10020040	70	-6.79	280184	72	-8.5	142	-30.58

4.3 Key Recovery Attacks

Finally, we demonstrate the concrete key recovery attack for the KATAN family in both related-key and single-key setting. [11] has already provided an optimized key recovery framework. Because each round is rather cheap for the KATAN family and we want to add many rounds in E_2, the differential pattern will be lost. This makes sieving techniques impossible. In other words, the key recovery technique in [11] is not related to the exact output difference values, thus it is easy to seamlessly apply here for a fair comparison. The principle of the attack and some facts of KATAN family used in the attack are listed below:

1. Use meet-in-the-middle approach to recover the key. This is achieved by storing all the ciphertexts pairs in a table, guessing the subkey bits for decryption then checking for matches in the table.
2. The differential state is known after $\#E_2$ rounds by only guessing $(\#E_2-4)$-round subkeys.

Table 4. Boomerang distinguisher for KATAN32/48/64 in the related-key setting

Ciphers	Total rounds	$\#E_0$	$\#E_1$	α	δ	Before ES($log2$)	After ES($log2$)	After SC	$\lambda_{E_0}/\lambda_{E_1}$ difference	key conditions	plaintext
KATAN32	154	70	84	1002 0040	280 184	-42.43	-29.72	-23.72	$2^{-24}/2^{-22}$	k_6, k_{25}	$L_2[1] = L_2[4] = L_2[8] = 0$
KATAN48	126	63	63	c00018 0c0600	800000 001051	-58.15	-46.40	-32.40	$2^{-22}/2^{-22}$	k_0, k_{19}	$L_2[0] = L_2[1] = L_2[2] = L_2[11] = L_2[17] = 0,$ $L_2[10] \neq L_2[18]$
KATAN64	116	56	60	1c00e 00000	100000 703800	-62.43	-50.84	-42.84	$2^{-18}/2^{-26}$	k_{11}	$L_2[9] = L_2[10] = L_2[11] = L_2[33] = 0$

3. A trade-off trick can be achieved by using the partial matching method which involves matching only part of the differential state instead of the whole. This technique is also known as the "early abort" mentioned in paper [17] and [18]. Denote P_r as the probability that a subkey candidate is the correct key, which is supposed to be $N^2 \times 2^{-2m}$, where N is the number plaintext pairs. Let r denote the number of rounds that we do not guess subkeys (except for the first skipped round, we guess 1 bit). By using the partial matching technique, we can improve the probability as follows:

(a) KATAN32: $P_r = N^2 \times 2^{-86+4r}$, $r \geq 6$, known difference bits when matching is $S_{matching} = 43 - 2r$.

(b) KATAN48: $P_r = N^2 \times 2^{-120+8r}$, $r \geq 4$, known difference bits when matching is $S_{matching} = 59 - 4r$.

(c) KATAN64: $P_r = N^2 \times 2^{-152+12r}$, $r \geq 3$, known difference bits when matching is $S_{matching} = 74 - 6r$.

$\#E_2$ denotes the number of rounds for the key recovery phase, then the subkey bits we need to guess is denoted by $2(\#E_2 - r) + 1$. Since N is the number plaintext pairs required, then we can generate N^2 quartets. To assure that the right quartet will appear, we set $N = 2^{\frac{m}{2}} \times P_r^{-1/2}$. Since we adapt the meet-in-the-middle approach, two pairs of plaintexts and ciphertexts need to be processed independently, thus the data complexity D is $2^{\frac{m}{2}+1} \times P_r^{-1/2}$. The key recovery steps are as follows:

1. Choose N plaintext pairs (P_1, P_2) and (P_3, P_4) such that $P_1 \oplus P_2 = P_3 \oplus P_4 = \alpha$, ask for ciphertexts C_1, C_2, C_3 and C_4 under secret key K_1, K_2, K_3 and K_4.
2. For each guess of $2(\#E_2 - r) + 1$ bits of subkey for K_i (Guess one K_i and others are determined), do the following:
   (a) For both (C_1, C_2), derive $S_{matching}$ bits of known differences by decrypting t rounds. XOR with δ and store in the big table.
   (b) For each pair (C_3, C_4), do
      i. Decrypt $\#E_2$ rounds and compute the $S_{matching}$ bits of the known difference.
      ii. Check if the value matches the ones stored in the table. If it exists, proceed the following step.
      iii. Brute force search the rest of the $80 - (2(\#E_2 - r) + 1) = 79 - 2(\#E_2 - r)$ unknown bits. Verify with fresh plaintext and ciphertext pairs, output the correct key if passed.

Step 2(a) and 2(b)-i requires to compute ($\frac{2^{2(\#E_2-r-1)} \times N \times 2 \times \#E_2}{\#E_0 + \#E_1 + \#E_2}$ $\#E_0 + \#E_1 + \#E_2$) rounds of KATAN32/48/64. Then after filtering, we have $2^{2(\#E_2-r)+1} \times P_r$ key candidates remaining. To brute force search the rest key bits, step(b)-iii takes $2^{2(\#E_2-r)+1} \times P_r \times 2^{79-2(\#E_2-r)} = 2^{80} \times P_r$. As a result, the total time complexity can be denoted as

$$T = 2 \times \frac{2^{2(\#E_2-r-1)} \times N \times 2 \times \#E_2}{\#E_0 + \#E_1 + \#E_2} + 2^{80} \times P_r$$

The memory complexity depends on Step2(a) where $2 \times N$ state values need to be stored.

Now based on the derived distinguishers for both single-key and related-key settings, we test all the possible variables for $\#E_2$ and r to derive the optimal results shown in Tables 5 and 6 respectively.

Table 5. Cryptanalysis results for KATAN family in the single-key setting

Ciphers	Total rounds	$\#E_0$	$\#E_1$	$\#E_2$	r	Dist Prob(log_2)	$T(log_2)$	$D(log_2)$	$MEM(bytes)$
KATAN32	117	35	48	34	7	-21.78	79.25	27.89	29.89
KATAN48	87	35	25	27	5	-23.36	78.00	36.68	39.26
KATAN64	72	30	26	16	3	-44.26	77.99	55.13	58.13

Table 6. Cryptanalysis results for KATAN family in the Related-key setting

Ciphers	Total rounds	$\#E_0$	$\#E_1$	$\#E_2$	r	Dist Prob(log_2)	$T(log_2)$	$D(log_2)$	$MEM(bytes)$
KATAN32	187	70	84	33	7	-23.72	78.39	31.86	33.86
KATAN48	150	63	63	24	4	-32.40	77.60	47.20	49.79
KATAN64	133	56	60	17	3	-42.84	78.46	58.42	61.42

5   Conclusion

In this paper, we investigated the extended boomerang attacks. Our study showed that by considering the extended version of the original boomerang attack, the efficiency of distinguishers can be greatly improved. For situations where the full differential distribution is not available or computing resources are limited, our results have shown that the extended boomerang attack can lead to strong results in practical cryptanalysis. Furthermore, we observed that the extended boomerang framework is able to amplify the effect of the conditional difference technique due to the large number of differential paths involved in the computation. As a result, we are able to derive the best cryptanalysis results by far on KATAN48/64 in the related-key setting. For all the other versions of the family, the best differential attacks are derived.

Acknowledgment. This work has been partly supported by the research funds of CCNU from colleges' basic research and operation of MOE under grand No. CCNU16A05040, and Fundamental Research Grant Scheme (FRGS - 203/PKOMP/6711427) funded by the Ministry of Higher Education of Malaysia (MOHE). The authors would like to thank anonymous reviewers for their comments. A special mention is needed for Jiqiang Lu for all the help and suggestions to improve this paper.

Appendix - Distinguisher Results in the Single-key Setting

By applying the same searching methodology, we derive the distinguishers for KATAN32/48/64 in the single-key setting as follows (Table 7).

Table 7. Boomerang distinguisher for KATAN32/48/64 in the single-key setting

Ciphers	Total rounds	$\#E_0$	$\#E_1$	α	δ	Before ES	After ES	$\lambda_{E_0}/\lambda_{E_1}$
KATAN32	83	35	48	8010	801081	-38.58	-21.78	$-17/-24$
KATAN48	60	35	25	904000	402000000	-36.60	-23.36	$-22/-18$
KATAN64	56	30	26	4002001	20110080000000	-52.52	-44.26	$-22/-22$

References

1. Ahmadian, Z., Rasoolzadeh, S., Salmasizadeh, M., Aref, M.R.: Automated Dynamic Cube Attack on Block Ciphers: Cryptanalysis of SIMON and KATAN. IACR Cryptology ePrint Archive 2015 (2015)
2. Albrecht, M.R., Leander, G.: An all-in-one approach to differential cryptanalysis for small block ciphers. In: Knudsen, L.R., Wu, H. (eds.) SAC 2012. LNCS, vol. 7707, pp. 1–15. Springer, Heidelberg (2013)
3. Biham, E., Dunkelman, O., Keller, N.: New results on boomerang and rectangle attacks. In: Daemen, J., Rijmen, V. (eds.) FSE 2002. LNCS, vol. 2365, pp. 1–16. Springer, Heidelberg (2002)
4. Biham, E., Dunkelman, O., Keller, N.: The rectangle attack - rectangling the serpent. In: Pfitzmann, B. (ed.) EUROCRYPT 2001. LNCS, vol. 2045, pp. 340–357. Springer, Heidelberg (2001)
5. Biham, E., Shamir, A.: Differential cryptanalysis of DES-like cryptosystems. In: Menezes, A., Vanstone, S.A. (eds.) CRYPTO 1990. LNCS, vol. 537, pp. 2–21. Springer, Heidelberg (1991)
6. Biryukov, A., Khovratovich, D.: Related-key cryptanalysis of the full AES-192 and AES-256. In: Matsui, M. (ed.) ASIACRYPT 2009. LNCS, vol. 5912, pp. 1–18. Springer, Heidelberg (2009)
7. Blondeau, C., Gérard, B.: Multiple differential cryptanalysis: theory and practice. In: Joux, A. (ed.) FSE 2011. LNCS, vol. 6733, pp. 35–54. Springer, Heidelberg (2011)
8. Blondeau, C., Nyberg, K.: New links between differential and linear cryptanalysis. In: Johansson, T., Nguyen, P.Q. (eds.) EUROCRYPT 2013. LNCS, vol. 7881, pp. 388–404. Springer, Heidelberg (2013)
9. De Cannière, C., Dunkelman, O., Knežević, M.: KATAN and KTANTAN — a family of small and efficient hardware-oriented block ciphers. In: Clavier, C., Gaj, K. (eds.) CHES 2009. LNCS, vol. 5747, pp. 272–288. Springer, Heidelberg (2009)
10. Fuhr, T., Minaud, B.: Match box meet-in-the-middle attack against KATAN. In: Cid, C., Rechberger, C. (eds.) FSE 2014. LNCS, vol. 8540, pp. 61–81. Springer, Heidelberg (2015)
11. Isobe, T., Sasaki, Y., Chen, J.: Related-key boomerang attacks on KATAN32/48/64. In: Boyd, C., Simpson, L. (eds.) ACISP. LNCS, vol. 7959, pp. 268–285. Springer, Heidelberg (2013)

12. Isobe, T., Shibutani, K.: All subkeys recovery attack on block ciphers: extending meet-in-the-middle approach. In: Knudsen, L.R., Wu, H. (eds.) SAC 2012. LNCS, vol. 7707, pp. 202–221. Springer, Heidelberg (2013)

13. Isobe, T., Shibutani, K.: Improved all-subkeys recovery attacks on FOX, KATAN and SHACAL-2 block ciphers. In: Cid, C., Rechberger, C. (eds.) FSE 2014. LNCS, vol. 8540, pp. 104–126. Springer, Heidelberg (2015)

14. Kelsey, J., Kohno, T., Schneier, B.: Amplified boomerang attacks against reduced-round MARS and serpent. In: Schneier, B. (ed.) FSE 2000. LNCS, vol. 1978, pp. 75–93. Springer, Heidelberg (2001)

15. Knellwolf, S., Meier, W., Naya-Plasencia, M.: Conditional differential cryptanalysis of NLFSR-based cryptosystems. In: Abe, M. (ed.) ASIACRYPT 2010. LNCS, vol. 6477, pp. 130–145. Springer, Heidelberg (2010)

16. Knellwolf, S., Meier, W., Naya-Plasencia, M.: Conditional differential cryptanalysis of trivium and KATAN. In: Miri, A., Vaudenay, S. (eds.) SAC 2011. LNCS, vol. 7118, pp. 200–212. Springer, Heidelberg (2012)

17. Lu, J., Kim, J.-S., Keller, N., Dunkelman, O.: Differential and rectangle attacks on reduced-round SHACAL-1. In: Barua, R., Lange, T. (eds.) INDOCRYPT 2006. LNCS, vol. 4329, pp. 17–31. Springer, Heidelberg (2006)

18. Lu, J., Kim, J.-S., Keller, N., Dunkelman, O.: Related-key rectangle attack on 42-round SHACAL-2. In: Katsikas, S.K., López, J., Backes, M., Gritzalis, S., Preneel, B. (eds.) ISC 2006. LNCS, vol. 4176, pp. 85–100. Springer, Heidelberg (2006)

19. Matsui, M.: On correlation between the order of S-Boxes and the strength of DES. In: De Santis, A. (ed.) EUROCRYPT 1994. LNCS, vol. 950, pp. 366–375. Springer, Heidelberg (1995)

20. Rasoolzadeh, S., Raddum, H.: Improved Multi-Dimensional Meet-in-the-Middle Cryptanalysis of KATAN. IACR Cryptology ePrint Archive 2016 (2016)

21. Sun, B., Liu, Z., Rijmen, V., Li, R., Cheng, L., Wang, Q., Alkhzaimi, H., Li, C.: Links among impossible differential, integral and zero correlation linear cryptanalysis. In: Gennaro, R., Robshaw, M. (eds.) Advances in Cryptology-CRYPTO 2015. LNCS, vol. 9215, pp. 95–115. Springer, Heidelberg (2015)

22. Wagner, D.: The boomerang attack. In: Knudsen, L.R. (ed.) FSE 1999. LNCS, vol. 1636, pp. 156–170. Springer, Heidelberg (1999)

23. Wei, L., Rechberger, C., Guo, J., Wu, H., Wang, H., Ling, S.: Improved meet-in-the-middle cryptanalysis of KTANTAN (Poster). In: Parampalli, U., Hawkes, P. (eds.) ACISP 2011. LNCS, vol. 6812, pp. 433–438. Springer, Heidelberg (2011)

24. Zhu, B., Gong, G.: Multidimensional meet-in-the-middle attack and its applications to KATAN32/48/64. Crypt. Commun. 6, 313–333 (2014)

Authenticated Encryption with Small Stretch (or, How to Accelerate AERO)

Kazuhiko Minematsu$^{(\boxtimes)}$

NEC Corporation, Kawasaki, Japan
k-minematsu@ah.jp.nec.com

Abstract. Standard form of authenticated encryption (AE) requires the ciphertext to be expanded by the nonce and the authentication tag. These expansions can be problematic when messages are relatively short and communication cost is high. To overcome the problem we propose a new form of AE scheme, MiniAE, which expands the ciphertext only by the single variable integrating nonce and tag. An important feature of MiniAE is that it requires the receiver to be stateful not only for detecting replays but also for detecting forgery of any type. McGrew and Foley already proposed a scheme having this feature, called AERO, however, there is no formal security guarantee based on the provable security framework.

We provide a provable security analysis for MiniAE, and show several provably-secure schemes using standard symmetric crypto primitives. This covers a generalization of AERO, hence our results imply a provable security of AERO. Moreover, one of our schemes has a similar structure as OCB mode of operation and enables rate-1 operation, i.e. only one blockcipher call to process one input block. This implies that the computation cost of MiniAE can be as small as encryption-only schemes.

Keywords: Authenticated encryption · Stateful decryption · Provable security · AERO · OCB

1 Introduction

Authenticated encryption (AE) is a symmetric-key cryptographic function for communication which provides both confidentiality and integrity of messages. A standard form of AE requires the ciphertext to be expanded by the amount of nonce, a never-repeating value maintained by the sender, and the authentication tag. This holds for popular schemes, such as CCM [1] and GCM [2]. The amount of expansion is small, say several dozen bytes. Nevertheless, it can be problematic when the messages are quite short. A typical example is wireless sensor network (WSN). For WSN, communication is much more energy-consuming than computation, and thus network packets are required to be very short. In fact, McGrew [3] provided examples of such real-life wireless protocols having maximum payload size ranging from 10 to 1K bytes. Struik [4] suggested that saving

© Springer International Publishing Switzerland 2016
J.K. Liu and R. Steinfeld (Eds.): ACISP 2016, Part II, LNCS 9723, pp. 347–362, 2016.
DOI: 10.1007/978-3-319-40367-0_22

8 bytes in communication may justify making encryption ten-times more expensive for WSN. Similar observation was given by Seys and Preneel [5]. Detailed energy cost evaluations for communication and cryptographic computation are given by [6,7].

As a solution to this problem, we propose MiniAE, a class of AE having smaller stretch than normal AEs. Its ciphertext is only expanded by the amount of single variable integrating nonce and tag. When ciphertext of MiniAE is stretched by s bits, it provides (about) s-bit authenticity and can securely encrypt at most 2^s messages, while nonce-based AE (NAE) needs $2s$-bit stretch for this purpose. A key difference from NAE is that MiniAE requires both sender and receiver to maintain a state (say counter), whereas NAE basically needs only the sender to be stateful. At first sight this might seem a big disadvantage, however, we remark that even NAE needs a stateful receiver when one wants to detect replays. In fact, replay detection via stateful receiver is employed by most of Internet protocols and wireless networks, such as Zigbee[1] and Bluetooth low energy (BLE)[2]. An important feature of MiniAE is that a receiver's state is not only used to detect replays but to detect forgeries of any other types. McGrew and Foley [3,8] already showed a similar idea and proposed a scheme called AERO. It can be seen as an encryption following encode-then-encipher (ETE) approach by Bellare and Rogaway [9], using XCB mode of operation [10] as its internal large keyed permutation. The approach of AERO is intuitively sound, however [3,8] do not provide a formal security analysis. As a consequence, it is not clear if ETE is essential for achieving the goal, i.e. small stretch. This is undesirable since these schemes are likely to be used by resource-constrained devices.

We provide a formal model of MiniAE and basic security notions, namely the confidentiality, integrity and replay protection, and show provably secure constructions. Our model is different from Bellare, Kohno and Namprempre [11], which proposes a security model with stateful decryption tailored to analyze (a generalization of) SSH Binary Packet Protocol. More specifically, we propose three MiniAE schemes with concrete security proofs. The first scheme is based on ETE and can be seen as a simple generalization of AERO. This shows that AERO is indeed secure for our security notions. The second scheme, which we call MiniCTR, is similar to a generic composition [12,13]. If it is instantiated by CTR mode encryption and a polynomial hash function, the computation cost of MiniCTR is almost the same as GCM [2]. The third scheme tries to further improve the efficiency. It is called MiniOCB for its structural similarity with OCB [14–16]. As well as OCB it is defined as a mode of tweakable blockcipher (TBC), and TBC can be instantiated by a blockcipher. It is parallelizable and rate-1, that is, it requires one blockcipher call for processing one plaintext block. The last two schemes show that ETE is not the exclusive approach to MiniAE, and a secure MiniAE can be as fast as nonce-based (unauthenticated) encryptions. We here stress that, unlike most NAEs, all our schemes are not capable of on-line encryption, and thus not desirable to handle long messages.

---

[1] http://www.zigbee.org.
[2] http://www.bluetooth.com.

We remark that our basic security notions in Sect. 3.2 are extensions of standard NAE security notions, hence do not consider *misuse*. According to [8] AERO is expected to have a certain *misuse-resistance* beyond NAE. To fill the gap, in the full version, we provide a short security analysis involving extended security notions covering misuse, and show a separation between the proposed schemes if we require these extended notions in addition to the basic ones.

2   Preliminaries

Let $\{0,1\}^*$ denote the set of all binary sequences including the empty string, ε. For $X \in \{0,1\}^*$, we write $|X|$ to denote the bit length of X, and let $|X|_n \overset{\text{def}}{=} \lceil |X|/n \rceil$. For $X, Y \in \{0,1\}^*$ we write $X\|Y$ to denote their concatenation. The first (last) i bits of X is denoted by $\mathtt{msb}_i(X)$ ($\mathtt{lsb}_i(X)$). We have $\mathtt{msb}_0(X) = \varepsilon$ and $\varepsilon \oplus X = \varepsilon$ for any X. For any $s > 0$, a partition of X into s-bit blocks is written as $(X[1], \ldots, X[x]) \overset{s}{\leftarrow} X$, where $|X[i]| = s$ for $i < x$ and $|X[x]| \leq s$. For $X = \varepsilon$, we let $X[1] \overset{s}{\leftarrow} X$ with $X[1] = \varepsilon$. Moreover, for X and Y such that $|X| \leq n$ and $|X| + |Y| \geq n$ we write $(\underline{X}, \underline{Y}) \overset{n}{\leftarrow} (X, Y)$ to denote the parsing into $\underline{X} = X\|\mathtt{msb}_{n-|X|}(Y)$ and $\underline{Y} = \mathtt{lsb}_{|Y|-(n-|X|)}Y$. The inverse parsing is written as $(X, Y) \overset{m}{\leftarrow} (\underline{X}, \underline{Y})$, where $|\underline{X}| \geq m$ and $X = \mathtt{msb}_m(\underline{X})$, $Y = \mathtt{lsb}_{|\underline{X}|-m}(\underline{X}\|\underline{Y})$. By writing $X10^*$ for $0 \leq |X| < n$ we mean a padding $10^{n-|X|-1}$ to X. We have $X10^* = X$ when $|X| = n$, and $\varepsilon 10^* = 10^{n-1}$. For a finite set $\mathcal{X}$ we write $X \overset{\$}{\leftarrow} \mathcal{X}$ to mean the uniform sampling of X over $\mathcal{X}$.

For keyed function $F : \mathcal{K} \times \mathcal{X} \to \mathcal{Y}$ with key $K \in \mathcal{K}$, we may simply write $F_K : \mathcal{X} \to \mathcal{Y}$ if key space is obvious, or even write as $F : \mathcal{X} \to \mathcal{Y}$ if being keyed is obvious. If $E_K : \mathcal{X} \to \mathcal{X}$ is a keyed permutation, or a blockcipher, E_K is a permutation over $\mathcal{X}$ for every $K \in \mathcal{K}$. Its inverse is denoted by E_K^{-1}. A tweakable keyed permutation or TBC [17], $\widetilde{E}_K : \mathcal{T} \times \mathcal{X} \to \mathcal{X}$, is a family of keyed permutation over $\mathcal{X}$ indexed by tweak $T \in \mathcal{T}$ and its encryption is written as $C = \widetilde{E}_K^T(M)$ for plaintext M, tweak T and ciphertext C. The decryption is written as $M = \widetilde{E}_K^{-1,T}(C)$. We consider $\mathcal{X}$ to be either a set of fixed length strings or variable length strings (though the original definition [17] assumes the fixed length). The latter is also called tweakable enciphering scheme (TES).

Random Functions. Let $\mathrm{Func}(n, m)$ be the set of all functions $\{0,1\}^n \to \{0,1\}^m$, and let $\mathrm{Perm}(n)$ be the set of all permutations over $\{0,1\}^n$. A uniform random function (URF) having n-bit input and m-bit output is a function family uniformly distributed over $\mathrm{Func}(n, m)$. It is denoted by $\mathsf{R} \overset{\$}{\leftarrow} \mathrm{Func}(n, m)$. An n-bit uniform random permutation (URP), denoted by P, is similarly defined as $\mathsf{P} \overset{\$}{\leftarrow} \mathrm{Perm}(n)$. We also define tweakable URP. Let $\mathcal{T}$ be a set of tweak and $\mathrm{Perm}^{\mathcal{T}}(n)$ be the set of all functions such that for any $f \in \mathrm{Perm}^{\mathcal{T}}(n)$ and $t \in \mathcal{T}$, $f(t, *)$ is a permutation. A tweakable n-bit URP with tweak $T \in \mathcal{T}$ is defined as $\widetilde{\mathsf{P}} \overset{\$}{\leftarrow} \mathrm{Perm}^{\mathcal{T}}(n)$.

Pseudorandom Function. For c oracles, $O_1, O_2, \ldots, O_c$, we write $\mathcal{A}^{O_1, O_2, \ldots, O_c}$ to represent the adversary $\mathcal{A}$ accessing these c oracles in an arbitrarily order.

If O and O' are oracles having the same input and output domains, we say they are compatible. Let $F_K : \{0,1\}^n \to \{0,1\}^m$ and $G_{K'} : \{0,1\}^n \to \{0,1\}^m$ be two compatible keyed functions, with $K \in \mathcal{K}$ and $K' \in \mathcal{K}'$ (key spaces are not necessarily the same). Let $\mathcal{A}$ be an adversary trying distinguish them using queries. Then the advantage of $\mathcal{A}$ is defined as

$$\mathrm{Adv}^{\mathrm{cpa}}_{F_K,G_{K'}}(\mathcal{A}) \overset{\mathrm{def}}{=} \Pr[\mathcal{A}^{F_K} \Rightarrow 1] - \Pr[\mathcal{A}^{G_{K'}} \Rightarrow 1],$$

$$\mathrm{Adv}^{\mathrm{cca}}_{F_K,G_{K'}}(\mathcal{A}) \overset{\mathrm{def}}{=} \Pr[\mathcal{A}^{F_K,F_K^{-1}} \Rightarrow 1] - \Pr[\mathcal{A}^{G_{K'},G_{K'}^{-1}} \Rightarrow 1],$$

where the latter is defined if F and G are keyed permutation, and probabilities are defined over uniform samplings of keys and internal randomness of $\mathcal{A}$. If F and G are tweakable, a tweak for a query is arbitrarily chosen by the adversary for both $\mathrm{Adv}^{\mathrm{cpa}}$ and $\mathrm{Adv}^{\mathrm{cca}}$. For URF R compatible to F, let $\mathrm{Adv}^{\mathrm{prf}}_{F_K}(\mathcal{A}) \overset{\mathrm{def}}{=} \mathrm{Adv}^{\mathrm{cpa}}_{F_K,\mathsf{R}}(\mathcal{A})$. In a similar manner, let tweakable URP $\widetilde{\mathsf{P}}$ compatible to TBC $\widetilde{E}_K$. Then we define

$$\mathrm{Adv}^{\mathrm{tprp}}_{\widetilde{E}_K}(\mathcal{A}) \overset{\mathrm{def}}{=} \mathrm{Adv}^{\mathrm{cpa}}_{\widetilde{E}_K,\widetilde{\mathsf{P}}}(\mathcal{A}), \text{ and } \mathrm{Adv}^{\mathrm{tsprp}}_{\widetilde{E}_K}(\mathcal{A}) \overset{\mathrm{def}}{=} \mathrm{Adv}^{\mathrm{cca}}_{\widetilde{E}_K,\widetilde{\mathsf{P}}}(\mathcal{A}),$$

We further extends these notions to the functions (or permutations) having variable-input length (VIL). For example, if F_K is a VIL keyed function: $\{0,1\}^* \to \{0,1\}^n$ we define $\mathrm{Adv}^{\mathrm{prf}}_{F_K}(\mathcal{A})$ as $\mathrm{Adv}^{\mathrm{cpa}}_{F_K,\mathsf{R}^*}(\mathcal{A})$, where R^* is an URF compatible to F_K which can be implemented by lazy sampling.

Time Complexity. If adversary $\mathcal{A}$ is with time complexity t, it means the total computation time and memory of $\mathcal{A}$ required for query generation and final decision, in some fixed model. If there is no description on time complexity of $\mathcal{A}$, it means $\mathcal{A}$ has no computational restriction. Conventionally we say F_K is a pseudorandom function (PRF) if $\mathrm{Adv}^{\mathrm{prf}}_{F_K}(\mathcal{A})$ is negligible for all practical adversaries (though the formal definition requires F_K to be a function family). Similarly we say F_K is a pseudorandom permutation (PRP) if $\mathrm{Adv}^{\mathrm{prp}}_{F_K}(\mathcal{A})$ is negligible and F_K is invertible. Strong PRP (SPRP), tweakable PRP (TPRP) and tweakable SPRP (TSPRP) are defined in a similar manner.

Universal Hash Function. Let $H : \mathcal{K} \times \mathcal{X} \to \{0,1\}^n$ be a keyed function, where key K is uniform over $\mathcal{K}$ and $\mathcal{X} \subseteq \{0,1\}^*$. We say H_K is $\epsilon(x)$-almost XOR universal (AXU) if

$$\max_{c \in \{0,1\}^n} \Pr_K[H_K(X) \oplus H_K(X') = c] \le \epsilon(x) \tag{1}$$

holds for any distinct $X, X' \in \mathcal{X}$ with $\max\{|X|_n, |X'|_n\} = x$ and for some $\epsilon(*)$. If input is divided into two parts, e.g. $X = (X_1, X_2)$, $|X|_n$ means $|X_1|_n + |X_2|_n$.

Building TBC. All our constructions will use TBC. It can be built from scratch [18–20] or from a blockcipher. Suppose we want a TBC of n-bit block and tweak space (which is assumed to be a set of binary strings) $\mathcal{T}$. From the result of [17], using an n-bit blockcipher E_K and an independently-keyed $\epsilon(x)$-AXU hash function, $H_{K'} : \mathcal{T} \to \{0,1\}^n$, we can build TBC as

$$\widetilde{E}^T_{K,K'}(M) = E_K(S \oplus M) \oplus S, \text{ where } S = H_{K'}(T) \tag{2}$$

for encryption of plaintext M and tweak T. This has a TSPRP-advantage of $O(\epsilon(\ell) \cdot q^2)$ plus a CCA-advantage of E_K, for any adversary with q CCA queries using tweak of maximum block length ℓ. Typically we can use a polynomial hash function defined over $\mathrm{GF}(2^n)$ as a universal hash fulfilling (1) with $\epsilon(x) = x/2^n$. Alternatively we can use PRF as a computational counterpart, say CMAC. In some cases the use of two keys in (2) can be reduced to one [15,21].

3 Definition of MiniAE

3.1 Basic Model

The encryption function of MiniAE accepts nonce N, associated data (AD) A, and plaintext M, and generates ciphertext C and *encrypted nonce* L, where $N, L \in \mathcal{N}_{ae} = \{0,1\}^\nu$ for some fixed ν, $A \in \mathcal{A}_{ae}$, $M \in \mathcal{M}_{ae}$ with $|C| = |M|$. Typically $\mathcal{A}_{ae} = \mathcal{M}_{ae} = \{0,1\}^*$ and we may simply write $\mathcal{M}$ for $\mathcal{M}_{ae}$. A message sent over a communication channel is (A, L, C). Thus the expansion is ν bits. AD A and plaintext M can be empty, and if M is empty the corresponding C is also empty. We require unique nonce for each encryption. We define nonce increment function $\mu : \mathcal{N}_{ae} \to \mathcal{N}_{ae}$, which is a permutation over $\mathcal{N}_{ae}$ and has single cycle of length $|\mathcal{N}_{ae}|$. We assume μ and initial nonce value are public and fixed. If N is the nonce last used in encryption, the next nonce is $\mu(N)$. Typically, μ is a counter increment $\mu(N) = N + 1$ where $+$ is modulo 2^ν. As mentioned earlier we assume stateful decryption. On receiving (A', L', C'), the stateful decryption function first computes the decrypted nonce $N' \in \mathcal{N}_{ae}$ using the key, and outputs the decrypted plaintext M' if N' is considered as valid, otherwise the default error symbol, $\bot$. The validity of N' is determined by comparison with the receiver state. Here stateful decryption is essential to detect replays, and we assume the receiver state is uniquely determined by the nonce in the previous successful decryption (thus a state is an element of $\mathcal{N}_{ae}$), which is typical in many replay protection schemes including AERO [8][3]. More generally, the receiver has a set of expected nonce values for each decryption. The set is defined as a function of the receiver state, and we write the function as $\rho : \mathcal{N}_{ae} \to 2^{\mathcal{N}_{ae}}$, where $2^{\mathcal{N}_{ae}}$ is the power set of $\mathcal{N}_{ae}$. The function ρ is public, and when N' is the value obtained by the decryption and $\widehat{N}$ is the last nonce accepted as valid, N' is determined as valid iff $N' \in \rho(\widehat{N})$ holds true. In this paper we assume $|\rho(N)| \le \omega$ holds for any N, where ω is called *verification range size*. Let us write i-th nonce used at encryption as N_i (e.g. $N_2 = \mu(N_1)$). Naturally we require that $N_{i+1}(= \mu(N_i)) \in \rho(N_i)$ for any i to accept the genuine ciphertext,

---

[3] Decryption of [8] also maintains the most recent invalid nonce, in order to do resynchronization.

and $N_j \notin \rho(N_i)$ for any $j \leq i$ to reject replays without fail. In practice ρ determines the resilience against packet loss. If the synchronization is perfect between the sender and receiver, the simplest setting as $\rho(N) = \mu(N)$ with $\omega = 1$ works fine. However we often need to include $\{N_j\}$ for some $j > i + 1$ for $\rho(N_i)$ when packets can lost in the channel. In this case $\rho(N) = \{\mu(N), \mu(\mu(N)), ...\}$ to tolerate the loss of consecutive $\omega - 1$ packets. This will increase a chance of success at forgery, roughly by a factor of ω.

Nonce Shorter than Block. As all of our constructions are defined over n-bit blocks for some n (say 128), we require $\nu \leq n$, and $|N| + |M| \geq n$ holds, which means if $\nu < n$ we have a nonzero limit on the minimum plaintext length, or, in practice we may pad as [8]. Throughout the paper, we may implicitly use $(\underline{N}, \underline{M})$ to denote the result of parsing $(\underline{N}, \underline{M}) \xrightarrow{n} (N, M)$, provided N and M are clear from the context. Similarly we may use $(\underline{L}, \underline{C})$ to denote the result of parsing $(\underline{L}, \underline{C}) \xrightarrow{n} (L, C)$. We remark that when $\nu = n$, we have $\underline{N} = N$, $\underline{M} = M$ and $\underline{L} = L$, $\underline{C} = C$.

3.2 Security Notions

Following NAE security notions, we introduce two security notions, namely privacy and authenticity, to model the security of MiniAE. Here privacy notion reflects the pseudorandomness of ciphertexts, and authenticity notion reflects the hardness of forgery even if the receiver state are chosen by the adversary. We think this form of authenticity will be beneficial for its simplicity, strong assurance, and independence of the details of state management[4]. Let **MiAE** be an MiniAE with ν-bit nonce (with some key $K \xleftarrow{\$} \mathcal{K}$). The encryption and decryption algorithms are **MiAE-$\mathcal{E}$** and **MiAE-$\mathcal{D}$**. Following Sect. 3.1, **MiAE-$\mathcal{E}$** takes (N, A, M) and returns (L, C) with $|M| = |C|$ and $|N| = |L| = \nu$. **MiAE-$\mathcal{D}$** takes $(\widehat{N}, A', L', C')$ with $|\widehat{N}| = |L'| = \nu$, where $\widehat{N}$ is a receiver state (i.e. a decrypted nonce) guessed by adversary. In practice $\widehat{N}$ is not sent over the communication channel. **MiAE-$\mathcal{D}$** then computes the decrypted nonce, N', and see if $N' \in \rho(\widehat{N})$. If true it returns a decrypted message $M' \in \mathcal{M}_{ae}$ and otherwise $\perp$. Thus we have

$$(L, C) \leftarrow \textbf{MiAE-}\mathcal{E}(N, A, M)$$
$$M'/\perp \leftarrow \textbf{MiAE-}\mathcal{D}(\widehat{N}, A', L', C').$$

Privacy Notion. Let $\mathcal{A}$ be a Priv-adversary who accesses **MiAE-$\mathcal{E}$** using q encryption queries with distinct nonces (i.e. nonce-respecting). Here we assume

---

[4] In this sense our notions are similar to Rogaway's nonce-based encryption [22] as it allows a provable security analysis without taking into account the details of nonce generation.

nonces are not necessarily updated[5] by μ, in the same manner to [22]. The privacy notion for Priv-adversary $\mathcal{A}$ is defined as

$$\mathrm{Adv}_{\mathbf{MiAE}}^{\mathrm{priv}}(\mathcal{A}) \overset{\mathrm{def}}{=} \Pr[\mathcal{A}^{\mathbf{MiAE}\text{-}\mathcal{E}} \Rightarrow 1] - \Pr[\mathcal{A}^{\$} \Rightarrow 1], \tag{3}$$

where random-bit oracle, $\$$, takes (N, A, M) and returns $(L, C) \overset{\$}{\leftarrow} \{0,1\}^{\nu} \times \{0,1\}^{|M|}$.

Authenticity Notion. Let $\mathcal{A}$ be an Auth-adversary against **MiAE**. We write q encryption queries as $(N_1, A_1, M_1), \ldots, (N_q, A_q, M_q)$, and q' decryption queries as $(\widehat{N}_1, A'_1, L'_1, C'_1), \ldots, (\widehat{N}_{q'}, A'_{q'}, L'_{q'}, C'_{q'})$. We may say verification queries instead of decryption queries. We also let $(L_1, C_1), \ldots, (L_q, C_q)$ be the corresponding oracle answers for encryption queries. We assume $\mathcal{A}$ follows the two conditions.

Condition 1: Adversary is nonce-respecting for encryption queries (i.e. $N_i \neq N_j$ for any $i \neq j$)

Condition 2: For all $i = 1, \ldots, q'$, $(A'_i, L'_i, C'_i) \neq (A_j, L_j, C_j)$ holds for all j-th encryption queries before the i-th decryption query.

As well as the privacy notion, nonces in the encryption queries are not necessarily generated by μ. The second condition excludes the adversary's trivial win including a replay, that is, a decryption query $(\widehat{N}, A', L', C')$ with $(A', L', C') = (A, L, C)$ with $N \in \rho(\widehat{N})$ for some previous encryption query (N, A, M) and response (L, C). This is because a replay is always detected at the decryption side in actual use of *any* MiniAE scheme following Sect. 3.1. We also excluded the case $N \notin \rho(\widehat{N})$, as it will be always rejected (thus trivial loss). The authenticity notion is defined as

$$\mathrm{Adv}_{\mathbf{MiAE}}^{\mathrm{auth}}(\mathcal{A}) \overset{\mathrm{def}}{=} \Pr[\mathcal{A}^{\mathbf{MiAE}\text{-}\mathcal{E}, \mathbf{MiAE}\text{-}\mathcal{D}} \text{ forges}], \tag{4}$$

where $\mathcal{A}$ forges if **MiAE**-$\mathcal{D}$ returns output other than $\perp$ for a decryption query.

For both privacy and authenticity notions, we write the total input blocks, denoted by σ, to mean $\sum_i |N_i|_n + |A_i|_n + |M_i|_n$ for the privacy notion, and $\sum_i |N_i|_n + |A_i|_n + |M_i|_n + \sum_j |L'_j|_n + |A'_j|_n + |C'_j|_n$ for the authenticity notion. **MiniAE as a large tweakable random permutation.** Since **MiAE** is a tweakable keyed permutation in general (where tweak is used for AD), we write $\mathrm{Adv}_{\mathbf{MiAE}}^{\mathrm{tprp}}(\mathcal{A})$ and $\mathrm{Adv}_{\mathbf{MiAE}}^{\mathrm{tsprp}}(\mathcal{A})$ to denote TPRP and TSPRP advantages of the underlying tweakable keyed permutation $\widetilde{\mathbf{E}}$. Note that $\widetilde{\mathbf{E}}$ is not always required to be strong with respect to these notions. In fact our results show that it can be much weaker.

IV-based Encryption. We also define IV-based encryption scheme: $\Pi_K : \mathcal{I} \times \mathcal{M} \to \mathcal{M}$ which is a permutation over $\mathcal{M}$ determined by $K \in \mathcal{K}$ and fixed-length initialization-vector (IV) $I \in \mathcal{I}$. Here IV is sampled uniformly random

---

[5] It is possible to define the adversary in our security notions strictly following the generation of nonce described at Sect. 3.1. Here we employ a more general definition for the simplicity.

for every encryption. Let Π_K oracle as the encryption oracle take $M \in \mathcal{M}$ and return (I, C), where $I \xleftarrow{\$} \mathcal{I}$ and $C \to \Pi_K(I, M)$. We remark that the adversary is not allowed to see I before querying M. We define the PRIV\$ advantage as the indistinguishability of Π_K from the random-bit oracle (\$), which returns $|I| + |M|$-bit random sequence, i.e.,

$$\text{Adv}_{\Pi_K}^{\text{priv\$}}(\mathcal{A}) \stackrel{\text{def}}{=} \Pr[\mathcal{A}^{\Pi_K} \Rightarrow 1] - \Pr[\mathcal{A}^{\$} \Rightarrow 1]. \qquad (5)$$

We say the total input block of $\mathcal{A}$ to mean the total number of plaintext blocks.

3.3   Remarks

Comparison with NAE security notions. Our security notions are quite similar to NAE security notions, e.g. [12,23]. For privacy notion, both NAE and MiniAE require that the outputs of encryption oracle are pseudorandom. For authenticity notion, both NAE and MiniAE require that a forgery is hard for nonce-respecting adversary. The standard authenticity notion for NAE considers stateless receiver, however if a certain NAE scheme is secure with respect to the standard authenticity notion, then it certainly detects replays if receiver is stateful and nonce is dealt with μ and ρ as described at Sect. 3.1. We remark that, when the receiver loses state NAE still can detect forgeries other than replays, while MiniAE can not: only unverified decryption is possible.

Comparison with Alternative Solutions. If sender and receiver are completely synchronized, we can use NAE and simply omit the nonce to be sent to save bandwidth (also called implicit sequence number [3]). However this is problematic when packets may lost. A mitigation is to send a partial information. This technique is employed by some popular protocols as [3] shows. Therefore it basically works for some settings, however it makes the messaging format dependent on the number of tolerable packet lost, which depends on the network condition and application and sometimes hard to determine in practice. Moreover, once the receiver loses the state, even the unverified decryption becomes impossible. In contrast, MiniAE allows ad-hoc mechanisms to handle packet lost without changing the message format, and unverified decryption without state, and allows efficient built-in resynchronization as shown by AERO.

Another solution to suppress expansion is Deterministic AE (DAE) proposed by Rogaway and Shrimpton [24]. In DAE there is no nonce and for plaintext M the encryption output is (C, T) where $|C| = |M|$ and T is the authentication tag of fixed length[6]. Since DAE encryption is deterministic, the standard privacy notion is impossible to achieve. DAE can prevent replay if the receiver keeps (hash values of) all received ciphertexts, or using Bloom filter allowing some false negatives. Either option requires much larger memories or computations than the verification of MiniAE. Table 1 summarizes encryption schemes in the presence of stateful receiver for replay protection.

---

[6] If DAE takes nonce as its input we call it MRAE (misuse-resistant AE) which has the same expansion as NAE.

Table 1. Comparison of encryption schemes.

Scheme	Expansion	Privacy	Authenticity	Replay protect	Dec w/o state
nonce-based Enc	$|N|$	✓	-	✓	✓
NAE	$|N| + |T|$	✓	✓	✓	✓
DAE	$|T|$	-	✓	difficult	✓
NAE+Nonce omit	$|T|$	✓	✓	✓	-
MiniAE	$|N|$	✓	✓	✓	✓

Applications to Low-power Wireless Sensor Network. To suppress communication overhead, link-layer security protocols for low-power WSN often employed NAE having a short nonce and short tag (see [25] for a good survey). For example, Zigbee and BLE use AES-CCM with 13-byte initial vector consisting of nonce and supplemental information, and 4-byte tag. If MiniAE is used instead, it enables stronger authenticity, say from 32-bit to 64-bit, while keeping the same ciphertext expansion, or, it is also possible to reduce the expansion, say by 4 bytes, while keeping the original level of authenticity and nonce space. More details are shown in the full version.

4 Building MiniAE

In this section we provide constructions of MiniAE. Throughout the section all schemes are assumed to have nonce of ν bits and verification range size ω. We assume ν and ω are fixed parameters, and also assume $\nu \leq n$ for some fixed block length n, and plaintext M used in a scheme satisfies $|M| \geq \nu - n$.

4.1 MiniAE from Large Tweakable Blockcipher

We start with a naive solution based on ETE approach mentioned earlier. We call the scheme MiniETE. More specifically, let $\widetilde{\mathbf{E}} : \mathcal{T} \times \mathcal{M} \to \mathcal{M}$ be a TBC, where $\mathcal{M} = \bigcup_{i \geq n} \{0, 1\}^i$. The encryption of MiniETE using $\widetilde{\mathbf{E}}$ is defined as $(L \| C) = \widetilde{\mathbf{E}}^A(N \| M)$. For decryption, we perform $(N' \| M') = \widetilde{\mathbf{E}}^{-1,A}(L \| C)$ and see if $N' \in \rho(\widehat{N})$. This scheme is provably secure if $\widetilde{\mathbf{E}}$ is a TSPRP. Concrete security bounds of MiniETE are shown in the following propositions. Here, the proof of Proposition 1 is trivial and that of Proposition 2 is easily obtained as a variant of the proof of Theorem 2 thus we omit it here.

Proposition 1. *Let* MiniETE[$\widetilde{\mathbf{E}}$] *be* MiniETE *using* $\widetilde{\mathbf{E}}$. *If* $\mathcal{A}$ *is a Priv-adversary with* q *encryption queries and* σ *total input blocks and time complexity* t, *we have*

$$\mathsf{Adv}^{\mathrm{priv}}_{\mathsf{MiniETE}[\widetilde{\mathbf{E}}]}(\mathcal{A}) \leq \mathsf{Adv}^{\mathrm{tprp}}_{\widetilde{\mathbf{E}}}(\mathcal{B}) + \frac{q^2}{2^{n+1}},$$

where $\mathcal{B}$ *uses* q *encryption queries with* σ *total input blocks and time complexity* $t' = t + O(\sigma)$.

Proposition 2. *Let $\mathcal{A}$ be an Auth-adversary with q encryption and q' decryption queries, σ total input blocks and time complexity t. We assume $(q + q') < 2^{\nu-1}$. Then we have*

$$\mathrm{Adv}^{\mathrm{auth}}_{\mathrm{MiniETE}[\widetilde{\mathbf{E}}]}(\mathcal{A}) \leq \mathrm{Adv}^{\mathrm{tsprp}}_{\widetilde{\mathbf{E}}}(\mathcal{B}) + \frac{2(q + q')(\omega + q')}{2^\nu},$$

where $\mathcal{B}$ uses q encryption queries and q' decryption queries with σ total input blocks and time complexity $t' = t + O(\sigma)$.

For instantiations of $\widetilde{\mathbf{E}}$, we could use known schemes [26–29] as internal wide-block TBC. As mentioned, this scheme is in fact a generalization of AERO which uses XCB [10] with AES-128. That is, AERO is provably secure in our security model, although there are minor differences and additional features[7]. MiniETE also has some similarities with ETE-based AE schemes, such as AEZ [30] and PIV [29].

4.2 MiniAE from encrypted counter

MiniETE is conceptually simple, however actual computation cost is rather high. A popular approach to $\widetilde{\mathbf{E}}$ shown by the seminal paper by Naor and Reingold [31] uses two universal hashing layers with one encryption layer, called Hash-Enc-Hash [26, 32, 33]. EME and CMC [27, 28] do not use universal hash but require two blockcipher calls for each n-bit input block.

To improve the efficiency, we present a two-pass scheme which we call MiniCTR. The name comes from that it consists of encryption of nonce and an additive encryption. Specifically, MiniCTR uses an n-bit block, variable-length tweak TBC $\widetilde{E}_K : \mathcal{T} \times \{0,1\}^n \to \{0,1\}^n$ and a keyed function of n-bit input and variable-length output, $F_{K'} : \{0,1\}^n \to \{0,1\}^*$. Here we assume $\mathcal{T}$ is sufficiently large to encode a pair $(A, \underline{M})$. Two keys, K and K', are assumed to be independent. The algorithms of MiniCTR are shown in Fig. 1 and the encryption is also shown in Fig. 2. We write $\Pi[F_{K'}]$ to denote the underlying additive encryption, where $\underline{L}$ is used as n-bit IV. In Theorems 1 and 2 below, we prove the security of MiniCTR when $\widetilde{E}$ is TSPRP-secure and $\Pi[F_{K'}]$ is PRIV\$-secure.

DAE does not work. The presented scheme has a similar structure as DAE schemes [24, 34, 35] or randomized encryption by Desai [36]. However we can not directly use them as MiniAE. For example, (a generic form of) DAE with n-bit tag is obtained by changing line 2 of Fig. 1 as a Feistel round $\underline{L} \leftarrow \underline{N} \oplus F'(A, M)$ with $\underline{N}$ fixed to 0^n using another PRF F'. However the privacy of this scheme is easily broken if we query (N, A, M) and $(N \oplus c, A, M)$ for some non-constant c: the corresponding pair of $\underline{L}$ has a fixed difference c.

Security. Let MiniCTR$[\widetilde{E}, F]$ be MiniCTR using TBC $\widetilde{E}_K$ and $F_{K'}$. The security bounds for MiniCTR$[\widetilde{E}, F]$ are presented in the following theorems.

---

[7] For instance AERO's nonce is a sequence number, and appended to the plaintext. Moreover the receiver additionally keeps the most recent sequence number value which was rejected, in order to do resynchronization.

Algorithm MiniCTR-$\mathcal{E}_{\widetilde{E},F}(N, A, M)$	Algorithm MiniCTR-$\mathcal{D}_{\widetilde{E},F}(\widehat{N}, A', L', C')$
1. $(\underline{N}, \underline{M}) \xleftarrow{n} (N, M)$	1. $(\underline{L'}, \underline{C'}) \xleftarrow{n} (L', C')$
2. $\underline{L} \leftarrow \widetilde{E}^{(A,\underline{M})}(\underline{N})$	2. $\underline{M'} \leftarrow F(\underline{L'}) \oplus \underline{C'}$
3. $\underline{C} \leftarrow F(\underline{L}) \oplus \underline{M}$	3. $\underline{N'} \leftarrow \widetilde{E}^{-1(A',\underline{M'})}(\underline{L'})$
4. $(L, C) \xleftarrow{v} (\underline{L}, \underline{C})$	4. if $\mathsf{msb}_\nu(\underline{N'}) \in \rho(\widehat{N})$ then
5. return (L, C)	5. $\quad (N', M') \xleftarrow{v} (\underline{N'}, \underline{M'})$
	6. $\quad$ return M'
	7. else return $\perp$

Fig. 1. Encryption and decryption algorithms of MiniCTR$[\widetilde{E}, F]$

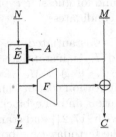

Fig. 2. The encryption algorithm of MiniCTR$[\widetilde{E}, F]$, except the pre- and post-parsings.

Theorem 1. *If $\mathcal{A}$ is a Priv-adversary with q encryption queries and σ total input blocks and time complexity t, we have*

$$\mathbf{Adv}^{\mathrm{priv}}_{\mathsf{MiniCTR}[\widetilde{E},F]}(\mathcal{A}) \le \mathbf{Adv}^{\mathrm{tprp}}_{\widetilde{E}}(\mathcal{B}) + \mathbf{Adv}^{\mathrm{priv\$}}_{\Pi[F]}(\mathcal{C}) + \frac{q^2}{2^{n+1}}.$$

where $\mathcal{B}$ uses q queries with total input blocks σ and time complexity $t' = t + O(\sigma)$, and $\mathcal{C}$ uses q queries and σ total input blocks with time complexity $t' = t + O(\sigma)$.

Theorem 2. *Let $\mathcal{A}$ be an Auth-adversary with q encryption queries, q' decryption queries, σ total input blocks, and time complexity t. We assume $(q + q') < 2^{\nu-1}$. Then we have*

$$\mathbf{Adv}^{\mathrm{auth}}_{\mathsf{MiniCTR}[\widetilde{E},F]}(\mathcal{A}) \le \mathbf{Adv}^{\mathrm{tsprp}}_{\widetilde{E}}(\mathcal{B}) + \frac{2(q + q')(\omega + q')}{2^\nu},$$

where $\mathcal{B}$ uses q encryption queries and q' decryption queries, having time complexity $t' = t + O(\sigma)$.

We remark that the authenticity does not require any security property of F here: the reason is simple, since the authenticity of N is guaranteed even when adversary can access the key of F.

Proof Overview. The proofs of Theorems 1 and 2 are deferred to the full version. Here we provide intuitions for them. For the privacy bound, we observe that the distinctness of N guarantees L to have a birthday-type collision probability, and the distinctness of L guarantees C to be uniform. For the authenticity, we observe that F has in fact no contribution to authenticity and thus the key of F can be given to the adversary. The resulting scheme is a variant of stateful message authentication code (MAC). Here the tag check procedure involves a comparison of decrypted nonce N' with a set of candidates of size ω (i.e. $\rho(\widehat{N})$). Defining bad event as a collision between N and N' or two N's, we perform an analysis of bad event probability. Note that a collision can occur either at an encryption or a decryption query, which makes the probability larger than $q'\omega/2^\nu$ (which is an obvious bound for guessing ν-bit random value with q' trials, with each trial consisting of ω candidates).

Instantiation. Typically, $\widetilde{E}$ is instantiated by n-bit blockcipher and n-bit polynomial hash with (2) and F is instantiated by CTR mode, e.g. $C = \Pi[F_{K'}](L, M)$ with $C[i] = E_{K'}(\underline{N} \oplus i) \oplus M[i]$ for $i = 1, 2, \ldots$ using blockcipher $E_{K'}$. In this case, the computation cost of MiniCTR for each n-bit plaintext block is one $GF(2^n)$ multiplication and one blockcipher call, which is roughly the same as GCM. Combined with [17,21] and standard security result for CTR mode, e.g. [37], we can prove the birthday-type bounds of MiniCTR comparable to those of GCM [38] both for privacy and authenticity[8]. For GCM, 12-byte nonce and 16-byte tag is a popular setting, and MiniCTR with 16-byte nonce will reduce the ciphertext expansion from 28 to 16 bytes keeping a comparable level of security.

4.3   MiniAE from OCB Mode

The computation cost of MiniCTR is similar to the generic composition of NAE, and thus there is still a significant difference from the nonce-based unauthenticated encryption. A natural question here is if we can further reduce the computation cost. We positively answer this question by showing a scheme achieving rate-1 operation, i.e. one blockcipher call per one input block. We call our proposal MiniOCB since the design is based on OCB [14–16]. MiniOCB is parallelizable for both encryption and decryption. MiniOCB uses n-bit TBC, $\widetilde{E}$, having variable-length tweak in $\mathcal{T} = \{0,1\}^n \times \mathcal{A}_{ae} \times \mathbb{N} \times \{0,1,2\}$ where $\mathbb{N} = \{1,2,\ldots\}$. The encryption and decryption algorithms of MiniOCB are shown in Figs. 3 and 4. It needs one TBC call to process one input block, and if TBC is instantiated by a blockcipher it is still rate-1 with respect to the underlying blockcipher (see below).

Design. While MiniOCB is based on OCB, it has an important difference. OCB uses a TBC (which is instantiated by XEX mode [15]) that takes a tweak involving the nonce, whereas MiniOCB can not explicitly use the nonce as a part of a tweak. This is because the nonce can not be present clear in a ciphertext and the decryption should be done so that any small change to a ciphertext will make

---

[8] Assuming GCM of ν-bit tag. We note that there is a difference in authentication strength due to the numerators of $1/2^\nu$, and GCM can be better e.g. when q' is huge.

Algorithm MiniOCB-$\mathcal{E}_{\widetilde{E}}(N, A, M)$	**Algorithm** MiniOCB-$\mathcal{D}_{\widetilde{E}}(\widehat{N}, A', L', C')$
1. $(\underline{N}, \underline{M}) \xleftarrow{n} (N, M)$	1. $(\underline{L'}, \underline{C'}) \xleftarrow{n} (L', C')$
2. $(M[1], M[2], \ldots, M[m]) \xleftarrow{n} \underline{M}$	2. $(C'[1], \ldots, C'[m']) \xleftarrow{n} \underline{C'}$
3. $\Sigma \leftarrow M[1] \oplus \ldots \oplus M[m]10^*$	3. **if** $|C'[m']| = n$ **then** $d' \leftarrow 0$
4. **if** $|M[m]| = n$ **then** $d \leftarrow 0$	4. **else** $d' \leftarrow 1$
5. **else** $d \leftarrow 1$	5. **for** $i = 1$ **to** $m' - 1$ **do**
6. $\underline{L} \leftarrow \widetilde{E}^{(\Sigma, A, m, d)}(\underline{N})$	6. $M'[i] \leftarrow \widetilde{E}^{-1(L', A', i, 2)}(C'[i])$
7. **for** $i = 1$ **to** $m - 1$ **do**	7. pad' $\leftarrow$ msb$_{|C'[m']|}(\widetilde{E}^{(L', A', m', 2)}(0^n))$
8. $C[i] \leftarrow \widetilde{E}^{(\underline{L}, A, i, 2)}(M[i])$	8. $M'[m'] \leftarrow C'[m'] \oplus$ pad'
9. pad $\leftarrow$ msb$_{|M[m]|}(\widetilde{E}^{(\underline{L}, A, m, 2)}(0^n))$	9. $\Sigma' \leftarrow M'[1] \oplus \ldots \oplus M'[m']10^*$
10. $C[m] \leftarrow M[m] \oplus$ pad	10. $\underline{N'} \leftarrow \widetilde{E}^{-1(\Sigma', A', m', d')}(\underline{L'})$
11. $\underline{C} \leftarrow (C[1], \ldots, C[m])$	11. **if** msb$_\nu(\underline{N'}) \in \rho(\widehat{N})$ **then**
12. $(L, C) \xleftarrow{\nu} (\underline{L}, \underline{C})$	12. $\underline{M'} \leftarrow (M'[1], \ldots, M'[m])$
13. **return** (L, C)	13. $(N', M') \xleftarrow{\nu} (\underline{N'}, \underline{M'})$
	14. **return** M'
	15. **else return** $\perp$

Fig. 3. Encryption and decryption algorithms of MiniOCB$[\widetilde{E}]$.

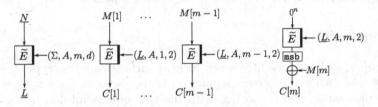

Fig. 4. The encryption algorithm of MiniOCB$[\widetilde{E}]$. Σ denotes the plaintext checksum, and d for encryption of $\underline{N}$ is 0 when $|M[m]| = n$ and 1 otherwise.

the decrypted nonce random. Instead we use encrypted nonce $\underline{L}$ to be a part of tweaks for plaintext encryption, and $\underline{L}$ is derived from an encryption of nonce with tweak involving the plaintext checksum, i.e., XOR of plaintext blocks, in the similar manner to OCB. A tweak of MiniOCB also contains $d = 0, 1, 2$ which is used to separate the roles of TBC calls. We remark that $\nu \leq n$ is required, as well as previous schemes.

We present security bounds of MiniOCB in the following theorems. For simplicity we here provide a security bound for the case of single decryption query.

Theorem 3. *Let $\widetilde{E}$ be a TBC with n-bit block with tweak space $\mathcal{T} = \{0, 1\}^n \times \mathcal{A}_{ae} \times \mathbb{N} \times \{0, 1, 2\}$, and let MiniOCB$[\widetilde{E}]$ be MiniOCB using $\widetilde{E}$ with ν-bit nonce and verification range size ω. Then, for any Priv-adversary $\mathcal{A}$ with $q < 2^{n-1}$ encryption queries and σ total input blocks and time complexity t, we have*

$$\mathrm{Adv}^{\mathrm{priv}}_{\mathrm{MiniOCB}[\widetilde{E}]}(\mathcal{A}) \leq \mathrm{Adv}^{\mathrm{tprp}}_{\widetilde{E}}(\mathcal{B}) + \frac{q^2}{2^n},$$

for an adversary $\mathcal{B}$ using σ encryption queries with $t + O(\sigma)$ time.

Theorem 4. *For any Auth-adversary $\mathcal{A}$ with $q < 2^{n-1}$ encryption queries with σ input blocks, and single decryption query with σ' input blocks, and time complexity t, we have*

$$\mathrm{Adv}^{\mathrm{auth}}_{\mathsf{MiniOCB}[\widetilde{E}]}(\mathcal{A}) \leq \mathrm{Adv}^{\mathrm{tsprp}}_{\widetilde{E}}(\mathcal{B}) + \frac{2.5q^2}{2^n} + \frac{2\omega}{2^\nu},$$

for an adversary $\mathcal{B}$ using σ encryption queries and σ' decryption queries with $t + O(\sigma + \sigma')$ time.

The proofs of these theorems are shown in the full version.

A blockcipher-based instantiation of $\widetilde{E}$ used in MiniOCB can use the construction of (2). One may wonder if every tweak update of $\widetilde{E}$ in MiniOCB requires computation proportional to $|A|$, since A is a part of tweak. However this is not true for most universal hash functions and PRFs, as we can cache the intermediate result depending only on A (e.g. CMAC). Tweak update with respect to third and fourth coordinates can be done without needing additional blockcipher calls (say) by using GF doubling technique [15]. Therefore once we process A, the cost of tweak update is quite small. In the full version, we provide a brief complexity analysis of our proposals with existing schemes.

5 Conclusion

In this paper, we have presented a new form of authenticated encryption scheme, called MiniAE, whose ciphertext expansion is the same as the length of single variable integrating nonce and tag, with the help of stateful decryption. While McGrew and Foley's AERO has the same feature, there is no formal treatment on the provable security. Focusing on the most fundamental security properties, i.e., pseudorandomness of ciphertexts under unique nonce, and a basic form of integrity protection including replay detection, we proposed three constructions of MiniAE, called MiniETE, MiniCTR and MiniOCB, where MiniETE is a generalization of AERO. Notably MiniOCB is based on OCB mode of operation and achieves rate-1 parallelizable encryption. This implies that MiniAE can be as efficient as nonce-based unauthenticated encryption.

Acknowledgements. The author would like to thank the anonymous reviewers of ACISP 2016 for useful comments, and Tetsu Iwata for fruitful discussions.

References

1. Dworkin, M.: Recommendation for Block Cipher Modes of Operation: The CCM Mode for Authentication and Confidentiality. NIST Special Publication 800-38C (2004)
2. Dworkin, M.: Recommendation for Block Cipher Modes of Operation: Galois/Counter Mode (GCM) and GMAC. NIST Special, Publication 800-38D (2007)

3. McGrew, D.: Low power wireless scenarios and techniques for saving bandwidth without sacrificing security. In: NIST Lightweight Cryptography Workshop 2015 (2015)

4. Struik, R.: Revisiting design criteria for AEAD ciphers targeting highly constrained networks. DIAC: Directions in Authenticated Ciphers (2013). http://2013.diac.cr.yp.to/

5. Seys, S., Preneel, B.: Power consumption evaluation of efficient digital signature schemes for low power devices. In: WiMob, vol. 1, pp. 79–86. IEEE (2005)

6. Singelée, D., Seys, S., Batina, L., Verbauwhede, I.: The communication and computation cost of wireless security: extended abstract. In: WISEC, pp. 1–4. ACM (2011)

7. de Meulenaer, G., Gosset, F., Standaert, F., Pereira, O.: On the energy cost of communication and cryptography in wireless sensor networks. In: WiMob, pp. 580–585. IEEE Computer Society (2008)

8. McGrew, D., Foley, J.: Authenticated Encryption with Replay prOtection (AERO). Internet-Draft (2013)

9. Bellare, M., Rogaway, P.: Encode-then-encipher encryption: how to exploit nonces or redundancy in plaintexts for efficient cryptography. In: Okamoto, T. (ed.) ASIACRYPT 2000. LNCS, vol. 1976, pp. 317–330. Springer, Heidelberg (2000)

10. McGrew, D.A., Fluhrer, S.R.: The security of the extended codebook (XCB) mode of operation. In: Adams, C., Miri, A., Wiener, M. (eds.) SAC 2007. LNCS, vol. 4876, pp. 311–327. Springer, Heidelberg (2007)

11. Bellare, M., Kohno, T., Namprempre, C.: Breaking and provably repairing the SSH authenticated encryption scheme: a case study of the Encode-then-Encrypt-and-MAC paradigm. ACM Trans. Inf. Syst. Secur. $7(2)$, 206–241 (2004)

12. Bellare, M., Namprempre, C.: Authenticated encryption: relations among notions and analysis of the generic composition paradigm. In: Okamoto, T. (ed.) ASIACRYPT 2000. LNCS, vol. 1976, pp. 531–545. Springer, Heidelberg (2000)

13. Bellare, M., Namprempre, C.: Authenticated encryption: relations among notions and analysis of the generic composition paradigm. J. Cryptol. $21(4)$, 469–491 (2008)

14. Rogaway, P., Bellare, M., Black, J.: OCB: a block-cipher mode of operation for efficient authenticated encryption. ACM Trans. Inf. Syst. Secur. $6(3)$, 365–403 (2003)

15. Rogaway, P.: Efficient instantiations of tweakable blockciphers and refinements to modes OCB and PMAC. In: Lee, P.J. (ed.) ASIACRYPT 2004. LNCS, vol. 3329, pp. 16–31. Springer, Heidelberg (2004)

16. Krovetz, T., Rogaway, P.: The software performance of authenticated-encryption modes. In: Joux, A. (ed.) FSE 2011. LNCS, vol. 6733, pp. 306–327. Springer, Heidelberg (2011)

17. Liskov, M., Rivest, R.L., Wagner, D.: Tweakable block ciphers. In: Yung, M. (ed.) CRYPTO 2002. LNCS, vol. 2442, pp. 31–46. Springer, Heidelberg (2002)

18. Schroeppel, R.: Hasty Pudding Cipher. AES Submission (1998). http://www.cs.arizona.edu/rcs/hpc/

19. Ferguson, N., Lucks, S., Schneier, B., Whiting, D., Bellare, M., Kohno, T., Callas, J., Walker, J.: Skein Hash Function. SHA-3 Submission (2008). http://www.skein-hash.info/

20. Jean, J., Nikolić, I., Peyrin, T.: Tweaks and keys for block ciphers: The TWEAKEY framework. In: Sarkar, P., Iwata, T. (eds.) ASIACRYPT 2014. LNCS, vol. 8874, pp. 274–288. Springer, Heidelberg (2014)

21. Minematsu, K.: Improved security analysis of XEX and LRW modes. In: Biham, E., Youssef, A.M. (eds.) SAC 2006. LNCS, vol. 4356, pp. 96–113. Springer, Heidelberg (2007)

22. Rogaway, P.: Nonce-based symmetric encryption. In: Roy, B., Meier, W. (eds.) FSE 2004. LNCS, vol. 3017, pp. 348–359. Springer, Heidelberg (2004)

23. Bellare, M., Rogaway, P., Wagner, D.: The EAX mode of operation. In: Roy, B., Meier, W. (eds.) FSE 2004. LNCS, vol. 3017, pp. 389–407. Springer, Heidelberg (2004)

24. Rogaway, P., Shrimpton, T.: A provable-security treatment of the key-wrap problem. In: Vaudenay, S. (ed.) EUROCRYPT 2006. LNCS, vol. 4004, pp. 373–390. Springer, Heidelberg (2006)

25. Jr., M.A.S., de Oliveira, B.T., Barreto, P.S.L.M., Margi, C.B., Carvalho, T.C.M.B., Näslund, M. : Comparison of authenticated-encryption schemes in wireless sensor networks. In: LCN, pp. 450–457. IEEE Computer Society (2011)

26. Chakraborty, D., Sarkar, P.: HCH: a new tweakable enciphering scheme using the hash-encrypt-hash approach. In: Barua, R., Lange, T. (eds.) INDOCRYPT 2006. LNCS, vol. 4329, pp. 287–302. Springer, Heidelberg (2006)

27. Halevi, S., Rogaway, P.: A tweakable enciphering mode. In: Boneh, D. (ed.) CRYPTO 2003. LNCS, vol. 2729, pp. 482–499. Springer, Heidelberg (2003)

28. Halevi, S., Rogaway, P.: A parallelizable enciphering mode. In: Okamoto, T. (ed.) CT-RSA 2004. LNCS, vol. 2964, pp. 292–304. Springer, Heidelberg (2004)

29. Shrimpton, T., Terashima, R.S.: A modular framework for building variable-input-length tweakable ciphers. In: Sako, K., Sarkar, P. (eds.) ASIACRYPT 2013, Part I. LNCS, vol. 8269, pp. 405–423. Springer, Heidelberg (2013)

30. Hoang, V.T., Krovetz, T., Rogaway, P.: Robust authenticated-encryption AEZ and the problem that it solves. In: Oswald, E., Fischlin, M. (eds.) EUROCRYPT 2015. LNCS, vol. 9056, pp. 15–44. Springer, Heidelberg (2015)

31. Naor, M., Reingold, O.: On the construction of pseudorandom permutations: Luby-Rackoff revisited. J. Cryptol. 12(1), 29–66 (1999)

32. Wang, P., Feng, D., Wu, W.: HCTR: a variable-input-length enciphering mode. In: Feng, D., Lin, D., Yung, M. (eds.) CISC 2005. LNCS, vol. 3822, pp. 175–188. Springer, Heidelberg (2005)

33. Halevi, S.: Invertible universal hashing and the TET encryption mode. In: Menezes, A. (ed.) CRYPTO 2007. LNCS, vol. 4622, pp. 412–429. Springer, Heidelberg (2007)

34. Iwata, T., Yasuda, K.: HBS: a single-key mode of operation for deterministic authenticated encryption. In: Dunkelman, O. (ed.) FSE 2009. LNCS, vol. 5665, pp. 394–415. Springer, Heidelberg (2009)

35. Iwata, T., Yasuda, K.: BTM: a single-key, inverse-cipher-free mode for deterministic authenticated encryption. In: Jacobson Jr., M.J., Rijmen, V., Safavi-Naini, R. (eds.) SAC 2009. LNCS, vol. 5867, pp. 313–330. Springer, Heidelberg (2009)

36. Desai, A.: New paradigms for constructing symmetric encryption schemes secure against chosen-ciphertext attack. In: Bellare, M. (ed.) CRYPTO 2000. LNCS, vol. 1880, pp. 394–412. Springer, Heidelberg (2000)

37. Bellare, M., Desai, A., Jokipii, E., Rogaway, P.: A concrete security treatment of symmetric encryption. In: FOCS, pp. 394–403. IEEE Computer Society (1997)

38. Niwa, Y., Ohashi, K., Minematsu, K., Iwata, T.: GCM security bounds reconsidered. In: Leander, G. (ed.) FSE 2015. LNCS, vol. 9054, pp. 385–407. Springer, Heidelberg (2015)

Impossible Differential Cryptanalysis of 14-Round Camellia-192

Keting Jia[1,4(✉)] and Ning Wang[2,3,4]

[1] Department of Computer Science and Technology,
Tsinghua University, Beijing 100084, China
ktjia@tsinghua.edu.cn
[2] Key Laboratory of Cryptologic Technology and Information Security,
Ministry of Education, Shandong University, Jinan 250100, China
wangning2012@mail.sdu.edu.cn
[3] School of Mathematics, Shandong University, Jinan 250100, China
[4] State Key Laboratory of Cryptology, P.O.Box 5159, Beijing 100878, China

Abstract. As an international standard by ISO/IEC, Camellia is a widely used block cipher, which has received much attention from cryptanalysts. The impossible differential attack is one of efficient methods to analyze Camellia. Liu et al. gave an 8-round impossible differential, of which the input and output differences depend on some weak keys. In this paper, we apply some key relations to build the precomputation table to reduce time complexity and give some relations between the size of weak key sets and the number of input and output differences of the impossible differentials, which are used to balance the time complexity and the fraction of key space attacked. Furthermore, we give an impossible differential attack on 14-round Camellia-192 with $2^{126.5}$ known plaintexts and $2^{189.32}$ encryptions. Our impossible differential attack works one more round than previous cryptanalysis results.

Keywords: Camellia · Block cipher · Impossible differential attack

1 Introduction

The block cipher Camellia was designed by Aoki et al. in 2000 [1], which is a Feistel-like construction with 128-bit block size. Nowadays Camellia has become an e-government recommended cipher by CRYPTREC, as well as one of NESSIE block cipher portfolio and international standard by ISO/IEC 18033-3 [9]. It has three versions with different key lengths and rounds, i.e. 18 rounds for a 128-bit key and 24 rounds for a 192 or 256-bit key corresponding to Camellia-128, Camellia-192 and Camellia-256, respectively. There is an interesting property for Camellia that FL/FL^{-1} layers are inserted every 6 rounds. The FL/FL^{-1} layers are used to resist the differential cryptanalysis by exploiting key-dependent

Supported by the National Natural Science Foundation of China (Grant No. 61133013 and 61402256) and the National Key Basic Research Program of China (Grant No. 2013CB834205).

J.K. Liu and R. Steinfeld (Eds.): ACISP 2016, Part II, LNCS 9723, pp. 363–378, 2016.
DOI: 10.1007/978-3-319-40367-0_23

functions across rounds. Therefore, some cryptanalyses on the simplified versions of Camellia without the FL/FL^{-1} layers are given, such as truncated differential attacks [11,22], linear and differential attacks [21], square attacks [13], and impossible differential attacks [16,17,20,23] etc.

In this paper, we focus on the original versions of Camellia with FL/FL^{-1} layers, which has been analysed by many cryptographers with various block cipher cryptanalysis methods. The square-type attacks were efficient to attack 9-round Camellia-128 and 10-round Camellia-256 [12]. The higher order differential attack was used to analyse the last 11 rounds Camellia-256 [8]. There is a little flaw in both the above attacks on reduced Camellia-256, which was corrected by Lu et al. [16]. The meet-in-the-middle (MITM) attacks on Camellia were given in [6,7,18,19], which were valid for 10-round Camellia-128, 12-round Camellia-192 and 13-round Camellia-256. The impossible differential attacks on 11/12/13-round Camellia-128/192/256 were given in [15], and recently improved by Boura *et al.* [4]. Besides, zero-correlation (ZC) cryptanalysis was utilized to attack 11-round Camellia-128 and 12-round Camellia-192 [3]. Recently, the truncated differential is used to attack 12-round Camellia-192 [14].

In this paper, we give the impossible differential attacks on Camellia with FL/FL^{-1} layers. There are some 7-round or 8-round impossible differentials introduced since Chen et al. presented the first 6-round impossible differential with FL/FL^{-1} layers [5]. Specially, Liu et al. proposed an 8-round impossible differential with FL/FL^{-1} layers after the first round and the 7-th round for some weak keys. Considering the 8-round impossible differentials without FL/FL^{-1} layers given by Wu et al. [23], we extend Liu et al's impossible differential. Since the input and output differences of the impossible differential depend on some weak keys, it requires different data complexity for different weak key sets. Hence, we study the relations between the size of weak key sets and the input and output differences of the impossible differentials, which are used to increase the fraction of key space attacked and reduce the time complexity. We give a 14-round impossible differential attack on a fraction of $2^{-2.92}$ of key space, which needs $2^{126.5}$ known plaintexts and $2^{181.40}$ encryptions. The current time complexity is about one in $2^{7.68}$ of the exhaustive search complexity for $2^{-2.92}$ weak key space. Applying four different impossible differentials and balancing the fraction of weak key space and the time complexity, we introduce the

Table 1. Summary of the attacks on reduced-round Camellia-192

Rounds	Whitening keys	Percentage of key space	Attack type	Data	Time (Enc)	Memory (Bytes)	Source
12	yes	100 %	ZC	$2^{125.7}$KP	$2^{188.8}$	2^{112}	[3]
12	yes	100 %	MITM	2^{113}CP	2^{180}	2^{158}	[7]
12	yes	100 %	Impossible Diff	$2^{119.7}$CP	$2^{161.06}$	$2^{154.7}$	[4]
12	yes	100 %	Truncated Diff	2^{117}CP	$2^{185.3}$	2^{119}	[14]
13(3–15)	no	100 %	Impossible Diff	$2^{118.59}$CP	$2^{182.10}$	$2^{124.0}$	[2]
14(2–15)	no	$2^{-2.92}$	Impossible Diff	$2^{126.5}$KP	$2^{181.4}$	2^{137}	Sect. 4
14(2–15)	no	41 %	Impossible Diff	$2^{126.5}$KP	$2^{184.98}$	$2^{137.0}$	Sect. 4
14(2–15)	no	100 %	Impossible Diff	$2^{126.5}$KP	$2^{189.32}$	$2^{137.0}$	Sect. 4

first impossible differential attack on 14-round Camellia-192 with $2^{126.5}$ known plaintexts and $2^{189.32}$ encryptions.

Table 1 summarizes our cryptanalysis results along with some previous results of reduced-round Camellia-192 with FL/FL^{-1}, where KP and CP represent known plaintexts and chosen plaintexts, respectively.

The rest of this paper is organized as follows. we list some notations and briefly describe the block cipher Camellia in Sect. 2. Section 3 presents some observations and impossible differentials of Camellia used in our cryptanalysis. We give impossible differential attacks on 14-round Camellia-192 in Sect. 4. In Sect. 5 we conclude this paper.

2   Preliminaries

In this section we list the notations used throughout this paper, and then give a brief description of the block cipher Camellia.

2.1   Notations

The following notations are used in this paper:

L_{r-1}	the left 64-bit half of the r-th round input
R_{r-1}	the right 64-bit half of the r-th round input
X_r	the state after the key addition layer of the r-th round
Y_r	the state after the substitution transformation layer of the r-th round
Z_r	the state after the diffusion layer of the r-th round
k_r	the subkey used in the r-th round
kf_i	the subkey used in the FL and FL^{-1} functions of Camellia, $i = 1, 2, 3, 4, 5, 6$
kw_i	the whitening key used in the begin and end of Camellia, $i = 1, 2, 3, 4$
$X[i]$	the i-th byte of a bit string X ($0 \leq i \leq 7$), where the left most byte is $X[0]$
$X[i \sim j]$	the $j - i + 1$ bytes of a bit string X starting from $X[i]$
$X_L (X_R)$	the left (right) half of a bit string X,
$X\{i\}$	the i-th most significant bit of a bit string $X (0 \leq i \leq 127)$, where the left-most bit is the most significant bit $X\{0\}$
$X\{i \sim j\}$	the $j - i + 1$ bit string of X from the i-th most significant bit
ΔX	the XOR difference of X and X', i.e., $\Delta X = X \oplus X'$
$ham(x)$	the hamming weight of x
$zero(x)$	the number of x's zero bits

$\oplus, \wedge, \vee$ bitwise exclusive OR (XOR), AND, OR
$\overline{x}$ binary complement of bit string x
$|S_{WK}|$ the size of the weak key set S_{WK}
$x\|y$ bit string concatenation of x and y
$x \lll l$ rotate x to the left by l bit

2.2 Brief Description of Block Cipher Camellia

Camellia [1] is a 128-bit block cipher with Feistel-like structure. There are three versions depending on the key size used, which are named as Camellia-128/192/256 with 18/24/24 rounds, respectively. Here, a brief description of the Camellia-192 is introduced.

Let $L_0\|R_0$ represent the XOR of 128-bit plaintext M and the whitening key $(kw_1\|kw_2)$. The encryption is given in the following (see Fig. 1).

– For $r = 1$ to 24, and $r \neq 6$, 12 and 18, do

$$L_r = R_{r-1} \oplus F(L_{r-1}, k_r), \quad R_r = L_{r-1}.$$

– For $r = 6$, 12 and 18, do

$$L_r^* = R_{r-1} \oplus F(L_{r-1}, k_r), \ R_r^* = L_{r-1},$$
$$L_r = FL(L_r^*, kf_{r/3-1}), \qquad R_r = FL^{-1}(R_r^*, kf_{r/3}),$$

– The 128-bit ciphertext $C = (R_{24}\|L_{24}) \oplus (kw_3\|kw_4)$.

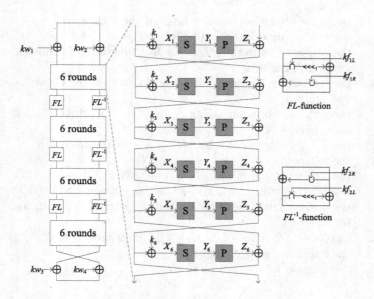

Fig. 1. The encryption of Camellia-192

The round function F includes there parts, i.e., a key-addition layer, a substitution transformation layer S and a diffusion layer P. The key-addition layer is the XOR between the left half input of the round function and the round subkey, i.e. $X_r = L_{r-1} \oplus k_r$ for the r-th round. The substitution transformation layer S contains four types of 8×8 S-boxes s_1, s_2, s_3 and s_4. Let the input of S in the r-th round be $X_r = (x_0, x_1, x_2, x_3, x_4, x_5, x_6, x_7)$, and then the output

$$Y_r = S(X_r) = \big(s_1(x_0), s_2(x_1), s_3(x_2), s_4(x_3), s_2(x_4), s_3(x_5), s_4(x_6), s_1(x_7)\big).$$

The linear transformation P is a diffusion component based on bytes. $Z_r = P(Y_r)$ and its inverse P^{-1} are defined in the following, where $Y_r = (y_0, y_1, y_2, y_3, y_4, y_5, y_6, y_7)$ is the input of P in r-th round, and $Z_r = (z_0, z_1, z_2, z_3, z_4, z_5, z_6, z_7)$ is the output.

$$
\begin{aligned}
z_0 &= y_0 \oplus y_2 \oplus y_3 \oplus y_5 \oplus y_6 \oplus y_7, & y_0 &= z_1 \oplus z_2 \oplus z_3 \oplus z_5 \oplus z_6 \oplus z_7, \\
z_1 &= y_0 \oplus y_1 \oplus y_3 \oplus y_4 \oplus y_6 \oplus y_7, & y_1 &= z_0 \oplus z_2 \oplus z_3 \oplus z_4 \oplus z_6 \oplus z_7, \\
z_2 &= y_0 \oplus y_1 \oplus y_2 \oplus y_4 \oplus y_5 \oplus y_7, & y_2 &= z_0 \oplus z_1 \oplus z_3 \oplus z_4 \oplus z_5 \oplus z_7, \\
z_3 &= y_1 \oplus y_2 \oplus y_3 \oplus y_4 \oplus y_5 \oplus y_6, & y_3 &= z_0 \oplus z_1 \oplus z_2 \oplus z_4 \oplus z_5 \oplus z_6, \\
z_4 &= y_0 \oplus y_1 \oplus y_5 \oplus y_6 \oplus y_7, & y_4 &= z_0 \oplus z_1 \oplus z_4 \oplus z_6 \oplus z_7, \\
z_5 &= y_1 \oplus y_2 \oplus y_4 \oplus y_6 \oplus y_7, & y_5 &= z_1 \oplus z_2 \oplus z_4 \oplus z_5 \oplus z_7, \\
z_6 &= y_2 \oplus y_3 \oplus y_4 \oplus y_5 \oplus y_7, & y_6 &= z_2 \oplus z_3 \oplus z_4 \oplus z_5 \oplus z_6, \\
z_7 &= y_0 \oplus y_3 \oplus y_4 \oplus y_5 \oplus y_6, & y_7 &= z_0 \oplus z_3 \oplus z_5 \oplus z_6 \oplus z_7,
\end{aligned}
$$

The FL function is a key-dependent boolean function inserted every 6 rounds. Let $(a_L \| a_R, kf_{iL} \| kf_{iR})$ and $(b_L \| b_R)$ be the input and output of FL, where $a_L, a_R, kf_{iL}, kf_{iR}, b_L$ and b_R are 32-bit words. The FL function is defined as

$$b_R = ((a_L \wedge kf_{iL}) \lll 1) \oplus a_R, \quad b_L = (b_R \vee kf_{iR}) \oplus a_L.$$

Key Schedule. Let the master key of Camellia be K, which generates the subkeys K_L and K_R. For Camellia-192, $K_L = K\{0 - 127\}$ is the left 128-bit of K, and $K_R = K\{128 - 191\} \| \overline{K\{128 - 191\}}$ is the concatenation of the right 64-bit of K and its binary complement. Two 128-bit subkeys K_A and K_B are derived from K_L and K_R by the computation of 6 round functions (see Fig. 4 in Appendix A). Then the whitening keys kw_i ($i = 1, ..., 4$), round subkeys k_r ($r = 1, ..., 24$) and kf_j ($j = 1, ..., 6$) are generated by rotating K_L, K_R, K_A or K_B (see Table 5 in Appendix A).

3 Impossible Differential Characteristics of Camellia

In this section, we give some observations of the block cipher Camellia, and present impossible differential characteristics for different key subsets.

3.1 Some Observations of Camellia

This section introduces some observations which help us to analyze the reduced-round Camellia-192.

Observation 1 [10]. *Let X, X', K be l-bit values, and $\Delta X = X \oplus X'$, then the differential properties of AND and OR operations are:*

$$(X \wedge K) \oplus (X' \wedge K) = \Delta X \wedge K,$$
$$(X \vee K) \oplus (X' \vee K) = \Delta X \oplus (\Delta X \wedge K).$$

Observation 2. *For S-boxes in Camellia, given an input and output differences pair (α, β), the probability that there exits x such that $s_i(x \oplus \alpha) \oplus s_i(x) = \beta$ (abbreviated by $\alpha \xrightarrow{s_i} \beta$) is 0.5, where $\alpha \neq 0$, $\beta \neq 0$, and $i = 1, 2, 3, 4$. And there exist 2 values of x when the input difference α can propagate β by S-boxes.*

We know there exist 127 non-zero output differences for a given non-zero input difference for any S-box in Camellia. Given (α, β), when $\alpha \neq 0$ and $\beta \neq 0$, the probability to make $s_i(x \oplus \alpha) \oplus s_i(x) = \beta$ hold is $127/255 \approx 0.5$ and there are averagely $256/127 \approx 2$ values of x. When α and β are any bytes, because there are 256×256 values of (α, x) and (α, β), respectively. There is a value of x such that $\alpha \xrightarrow{s_i} \beta$ on average.

Observation 3 [20]. *For Camellia-192/256, if a value of (K_B, K_R) is given, then the corresponding value for (K_L, K_A) can be obtained with a computational complexity of approximately 6 one-round Camellia computations.*

Observation 4. *For Camellia-192/256, if a value for (K_{BR}, K_{RL}) is given, then there is a linear relation between K_{AL} and K_{BL} in the following.*

$$K_{BL} \oplus K_{AL} = K_{RL} \oplus F(K_{BR}, \Sigma_6). \tag{1}$$

This property is obviously deduced by the key schedule of Camellia-192/256.

3.2   8-Round Impossible Differential Characteristics

Wu et al. proposed 4 8-round impossible differential characteristics for Camellia without FL/FL^{-1} layers as follows:

$$(0,0,0,0,0,0,0,0,\ a,0,0,0,0,0,0,0) \xrightarrow{8r} (h,0,0,0,0,0,0,0,\ 0,0,0,0,0,0,0,0),$$
$$(0,0,0,0,0,0,0,0,\ 0,a,0,0,0,0,0,0) \xrightarrow{8r} (0,h,0,0,0,0,0,0,\ 0,0,0,0,0,0,0,0),$$
$$(0,0,0,0,0,0,0,0,\ 0,0,a,0,0,0,0,0) \xrightarrow{8r} (0,0,h,0,0,0,0,0,\ 0,0,0,0,0,0,0,0),$$
$$(0,0,0,0,0,0,0,0,\ 0,0,0,a,0,0,0,0) \xrightarrow{8r} (0,0,0,h,0,0,0,0,\ 0,0,0,0,0,0,0,0),$$

where $a \neq 0$, $h \neq 0$.

For some weak keys, Liu et al. extend the 8-round impossible differential characteristic with two FL/FL^{-1} layers inserted after the first and seventh rounds, i.e.,

$$D1 : (0,0,0,0,0,0,0,0,\ a,0,0,0,a',0,0,0) \xrightarrow{8r} (b,0,0,0,b',0,0,0,\ 0,0,0,0,0,0,0,0,),$$

where $a \neq 0, b \neq 0$, a' and b' are any values of byte [15], see Fig. 2. Here we only considering the case $a' = 0, b' = 0$, which is described in Observation 5.

Observation 5. *For an 8-round Camellia encryption with two FL/FL^{-1} layers inserted after the first and seventh rounds, in which four subkeys $kf_j(j = 1, 2, 3, 4)$ are used. Let the input differences of the first round be $\Delta L_0 = 0$, $\Delta R_0 = (a, 0, 0, 0, 0, 0, 0, 0, 0)$, and the output differences of the 8-th round be $\Delta L_8 = (h, 0, 0, 0, 0, 0, 0, 0, 0)$, $\Delta R_8 = 0$. Then $(\Delta L_0, \Delta R_0) \xrightarrow{8 \ rounds} (\Delta L_8, \Delta R_8)$ are 8-round impossible differentials when $kf_1[0] \wedge a = 0$ and $kf_4[0] \wedge h = 0$, $a \neq 0, h \neq 0$.*

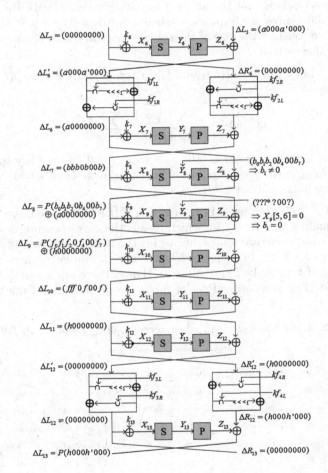

Fig. 2. 8-round Impossible Differential of Camellia in [15]

Considering the above 8-round impossible differentials without FL/FL^{-1} layers, we extend Liu et al's impossible differential. Similarly, there are another three 8-round impossible differentials in the following, where $a \neq 0, h \neq 0$.

$D2 : (0,0,0,0,0,0,0,0,\ 0,a,0,0,0,0,0,0) \xrightarrow{8r} (0,h,0,0,0,0,0,0,\ 0,0,0,0,0,0,0,0),$
where $kf_1[1] \wedge a = 0, kf_4[1] \wedge h = 0;$

$D3 : (0,0,0,0,0,0,0,0,\ 0,0,a,0,0,0,0,0) \xrightarrow{8r} (0,0,h,0,0,0,0,0,\ 0,0,0,0,0,0,0,0),$
where $kf_1[2] \wedge a = 0, kf_4[2] \wedge h = 0;$

$D4 : (0,0,0,0,0,0,0,0,\ 0,0,0,a,0,0,0,0) \xrightarrow{8r} (0,0,0,h,0,0,0,0,\ 0,0,0,0,0,0,0,0),$
where $kf_1[3] \wedge a = 0, kf_4[3] \wedge h = 0.$

However, it is obvious that the above 8-round differentials with the same input and output differences are impossible when $a = 0, h \neq 0$ or $a \neq 0, h = 0$ for any key. Hence, we consider the size of the subkey space in which there exist 8-round impossible differentials.

Property 1. Let $S_{WK_{i,j}} = \{(kf_1[0], kf_4[0]) | zero(kf_1[0]) \geq i, zero(kf_4[0]) \geq j\}$. Then the size of $S_{WK_{i,j}}$ is

$$|S_{WK_{i,j}}| = \sum_{i \leq x \leq 8} C_8^x \times \sum_{j \leq x \leq 8} C_8^x. \qquad (2)$$

The set $S_{WK_{i,j}}$ covers a fraction of $Pr_{i,j} = |S_{WK_{i,j}}|/2^{16}$ of the key space. For an element of $S_{WK_{i,j}}$, the least number of (a, h) to make both $kf_1[0] \wedge a = 0$ and $kf_4[0] \wedge h = 0$ hold is about 2^{i+j}.

For $k = 0, \ldots, 7$, $a\{k\}$ must be 0 when $kf_1[0]\{k\} = 1$. Since there are at most $8 - i$ bits equaling to 1 for $kf_1[0]$ which means the corresponding $8 - i$ bits of a must be zero and there are no conditions for the remaining i bits of a. Then the least number of a is $2^i - 1$ to make $kf_1[0] \wedge a = 0$. Similarly, there are at least $2^j - 1$ values of h to make $kf_4[0] \wedge h = 0$. Hence, there are about 2^{i+j} values of (a, h) at least. The percentage $Pr_{i,j}$ of $S_{WK_{i,j}}$ is presented in Table 2.

Table 2. The percentage $Pr_{i,j}$ when $zero(kf_1[0]) \geq i$ and $zero(kf_4[0]) \geq j$

(i,j)	0	1	2	3	4	5	6	7	8
0	1	$2^{-0.01}$	$2^{-0.05}$	$2^{-0.23}$	$2^{-0.65}$	$2^{-1.46}$	$2^{-2.79}$	$2^{-4.83}$	$2^{-8.00}$
1	$2^{-0.01}$	$2^{-0.01}$	$2^{-0.06}$	$2^{-0.23}$	$2^{-0.66}$	$2^{-1.47}$	$2^{-2.80}$	$2^{-4.84}$	$2^{-8.01}$
2	$2^{-0.05}$	$2^{-0.06}$	$2^{-0.10}$	$2^{-0.28}$	$2^{-0.70}$	$2^{-1.51}$	$2^{-2.84}$	$2^{-4.88}$	$2^{-8.05}$
3	$2^{-0.23}$	$2^{-0.23}$	$2^{-0.28}$	$2^{-0.45}$	$2^{-0.88}$	$2^{-1.69}$	$2^{-3.02}$	$2^{-5.06}$	$2^{-8.23}$
4	$2^{-0.65}$	$2^{-0.66}$	$2^{-0.70}$	$2^{-0.88}$	$2^{-1.30}$	$2^{-2.11}$	$2^{-3.44}$	$2^{-5.48}$	$2^{-8.65}$
5	$2^{-1.46}$	$2^{-1.47}$	$2^{-1.51}$	$2^{-1.69}$	$2^{-2.11}$	$2^{-2.92}$	$2^{-4.25}$	$2^{-6.29}$	$2^{-9.46}$
6	$2^{-2.79}$	$2^{-2.80}$	$2^{-2.84}$	$2^{-3.02}$	$2^{-3.44}$	$2^{-4.25}$	$2^{-5.58}$	$2^{-7.62}$	$2^{-10.79}$
7	$2^{-4.83}$	$2^{-4.84}$	$2^{-4.88}$	$2^{-5.06}$	$2^{-5.48}$	$2^{-6.29}$	$2^{-7.62}$	$2^{-9.66}$	$2^{-12.83}$
8	$2^{-8.00}$	$2^{-8.01}$	$2^{-8.05}$	$2^{-8.23}$	$2^{-8.65}$	$2^{-9.46}$	$2^{-10.79}$	$2^{-12.83}$	$2^{-16.00}$

Given a byte a, let $zero(\cdot)$ represent the number of zero bits, and $ham(\cdot)$ mean the number of bits equaling to 1. It is obvious that $ham(a) + zero(a) = 8$.

Property 2. Let the number of zero bits of the byte b satisfy $zero(b) \geq i$, and the hamming weight of a non-zero byte a satisfy $ham(a) \leq i$, where $1 \leq i \leq 8$. The probability P_i to make $a \wedge b = 0$ and $zero(b) \geq i$ for a given $a(a \neq 0)$ with $ham(a) \leq i$ is:

$$P_i = P\{a \wedge b = 0, zero(b) \geq i | a \neq 0, ham(a) \leq i, b = 0, \ldots, 255\}$$

$$= \frac{\sum_{i \leq t \leq 8} \left(C_8^t \times \left(\sum_{i \leq x \leq 8} C_{8-t}^{x-t} \times 2^{-8} \right) \right)}{\sum_{1 \leq t \leq i} C_8^t}, \tag{3}$$

where $i = 1, \ldots, 7$.

Proof. Let $ham(a) = t \leq i$. Then there are t zero bits of b to make $a \wedge b = 0$. Since $zero(b) \geq i$, there are at least $i - t$ zero bits for the remaining $8 - t$ bits of b. Hence,

$$P\{a \wedge b = 0, zero(b) \geq i | a \neq 0, ham(a) = t, b = 0, \ldots, 255\} = \sum_{i \leq x \leq 8} C_{8-t}^{x-t} \times 2^{-8}.$$

There are C_8^t values of a such that $ham(a) = t$, and $\sum_{1 \leq x \leq i} C_8^x$ values of a to make $ham(a) \leq i$. Thus, we have Eq. (3) to compute the probability P_i.   □

The values of P_i for $i = 1, \ldots, 8$ see Table 3, which are also obtained by enumerating all a and b satisfying constraints and checking the conditions.

Table 3. The probability P_i obtained from the property 2

i	1	2	3	4	5	6	7	8
P_i	2^{-1}	$2^{-1.71}$	$2^{-2.38}$	$2^{-2.98}$	$2^{-3.59}$	$2^{-4.38}$	$2^{-5.68}$	2^{-8}

4 Impossible Differential Attack on 14-Round Camellia-192

In this section, we mount the 8-round impossible differential by Observation 5 from rounds 6–13, and extend 4 rounds on the top and 2 rounds on the bottom to attack 14-round Camellia-192 (see Fig. 3). By the key schedule, we know $kf_1[0] = K_R\{30 \sim 37\}, kf_4[0] = K_L\{124 \sim 127, 0 \sim 3\}$ (see Table 5 in Appendix A). Let the input and output differences of the 8-round impossible differential be

$$(\Delta L_5, \Delta R_5) = (0,0,0,0,0,0,0,0,\ a,0,0,0,0,0,0,0),$$
$$(\Delta L_{13}, \Delta R_{13}) = (h,0,0,0,0,0,0,0,\ 0,0,0,0,0,0,0,0).$$

Let $S_{WK_{i,j}}$ be the weak key set. Then we know $ham(a) \leq i$, $ham(h) \leq j$ in order to generate the impossible differential based on Observation 5.

Precomputation. In order to reduce the time complexity, we build a table to store some intermediated values and differences which has been used to eliminate the wrong keys more efficiently based on the key relation $k_3 = \overline{k_4}$ and the difference propagation in the extended top rounds.

Given $(y_0, y_1, y_5, y_6, y_7)$, we know the following equations by the linear transformation $Z_r = P(Y_r)$,

- $y_0 \oplus y_6 = z_1 \oplus z_4 \oplus z_7$;
- $y_0 \oplus y_1 \oplus y_5 = z_0 \oplus z_2 \oplus z_7$;
- $y_6 \oplus y_7 = z_0 \oplus z_2 \oplus z_4 \oplus z_7$;

where $Y_r = (y_0, y_1, y_2, y_3, y_4, y_5, y_6, y_7)$ and $Z_r = (z_0, z_1, z_2, z_3, z_4, z_5, z_6, z_7)$. It is obvious that these equations are independent of (z_3, z_5, z_6) and we can get (z_1, z_4, z_7) by solving the above equation systems when we know (z_0, z_2).

From Fig. 3, we know $\Delta L_2 = P(\alpha_0 \alpha_1 \alpha_2 0 \alpha_4 0 0 \alpha_7) \oplus P(0aaaa00a)$, $\Delta L_3 = (\alpha a \alpha 0 \alpha 00 \alpha)$, $\Delta L_4 = (a0000000)$, $\Delta R_2 = (????????)$, where $ham(a) \leq i$. We traverse $\Delta L_2, \Delta L_3, \Delta L_4, \Delta R_2$, Then we deduce ΔX_4, ΔY_4, ΔX_3, ΔY_3 by partial encryption. Furthermore, we get X_3 and Y_3, $X_4[0, 1, 2, 4, 7]$ by the input and output differences of S-boxes. For all $k_3[0, 1, 2, 4, 7](K_R\{15 \sim 38, 47 \sim 54, 7 \sim 14\})$ which make $kf_1[0] \wedge a = 0$ $(kf_1[0] = k_3\{15 \sim 22\})$, we compute $R_2[0, 1, 2, 4, 7]$ and $L_2[0, 1, 2, 4, 7]$ as a result of $k_4 = \overline{k_3}$. We build a table T_1 to store the $(k_3[0, 1, 2, 4, 7], X_3[3, 5, 6], L_2[0, 2], \alpha, \alpha_2, a, \alpha_4)$ indexed by $(\Delta R_2, R_2[0, 1, 2, 4, 7], \alpha_0, \alpha_1, \alpha_7, L_2[1] \oplus L_2[4] \oplus L_2[7], L_2[0] \oplus L_2[2] \oplus L_2[7], L_2[0] \oplus L_2[2] \oplus L_2[4] \oplus L_2[7])$.

Since there are at least $8 - i$ zero bits for a, the number of a is $n_a = C_8^1 + \cdots + C_8^i$. There are $2^{14 \times 8} \times n_a$ values for $(\Delta L_2, \Delta L_3, \Delta L_4, \Delta R_2)$ and 2^{40} values for $k_3[0, 1, 2, 4, 7]$. The probability such that $kf_1[0] \wedge a = 0$ and $zero(kf_1[0]) \geq i$ by Property 2 is P_i. Therefore, there are about $\frac{2^{19 \times 8} \times n_a}{2^{19 \times 8}} \times P_i = n_a \times P_i$ values for each index. The complexity of building the table is less than $2^{20 \times 8}$ encryptions.

We demonstrate the attack on 14-round Camellia-192 in a known plaintexts attack scenario as follows. Here the early abort technique from [17] is used to reduce the time complexity.

Data Collection. For 2^n plaintexts, ask for the encryption of these plaintexts, and store the corresponding ciphertexts in a hash table H indexed by 72-bit $(R_{15}[3, 5, 6], R_{15}[0] \oplus R_{15}[1], R_{15}[0] \oplus R_{15}[2], R_{15}[0] \oplus R_{15}[4], R_{15}[0] \oplus R_{15}[7], P^{-1}(L_{15})[5, 6])$. Then, we get 2^{2n-73} pairs, which satisfy

$$\Delta P^{-1}(L_{15}) = (*, *, *, h, *, 0, 0, *), \Delta R_{15} = (g, g, g, 0, g, 0, 0, g),$$

where $h \neq 0, g \neq 0$. Since $\Delta Y_2 = P^{-1}(\Delta R_1 \oplus \Delta L_2)$, then we would compute $\Delta Y_2[5, 6] = P^{-1}(\Delta R_1)[5, 6]$, and ΔY_{15} would be deduced from ΔL_{15} (see Fig. 3). Then we get the input and output differences of 7 active S-boxes in the 2-nd round and 15-th the round in total. For an active S-box, let the input difference be α, the output difference be β, the pairs which make the differential transition $\alpha \xrightarrow{S\text{-}box} \beta$ would remain, where $\alpha \neq 0$ and $\beta \neq 0$. There are about 2^{2n-80} pairs

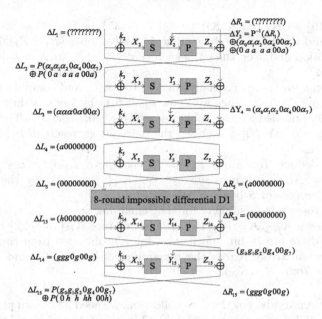

Fig. 3. The attack on 14-round Camellia-192

left by Observation 2. Then we filter out the pairs in which there are at least $8 - j$ zero bits for h, i.e., $ham(h) \leq j$. The number of h is $n_h = C_8^1 + \cdots + C_8^j$. There are about $2^{2n-80} \times n_h \times 2^{-8} = 2^{2n-88} \times n_h$ remaining pairs on average.

Key Recovery. We apply the following procedure to eliminate the wrong sub-keys, and find the right key.

1. For each pair, according to the input and output differences of 7 active S-boxes in the 2-nd round and 15-th round obtained in data collection, we deduce the subkey $k_{15}[0,1,2,4,7]$ ($K_B\{60 \sim 83, 92 \sim 99, 116 \sim 123\}$) and $k_2[5,6]$($K_B\{104 \sim 119\}$) by accessing the difference distribution table of S-boxes. If $k_2[6]\{4 \sim 7\} = k_{15}[7]\{0 \sim 3\}$, keep the pairs. There are about $2^{2n-90}\times n_h{}^1$ pairs left, which are corresponding to 2^5 values of 52-bit $K_B\{60 \sim 83, 92 \sim 99, 104 \sim 123\}$ on average.
2. Guessing 2^4 values of $K_B\{124 \sim 127\}$, we know $k_2[0,1,5,6,7]$ and then deduce $\Delta Y_2[0,1,7]$ and $Y_2[0,1,5,6,7]$ to compute $Y_2[0]\oplus Y_2[6]\oplus P^{-1}(\Delta L_2)[0]\oplus P^{-1}(\Delta L_2)[6]$, $Y_2[0] \oplus Y_2[1] \oplus P^{-1}(\Delta L_2)[0] \oplus P^{-1}(\Delta L_2)[1]$, $Y_2[6] \oplus Y_2[7] \oplus P^{-1}(\Delta L_2)[6] \oplus P^{-1}(\Delta L_2)[7]$. By partial encryption, we get $\Delta R_2, R_2$. Hence, we obtain $k_3[0,1,2,4,7]$, $X_3[3,5,6]$, $L_2[0,2]$, $P^{-1}(\Delta L_2)[2,3,4]$, $L_2[0,2]$ and ΔL_3 by accessing table T_1. And then we compute $\Delta Y_2[2,3,4]$ and deduce $k_2[2,3,4]$ by the input and output differences of S-boxes in round 2. If

---

[1] There are 2 values for $k_2[6]$ and $k_{15}[7]$, respectively. Hence for a given pair, the probability $\Pr\{k_2[6]\{4 \sim 7\} = k_{15}[7]\{0 \sim 3\}\} = 2 \times 2 \times 2^{-4} = 2^{-2}$. Hence, there are about $2^{2n-90} \times n_h$ remaining pairs.

$k_2\{16 \sim 19\} = K_B\{80 \sim 83\}$ or $k_2\{32 \sim 35\} = K_B\{96 \sim 99\}$, we store the pairs and the corresponding subkeys. We compute $(R_1 \oplus Z_2)[0,2]$ by partial encryption and keep the pairs such that $(R_1 \oplus Z_2)[0,2] = L_2[0,2]$. There are about $2^{2n-90+5+4-24} = 2^{2n-105} \times n_h \times n_a \times P_i$ pairs left.

3. For the remaining pairs, partially encrypt to get L_2 and compute $k_3[3,5,6] = L_2[3,5,6] \oplus X_3[3,5,6]$. Since we know $k_{15}[3,5,6]$ by key schedule, then compute $L_{13}[0]$, and deduce the subkey $k_{14}[0](K_R\{60 \sim 63, 0 \sim 3\})$ as a result of $\Delta L_{13}[0] = h, \Delta Y_{14}[0] = g$. Keep the pairs which result in $k_3\{45 \sim 52\} = \overline{k_{14}[0]}$.

4. Then we deduce L_3. Since $k_4 = \overline{k_3}$, compute $L_4[0]$. Since $\Delta X_5[0] = a, \Delta Y_5[0] = \Delta L_3[0]$, deduce subkey $k_5[0](K_A\{15 \sim 22\})$ by the input and output differences of S-boxes in the 5-th round.

5. Eliminate these wrong subkeys for the remaining pairs.

6. For the known $K_{BR}, K_R, K_A\{15 \sim 22\}$, we deduce $K_B\{15 \sim 22\}$ by equation (1). Then there are 76-bit information for K_B obtained from the equivalent subkeys, exhaustively search the remaining 52 bits of K_B and deduce the master key from (K_B, K_R).

Complexity Analysis. For the data collection, we need 2^n known plaintexts, 2^n encryptions and $2^{2n-73}(1 + 2^{-1} + \cdots + 2^{-6}) \times 1/8 = 2^{2n-75}$ one-round encryptions. In the key recovery procedure, we spend $2^{2n-88} \times n_h \times 1/8 = 2^{2n-91} \times n_h$ one-round encryptions in step 1. In step 2, $2^{2n-90} \times n_h \times 2^5 \times 2^4 = 2^{2n-81} \times n_h$ memory accesses and $2^{2n-81} \times n_h \times n_a \times P_i \times 3/8 + 2^{2n-81} \times n_h \times n_a \times P_i \times 2^{-8} = 2^{2n-82.4} \times n_a \times n_h \times P_i$ one-round encryptions are needed. There are $2^{2n-105} \times n_h \times n_a \times P_i$ and $2^{2n-113} \times n_h \times n_a \times P_i$ one-round encryptions in steps 3 and 4, respectively. It costs $2^{2n-113} \times n_h \times n_a \times P_i$ one-round encryptions and memory accesses in step 5. The computation complexities of first 5 steps is denoted by $TC_0 \approx 2^{2n-91}(2^{16} + n_h + 2^{8.6} \times n_a \times n_h \times P_i)/14 + 2^{2n-81} \times n_h$ encryptions[2]. There are 140 unknown bits of (K_B, K_R) which may lead to the impossible differential. Since we choose the weak key set $S_{WK_{i,j}}$, it is expected that there remain $\epsilon = 2^{140} \times \text{Pr}_{i,j} \times (1 - 2^{-168})^{2^{2n-73-(8-i)-(8-j)}}$ possible values for the 140-bit subkey. The complexity of last step is $TC_1 = 2^{52}\epsilon$ encryptions. The time complexity represents $TC_{all} = TC_0 + TC_1$.

We choose i, j, n to balance the size of weak key set attacked and the time complexity see Table 4. Let $i = 5, j = 5, n = 126.5$, which covers a fraction of $2^{-2.92}$ of key space. The data complexity is about $2^{126.5}$ known plaintexts. The time complexity of the 5 steps is $2^{180.36}$ encryptions, and exhaustive search of the last step needs $2^{180.44}$ encryptions. Hence the time complexity is about $2^{181.40}$ encryptions.

Attack for the Whole Key Space. We apply four impossible differentials to attack 14-round Camellia-192, which take similar data collection and key recovery procedure. The four attacks cover the fraction of key space is $1 - (1 - WK_{i,j})^4$. Then we need to exhaustive search the remaining $(1 - WK_{i,j})^4$ fraction of key

---

[2] It is convenient to calculate, we take a memory access as a 14-round encryption.

Table 4. The complexities for different key spaces

i	j	Percentage of key space	Data complexity	TC_1	TC_0	TC_{all}
1	1	1	2^{128}	$2^{190.55}$	$2^{178.75}$	$2^{190.55}$
1	1	1	2^{127}	$2^{193.43}$	$2^{176.75}$	$2^{193.43}$
4	4	$2^{-1.3}$	$2^{126.5}$	$2^{184.94}$	2^{180}	$2^{184.98}$
5	5	$2^{-2.92}$	$2^{126.5}$	$2^{180.44}$	$2^{180.36}$	$2^{181.40}$
6	6	$2^{-5.58}$	$2^{125.5}$	$2^{177.78}$	$2^{178.36}$	$2^{179.10}$
8	8	2^{-16}	2^{122}	$2^{171.68}$	$2^{171.06}$	$2^{171.4}$

space. When the percentage of weak key space $WK_{i,j}$ is less, the complexity of exhaustively search the remaining fraction of key space is larger. The attacks on some weak key space can not be transformed to attacks on the whole key space as a result of the high exhaustively search complexity. By balance, we choose $i = 4, j = 4, n = 126.5$, each attack needs $2^{184.94}$ encryptions for $2^{126.5}$ known plaintexts. The four impossible differentials cover the fraction of key space is $1 - (1 - 0.41)^4 = 87.50\%$. Then we exhaustive search the remaining $(1 - 0.41)^4 = 2^{-3}$ fraction of key space, which needs $2^{192-3} = 2^{189}$ encryptions. Hence the time complexity of the impossible differential attack on 14-round Camellia-192 for the whole key space is $2^{184.98} \times 4 + 2^{189} = 2^{189.32}$ encryptions.

5 Conclusion

In this paper, we improve the impossible differential attacks on reduced-round Camellia-192 with one more round than previous results based on 8-round impossible differential given by Liu et al. Because the input and output differences of the impossible differential depends on the weak keys. Hence, we classify the key space into different weak key sets, which corresponds to a set of input and output differences. Then we present some relations between the size of weak key sets and the number of input and output differences of the impossible differentials, which are used to reduce the time complexity and increase the fraction of key space attacked. Finally, combining with key relations and pre-computation techniques, we give the first impossible differential attack on 14-round Camellia-192. The impossible differential attack on 14-round Camellia-192 needs $2^{126.5}$ known plaintexts and $2^{189.32}$ encryptions.

Acknowledgments. We would like to thank anonymous reviewers and the shepherd Jiqiang Lu for their very helpful comments on the paper.

A Key Schedule for Camellia-192

Here, we introduce the key schedule of Camellia in Fig. 4 and subkeys for Camellia-192 in Table 5.

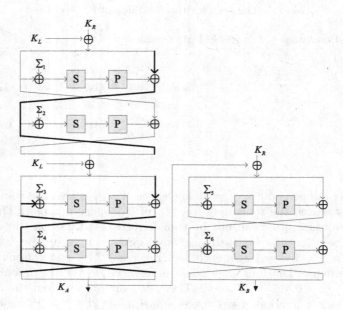

Fig. 4. The key schedule of Camellia

Table 5. Subkeys for Camellia-192 from Round 1 to Round 24

	Subkey	Value		Subkey	Value
Round 1	k_1	$(K_B \lll 0)_L$	Round 13	k_{13}	$(K_R \lll 60)_L$
Round 2	k_2	$(K_B \lll 0)_R$	Round 14	k_{14}	$(K_R \lll 60)_R$
Round 3	k_3	$(K_R \lll 15)_L$	Round 15	k_{15}	$(K_B \lll 60)_L$
Round 4	k_4	$(K_R \lll 15)_R$	Round 16	k_{16}	$(K_B \lll 60)_R$
Round 5	k_5	$(K_A \lll 15)_L$	Round 17	k_{17}	$(K_L \lll 77)_L$
Round 6	k_6	$(K_A \lll 15)_R$	Round 18	k_{18}	$(K_L \lll 77)_R$
FL	kf_1	$(K_R \lll 30)_L$	FL	kf_5	$(K_A \lll 77)_L$
FL^{-1}	kf_2	$(K_R \lll 30)_R$	FL^{-1}	kf_6	$(K_A \lll 77)_R$
Round 7	k_7	$(K_B \lll 30)_L$	Round 19	k_{19}	$(K_R \lll 94)_L$
Round 8	k_8	$(K_B \lll 30)_R$	Round 20	k_{20}	$(K_R \lll 94)_R$
Round 9	k_9	$(K_L \lll 45)_L$	Round 21	k_{21}	$(K_A \lll 94)_L$
Round 10	k_{10}	$(K_L \lll 45)_R$	Round 22	k_{22}	$(K_A \lll 94)_R$
Round 11	k_{11}	$(K_A \lll 45)_L$	Round 23	k_{23}	$(K_L \lll 111)_L$
Round 12	k_{12}	$(K_A \lll 45)_R$	Round 24	k_{24}	$(K_L \lll 111)_R$
FL	kf_3	$(K_L \lll 60)_L$			
FL^{-1}	kf_4	$(K_L \lll 60)_R$			

References

1. Aoki, K., Ichikawa, T., Kanda, M., Matsui, M., Moriai, S., Nakajima, J., Tokita, T.: *Camellia*: a 128-bit block cipher suitable for multiple platforms - design and analysis. In: Stinson, D.R., Tavares, S. (eds.) SAC 2000. LNCS, vol. 2012, p. 39. Springer, Heidelberg (2001)
2. Blondeau, C.: Impossible differential attack on 13-round camellia-192. Inf. Process. Lett. **115**(9), 660–666 (2015)
3. Bogdanov, A., Geng, H., Wang, M., Wen, L., Collard, B.: Zero-correlation linear cryptanalysis with FFT and improved attacks on ISO Standards Camellia and CLEFIA. In: Lange, T., Lauter, K., Lisoněk, P. (eds.) SAC 2013. LNCS, vol. 8282, pp. 306–323. Springer, Heidelberg (2014)
4. Boura, C., Naya-Plasencia, M., Suder, V.: Scrutinizing and improving impossible differential attacks: applications to CLEFIA, Camellia, LBlock and SIMON. In: Sarkar, P., Iwata, T. (eds.) ASIACRYPT 2014. LNCS, vol. 8873, pp. 179–199. Springer, Heidelberg (2014)
5. Chen, J., Jia, K., Yu, H., Wang, X.: New impossible differential attacks of reduced-round Camellia-192 and Camellia-256. In: Parampalli, U., Hawkes, P. (eds.) ACISP 2011. LNCS, vol. 6812, pp. 16–33. Springer, Heidelberg (2011)
6. Chen, J., Li, L.: Low data complexity attack on reduced Camellia-256. In: Susilo, W., Mu, Y., Seberry, J. (eds.) ACISP 2012. LNCS, vol. 7372, pp. 101–114. Springer, Heidelberg (2012)
7. Dong, X., Li, L., Jia, K., Wang, X.: Improved attacks on reduced-round Camellia-128/192/256. In: Nyberg, K. (ed.) CT-RSA 2015. LNCS, vol. 9048, pp. 59–83. Springer, Heidelberg (2015)
8. Hatano, Y., Sekine, H., Kaneko, T.: Higher order differential attack of Camellia (II). In: Nyberg, K., Heys, H.M. (eds.) SAC 2002. LNCS, vol. 2595. Springer, Heidelberg (2003)
9. International Organization for Standardization(ISO): International Standard-ISO/IEC 18033-3, Information technology-Security techniques-Encryption algorithms-Part 3: Block ciphers (2010)
10. Kühn, U.: Improved cryptanalysis of MISTY1. In: Daemen, J., Rijmen, V. (eds.) FSE 2002. LNCS, vol. 2365, p. 61. Springer, Heidelberg (2002)
11. Lee, S., Hong, S.H., Lee, S.-J., Lim, J.-I., Yoon, S.H.: Truncated differential cryptanalysis of Camellia. In: Kim, K. (ed.) ICISC 2001. LNCS, vol. 2288, p. 32. Springer, Heidelberg (2002)
12. Lei, D., Chao, L., Feng, K.: New observation on Camellia. In: Preneel, B., Tavares, S. (eds.) SAC 2005. LNCS, vol. 3897, pp. 51–64. Springer, Heidelberg (2006)
13. Duo, L., Li, C., Feng, K.: Square like attack on Camellia. In: Qing, S., Imai, H., Wang, G. (eds.) ICICS 2007. LNCS, vol. 4861, pp. 269–283. Springer, Heidelberg (2007)
14. Li, L., Jia, K., Wang, X., Dong, X.: Meet-in-the-middle technique for truncated differential and its applications to CLEFIA and Camellia. In: Leander, G. (ed.) FSE 2015. LNCS, vol. 9054, pp. 48–70. Springer, Heidelberg (2015)
15. Liu, Y., Li, L., Gu, D., Wang, X., Liu, Z., Chen, J., Li, W.: New observations on impossible differential cryptanalysis of reduced-round Camellia. In: Canteaut, A. (ed.) FSE 2012. LNCS, vol. 7549, pp. 90–109. Springer, Heidelberg (2012)
16. Lu, J., Wei, Y., Fouque, P.A., Kim, J.: Cryptanalysis of reduced versions of the camellia block cipher. IET Inf. Secur. **6**(3), 228–238 (2012)

17. Lu, J., Kim, J.-S., Keller, N., Dunkelman, O.: Improving the efficiency of impossible differential cryptanalysis of reduced Camellia and MISTY1. In: Malkin, T. (ed.) CT-RSA 2008. LNCS, vol. 4964, pp. 370–386. Springer, Heidelberg (2008)

18. Lu, J., Wei, Y., Kim, J., Pasalic, E.: The higher-order meet-in-the-middle attack and its application to the Camellia block cipher. In: Nandi, M., Galbraith, S. (eds.) INDOCRYPT 2012. LNCS, vol. 7668, pp. 244–264. Springer, Heidelberg (2012)

19. Lu, J., Wei, Y., Pasalic, E., Fouque, P.-A.: Meet-in-the-middle attack on reduced versions of the Camellia block cipher. In: Hanaoka, G., Yamauchi, T. (eds.) IWSEC 2012. LNCS, vol. 7631, pp. 197–215. Springer, Heidelberg (2012)

20. Mala, H., Shakiba, M., Dakhilalian, M., Bagherikaram, G.: New results on impossible differential cryptanalysis of reduced–round Camellia–128. In: Jacobson Jr., M.J., Rijmen, V., Safavi-Naini, R. (eds.) SAC 2009. LNCS, vol. 5867, pp. 281–294. Springer, Heidelberg (2009)

21. Shirai, T.: Differential, linear, boomerang and rectangle cryptanalysis of reduced-round Camellia. In: The Third NESSIE Workshop (2002)

22. Sugita, M., Kobara, K., Imai, H.: Security of reduced version of the block cipher Camellia against truncated and impossible differential cryptanalysis. In: Boyd, C. (ed.) ASIACRYPT 2001. LNCS, vol. 2248, p. 193. Springer, Heidelberg (2001)

23. Wu, W., Zhang, L., Zhang, W.: Improved impossible differential cryptanalysis of reduced-round Camellia. In: Avanzi, R.M., Keliher, L., Sica, F. (eds.) SAC 2008. LNCS, vol. 5381, pp. 442–456. Springer, Heidelberg (2009)

Automatic Differential Analysis of ARX Block Ciphers with Application to SPECK and LEA

Ling Song[1,2,3], Zhangjie Huang[1,2(✉)], and Qianqian Yang[1,2]

[1] State Key Laboratory of Information Security,
Institute of Information Engineering, Chinese Academy of Sciences,
Beijing 100093, China
{songling,huangzhangjie,yangqianqian}@iie.ac.cn
[2] Data Assurance and Communication Security Research Center,
Chinese Academy of Sciences, Beijing 100093, China
[3] Nanyang Technological University, Singapore, Singapore

Abstract. In this paper, we focus on the automatic differential cryptanalysis of ARX block ciphers with respect to XOR-difference, and develop Mouha et al.'s framework for finding differential characteristics by adding a new method to construct long characteristics from short ones. The new method reduces the searching time a lot and makes it possible to search differential characteristics for ARX block ciphers with large word sizes such as $n = 48, 64$. What's more, we take the differential effect into consideration and find that the differential probability increases by a factor of $4 \sim 16$ for SPECK and more than 2^{10} for LEA when multiple characteristics are counted in. The efficiency of our method is demonstrated by improved attacks of SPECK and LEA, which attack 1, 1, 4 and 6 more rounds of SPECK48, SPECK64, SPECK96 and SPECK128, respectively, and 2 more rounds of LEA than previous works.

Keywords: Differential cryptanalysis · Automatic search · ARX · SPECK · LEA

1 Introduction

ARX ciphers are a broad class of symmetric-key cryptographic algorithms that only consists of three operations: additions modulo 2^n, bit rotations and XORs. Some examples of ARX ciphers are: the block ciphers SPECK [3], LEA [13], Chaskey [16], the stream cipher Salsa20 [4], and the SHA-3 finalists

Supported by the National Key Basic Research Program of China (2013CB834203), the National Natural Science Foundation of China (Grants 61402469 and 61272477), the Strategic Priority Research Program of Chinese Academy of Sciences under Grant XDA06010702, and the State Key Laboratory of Information Security, Chinese Academy of Sciences.

© Springer International Publishing Switzerland 2016
J.K. Liu and R. Steinfeld (Eds.): ACISP 2016, Part II, LNCS 9723, pp. 379–394, 2016.
DOI: 10.1007/978-3-319-40367-0_24

Skein [10] and Blake [2]. To evaluate the security of an ARX cipher, differential cryptanalysis [5] is one of the most important attacks that should be considered.

Even though ARX ciphers have a long history for use, their security analysis are lagging behind. For S-box based symmetric-key ciphers, their security against differential cryptanalysis is measured by the number of active S-boxes. On the contrary, there is no rigorous security proof of ARX ciphers against differential cryptanalysis in existing literature, so searching optimal differentials becomes the only way for evaluation. In 2013, Mouha et al. introduce a framework [17] for searching optimal differential characteristics of ARX ciphers, assuming all the operations in the cipher are independent. From the application to Salsa20, the assumption is shown to be invalid sometimes. In [6,7], Biryukov et al. proposed a tool for automatically searching differential characteristics in ARX ciphers based on Matsui's algorithm and partial difference distribution tables. This tool suits differential search with respect to both XOR- and ADD- differences. However, the it is not applicable for cases where the block size is too large, such as $n = 48, 64$.

In this paper, we focus on the automatic differential cryptanalysis of ARX block ciphers with respect to XOR-difference. We apply Mouha et al.'s framework of finding differential characteristics to ARX block ciphers assuming additions are independent, and develop the framework by adding a new method for constructing long characteristics from short ones. The new method reduces the searching time, especially for a large word size such as $n = 64$. Besides, we take the differential effect into consideration and find that the differential probability increases by a factor of $4 \sim 2^{10}$ when multiple characteristics are counted in. The efficiency of our new method can be demonstrated by the application to two block ciphers: SPECK and LEA, in which better differentials are found and differential attacks against them are improved. The results are summarized in Table 1 and compared with the best ones of previous works. As can be seen, for SPECK we reduce the complexities of differential attack on SPECK32/64, and attack 1, 1, 4 and 6 more rounds against SPECK48, SPECK64, SPECK96 and SPECK128, respectively; for LEA, except the attacks in the specification we provide the first differential analysis for it and attack 13, 13 and 15 rounds of LEA-128, LEA-192 and LEA-256, respectively.

During the submission of this paper, there are another two related papers presented on FSE 2016 [8,11]. In [11] Fu et al. extend Sun's MILP-based automatic search algorithms for differential and linear trails [20] from Sbox-based block ciphers to ARX block ciphers and improve the differential and linear attacks on SPECK. In the other paper, Biryukov et al. [8] propose the first adaptation of Matsuis algorithm for finding the best differential and linear trails in ARX ciphers and the adapted algorithm is also applied to SPECK. Still the differential characteristics of SPECK96 and SPECK128 in this paper are the best in terms of the number of rounds, and the ones of SPECK32, SPECK48 and SPECK64 are the best in terms of probabilities because we take differential effect into account.

The rest of this paper is organized as follows. Section 2 provides a background of differential cryptanalysis; Sect. 3 elaborates on searching method developed in this paper; Sect. 4 briefly describes the two block ciphers SPECK and LEA;

Table 1. Previous attacks and our new attacks on SPECK.

Variant	Rounds attacked/ Total rounds	Time	Data (CP)	Memory	Reference
SPECK32/64	14/22	2^{63}	2^{31}	2^{22}	[9]
	14/22	$2^{61.41}$	$2^{29.41}$	2^{22}	This paper
SPECK48/72	14/22	2^{65}	2^{41}	2^{22}	[9]
	15/22	$2^{68.31}$	$2^{44.31}$	2^{22}	This paper
SPECK48/96	15/23	2^{89}	2^{41}	2^{22}	[9]
	16/23	$2^{92.31}$	$2^{44.31}$	2^{22}	This paper
SPECK64/96	18/26	2^{93}	2^{61}	2^{22}	[9]
	19/26	$2^{92.56}$	$2^{60.56}$	2^{22}	This paper
SPECK64/128	19/27	2^{125}	2^{61}	2^{22}	[9]
	20/27	$2^{124.56}$	$2^{60.56}$	2^{22}	This paper
SPECK96/96	16/28	2^{85}	2^{85}	2^{22}	[9]
	18/28	2^{85}	2^{85}	2^{22}	This paper
	20/28	$2^{94.94}$	$2^{94.94}$	2^{22}	This paper
SPECK96/144	17/29	2^{133}	2^{85}	2^{22}	[9]
	19/29	2^{133}	2^{133}	2^{22}	This paper
	21/29	$2^{142.94}$	$2^{94.94}$	2^{22}	This paper
SPECK128/128	17/32	2^{113}	2^{113}	2^{22}	[9]
	23/32	$2^{124.35}$	$2^{124.35}$	2^{22}	This paper
SPECK128/192	18/33	2^{177}	2^{113}	2^{22}	[9]
	24/33	$2^{188.35}$	$2^{124.35}$	2^{22}	This paper
SPECK128/256	19/34	2^{241}	2^{113}	2^{22}	[9]
	25/34	$2^{252.35}$	$2^{124.35}$	2^{22}	This paper
LEA-128	12/24	2^{84}	2^{100}	2^{76}	[13]
LEA-128	14/24	$2^{124.02}$	$2^{124.02}$	2^{22}	This paper
LEA-192	14/28	$2^{124.02}$	$2^{124.02}$	2^{22}	This paper
LEA-256	15/32	$2^{252.02}$	$2^{124.02}$	2^{22}	This paper

in Sect. 5 we provide the searching results for differentials of SPECK and LEA, on which attacks are launched; Sect. 6 is a short discussion; and finally, the last section is the conclusion.

A few words on notations: differences here are expressed using XOR; values for differences are represented in hexadecimal.

2   Background

This section briefly reviews the differential cryptanalysis and differential properties of addition. At the end of this section, the assumption we take in this paper is clarified.

2.1 Differential Cryptanalysis

Differential cryptanalysis was introduced by Biham and Shamir in [5]. For block ciphers, it is used to analyze how input differences lead to output differences. If certain input/output difference happens in a non-random way, it can be used to build a distinguisher or even to recover keys.

To consider the security of iterated block ciphers against differential cryptanalysis, Lai et al. first introduced the theory of Markov ciphers and made a distinction between a differential and a differential characteristic [14]. A differential is a difference propagation from an input difference to an output difference, while a differential characteristic specifies not only the input/output difference, but also all the internal differences after each round. For a Markov cipher, the probability of a differential characteristic is the multiplication of difference transition probabilities of each round, and the probability of a differential is equal to the sum of the probabilities of all differential characteristics which correspond to the differential.

2.2 Estimating Differential Probabilities for ARX Ciphers

For ARX block ciphers, only additions modulo 2^n are non-linear operations and propagate differences indefinitely. So we focus on calculating differential probability of addition. In [15], Lipmaa and Moriai study the differential properties of addition. Let $\mathrm{xdp}^+(\alpha, \beta \to \gamma)$ be the XOR-differential probability of addition modulo 2^n, with input differences α, β and output difference γ. The authors prove that the differential $(\alpha, \beta \to \gamma)$ is valid if and only if

$$\mathrm{eq}(\alpha \ll 1, \beta \ll 1, \gamma \ll 1) \wedge (\alpha \oplus \beta \oplus \gamma \oplus (\beta \ll 1)) = 0, \tag{1}$$

where

$$\mathrm{eq}(x, y, z) := (\neg x \oplus y) \wedge (\neg x \oplus z). \tag{2}$$

For every valid differential $(\alpha, \beta \to \gamma)$, the weight $w(\alpha, \beta \to \gamma)$ is defined as follows:

$$w(\alpha, \beta \to \gamma) := -\log_2(\mathrm{xdp}^+(\alpha, \beta \to \gamma)).$$

The weight of a valid differential can be calculated as:

$$w(\alpha, \beta \to \gamma) = h(\neg\mathrm{eq}(\alpha, \beta, \gamma)), \tag{3}$$

where $h(x)$ denotes the number of non-zero bits in x except the most significant bit.

Assumption of Independent Additions. In this paper, we assume that additions in the block cipher are independent of each other with regard to XOR-difference due to the use of round keys. Under this assumption, the probability of a differential characteristic is equal to the multiplication of the probabilities of all addition operations. Specifically, we calculate the weight of a differential characteristic as the sum of weights of all addition operations.

3   Automatic Search for Characteristics and Differentials in ARX Block Ciphers

In this section we elaborate on the searching method used in this paper.

3.1   Mouha's Framework for Searching Differential Characteristics of ARX Ciphers

In [17], Mouha and Preneel construct a framework to search for optimal differential characteristics of ARX ciphers and apply it to Salsa20. In their framework, a typical Satisfiability Modulo Theory (SMT) solver STP [12] is used. STP is built upon a SAT solver. Since many word-wise operations are included in its input language, it is suitable for searching problems of ARX ciphers.

In the framework, they find differential characteristics up to a certain weight W with STP. First, they write simple equations with respect to XOR-difference for every addition, rotation and XOR of an ARX cipher as follows.

- Use n-bit variables to represent input difference words.
- Introduce additional n-bit variables to represent the differences after the addition, XOR, and rotation operations when required.
- Use Eqs. (1) and (2) for every addition modulo 2^n of the cipher to ensure that the input and output differences correspond to a valid differential of the addition operation.
- Include Eq. (3) to calculate the weight of each addition operation, and represent the sum of weights of all additions with W, which corresponds to the weight of the differential characteristics under consideration.
- Specify that input difference is non-zero and restrict W to a maximum of a certain number.

Second, they feed the equations generated into STP. STP converts these equations into formulae of conjunctive normal form (CNF), and then invokes an underlying SAT solver to find solutions.

Although Mouha's framework that multiplies the differential probabilities of all additions was originally applied to a stream cipher, it is more suitable for ARX block ciphers where a round key is XORed each round. The reason is that additions in an ARX stream cipher are usually not independent, while additions in an ARX block cipher may be independent due to the use of round keys.

3.2   Obtaining a Long Characteristic from Two Short Ones

Mouha's framework can be applied directly to ARX block ciphers where additions are independent with regard to XOR-difference. However, due to the limitation of computation power, it takes too much time to find a long characteristic. In this paper, we introduce a method to obtain a long characteristic from two short ones. The method lies in searching differential characteristics from an internal difference which has only one active bit. This idea for searching long characteristics was inspired by the phenomenon that many optimal characteristics obtained have a special internal difference with only one active bit which usually leads to a differential transition of the nearest round with probability 1.

The method for obtaining long characteristics is illustrated in Fig. 1. First, we set an internal difference after some rounds D to be a value where only one bit is nonzero, and then search forward and backward independently to get two short characteristics. After that we combine these two short characteristics together to get a long one. Since either the input or output difference is fixed, two short characteristics with best probability can be easily searched. Note that this method saves much time for searching long characteristics, but does not always guarantee best characteristics.

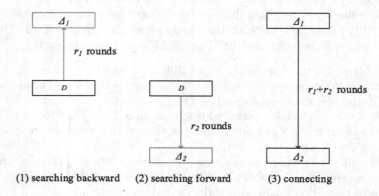

(1) searching backward   (2) searching forward   (3) connecting

Fig. 1. Obtaining a longer characteristic from two shorter ones.

This method in differential attack resembles the one used in boomerang attack [21]. However, conditions for the two short characteristics are different. Suppose the probabilities of the two short characteristics are p and q respectively, and the block size is N. For standard differential attacks, $pq > 2^{-N}$ and the two short characteristics must be connected, while for boomerang attacks $pq > 2^{-N/2+1}$ and the two short characteristics are independent.

3.3 Characteristics to Differentials

For ARX ciphers, the probability of one characteristic cannot well approximate the probability of the corresponding differential because of a strong differential effect, that is, between the input difference and the output difference there are many characteristics.

To calculate the differential probability as accurately as possible, more characteristics sharing the same input and output difference should be counted in. After a good characteristic is obtained, we fix the input and output difference, and search all characteristics with probability less or equal than that of the one obtained. More precisely, if the characteristic obtained has a weight W, we search all characteristics with the same input and output difference where the weight is $W, W + 1, W + 2, \cdots$, and add the probabilities of all these characteristics together. Note that STP just outputs one solution. To find all solutions, the user can tell STP to generate the CNF formulae and exit. A special SAT solver, such as CryptoMiniSat [19], can then be used to get all solutions.

4 Description of SPECK and LEA

4.1 SPECK

SPECK is a family of lightweight block ciphers designed by researchers from the U.S. National Security Agency (NSA) [3]. It contains 10 variants, each of which is characterized by its block size $2n$ and key size mn. For example, SPECK32/64 refers to the SPECK block cipher with block size 32 bits and key size 64 bits. The parameters of SPECK are listed in Table 4.

The SPECK$2n$ encryption maps a plaintext of two n-bit words (x_0, y_0) into a ciphertext (x_T, y_T), using a sequence of T rounds. The key-dependent round function is defined as

$$R^k(x, y) = (((x \ggg \alpha) \boxplus y) \oplus k, (y \lll \beta) \oplus ((x \ggg \alpha) \boxplus y) \oplus k),$$

where k is the round key, and rotation constants α and β are given in Table 4.

The SPECK key schedule reuses the round function to generate the round keys $k_0, \cdots, k_T$. The m-word master key $K = (l_{m-2}, \cdots, l_0, k_0)$ are used as follow:

$$l_{i+m-1} = (k_i \boxplus (l_i \ggg \alpha)) \oplus i$$
$$k_{i+1} = (k_i \lll \beta) \oplus l_{i+m-1}.$$

Figure 2 provides a schematic view on the round function and the key schedule of SPECK.

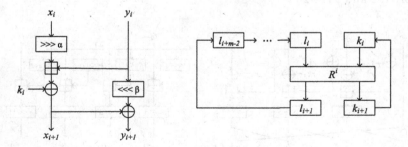

Fig. 2. The round function and the key schedule of SPECK. R^i is the SPECK round function with i acting as the round key.

4.2 LEA

LEA is an ARX block cipher designed by Hong et al. [13] and provides a high-speed software encryption on general-purpose processors. It has the block size of 128 bits and the key size of 128, 192, or 256 bits. We denote the algorithms with 128-bit, 192-bit, and 256-bit keys by LEA-128, LEA-192, and LEA-256, respectively.

The encryption of LEA maps a plaintext of four 32-bit words $(x_0^0, x_1^0, x_2^0, x_3^0)$ into a ciphertext $(x_0^r, x_1^r, x_2^r, x_3^r)$ using a sequence of r rounds, where $r = 24$ for LEA-128, $r = 28$ for LEA-192 and $r = 32$ for LEA-256. The round function for round $i, 0 \leq i < r$ is defined as follows:

$$x_0^{i+1} \leftarrow ((x_0^i \oplus rk_0^i) \boxplus (x_1^i \oplus rk_1^i)) \lll 9,$$
$$x_1^{i+1} \leftarrow ((x_1^i \oplus rk_2^i) \boxplus (x_2^i \oplus rk_3^i)) \ggg 5,$$
$$x_2^{i+1} \leftarrow ((x_2^i \oplus rk_4^i) \boxplus (x_3^i \oplus rk_5^i)) \ggg 3,$$
$$x_3^{i+1} \leftarrow x_0^i.$$

where $rk^i = (rk_0^i, rk_1^i, rk_2^i, rk_3^i, rk_4^i, rk_5^i)$ is the round key, which is generated by a key schedule. We take LEA-128 as an example. Let $K = (k_0, k_1, k_2, k_3)$ be a 128-bit key. We set $t_i^0 = k_i$ for $0 \leq i < 4$. For round $i, 0 \leq i < r$, rk^i is produced through following relations:

$$t_0^{i+1} \leftarrow (t_0^i \boxplus (\delta^i \lll i)) \lll 1,$$
$$t_1^{i+1} \leftarrow (t_1^i \boxplus (\delta^i \lll i+1)) \lll 3,$$
$$t_2^{i+1} \leftarrow (t_2^i \boxplus (\delta^i \lll i+2)) \lll 6,$$
$$t_3^{i+1} \leftarrow (t_3^i \boxplus (\delta^i \lll i+3)) \lll 11,$$
$$rk^i \leftarrow (t_0^{i+1}, t_1^{i+1}, t_2^{i+1}, t_1^{i+1}, t_3^{i+1}, t_1^{i+1}).$$

where δ^i is the constant for round i. Figure 3 provides a schematic view on the round function of LEA and the key schedule of LEA-128. We omit key schedules of LEA-192 and LEA-256.

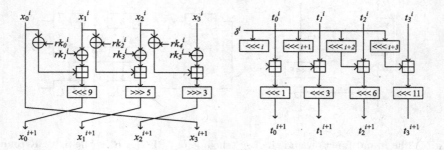

Fig. 3. The round function of LEA and the key schedule of LEA-128.

5 Searching Results and Attacks of SPECK and LEA

In this section we apply the searching method explained in Sect. 3 to SPECK and LEA. For five versions of SPECK (in respect of block size) and LEA, we would like to find the longest characteristics. To this goal, we need to find the minimal weight of differential characteristics with given number of rounds. Suppose the block size is N. If the weight of an r-round differential characteristic is less than N, then the corresponding differential characteristic can be used to build a distinguisher or to recover the key. On the contrary, if the minimal weight of all r-round differential characteristics is no less than N, then no useful differential characteristic exists for that r-round cipher. However, even though the weight of some characteristics is larger than N, the weight of the corresponding differential may be less than N. Therefore, we also evaluate the probability of the corresponding differential by counting in more characteristics which share the same input and output difference. For a differential, as long as its weight is less than N, it is useful, and our attacks in this paper are mounted based on differentials. Note that all of the characteristics are searched with STP2.0 on a 3.4 GHz Intel Core i7-2600 processor, and CryptoMiniSat4 is used as the underlying solver of STP.

5.1 Characteristics and Differentials of SPECK

Characteristics of SPECK32 and SPECK48. We directly apply Mouha's framework to SPECK with block size $2n = 32, 48$. For SPECK32, the best 9-round characteristic obtained has a weight of 30, which coincides with that of [6]. We provides the source code for searching 9-round characteristics of SPECK32 in the extension of this paper [18] for verification. In addition, from a 10-round characteristic with weight 35 as shown in Table 5, we get the corresponding differential $(0040, 2040) \rightarrow (A840, 0800)$ with weight 31. As far as we know, this 10-round characteristic is the longest distinguisher for SPECK32 in the literature. For SPECK48, our computer takes 12.5 days to find a 11-round characteristic with weight 46, and the corresponding differential has a weight of 43.31. In [11] another 11-round characteristic with weight 45 is provided. According to our computation its corresponding differential has a weight of 42.38, which is better than ours.

Characteristics of SPECK64, SPECK96 and SPECK128. We construct long characteristics for these versions where $2n = 64, 96, 128$ from two short ones. Take SPECK64 as an example. We set an internal difference to be $(00000080, 00000000)$ and search forward and backward independently. According to experiments, a 4-round forward characteristic with weight 9 and an 11-round backward characteristic with weight 53 can be combined to get a 15-round characteristic of weight 62. The corresponding differential has a weight less than 59.56. For SPECK96 and SPECK128, the searching works similarly. However, for both of them, differentials are derived from characteristics with weight equal to the block size. Specifically, from a 17-round characteristic of SPECK96 with weight 96 we get a 17-round differential with weight less than 93.94; from a

20-round characteristic of SPECK128 with weight 128, we obtain a 20-round differential with weight less than 123.35. The times for searching long characteristics for SPECK64, SPECK96 and SPECK128 are 0.9 h, 11.3 h and 5.2 h respectively, which are much less compared with the time for directly searching characteristics of SPECK48.

Comparison. Table 2 compares the differentials of SPECK we find with the ones in the literature. For SPECK32, we find a 10-round differential with probability $2^{-31.02}$, the best distinguisher of SPECK32 to date. We also find a 9-round characteristic of SPECK32 that coincides with that of [6] but has a tighter estimation of differential probability. For SPECK48, we obtain an 11-round characteristic with a better weight. For SPECK64, SPECK96 and SPECK128, the characteristics cover 1, 4 and 5 more round(s) than previous works.

Table 2. Comparison of our differentials of SPECK with previous ones.

Block size	Rounds r	Prob.	Input difference	Output difference	Reference
32	9	2^{-30}	(8054, A900)	(0040, 0542)	[6]
	9	$2^{-28.41}$	(8054, A900)	(0040, 0542)	This paper
	10	$2^{-31.01}$	(0040, 2040)	(A840, 0800)	This paper
48	11	$2^{-46.48}$	(202040, 082921)	(808424, 84A905)	[6]
	11	$2^{-43.31}$	(504200, 004240)	(202001, 202000)	This paper
64	14	$2^{-59.02}$	(00000009, 01000000)	(00040024, 04200D01)	[6]
	15	$2^{-59.56}$	(04092400, 20040104)	(808080A0, A08481A4)	This paper
96	13	2^{-84}	(2A20200800A2, 322320680801)	(1008004C804, C0180228C60)	[1]
	15	2^{-84}	(000900000000, 000001000000)	(A0A000008880, 81A02004C88C)	This paper
	17	$2^{-93.94}$	(240004000009, 010420040000)	(A0A000008880, 81A02004C88C)	This paper
128	15	$2^{-117.28}$	(0640240804002440, 6004400C20040004)	(828028080A080888, E88C81A4A0924B2C)	[1]
	18	$2^{-117.75}$	(0202000000000080, 8012020000000480)	(0800002080820808, 48080124A0924A08)	This paper
	20	$2^{-123.35}$	(0124000400000000, 0801042004000000)	(8004000080000124, 8420040080000801)	This paper

5.2   Characteristics and Differentials of LEA

Characteristics of LEA. We construct long characteristics for LEA from two short ones. We set an internal difference to be (00000100, 00000000, 00000000, 000 00000) and search forward and backward independently. A 12-round characteristic of weight 112 can be constructed by combining two short ones of 6 forward rounds and 6 backward rounds respectively. From this characteristic we derive a 12-round differential

$$(10401080, 0A001080, 02041208, 00049228)$$
$$\rightarrow (88008008, 88A2A00A, 22020060, 00000010)$$

with weight less than 101.71. Also, a 13-round characteristic can be constructed by connecting two short ones of 6 forward rounds and 7 backward rounds and its weight is 134. From this characteristic a 13-round differential

$$(00049018, 40049000, 10220041, 00028001)$$
$$\rightarrow (88008008, 88A2A00A, 22020060, 00000010)$$

of weight less than 123.02 is derived.

The details of these two characteristics are shown in Table 7. Compared with the only differential analysis in the specification of LEA, the differential in this paper covers two more rounds Tables 3 and 6.

Table 3. Comparison of our differentials of LEA with previous ones.

#Rounds	Prob.	Reference
11	2^{-98}	[13]
12	2^{-128}	[13]
12	$\mathbf{2^{-101.71}}$	**This paper**
13	$\mathbf{2^{-123.02}}$	**This paper**

5.3 Differential Attacks on SPECK and LEA

Differential attacks on SPECK. In [9] Dinur proposed an enumeration technique for key recovery in differential attacks against SPECK. Given a differential characteristic for SPECK$2n/mn$ that covers r rounds of the cipher with probability $p > 2 \cdot 2^{-2n}$, the enumeration technique can be used to recover the key of a variant with $(r + m)$ rounds with $2 \cdot p^{-1}$ chosen plaintexts, in an average time complexity of $2 \cdot p^{-1} \cdot 2^{(m-2)n}$ encryptions. The required memory is constant for all versions of SPECK, which is 2^{22} bytes, i.e. only a few megabytes.

Adding one round for free. We use the r-round differential $(\alpha \rightarrow \beta)$ over rounds $2 \sim (r + 1)$, and choose pairs of plaintexts such that their difference after the first round is α. In this way, one more round can be extended for free. This idea was also adopted by Abed et al. in [1]. Consequently, given an r-round differential, the attack can cover $(r + m + 1)$ rounds.

For SPECK32/64, we use the same 9-round differential as in [1,6]. According to our experiments, the differential holds with probability at least $2^{-28.41}$, which is much larger than 2^{-30}, the probability of the best characteristic of the differential. This indicates that the complexities of the attack can be reduced with a tighter estimation of the probability of the differential. Combined with Dinur's enumeration technique for key recovery, the differential can be used to attack a 14-round SPECK32/64 at a cost of $2 \cdot 2^{28.41} = 2^{29.41}$ plaintexts and $2 \cdot 2^{28.41} \cdot 2^{32} = 2^{61.41}$ encryptions.

Differential attacks for the rest variants are similar to that of SPECK32/64, so we omit the details on calculation of the complexities. The attacks are mounted based on the differentials in Table 2 and the results are summarized in Table 1. Compared with the previous works, the attacks on SPECK48, SPECK64, SPCKE96, SPECK128 extend 1, 1, 4 and 6 more round(s) respectively.

Differential Attacks on LEA. Since the differential equations of addition in the key recovery of LEA are similar to that of SPECK, Dinur's enumeration technique can be adapted to LEA. Given an r-round differential characteristic of LEA with probability $p > 2 \cdot 2^{-N}$ where N is the block size, for LEA-128 and LEA-192, the attack recovers the key of a variant of $(r + 1)$ rounds with $2 \cdot p^{-1}$ plaintexts, in expected time complexity of $2 \cdot p^{-1}$ encryptions, while $(r+2)$ rounds of LEA-256 can be attacked with $2 \cdot p^{-1}$ plaintexts and $2 \cdot p^{-1} \cdot 2^N$ encryptions in average. The attacks are summarized in Table 1.

6   Discussion

Differential Effect. Experimental results confirm the strong differential effect of ARX block ciphers. When the characteristics sharing the same input and output difference are counted in, the differential probability increases by a factor of $4 \sim 16$ for SPECK and by a factor more than 2^{10} for LEA. Due to this differential effect, the probability of a characteristic shouldn't be simply taken as the differential probability for these ARX block ciphers.

Limitation of Our Searching Method. The searching method discussed in this paper takes the assumption of independent additions with respect to XOR-difference. However, additions are not independent in most ARX block ciphers, such as TEA [22], and Chaskey [16], to which our searching method can not be applied directly. One of our future work is to deal with the dependency among additions.

7   Conclusion

In this paper, we apply Mouha's framework of finding differential characteristics to ARX block ciphers where the additions are independent with respect to XOR differences, and develop this framework by adding a new method for constructing long characteristics from short ones. This new method reduces the searching time a lot and makes it possible to search differential characteristics for ARX block ciphers with large word size such as $n = 64$. In addition, we take the differential effect into consideration and the results show the probability of a characteristic shouldn't be simply taken as the differential probability for these ARX block ciphers. The efficiency of our method is demonstrated by improved attacks of SPECK and LEA. One of our future work is to deal with the dependency among additions which are common in most ARX ciphers.

Acknowledgement. The authors would like to thank Jian Guo for his valuable suggestions and thank the anonymous reviewers for their valuable comments and suggestions.

A   Parameters of SPECK

Table 4. The SPECK parameters.

Block size $2n$	Key size mn	Word size n	Key words m	Rounds T	α	β
32	64	16	4	22	7	2
48	72	24	3	22	8	3
	96		4	23	8	3
64	96	32	3	26	8	3
	128		4	27	8	3
96	96	48	2	28	8	3
	144		3	29	8	3
128	128	64	2	32	8	3
	192		3	33	8	3
	256		4	34	8	3

B   Differential Characteristics of SPECK and LEA

Table 5. Differential characteristics for SPECK32, SPECK48 and SPECK64.

r	SPECK32			SPECK48			SPECK64		
	Δx	Δy	$\log_2 p$	Δx	Δy	$\log_2 p$	Δx	Δy	$\log_2 p$
0	2040	0040		504200	004240		04092400	20040104	
1	8000	8100	−1	001202	020002	−5	20000820	20200001	−6
2	8000	8402	−1	000010	100000	−3	00000009	01000000	−4
3	8D02	9D08	−4	000000	800000	−1	08000000	00000000	−2
4	6002	1420	−9	800000	800004	0	00080000	00080000	−1
5	1060	40E0	−5	808004	808020	−2	00080800	00480800	−2
6	0380	0001	−6	8400A0	8001A4	−4	00480008	02084008	−4
7	0004	0000	−3	608DA4	608080	−9	06080808	164A0848	−7
8	0800	0800	−1	042003	002400	−11	F2400040	40104200	−13
9	0810	2810	−2	012020	000020	−5	00820200	00001202	−8
10	0800	A840	−3	200100	200000	−3	00009000	00000010	−4
11				202001	202000	−3	00000080	00000000	−2
12							80000000	80000000	0
13							80800000	80800004	−1
14							80008004	84008020	−3
15							808080A0	A08481A4	−5
$\Sigma_r \log_2 p_r$			−35			−46			−62
$\log_2 p_{\text{diff}} >$			−31.01			−43.31			−59.56

Table 6. Differential characteristics for SPECK96 and SPECK128.

r	SPECK96			SPECK128		
	Δx	Δy	$\log_2 p$	Δx	Δy	$\log_2 p$
0	240004000009	010420040000		0124000400000000	0801042004000000	
1	082020000000	000120200000	-6	0800202000000000	4808012020000000	-6
2	000900000000	000001000000	-4	4800010000000000	0840080100000002	-6
3	000008000000	000000000000	-2	080808000000006	4A08480800000016	-7
4	000000080000	000000080000	-1	4000400000000032	1042004000000080	-12
5	000000080800	000000480800	-2	0202000000000080	8012020000000480	-7
6	000000480008	000002084008	-4	0010000000000480	0080100000002084	-5
7	0800FE080808	0800EE4A0848	-12	8080000000006080	84808000000164A0	-6
8	000772400040	400000104200	-21	0400000000032400	2004000000080104	-11
9	000000820200	000000001202	-11	2000000000080020	2020000000480801	-7
10	000000009000	000000000010	-4	0000000000480001	0100000002084008	-6
11	000000000080	000000000000	-2	00000000E080808	080000001E4A0848	-8
12	800000000000	800000000000	0	00000000F2400040	4000000000104200	-15
13	808000000000	808000000004	-1	0000000000820200	0000000000001202	-8
14	800080000004	840080000020	-3	0000000000009000	0000000000000010	-4
15	808080800020	A08480800124	-5	0000000000000080	0000000000000000	-2
16	800400008124	842004008801	-9	8000000000000000	8000000000000000	0
17	A0A000008880	81A02004C88C	-9	8080000000000000	8080000000000004	-1
18				8000800000000004	8400800000000020	-3
19				8080808000000020	A084808000000124	-5
20				8004000080000124	8420040080000801	-9
$\Sigma_r \log_2 p_r$			-96			-128
$\log_2 p_{\text{diff}} >$			-93.94			-123.35

Table 7. Differential characteristics for LEA.

r	12-round		13-round	
	$\Delta x_0 \parallel \Delta x_1 \parallel \Delta x_2 \parallel \Delta x_3$	$\log_2 p$	$\Delta x_0 \parallel \Delta x_1 \parallel \Delta x_2 \parallel \Delta x_3$	$\log_2 p$
0	104010800A0010800204120800049228		0004901840049000002800110220041	
1	80000014404020140040100410401080	-20	104010800A0010800204100800049018	-20
2	80400080860000808200001080000014	-16	800000144040200C0040100410401080	-20
3	8000000C8040000C8040000480400080	-14	80400080860000808200001080000014	-18
4	800000008000000080000108000000C	-10	8000000C8040000C8040000480400080	-14
5	00000000080000000800000080000000	-4	800000008000000080000108000000C	-10
6	00000100000000000000000000000000	0	00000000080000000800000080000000	-4
7	00020000000000000000000000000100	-1	00000100000000000000000000000000	-0
8	04000000000000000000002000020000	-2	00020000000000000000000000000100	-1
9	00000000800000070000040404000000	-6	04000000000000000000002000020000	-2
10	00000200080002008080080000000008	-11	00000000800000070000040404000000	-6
11	00000010044400501010010100000200	-9	00000200080002008080080000000008	-11
12	8800800888A2A00A2202006000000010	-19	00000010044400501010010100000200	-9
13			8800800888A2A00A2202006000000010	19
$\Sigma_r \log_2 p_r$		-112		-134
$\log_2 p_{\text{diff}} >$		-101.71		-123.02

References

1. Abed, F., List, E., Lucks, S., Wenzel, J.: Differential cryptanalysis of round-reduced simom and speck. In: Carlos, C., Christian, R. (eds.) Fast Software Encryption - FSE 2014. Lecture Notes in Computer Science, vol. 8540, pp. 525–545. Springer, Heidelberg (2014)
2. Aumasson, J.-P., Henzen, L., Meier, W., Phan, R.C.-W.: Sha-3 proposal blake. Technical report, Submission to the NIST SHA-3 Competition (Round 2) (2008)
3. Beaulieu, R., Shors, D., Smith, J., Treatman-Clark, S., Weeks, B., Wingers, L.: The simon and speck families of lightweight block ciphers. Technical report, Cryptology ePrint Archive, Report 2013/404 (2013)
4. Bernstein, D.J.: The Salsa20 family of stream ciphers. In: Robshaw, M., Billet, O. (eds.) New Stream Cipher Designs. LNCS, vol. 4986, pp. 84–97. Springer, Heidelberg (2008)
5. Biham, E., Shamir, A.: Differential cryptanalysis of DES-like cryptosystems. J. Cryptol. 4(1), 3–72 (1991)
6. Biryukov, A., Roy, A., Velichkov, V.: Differential analysis of block ciphers SIMON and SPECK. In: Cid, C., Rechberger, C. (eds.) FSE 2014. LNCS, vol. 8540, pp. 546–570. Springer, Heidelberg (2015)
7. Biryukov, A., Velichkov, V.: Automatic search for differential trails in ARX ciphers. In: Benaloh, J. (ed.) CT-RSA 2014. LNCS, vol. 8366, pp. 227–250. Springer, Heidelberg (2014)
8. Biryukov, A., Velichkov, V., Le Corre, Y.: Milp-based automatic search algorithms for differential and linear trails for speck. In: Peyrin, T. (ed.) Fast Software Encryption - FSE 2016 (2016). (to appear in FSE 2016)
9. Dinur, I.: Improved differential cryptanalysis of round-reduced speck. In: Joux, A., Youssef, A. (eds.) SAC 2014. LNCS, vol. 8781, pp. 147–164. Springer, Heidelberg (2014)
10. Ferguson, N., Lucks, S., Schneier, B., Whiting, D., Bellare, M., Kohno, T., Callas, J., Walker, J.: The skein hash function family. Technical report, Submission to the NIST SHA-3 Competition (Round 2) (2009)
11. Kai, F., Wang, M., Guo, Y., Sun, S., Lei, H.: Automatic search for the best trails in arx: application to block cipher speck. In: Peyrin, T. (ed.) Fast Software Encryption - FSE 2016 (2016). (to appear in FSE 2016)
12. Ganesh, V., Dill, D.L.: A decision procedure for bit-vectors and arrays. In: Damm, W., Hermanns, H. (eds.) CAV 2007. LNCS, vol. 4590, pp. 519–531. Springer, Heidelberg (2007)
13. Hong, D., Lee, J.-K., Kim, D.-C., Kwon, D., Ryu, K.H., Lee, D.-G.: LEA: A 128-bit block cipher for fast encryption on common processors. In: Kim, Y., Lee, H., Perrig, A. (eds.) WISA 2013. LNCS, vol. 8267, pp. 1–24. Springer, Heidelberg (2014)
14. Lai, X., Massey, J.L.: Markov ciphers and differential cryptanalysis. In: Davies, D.W. (ed.) EUROCRYPT 1991. LNCS, vol. 547, pp. 17–38. Springer, Heidelberg (1991)
15. Lipmaa, H., Moriai, S.: Efficient algorithms for computing differential properties of addition. In: Matsui, M. (ed.) FSE 2001. LNCS, vol. 2355, pp. 336–350. Springer, Heidelberg (2002)
16. Mouha, N., Mennink, B., Van Herrewege, A., Watanabe, D., Preneel, B., Verbauwhede, I.: Chaskey: an efficient mac algorithm for 32-bit microcontrollers. In: Joux, A., Youssef, A. (eds.) SAC 2014. LNCS, vol. 8781, pp. 306–323. Springer, Heidelberg (2014)

17. Mouha, N., Preneel, B.: Towards finding optimal differential characteristics for arx: Application to salsa20. Technical report, Cryptology ePrint Archive, Report 2013/328 (2013)
18. Song, L., Huang, Z., Yang, Q.: Automatic differential analysis of arx block ciphers with application to speck and lea. Technical report, Cryptology ePrint Archive, Report 2016/209 (2016)
19. Soos, M., Nohl, K., Castelluccia, C.: Extending SAT solvers to cryptographic problems. In: Kullmann, O. (ed.) SAT 2009. LNCS, vol. 5584, pp. 244–257. Springer, Heidelberg (2009)
20. Sun, S., Hu, L., Wang, P., Qiao, K., Ma, X., Song, L.: Automatic security evaluation and (related-key) differential characteristic search: application to SIMON, PRESENT, LBlock, DES(L) and other bit-oriented block ciphers. In: Sarkar, P., Iwata, T. (eds.) ASIACRYPT 2014. LNCS, vol. 8873, pp. 158–178. Springer, Heidelberg (2014)
21. Wagner, D.: The boomerang attack. In: Knudsen, L.R. (ed.) FSE 1999. LNCS, vol. 1636, pp. 156–170. Springer, Heidelberg (1999)
22. Wheeler, D.J., Needham, R.M.: TEA, a tiny encryption algorithm. In: Preneel, B. (ed.) FSE 1994. LNCS, vol. 1008. Springer, Heidelberg (1995)

On the Security of the LAC Authenticated Encryption Algorithm

Jiqiang Lu[✉]

Infocomm Security Department,
Institute for Infocomm Research,
Agency for Science, Technology and Research, 1 Fusionopolis Way,
Singapore 138632, Singapore
jlu@i2r.a-star.edu.sg, lvjiqiang@hotmail.com

Abstract. The LAC authenticated encryption algorithm was a candidate to the CAESAR competition on authenticated encryption, which follows the design of the ALE authenticated encryption algorithm. In this paper, we show that the security of LAC depends greatly on the parameter of the maximum message length and the order of padding the last message block, by cryptanalysing its variants that differ from the original LAC only in the above-mentioned two points. For the LAC variants, we present a structural state recovery attack in the nonce-respecting scenario, which is independent from the underlying block cipher, which requires only chosen queries to their encryption and tag generation oracles and can recover an internal state of the initialization phase for one of some used Public Message Numbers (PMNs) more advantageously than exhaustive key search; and the recovered internal state can be used to make an existential forgery attack under this PMN. Besides, slightly inferior to exhaustive key search, the state recovery attack can apply to the LAC variant that differs from LAC only in the order of padding the last message block. Although the state recovery attack does not apply to the original LAC, it sheds some light on this type of interesting structures, and shows that an authenticated encryption algorithm with a such or similar structure may be weakened when it is misused deliberately or accidentally with the reverse message padding order and a different maximum message length, and users should be careful about the two points when employing such a structure in reality.

Keywords: Authenticated encryption algorithm · LAC · State recovery attack · Forgery attack

1 Introduction

A (symmetric) authenticated encryption algorithm is an algorithm that transforms an arbitrary-length data stream (below an upper bound generally), called a message or plaintext, into another data stream of the same length, called a ciphertext, and generates an authentication tag for the message at the same

© Springer International Publishing Switzerland 2016
J.K. Liu and R. Steinfeld (Eds.): ACISP 2016, Part II, LNCS 9723, pp. 395–408, 2016.
DOI: 10.1007/978-3-319-40367-0_25

time, under the control of a secret key. We refer the reader to Bellare and Nam-prempre's work [1] for an introduction to authenticated encryption.

LAC [9] is a block-cipher-based lightweight authenticated encryption algorithm, which has a similar structure to the ALE [3] authenticated encryption algorithm. Built on a variant called LBlock-s of the LBlock lightweight block cipher [8], LAC takes as input an 80-bit user key, a 64-bit public message number (nonce) and a plaintext as well as associated data, and outputs a ciphertext of the same length as the plaintext and a 64-bit authentication tag. In 2014, LAC was submitted to the Competition for Authenticated Encryption: Security, Applicability, and Robustness (CAESAR) [4], however, Leurent [5] described an (existential) forgery attack on the full LAC algorithm, by showing that there exist 16-round differentials [2] with a probability of $2^{-61.52}$ in the LBlock-s cipher, which is slightly larger than the expected bound 2^{-64}. It is worthy to mention that the full ALE algorithm was shown in 2013 by Wu et al. [7] to suffer from an (existential) forgery attack based on differential cryptanalysis.

Leurent's attack on LAC as well as Wu et al.'s attack on ALE is mainly due to a security weakness of the underlying round-reduced block cipher, specifically the number of rounds is too small to be sufficient; otherwise, the attack would not work. In this paper, we analyse the security of LAC from a structural perspective, by focusing on its structure without exploiting any security weakness of the underlying block cipher, that is, we treat the block cipher as a sound pseudo-random permutation. We find that the security of LAC (in the nonce-respecting scenario) depends greatly on the parameter of the maximum message length and the order of padding the last message block (or equivalently the order of the two halves of the leaked 48-bit output), by presenting a state recovery attack on the LAC variants that differ from the original LAC only in that a different value is used for the parameter of the maximum message length and that the reverse order for padding the last message block is used. The attack on the LAC variants requires only chosen queries to their encryption and tag generation oracles, and can recover an internal state of the initialization phase for one of some used Public Message Numbers (PMNs) more advantageously than exhaustive key search. The recovered internal state can be used to make an existential forgery attack on the LAC variants under this PMN. Besides, slightly inferior to exhaustive key search, the attack can apply to the LAC variant that differs from LAC only in the reverse order of padding the last message block.

Our attack may apply to other authenticated encryption algorithms with similar structures, for example, it may apply to similar variants of ALE [6]. In reality, particularly in industry, a cryptographic algorithm is sometimes misused deliberately or accidentally, due to various practical reasons, say, being slightly modified for a particular application requirement, being modified with a different block cipher in place of the underlying block cipher, being confused with big- and little-endian formats, etc. As a result, although our attack does not apply to the original LAC, it sheds some light on this type of interesting structures, and shows that an authenticated encryption algorithm with a such or similar structure may be weakened when it is misused with the reverse message padding order and a different maximum message length. Thus, users should be very careful about the two points when employing such a structure in reality, even when the underlying round-reduced block cipher has a sufficient number of rounds in the sense of security.

The remainder of the paper is organised as follows. In the next section, we give the notation and describe the LAC algorithm and the variants for our attacks. We present our state recovery attack and existential forgery attack on the LAC variants in Sects. 3 and 4, respectively. Section 5 concludes this paper.

2   Preliminaries

In this section, we give the notation used throughout this paper, and briefly describe the LAC algorithm and the variants for our attacks.

2.1   Notation

In all descriptions we assume that the bits of a value are numbered from right to left (or sometimes from top to bottom), starting with 1, with the first bit being the least significant bit. We use the following notation.

$\oplus$	bitwise logical exclusive OR (XOR) operation of two bit strings of the same length
$\|\|$	string concatenation
$\|X\|$	the number of elements when X is a set, or the bit length when X is a value
e	the base of the natural logarithm ($e = 2.71828\cdots$)
$\lceil X \rceil$	the smallest integer that is larger than or equal to a value X
$\mathcal{O}(X)$	a value that is of the same order as a value X

2.2   The LAC Authenticated Encryption Algorithm

The message encryption and tag generation procedure of LAC [9] consists of four phases: initialization, processing associated data, message encryption, and tag generation, as depicted in Fig. 1, where

- PMN is a 64-bit Public Message Number (PMN), serving as a nonce. The designers require that a PMN should be used (at most) only once under the same key, that is, LAC works in a nonce-respecting scenario.
- **E** is a simplified version LBlock-s of the LBlock [8] block cipher, that has a 64-bit block length, an 80-bit user key K and a total of 32 rounds;
- **G** is a 16-round reduced version of the **E** block cipher, with the 16 round subkeys generated from the key schedule **KS**;
- $\widehat{\mathbf{G}}$ is the version of **G** that not only outputs a normal 64-bit ciphertext but also outputs the most significant 24 bits of the left half X_9 of the output of the eighth round of the **G** cipher and the most significant 24 bits of the left half X_{17} of the output of the sixteenth round of the **G** cipher (i.e., the output of **G**), (the 48 bits serve as a keystream block);
- 0^{16} is a binary string of 16 zeros;

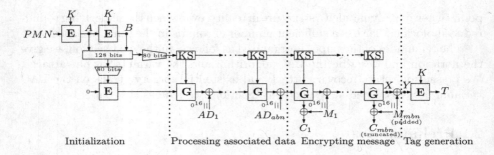

Fig. 1. The message encryption and tag generation procedure of LAC

- $(AD_1, AD_2, \cdots, AD_{abn})$ is an associated data of abn 48-bit blocks;
- $(M_1, M_2, \cdots, M_{mbn})$ is a message of mbn 48-bit blocks;
- $(C_1, C_2, \cdots, C_{mbn})$ is the ciphertext for $(M_1, M_2, \cdots, M_{mbn})$; and
- T is the tag for $(M_1, M_2, \cdots, M_{mbn})$.

During the initialization phase, a PMN passes through a cascade of two applications of the **E** block cipher with the user key K, and the concatenation of the outputs of the two applications of the **E** block cipher constitutes a 128-bit internal state. Then, the most significant 80 bits of the 128-bit internal state are used as the key for encrypting a 64-bit zero string with **E** to produce the initial data state; and the least significant 80 bits of the 128-bit internal state are to be used as the initial key state. During the phase of processing associated data, the key state is updated iteratively, and the data state is updated iteratively by first applying the **G** operation with the corresponding key state as the key, and then XORing with the corresponding block of associated data. During the phase of encrypting message, the key state is updated likewise, but the data state is updated iteratively by first applying the $\widehat{\mathbf{G}}$ operation with the corresponding key state as the key, and then XORing with the corresponding message block, and the 48-bit output leaked from $\widehat{\mathbf{G}}$ is XORed with the message block to produce the corresponding ciphertext block. Finally, the data state is encrypted with **E** under the user key K to generate an authentication tag. We refer the reader to [9] for the specification of LAC.

Denote the bit length of a message by msl. The message padding of LAC will append the smallest number u of zeros such that $(u + msl + 40) \bmod 48 = 0$ and then append the message length msl on the subsequent 40 bits (the length of a message is limited to be at most 2^{40} bits long). Accordingly, the $40 + u$ bits of the last one or two ciphertext blocks that correspond to the u bit positions of the appended u zeros and the 40 bit positions for message length msl will be truncated. In particular, when the last message block is full, LAC will make an additional 48-bit message block of the form $0^8 \| msl$, and the resulting ciphertext block will be discarded without transmission.

More specifically, suppose m is the last message block of a message, then the padding is of the form $m \| \underbrace{0 \cdots 0}_{u} \| msl$, such that $(u + |m| + 40) \bmod 48 = 0$.

Suppose the 64-bit output of the last $\widehat{\mathbf{G}}$ operation is $X_{17}||X_{16}$ and its 48-bit output is $X_9[9 \sim 32]||X_{17}[9 \sim 32]$, where X_9, X_{16}, X_{17} are 32-bit blocks, $X_9[9 \sim 32]$ represents bits $(9, 10, \cdots, 32)$ of X_9, and so on. If $|m| \leq 8$, then the last ciphertext block before truncation is $(X_9[9 \sim 32]||X_{17}[9 \sim 32]) \oplus (m||\underbrace{0 \cdots 0}_{u}|msl)$, and

the bits corresponding to $(\underbrace{0 \cdots 0}_{u}|msl)$ will be truncated before transmission.

Padding is similar if the bit length of the associated data is not a multiple of 48.

2.3   Variants of LAC

Denote by mml the bit number of the maximum message length. (CAESAR requires that a maximum message length must not be smaller than 65536 bytes [4]). Now we define some variants of LAC as follows:

- $24 \leq mml \leq 31$ is used. Thus, the resulting message padding is to append the smallest number u of zeros such that $(u + msl + mml) \bmod 48 = 0$ and the message length msl on the subsequent mml bits. ($mml = 40$ for LAC.)
- For the last block m of a message of msl bits long, the padding is of the form $msl||\underbrace{0 \cdots 0}_{u}||m$, such that $(u + msl + mml) \bmod 48 = 0^1$. This is the reverse order of the original LAC.
- All the other specifications of the variants are exactly the same as LAC, (including that when the last message block is full, the variants will make an additional 48-bit message block and the resulting ciphertext block will be discarded without transmission).

The first two points may be easily made in reality, due to various reasons, for example, the first point may be deliberate to meet the different message length of a particular application, and the second point may be accidental due to a confusion with endianness, particularly when employing a different cipher.

We note that for our attacks, there are some trivial equivalents to the above variants, for example, a variant assuming that there is no message padding if the last message block is full — a popular manner for message padding for message authentication schemes, and another variant assuming that the last ciphertext block for the padded message block will be transmitted without truncation.

We denote by $\widehat{\text{LAC}}$ the variants of LAC, as well as their equivalents with respect to our attacks. To make it easier to describe our attacks, we define four 64-bit (secret) parameters A, B, X, Y to represent the values at the four internal states marked in Fig. 1, that is, A is the output of the first $\mathbf{E}$ operation; B is the output of the second $\mathbf{E}$ operation; X is the output of the last $\widehat{\mathbf{G}}$ operation; and Y is the input to the last $\mathbf{E}$ operation.

---

[1] An equivalent of this point under our attack is that the position of the most significant 24 bits of the output of the eighth round of the $\widehat{\mathbf{G}}$ operation is exchanged with the position of the most significant 24 bits of the output of the sixteenth round of the $\widehat{\mathbf{G}}$ operation, (without reversing the message padding order), that is $(X_{17}[9 \sim 32]||X_9[9 \sim 32])$.

3   State Recovery Attack on $\widehat{\text{LAC}}$

In this section, we present a state recovery attack on $\widehat{\text{LAC}}$ in a nonce-respecting scenario (under the same key). The attack requires only chosen queries to the encryption and tag generation oracle of $\widehat{\text{LAC}}$, and it can recover the 128-bit internal state immediately after the first two $\mathbf{E}$ operations for one of some used PMNs, more advantageously than exhaustive key search.

3.1   Attack Procedure

The attack procedure is made up of three phases, to be described in Subsects. 3.1.1, 3.1.2 and 3.1.3. Observe that for a message of msl bits long such that $msl \bmod 48 = 48 - mml$, the last-block message-ciphertext pair reveals $(48 - mml)$ bits of the 64-bit output of the last $\widehat{\mathbf{G}}$ operation, by the specification of $\widehat{\text{LAC}}$.

3.1.1   Phase I

This phase works in a chosen-message and known-nonce scenario with fixed associated data, which is illustrated in Fig. 2.

(a) Choose an arbitrary message M of msl bits long such that $msl \bmod 48 = 48 - mml$, and represent it as $(M_1, M_2, \cdots, M_{mbn})$, where the first $mbn - 1$ blocks are 48 bits long each, and $mbn = \lceil \frac{msl}{48} \rceil < \frac{2^{mml}}{48}$. Query the $\widehat{\text{LAC}}$ encryption and tag generation oracle with the message M and associated data $(AD_1, AD_2, \cdots, AD_{abn})$ of abn 48-bit blocks long for 2^ϕ times ($abn \geq 0$, and the last one or two blocks are padded ones), where ϕ meets the following Condition (1), and ϕ and mbn meet the following Condition (2):

$$2^{\phi + mml - 64} \ll 1 - e^{-2^{2\phi - 64}};\tag{1}$$
$$2^{2\phi + 2 \times mml - 48 \times mbn + 32} \ll 1 - e^{-2^{2\phi - 64}}.\tag{2}$$

For the i-th query ($i = 1, 2, \cdots, 2^\phi$), we denote by:
- PMN_i the PMN used;
- $C^{(i)} = (C_1^{(i)}, C_2^{(i)}, \cdots, C_{mbn}^{(i)})$ the ciphertext, where the first $mbn-1$ blocks are 48 bits long each, and the last block $C_{mbn}^{(i)}$ is $msl \bmod 48 = 48 - mml$ bits long;
- T_i the tag; and
- A_i, B_i, X_i, Y_i respectively for the four parameters A, B, C, D defined in Sect. 2.3.

Observe that

$$X_i[41 \sim (88 - mml)] = (M_{mbn} \oplus C_{mbn}^{(i)})[1 \sim (48 - mml)],$$
$$Y_i = X_i \oplus (0^{16 + mml} \| M_{mbn}).$$

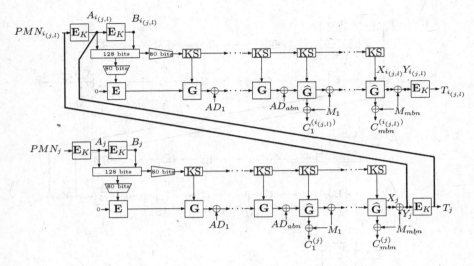

Fig. 2. Phase I of the state recovery attack on $\widehat{\text{LAC}}$

(b) For each permutation (PMN_i, PMN_j) of two PMNs PMN_i and PMN_j,[2] $(1 \leq i, j \leq 2^\phi, j \neq i)$, check whether $PMN_i = Y_j$ partially by checking whether

$$
\begin{aligned}
& PMN_i[41 \sim (88 - mml)] \\
&= Y_j[41 \sim (88 - mml)] \\
&(= X_j[41 \sim (88 - mml)] \oplus (0^{16+mml} || M_{mbn})[41 \sim (88 - mml)]) \\
&(= (M_{mbn} \oplus C_{mbn}^{(j)})[1 \sim (48 - mml)] \oplus \\
&\quad (0^{16+mml} || M_{mbn})[41 \sim (88 - mml)]),
\end{aligned}
\tag{3}
$$

which can be done efficiently by storing PMN_j in a table indexed by $Y_j[41 \sim (88 - mml)]$. Keep only the qualified permutations (PMN_i, PMN_j), and we denote by $PMN_{i_{(j,l)}}$ the qualified PMNs PMN_i for PMN_j, where l is the number of qualified PMNs PMN_i. Thus, we have $PMN_{i_{(j,l)}}[41 \sim (88 - mml)] = Y_j[41 \sim (88 - mml)]$. Furthermore, we have:

$$\text{if } PMN_{i_{(j,l)}} = Y_j, \text{then } A_{i_{(j,l)}} = T_j.$$

3.1.2   Phase II
This phase works in a chosen-message and chosen-nonce scenario with arbitrary associated data, which is illustrated in Fig. 3.

---

[2] Note that (PMN_i, PMN_j) is a permutation, rather than a combination. Thus, (PMN_i, PMN_j) and (PMN_j, PMN_i) are different.

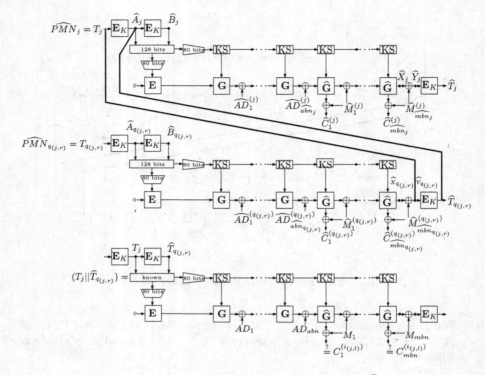

Fig. 3. Phase II of the state recovery attack on $\widehat{\mathrm{LAC}}$

(a) Let $\mathcal{S} = \{T_j$ such that $|PMN_{i_{(j,l)}}| > 0, j = 1, 2, \cdots, 2^{\phi}\}$, and $|\mathcal{S}| = 2^{\beta}$. Query the $\widehat{\mathrm{LAC}}$ encryption and tag generation oracle with an arbitrary associated data for any PMN $PMN = T_j \in \mathcal{S}$ in a chosen-nonce scenario. For $PMN = T_j$, we denote

- the PMN by $\widehat{PMN}_j (= T_j)$;
- the associated data by $(\widehat{AD}_1^{(j)}, \widehat{AD}_2^{(j)}, \cdots, \widehat{AD}_{\widehat{abn}_j}^{(j)})$, that is $\widehat{abn}_j$ 48-bit blocks long, $(\widehat{abn}_j \geq 0, \widehat{abn}_j$ can be different one another, and the last one or two blocks are padded ones);
- by $\widehat{M}^{(j)} = (\widehat{M}_1^{(j)}, \widehat{M}_2^{(j)}, \cdots, \widehat{M}_{\widehat{mbn}_j}^{(j)})$ the message of $\widehat{msl}_j$ bits long such that $\widehat{msl}_j \bmod 48 = 48 - mml$, where $\widehat{mbn}_j = \lceil \frac{\widehat{msl}_j}{48} \rceil < \frac{2^{mml}}{48}$, the first $\widehat{mbn}_j - 1$ blocks are 48 bits long each, $(\widehat{mbn}_j$ can be different one another);
- the ciphertext by $\widehat{C}^{(j)} = (\widehat{C}_1^{(j)}, \widehat{C}_2^{(j)}, \cdots, \widehat{C}_{\widehat{mbn}_j}^{(j)})$, where the first $\widehat{mbn}_j - 1$ blocks are 48 bits long each, and the last block $\widehat{C}_{\widehat{mbn}_j}^{(j)}$ is $\widehat{msl}_j \bmod 48 = 48 - mml$ bits long;

– the tag by $\widehat{T}_j$; and

– $\widehat{A}_j$, $\widehat{B}_j$, $\widehat{X}_j$, $\widehat{Y}_j$ respectively for the four parameters A, B, C, D defined in Sect. 2.3.

Note that if $\widehat{PMN}_j(= T_j)$ happens to appear in Step I-(a) we can reuse the corresponding associated data, message, ciphertext and tag, (without querying for $\widehat{PMN}_j$ here).

(b) For each permutation $(\widehat{PMN}_p, \widehat{PMN}_q)$ of two PMNs $\widehat{PMN}_p$ and $\widehat{PMN}_q$,[3] $(1 \le p \ne q \le 2^\beta)$, check whether $\widehat{PMN}_p = \widehat{Y}_q$ partially by checking whether

$$\widehat{PMN}_p[41 \sim (88 - mml)]$$
$$= \widehat{Y}_q[41 \sim (88 - mml)]$$
$$(= \widehat{X}_q[41 \sim (88 - mml)] \oplus (0^{16+mml}||\widehat{M}^{(q)}_{mbn_q})[41 \sim (88 - mml)])$$
$$(= (\widehat{M}^{(q)}_{mbn_q} \oplus \widehat{C}^{(q)}_{mbn_q})[1 \sim (48 - mml)] \oplus$$
$$(0^{16+mml}||\widehat{M}^{(q)}_{mbn_q})[41 \sim (88 - mml)]),$$

which can be similarly done efficiently by storing $\widehat{PMN}_p$ in a table indexed by $\widehat{Y}_p[41 \sim (88 - mml)]$. Keep only the qualified permutations $(\widehat{PMN}_p, \widehat{PMN}_q)$. In particular, for $\widehat{PMN}_j(= T_j)$, we denote by $\widehat{PMN}_{q(j,r)}(= T_{q(j,r)})$ the qualified PMNs, where r is the number of qualified PMNs for $\widehat{PMN}_j$. Thus, we have

$$\widehat{PMN}_j[41 \sim (88 - mml)]$$
$$= \widehat{Y}_{q(j,r)}[41 \sim (88 - mml)] \tag{4}$$
$$(= \widehat{X}_{q(j,r)}[41 \sim (88 - mml)] \oplus (0^{16+mml}||\widehat{M}^{(q(j,r))}_{mbn_{q(j,r)}})[41 \sim (88 - mml)])$$
$$(= (\widehat{M}^{(q(j,r))}_{mbn_{q(j,r)}} \oplus \widehat{C}^{(q(j,r))}_{mbn_{q(j,r)}})[1 \sim (48 - mml)] \oplus$$
$$(0^{16+mml}||\widehat{M}^{(q(j,r))}_{mbn_{q(j,r)}})[41 \sim (88 - mml)]),$$

and if $\widehat{PMN}_j = \widehat{Y}_{q(j,r)}$, then $\widehat{A}_j = \widehat{T}_{q(j,r)}$.

(c) For any $(\widehat{PMN}_j(= T_j), \widehat{PMN}_{q(j,r)}(= T_{q(j,r)}))$, treat the corresponding value $(T_j||\widehat{T}_{q(j,r)})$ as the 128-bit secret state immediately after the first two **E** operations of $\widehat{LAC}$, then compute the resulting ciphertext for message $M = (M_1, M_2, \cdots, M_{mbn})$ under the associated data $(AD_1, AD_2, \cdots, AD_{abn})$, and finally check whether the mbn ciphertext blocks respectively match the

---

[3] Likewise, $(\widehat{PMN}_p, \widehat{PMN}_q)$ is a permutation, so $(\widehat{PMN}_p, \widehat{PMN}_q)$ and $(\widehat{PMN}_q, \widehat{PMN}_p)$ are different.

mbn ciphertext blocks of some $C^{(i_{(j,l)})}$ such that $(PMN_{i_{(j,l)}}, PMN_j)$ is a qualified permutation in Phase I. Record the qualified triples $(PMN_{i_{(j,l)}}, \widehat{PMN}_j, \widehat{PMN}_{q_{(j,r)}})$ only.

3.1.3   Phase III

For a recorded $(PMN_{i_{(j,l)}}, \widehat{PMN}_j, \widehat{PMN}_{q_{(j,r)}})$ in Step II-(c), output $(T_j \| \widehat{T}_{q_{(j,r)}})$ as the 128-bit secret state just after the first two $\mathbf{E}$ operations under $PMN = PMN_{i_{(j,l)}}$. As a consequence, we can generate all subsequent internal states except the last $\mathbf{E}_K$ operation under $PMN = PMN_{i_{(j,l)}}$.

3.2   Complexity Analysis

In Step I-(b), for every PMN PMN_j, it is expected that there are $\frac{2^\phi - 1}{2^{64}} \approx 2^{\phi - 64}$ qualified PMNs PMN_i such that $PMN_i = Y_j$, and there are $\frac{2^\phi - 1}{2^{48 - mml}} \approx 2^{\phi + mml - 48}$ qualified PMNs PMN_j such that Eq. (3) holds, that is $l \approx 2^{\phi + mml - 48}$ on average; and the $2^{\phi - 64}$ qualified PMNs PMN_i must be among the $2^{\phi + mml - 48}$ qualified PMNs $PMN_{i_{(j,l)}}$. Since $\phi \geq 24$ (from Condition (1)) generally, it is expected that $\beta = \phi$ in Phase II. The probability that there exists a qualified permutation (PMN_i, PMN_j) such that $PMN_i = Y_j$ holds is $1 - (1 - \frac{1}{2^{64}})^{2^\phi \times (2^\phi - 1)} \approx 1 - e^{-2^{2\phi - 64}}$.

In Step II-(b), the expected number of distinct $\widehat{PMN}_p$ is 2^β; for every $\widehat{PMN}_p$, it is expected that there are approximately $\frac{2^\beta - 1}{2^{64}} \approx 2^{\beta - 64}$ qualified PMNs $\widehat{PMN}_q$ such that $\widehat{PMN}_p = \widehat{Y}_q$; and for every $\widehat{PMN}_j (= T_j)$, it is expected that there are approximately $\frac{2^\beta - 1}{2^{48 - mml}} \approx 2^{\beta + mml - 48}$ qualified PMNs $\widehat{PMN}_{q_{(j,r)}} (= T_{q_{(j,r)}})$ such that Eq. (4) holds, that is $r \approx 2^{\beta + mml - 48}$ on average; and the $2^{\beta - 64}$ qualified PMNs $\widehat{PMN}_q$ must be among the $2^{\beta + mml - 48}$ qualified PMNs $\widehat{PMN}_{q_{(j,r)}}$. Hence, the expected number of the set $\{(\widehat{PMN}_j (= T_j), \widehat{PMN}_{q_{(j,r)}} (= T_{q_{(j,r)}})) | j = 1, 2, \cdots, 2^\beta\}$ is $2^\beta \times 2^{\beta + mml - 48} = 2^{2\beta + mml - 48}$.

In Step II-(c), for a permutation $(\widehat{PMN}_j, \widehat{PMN}_{q_{(j,r)}})$, the resulting ciphertext matches the ciphertext of some $C^{(i_{(j,l)})}$ such that $(PMN_{i_{(j,l)}}, PMN_j)$ is a qualified permutation in Phase I is expected to be approximately $2^{\phi + mml - 48} \times (2^{-48})^{mbn} = 2^{\phi + mml - 48 \times (mbn + 1)}$. Hence, the expected number of the recorded $(PMN_{i_{(j,l)}}, \widehat{PMN}_j, \widehat{PMN}_{q_{(j,r)}})$ is

$$2^{2\beta + mml - 48} \times 2^{\phi + mml - 48 \times (mbn + 1)} = 2^{3\phi + 2 \times mml - 48 \times (mbn + 2)}.$$

On the other hand, a permutation $(PMN_{i_{(j,l)}}, \widehat{PMN}_j, \widehat{PMN}_{q_{(j,r)}})$ such that both $PMN_{i_{(j,l)}} = Y_j$ and $\widehat{PMN}_j = \widehat{Y}_{q_{(j,r)}}$ hold is expected to be correct, and thus can pass the filtering condition with probability one. For a permutation $(PMN_{i_{(j,l)}}, PMN_j)$ such that $PMN_{i_{(j,l)}} = Y_j$ holds, the probability that there is a qualified permutation $(\widehat{PMN}_j (= T_j), \widehat{PMN}_{q_{(j,r)}} (= T_{q_{(j,r)}}))$ such that

$\widehat{PMN}_j = \widehat{Y}_{q(j,r)}$ holds is $1 - (1 - \frac{1}{2^{64}})^{2^\beta - 1} \approx 2^{\beta - 64}$, as $\beta = \phi < 64$. Hence, the probability that there is a permutation $(PMN_{i_{(j,l)}}, \widehat{PMN}_j, \widehat{PMN}_{q(j,r)})$ such that both $PMN_{i_{(j,l)}} = Y_j$ and $\widehat{PMN}_j = \widehat{Y}_{q(j,r)}$ hold is $(1 - e^{-2^{2\phi - 64}}) \times 2^{\beta - 64} = (1 - e^{-2^{2\phi - 64}}) \times 2^{\phi - 64}$.

Step I-(a) requires 2^ϕ queries and a memory of approximately $2^\phi \times (mbn \times \frac{48}{8} + 8 \times 2 + 3 \times 2) = 2^\phi \times (6 \times mbn + 22)$ bytes, and Step I-(b) has a computational complexity of approximately $2^\phi \times 2^{\phi + mml - 48} = 2^{2\phi + mml - 48}$ memory accesses to retrieve $(PMN_{i_{(j,l)}}, PMN_j)$. Step II-(a) requires 2^β queries and a memory of $\sum_{i=1}^{2^\beta} (\widehat{abn}_i \times \frac{48}{8} + 2 \times \widehat{mbn}_i \times \frac{48}{8} + 8 \times 2 + 3 \times 2)$ bytes (it can be reduced by using the same set of associated data and message), and Step II-(b) has a computational complexity of approximately $2^{2\beta + mml - 48}$ memory accesses to retrieve $(\widehat{PMN}_j, \widehat{PMN}_{q(j,r)})$. Step II-(c) has a computational complexity of approximately $2^{2\beta + mml - 48} = 2^{2\phi + mml - 48}$ computations of $\widehat{LAC}$.

The attack is valid if:

1. the expected number of correct $(PMN_{i_{(j,l)}}, \widehat{PMN}_j, \widehat{PMN}_{q(j,r)})$ recorded in Step II-(c) (that meets both $PMN_{i_{(j,l)}} = Y_j$ and $\widehat{PMN}_j = \widehat{Y}_{q(j,r)}$) is much more than the expected number of wrong $(PMN_{i_{(j,l)}}, \widehat{PMN}_j, \widehat{PMN}_{q(j,r)})$ recorded in Step II-(c), that is

$$2^{3\phi + 2 \times mml - 48 \times (mbn + 2)} \ll (1 - e^{-2^{2\phi - 64}}) \times 2^{\phi - 64},$$

   which corresponds to Condition (2); and
2. the expected computational complexity for the attack to recover an internal state is less than the computational complexity of a generic attack (e.g. exhaustive key search) recovering an internal state, that is

$$\frac{2^{2\phi + mml - 48}}{(1 - e^{-2^{2\phi - 64}}) \times 2^{\phi - 64}} \ll 2^{80},$$

   which corresponds to Condition (1).

A simple analysis of Conditions (1) and (2) reveals that there is a solution for ϕ and mbn when $(24 \leq) mml \leq 31$. Therefore, working in the nonce-respecting scenario, the state recovery attack requires $2^{\phi + 1}$ queries on the $\widehat{LAC}$ encryption and tag generation oracle and a memory of $\mathcal{O}(2^{\phi + 1})$ bytes, and has a computational complexity of approximately $2^{2\phi + mml - 48}$ computations of $\widehat{LAC}$, with a success probability of $(1 - e^{-2^{2\phi - 64}}) \times 2^{\phi - 64}$. In particular, when $mml = 30$, we can set $\phi = 32$ and $mbn \geq 4$, and the attack requires 2^{33} queries and a memory of $\mathcal{O}(2^{33})$ bytes, and has a computational complexity of approximately 2^{46} computations of $\widehat{LAC}$, with a success probability of about $2^{-32.7}$. When $mml = 24$, we can set $\phi = 32$ and $mbn \geq 2$, and the attack requires 2^{33} queries and a memory of $\mathcal{O}(2^{33})$ bytes, and has a computational complexity of approximately 2^{40}

406 J. Lu

computations of $\widehat{\mathrm{LAC}}$, with a success probability of about $2^{-32.7}$. Obviously, the memory can be reused if we want to repeat the attack with many times, e.g. for different keys.

Note that the attack can apply to the case with $mml = 40$ for the original LAC, but it is slightly inferior to exhaustive key search, for example, when we set $\phi = 32$ and $mbn \geq 4$, the attack requires 2^{33} queries and a memory of $\mathcal{O}(2^{33})$ bytes, and has a computational complexity of approximately 2^{56} computations, with a success probability of about $2^{-32.7}$.

4 Existential Forgery Attack on $\widehat{\mathrm{LAC}}$

Once a concerned 128-bit internal state is recovered by the above state recovery attack, we can make an existential forgery attack on $\widehat{\mathrm{LAC}}$ without any further queries, under the PMN corresponding to the recovered internal state.

For a permutation $(PMN_{i_{(j,l)}}, \widehat{PMN}_j(= T_j), \widehat{PMN}_{q_{(j,r)}}(= T_{q_{(j,r)}}))$ outputted in the above state recovery attack, the corresponding 128-bit secret state just after the first two $\mathbf{E}$ operations is $(T_j\|\widehat{T}_{q_{(j,r)}})$. We can choose a message $(\widetilde{M}_1, \widetilde{M}_2, \cdots, \widetilde{M}_{\widetilde{mbn}})$ of $\widetilde{mbn}(\geq 3)$ 48-bit blocks long, and then produce its ciphertext $(\widetilde{C}_1, \widetilde{C}_2, \cdots, \widetilde{C}_{\widetilde{mbn}})$ and tag $\widetilde{T}$ under $PMN = PMN_{i_{(j,l)}}$, for example, in the following way as illustrated in Fig. 4:

1. Compute the first $(\widetilde{mbn} - 3)$ ciphertext blocks $(\widetilde{C}_1, \widetilde{C}_2, \cdots, \widetilde{C}_{\widetilde{mbn}-3})$ for the first $(\widetilde{mbn} - 3)$ message blocks $(\widetilde{M}_1, \widetilde{M}_2, \cdots, \widetilde{M}_{\widetilde{mbn}-3})$ until immediately after the output of the last third $\widehat{\mathbf{G}}$ operation.
2. Let $\widetilde{Y} = PMN_{i_{(j,l)}}$ (or T_j). Choose and pad the last message block to form $\widetilde{M}_{\widetilde{mbn}}$, then compute $\widetilde{X} = (0^{16}\|\widetilde{M}_{\widetilde{mbn}}) \oplus \widetilde{Y}$, decrypt $\widetilde{X}$ through the last $\widehat{\mathbf{G}}$ operation, and we denote the resulting value by $\widetilde{Z}$ (that is the input to the last $\widehat{\mathbf{G}}$ operation), finally compute the last ciphertext block $\widetilde{C}_{\widetilde{mbn}}$.
3. For $t = 1, 2, \cdots, 2^{16}$, choose randomly at uniform the last second message block $\widetilde{M}^{(t)}_{\widetilde{mbn}-1}$, and do as follows:
   (a) Decrypt $(0^{16}\|\widetilde{M}^{(t)}_{\widetilde{mbn}-1}) \oplus \widetilde{Z}$ through the last second $\widehat{\mathbf{G}}$ operation, and check whether the most significant 16 bits of the resulting value correspond to the most significant 16 bits of the 64-bit output of the last third $\widehat{\mathbf{G}}$ operation that is generated in Step 1. If yes, go to the next sub-step; otherwise, repeat Step 3 with a different t.
   (b) Compute the last third message block $\widetilde{M}_{\widetilde{mbn}-2}$ from the output of the last third $\widehat{\mathbf{G}}$ operation and the input to the last second $\widehat{\mathbf{G}}$ operation, and compute the last second and third ciphertext blocks $\widetilde{C}_{\widetilde{mbn}-1}$ and $\widetilde{C}_{\widetilde{mbn}-2}$. The corresponding tag $\widetilde{T} = T_j$ (respectively $\widehat{T}_{q_{(j,r)}}$).

Observe that $\widetilde{Y}$ can be that value corresponding to a different permutation outputted in the above state recovery attack, and $\widetilde{T}$ will be the corresponding value as well.

The attack has a computational complexity of 2^{16} computations of the $\widehat{\mathbf{G}}$ operation to obtain a forgery for a message under $PMN = PMN_{i_{(j,l)}}$, with a success probability of $(1 - 2^{-16})^{2^{16}} \approx 63\%$, (a larger success probability can be achieved by using a larger t). Once made, the forgery can replace the original ciphertext-tag pair under $PMN = PMN_{i_{(j,l)}}$ during online communications, and thus will pass the decryption and tag verification phase of $\widehat{\mathrm{LAC}}$, in the nonce-respecting scenario that does not allow to use a nonce twice in the decryption and tag verification phase.

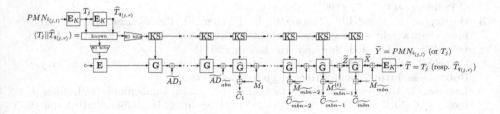

Fig. 4. Existential forgery attack on $\widehat{\mathrm{LAC}}$

Note that the forgery attack that includes the phases of the state recovery attack as a step is meaningless if a forgery is the sole attack goal, because it is slower than a generic attack on a 64-bit tag size. It is a side result of the state recovery attack presented in Sect. 3.

5   Concluding Remarks

In this paper, we have shown that the security of the LAC authenticated encryption algorithm depends greatly on the parameter of the maximum message length and the order of padding the last message block (or equivalently the order of the two halves of the leaked 48-bit output), by presenting a structural state recovery attack on its variants that differ from the original LAC only in the two points. Furthermore, slightly inferior to exhaustive key search, the attack can apply to the LAC variant that differs from the original LAC only in the reverse order of padding the last message block. The attack is only based on the structure of the LAC variants, and may apply to other authenticated encryption algorithms with similar structures. Therefore, an authenticated encryption algorithm with a such or similar structure may be weakened when it is misused with the reverse message padding order (or equivalently the reverse order of the two halves of the leaked output) and different maximum message lengths, and thus users should be very careful about the two points when employing such a structure in reality.

Acknowledgments. The author is grateful to Prof. Wenling Wu and Lei Zhang for their discussions on an earlier version of this work, and to Prof. Yongzhuang Wei and the Natural Science Foundation of China (No. 61572148) for their support.

References

1. Bellare, M., Namprempre, C.: Authenticated encryption: relations among notions and analysis of the generic composition paradigm. J. Cryptology **21**(4), 469–491 (2008)
2. Biham, E., Shamir, A.: Differential cryptanalysis of DES-like cryptosystems. J. Cryptology **4**(1), 3–72 (1991). Springer
3. Bogdanov, A., Mendel, F., Regazzoni, F., Rijmen, V., Tischhauser, E.: ALE: AES-based lightweight authenticated encryption. In: Moriai, S. (ed.) FSE 2013. LNCS, vol. 8424, pp. 447–466. Springer, Heidelberg (2014)
4. CAESAR – Competition for Authenticated Encryption: Security, Applicability, and Robustness. http://competitions.cr.yp.to/caesar.html
5. Leurent, G.: Differential forgery attack against LAC. In: Dunkelman, O., Keliher, L. (eds.) SAC 2015. LNCS, vol. 9566, pp. 217–224. Springer, Heidelberg (2016). doi:10. 1007/978-3-319-31301-6_13
6. Lin, L.: Private communications (2014)
7. Wu, S., Wu, H., Huang, T., Wang, M., Wu, W.: Leaked-state-forgery attack against the authenticated encryption algorithm ALE. In: Sako, K., Sarkar, P. (eds.) ASIACRYPT 2013, Part I. LNCS, vol. 8269, pp. 377–404. Springer, Heidelberg (2013)
8. Wu, W., Zhang, L.: LBlock: a lightweight block cipher. In: Lopez, J., Tsudik, G. (eds.) ACNS 2011. LNCS, vol. 6715, pp. 327–344. Springer, Heidelberg (2011)
9. Zhang, L., Wu, W., Wang, Y., Wu, S., Zhang, J.: LAC: a lightweifht authenticated encryption cipher version 1, Submission to the CAESAR competition, 15 March 2014. http://competitions.cr.yp.to/round1/lacv1.pdf

Linear Hull Attack on Round-Reduced Simeck with Dynamic Key-Guessing Techniques

Lingyue Qin[1], Huaifeng Chen[3], and Xiaoyun Wang[2,3(✉)]

[1] Department of Computer Science and Technology, Tsinghua University,
Beijing 100084, China
qly14@mails.tsinghua.edu.cn
[2] Institute of Advanced Study, Tsinghua University, Beijing 100084, China
xiaoyunwang@mail.tsinghua.edu.cn
[3] Key Laboratory of Cryptologic Technology and Information Security,
Ministry of Education, Shandong University, Jinan 250100, China
hfchen@mail.sdu.edu.cn

Abstract. Simeck is a new family of lightweight block cipher proposed
by Yang *et al.* in CHES'15, which performs efficiently in hardware implementation. In this paper, we search out Simeck's differentials with low
Hamming weight and high probability using Kölbl's tool, then exploit
the links between differentials and linear characteristics to construct linear hulls for Simeck. We give improved linear hull attack with dynamic
key-guessing techniques on Simeck on the basis of round function's property. Our results cover Simeck 32/64 reduced to 23 rounds, Simeck 48/96
reduced to 30 rounds, Simeck 64/128 reduced to 37 rounds, which are
the best known results so far for any variant of Simeck.

Keywords: Simeck · Linear cryptanalysis · Differential cryptanalysis ·
Linear hull · Dynamic key-guessing

1 Introduction

Simeck [19] is a new family of lightweight block cipher proposed in CHES'15
by Yang, Zhu, Suder, Aagaard and Gongbased. They combined the Simon and
Speck block ciphers designed by NSA in [8], using a different set of rotation
constants of Simon's round function and the key schedule of Speck. The round
function of Simeck only contains the AND operation, left rotation and the XOR
operation, leading to a more compact and efficient implementation in hardware.
The Simeck family has three variants with different block size and key size,
including Simeck32/64, Simeck48/96, Simeck64/128.

Related Works. Many cryptanalysis techniques of Simon can be used to attack
Simeck due to their similarity, including differential [3,5,9], linear [2,4] cryptanalysis and so on. For Simon, Wang *et al.* [18] improved the differential attack

© Springer International Publishing Switzerland 2016
J.K. Liu and R. Steinfeld (Eds.): ACISP 2016, Part II, LNCS 9723, pp. 409–424, 2016.
DOI: 10.1007/978-3-319-40367-0_26

results by dynamic key-guessing techniques. Then basing on the dynamic key-guessing techniques in the linear hull cryptanalysis, Chen *et al.* [10] applied the Guess, Split and Combine technique to reduce the time complexity in the calculation of the empirical correlations. They can attack one or two more rounds for all versions of Simon than Wang *et al.*'s results.

For Simeck, there are only a few cryptanalysis results so far. Kölbl *et al.* [12] compared Simon and Simeck on the lower bound of differential and linear characteristic and presented some differentials to attack 19/26/33 rounds of Simeck32/48/64. Bagheri *et al.* [7] analyzed Simeck's security against linear cryptanalysis. With Matsui's algorithm 2, they can attack 18/23/27 rounds for Simeck32/48/64. Zhang *et al.* evaluated the security of 20/24/27 rounds of Simeck32/48/64 against zero correlation linear cryptanalysis [20]. Qiao *et al.* [15] used differential cryptanalysis with dynamic key-guessing techniques to attack Simeck and improved the previously best results on all versions by 2 rounds.

Table 1. Summary of cryptanalysis results on Simeck

Cipher	Round	Data complexity	Time complexity	Reference
Simeck32/64	18	2^{31}	$2^{63.5}$	[7]
	19	2^{31}	2^{36}	[12]
	20	2^{32}	$2^{56.65}$	[20]
	22	2^{32}	$2^{57.9}$	[15]
	23	$2^{31.91}$	$2^{61.78}A^{\mathrm{a}} + 2^{56.41}E^{\mathrm{b}}$	Sect. 4.1
Simeck48/96	24	2^{45}	2^{94}	[7]
	24	2^{48}	$2^{91.6}$	[20]
	26	2^{47}	2^{62}	[12]
	28	2^{46}	$2^{68.3}$	[15]
	30	$2^{47.66}$	$2^{92.2}A + 2^{88.04}E$	Sect. 4.2
Simeck64/128	27	2^{61}	$2^{120.5}$	[7]
	27	2^{64}	$2^{112.79}$	[20]
	33	2^{63}	2^{96}	[12]
	35	2^{63}	$2^{116.3}$	[15]
	37	$2^{63.09}$	$2^{111.44}A + 2^{121.25}E$	Sect. 4.3

[a] additions.

[b] encryption of attacked rounds.

Our Contributions. This paper analyzes the security of Simeck against improved linear hull cryptanalysis with dynamic key-guessing techniques. At first using Kölbl's tool, we search out better differentials than the previous results. The probability of Simeck32/64 is more accurate with searching more differential characteristics. For Simeck48/96 and Simeck64/128, the differentials with less active bits are preferred so we can extend the trails for more rounds and attack more rounds. Then we take advantage of the links between linear characteristic and differential characteristic to construct linear hull distinguishers for the Simeck family. After getting the boolean expressions for the parity bits of the distinguishers, we use the Guess, Split and Combine technique to calculate the empirical correlations, which reduces the time complexity greatly. As a result, 23/30/37 rounds of Simeck32/48/64 can be attacked (Table 1), which are the best results so far. We also do some experiments to verify our results. The experiment on the bias of the linear hull for Simeck32/64 meets our expectation and 48.4 % of the results have a bias higher than we expect. Due to the time limitation, we implement the attack on 21-round Simeck32/64 to recover 8-bit information of 32-bit subkeys. The success rate is 45.6 % corresponding to our estimated value, which proves our algorithm is effective.

Outline. This paper is organized as follows. Section 2 gives a brief description of the Simeck family and dynamic key-guessing techniques in the linear hull cryptanalysis. In Sect. 3, we introduce some new differentials and linear hulls from the differentials. Then linear hull cryptanalysis with the dynamic key-guessing techniques are applied to attack all versions of Simeck in Sect. 4. Finally we conclude in Sect. 5.

2 Preliminaries

2.1 The Simeck Family

The Simeck family with Feistel structure is proposed in CHES'15. The cipher with $2n$-bit block and mn-bit key will be referred to as Simeck$2n/mn$. There are three versions of Simeck, including Simeck32/64 (32 rounds), Simeck48/96 (36 rounds) and Simeck64/128 (44 rounds). In this paper, we use the notations as follows.

X^r $2n$-bit output of round r (input of round $r+1$)
X_L^r left n-bit of X^r
X_R^r right n-bit of X^r
K^r n-bit subkey of round $r+1$
$X \lll i$ cycle shift of X to the left by i bits
$\oplus$ bitwise XOR
$\&$ bitwise AND

Round Function. The round function is described in Fig. 1. The $(r+1)$ round's input is $(X_L^r \| X_R^r)$ and output is $(X_L^{r+1} \| X_R^{r+1})$. The round function is

$$X_L^{r+1} = F(X_L^r) \oplus X_R^r \oplus K^r, \quad X_R^{r+1} = X_L^r,$$

where function $F(X) = ((X \lll 5)\&X) \oplus (X \lll 1)$. We can also present the round function for single bit, which we will use in the rest of the paper. Let $X_L^r = \{X_{L,n-1}^r, X_{L,n-2}^r, ..., X_{L,0}^r\}$, $X_R^r = \{X_{R,n-1}^r, X_{R,n-2}^r, ..., X_{R,0}^r\}$, and the round function can be denoted as

$$X_{L,i}^{r+1} = (X_{L,(i-5+n)\%n}^r \& X_{L,i}^r) \oplus X_{L,(i-1+n)\%n}^r \oplus X_{R,i}^r \oplus K_i^r, \quad X_{R,i}^{r+1} = X_{L,i}^r,$$

where $i = 0, 1, ..., n-1$, and $X_{L,0}^r$, $X_{R,0}^r$ is the LSB of X_L^r and X_R^r.

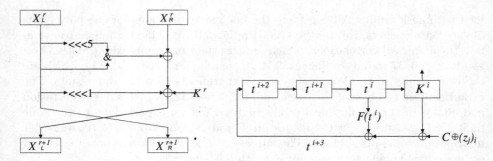

Fig. 1. The round function of Simeck   **Fig. 2.** The key schedule of Simeck

Key Schedule. The key schedule of Simeck (Fig. 2) is similar with Speck. We describe it briefly. To generate a sequence of round keys $\{K^0, ..., K^{n_r-1}\}$ from the master key, the states $\{t^2, t^1, t^0, K^0\}$ are initialized with the master key at first. Then the registers are updated to generate the round keys used in all n_r-round encryption. The updating process is

$$K^{i+1} = t^i, \quad t^{i+3} = F(t^i) \oplus K^i \oplus C \oplus (z_j)_i,$$

where $0 \leq i \leq n_r - 1$, $C = 2^n - 4$ (n is the word size), $(z_j)_i$ is the i-th bit of z_j. For Simeck32/64 and Simeck48/96, the sequence z_j is generated by the primitive polynomial $X^5 + X^2 + 1$ with the initial states $(1, 1, 1, 1, 1)$. And for Simeck64/128, the z_j is generated by the primitive polynomial $X^6 + X + 1$ with the initial states $(1, 1, 1, 1, 1, 1)$.

2.2 Linear Cryptanalysis

We first give the calculation formula of the correlation for boolean function. Let $g(x) : F_2^n \rightarrow F_2$ is a boolean function and $B(g) = \sum_{x \in F_2^n} (-1)^{g(x)}$, so the correlation $c(g)$ is

$$c(g) = \frac{1}{2^n} B(g) = \frac{1}{2^n} \sum_{x \in F_2^n} (-1)^{g(x)}.$$

Then the bias of $g(x)$ is $\epsilon(g) = \frac{1}{2} c(g)$. In the rest of the paper, we use the $B(g)$ as correlation for simplicity of description in some situations.

Linear cryptanalysis [13] is an important known plaintext cryptanalytic technique, and it tries to find a highly probable expression with plaintexts P, ciphertexts C and key bits K as

$$\alpha \cdot P \oplus \beta \cdot C = \gamma \cdot K,$$

where α, β, γ are masks. The bias of the expression is $\varepsilon(\alpha \cdot P \oplus \beta \cdot C \oplus \gamma \cdot K)$, so at least $O(\frac{1}{\epsilon^2})$ plaintexts are needed in the key recovery attack.

The linear hull [14] is a set of linear approximations with the same input mask and output mask, and the potential of a linear hull with mask α and β is

$$ALH(\alpha, \beta) = \sum_{\gamma} \epsilon^2(\alpha \cdot P \oplus \beta \cdot C \oplus \gamma \cdot K) = \bar{\epsilon}^2.$$

Notice the $\bar{\epsilon}^2$ may be higher than ϵ^2 in most situations, so there needs less plaintexts in the linear hull cryptanalysis than linear cryptanalysis.

2.3 Linear Compression and Dynamic Key-Guessing Techniques

To reduce the time complexity of calculating the correlation in the linear hull cryptanalysis, the linear part of the function can be compressed at first. Let $y = f(x, k)$ is a boolean function, and x is l_1-bit plaintext, k is l_2-bit key, the counter vector $V[x]$ denotes the number of x. If $y = f(x, k) = x_0 \oplus k_0 \oplus f'(x', k')$, we can generate a new counter vector $V'[x'] = \sum_{x_0 \in F_2} (-1)^{x_0} V[x_0 || x']$, so the correlation of y under some k guess is

$$B^k(y) = \sum_x (-1)^{f(x,k)} V[x] \Rightarrow B^k(y) = (-1)^{k_0} \sum_{x'} (-1)^{f'(x', k')} V'[x'].$$

Since the k_0 value doesn't affect the absolute value of $B^k(y)$, k_0 is called related bit and doesn't need to be guessed. So there needs $2^{l_1 + l_2 - 2}$ computations, less than $2^{l_1 + l_2}$. If $y = f(x, k)$ has multiple linear bits of x, k, we can also compress them using above method.

Besides, Chen et $al.$ in [10] introduced the Guess, Split and Combine technique to reduce the time complexity based on the dynamic key-guessing techniques. In the calculation of $B^k(y) = \sum_x (-1)^{f(x,k)} V[x]$, let $k = k_G || k_A || k_B || k_C$ ((k_G, k_A, k_B, k_C) are $l_2^G, l_2^A, l_2^B, l_2^C$-bit) and guess the k_G at first. Then all the x values are split into two sets S_A and S_B. For N_A values of $x \in S_A$, $f(x) = f_A(x, k_A || k_C)$, and for N_B values of $x \in S_B$, $f(x) = f_B(x, k_B || k_C)$,

$$B^k(y) = \sum_{x \in S_A} (-1)^{f_A(x, k_A || k_C)} V_A[x] + \sum_{x \in S_B} (-1)^{f_B(x, k_B || k_C)} V_B[x].$$

One needs $N_A 2^{l_2^G + l_2^A + l_2^C} + N_B 2^{l_2^G + l_2^B + l_2^C} + 2^{l_2}$ additions in the Guess, Split and Combine process, which takes less time than the general method with $2^{l_1 + l_2}$.

For example, we use the Guess, Split and Combine technique to calculate the correlation $B^{k_1, k_2}(y)$ of $f_1 = (x_1 \oplus k_1)\&(x_2 \oplus k_2)$ with the counter $V[x_1, x_2]$.

1. Guess k_1 at first.
2. Split the $x = x_1 || x_2$ into two cases according the value of $(x_1 \oplus k_1)$.
   (a) For x_1 that satisfies $x_1 \oplus k_1 = 0$, $f_1 = 0$. It is necessary to generate a new counter $V_1 = \sum_{x_2 \in F_2} V[x_1 = k_1, x_2]$.
   (b) For x_1 that satisfies $x_1 \oplus k_1 = 1$, $f_1(x, k) = (x_2 \oplus k_2)$. It is necessary to generate a new counter $V_2 = \sum_{x_2 \in F_2} (-1)^{x_2} V[x_1 = k_1 \oplus 1, x_2]$, and k_2 is related bit.
3. Combine the two cases, $B^{k_1, k_2}(y) = V_1 + (-1)^{k_2} V_2$.

Step 2.(a)/2.(b) needs 1 addition, and step 3 needs 2 additions. So in total there needs $2 \times (1 + 1 + 2) = 2^3$ additions to compress x_1, x_2, less than the general method.

3   The Linear Hull Distinguishers of Simeck

This section first gives some good differentials searched by Kölbl's tool, then derives equivalent linear hulls from the differentials. We also do an experiment on the 13-round linear hull for Simeck32/64 to verify the bias in Sect. 3.2.

3.1   Differential Distinguishers of Simeck

Differential cryptanalysis is a chosen plaintext/ciphertext cryptanalytic technique. In the round function of Simeck, the only non-linear operation is the AND operation. For the single bit x and y, the probability of $(x\&y) = 0$ is 0.75. We can extract highly probable differential expressions of the function $F(X)$ as

Differential Characteristic 1 : $\Pr[(\Delta X))_i \rightarrow (\Delta F(X))_{i+1}] = 0.5,$

Differential Characteristic 2 : $\Pr[(\Delta X))_i \rightarrow (\Delta F(X))_{i+1,i}] = 0.5,$

Differential Characteristic 3 : $\Pr[(\Delta X))_i \rightarrow (\Delta F(X))_{i+1,i+5}] = 0.5,$

Differential Characteristic 4 : $\Pr[(\Delta X))_i \rightarrow (\Delta F(X))_{i+1,i,i+5}] = 0.5,$

where the $(\Delta F(X))_{i+1}$ denotes the $(i+1)$-th bit is 1 and the others are 0.

In [11], Kölbl introduced a tool for cryptanalysis of symmetric primitives based on SMT/SAT solvers. We use the tool to search the differentials which have a balance between low Hamming weight and high probability to attack more rounds using less plaintexts. The differentials we choose are listed in Table 2.

Table 2. The differentials of Simeck

Cipher	Round	Δ_{in}	Δ_{out}	log_2diff	Reference
Simeck32/64	13	$(0x0, 0x2)$	$(0x2, 0x0)$	-29.64	[15]
Simeck32/64	13	$(0x0, 0x2)$	$(0x2, 0x0)$	-28.91	this paper
Simeck48/96	20	$(0x400000, 0xE00000)$	$(0x400000, 0x200000)$	-43.65	[12]
Simeck48/96	20	$(0x400000, 0xA00000)$	$(0x400000, 0x200000)$	-43.66	this paper
Simeck64/128	26	$(0x0, 0x4400000)$	$(0x8800000, 0x400000)$	-60.02	[12]
Simeck64/128	26	$(0x0, 0x4400000)$	$(0x800000, 0x400000)$	-60.09	this paper

For Simeck32/64, by searching all the characteristics with probability higher than 2^{-52}, we get more accurate result than [15]. For Simeck48/96 and Simeck64/128, the differentials with less active bits in the input difference and output difference are preferred, since less key bits are involved in the attack. At the same time, the probability of the differentials must be higher than 2^{-45} or 2^{-61}, to ensure the data complexity and success rate can be achieved (If we search more time, the probability will be equivalent to the result in [12]).

3.2 Linear Hull Distinguishers of Simeck

In [4], Alizadeh *et al.* noticed each differential characteristic can be mapped into a linear approximation for Simon. The property is based on the round function of Simon, so we can use the similar property for Simeck to construct an equivalent linear characteristic from a differential characteristic. The relation between the probability p of a differential and the potential $\bar{\epsilon}^2$ of a linear hull is $\bar{\epsilon}^2 = 2^{-2}p$. The linear approximation expressions of the function $F(X)$ for Simeck are

Linear Approxiamtion 1 : $\Pr[(F(X))_i = (X)_{i-1}] = 0.75,$

Linear Approxiamtion 2 : $\Pr[(F(X))_i = (X)_{i-1} \oplus (X)_i] = 0.75,$

Linear Approxiamtion 3 : $\Pr[(F(X))_i = (X)_{i-1} \oplus (X)_{i-5}] = 0.75,$

Linear Approxiamtion 4 : $\Pr[(F(X))_i = (X)_{i-1} \oplus (X)_i \oplus (X)_{i-5}] = 0.25.$

[1,6,17] gave some other methods to find linear hulls for Simon, including correlation matrix, Mixed Integer Programming (MIP) and so on. In this paper, we use the differential characteristics to get linear characteristics. The used linear approximations (Used App) can be found above. The details for Simeck32/64 are listed in Table 3. For Simeck48/96 and Simeck64/128, the details of the calculation process are similar with Simeck32/64 that we omit them in this paper. The linear hulls for all versions of Simeck can be seen in Table 4.

Table 3. Linear hull based on the differential for Simeck32/64

r	Differential		Linear		
	Δ_L	Δ_R	X_L	X_R	Used app
0	–	1	1	–	–
1	1	–	–	1	1
2	2	1	1	0	1
3	1,3	2	0	1,15	1 : 1
4	4	1,3	1,15	14	1
5	1,3,5	4	14	1,13,15	3 : 1 : 2
6	2,3	1,3,5	1,13,15	0,15	1 : 1
7	1,4,5	2,3	0,15	1,13,14	3 : 2 : 2
8	3,4	1,4,5	1,13,14	14,15	1 : 2
9	1,3	3,4	14,15	1,15	1 : 2
10	2	1,3	1,15	0	1
11	1	2	0	1	1
12	–	1	1	–	–
13	1	–	–	1	–
	$\sum_r \log_2 pr = -38$		$\log_2 \varepsilon^2 = -40$		
	$\log_2 p_{diff} = -28.91$		$\log_2 \bar{\varepsilon}^2 = -30.91$		
	$\#trails = 1846518$		$\#characteristics = 1846518$		

Table 4. The linear hulls for Simeck

Cipher	Round	Input Active bits	Output Active bits	ALH
Simeck32/64	13	$X_{L,1}^r$	$X_{R,1}^{r+13}$	−30.91
Simeck48/96	20	$X_{L,19}^r, X_{L,21}^r, X_{R,20}^r$	$X_{L,21}^{r+20}, X_{R,20}^{r+20}$	−45.66
Simeck64/128	26	$X_{L,18}^r, X_{L,22}^r$	$X_{L,22}^{r+26}, X_{R,21}^{r+26}$	−62.09

Experiments for Simeck32/64. Since the block of Simeck32/64 only contains 32 bits, we can iterate over the 2^{32} possible plaintexts to validate the bias $(\bar{\varepsilon}^2)$ of the 13-round linear hull. Randomly select 1000 keys and the experimental results are listed in Table 5. In the experiments, 48.4 % of the keys have a bias higher than $2^{-30.91}$, which is corresponding to the linear hull's $ALH = 2^{-30.91}$.

Table 5. Bias of the 13-round linear hull

$log_2(\bar{\varepsilon}^2)$	Num	Probability	$log_2(\bar{\varepsilon}^2)$	Num	Probability
$[-27.91, 0)$	56	0.056	$[-30.91, -29.91)$	151	0.151
$[-28.91, -27.91)$	123	0.123	$[-31.91, -30.91)$	144	0.144
$[-29.91, -28.91)$	154	0.154	$(-\infty, -31.91)$	372	0.372

4   Key Recovery Attack on Simeck

In this section, we discuss key recovery attack on all three versions of Simeck, and implement the 21-round attack for Simeck32/64 to verify our algorithm.

4.1   Key Recovery Attack on Simeck32/64

We use the 13-round linear hull

$$X_{L,1}^r \to X_{R,1}^{r+13}$$

obtained in Sect. 3.2 to attack Simeck32/64. At first four more rounds before and four more rounds after the linear hull are added to get a 21-round distinguisher. Take some plaintexts or subkeys as a whole, we can get the expression for $X_{L,1}^r$ as $f(x,k) = x_0 \oplus k_0 \oplus f'(x',k')$, where

$$f'(x',k') = ((x_1 \oplus k_1)\&(x_2 \oplus k_2)) \oplus ((x_3 \oplus k_3)\&(x_4 \oplus k_4))\oplus$$
$$[(x_5 \oplus k_5 \oplus (x_6 \oplus k_6)\&(x_7 \oplus k_7))\&(x_8 \oplus k_8 \oplus (x_7 \oplus k_7)\&(x_9 \oplus k_9))]$$
$$\oplus \{\{(x_{10} \oplus k_{10} \oplus (x_6 \oplus k_6)\&(x_7 \oplus k_7))\oplus$$
$$[(x_{11} \oplus k_{11} \oplus (x_{12} \oplus k_{12})\&(x_{13} \oplus k_{13}))\&(x_{14} \oplus k_{14} \oplus (x_3 \oplus k_3)\&(x_{13} \oplus k_{13}))]\}$$
$$\&\{(x_{15} \oplus k_{15} \oplus (x_7 \oplus k_7)\&(x_9 \oplus k_9))\oplus$$
$$[(x_{14} \oplus k_{14} \oplus (x_{13} \oplus k_{13})\&(x_3 \oplus k_3))\&(x_{16} \oplus k_{16} \oplus (x_3 \oplus k_3)\&(x_4 \oplus k_4))]\}\}.$$

In the expression, $x' = \{x_1, ..., x_{16}\}$ and $k' = \{k_1, ..., k_{16}\}$. The details of $\{x_0, x_1, ..., x_{16}\}$, $\{k_0, k_1, ..., k_{16}\}$ are given in Table 6. Notice $x_{10} = x_3 \oplus x_5$ and $x_{15} = x_4 \oplus x_8$, so there are 15 independent bits of x and 17 independent bits of k. The $X_{R,1}^{r+13}$ also can be represented as $f(x, k)$ where x, k have similar expressions as that in Table 6. (The expressions of x, k for $X_{R,1}^{r+13}$ is so similar to Table 6 that we omit them in this paper).

Table 6. The expressions for $X_{L,1}^r$

x	Expression of x	k	Expression of k
x_0	$X_{L,1}^{r-4} \oplus X_{L,15}^{r-4}$ $\oplus (X_{L,9}^{r-4} \& \oplus X_{L,14}^{r-4}) \oplus X_{L,13}^{r-4} \oplus X_{R,14}^{r-4}$	k_0	$K_1^{r-1} \oplus K_0^{r-2} \oplus K_1^{r-3}$ $\oplus K_{15}^{r-3} \oplus K_{14}^{r-4}$
x_1	$(X_{L,5}^{r-4} \& \oplus X_{L,10}^{r-4}) \oplus X_{L,9}^{r-4} \oplus X_{R,10}^{r-4}$	k_1	K_{10}^{r-4}
x_2	$(X_{L,10}^{r-4} \& \oplus X_{L,15}^{r-4}) \oplus X_{L,14}^{r-4} \oplus X_{R,15}^{r-4}$	k_2	K_{15}^{r-4}
x_3	$(X_{L,7}^{r-4} \& \oplus X_{L,12}^{r-4}) \oplus X_{L,11}^{r-4} \oplus X_{R,12}^{r-4}$	k_3	K_{12}^{r-4}
x_4	$(X_{L,12}^{r-4} \& \oplus X_{L,1}^{r-4}) \oplus X_{L,0}^{r-4} \oplus X_{R,1}^{r-4}$	k_4	K_1^{r-4}
x_5	$(X_{L,5}^{r-4} \& \oplus X_{L,10}^{r-4}) \oplus X_{L,9}^{r-4} \oplus X_{R,10}^{r-4} \oplus X_{L,11}^{r-4}$	k_5	$K_{10}^{r-4} \oplus K_{11}^{r-3}$
x_6	$(X_{L,1}^{r-4} \& \oplus X_{L,6}^{r-4}) \oplus X_{L,5}^{r-4} \oplus X_{R,6}^{r-4}$	k_6	K_6^{r-4}
x_7	$(X_{L,6}^{r-4} \& \oplus X_{L,11}^{r-4}) \oplus X_{L,10}^{r-4} \oplus X_{R,11}^{r-4}$	k_7	K_{11}^{r-4}
x_8	$(X_{L,10}^{r-4} \& \oplus X_{L,15}^{r-4}) \oplus X_{L,14}^{r-4} \oplus X_{R,15}^{r-4} \oplus X_{L,0}^{r-4}$	k_8	$K_{15}^{r-4} \oplus K_0^{r-3}$
x_9	$(X_{L,11}^{r-4} \& \oplus X_{L,0}^{r-4}) \oplus X_{L,15}^{r-4} \oplus X_{R,0}^{r-4}$	k_9	K_0^{r-4}
x_{10}	$x_3 \oplus x_5$	k_{10}	$k_3 \oplus k_5 \oplus K_{12}^{r-2}$
x_{11}	$(X_{L,1}^{r-4} \& \oplus X_{L,6}^{r-4}) \oplus X_{L,5}^{r-4} \oplus X_{R,6}^{r-4} \oplus X_{L,7}^{r-4}$	k_{11}	$K_6^{r-4} \oplus K_7^{r-3}$
x_{12}	$(X_{L,13}^{r-4} \& \oplus X_{L,2}^{r-4}) \oplus X_{L,1}^{r-4} \oplus X_{R,2}^{r-4}$	k_{12}	K_2^{r-4}
x_{13}	$(X_{L,2}^{r-4} \& \oplus X_{L,7}^{r-4}) \oplus X_{L,6}^{r-4} \oplus X_{R,7}^{r-4}$	k_{13}	K_7^{r-4}
x_{14}	$(X_{L,6}^{r-4} \& \oplus X_{L,11}^{r-4}) \oplus X_{L,10}^{r-4} \oplus X_{R,11}^{r-4} \oplus X_{L,12}^{r-4}$	k_{14}	$K_{11}^{r-4} \oplus K_{12}^{r-3}$
x_{15}	$x_4 \oplus x_8$	k_{15}	$k_4 \oplus k_8 \oplus K_1^{r-2}$
x_{16}	$(X_{L,11}^{r-4} \& \oplus X_{L,0}^{r-4}) \oplus X_{L,15}^{r-4} \oplus X_{R,0}^{r-4} \oplus X_{L,1}^{r-4}$	k_{16}	$K_0^{r-4} \oplus K_1^{r-3}$

The x denotes the plaintexts or ciphertexts and the k denotes the subkey bits. We use $x_p = \{x_{p,0}, ..., x_{p,16}\}$ and $k_p = \{k_{p,0}, ..., k_{p,16}\}$ to represent the x, k for $X_{L,1}^r$. For $X_{R,1}^{r+13}$, we use x_c and k_c. Then the $X_{L,1}^r$ can be denoted by $f(x_p, k_p)$ and the $X_{R,1}^{r+13}$ can be denoted by $f(x_c, k_c)$.

Let the plaintexts $P = X^{r-4}$ and the ciphertexts $C = X^{r+17}$. We can compress the N pairs (P, C) into a counter vector $V[x_p, x_c]$ of size $2^{15+15} = 2^{30}$. Then the empirical correlation under some subkey k_p and k_c is

$$\overline{c}_{k_p, k_c} = \frac{1}{N} \sum_{x_p, x_c} (-1)^{f(x_p, k_p) \oplus f(x_c, k_c)} V[x_p, x_c].$$

As we can see, $f(x, k) = x_0 \oplus k_0 \oplus f'(x', k')$ is linear with $x_0 \oplus k_0$. So the $x_{p,0}$ and $x_{c,0}$ can be compressed at first as following

$$V_1[x'_p, x'_c] = \sum_{x_{p,0}, x_{c,0} \in F_2} (-1)^{x_{p,0} \oplus x_{c,0}} V[x_p, x_c].$$

The target correlation becomes

$$\bar{c}_{k'_p, k'_c} = \frac{1}{N} \sum_{x'_c} (-1)^{f'(x'_c, k'_c)} \sum_{x'_p} (-1)^{f'(x'_p, k'_p)} V_1[x'_p, x'_c],$$

and the $k_{p,0}$, $k_{c,0}$ can be regarded as related bits and omitted in the calculation. We introduce how to calculate the $B^{k'}(y) = \sum_{x'} (-1)^{f'(x', k')} V'[x']$ efficiently using dynamic key-guessing techniques in the following Procedure A, where $y = f'(x', k')$ and $V'[x']$ is the num of x'. The calculation of $B^{k'_p}(y) = \sum_{x'_p} (-1)^{f'(x'_p, k'_p)} V_1[x'_p, x'_c]$ for constant x'_c is same with $B^{k'}(y)$, so calculating the $\bar{c}_{k'_p, k'_c}$ needs to call Procedure A twice.

Procedure A. The expression of $f'(x', k')$ is the same with the expression for Simon32/64, so the calculation process is similar. The details can be seen in the Sect. 4.2 of [10], and we gives the basic ideas in the following. There are only 14 independent bits for $\{x_1, \ldots x_{16}\}$ and 16 independent bits for $\{k_1, \ldots, k_{16}\}$. We introduces the procedure briefly.

1. Guess k_1, k_3, k_7 at first.
2. Split the $f'(x', k')$ into 8 cases according to the values of $\{x_1 \oplus k_1, x_3 \oplus k_3, x_7 \oplus k_7\}$. For each case, there needs $2^8 \times 7$ additions to generate a new counter vector. Then also apply the Guess, Split and Combine technique to calculate the partial correlation of each case, and the time complexity is $2^{11.19}$ additions each.
3. Combine the 8 cases to get the final correlation, there needs $2^{13} \times 7$ additions.

The total time of Procedure A is

$$T = 2^3 \times (8 \times (2^8 \times 7 + 2^{11.19}) + 2^{13} \times 7) = 2^{19.46}.$$

Attack on 23 Rounds. We add one more round before and one more round after the 21-round distinguisher. According the plaintexts and ciphertexts involved in the 21-round distinguisher, there needs to guess 13-bit keys in $(r - 5)$-th round and 13-bit keys in $(r + 17)$-th round. The estimated potential $\bar{\varepsilon}^2$ of the linear hull is $2^{-30.91}$. Set the advantage $a = 8$ and data complexity $N = 2 \times 2^{30.19} = 2^{31.19} = c_N \cdot \bar{\varepsilon}^2$. According to the experiments on the bias of the 13-round linear hull in the Sect. 3.2 and the theory of success rate in [16], we can get the range of the success rate $(0.411, 0.532)$ of the attack in Table 7.

Table 7. Experimental results for the 13-round linear hull of Simeck32/64

$log_2(\bar{\varepsilon}^2)$	Prob.(p)	c_N	Lower success-rate(s_l)	Upper success-rate(s_u)
$[-27.91, 0)$	0.056	$c_N \geq 16$	1	1
$[-28.91, -27.91)$	0.123	$8 \leq c_N < 16$	0.997	1
$[-29.91, -28.91)$	0.154	$4 \leq c_N < 8$	0.867	0.997
$[-30.91, -29.91)$	0.151	$2 \leq c_N < 4$	0.477	0.867
$[-31.91, -30.91)$	0.144	$1 \leq c_N < 2$	0.188	0.477
			$\sum p \cdot s_l = 0.411$	$\sum p \cdot s_u = 0.532$

The details of the attack are as follows.

1. Guess 13 bits $\{K_0^{r-5} - K_2^{r-5}, K_5^{r-5} - K_7^{r-5}, K_9^{r-5} - K_{15}^{r-5}\}$ and 13 bits $\{K_0^{r+17} - K_2^{r+17}, K_5^{r+17} - K_7^{r+17}, K_9^{r+17} - K_{15}^{r+17}\}$. For each of the 2^{26} values,
   a. Encrypt the plaintexts by one round and decrypt the ciphertexts by one round to get the X^{r-4} and X^{r+17}. Then compress the N pairs (X^{r-4}, X^{r+17}) into a counter vector $V_1[x'_p, x'_c]$ of size $2^{14+14} = 2^{28}$. This step takes $N = 2^{31.91}$ times two-round encryptions and compressions.
   b. For each of 2^{14} x'_c, call Procedure A to calculate the correlation for different k'_p and constant x'_c. Now we have 2^{16+14} counters of 14 bits x'_c and 16 bits k'_p. This step needs $2^{14} \times 2^{19.46}$ times additions.
   c. For each of 2^{16} k'_p, call Procedure A to calculate the correlation for different k'_c. Now we have 2^{16+16} counters of 16 bits k_p and 16 bits k'_c. This step needs $2^{16} \times 2^{19.46}$ additions.

   In total, there needs $2^{26} \times 2^{31.91}$ times two-round encryptions and $2^{26} \times (2^{33.46} + 2^{35.46}) = 2^{61.78}$ additions.
2. We have $2^{26+32} = 2^{58}$ counters now. Since the advantage is 8, so the key ranked in the largest 2^{58-8} counters can be the right key. Get 2^{56} candidates of the master key according to the the key schedule and do exhaustive search to find the right key. There needs 2^{56} times 23-round encryptions.

Attack complexity: $2^{61.78}$ additions and $2^{56.41}$ 23-round encryptions.

Implementation of the 21-Round Attack. If we don't consider the $(r-5)$-th round and $(r+17)$-th round in the 23-round attack, the 21-round attack needs $2^{35.78}$ additions to get 2^{24} possible values of 32 subkey bits. (Due to the time limitation, we don't do the exhaustive search to recover the whole master key).

We randomly select the master key to do experiments on the recovery of 8-bit key information for the 32 bits subkey involved in the 21-round attack. If the correct subkey bits are in the first 2^{24} counters of all the 2^{32} counters in descending order, we believe the attack is successful and can recover the correct key bits. There are 1000 master keys tested and the success rate is 0.456, which meets our expectation $(0.411, 0.531)$ and our attack algorithm is effective.

4.2   Key Recovery Attack on Simeck48/96

We use the 20-round linear hull

$$X_{L,19}^r \oplus X_{L,21}^r \oplus X_{R,20}^r \to X_{L,21}^{r+20} \oplus X_{R,20}^{r+20}$$

obtained in Sect. 3.2 to attack Simeck48/96. Add 4 rounds before r-th round, we get the expression $f_B(x_B, k_B)$ for $X_{L,19}^r \oplus X_{L,21}^r \oplus X_{R,20}^r$. Add 4 rounds after $(r+20)$-th round, we get the expression $f_C(x_C, k_C)$ for $X_{L,21}^{r+20} \oplus X_{R,20}^{r+20}$.(We give expressions of $f_B(x_B, k_B)$ and $f_C(x_C, k_C)$ and details of $\{x_B, k_B\}$ and $\{x_C, k_C\}$ are similar with Table 6 that we omit them in this paper.). Then we can get a 28-round distinguisher for Simeck48/96.

Table 8. Time complexity for some functions

Case	Expression	Time
f_1	$(x_1 \oplus k_1 \oplus (x_2 \oplus k_2)\&(x_3 \oplus k_3))\&(x_4 \oplus k_4 \oplus (x_2 \oplus k_2)\&(x_5 \oplus k_5))$	$2^{6.46}$
f_2	$[x_1 \oplus k_1 \oplus (x_2 \oplus k_2)\&(x_3 \oplus k_3)\oplus$ $(x_4 \oplus k_4 \oplus (x_5 \oplus k_5)\&(x_6 \oplus k_6))\&(x_7 \oplus k_7 \oplus (x_6 \oplus k_6)\&(x_8 \oplus k_8))]$ $\&[x_9 \oplus k_9 \oplus (x_3 \oplus k_3)\&(x_{10} \oplus k_{10})\oplus$ $(x_7 \oplus k_7 \oplus (x_6 \oplus k_6)\&(x_8 \oplus k_8))\&(x_{11} \oplus k_{11} \oplus (x_8 \oplus k_8)\&(x_{12} \oplus k_{12}))]$	$2^{15.99}$
f_3	$f_2 \oplus ((x_8 \oplus k_8)\&(x_{12} \oplus k_{12}))$	$2^{15.99}$
f_4	$f_2 \oplus ((x_{13} \oplus k_{13})\&(x_{14} \oplus k_{14})) \oplus ((x_8 \oplus k_8)\&(x_{12} \oplus k_{12}))\oplus$ $(x_{15} \oplus k_{15} \oplus (x_2 \oplus k_2)\&(x_3 \oplus k_3))\&(x_{16} \oplus k_{16} \oplus (x_{10} \oplus k_{10})\&(x_3 \oplus k_3))$ $Notice: x_1 = x_8 \oplus x_{15}, x_9 = x_{12} \oplus x_{16}$	$2^{19.46}$
f_5	$f_4 \oplus ((x_8 \oplus k_8)\&(x_{12} \oplus k_{12}))$	$2^{19.46}$

For simplicity, we give the time complexity of calculating the correlation for some common boolean functions in Table 8. Case f_1 and f_2 can be found in [10] and the time complexity is $2^{6.46}$ and $2^{15.99}$. There is little difference between case f_2 and f_3, where $f_3 = f_2 \oplus ((x_8 \oplus k_8)\&(x_{12} \oplus k_{12}))$. Because the x_8, x_{12} and k_8, k_{12} are also involved in f_2 and compressed at first, so in the calculation the only change is the method of generating the new counter vector, and the time complexity is equal for the two cases. The case f_4 is same with the Procedure A in Sect. 4.1 and the time complexity is $2^{19.46}$. For the similar reason like f_2 and f_3, the f_5 have a time complexity of $2^{19.46}$ as f_4.

Procedure B. Here we discuss how to calculate $B^{k_B}(y) = \sum_{x_B} (-1)^{f_B(x_B, k_B)}$

$$f_B(x_B, k_B) = x_0 \oplus k_0 \oplus (x_1 \oplus k_1)\&(x_2 \oplus k_2)$$
$$\oplus (x_3 \oplus k_3)\&(x_4 \oplus k_4) \oplus (x_5 \oplus k_5)\&(x_6 \oplus k_6)$$
$$\oplus [(x_7 \oplus k_7 \oplus (x_8 \oplus k_8)\&(x_9 \oplus k_9))\&(x_{10} \oplus k_{10} \oplus (x_9 \oplus k_9)\&(x_{11} \oplus k_{11}))]$$
$$\oplus \{[x_{12} \oplus k_{12} \oplus (x_8 \oplus k_8)\&(x_9 \oplus k_9)\oplus$$

$(x_{13} \oplus k_{13} \oplus (x_{14} \oplus k_{14}) \& (x_{15} \oplus k_{15})) \& (x_{16} \oplus k_{16} \oplus (x_3 \oplus k_3) \& (x_{15} \oplus k_{15}))]$
$\& [x_{17} \oplus k_{17} \oplus ((x_9 \oplus k_9) \& (x_{11} \oplus k_{11})) \oplus$
$(x_{16} \oplus k_{16} \oplus (x_3 \oplus k_3) \& (x_{15} \oplus k_{15})) \& (x_{18} \oplus k_{18} \oplus (x_3 \oplus k_3) \& (x_4 \oplus k_4))]\}$
$\oplus \{[x_{19} \oplus k_{19} \oplus (x_{20} \oplus k_{20}) \& (x_{21} \oplus k_{21}) \oplus$
$(x_{22} \oplus k_{22} \oplus (x_{23} \oplus k_{23}) \& (x_{24} \oplus k_{24})) \& (x_{25} \oplus k_{25} \oplus (x_5 \oplus k_5) \& (x_{24} \oplus k_{24}))]$
$\& [x_{26} \oplus k_{26} \oplus (x_{21} \oplus k_{21}) \& (x_{27} \oplus k_{27}) \oplus$
$(x_{25} \oplus k_{25} \oplus (x_5 \oplus k_5) \& (x_{24} \oplus k_{24})) \& (x_{28} \oplus k_{28} \oplus (x_5 \oplus k_5) \& (x_6 \oplus k_6))]\}$

$V_B[x]$ efficiently using dynamic key-guessing techniques. Compress the plaintexts of r-th round into a counter $V_B[x_1, ..., x_{28}]$. Since $x_{12} = x_3 \oplus x_7, x_{17} = x_4 \oplus x_{10}$, there are only 26 independent x bits.

1. Compress $\{x_1 - x_4, x_7 - x_{18}\}$ as case f_4 for each $\{x_5, x_6, x_{19} - x_{28}\}$, the time complexity is $2^{19.46}$ each. This step needs $2^{12} \cdot 2^{19.46} = 2^{31.46}$ additions in total. Now we have a counter vector for 16 bits keys and 12 bits x.
2. Compress $\{x_5, x_6, x_{19} - x_{28}\}$ as case f_3 for each $\{k_1 - k_4, x_7 - x_{18}\}$, the time complexity is $2^{15.99}$ each. This step needs $2^{16} \cdot 2^{15.99} = 2^{31.99}$ additions in total. Now we have a counter vector for 28 bits keys.

In total, the time complexity of procedure B is $2^{31.46} + 2^{31.99} = 2^{32.75}$ additions.

Procedure C. Here we discuss how to calculate $B^{k_C}(y) = \sum_{x_C} (-1)^{f_C(x_C, k_C)}$ $V_C[x]$ efficiently using dynamic key-guessing techniques. Compress the ciphertexts of $(r+20)$-th round into a counter $V_C[x_1, ..., x_{21}]$, since $x_{13} = x_8 \oplus x_{18}, x_{19} = x_{11} \oplus x_{21}$, there are only 19 independent x bits.

$f_C(x_C, k_C) = x_0 \oplus k_0 \oplus ((x_1 \oplus k_1) \& (x_2 \oplus k_2))$
$\oplus [(x_3 \oplus k_3 \oplus (x_4 \oplus k_4) \& (x_5 \oplus k_5)) \& (x_6 \oplus k_6 \oplus (x_5 \oplus k_5) \& (x_7 \oplus k_7))]$
$\oplus [(x_8 \oplus k_8 \oplus (x_9 \oplus k_9) \& (x_{10} \oplus k_{10})) \& (x_{11} \oplus k_{11} \oplus (x_{10} \oplus k_{10}) \& (x_{12} \oplus k_{12}))]$
$\oplus \{[x_{13} \oplus k_{13} \oplus ((x_9 \oplus k_9) \& (x_{10} \oplus k_{10})) \oplus$
$(x_{14} \oplus k_{14} \oplus (x_{15} \oplus k_{15}) \& (x_{16} \oplus k_{16})) \& (x_{17} \oplus k_{17} \oplus (x_{16} \oplus k_{16}) \& (x_{18} \oplus k_{18}))]$
$\& [x_{19} \oplus k_{19} \oplus ((x_{10} \oplus k_{10}) \& (x_{12} \oplus k_{12})) \oplus$
$(x_{17} \oplus k_{17} \oplus (x_{16} \oplus k_{16}) \& (x_{18} \oplus k_{18})) \& (x_{20} \oplus k_{20} \oplus (x_{18} \oplus k_{18}) \& (x_{21} \oplus k_{21}))]\}$

1. Compress $\{x_3 - x_7\}$ as case f_1 for each $\{x_1, x_2, x_8 - x_{21}\}$, the time complexity is $2^{6.46}$ each. This step needs $2^{14} \cdot 2^{6.46} = 2^{20.46}$ additions in total. Now we have a counter vector for 5 bits keys and 14 bits x.
2. Compress $\{x_1, x_2, x_8 - x_{21}\}$ as case f_5 for each $\{k_3 - k_7\}$, the time complexity is $2^{19.46}$ each, and this step needs $2^5 \cdot 2^{19.46} = 2^{24.46}$ additions in total. Now we have a counter vector for 21 bits keys.

In total, the time complexity of procedure C is $2^{20.46} + 2^{24.46} = 2^{24.55}$ additions.

Attack on 30 Rounds. We add one more round before and one more round after the 28-round distinguisher. According the plaintexts and ciphertexts involved in the 28-round distinguisher, there needs to guess 21-bit keys in $(r-5)$-th round and 18-bit keys in $(r+24)$-th round. The estimated potential of this linear hull is $2^{-45.66}$. Set the advantage $a = 8$ and data complexity $N = 4 \times 2^{45.66} = 2^{47.66}$, the success rate is 0.867.

1. Guess 21 bits $\{K_1^{r-5}, K_3^{r-5} - K_{21}^{r-5}, K_{23}^{r-5}\}$ and 18 bits $\{K_0^{r+24}, K_4^{r+24} - K_6^{r+24}, K_8^{r+24} - K_{21}^{r+24}\}$. For each of 2^{39} values,
   a. Encrypt the plaintexts by one round and decrypt the ciphertexts by one round to get the X^{r-4} and X^{r+24}. Then compress the N pairs (X^{r-4}, X^{r+24}) into a counter vector of size 2^{45}. This step takes $N = 2^{47.66}$ times two-round encryptions and compressions.
   b. For each of 2^{19} x_C in f_C, call Procedure B. Now we have 2^{19+28} counters of 19 bits x_C and 28 bits k_B. This step needs $2^{19} \times 2^{32.75}$ additions.
   c. For each of 2^{28} k_B, call Procedure C. Now we have 2^{28+21} counters of 28 bits k_B and 21 bits k_C. This step needs $2^{28} \times 2^{24.55}$ additions.
   In total, this step needs $2^{39} \times 2^{47.66}$ times two-round encryptions and $2^{39} \times 2^{53.2}$ additions.
2. We have $2^{39+49} = 2^{88}$ counters in total and the key ranked in the largest 2^{88-8} counters can be the right key. Get 2^{88} candidates of the master key according to the the key schedule and do exhaustive search to find the right key.

Attack complexity: $2^{92.2}$ additions and $2^{88.04}$ 30-round encryptions.

4.3   Key Recovery Attack on Simeck64/128

We use the 26-round linear hull

$$X_{L,18}^r \oplus X_{L,22}^r \to X_{L,22}^{r+26} \oplus X_{R,21}^{r+26}$$

obtained in Sect. 3.2 to attack Simeck64/128. Add four more rounds on the top and four more rounds on the bottom to get a 34-round distinguisher. The expression for the parity bits $X_{L,18}^r \oplus X_{L,22}^r$ and $X_{L,22}^{r+26} \oplus X_{R,21}^{r+26}$ are also similar with the other two situations that we omit the details in this paper.

Then adding two more rounds before and one more round after the 34-round distinguisher we can attack the 37-round Simeck64/128. The procedure is similar with the attack on Simeck32/64 and Simeck48/96, and due to the space limitation we will not repeat it. The estimated potential of this linear hull is $2^{-62.09}$. Set the advantage $a = 8$ and data complexity $N = 2 \times 2^{62.09} = 2^{63.09}$, the success rate is 0.477. The time complexity of the 37-round attack is $2^{111.44}$ additions and $2^{121.25}$ 37-round encryptions.

5   Conclusion

In this paper, we analyzed the security of Simeck against improved linear hull cryptanalysis with dynamic key-guessing techniques. We searched out better differentials using Kölbl's tool, then got linear hulls for all versions of Simeck. With Chen *et al.*'s Guess, Split, Combine technique to reduce the time complexity in the calculation of empirical correlations, we made the improved linear hull attack on Simeck. As a result, we can attack 23-round Simeck32/64, 30-round Simeck48/96 and 37-round Simeck64/128, which are the best results so far from the point of rounds attacked. The experiments on the bias of the linear hull for Simeck32/64 met our expectation and 48.4 % of the results have a bias higher than we expected. We also implemented the attack on 21-round Simeck32/64, and the success rate is 45.6 % corresponding to our estimated value, which proves our algorithm is effective.

In the future, we will try to search better linear hulls for Simeck using other methods like correlation matrix, Mixed Integer Programming (MIP) and so on. Then we will apply the improved linear hull attack with dynamic key-guessing techniques to other bit-oriented block ciphers.

Acknowledgement. This research was partially supported by the National Natural Science Foundation of China (Grant No. 61133013) and also supported by National Key Basic Research Program of China (Grant No. 2013CB834205).

References

1. Abdelraheem, M.A., Alizadeh, J., Alkhzaimi, H.A., Aref, M.R., Bagheri, N., Gauravaram, P.: Improved linear cryptanalysis of reduced-round simon-32 and simon-48. In: Biryukov, A., Goyal, V. (eds.) Progress in Cryptology-INDOCRYPT 2015. LNCS, pp. 153–179. Springer, Heidelberg (2015)
2. Abdelraheem, M.A., Alizadeh, J., Alkhzaimi, H.A., Aref, M.R., Bagheri, N., Gauravaram, P., Lauridsen, M.M.: Improved linear cryptanalysis of reduced-round simon. Technical report, Cryptology ePrint Archive, Report 2014/681 (2014). http://eprint.iacr.org
3. Abed, F., List, E., Lucks, S., Wenzel, J.: Differential cryptanalysis of round-reduced simon and speck. In: Cid, C., Rechberger, C. (eds.) FSE 2014. LNCS, vol. 8540, pp. 525–545. Springer, Heidelberg (2015)
4. Alizadeh, J., Alkhzaimi, H.A., Aref, M.R., Bagheri, N., Gauravaram, P., Kumar, A., Lauridsen, M.M., Sanadhya, S.K.: Cryptanalysis of SIMON variants with connections. In: Sadeghi, A.-R., Saxena, N. (eds.) RFIDSec 2014. LNCS, vol. 8651, pp. 90–107. Springer, Heidelberg (2014)
5. AlKhzaimi, H., Lauridsen, M.M.: Cryptanalysis of the simon family of block ciphers. IACR Cryptology ePrint Archive, 2013:543 (2013)
6. Ashur, T.: Improved linear trails for the block cipher simon. IACR Cryptology ePrint Archive, 2015:285 (2015)
7. Bagheri, N.: Linear cryptanalysis of reduced-round simeck variants. In: Goyal, V., Biryukov, A. (eds.) Progress in Cryptology-INDOCRYPT 2015. LNCS, pp. 140–152. Springer, Heidelberg (2015)

8. Ray, B., Douglas, S., Jason, S., Stefan, T.-C., Bryan, W., Louis, W.: The simon and speck families of lightweight block ciphers. IACR Cryptology ePrint Archive, 2013:404 (2013)

9. Biryukov, A., Roy, A., Velichkov, V.: Differential analysis of block ciphers SIMON and SPECK. In: Cid, C., Rechberger, C. (eds.) FSE 2014. LNCS, vol. 8540, pp. 546–570. Springer, Heidelberg (2015)

10. Chen, H., Wang, X.: Improved linear hull attack on round-reduced simon with dynamickey-guessing techniques.Technical report, Cryptology ePrint Archive, Report 2015/666, July 2015. http://eprint.iacr.org/2015/666.pdf

11. Kölbl, S., Leander, G., Tiessen, T.: Observations on the simon block cipher family. In: Gennaro, R., Robshaw, M. (eds.) Advances in Cryptology-CRYPTO 2015. LNCS, pp. 161–185. Springer, Heidelberg (2015)

12. Kölbl, S., Roy, A.: A brief comparison of simon and simeck. Technical report, Cryptology ePrint Archive, Report 2015/706 (2015)

13. Matsui, M.: Linear cryptanalysis method for DES cipher. In: Helleseth, T. (ed.) EUROCRYPT 1993. LNCS, vol. 765, pp. 386–397. Springer, Heidelberg (1994)

14. Nyberg, K.: Linear approximation of block ciphers. In: Santis, A. (ed.) EUROCRYPT 1994. LNCS, vol. 950, pp. 439–444. Springer, Heidelberg (1995)

15. Qiao, K., Hu, L., Sun, S.: Differential analysis on simeck and simon with dynamic key-guessing techniques. Cryptology ePrint Archive, Report 2015/902 (2015). http://eprint.iacr.org/

16. Selçuk, A.A., Biçak, A.: On Probability of Success in Linear and Differential Cryptanalysis. In: Cimato, S., Galdi, C., Persiano, G. (eds.) SCN 2002. LNCS, vol. 2576, pp. 174–185. Springer, Heidelberg (2003)

17. Shi, D., Hu, L., Sun, S., Song, L., Qiao, K., Ma, X.: Improved linear (hull) cryptanalysis of round-reduced versions of simon. Technical report, IACR Cryptology ePrint Archive, Report 2014/973 (2014). http://eprint.iacr.org/2014/973

18. Wang, N., Wang, X., Jia, K., Zhao, J.: Differential attacks on reduced simon versions with dynamic key-guessing techniques. Technical report, Cryptology ePrint Archive, Report 2014/448 (2014)

19. Yang, G., Zhu, B., Suder, V., Aagaard, M.D., Gong, G.: The simeck family of lightweight block ciphers. In: Güneysu, T., Handschuh, H. (eds.) CHES 2015. LNCS, vol. 9293, pp. 307–329. Springer, Heidelberg (2015)

20. Zhang, K., Guan, J., Hu, B., Lin, D.: Security evaluation on simeck against zero correlation linear cryptanalysis. Cryptology ePrint Archive, Report 2015/911 (2015). http://eprint.iacr.org/

Short Papers-Public Key
and Identity-Based Encryption

Reducing the Key Size
of the SRP Encryption Scheme

Dung Hoang Duong[1,2(✉)], Albrecht Petzoldt[1], and Tsuyoshi Takagi[1,2]

[1] Institute of Mathematics for Industry, Kyushu University,
744 Motooka, Nishi-ku, Fukuoka 819-0395, Japan
{duong,petzoldt,takagi}@imi.kyushu-u.ac.jp
[2] JST, CREST, 4-1-8 Honcho, Kawaguchi, Saitama 332-0012, Japan

Abstract. Multivariate Public Key Cryptography (MPKC) is one of
the main candidates for secure communication in a post-quantum era.
Recently, Yasuda and Sakurai proposed in [8] a new multivariate encryption scheme called SRP, which is very efficient and resists all known
attacks against multivariate schemes. However, the key sizes of the
scheme are quite large. In this paper we propose a new strategy to reduce
the key size of the SRP scheme, which enables us to reduce the size of the
public key by up to 54 %. Furthermore, we can use the additional structure in the public key polynomials to speed up the encryption process of
the scheme by up to 50 %. We show by experiments that our modifications do not weaken the security of the scheme.

Keywords: Multivariate cryptography · SRP encryption scheme ·
Key size reduction · Efficiency

1 Introduction

Multivariate cryptography is one of the main candidates to guarantee the security of communication in the post-quantum era. Multivariate schemes are in
general very fast and require only modest computational resources, which makes
them attractive for the use on low cost devices like RFIDs or smart cards. While
there exist many practical multivariate *signature* schemes such as UOV, Rainbow
and Gui, the number of candidates for practical multivariate *encryption* schemes
is quite limited. Therefore, the development of secure and efficient multivariate
encryption schemes is an important research topic.

Recently, Yasuda and Sakurai proposed in [8] a new multivariate encryption
scheme called SRP, which is very efficient and resists all known attacks against
multivariate schemes. However, similar to other multivariate schemes, the sizes
of the public and private key of SRP are quite large.

In this paper we propose a technique to reduce the public key size of the
SRP scheme, by which we achieve a reduction of the public key size of SRP by
up to 54 %. Furthermore, the additional structure in the public key polynomials
allows us to speed up the encryption process of the scheme by up to 50 %.

© Springer International Publishing Switzerland 2016
J.K. Liu and R. Steinfeld (Eds.): ACISP 2016, Part II, LNCS 9723, pp. 427–434, 2016.
DOI: 10.1007/978-3-319-40367-0_27

We show by experiments that the security of the SRP scheme is not weakened by our modifications. Our technique is the first approach to reduce the public key size of a multivariate *encryption* scheme.

By our modifications, we obtain a very efficient multivariate encryption scheme. The public key size of the scheme is about 50% smaller than that of other multivariate encryption schemes such as ABC and ZHFE. The encryption process is about twice as fast as that of the other schemes.

Our paper is organized as follows. In Sect. 2, we recall the basic concepts of multivariate public key cryptography and the SRP encryption scheme. Section 3 presents the construction of our CyclicSRP scheme and analyzes the security of our construction. In Sect. 4 we give concrete parameter sets for our scheme and compare it with the standard SRP scheme with regard to key sizes and efficiency of the encryption process. Finally, Sect. 5 concludes the paper.

2   The SRP Encryption Scheme

In this section, we recall the basic SRP scheme of [8]. Before we come to the description of the scheme itself, we start with a short overview of the basic concepts of multivariate cryptography.

2.1   Multivariate Cryptography

The basic objects of multivariate cryptography are systems of multivariate quadratic polynomials over a finite field. The security of multivariate schemes is based on the *MQ Problem* of solving such a system, which has been proven to be NP-Hard.

To build a multivariate public key cryptosystem (MPKC), one starts with an easily invertible quadratic map $\mathcal{F} : \mathbb{F}^n \to \mathbb{F}^m$ (*central map*). To hide the structure of $\mathcal{F}$ in the public key, we compose it with two invertible affine (or linear) maps $\mathcal{S} : \mathbb{F}^m \to \mathbb{F}^m$ and $\mathcal{T} : \mathbb{F}^n \to \mathbb{F}^n$. The *public key* of the scheme is therefore given by $\mathcal{P} = \mathcal{S} \circ \mathcal{F} \circ \mathcal{T} : \mathbb{F}^n \to \mathbb{F}^m$. The *private key* consists of the three maps $\mathcal{S}, \mathcal{F}$ and $\mathcal{T}$ and therefore allows to invert the public key. To *encrypt* a message $M \in \mathbb{F}^n$, one simply computes $C = \mathcal{P}(M) \in \mathbb{F}^m$. To *decrypt* a ciphertext $C \in \mathbb{F}^m$, one computes recursively $\mathbf{x} = \mathcal{S}^{-1}(C) \in \mathbb{F}^m$, $\mathbf{y} = \mathcal{F}^{-1}(\mathbf{x}) \in \mathbb{F}^n$ and $M = \mathcal{T}^{-1}(\mathbf{y})$. $M \in \mathbb{F}^n$ is the plaintext corresponding to the ciphertext C.

2.2   SRP

The SRP encryption scheme was proposed by Yasuda and Sakurai in [8] by combining the Square encryption scheme [3], the Rainbow signature scheme [5] and the Plus method [4]. By combining Square and Rainbow to one scheme, several attacks against the single schemes are not longer applicable. Furthermore, since both Square and Rainbow are very efficient, the same holds for the SRP scheme.

Let $\mathbb{F}$ be a finite field with q elements ($q \equiv 3 \bmod 4$), $\mathbb{E}$ be a degree d extension field of $\mathbb{F}$ (d odd), and ϕ be an isomorphism between the field $\mathbb{E}$ and the vector space $\mathbb{F}^d$. Moreover, let o, r, s and l be non-negative integers.

Key Generation. Let $n = d + o - l$, $n' = d + o$ and $m = d + o + r + s$. The *central map* $\mathcal{F} : \mathbb{F}^{n'} \to \mathbb{F}^m$ of the scheme is the concatenation of three maps $\mathcal{F}_S$, $\mathcal{F}_R$, and $\mathcal{F}_P$. These maps are defined as follows.

(i) The Square part $\mathcal{F}_S : \mathbb{F}^{n'} \to \mathbb{F}^d$ is the composition of the maps

$$\mathbb{F}^{d+o} \xrightarrow{\pi_d} \mathbb{F}^d \xrightarrow{\phi^{-1}} \mathbb{E} \xrightarrow{X \mapsto X^2} \mathbb{E} \xrightarrow{\phi} \mathbb{F}^d.$$

Here $\pi_d : \mathbb{F}^{d+o} \to \mathbb{F}^d$ is the projection to the first d coordinates.

(ii) The UOV (Rainbow) part $\mathcal{F}_R = (f^{(1)}, \ldots, f^{(o+r)}) : \mathbb{F}^{n'} \to \mathbb{F}^{o+r}$ is constructed as for the usual UOV signature scheme: let $V = \{1, \ldots, d\}$ and $O = \{d+1, \ldots, d+o\}$. For every $k \in \{1, \ldots, o+r\}$, the quadratic polynomial $f^{(k)}$ is of the form

$$f^{(k)}(x_1, \ldots, x_{n'}) = \sum_{i \in O, j \in V} \alpha_{i,j}^{(k)} x_i x_j + \sum_{i,j \in V, i \leq j} \beta_{i,j}^{(k)} x_i x_j + \sum_{i \in V \cup O} \gamma_i^{(k)} x_i + \eta^{(k)},$$

where $\alpha_{i,j}^{(k)}, \beta_{i,j}^{(k)}, \gamma_i^{(k)}, \eta^{(k)}$ are randomly chosen $\mathbb{F}$-elements.

(iii) The Plus part $\mathcal{F}_P = (g^{(1)}, \ldots, g^{(s)}) : \mathbb{F}^{n'} \to \mathbb{F}^s$ consists of s randomly chosen quadratic polynomials $g^{(1)}, \ldots, g^{(s)}$.

We additionally choose an affine embedding $\mathcal{T} : \mathbb{F}^n \hookrightarrow \mathbb{F}^{n'}$ of full rank and an affine isomorphism $\mathcal{S} : \mathbb{F}^m \to \mathbb{F}^m$. The *public key* is given by $\mathcal{P} = \mathcal{S} \circ \mathcal{F} \circ \mathcal{T} : \mathbb{F}^n \to \mathbb{F}^m$ and the *private key* consists of $\mathcal{S}, \mathcal{F}$ and $\mathcal{T}$.

Encryption: Given a message $M \in \mathbb{F}^n$, the ciphertext C is computed as $C = \mathcal{P}(M) \in \mathbb{F}^m$.

Decryption: Given a ciphertext $C \in \mathbb{F}^m$, the decryption is executed as follows.

(1) Compute $\mathbf{x} = (x_1, \ldots, x_m) = \mathcal{S}^{-1}(C)$ and $X = \phi^{-1}(x_1, \ldots, x_d)$.
(2) Compute $R_{1,2} = \pm X^{(q^d+1)/4}$ and set $\mathbf{y}^{(i)} = (y_1^{(i)}, \ldots, y_d^{(i)}) = \phi(R_i)$ $(i = 1, 2)$.
(3) Given the vinegar values $y_1^{(i)}, \ldots, y_d^{(i)}$ $(i = 1, 2)$, solve the two systems of $o + r$ linear equations in $n' - d = o$ variables $u_{d+1}, \ldots, u_{n'}$ given by

$$f^{(k)}(y_1^{(i)}, \ldots, y_d^{(i)}, u_{d+1}, \cdots, u_{n'}) = x_{d+k} \quad (i = 1, 2)$$

for $k = 1, \cdots, o + r$. The solution is denoted by $(y_{d+1}, \cdots, y_{n'})$.[1]
(4) Compute the plaintext $M \in \mathbb{F}^n$ by finding the pre-image of $(y_1, \cdots, y_{n'})$ under the affine embedding $\mathcal{T}$.

Note that the only part of the central map needed for decryption are the coefficients of the Rainbow polynomials $f^{(1)}, \ldots, f^{(o+r)}$.

In the following, we restrict to a homogeneous quadratic map $\mathcal{F}$ as well as to linear maps $\mathcal{S}$ and $\mathcal{T}$. Therefore, the public key $\mathcal{P}$ of the scheme will be a homogeneous quadratic system, too. The number of terms in each component of the public key is given by $\frac{n \cdot (n+1)}{2} =: D$.

---

[1] By increasing r, the probability of both $(y_1^{(1)}, \ldots, y_d^{(1)})$ and $(y_1^{(2)}, \ldots, y_d^{(2)})$ leading to a solution of the linear system can be reduced arbitrarily.

3   Our Improved Scheme

In this section, we present our technique to generate a key pair for SRP with a structured public key. In particular we are able to construct a public key of the form shown in Fig. 1.

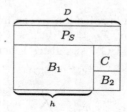

Fig. 1. Structure of the public key $\mathcal{P}$

Here, the matrices $B_1 \in \mathbb{F}^{(m-d) \times h}$ and $B_2 \in \mathbb{F}^{s \times (D-h)}$ can be arbitrarily chosen by the user, and the parameter h is given by $h = \frac{d \cdot (d+1)}{2} + d \cdot (o - l)$.

In the following, we choose the matrices B_1 and B_2 in a "cyclic" way. In particular, we choose two random vectors $\mathbf{b}_1 \in \mathbb{F}^h$ and $\mathbf{b}_2 \in \mathbb{F}^{D-h}$. The first row of the matrix B_1 is just the vector $\mathbf{b}_1$, while the i-th row of B_1 corresponds to a cyclic right shift of the vector $\mathbf{b}_1$ by $i - 1$ positions ($i = 2, \ldots, m - d$). Analogously, the first row of the matrix B_2 corresponds to the vector $\mathbf{b}_2$ and the i-th row of this matrix is the cyclic right shift of $\mathbf{b}_2$ by $i - 1$ positions.

By choosing the matrices B_1 and B_2 in this way, we have to store only the two vectors $\mathbf{b}_1$ and $\mathbf{b}_2$ in order to recover the matrices B_1 and B_2. Therefore, the public key size of the scheme is reduced significantly (see Sect. 4). Furthermore, we can use the structure in the matrices B_1 and B_2 to speed up the encryption process of the scheme. The resulting scheme is called CyclicSRP.

3.1   Notations

Let $\mathcal{Q} = \mathcal{F} \circ \mathcal{T}$. For the maps $\mathcal{F}, \mathcal{Q}$ and $\mathcal{P}$ we denote the coefficients of the monomial $x_i \cdot x_j$ in the k-th component of the maps by $f_{ij}^{(k)}$, $q_{ij}^{(k)}$ and $p_{ij}^{(k)}$ respectively. We write these coefficients down into matrices F, Q and P and divide these matrices into submatrices as shown in Fig. 2.

Furthermore, let $S = (s_{ij})_{1 \leq i \leq m}^{1 \leq j \leq m}$ and $T = (t_{ij})_{1 \leq i \leq n'}^{1 \leq j \leq n}$ be the matrix representations of the linear maps $\mathcal{S}$ and $\mathcal{T}$ respectively.

Additionally, we define $Q_S = (Q_{Sh} \| Q_S') \in \mathbb{F}^{d \times D}$ and $Q_{RPh} = \begin{pmatrix} Q_{Rh} \\ Q_{Ph} \end{pmatrix} \in$
$\mathbb{F}^{(o+r+s) \times h}$.

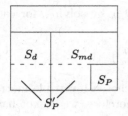
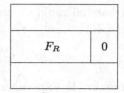

Q_{Sh}	Q'_S
Q_{Rh}	Q'_R
Q_{Ph}	Q'_P

| F_R | 0 |

Fig. 2. Layout of the matrices S, Q and F

3.2 Construction

After fixing the matrices S, T, B_1 and B_2, the entries of the matrix Q_S (i.e. the coefficients of the map Q referring to the Square part of SRP) are determined by the equation

$$Q_S(\mathbf{x}) = \phi\left((\phi^{-1} \circ \pi_d \circ \mathcal{T}(\mathbf{x}))^2\right) = (q^{(1)}(\mathbf{x}), \ldots, q^{(d)}(\mathbf{x})). \qquad (1)$$

From $\mathcal{P} = \mathcal{S} \circ \mathcal{Q}$ it follows directly that $P = S \cdot Q$. Therefore we obtain $B_1 = S_d \cdot Q_{Sh} + S_{md} \cdot Q_{RPh}$ which, under the assumption of S_{md} being invertible, yields

$$Q_{RPh} = S_{md}^{-1} \cdot (B_1 - S_d \cdot Q_{Sh}). \qquad (2)$$

Furthermore, from $\mathcal{Q} = \mathcal{F} \circ \mathcal{T}$ we obtain the relation

$$q_{ij}^{(k)} = \sum_{r=1}^{n'} \sum_{s=r}^{n'} \alpha_{ij}^{rs} f_{rs}^{(k)} \quad (1 \leq i \leq j \leq n) \qquad (3)$$

for each $k = 1, \ldots, m$, where

$$\alpha_{ij}^{rs} = \begin{cases} t_{ri} t_{si} & \text{if } i = j \\ t_{ri} t_{sj} + t_{rj} t_{si} & \text{otherwise.} \end{cases}$$

We consider the $m - d - s = o + r$ equations from (3) for $k = d+1, \ldots, m-s$; those correspond to the UOV part of SRP. Due to the special structure of the UOV polynomials, we have

$$q_{ij}^{(k)} = \sum_{r=1}^{d} \sum_{s=r}^{n'} \alpha_{ij}^{rs} f_{rs}^{(k)} \quad (1 \leq i \leq j \leq n, \; d+1 \leq k \leq m-s). \qquad (4)$$

Let A be the $(d(d+1)/2 + od) \times h$ matrix containing the coefficients α_{ij}^{rs} of Eq. (4) for $1 \leq r \leq d, r \leq s \leq n'$ for the rows and $1 \leq i \leq d, i \leq j \leq n$ for the columns. With this notation, Eq. (4) yields

$$Q_{Rh} = F_R \cdot A. \qquad (5)$$

If A has full rank, we therefore can recover F_R from Q_{Rh} by solving, for each $k \in \{d+1, \ldots, m-s\}$, a linear system of the form

$$(q_{11}^{(k)}, q_{12}^{(k)}, \ldots, q_{dn}^{(k)}) = (f_{11}^{(k)}, f_{12}^{(k)}, \ldots, f_{dn'}^{(k)}) \cdot A. \tag{6}$$

Remark: (1) Experiments show that, for a randomly chosen invertible matrix T, the probability of A having rank h is quite high. Therefore, we do not have to test many matrices T to find a matrix A of full rank.

(2) The linear systems in Eq. (6) have multiple solutions. We just randomly choose one of these solutions and put it into the matrix F_R.

Having recovered the coefficients of the Rainbow central map, we can easily compute the elements of the matrix Q_R' by using the relation $\mathcal{Q} = \mathcal{F} \circ \mathcal{T}$.

The last submatrix of Q still unknown is now Q_P'. Under the assumption of S_P being invertible we can recover it by

$$Q_P' = S_P^{-1} \cdot \left(B_2 - S_P' \cdot \begin{pmatrix} Q_S' \\ Q_R' \end{pmatrix} \right). \tag{7}$$

Having therefore recovered the whole matrix Q, it is easy to compute the coefficient matrix of the public key by

$$P = S \cdot Q. \tag{8}$$

Note that the so computed matrix P will have the structure shown in Fig. 1.

We publish P as the *public key* of our scheme, while the *private key* consists of S, T and F_R. Algorithm 1 shows this key generation process in compact form.

Algorithm 1. Key Generation of CyclicSRP

Input: SRP parameters q, d, o, r, s, l, matrices $B_1 \in \mathbb{F}^{(m-d) \times h}$ and $B_2 \in \mathbb{F}^{s \times (D-h)}$.
Output: SRP key pair $((S, F_R, T), P)$ with P of the form of Figure 1.

1: Choose an invertible matrix $S \in \mathbb{F}^{m \times m}$ such that the submatrices $S_{md} \in \mathbb{F}^{(m-s) \times (m-s)}$ and $S_p \in \mathbb{F}^{s \times s}$ are invertible.
2: Choose a full rank matrix $T \in \mathbb{F}^{n' \times n}$ such that the matrix A has full rank.
3: Compute Q_S by equation (1).
4: Compute Q_{RPh} by equation (2).
5: Compute F_R by solving the linear systems of equation (6).
6: Compute Q_R using the relation $\mathcal{Q} = \mathcal{F} \circ \mathcal{T}$.
7: Compute Q_P' by equation (7).
8: Compute $P = S \cdot Q$.
9: **return** $((S, F_R, T), P)$

3.3   Security

The security analysis of our scheme runs in the same way as for the standard SRP scheme of [8]. We therefore refer to [8] regarding an analysis of our scheme against structural attacks [1,6], and only cover here direct attacks [4].

Direct Attacks. The direct attack tries to recover the plaintext M by solving the public system $\mathcal{P}(M) = C$ as an instance of the MQ Problem using an algorithm like XL or a Gröbner Basis method.

To study the security of the CyclicSRP scheme against direct attacks, we carried out a large number of experiments with MAGMA, which contains an efficient implementation of Faugéres F_4-algorithm for computing Gröbner Bases. Table 1 shows the results of our experiments against random systems, the SRP scheme and our scheme.

Table 1. Results of experiments with direct attacks

Parameters		CyclicSRP		SRP		Random system	
q, d, o, r, s, l	m, n	d_{reg}	time (s)	d_{reg}	time (s)	d_{reg}	time (s)
$31, 11, 10, 5, 4, 6$	$30, 15$	4	3.2	4	3.2	4	3.2
$31, 11, 10, 5, 4, 4$	$30, 17$	5	91.8	5	92.7	5	94.0
$31, 11, 10, 5, 4, 2$	$30, 19$	6	4,646	6	4,650	6	5,785

As the table shows, the F_4 algorithm can not solve our systems significantly faster than those of the standard SRP scheme.

4 Results

In this section we compare our scheme with the standard SRP scheme of [8]. We use the three parameter sets proposed in [8], i.e.

(A) $(q, d, o, r, s, l) = (31, 33, 32, 16, 5, 16)$ providing 80 bit of security

(B) $(q, d, o, r, s, l) = (31, 47, 47, 22, 5, 22)$ providing 112 bit of security and

(C) $(q, d, o, r, s, l) = (31, 71, 71, 32, 5, 32)$ proving a security level of 160 bit.

Table 2. Comparison between SRP and CyclicSRP regarding key sizes and efficiency of the encryption process

		(A)	(B)	(C)
Parameters	q, d, o, r, s, l	$31, 33, 32, 16, 5, 16$	$31, 47, 47, 22, 5, 22$	$31, 71, 71, 32, 5, 32$
	m, n	$86, 49$	$121, 72$	$179, 110$
Public key size	Standard SRP	$105, 350$	$317, 988$	$1, 092, 795$
	CyclicSRP	$48, 178$	$148, 569$	519.900
	Reduction	54.3%	53.3%	52.4%
# field mult.	Standard SRP	106,575	320,616	1,098,900
during	CyclicSRP	54,068	160,587	546,875
encryption	Reduction	49.3%	49.9%	50.2%

Table 2 gives a comparison between the standard SRP scheme and our scheme with regard to the public key size.

Additionally to the key size reduction, we can use the structure in the public key of CyclicSRP to reduce the number of multiplications needed in the encryption process significantly. However, due to lack of space, we can not describe the details of this technique here (see the extended version of this paper [2]) and just present the results (see Table 2).

5   Conclusion

In this paper we investigated the recent multivariate encryption scheme SRP [8] which is a good candidate for post-quantum encryption schemes. We proposed a technique to reduce the public key size of this scheme. The resulting scheme, CyclicSRP, reduces the size of the public key by up to 54 % and the number of field multiplications needed during the encryption process by 50 %. By our technique we therefore help to solve one of the biggest problems of multivariate schemes, namely the large size of the public keys. To our knowledge, our proposal is the first application of such a technique to a multivariate encryption scheme.

Acknowledgements. This research is supported by JSPS KAKENHI no. 15F15350 and 16K17644.

References

1. Billet, O., Gilbert, H.: Cryptanalysis of rainbow. In: De Prisco, R., Yung, M. (eds.) SCN 2006. LNCS, vol. 4116, pp. 336–347. Springer, Heidelberg (2006)
2. Duong, D.H., Petzoldt, A., Takagi, T.: Reducing the Key Size of the SRP Encryption Scheme - Extended Version. IACR eprint, https://eprint.iacr.org/2016/383.pdf
3. Clough, C., Baena, J., Ding, J., Yang, B.Y., Chen, M.S.: Square, a new multivariate encryption scheme. In: Fischlin, M. (ed.) CT-RSA 2009. LNCS, vol. 5473, pp. 252–264. Springer, Heidelberg (2009)
4. Ding, J., Gower, J.E., Schmidt, D.S.: Multivariate Public Key Cryptosystems. Advances in Information Security, vol. 25. Springer US, New York (2006)
5. Ding, J., Schmidt, D.: Rainbow, a new multivariable polynomial signature scheme. In: Ioannidis, J., Keromytis, A.D., Yung, M. (eds.) ACNS 2005. LNCS, vol. 3531, pp. 164–175. Springer, Heidelberg (2005)
6. Ding, J., Yang, B.Y., Chen, C.H.O., Chen, M.S., Cheng, C.M.: New differential-algebraic attacks and reparametrization of rainbow. In: Bellovin, S.M., Gennaro, R., Keromytis, A.D., Yung, M. (eds.) ACNS 2008. LNCS, vol. 5037, pp. 242–257. Springer, Heidelberg (2008)
7. Petzoldt, A., Bulygin, S., Buchmann, J.: CyclicRainbow – a multivariate signature scheme with a partially cyclic public key. In: Gong, G., Gupta, K.C. (eds.) INDOCRYPT 2010. LNCS, vol. 6498, pp. 33–48. Springer, Heidelberg (2010)
8. Yasuda, T., Sakurai, K.: A multivariate encryption scheme with rainbow. In: Qing, S., et al. (eds.) ICICS 2015. LNCS, vol. 9543, pp. 236–251. Springer, Heidelberg (2016). doi:10.1007/978-3-319-29814-6_19

Short Papers-Biometric Security

Biometric Access Control with High Dimensional Facial Features

Ying Han Pang[✉], Ean Yee Khor, and Shih Yin Ooi

Faculty of Information Science and Technology, Multimedia University,
Cyberjaya, Malaysia
{yhpang,syooi}@mmu.edu.my, eanyeekhor@gmail.com

Abstract. Access control is vital to prevent adversary from stealing resources from data centres. The security of traditional authentication means, such as password and Personal Identification Number (PIN), are imperfect for access control. In this paper, a reliable facial biometric access control with promising authentication performance is proposed. In our study, facial feature representation is computed based on ICA modelling, descriptor binarization, bitwise operation on the bit maps and effective compression via whitening PCA. The proposed technique is namely Binarized Independent Component Pattern (BICP). BICP training module integrates ICA methodology to construct ICA filter bank from natural image patches. Each face image is convoluted with the filters for the corresponding ICA responses. The ICA responses are further processed via feature binarization, and XOR bitwise operation before convert to code map. Next, block-wise histogramming is applied on each code map. By concatenating the regional histograms, it produces a set of high dimensional BICP descriptor, which will be further scaled and compressed. Empirical results show the remarkable performance of BICP on facial expression, illumination, time span and facial makeup effects.

Keywords: Access control · Face biometric · ICA filters · XOR operation · Binary pattern

1 Introduction

Access control is an absolute necessity to prevent adversary to view and exploit resources in a computing environment. The widely used authentication means for access control are Personal Identification Number and passwords. These knowledge-based authentication systems are sub-reliable, considering their vulnerability of getting stolen or cracked. In the recent decade, biometrics has gradually overtaken these methods due to its high accuracy and reliability. Biometric-based access control systems include but not limited to palm vein recognition system proposed by Sonal et al. [1], finger knuckle print recognition proposed by Zhang et al. [2], multimodal biometric identification system which combining palm veins and palm print proposed by Wang et al. [3] and facial biometric access control system that to be implemented by HSBC [4].

© Springer International Publishing Switzerland 2016
J.K. Liu and R. Steinfeld (Eds.): ACISP 2016, Part II, LNCS 9723, pp. 437–445, 2016.
DOI: 10.1007/978-3-319-40367-0_28

HSBC rolls out facial recognition technology at its data centres to protect sensitive information [4]. The fond of a facial biometric solution is due to its wide public acceptance and its inheritably non-intrusive nature. There are four modules in the face recognition methodology, namely: (1) face detection, (2) preprocessing, (3) feature representation, and (4) classification. During the phase of face detection, facial region is detected and extracted. The image quality is enhanced by minimizing the induced noise, adjusting the placement and orientation of the facial region for rotational and translational invariance, and normalizing the image intensity in the preprocessing step. Feature representation module extracts the dominant information from the previously preprocessed data, and also to discard the redundant data. Lastly, the computed feature representation is evaluated by matching it with the stored feature templates. Feature representation learning is essential for promising performance. Hence, numerous researchers have putted forth major efforts on this area.

Recent literatures demonstrate the great potential of high dimensional feature representations in object recognition context. Chen et al. [5] made evident the ever-increasing recognition accuracy along the feature dimensionality in Local Binary Pattern (LBP) [6], Scale Invariant Feature Transform (SIFT) [7], Histograms of Oriented Gradients (HOG) [8], Gabor [9] and Learning-based Descriptor (LE) [10]. Hussain et al. proposed a new high dimensional face representation based on Local Quantized Patterns (LQP) [11]. LQP is a generalization of local pattern features that adopts vector quantization and lookup table for more pixels and quantization levels in local pattern features. Furthermore, Barkan et al. is another group of researchers that utilizes high dimensional feature for face representation [12]. In their proposed technique, the calculation of LBP histograms is performed block-wise. To be specific, face images are segmented into multiple overlapping blocks. Then, the histograms of all the segmented blocks are computed and concatenated to form the final descriptor.

Kannala and Rahtu proposed a learning technique by encoding a binary code for each pixel through thresholding the outputs of the linear projection of local image patches onto an independent component subspace [13]. The basis vectors in the subspace are learnt via Independent Component Analysis (ICA) from natural image resemble. Empirical results demonstrate the superiority of the proposed Binarized Statistical Image Features (BSIF) in texture classification and face recognition. Ylioinas et al. improved BSIF for application specific learning. Filters are learnt from different face regions based on training face image patches [14]. Besides, a simple matrix-vector production is introduced to smooth each region histogram.

2   Motivations and Contributions

The independent component model is one of the most ecologically inspired models for understanding image representation in the array of simple cells in the human primary cortex [15]. Hence, the contribution of independent component methodology in image understanding is being notarized [13, 14]. In addition, binary feature descriptor is preferable for the sake of memory efficiency, speedy computation and local variation robustness [16]. The instances of binary code learners are works of [17, 18].

In this paper, we propose a high dimensional face representation, coined as Binarized Independent Component Pattern (BICP). It is a hybrid model of ICA model, feature binarization and bitwise operation. The major contributions of this work includes:

1. A high dimensional face representation by exploiting ICA filters. In conjunction with ICA characteristics, the face representation carries features that are similar to the pattern of the human primary visual [15]. This feature could assure the performance of BICP in face recognition at a certain level.
2. BICP consolidates ICA response invariance through feature binarizing, XOR bitwise operation, block-wise histogramming and descriptor regularization. These processes allow nonlinear operation in BICP which boosts the discriminating capability. Besides, the histogramming tenders certain degree of translation invariance in the features, and feature regularization suppresses those numerically dominating entries caused by the zero padding in the block-wise histogramming, particularly at the cell boundaries padded with zero.
3. Extensive experimental results are presented to study the performance of BICP in face recognition under various scenarios such as variations in facial expression, illumination, time span as well as facial makeup effect.

3   Binarized Independent Component Pattern

Figure 1 illustrates the framework of BICP. BICP training module integrates ICA methodology for generating ICA filters from natural image patches. Then, each face image is convoluted with the ICA filters to construct the corresponding ICA responses. The ICA responses, as well as their mean μ, will be further processed via feature binarization, XOR operation and conversion to code map. Next, block-wise histogramming is performed on each code map that corresponds to each face image. Concatenating the regional histograms produces high dimensional BICP learned face representation. Lastly, the representation is scaled using a signed square root normalization and compressed via WPCA for better discriminating capability.

3.1   Constructing ICA Responses

The same ICA filters learnt from 13 natural images shared by authors of [19] is adopted. ICA filters are in different filter sizes $l \times l$. Each filter set is learnt using 50,000 image patches. The procedure of ICA filter learning is as follows: (1) subtraction of patch intensity mean, (2) dimension reduction and whitening via PCA, and (3) independent component estimation. Figure 2 illustrates some samples of filters with 7×7 size and number of filters, $b = 3$.

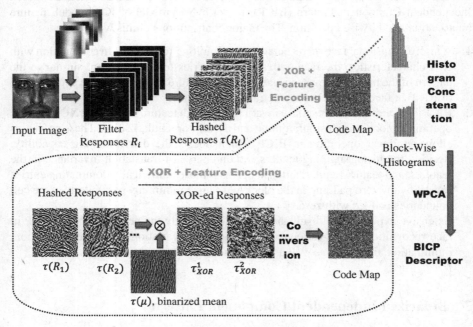

ICA Filter Bank

Input Image | Filter Responses R_i | Hashed Responses $\tau(R_i)$ | Code Map | Block-Wise Histograms

* XOR + Feature Encoding

Histo gram Conc atena tion

WPCA

BICP Descriptor

Fig. 1. BICP Framework

Fig. 2. Samples of ICA Filters with 7×7 size and $b = 3$

Given an image I_j of size $w \times h$ and ICA filter $W_i \in \mathbb{R}^{l \times l}$, ICA response R_i^j is,

$$R_i^j = \{I_j * W_i\}, \quad i = 1, \ldots, b \text{ and } j = 1, \ldots, N \tag{1}$$

where * is convolution, N is the total images and b is the total filters.

3.2   Binarizing ICA Responses and XOR Bitwise Operation

There are b ICA responses R_i where $i = 1, .., b$ for each image since there are b number of ICA filters. ICA response mean is generated, i.e. $\mu = \frac{1}{b} \sum_{i=1}^{b} R_i$, then further binarized,

i.e. $\tau(\mu) = \begin{cases} 1 & if \, \mu > 0 \\ 0 & otherwise \end{cases}$.

Each response is binarized via $\tau(R_i) = \begin{cases} 1 & if R_i > \mu \\ 0 & otherwise \end{cases}$ to obtain binary pattern. Next, XOR operation is performed on the binarized ICA patterns and response mean $\tau(\mu)$. After that, the resulting XOR-ed patterns are considered in the binary to decimal value conversion to generate code map via $\sum_{i=1}^{b} \tau_{XOR}^i \times 2^{i-1}$.

3.3 BICP Descriptor

In this step, blockwise histogramming is performed. In details, each of the code map is segmented into B non-overlapping blocks. Histogram of each block is computed and concatenated to construct a final descriptor. It is worth noting that the generated descriptor is in high dimension. Hence, a compression is needed for computation efficiency. Prior to WPCA compression, the descriptor is regulated via a signed square root normalization operation.

4   Experimental Results and Discussions

In this study, facial biometric authentication under various scenarios is considered for performance evaluation. These include facial expression variation, illumination variation, time span between the gallery and probe data as well as facial makeup effect. Moreover, some state of the art learning techniques, including but not limited to LBP [6], HOG [8], Gabor [9], LQP [11], BSIF [13], LGBPHS [20], DLBP [21] and DFD [22], are considered for benchmarking. Here, we consider face identification mode. In other word, rank-1 identification rate is measured as performance metric. As in [23], face images are preprocessed accordingly for illumination normalization [24]. In the experiments, the size of block-wise histogram is set to 13×13 and the WPCA transform is computed using all the gallery data. Nearest neighbour classifier with cosine distance metric is adopted in the experiments.

4.1 Performance on Facial Expression, Illumination and Time Span Effects

We employ FERET database for the facial expression variation, illumination variation and time span effect. FERET subset *fa*, containing 1196 images with regular facial expression from 1196 subjects, is used as gallery data. For probes, FERET subsets: (1) *fb* containing 1195 images with varying facial expressions, (2) *fc* containing 194 images with varying illuminations, (3) *dup1* containing 722 images taken between one minute and 1031 days after their respective gallery matches and *dup2* containing 234 images taken at least 18 months after their gallery entries, are used to study the effects of facial expression variation, illumination variation and time span effect respectively. All face images in the gallery, which are 1196 images, are used to compute 1195-dimensional WPCA transform.

Table 1 records the face identification performance on the effects of facial expression (*fb*), illumination (*fc*) and time span between gallery and probe data (*dup1* and *dup2*) of BICP compared with other popular face learning techniques. BICP achieves state of the art accuracy in *fb* and *fc* subsets. This indicates that BICP is able to extract discriminative clues for face authentication. In conjunction with a simple model of simple cells in the human primary cortex (i.e. ICA filters), XOR operation, signed square root based histogram normalization and WPCA, BICP demonstrates its superiority to face appearance variations, especially to aging effect. BICP could even sustain its performance to face images taken at least one and a half years apart.

Table 1. Performance to the effects of facial expression, illumination and time span

Techniques	Rank-1 Rate (%)				
	fb	*fc*	*dup1*	*dup2*	*mean*
LBP [a] [6]	97	79	66	64	76.5
LQP[a] [11]	99.2	69.6	65.8	48.3	70.7
BSIF[a] [13]	97.9	100	84.3	82.9	91.3
LGBPHS[a] [20]	98	97	74	71	85
DLBP[a] [21]	99	99	86	85	92.25
DFD[a] [22]	99.2	98.5	85	82.9	91.4
POEM[a] [25]	97.6	95	77.6	76.2	86.6
LQP+WPCA[a] [11]	99.8	94.3	85.5	78.6	89.55
POEM+WPCA[a] [25]	99.6	99.5	88.8	85	93.3
BSIF+WPCA[b]	98.91	100	91.83	90.6	95.33
BICP	**99.16**	**100**	**93.49**	**92.31**	**96.24**

[a]The experimental results are extracted from the original papers.
[b]Re-implemented based on the optimal parameters, with illumination normalization [24]

4.2 Performance on Facial Makeup Effect

Facial makeup is a socially acceptable approach that could make a woman appears more attractive and boosts her sense of confidence. Evidently, facial makeup alters the perceived shape and texture of a face [26, 27]. Dantcheva et al. highlights the severe negative impact of facial makeup towards the recognition performance of the existing face matching methods [26, 28]. Hence, recently a group of researchers is endeavouring for best solutions to address the issue of facial makeup [27, 29]. In this section, we study the performance of BICP in facial makeup effect.

Youtube Makeup (YMU) database is adopted to study the facial makeup effect. YMU is a publicly available makeup face repository. There are 151 Caucasian female subjects in this database. Each subject consists of two (2) non-makeup images and two (2) makeup images, resulting total of 604 face images. Two testing protocols are experimented in this paper: non-makeup (NM) versus makeup (M) and makeup (M) versus non-makeup (NM) matchings. In the first protocol, NM set is used as gallery data and M set as probes; and vice versa in the second protocol. All face images in the gallery are used to compute 301-dimensional WPCA transform.

From Table 2, it is observed that BICP contributes a performance advantage as observed in YMU experiments in both NM versus M and M versus NM matchings. To conclude, despite achieving notable performance from facial biometric access control authentication with facial expression variation, illumination variation and time span, the proposed BICP also endorses its discriminating capability in the facial makeup effect.

Table 2. Performance to the effects of makeup

Techniques	Rank-1 Rate (%)		
	NM versus M	M versus NM	Mean
LBP[c] [6]	54.64	54.97	54.81
HOG[c] [8]	48.34	42.38	45.36
Gabor[c] [9]	38.74	34.11	36.43
LGBP[c] [20]	42.05	38.04	40.05
BSIF+WPCA[c]	69.54	72.19	70.87
BICP	**76.82**	**75.83**	**76.32**

[c]Re-implemented based on the optimal parameters, with illumination normalization [24]

5 Conclusion

This paper presents a facial biometric access control system by using a high dimensional face representation by exploiting ICA filters. The technique is dubbed as Binarized Independent Component Pattern (BICP). In conjunction with ICA characteristics, the proposed face representation carries features that are similar to the pattern of the human primary visual. This feature guarantees the performance of BICP in face recognition at a certain level. Besides, BICP consolidates ICA response invariance through feature binarization, XOR bitwise operation, block-wise histogramming and descriptor regularization. Empirical results show the remarkable performance of BICP on facial expression, illumination, time span and facial makeup effects.

References

1. Sonal, S.A., Dhiraj, P., Pallavi, D., Yogesh, H.D.: Hardware implementation of palm vein biometric modality for access control in multilayered security system. In: Second International Symposium on Computer Vision and the Internet, pp. 492–498 (2015)
2. Zhang, L., Zhang, L., Zhang, D., Guo, Z.: Phase congruency induced local features for finger-knuckle-print recognition. ELSEVIERScienceDirect Pattern Recogn. **45**, 2522–2531 (2012)
3. Wang, J.G., Yau, W.Y., Suwandy, A., Sung, E.: Person recognition by fusing palmprint and palm vein images based on "Laplacianpalm" representation. ELSEVIER-ScienceDirect Pattern Recogn. **41**, 1514–1527 (2008)
4. Karl, F.: HSBC uses biometrix to protect data. Infosecurity **5**(8), 9 (2008)
5. Chen, D., Cao, X., Wen, F., Sun, J.: Blessing of dimensionality: high-dimensional feature and its efficient compression for face verification. In: 2013 IEEE Conference on Computer Vision and Pattern Recognition (CVPR), pp. 3025–3032 (2013)
6. Ahonen, T., Hadid, A., Pietikainen, M.: Face description with local binary patterns: application to face recognition. IEEE Trans. Pattern Anal. Mach. Intell. **28**(12), 2037–2041 (2006)

7. Bicego, M., Lagorio, A., Grosso, E., Tistarelli, M.: On the use of SIFT features for face authentication. In: Conference on Computer Vision and Pattern Recognition Workshop, CVPRW 2006, p. 35 (2006)
8. Déniz, O., Bueno, G., Salido, J., De la Torre, F.: Face recognition using histograms of oriented gradients. Pattern Recogn. Lett. **32**(12), 1598–1603 (2011)
9. Shen, L., Bai, L.: A review on Gabor wavelets for face recognition. J. Pattern Anal. Appl. **9**(2–3), 273–292 (2006)
10. Cao, Z., Yin, Q., Tang, X., Sun, J.: Face recognition with learning-based descriptor. In: IEEE Conference on Computer Vision and Pattern Recognition (CVPR), pp. 2707–2714 (2010)
11. Hussain, S.U., Napoléon, T., Jurie, F.: Face recognition using local quantized patterns. In: British Machive Vision Conference, 11 p. (2012)
12. Barkan, O., Weill, J., Wolf, L., Aronowitz, H.: Fast high dimensional vector multiplication face recognition. In: IEEE International Conference on Computer Vision (ICCV), pp. 1960–1967 (2013)
13. Kannala, J., Rahtu, E.: Bsif: Binarized statistical image features. In: 21st International Conference on Pattern Recognition (ICPR), pp. 1363–1366 (2012)
14. Ylioinas, J., Kannala, J., Hadid, A., Pietikäinen, M.: Face recognition using smoothed high-dimensional representation. In: Paulsen, R.R., Pedersen, K.S. (eds.) SCIA 2015. LNCS, vol. 9127, pp. 516–529. Springer, Heidelberg (2015)
15. van Hateren, J.H., van der Schaaf, A.: Independent component filters of natural images compared with simple cells in primary visual cortex. Proc. Royal Soc. London B: Biol. Sci. **265**(1394), 359–366 (1998)
16. Lu, J., Liong, V.E., Zhou, X., Zhou, J.: Learning compact binary face descriptor for face recognition. IEEE Trans. Pattern Anal. Machine Intell. **37**(10), 2041–2056 (2015)
17. Gong, Y., Lazebnik, S.: Iterative quantization: a procrustean approach to learning binary codes. In: IEEE Conference on Computer Vision and Pattern Recognition (CVPR), pp. 817–824 (2011)
18. Trzcinski, T., Lepetit, V.: Efficient discriminative projections for compact binary descriptors. In: Fitzgibbon, A., Lazebnik, S., Perona, P., Sato, Y., Schmid, C. (eds.) ECCV 2012, Part I. LNCS, vol. 7572, pp. 228–242. Springer, Heidelberg (2012)
19. Hyvärinen, A., Hurri, J., Hoyer, P. O.: Natural Image Statistics: A Probabilistic Approach to Early Computational Vision, vol. 39. In: Springer Science and Business Media (2009)
20. Zhang, W., Shan, S., Gao, W., Chen, X., Zhang, H.: Local gabor binary pattern histogram sequence (lgbphs): a novel non-statistical model for face representation and recognition. In: Tenth IEEE International Conference on Computer Vision, vol. 1, pp. 786–791 (2005)
21. Maturana, D., Mery, D., Soto, A.: Learning discriminative local binary patterns for face recognition. In: IEEE International Conference on Automatic Face and Gesture Recognition and Workshops (FG 2011), pp. 470–475 (2011)
22. Lei, Z., Pietikainen, M., Li, S.Z.: Learning discriminant face descriptor. IEEE Trans. Pattern Anal. Mach. Intell. **36**(2), 289–302 (2014)
23. Ahonen, T., Rahtu, E., Ojansivu, V., Heikkilä, J.: Recognition of blurred faces using local phase quantization. In: 19th International Conference on Pattern Recognition, pp. 1–4 (2008)
24. Tan, X., Triggs, B.: Enhanced local texture feature sets for face recognition under difficult lighting conditions. IEEE Trans. Image Proc. **19**(6), 1635–1650 (2010)
25. Vu, N.S., Caplier, A.: Enhanced patterns of oriented edge magnitudes for face recognition and image matching. IEEE Trans. Image Proc. **21**(3), 1352–1365 (2012)
26. Dantcheva, A., Chen, C., Ross, A.: Makeup challenges automated face recognition systems. In: SPIE Newsroom, pp. 1–4 (2013)

27. Wen, L., Guo, G.D.: Dual attributes for face verification robust to facial cosmetics. J Comput. Vis. Image Process. **3**(1), 63–73 (2013)
28. Dantcheva, A., Chen, C., Ross, A.: Can facial cosmetics affect the matching accuracy of face recognition systems?. In: IEEE Fifth International Conference on Biometrics: Theory, Applications and Systems, pp. 391–398 (2012)
29. Guo, G., Wen, L., Yan, S.: Face Authentication with makeup changes. IEEE Trans. Circ. Syst. Video Technol. **24**(5), 814–825 (2014)

Security Analysis on Privacy-Preserving Cloud Aided Biometric Identification Schemes

Shiran Pan[1,2,3], Shen Yan[1,2,3], and Wen-Tao Zhu[1,2(✉)]

[1] State Key Laboratory of Information Security,
Institute of Information Engineering, Chinese Academy of Sciences, Beijing, China
{panshiran,yanshen}@iie.ac.cn, wtzhu@ieee.org
[2] Data Assurance and Communication Security Research Center,
Chinese Academy of Sciences, Beijing, China
[3] University of Chinese Academy of Sciences, Beijing, China

Abstract. Biometric identification (BI) is the task of searching a pre-established biometric database to find a matching record for an enquiring biometric trait sampled from an unknown individual of interest. This has recently been aided with cloud computing, which brings a lot of convenience but simultaneously arouses new privacy concerns. Two cloud aided BI schemes pursuing privacy preserving have recently been proposed by Wang et al. in ESORICS '15. In this paper, we propose several elaborately designed attacks to reveal the security breaches in these two schemes. Theoretical analysis is given to validate our proposed attacks, which indicates that via such attacks the cloud server can accurately infer the outsourced database and the identification request.

Keywords: Biometric identification · Cloud computing · Security breaches · Privacy preserving

1 Introduction

Biometric identification (BI) is to identify an individual of interest by searching a pre-established biometric database to find a matching record for an enquiring user's biometric trait sampled from an unknown individual. Due to the universality, uniqueness, and permanence of the biometric data [1], BI has been wildly used in identifying an individual's identity (e.g., in forensic scenarios). There have been several kinds of BI systems in practical applications, such as fingerprint, voice pattern, and facial pattern recognition systems [2].

As cloud computing is now gaining much momentum, individuals, companies, and governments are motivated to outsource their data to the cloud to enjoy the benefits of high flexibility and cost-saving feature of the cloud computing [3]. As far as the BI system is concerned, the database owner may desire to outsource the biometric database to the cloud and enjoy the cloud aided identification service, which can relieve the database owner of the local storage burden and the high computation overhead introduced by searching over the large-scale database. However, the proliferation of cloud aided biometric identification (CABI)

© Springer International Publishing Switzerland 2016
J.K. Liu and R. Steinfeld (Eds.): ACISP 2016, Part II, LNCS 9723, pp. 446–453, 2016.
DOI: 10.1007/978-3-319-40367-0_29

also attracts increasing concerns on its security [4] and privacy [5], since the biometric data is highly sensitive and is impossible to be revoked and replaced once leaked. Therefore, appropriate protection mechanism should be carefully placed in CABI systems in order to combat unsolicited access and inadvertent information disclosure.

Several CABI schemes [6,7] have recently been proposed but these schemes are not appropriate for real-world cloud aided applications, since they will be cracked down when there exists collusion between the system participants. Focused on the collusion resistance, some other schemes have been proposed by Yuan et al. [8] and Wang et al. [9]. Yuan et al. [8] claimed that their scheme is secure under the known-plaintext attack (KPA) and even the chosen-plaintext attack (CPA). However, Wang et al. [9] observed that it is not the case and presented some attacks to show that the scheme proposed in [8] can be broken by KPA and CPA. As a following study, in ESORICS '15 Wang et al. [9] proposed two new CABI schemes considering the semi-honest participants. Wang et al. claimed their schemes achieve higher security since the proposed basic scheme is resilient to the known-sample attack (KSA), while the enhanced scheme can additionally defend against the collusion attack of the cloud server and some enquiring user. However, we observe that both schemes are vulnerable, even to exactly the adversaries designated in [9]. Specifically, we present several elaborately designed attacks that will completely break these schemes [9].

Our technical contributions can be summarized as follows:

– We propose several elaborately designed attacks to reveal the inherent security breaches in the two schemes proposed in [9].
– Theoretical analysis is given to validate our proposed attacks, which indicates that via such attacks the cloud server can accurately infer the outsourced database and the identification request.

The rest of the paper is organized as follows: In Sect. 2, we review Wang et al.'s schemes [9]. We propose several attacks on these schemes [9] in Sect. 3. The paper is concluded in Sect. 4.

2   Review of Wang et al.'s Two Schemes

Recently, Wang et al. [9] proposed two CABI schemes that focus on the fingerprint identification. Following [5,8], Wang et al. assumed that both the biometric records in the database and the biometric trait submitted by the enquiring user are represented by feature vectors. In this section, we will review these two schemes by describing their main bodies.

2.1   CloudBI-I: The Basic Scheme

We first describe Wang et al.'s basic scheme CloudBI-I. For the fingerprints collected from m individuals, the biometric database owner first generates the corresponding biometric records denoted as $\{b_i\}_{i=1}^m$, which form the biometric database $\mathcal{D}$. Each $\boldsymbol{b}_i$ is set to an n-dimensional vector, i.e., $\boldsymbol{b}_i = (b_{i1}, b_{i2}, \cdots, b_{in})$, with each entry b_{ij} lying in a pre-determined domain. To facilitate the identification, $\boldsymbol{b}_i$ will be extended to $\hat{\boldsymbol{b}}_i = (b_{i1}, b_{i2}, \cdots, b_{in}, b_{i,n+1}, 1)$, where $b_{i,n+1} = -(b_{i1}^2 + b_{i2}^2 + \cdots + b_{in}^2)/2$. The database owner then accordingly generates a diagonal matrix $\boldsymbol{B}_i$ with the diagonal entries set to $\{b_{i1}, b_{i2}, \cdots, b_{in}, b_{i,n+1}, 1\}$ (i.e., the entries of $\hat{\boldsymbol{b}}_i$).

Subsequently, the database owner randomly selects two $(n+2) \times (n+2)$ invertible matrices $\boldsymbol{M}_1$ and $\boldsymbol{M}_2$ as the encryption keys, and encrypts each $\boldsymbol{B}_i$ by computing

$$C_i = M_1 B_i M_2. \tag{1}$$

After encryption, the database owner outsources the encrypted database $\mathcal{C} = \{C_i\}_{i=1}^m$ to the cloud server. When an enquiring user has a fingerprint to be identified, he first locally generates the corresponding biometric trait $\boldsymbol{b}_t = (b_{t1}, b_{t2}, \cdots, b_{tn})$ that is also an n-dimensional vector, and then submits it to the database owner who will select a random number r_t and extend $\boldsymbol{b}_t$ to $\hat{\boldsymbol{b}}_t = (b_{t1}, b_{t2}, \cdots, b_{tn}, 1, r_t)$. The database owner then generates a diagonal matrix $\boldsymbol{B}_t$ with the diagonal entries set to $\{b_{t1}, b_{t2}, \cdots, b_{tn}, 1, r_t\}$ (i.e., the entries of $\hat{\boldsymbol{b}}_t$), and subsequently encrypts $\boldsymbol{B}_t$ by computing

$$C_T = M_2^{-1} B_t M_1^{-1}.$$

Then $\boldsymbol{C}_T$ is submitted to the cloud server for identification. Upon receiving $\boldsymbol{C}_T$, the cloud server compares the Euclidean distance between each $\boldsymbol{b}_i$ and $\boldsymbol{b}_t$ by computing the trace (denoted as $\boldsymbol{tr}(\cdot)$) of the following matrix $\boldsymbol{P}_i$:

$$P_i = C_i C_T = M_1 B_i M_2 M_2^{-1} B_t M_1^{-1} = M_1 B_i B_t M_1^{-1}.$$

Due to the property of matrix similarity transformation [10], $\boldsymbol{tr}(\boldsymbol{P}_i)$ is thus equal to $\boldsymbol{tr}(\boldsymbol{B}_i \boldsymbol{B}_t)$, i.e., $\boldsymbol{tr}(\boldsymbol{P}_i)$ equals $(\sum_{j=1}^n b_{ij} b_{tj} + b_{i,n+1} + r_t)$. The cloud server then sorts these values $\{\boldsymbol{tr}(\boldsymbol{P}_i)\}_{i=1}^m$ and accordingly returns the candidate results to the database owner. Here we omit other details of this scheme, since they are irrelevant to our proposed attacks.

2.2   CloudBI-II: The Enhanced Scheme

Wang et al. claimed that CloudBI-I can resist KSA but will be broken by the collusion between the cloud server and some enquiring user. Therefore, Wang et al. proposed an enhanced scheme CloudBI-II. The main idea is to introduce more randomness into the database encryption and the query encryption. Specifically, for each $\boldsymbol{B}_i$, the database owner additionally selects a random lower triangular matrix $\boldsymbol{Q}_i$ with the diagonal entries set to all 1's, and then encrypts $\boldsymbol{B}_i$ by computing

$$C_i = M_1 Q_i B_i M_2.$$

Similarly, the database owner generates the encrypted identification query for the enquiring user as

$$C_T = M_2^{-1} B_t Q_t M_1^{-1}, \tag{2}$$

where Q_t is also a random lower triangular matrix with the diagonal entries set to all 1's. The remaining operations are the same as the basic scheme CloudBI-I.

3   Proposed Attacks

In this section, we will propose several elaborately constructed attacks by exploiting the inherent structure of the biometric data and some important properties of matrix transformation.

3.1   Modified Signature Linking Attack on CloudBI-I

Wang et al. [9] claimed that their basic scheme CloudBI-I is resilient to KSA because the techniques they used for designing the scheme are not belong to distance-preserving transformation (DPT) [11], i.e., the Euclidean distances between any two plaintext biometric records will not be preserved after encryption. Therefore, according to the analysis presented in [12], the PCA attack [13] and the signature linking attack [12] will fail to attack CloudBI-I. However, we observe that the above reasoning is not rigorous and we will demonstrate a so-called modified signature linking attack (MSLA), which bypasses the computation on the Euclidean distances, to recover the outsourced database in CloudBI-I.

According to the definition of KSA, the adversary has some samples in the plaintext database $\mathcal{D}$. Without loss of generality, we assume that the knowledge of the adversary is $\mathcal{G} = \{b_i\}_{i=1}^{k} \subseteq \mathcal{D}$ so that he can naturally generate $\{B_i\}_{i=1}^{k}$ without knowing any of the corresponding encrypted values $\{C_i\}_{i=1}^{k}$. As shown in Eq. 1, due to the property of matrix similarity transformation [10], we have

$$tr\left(C_i^{-1}C_j\right) = tr\left(M_2^{-1}B_i^{-1}B_jM_2\right) = tr\left(B_i^{-1}B_j\right). \tag{3}$$

Although the Euclidean distances between the encrypted records are not preserved, we can define the signature of $\mathcal{G}$ as

$$sig(\mathcal{G}) = \{tr\left(B_1^{-1}B_2\right), \cdots, tr\left(B_1^{-1}B_k\right), tr\left(B_2^{-1}B_3\right), \cdots, tr\left(B_{k-1}^{-1}B_k\right)\}.$$

In MSLA, the adversary aims to find an ordered set of encrypted records $\mathcal{H} \subseteq \mathcal{C} = \{C_i\}_{i=1}^{m}$, such that $\mathcal{H}$ has the same size and gives the same signature as $\mathcal{G}$. Let $\mathcal{H} = \{C_{1'}, C_{2'}, \cdots, C_{k'}\}$ so that the signature of $\mathcal{H}$ is

$$sig(\mathcal{H}) = \{tr\left(C_{1'}^{-1}C_{2'}\right), \cdots, tr\left(C_{1'}^{-1}C_{k'}\right), tr\left(C_{2'}^{-1}C_{3'}\right), \cdots, tr\left(C_{(k-1)'}^{-1}C_{k'}\right)\}.$$

If there is only one set $\mathcal{H}$ with a matching signature, the adversary can conclude that $C_{i'}$ is the encrypted value of b_i. Then the adversary try to solve any plaintext biometric record b_j correspond to C_j by solving the following linear equations:

$$tr(B_i^{-1}B_j) = tr(C_i^{-1}C_j), \quad i = 1, \cdots, k.$$

Particularly, there are $(n + 2)$ unknowns in each linear equation so that the adversary will successfully recover $\boldsymbol{B}_j$ if $k \geq (n + 2)$ holds.

The main issue that the success of proposed MSLA rests on is whether there exists a signature collision, i.e., whether it is likely to find another set, which is not the encrypted values of $\mathcal{G}$ but happens to give the same signature as $\mathcal{G}$. As shown in the following theorem, the probability of the signature collision is very small and we can well control it by increasing the size k of $\mathcal{G}$.

Theorem 1. *Let α be the probability of an n-dimensional vector contained in $\mathcal{D}$. Assume the knowledge of the adversary is $\mathcal{G} = \{\boldsymbol{b}_i\}_{i=1}^{k} \subseteq \mathcal{D}, \forall \epsilon > 0$, if $k \geq n + 1 + \ln \epsilon / \ln \alpha$, then $Pr(signature\ collision) < \epsilon$.*

Due to the space limit, here we omit the proof. Note that MSLA will also work for CloudBI-II [9] since Eq. 3 still holds. In conclusion, via MSLA the adversary can obtain the corresponding relationships between the plaintext and the encrypted biometric records, and further construct linear equations to get the plaintext database. Next, we will show other two attacks on CloudBI-II.

3.2   Two Attacks on CloudBI-II

In the design of CloudBI-II [9], several random lower triangular matrices $\{\boldsymbol{Q}_i\}_{i=1}^{m}$ and $\boldsymbol{Q}_c$ are introduced into the database encryption and the query encryption. Wang et al. claimed that such randomness makes it impossible for the adversary to figure out either the biometric records $\boldsymbol{b}_i$ in $\mathcal{D}$ or the biometric traits $\boldsymbol{b}_t$ submitted by non-colluding enquiring users, even the adversary can collude with some user and independently select the biometric traits submitted to the database owner. Therefore, Wang et al. asserted that CloudBI-II can defend against the collusion attack of the cloud server and some enquiring user.

Next we will demonstrate two attacks, which rely on the collusion ability of the adversary designated in [9], to break the scheme CloudBI-II. Via these two attacks, the adversary can obtain some certain information about the randomness that are added into the database encryption and the query encryption, and further recover the plaintext biometric records and the enquiring biometric traits.

We begin by describing an attack to recover the biometric records in the database. As defined in [9], the cloud server (i.e., the colluding adversary in the BI system) can independently select several vectors as the biometric traits to be identified. Without loss of generality, we assume that the cloud server selects $(n + 2)$ vectors $\{\boldsymbol{b}_t^{(i)}\}_{i=1}^{n+2}$ to be submitted to the database owner, where $\boldsymbol{b}_t^{(i)} = (b_{t1}^{(i)}, b_{t2}^{(i)}, \cdots, b_{tn}^{(i)})$. Upon receiving these vectors, the database owner will encrypt them and send the encrypted values $\{\boldsymbol{C}_T^{(i)}\}_{i=1}^{n+2}$ to the cloud server, here $\boldsymbol{C}_T^{(i)} = \boldsymbol{M}_2^{-1} \boldsymbol{B}_t^{(i)} \boldsymbol{Q}_t^{(i)} \boldsymbol{M}_1^{-1}$ as shown in Eq. 2. Notice that, the cloud server knows all these $\{\boldsymbol{b}_t^{(i)}\}_{i=1}^{n+2}$ but does not know the randomness $\{r_t^{(i)}\}_{i=1}^{n+2}$ that are added into $\{\boldsymbol{C}_T^{(i)}\}_{i=1}^{n+2}$ by the database owner. However, the cloud server can obtain the proportional relationships between $\{r_t^{(i)}\}_{i=1}^{n+2}$ by computing

$$tr((C_T^{(i)})^{-1}C_T^{(j)}) - (1/b_t^{(i)})(b_t^{(j)})^{\mathrm{T}} - 1$$

$$= tr(M_1(Q_t^{(i)})^{-1}(B_t^{(i)})^{-1}M_2M_2^{-1}B_t^{(j)}Q_t^{(j)}M_1^{-1}) - (1/b_t^{(i)})(b_t^{(j)})^{\mathrm{T}} - 1$$

$$= tr(M_1(Q_t^{(i)})^{-1}(B_t^{(i)})^{-1}B_t^{(j)}Q_t^{(j)}M_1^{-1}) - (1/b_t^{(i)})(b_t^{(j)})^{\mathrm{T}} - 1. \qquad (4)$$

Due to the property of matrix similarity transformation and the fact that the inverse matrix of a unit lower triangular matrix is also a unit lower triangular matrix [10], $tr(M_1(Q_t^{(i)})^{-1}(B_t^{(i)})^{-1}B_t^{(j)}Q_t^{(j)}M_1^{-1})$ is therefore equal to $tr((B_t^{(i)})^{-1}B_t^{(j)})$. Since the matrix $(B_t^{(i)})^{-1}B_t^{(j)}$ has the following structure:

$$(B_t^{(i)})^{-1}B_t^{(j)} = \begin{pmatrix} b_{t1}^{(j)}/b_{t1}^{(i)} & 0 & \cdots & \cdots & 0 & 0 \\ 0 & b_{t2}^{(j)}/b_{t2}^{(i)} & \cdots & \cdots & 0 & 0 \\ \vdots & \vdots & \ddots & \vdots & \vdots & \vdots \\ 0 & \cdots & 0 & b_{tn}^{(j)}/b_{tn}^{(i)} & 0 & 0 \\ 0 & \cdots & 0 & 0 & 1 & 0 \\ 0 & \cdots & 0 & 0 & 0 & r_t^{(j)}/r_t^{(i)} \end{pmatrix}$$

the result of Eq. 4 is thus equal to $r_t^{(j)}/r_t^{(i)}$ denoted as r_{ji}. By such computations, the cloud server can get a set of ratios $\{r_{j1}\}_{j=2}^{n+2}$, and further generate a novel matrix D for attacking as

$$D = \begin{pmatrix} b_{t1}^{(1)} & b_{t2}^{(1)} & \cdots & b_{tn}^{(1)} & 1 & 1 \\ b_{t1}^{(2)} & b_{t2}^{(2)} & \cdots & b_{tn}^{(2)} & 1 & r_{21} \\ \vdots & \vdots & \vdots & \vdots & \vdots & \vdots \\ b_{t1}^{(n+2)} & b_{t2}^{(n+2)} & \cdots & b_{tn}^{(n+2)} & 1 & r_{n+2,1} \end{pmatrix}.$$

With this matrix, the cloud server can figure out the biometric record b_i corresponding to C_i by solving the following linear equation:

$$Dy = \left(tr(C_iC_T^{(1)}), tr(C_iC_T^{(2)}), \cdots, tr(C_iC_T^{(n+2)})\right)^{\mathrm{T}}. \qquad (5)$$

The biometric record b_i corresponding to C_i actually consists of the first n entries of the solution y to Eq. 5. In this way, the cloud server can recover all the biometric records in the database. For the correctness, we present the following theorem.

Theorem 2. *If the matrix rank of D (denoted as $rk(D)$) equals $(n+2)$, then b_i consists of the first n entries of the solution y to Eq. 5.*

Proof. Eq. 5 can be rewritten as $Dy = \gamma$, where the augmented matrix can be denoted as $\tilde{D} = (D, \gamma)$. Since $rk(\tilde{D}) = rk(D) = n + 2$, we can conclude that there exists a unique solution to Eq. 5. We assume the corresponding biometric record of C_i is $b_i = (b_{i1}, b_{i2}, \cdots, b_{in})$, which will be extended to

$\hat{b}_i = (b_{i1}, b_{i2}, \cdots, b_{in}, b_{i,n+1}, 1)$ for the encryption, where $b_{i,n+1} = -(b_{i1}^2 + b_{i2}^2 + \cdots + b_{in}^2)/2$. We now consider the vector $y^* = (b_{i1}, b_{i2}, \cdots, b_{in}, b_{i,n+1}, r_t^{(1)})^{\mathrm{T}}$, here $r_t^{(1)}$ is the random number added into the generation of $C_T^{(1)}$ by the database owner. As introduced in Sect. 2.1, we have

$$Dy^* = \begin{pmatrix} b_{t1}^{(1)} & b_{t2}^{(1)} & \cdots & b_{tn}^{(1)} & 1 & 1 \\ b_{t1}^{(2)} & b_{t2}^{(2)} & \cdots & b_{tn}^{(2)} & 1 & r_{21} \\ \vdots & \vdots & \vdots & \vdots & \vdots & \vdots \\ b_{t1}^{(n+2)} & b_{t2}^{(n+2)} & \cdots & b_{tn}^{(n+2)} & 1 & r_{n+2,1} \end{pmatrix} \begin{pmatrix} b_{i1} \\ b_{i2} \\ \vdots \\ r_t^{(1)} \end{pmatrix} = \begin{pmatrix} tr(C_i C_T^{(1)}) \\ tr(C_i C_T^{(2)}) \\ \vdots \\ tr(C_i C_T^{(n+2)}) \end{pmatrix} = \gamma.$$

As shown above, we can conclude that y^* is actually the unique solution to Eq. 5. Therefore, b_i consists of the first n entries of the solution to Eq. 5.

Based on the ratios r_{ji} calculated by Eq. 4, we can design another attack on CloudBI-II so that the cloud server can recover all the biometric traits submitted by non-colluding enquiring users. Specifically, the adversary can construct another matrix A for attacking as

$$A = \begin{pmatrix} 1/b_{t1}^{(1)} & 1/b_{t2}^{(1)} & \cdots & 1/b_{tn}^{(1)} & 1 \\ 1/b_{t1}^{(2)} & 1/b_{t2}^{(2)} & \cdots & 1/b_{tn}^{(2)} & 1/r_{21} \\ \vdots & \vdots & \vdots & \vdots & \vdots \\ 1/b_{t1}^{(n+1)} & 1/b_{t2}^{(n+1)} & \cdots & 1/b_{tn}^{(n+1)} & 1/r_{n+1,1} \end{pmatrix}.$$

Upon receiving a new encrypted query C_T^* submitted by the database owner, the cloud server can figure out the corresponding enquiring biometric trait b_t^* by solving the following linear equation:

$$Ax = \left(tr((C_T^{(1)})^{-1}C_T^*) - 1, tr((C_T^{(2)})^{-1}C_T^*) - 1, \cdots, tr((C_T^{(n+1)})^{-1}C_T^*) - 1\right)^{\mathrm{T}}. \tag{6}$$

The vector that consists of the first n entries of the solution x to Eq. 6 is exactly the b_t^* corresponding to C_T^*. Similarly, we have the following theorem.

Theorem 3. *If $rk(A)$ equals $(n+1)$, then b_t^* consists of the first n entries of the solution x to Eq. 6.*

The proof of Theorem 3 is similar to that of Theorem 2. Here we omit the proof due to the space limit.

4   Conclusion

In this paper, we have proposed several elaborately designed attacks to reveal the inherent security breaches in the two CABI schemes proposed by Wang et al. [9]. Additionally, theoretical analysis has been given to validate our proposed attacks. As our future work, we will address the privacy-preserving CABI problem by constructing new encryption algorithms for the biometric data.

Acknowledgment. The authors would like to thank the anonymous reviewers for their valuable comments. This work was supported by the National Natural Science Foundation of China under Grant 61272479, the National 973 Program of China under Grant 2013CB338001, and the Strategic Priority Research Program of Chinese Academy of Sciences under Grant XDA06010702

References

1. Bolle, R., Pankanti, S.: Biometrics: Personal Identification in Networked Society. Kluwer Academic Publishers, Norwell (1998)
2. Jain, A.K., Hong, L., Pankanti, S.: Biometric identification. Commun. ACM **43**, 90–98 (2000)
3. Marstona, S., Li, Z., Bandyopadhyay, S., Zhang, J., Ghalsasi, A.: Cloud computing - The business perspective. Decis. Support Syst. **51**, 176–189 (2011)
4. Al-Assam, H., Jassim, S.: Security evaluation of biometric keys. Comput. Secur. **31**, 151–163 (2012)
5. Huang, Y., Malka, L., Evans, D., Katz, J.: Efficient privacy-preserving biometric identification. In: 18th Annual Network & Distributed System Security Symposium NDSS 2011, February 2011
6. Blanton, M., Aliasgari, M.: Secure outsourced computation of iris matching. J. Comput. Secur. **20**, 259–305 (2012)
7. Chun, H., Elmehdwi, Y., Li, F., Bhattacharya, P., Jiang, W.: Outsourceable two-party privacy-preserving biometric authentication. In: 9th Symposium on Information, Computer and Communications Security ASIACCS 2014, pp. 401–412. ACM (2014)
8. Yuan, J., Yu, S.: Efficient privacy-preserving biometric identification in cloud computing. In: 32nd IEEE International Conference on Computer Communications INFOCOM 2013, pp. 2652–2660. IEEE (2013)
9. Wang, N., Hu, S., Ren, K., He, M., Du, M., Wang, Z.: CloudBI: practical privacy-preserving outsourcing of biometric identification in the cloud. In: Pernul, G., Ryan, P.Y.A., Weippl, E. (eds.) ESORICS 2015. LNCS. Springer, Heidelberg (2015)
10. Strang, G.: Introduction to Linear Algebra. Wellesley, Cambridge (2009)
11. Oliveira, S.R.M., Zaiane, O.R.: Privacy preserving clustering by data transformation. J. Inf. Data Manag. **1**, 53–56 (2010)
12. Wong, W.K., Cheung, D.W., Kao, B., Mamoulis, N.: Secure kNN computation on encrypted databases. In: 28th ACM International Conference on Management of Data, SIGMOD 2009, pp. 139–152. ACM (2009)
13. Liu, K., Giannella, C.M., Kargupta, H.: An attacker's view of distance preserving maps for privacy preserving data mining. In: Fürnkranz, J., Scheffer, T., Spiliopoulou, M. (eds.) PKDD 2006. LNCS (LNAI), vol. 4213, pp. 297–308. Springer, Heidelberg (2006)

Short Papers-Digital Forensics

Interest Profiling for Security Monitoring and Forensic Investigation

Min Yang[1], Fei Xu[2(✉)], and Kam-Pui Chow[1]

[1] Department of Computer Science, The University of Hong Kong,
Hong Kong, China
{myang,chow}@cs.hku.hk
[2] Institute of Information Engineering,
Chinese Academy of Sciences, Beijing, China
xufei@iie.ac.cn

Abstract. User interest profiles are of great importance for security monitoring and forensic investigation. Once a specific topic becomes sensitive or suspected, being able to quickly determine who has shown an interest in that topic can assist investigators to focus their attention from massive data and develop effective investigation strategies. To automatically generate user interest profiles, we extend Author Topic model to explicitly model user's dynamic interest based on the text information posted by the user. Our model is able to monitor the evolution of user interest from time-stamped documents. Moreover, instead of modeling a topic as a multinomial distribution over words, we develop a model that can discover and output multi-word phrases to describe topics, which facilitates the human interpretation of unorganized texts. Therefore, our technique has the potential to reduce the cost of investigation and discover latent evidence that is often missed by expression-based searches. We evaluate the effectiveness and performance of our algorithm on a real-life forensic dataset Enron. The experiment results demonstrate that our algorithm can effectively discover user's dynamic interest. The generated user interest profiles can further assist investigator to discover the latent evidence effectively from textual forensic data and perform security monitoring.

Keywords: User interest · Interest profiling · Forensic investigation · Security monitoring

1 Introduction

The development of information technology has led to an explosion of the evidence set that may contain thousands of documents per suspect. However, only a very small proportion of these documents are relevant. Given the limit of time, it is hard for forensic investigator to discover actionable evidence manually from thousands of text documents. On the other hand, social media provides a flexible communication channel for individuals. It is crucial for law enforcement agencies

© Springer International Publishing Switzerland 2016
J.K. Liu and R. Steinfeld (Eds.): ACISP 2016, Part II, LNCS 9723, pp. 457–464, 2016.
DOI: 10.1007/978-3-319-40367-0_30

to discover potential criminal activities before they occur, which can be done by analyzing the suspect's online documents.

User interest profiling is the process of acquiring and maintaining the knowledge related to the interests or needs of a specific user [4,6,10,16,21]. User interest profiles are of great importance for security monitoring and forensic investigation. Once a specific topic becomes sensitive or suspected, being able to quickly determine who has shown an interest in that topic can assist investigators to focus their attention from massive data, so that they can develop effective investigation strategies. For example, to address the insider threat of commercial and government organizations before it occurs, interest profiling of the employees based on their emails can assist investigators filtering the number of suspects to a manageable number [5].

Latent Dirichlet Allocation (LDA) [3] is a type of statistical model for discovering the abstract "topics" that occur in a collection of documents. [15] extend LDA to include authorship information to model the interests of users. Topic models has the potential to discover latent evidences. Topic model is a type of statistical model for discovering the abstract "topics" that occur in a collection of documents.

In this paper, we propose a Multiword Dynamic Author Topic Model (M-DATM) inspired by the work of [2,15] for modeling the dynamic evolution of individual author's interest. We first use a frequent phrase mining algorithm to merge tokens within the document into human-interpretable phrases. Instead of modeling a topic as a multinomial distribution over words, our model can directly output phrases and the latent topic assignment in order to facilitate the human interpretation of the large amount of unorganized texts. Second, we extend Author Topic model [15] to include temporal information, which captures the evolution of topics in a sequentially organized corpus of documents. The temporal information captured by M-DATM plays a very important role in forming meaningful time-sensitive topics. Using such an approach, we can find evidence faster, and spot evidence patterns that would not even have been found otherwise.

We evaluate the effectiveness and performance of our algorithm on a real-life forensic dataset Enron. The experiment results demonstrate that our algorithm has the potential to assist security monitoring and forensic investigation.

2   Related Work

Attempting to understand the meaning of the forensic data, especially when the user has limited insight into the collection, is a difficult task. In the past decades, a various of text analysis approaches have been proposed for forensic investigation [11,14,18,19]. Among these methods, topic modeling has the potential to discovery latent evidences and build user profiles. For example, Okolica et al. [14] discern employees interests from email using an extended version of Probabilistic Latent Semantic Indexing (PLSI). These interests are transformed into implicit and explicit social network graphs, which are used to locate potential insiders by identifying individuals who have a hidden interest in a sensitive topic. In another work [8], LDA is applied to forensic data. No evidence was discovered in this specific case, but the analysis indicates that topic modeling can be very useful in discovering the semantic context of text documents and for summarizing document content.

As author's personal interests are important for user-centric applications, a variety of LDA extensions have been proposed to incorporate authorship information into the text [15]. The Author-Topic model [15] is the first generative model that simultaneously models the content of documents and the interests of authors. To characterize topics and their changes over time, there are other extensions of LDA which use information in the timestamps. Lei and Lafferty [2] propose a dynamic topic model (DTM) which jointly models word co-occurrence and time. Wang and McCallum [17] propose a non-Markov continuous-time model, called ToT. These models are able to capture the evolution of topics, but they do not consider authorship information.

There are recent works taking both the time stamp and the authorship of documents into account, such as the Temporal-Author-Topic (TAT) model [7]. Nevertheless, these models do not characterize the drift of the individual author's interests. In addition, none of these methods consider outputting phrases to represent latent topics.

3   Methodology

The amount of digital data associated with individuals users has grown tremendously in recent years. Since user interests guide their activities, it plays an important role in the assessment of whether an event is relevant to a particular person. As a consequence, interest profiles can help to summarize a large amounts of information available from a user. We propose M-DATM to build user interest profiles by extending Author Topic model to extract topical phrases and include temporal information. This model captures not only the topics of the data, but also how the topics of interest change over time. In the rest of this section, we formally present the M-DATM in details.

3.1   Frequent Phrase Mining

Most topic modeling algorithms simply lists the most probable topical terms, but we notice that the human interpretation often relies on inherent grouping of terms into phrase. In this subsection, we identify topic-representative phrases instead of single words because single words usually cannot deliver sufficient information for the topics and can sometimes even be ambiguous. For example, a single word "California" or "crisis" alone cannot convey the full meaning of the phrase "California crisis".

Following the definition in [9], the valid candidate phrases need to have the following properties: 1) A phrase that is important to a topic should be frequent within that topic; 2) The tokens in that phrase should have a co-occurrence frequency that is significantly higher than the average.

Before performing topic modeling, we apply a phrase-mining algorithm [9] to merges the tokens within the document into human-interpretable phrases. We extract high-quality frequent phrases through collecting aggregate counts for all contiguous words in a corpus that satisfy a certain minimum support threshold. There are two properties for efficiently mining these frequent phrases, which were first introduced for mining frequent patterns using the Apriori algorithm [1]: (1) If a phrase P is not frequent, then any super-phrase of P is guaranteed to be not frequent; (2) If a document contains no frequent phrases of length n, the document does not contain frequent phrases of length $\geq n$. Thus, if the document we are considering has been deemed to contain no more phrases of a certain length, then the document is guaranteed to contain no phrases of a longer length. We can safely remove it from any further consideration. The readers can refer to the paper [1,9] for the implementation details about frequent phrase mining. Different from general frequent transaction pattern mining, we take an increasing-size sliding window over the corpus to generate candidate phrases since we only consider contiguous tokens.

3.2   M-DATM Model

LDA is a three-level hierarchical Bayesian model. Each document is modeled as a finite mixture φ_d over an underlying set of topics. Each topic θ_k is, in turn, modeled as an finite mixture over an underlying set of word probabilities. LDA is not aware of the document timestamps and the authorship. It implicitly assumes that the documents are drawn exchangeably from an invariant set of topics. However, for many collections (e.g. emails, news articles and search query logs), the timestamps and the authorship information associated with the documents reflects an evolving set of topics. This is the motivation of our M-DATM model.

The M-DATM model is an extension of Author Topic model to incorporate the temporal information, which monitors the evolution of author interest in time-stamped documents. Below is a description of the generative model:

1. For each topic $k \in [1, K]$:
   (a) Draw a topic-word distribution $\varphi_k \sim \text{Dirichlet}(\beta)$
2. For each author $a \in [1, A]$:
   (a) draw an author-topic distribution $\theta_a \sim \text{Dirichlet}(\alpha)$
3. For each i-th token w_{di} in document $d \in [1, D]$:
   (a) Draw an author a from an author set A_d uniformly
   (b) Draw a topic $z_{di} \sim \text{Multinomial}(\theta_a)$
   (c) Draw a token $w_{di} \sim \text{Multinomial}(\theta_{z_{di}})$
   (d) Draw a timestamp $t_{di} \sim \text{Beta}(\psi_{z_{di}})$

We use Gibbs Sampling [12] for parameter estimation. It provides a simple scheme for obtaining parameter estimates under Dirichlet priors and allows combination of estimates from several local maximas of the posterior distribution. The reader may refer to [7,15,20] for a detailed derivation of the sampling procedure.

With M-DATM, we can not only answer questions like "what is the topic of a given document" and "what are the top words in a given topic", but also answer questions like "list the top words of a given topic in a certain time slice" (by examining $(\theta_{z_{d,n}}, t)$ or "list the topics that reflect somebody's interest over time" (by examining the $\varphi_{x_{d,n}}$ of different topics over time).

4 Experiments and Analysis

4.1 Data Sets Description

We use the Enron corpus as the experiment dataset. The Enron corpus is the only publicly available large corpus of real-world email traffic. This data was published by the Federal Energy Regulatory Commission during its investigation. The raw Enron corpus contains 619,446 messages belonging to 158 user. Klimt et al. [13] then cleaned it by removing certain folders. These removed folder did not appear to be used directly by the users, but rather were computer generated. In the cleaned Enron corpus, there are 200,399 messages belonging to 158 users with an average of 757 messages per user[1]. Each message in the dataset includes: the email addresses of the sender and receiver, date and time, the subject, the body text.

4.2 Data Preprocessing

We preprocess the data before applying the M-DATM. The texts are first tokenized using the natural language toolkit NLTK[2]. Then, we remove non-alphabet characters, numbers, pronoun, words with two characters or less, punctuation and stop words[3] (common words appearing frequently in the text) from the text. Finally, the WordNet stemmer[4] is applied to reduce the vocabulary size and settle the issue of data spareness.

4.3 Experiment Results

Topic modeling can assist digital forensic investigators and security monitoring in several ways. For large-scale dataset, performing topic modeling on natural language data can provide analysts and investigators with valuable information about the semantic context of the data. In this section, we present the topics discovered by M-DATM and analyze the change curve of these topics over time. We also demonstrate the ability of M-DATM algorithm to discover user's interest over time.

Our experiments use M-DATM as the topic model, in which the topic discovery is affected by the temporal and authorship information. In this experiment,

---

[1] http://www.cs.cmu.edu/enron/.
[2] http://www.nltk.org.
[3] http://www.ranks.nl/stopwords.
[4] http://wordnet.princeton.edu/.

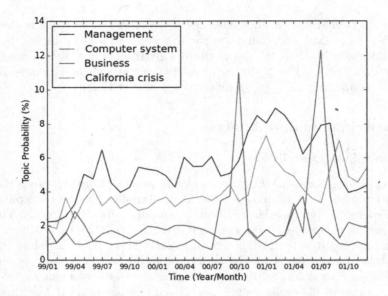

Fig. 1. Change curve of the selected topics (Color figure online)

the *minsupport* for frequent phrase mining is 150. We choose topic number $K = 50$, and hyperparameters $\alpha = 0.1$, $\beta = 0.5$ and $\lambda = 0.25$. The M-DATM algorithm is implemented based on the publicly available code[5].

Since the semantics of the topics can reflect peoples interests, the significant change of the topics usually indicates the occurrence and the end of events. Figure 1 presents the change curve of these four topics from January, 1999 to December, 2001. As shown in Fig. 1, the Computer System topic has its peak around October, 2000 and July, 2001. After examining relevant emails, it appears that there are two serious outage around October, 2000 and July, 2001, respectively. We can also infer these two events from the list of top words of the topic of Computer System in October, 2000 and July, 2001. The word "outage" has the highest priority in these timestamps. The California Crisis topic has its peak around January, 2001 and August, 2001, since California governor Davis declares a state of emergency in January and the energy prices normalized in September. The peaks of the Business topic indicates two events: first, Enron's Board of Directors exempted CFO Fastow from the company's code of ethics so that he can run a private equity fund – LJM1 that will raise money for and do deals with Enron in June, 1999. The LJM Funds become one of the key tools for Enron to manage its balance sheet. Second, in March 2001, Enron scheduled unusual analyst conference call to boost the stock. For the Management topic, we cannot explain the change curve in details since we have no idea about the personnel changes in Enron. Nevertheless, we know that Enron's Board of Directors exempted CFO Fastow from the company's code of ethics in June, 1999 and

---

[5] http://web.engr.illinois.edu/~elkishk2/.

Table 1. Top five individuals who are interested in the selected topics

California crisis topic	Management topic
James Steffes, VP, government affairs	Sally Beck, Chief operating officer
Mary Hain, In house lawyer	David Delainey, CEO (Enron N.A. & E.energy)
Michelle Lokay, Administrative assistant	Rick Buy, Chief risk management
Lindy Donoho, Employee	TWMark McConnell, Manager, TW
Richard Shapiro, VP, regulatory affairs	Louise Kitchen, President (Enron Online)

Lay retired as CEO and was replaced by Skilling in February, 2001. The change curve of Management topic precisely reflects these two event.

We are interested in those individuals who have an interest in the selected topics. This has potential to assist investigator finding criminal activities such as insider threats. It is done by calculating the average interest in a topic (indicated by $p(topic|user)$) and then finding those individuals who have an interest in the topic greater than 95 % of the population. These individuals with the highest interest in the selected topics are shown in Table 1. By examining the individuals positions in Enron, most of their interests are interpretable. Taking the Management topic as an example, almost all of the individuals listed are senior management team members of Enron. Our model produces similar results for California crisis topic.

5   Conclusions and Future Work

In this paper, we presented a Multiword Dynamic Author Topic model to discover user profiles (i.e. topics of interest), explicitly modeling time jointly with word co-occurrence patterns. With M-DATM, we not only discover the hot topics of interest from the whole dataset, but also find the individuals who have an interest in a selected topic. We are able to observe user's interest over time and monitor the change of the user's interest. We evaluate the performance of our model on a real-life forensic dataset Enron. The experiment results demonstrate that our algorithm has the potential to assist security monitoring and forensic investigation.

Acknowledgements. This work is supported by the Strategic Priority Research Program of the Chinese Academy of Sciences (No. XDA06030200).

References

1. Agrawal, R., Srikant, R., et al.: Fast algorithms for mining association rules. In: Proceedings of the 20th International Conference of Very Large Data Bases, VLDB, vol. 1215, pp. 487–499 (1994)

2. Blei, D.M., Lafferty, J.D.: Dynamic topic models. In: Proceedings of the 23rd International Conference on Machine Learning, pp. 113–120. ACM (2006)
3. Blei, D.M., Ng, A.Y., Jordan, M.I.: Latent Dirichlet allocation. J. Mach. Learn. Res. **3**, 993–1022 (2003)
4. Chen, Y.S., Shahabi, C.: Automatically improving the accuracy of user profiles with genetic algorithm. In: Proceedings of IASTED International Conference on Artificial Intelligence and Soft Computing, pp. 283–288 (2001)
5. Claypool, M., Brown, D., Le, P., Waseda, M.: Inferring user interest. IEEE Internet Comput. **5**(6), 32–39 (2001)
6. Daoud, M., Lechani, L.T., Boughanem, M.: Towards a graph-based user profile modeling for a session-based personalized search. Knowl. Inf. Syst. **21**(3), 365–398 (2009)
7. Daud, A.: Using time topic modeling for semantics-based dynamic research interest finding. Knowl.-Based Syst. **26**, 154–163 (2012)
8. de Waal, A., Venter, J., Barnard, E.: Applying topic modeling to forensic data. In: Ray, I., Shenoi, S. (eds.) Advances in Digital Forensics IV. IFIP, vol. 285, pp. 115–126. Springer US, New York (2008)
9. El-Kishky, A., Song, Y., Wang, C., Voss, C.R., Han, J.: Scalable topical phrase mining from text corpora. Proc. VLDB Endowment **8**(3), 305–316 (2014)
10. Fawcett, T., Provost, F.J.: Combining data mining and machine learning for effective user profiling. In: KDD, pp. 8–13 (1996)
11. Garfinkel, S.L.: Digital forensics research: the next 10 years. Digit. Invest. **7**, S64–S73 (2010)
12. Griffiths, T.L., Steyvers, M.: Finding scientific topics. Proc. Nat. Acad. Sci. **101**(suppl 1), 5228–5235 (2004)
13. Klimt, B., Yang, Y.: Introducing the enron corpus. In: CEAS (2004)
14. Okolica, J.S., Peterson, G.L., Mills, R.F.: Using PLSI-U to detect insider threats by datamining e-mail. Int. J. Secure. Network. **3**(2), 114–121 (2008)
15. Rosen-Zvi, M., Griffiths, T., Steyvers, M., Smyth, P.: The author-topic model for authors and documents. In: Proceedings of the 20th Conference on Uncertainty in Artificial Intelligence, pp. 487–494. AUAI Press (2004)
16. Turvey, B.E.: Criminal Profiling: An Introduction to Behavioral Evidence Analysis. Academic press, San Diego (2011)
17. Wang, X., McCallum, A.: Topics over time: a non-Markov continuous-time model of topical trends. In: Proceedings of the 12th ACM SIGKDD International Conference on Knowledge Discovery and Data Mining, pp. 424–433. ACM (2006)
18. Yang, M., Chow, K.-P.: Authorship attribution for forensic investigation with thousands of authors. In: Cuppens-Boulahia, N., Cuppens, F., Jajodia, S., Abou El Kalam, A., Sans, T. (eds.) SEC 2014. IFIP AICT, vol. 428, pp. 339–350. Springer, Heidelberg (2014)
19. Yang, M., Chow, K.P.: An information extraction framework for digital forensic investigations. In: Peterson, G., et al. (eds.) Advances in Digital Forensics XI. IFIP AICT, vol. 462, pp. 61–76. Springer, Heidelberg (2015). doi:10.1007/978-3-319-24123-4_4
20. Yang, M., Zhu, D., Chow, K.P.: A topic model for building fine-grained domain-specific emotion lexicon. In: ACL (2), pp. 421–426 (2014)
21. Zhou, X., Wu, S.-T., Li, Y., Xu, Y., Lau, R.Y.K., Bruza, P.D.: Utilizing search intent in topic ontology-based user profile for web mining. In: IEEE/WIC/ACM International Conference on Web Intelligence, WI 2006, pp. 558–564. IEEE (2006)

Short Papers-National Security Infrastructure

Pseudonymous Signature on eIDAS Token – Implementation Based Privacy Threats

Mirosław Kutyłowski[✉], Lucjan Hanzlik, and Kamil Kluczniak

Faculty of Fundamental Problems of Technology,
Politechnika Wrocławska, Wrocław, Poland
{miroslaw.kutylowski,lucjan.hanzlik,kamil.kluczniak}@pwr.edu.pl

Abstract. We investigate eIDAS Token specification for Pseudonymous Signature published recently by German security authority BSI, German Federal Office for Information Security. We analyze how far the current specification prevents privacy violations by the Issuer by malicious or simply careless implementation. We find that, despite the declared design goal of protecting privacy of the citizens, it is quite easy to convert the system into a "Big Brother" system and enable spying the citizens by third parties.

We show that there is a simple and elegant way for preventing all attacks of the kind described. Moreover, we show that it is possible with relatively small amendments to the scheme.

1 Introduction

Personal identity documents are more and more frequently equipped with an electronic layer. The primary goal of this layer was to prevent forgeries by providing key data digitally signed by the document issuer. However, there is an opportunity to use it for e-services such as authentication on a (remote) terminal. This has attracted a lot of attention recently, see the eIDAS regulation of European Union [6]. It aims to create common trust levels and fundamental mechanisms enabling interoperability of authentication services. It supports many novel services and features, including use of pseudonyms.

Privacy-by-design principle introduced by new personal data protection law is another driving force in Europe. It says that the information processing systems must be based on technical security (the former approach was based on penalties for unauthorized data processing).

Privacy Protection via Unlinkability. One of the ideas to achieve privacy-by-design is to eliminate unnecessary data disclosure via authentication. In the traditional setting we authenticate ourselves with full identity and then our rights

---

This research has been supported by the Polish National Science Centre, project HARMONIA, DEC-2013/08/M/ST6/00928.

J.K. Liu and R. Steinfeld (Eds.): ACISP 2016, Part II, LNCS 9723, pp. 467–477, 2016.
DOI: 10.1007/978-3-319-40367-0_31

are determined based on this identity. In many cases a pseudonymous identity would be enough. However, it is not just replacing the regular identity with a pseudonymous one. The problem is that:

- in many cases the user must not be able to appear under two pseudonyms in the same system (i.e. Sybil attacks must be impossible),
- user's activities in different systems must not be linkable – the colluding systems cannot link the pseudonyms of the same person.

Restricted Identification [5] is a mechanism that aims to replace the insecure login-password mechanism and has been implemented on the German personal identity card. It creates a unique password for each *sector* in a strong cryptographic way.

Pseudonymous Signature. This is one of the mechanisms on the eIDAS Token, which has been designed presumably as a replacement for Restricted Identification. It has certain advantages:

- it does not enable to impersonate a user by an adversary knowing a so-called *group key* (see [7]),
- it enables Chip Authentication in a way that creates an undeniable evidence for later disputes.

There are also some disadvantages:

- the last property can be regarded as a disadvantage as well. Previously simultability was frequently declared as a strong privacy protection feature – an authentication proof was not transferable and therefore useless for illegal data trade,
- the seclusiveness problem has not been solved so far.

The Problem. There are two critical security assumptions behind the design of [5]: the eID chips are tamper resistant,and the Issuer of eID is trustworthy. The first assumption is critical in the sense that it is not known how to improve the scheme to make it immune against chip compromise. Some authors provide the same functionality resistant to compromise of eID chips (see e.g. [4] or [8]), but completely new protocols are used (with other disadvantages, like use of pairings). In this paper we focus on the second assumption and ask *how secure are the citizens using eIDAS token from* [5] *in case of rogue authorities?*

Even if in many cases the authorities and manufacturers are trustworthy, the eIDAS token solution might become an international standard. Therefore we cannot exclude an application of this technology in case where the Issuer cannot be trusted.

Paper Overview. In Sect. 2 we recall the technical specification of Pseudonymous Signature from [5]. In Sect. 3 we present some scenarios for rogue implementation of the Issuer in such a way that not only the Issuer can deanonymize users, but also may delegate these possibilities to third parties without giving the private keys of the users. In Sect. 4 we show a relatively simple and elegant solution to prevent all attacks of this kind in a way compliant with the specification of Pseudonymous Signatures from [5].

2   Pseudonymous Signature on eIDAS Token

Here we recall the Pseudonymous Signature from [5]. We follow the notation from [5] in order to make a direct reference to this de facto standard.

System Setup. The system is based on a cyclic group $\mathcal{G}$ of a prime order p (the specification also refers to EC groups). Let g denote a fixed generator of $\mathcal{G}$. There is a pair of keys: the secret key SK_M and the matching public key $PK_M = g^{SK_M}$.

Group Setup. For a group of eID documents the Issuer uses a pair of keys: a secret key SK_{ICC} and the public key $PK_{ICC} = g^{SK_{ICC}}$. The size of a group is a compromise between the size of anonymity set (the number of eIDs based on the same PK_{ICC}) and the cost of revocation of all eIDs using PK_{ICC} in case of leaking SK_{ICC}.

Domain Setup. For a domain *sector* there is a public key PK_{sector} generated by a trusted third party. For application scenarios requiring that the trusted authority can be asked to deanonymize a domain pseudonym of a user, the trusted authority generates PK_{sector} as $g^{SK_{sector}}$. Otherwise, "the third party SHALL generate Sector Public Keys in a way that the corresponding private keys are unknown". A common way to achieve this is to create PK_{sector} via a hash function from the domain identifier.

Issuing an ID Document. For the sake of Pseudonymous Signatures of user U the Issuer generates at random a key $SK_{ICC,2,U} < p^1$. The second private key $SK_{ICC,1,U}$ is

$$SK_{ICC} := SK_{ICC,1,U} + SK_M \cdot SK_{ICC,2,U} \bmod p$$

The corresponding public keys $PK_{ICC,1,U} = g^{SK_{ICC,1,U}}$ and $PK_{ICC,2,U} = g^{SK_{ICC,2,U}}$ might be stored by the Issuer for the sake of deanonymization. The keys $SK_{ICC,1}, SK_{ICC,2}$ are stored on the eID document. (The keys $PK_{ICC,1}, PK_{ICC,2}$ need not to be stored there.)

Creation of Pseudonyms for a Domain. An eID document holding the private keys $SK_{ICC,1,U}$, $SK_{ICC,2,U}$ creates the pseudonyms for the sector with the public key PK_{sector}:

$$I^{sector}_{ICC,1,U} := PK^{SK_{ICC,1,U}}_{sector} \quad \text{and} \quad I^{sector}_{ICC,2,U} := PK^{SK_{ICC,2,U}}_{sector} \ .$$

---

[1] We change the notation from [5] and indicate explicitly the key owner.

Creation of a Pseudonymous Signature for a Domain. (We present a simplified version without some irrelevant implementation details.)

The following steps are executed by user M for signing a message M:

1. choose k_1, k_2 at random,
2. compute $Q_1 := g^{k_1} \cdot PK_M^{k_2}$,
3. [optional] compute $A_1 := PK_{sector}^{k_1}$,
4. [optional] compute $A_2 := PK_{sector}^{k_2}$,
5. compute $c := \mathrm{Hash}(Q_1, I_{ICC,1,U}^{sector}, A_1, I_{ICC,2,U}^{sector}, A_2, PK_{sector}, params, M)$.
   (the parameters $I_{ICC,1,U}^{sector}, A_1$ and $I_{ICC,2,U}^{sector}, A_2$ are optional and omitted when, respectively, A_1 or A_2 are not computed). The argument *params* stands for some additional parameters which are not important from our point of view.
6. compute $s_1 := k_1 - c \cdot SK_{ICC,1,U} \bmod p$ and $s_2 := k_2 - c \cdot SK_{ICC,2,U} \bmod p$.
7. output the signature (c, s_1, s_2).

Signature Verification. Given a signature (c, s_1, s_2), the pseudonyms $I_{ICC,1,U}^{sector}$, $I_{ICC,2,U}^{sector}$ are to be attached, if A_1 and, respectively, A_2 have been used for signature creation.

The verification procedure looks as follows:

1. recompute Q_1 as $Q_1' := PK_{ICC}^c \cdot g^{s_1} \cdot PK_M^{s_2}$,
2. [optional] recompute A_1 as $A_1' := (I_{ICC,1,U}^{sector})^c \cdot PK_{sector}^{s_1}$,
3. [optional] recompute A_2 as $A_2' := (I_{ICC,2,U}^{sector})^c \cdot PK_{sector}^{s_2}$,
4. recompute c as $c' := \mathrm{Hash}(Q_1', I_{ICC,1,U}^{sector}, A_1', I_{ICC,2,U}^{sector}, A_2', PK_{sector}, params, M)$ (if some arguments are omitted during signature creation, then the same arguments should be omitted here).
5. accept if $c' = c$.

Note that the verification will yield the positive result, if the signer follows the protocol:

$$Q_1' = PK_{ICC}^c \cdot g^{s_1} \cdot PK_M^{s_2} = PK_{ICC}^c \cdot g^{k_1 - c \cdot SK_{ICC,1,U}} \cdot PK_M^{k_2 - c \cdot SK_{ICC,2,U}}$$
$$= g^{k_1} \cdot PK_M^{k_2} \cdot \left(PK_{ICC} \cdot g^{-SK_{ICC,1,U}} \cdot PK_M^{-SK_{ICC,2,U}}\right)^c$$
$$= Q_1 \cdot \left(g^{SK_{ICC}} \cdot g^{-(SK_{ICC,1,U} + SK_M \cdot SK_{ICC,2,U})}\right)^c = Q_1 \cdot 1^c = Q_1 \ .$$
$$A_1' = (I_{ICC,1,U}^{sector})^c \cdot PK_{sector}^{s_1} = PK_{sector}^{c \cdot SK_{ICC,1,U}} \cdot PK_{sector}^{k_1 - c \cdot SK_{ICC,1,U}} = PK_{sector}^{k_1} = A_1 \ ,$$
$$A_2' = (I_{ICC,2,U}^{sector})^c \cdot PK_{sector}^{s_2} = PK_{sector}^{c \cdot SK_{ICC,2,U}} \cdot PK_{sector}^{k_2 - c \cdot SK_{ICC,2,U}} = PK_{sector}^{k_2} = A_2 \ .$$

Differences with the Protocol from [2]. The version presented in [2] is the protocol described above with the following choice of options[2]:

---

[2] The description of NymVf contains a misprint: y should be replaced by g_2, which corresponds to PK_M in [5].

- the optional parameters $I^{sector}_{ICC,1,U}$, A_1 <u>are used</u>,
- the optional parameters $I^{sector}_{ICC,2,U}$, A_2 <u>are not used</u>,
- the discrete logarithm of PK_{sector} is always known to the Issuer.

For the protocol described in [2] certain security proofs have been given (there are some problems with them [9]). The recommendation [5] contains neither formal security proofs nor a design rationale.

3   Rogue Issuing Authority

The main purpose of Pseudonymous Signature is to protect signer's privacy. Definitely, we have to trust the Issuer, as according to [5] it creates the secret keys of each single user. The Issuer can retain these keys and use later to deanonymize the users. A silent assumption in [5] as well as in [2,3] is that this is inevitable. In Sect. 4 we show that this is not the case as we can secure the users against the Issuer.

The main problem that we discuss in this section is "delegation" of the ability to deanonymize the users. Is it easy to reveal some data to a third party, called Tracer, so that it can deanonymize as well? The volume of data forwarded to the Tracer counts very much, since the leakage can be created by rogue software installed by the honest Issuer, who himself becomes a victim of the attack: it is much easier to leak a few keys than to hand over the whole database.

In certain situations the Issuer might be forced to provide deanonymization tools to the Tracer. In this case it is important to limit the possibilities of the Tracer. For instance, it should be impossible for the Tracer to create valid secret keys for new users or to forge signatures of the existing users.

The situation described above may concern the state authorities: the Issuer of a country A might be forced to provide deanonymization tools for the security authorities of a country B due to political dependence or in course of trading secrets. However, we have to be aware that a leakage may also concern data transfer to the organized crime. This is particularly dangerous, since the signers may falsely assume that their anonymity is well protected, while it might be not true in case of their biggest foes. Protection against authorities should also be considered. For instance, if Pseudonymous Signatures are used for the sake of electronic voting, some regimes might be tempted to deanonymize the voter supporting the opposition.

Below we show methods for tracing the users of Pseudonymous Signatures.

3.1   Scenario 1: The Issuer Creates Users' Private Keys according to the Protocol

The protocol description in [5] says that the user may authenticate himself with only one pseudonym (or none of them). First let us make the following observation:

Proposition 1. *Assume that the Tracer knows SK_M and holds at least one identity document. Then given one pseudonym of a user U in a domain, he can compute the second pseudonym of U in this domain.*

Proof. First the Tracer can compute $PK_{sector}^{SK_{ICC}}$. Namely, he generates own pseudonyms $I_{ICC,1,T}^{sector}$, $I_{ICC,2,T}^{sector}$ and computes $I_{ICC,1,T}^{sector} \cdot (I_{ICC,2,T}^{sector})^{SK_M}$. Note that

$$I_{ICC,1,T}^{sector} \cdot (I_{ICC,2,T}^{sector})^{SK_M} = (PK_{sector})^{SK_{ICC,1,T}} \cdot (PK_{sector})^{SK_{ICC,2,T} \cdot SK_M} = (PK_{sector})^{SK_{ICC}}$$

Now, given the pseudonym $I_{ICC,1,U}^{sector}$, the Tracer can derive $I_{ICC,2,U}^{sector}$ as

$$(PK_{sector})^{SK_{ICC}} / I_{ICC,1,U}^{sector})^{SK_M^{-1}} \bmod p$$

Similarly, one can derive $I_{ICC,1,U}^{sector}$ from $I_{ICC,2,U}^{sector}$ as

$$(PK_{sector})^{SK_{ICC}} / (I_{ICC,2,U}^{sector})^{SK_M}.$$

□

By Proposition 1 separation of user's signatures based on the pseudonym $I_{ICC,1,U}^{sector}$ and the signatures based on the pseudonym $I_{ICC,2,U}^{sector}$ is not strict, even if the user never creates signatures based on both pseudonyms.

Remark 1. The proof does not work if we replace SK_M by SK_{ICC} in Proposition 1.

It seems that in order to trace a user U, the Issuer has to give the Tracer either $SK_{ICC,1,U}$ or $SK_{ICC,2,U}$. Since the key $SK_{ICC,2,U}$ has to be chosen at random, the Issuer has to leak the key separately for each user. This is somewhat difficult, leaking a single secret key is much easier, e.g. it can be copied to a piece of paper and taken away.

Note that revealing both private keys for 2 different users would mean revealing the system keys SK_M and SK_{ICC} and thereby would delegate the right to issue eID documents as well – which is perhaps much more than the Issuer might agree upon. Unfortunately, it is hard to exclude that the Tracer has broken two different identity documents and therefore was able to derive SK_M and SK_{ICC}. In this case leaking one of the keys $SK_{ICC,1,U}$ and $SK_{ICC,2,U}$ is enough to leak both keys. Then the Tracer would be able to impersonate a given user as well. So this kind of leakage is probably unacceptable for the Issuer.

3.2 Scenario 2: The Issuer Creates the Users' Private keys with a PRNG

Generation of private keys by the Issuer can be implemented in the following way. The Issuer holds a secret random seed s for a cryptographically secure Pseudorandom Number Generator (PRNG) creating numbers in the range $[0, p-1]$. Then the Issuer computes $SK_{ICC,2,U} := \mathrm{PRNG}(s, \mathrm{ID}_U)$, where ID_U is the identifier of U.

Note that having s alone enables the third party to recompute $SK_{ICC,2,U}$ for each user U and thereby to compute the second pseudonym $I^{sector}_{ICC,2,U} = PK^{SK_{ICC,2,U}}_{sector}$ of U in the sector with the public key PK_{sector}.

An implementation based on Scenario 2 can be well justified. Namely, it eliminates problems related to weak sources of randomness. (Note that if the randomness is weak and $SK_{ICC,2,U}$ predictable in some sense, then a party knowing the weakness can extract the candidate keys $SK_{ICC,2,U}$ and check them against the pseudonyms.) Deploying an PRNG is also recommended by NIST [10] – no nondeterministic RNG is recommended for use (of course, the FIPS specification of DRNG requires input of entropy bits, but an external observer cannot test whether these entropy bits are really used).

Such a scenario is still problematic, as the Tracer getting s can compute $SK_{ICC,2,U}$ for any user U. A much better choice would be to enable to trace selectively some users.

3.3   Scenario 3: $SK_{ICC,1,U}$ and $SK_{ICC,2,U}$ with a hidden relationship.

For each user U there are parameters x_U and s_U generated in pseudorandom way. Then

$$\begin{cases} x_U & = SK_{ICC,1,U} + SK_{ICC,2,U} \cdot s_U \mod p, \\ SK_{ICC} = SK_{ICC,1,U} + SK_{ICC,2,U} \cdot SK_M \mod p, \end{cases} \quad (1)$$

The service dependent trapdoor is $T_{sector,U} = PK^{x_U}_{sector}$. The Tracer gets $T_{sector,U}$ and s_U from the Issuer in order to trace the user U in this sector. The test is:

$$T_{sector,U} \stackrel{?}{=} I^{sector}_{ICC,1,U} \cdot (I^{sector}_{ICC,2,U})^{s_U}$$

Note that even if the Tracer learns SK_M, SK_{ICC}, s_U and $T_{sector,U}$, then he still cannot solve the above system of linear Eq. (1) as there are three unknowns: $SK_{ICC,1,U}$, $SK_{ICC,2,U}$ and x_U (note that x_U cannot be extracted from $T_{sector,U}$).

The question is whether additional input would ease forging pseudonymous signatures. This seems not to be the case by the following argument:

given an instance – an input given to an adversary in a standard case, then the adversary can choose an a at random, put

$$T_{sector,U} := I^{sector}_{ICC,1,U} \cdot (I^{sector}_{ICC,2,U})^a$$

and perform the attack using such $T_{sector,U}$. There are two cases: If for $T_{sector,U}$ constructed in this way the attack yields noticeably different results than in the real case, then we can easily build a distinguisher between the output of the PRNG and random numbers. Of course, if we apply a good PRNG, this should not be the case. The other option is that the attack based on such $T_{sector,U}$ works like for the real case. So we see that if it is possible to mount a forgery based on enhanced data, then we can mount a similar attack for the regular case.

Remarks. Note that the leakage could be selective (the Issuer betrays s_U, x_U for some users) or a global one (the Issuer betrays the secret seed s for all of them). Moreover, we may arrange the process of creating the secrets s_U in a tree-like fashion so that one can betray only the secrets from a subtree.

The above attack does not work for the former version described in [2,3], as in this case $I^{sector}_{ICC,2,U}$ is not available.

Note that the Tracer cannot learn the pseudonym of a user in a sector, if the user does not create it. The capability of the Tracer seems to be limited to deanonymization of the users which are active in a sector.

3.4   Scenario 4: Tracing with One Pseudonym

The attacks described above require both domain pseudonyms to deanonymize a user. So one may hope that if we retreat to the setting from [2], then we are again secure against deanonymization attacks enabled by a rogue Issuer. Unfortunately, we show that this is not the case.

In order to enable tracing a user U, the Tracer gets a special *shadow eID*, say for a user U'. Namely, the Issuer creates $SK_{ICC,1,U'}$, $SK_{ICC,2,U'}$ so that:

$$\begin{cases} SK_{ICC,1,U} = s_U \cdot (SK_{ICC,1,U'})^2 & \mod p\ , \\ SK_{ICC} = SK_{ICC,1,U'} + SK_{ICC,2,U'} \cdot SK_M \mod p\ . \end{cases} \tag{2}$$

Now, given PK_{sector}, the user U' can compute the pseudonym $I^{sector}_{ICC,1,U}$ of the user U in the following way:

1. compute its own pseudonym $I'' = I^{sector}_{ICC,1,U'}$ for PK_{sector},
2. compute $I' := (I'')^{s_U}$,
3. feed own eID with I' as the public key of a sector, consequently the eID returns $I = (I')^{SK_{ICC,1,U'}}$,
4. output I.

Note that the output is correct, since

$$(I')^{SK_{ICC,1,U'}} = PK^{s_U \cdot (SK_{ICC,1,U'})^2}_{sector} = PK^{SK_{ICC,1,U}}_{sector} = I^{sector}_{ICC,1,U}\ .$$

In the above procedure the role of s_U is to prevent detection that the eID U' is rogue. Indeed, for $s_U = 1$ an inspector holding the eID of user U' could run the above procedure and check the results. The secret s_U guarantees that such an inspection is infeasible - the holder of eID U' may deny to know any such secret.

On the other hand, even if $I^{sector}_{ICC,1,U'}$ and s_U are known, it is infeasible to compute $PK^{s_U \cdot (SK_{ICC,1,U'})^2}_{sector}$ without knowing $SK_{ICC,1,U'}$. Indeed, this is equivalent to Square Diffie-Hellman problem, which is equivalent to CDH [1]. So if the shadow user U' is behaving in a regular way, it is infeasible to derive the pseudonym of U.

It is also worth to note that $SK_{ICC,1,U'}$ can be chosen at random – then s_U is derived as $SK_{ICC,1,U}/(SK_{ICC,1,U'})^2$. So the probability distribution of the keys for the shadow user U' is the same as for the case when it is not used for tracing U. Of course, U' can trace many users: the Issuer gives U' the secret s_U for each traced user U.

4   Protection Against Rogue Issuers

If the Issuer creates the users' secret keys, we cannot exclude leaking them. Therefore, the only really effective solution would be to prevent the Issuer to know the private keys of the users. Below we propose a method that achieves this goal.

Secure Setup of Pseudonymous Signatures.
Secure initialization of the eID of a user U consists of the following steps:

1. After manufacturing time the eID chip stores two pairs of *prekeys*: $(x_{1,1}, x_{2,1})$ and $(x_{1,2}, x_{2,2})$. They satisfy the equations
$SK_{ICC} = x_{1,i} + x_{2,i} \cdot SK_M$ for $i = 1, 2$.
2. The eID document reaches the user U in the *initialization mode*. In the first step the eID document presents the following *pre-identifiers* to the document owner U:

$$IN_{1,1} = g^{x_{1,1}}, \quad IN_{2,1} = g^{x_{2,1}}, \quad IN_{1,2} = g^{x_{1,2}}, \quad IN_{2,2} = g^{x_{2,2}} .$$

3. The eID document owner U chooses a, b such that $a + b = 1 \bmod p$ and presents them to the eID document. Thereby he requests the eID chip to hold

$$SK_{ICC,1,U} := a \cdot x_{1,1} + b \cdot x_{1,2} \bmod p ,$$
$$SK_{ICC,2,U} := a \cdot x_{2,1} + b \cdot x_{2,2} \bmod p$$

as the private key for Pseudonymous Signature. Note that

$$SK_{ICC,1} + SK_{ICC,2} \cdot SK_M = a \cdot x_{1,1} + b \cdot x_{1,2} + (a \cdot x_{2,1} + b \cdot x_{2,2}) \cdot SK_M$$
$$= a \cdot (x_{1,1} + x_{2,1} \cdot SK_M) + b \cdot (x_{1,2} + x_{2,2} \cdot SK_M)$$
$$= a \cdot SK_{ICC} + b \cdot SK_{ICC} = SK_{ICC} ,$$

so the derived private keys are correct. Also, for any y_1, y_2 satisfying $SK_{ICC} = y_1 + y_2 \cdot SK_M$, there is exactly one pair (a, b) such that

$$\begin{cases} y_1 = a \cdot x_{1,1} + b \cdot x_{1,2} \bmod p, \\ y_2 = a \cdot x_{2,1} + b \cdot x_{2,2} \bmod p, \end{cases} \tag{3}$$

and $a + b = 1 \bmod p$. Indeed,

$$\begin{vmatrix} x_{1,1} & x_{1,2} \\ x_{2,1} & x_{2,2} \end{vmatrix} = \begin{vmatrix} x_{1,1} + x_{2,1} \cdot SK_M & x_{1,2} + x_{2,2} \cdot SK_M \\ x_{2,1} & x_{2,2} \end{vmatrix}$$
$$= \begin{vmatrix} SK_{ICC} & SK_{ICC} \\ x_{2,1} & x_{2,2} \end{vmatrix} = SK_{ICC} \cdot (x_{2,2} - x_{2,1}) \neq 0 \bmod p$$

so there are a and b that satisfy (3). Moreover,

$$SK_{ICC} = y_1 + SK_M \cdot y_2 = (a \cdot x_{1,1} + b \cdot x_{1,2}) + SK_M \cdot (a \cdot x_{2,1} + b \cdot x_{2,2})$$
$$= a \cdot (x_{1,1} + SK_M \cdot x_{2,1}) + b \cdot (x_{1,2} + SK_M \cdot x_{2,2}) = a \cdot SK_{ICC} + b \cdot SK_{ICC} \bmod p$$

Hence $a + b = 1 \bmod p$. Finally we may conclude that the key pair $(SK_{ICC,1,U}, SK_{ICC,2,U})$ is uniformly distributed in the set of all private key pairs.

4. For the future use the eID document owner retains

$$I_1 := IN_{1,1}^a \cdot IN_{1,2}^b, \quad I_2 := IN_{2,1}^a \cdot IN_{2,2}^b \ .$$

5. At this moment the eID document erases the pre-keys, the initialization procedure terminates and the eID document can create pseudonymous signatures with the keys $SK_{ICC,1,U}$, $SK_{ICC,2,U}$.

Anytime the user U can test whether the keys $SK_{ICC,1,U}$, $SK_{ICC,2,U}$ are really used by his eID document. For this purpose the user U asks for identifiers for a sector with $PK_{sector} = g^h$, where h is known to him. The pseudonyms $I_{ICC,1}^{sector}$, $I_{ICC,2}^{sector}$ returned by the eID chip should satisfy the following equalities:

$$I_{ICC,1,U}^{sector} = PK_{sector}^{SK_{ICC,1,U}} = PK_{sector}^{a \cdot x_{1,1} + b \cdot x_{1,2}} = g^{h \cdot a \cdot x_{1,1}} \cdot g^{h \cdot b \cdot x_{1,2}} = IN_{1,1}^{h \cdot a} \cdot IN_{1,2}^{h \cdot b} = I_1^h$$
$$I_{ICC,2,U}^{sector} = PK_{sector}^{SK_{ICC,2,U}} = PK_{sector}^{a \cdot x_{2,1} + b \cdot x_{2,2}} = g^{h \cdot a \cdot x_{2,1}} \cdot g^{h \cdot b \cdot x_{2,2}} = IN_{2,1}^{ha} \cdot IN_{2,2}^{hb} = I_2^h$$

So the document owner performs the test

$$I_{ICC,1}^{sector} \stackrel{?}{=} I_1^h \quad \text{and} \quad I_{ICC,2}^{sector} \stackrel{?}{=} I_2^h \tag{4}$$

If the test fails, then the eID chip is cheating about the choice of the private key.

The eID chip may attempt to guess the moment of the test. However, this would be equivalent to guessing whether the document owner knows the discrete logarithm of the element presented as the public key of a sector. Since deanonymization requires that somebody knows this discrete logarithm, it is infeasible to demand from the owner a proof that he does not know the discrete logarithm.

Note that the above method works also for the original scheme from [3]. Then the test concerns only one equality.

The only problem with the above approach is that it precludes deanonymization. In order to enable it, one can extend the protocol so that the life-cycle of an eID document consists of the configuration phase and the application phase. After the configuration phase the eID document enters the application phase and there is no way back to the configuration phase. The configuration phase consists of the following steps:

- generate the private keys $SK_{ICC,1,U}$, $SK_{ICC,2,U}$ as described above,
- generate the pseudonyms $P_1 = g^{SK_{ICC,1,U}}$, $P_2 = g^{SK_{ICC,2,U}}$ and a Pseudonymous Signature for $PK_{sector} = g$, send the pseudonyms and the signature to the Issuer over a secure channel,

- enter the application phase after receiving an acknowledgement of the Issuer confirming P_1 and P_2.

Given P_1, P_2, deanonymization may be executed as for the original eIDAS token [5].

5 Conclusions

Despite the careful design of [5], it turns out that some details of the specification need to be carefully reviewed. We need a complete system description with a corresponding security model taking into account malicious behavior of protocol participants. Potential mistakes may have deep impact, as decisions concerning electronic identity documents have their long term consequences due to the typical exchange period of 10 years.

References

1. Bao, F., Deng, R.H., Zhu, H.: Variations of Diffie-Hellman problem. In: Qing, S., Gollmann, D., Zhou, J. (eds.) ICICS 2003. LNCS, vol. 2836, pp. 301–312. Springer, Heidelberg (2003)
2. Bender, J., Dagdelen, Ö., Fischlin, M., Kügler, D.: Domain-specific pseudonymous signatures for the German identity card. IACR Cryptology ePrint Archive **2012**, 558 (2012)
3. Bender, J., Dagdelen, Ö., Fischlin, M., Kügler, D.: Domain-specific pseudonymous signatures for the German identity card. In: Gollmann, D., Freiling, F.C. (eds.) ISC 2012. LNCS, vol. 7483, pp. 104–119. Springer, Heidelberg (2012)
4. Bringer, J., Chabanne, H., Lescuyer, R., Patey, A.: Efficient and strongly secure dynamic domain-specific pseudonymous signatures for ID documents. In: Christin, N., Safavi-Naini, R. (eds.) FC 2014. LNCS, vol. 8437, pp. 252–269. Springer, Heidelberg (2014)
5. BSI: Advanced Security Mechanisms for Machine Readable Travel Documents and eIDAS Token 2.20. Technical Guideline TR-03110-2 (2015)
6. European Parliament the Council: Regulation (EU) No 910/2014 of the European Parliament and of the Council on electronic identification and trust services for electronic transactions in the internal market and repealing Directive 1999/93/EC (2014)
7. Hanzlik, L., Kutyłowski, M.: Insecurity of anonymous login with German personal identity cards. In: Security and Privacy in Social Networks and Big Data (SocialSec), pp. 39–43. IEEE Computer Society (2015)
8. Kluczniak, K.: Anonymous authentication using electronic identity documents. Ph.D. Dissertation, submitted (2016)
9. Kluczniak, K.: Domain-specific pseudonymous signatures revisited. IACR Cryptology ePrint Archive **2016**, 70 (2016)
10. NIST: Annex C: Approved random number generators for FIPS PUB 140–2, security requirements for cryptographic modules, January 2016. http://csrc.nist.gov/publications/fips/fips140-2/fips1402annexc.pdf

Short Papers-Mobile Security

A Feasible No-Root Approach on Android

Yao Cheng[✉], Yingjiu Li, and Robert H. Deng

School of Information Systems, Singapore Management University,
Singapore, Singapore
{ycheng,yjli,robertdeng}@smu.edu.sg

Abstract. Root is the administrative privilege on Android, which is however inaccessible on stock Android devices. Due to the desire for privileged functionalities and the reluctance of rooting their devices, Android users seek for no-root approaches, which provide users with part of root privileges without rooting their devices. In this paper, we newly discover a feasible no-root approach based on the ADB loopback. To ensure such no-root approach is not misused proactively, we examine its dark side, including privacy leakage via logs and user input inference. Finally, we discuss the solutions and suggestions from different perspectives.

Keywords: No-Root approach · Android Debug Bridge (ADB) · Privacy leakage · Exploit analysis

1 Introduction

Android is a Linux based system with discretionary access control enforcement. Root access, which is part of traditional Linux systems, is blocked on stock Android devices for security reasons. If users would like to gain complete control over their Android devices with administrative permissions, they could root their devices at their own risks, such as device bricking and warranty turning void.

To avoid the risks of rooting their Android devices, users turn to no-root approaches which enable them to attain their desired permissions but without rooting their devices. The motivation of using no-root approaches might be strong since Android do not always provide all easy-to-use but desperately needed features. Some popular no-root applications [1,2], even paid ones [3], have achieved millions of downloads and high reputations in Google Play.

The existing no-root applications ("apps") primarily use Android Debug Bridge (ADB) [4] to launch a separate privileged executable program as background service on the target device. The background service is designed to respond to user's requests made from the no-root app and perform certain privileged tasks which the no-root app is not authorized to perform.

In this paper, we newly discover a feasible no-root approach leveraging the new ADB functionality provided on Android versions 4.x and 5.x which take up to 95.7 % in the distribution of Android devices according to the official statistics [5]. To our best knowledge, we are the first to discover such no-root

© Springer International Publishing Switzerland 2016
J.K. Liu and R. Steinfeld (Eds.): ACISP 2016, Part II, LNCS 9723, pp. 481–489, 2016.
DOI: 10.1007/978-3-319-40367-0_32

approach. This no-root approach has its advantage compared to the other no-root approaches in that it creates an ADB *loopback* instead of introducing a separate service. After the ADB loopback is created, a no-root app on the target device can run as a debugger to execute ADB commands to accomplish the privileged operations.

Though, we have not found any wild samples using this no-root approach yet, they may appear in the market at any time in any form, e.g., malicious apps pretending to be no-root apps. To ensure that such no-root approach is not misused in a proactive instead of reactive manner, we examine the dark side of this approach and reveal that the attacks leveraging this no-root approach can be launched from an app on a standalone victim device instead of on a development computer connected to the victim device. We reported the issue to Android. The latest Android 6.0 takes action to remove ADB client and ADB server on the latest Android 6.0 to avoid the attacks.

2   A Feasible No-Root Approach

2.1   ADB

ADB [4] is a debug system for Android that allows developers to connect development computers and Android devices/emulators. Developers can debug Android devices on separate development computers via ADB. ADB includes three components as shown in Fig. 1 (the components not in red), i.e., ADB client, ADB server[1], and ADB daemon. A developer issues an ADB command via an ADB client on a development computer. An ADB server on the development computer, passes the command from ADB client to an ADB daemon which runs on a target Android device. The response to the command is passed back to the developer along the same route. Before debugging, there is a switch to be enabled in the Settings→Developer options. Since Android 4.2.2, at the first time a development commuter connects the target Android device, a confirmation dialog showing the MD5 hash of an RSA public key of the development computer is prompted to obtain the explicit confirmation from the device owner.

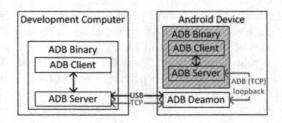

Fig. 1. ADB architecture.

---

[1] In practice, ADB server is implemented in the same binary as ADB client.

After the connection established, two categories of commands can be issued from the developer computer to the connected Android device, i.e., ADB commands and shell commands. ADB commands fulfil the functionalities for debugging purpose, such as device connection, app (un)installing, data transfer, and shell starting. Shell commands can be used after the shell starting, when a shell user, whose UID is 2000 on Android, is born with shell permissions. The majority of shell permissions [6] have protection levels equal to or higher than "dangerous". Note that any permissions higher than "dangerous" level are either hidden or not for use by third-party apps.

2.2 The Existing No-Root Approach

The existing no-root apps adopt ADB to launch a separate service in their pre-processing, and delegate the privileged tasks to this service during runtime. The preprocessing usually includes two manual operations. The first is to connect a mobile device to a development computer and switch on the debug mode. The second is to run a provisioned enabler on the development computer which has been downloaded separately from a no-root app's website. To understand the purpose of using an enabler, we introduce a typical enabler script as shown in Listing 1. In Listing 1, "svc" denotes the native service that performs a target task which requires certain high-level permissions. The executable service is pushed to the device (Line 1) and started by ADB shell (Line 3) so that it inherits the shell permissions for exercising some privileged functionalities. After that, the no-root app which directly interacts with users, is able to work by delegating some of its tasks to the running service through sockets. The service needs to be restarted once the Android device is rebooted, i.e., to run the enabler again.

2.3 A Feasible No-Root Approach Based on ADB Loopback

Different from the existing approach, whose privilege resides in a separate service, we newly discover a feasible no-root approach based on ADB loopback and requiring no separate service.

An Android device of versions from 4.x to 5.x can debug another Android device, because these new versions have introduced the ADB components, which are originally on development computers, to Android systems, i.e., ADB client and ADB server (the dashed components in Fig. 1). In addition, the connection mode is not limited to USB cable. A new TCP mode allows a development computer using TCP links to connect to the target Android device. However, an inconspicuous side consequence is that an Android device gains the capability of debugging itself by connecting its ADB server to its local ADB daemon via TCP mode (the loopback in Fig. 1). Based on such ADB loopback, we discover a new feasible no-root approach.

Listing 1. The existing no-root script.

```
1   adb push ./svc /data/local/svc
2   adb shell chmod 777 /data/local/svc
3   adb shell /data/local/svc &
```

Listing 2. The core snippet of Looper.

```
1   adb tcpip 5555
2   adb shell adb kill-server
3   adb shell HOME=/sdcard adb start-
    ↪  server &
```

It takes a simple preprocessing to establish the ADB loopback. What a user needs to do in this preprocessing is to run a script, which we name as *"Looper"*, on a development computer connected to the target Android device. Listing 2 shows the core snippet of Looper. Looper turns on the TCP mode at port 5555 on the target Android device (Line 1). Then, it restarts the ADB server setting "/sdcard" as HOME folder (Line 2 and Line 3). The purpose of changing HOME folder is to guarantee that Looper could work as well on Android 4.2.2 and higher. This is because since Android 4.2.2, ADB introduces the RSA authentication that stores its key pair in the HOME folder. Looper changes the HOME folder to a shell-user-accessible folder, so that the RSA key pair of the ADB server can be stored successfully for later authentication. After confirming the dialogs requiring the explicit confirmation from the device owner, the ADB loopback is established, and its effect lasts till the Android device is rebooted.

After ADB loopback is established, a no-root app with the permission to connect to local TCP ports can play the role of a debugger. The permissions of ADB that are intended for remote development computers are now available on stand-alone Android devices. As a result, by using ADB loopback, no-root apps can perform privileged tasks as intended.

3   Exploits on the Dark Side

No-root has always been a double-edged sword[2]. It is important to explore its dark side proactively. In this section, we demonstrate two typical exploits on such no-root approach.

3.1   Adversary Model

The scenario of our investigation is that a user has an Android device which is *not* rooted. (S)he has installed a no-root app that adopts the newly-discovered no-root approach on his/her device for the purpose of enjoying privileged functions without rooting the device. We investigate the potential threats causing by a malicious app only with the internet permission, which can be the no-root app itself or other apps on the same device.

---

[2] The existing no-root approach could lead to privacy leakage due to the insecure socket communication between the no-root app and its native service [7].

3.2   Privacy Leakage via Application Logs

Android provides a logging system for inspecting debugging outputs. The access to log messages is regulated by callers' UIDs. Normal users, i.e., third-party apps without root privilege, can only access the logs related to themselves. However, an app, leveraging the no-root approach we discover, can get system-wide logs using "logcat" which is the official tool for dumping log messages.

If there is no sensitive information being logged, there should be no information leakage via logs. Android documents have suggested that logs should be managed, e.g., removed in release versions, according to their types [8]. Even though, it happened that some informative data is logged [9]. We are interested in whether developers manage sensitive logs properly nowadays, since private log may become readable to other apps in this scenario.

The sensitive information on mobile devices is classified into four categories. The device parameters reflect the characteristics of devices, including Android version, device model, manufacturer, root status, and phone service information (phone number, IMEI, and IMSI). The app account information is on the application level, which includes account ID, account credential, and personal profile. The user interaction indications indicate the operations a user performs, such as opening an activity and inputting a password. Finally, geographic data, network information, and others are classified into the last category.

The top-ranked 10 account-sensitive free apps from Google Play and Anzhi Market are examined, respectively. The observation shows that 11 of the 20 top-ranked apps log some sensitive data in Table 1.

Table 1. The sensitive information collected from log messages.

Applications	Device params	Account info	User interaction	Others
org.mozilla.firefox (G)	✓	✓	-	-
com.tencent.mtt (A)	-	✓	-	-
com.taobao.taobao (A)	✓	✓	-	-
com.sinovatech.unicom.ui (A)	✓	✓	✓	✓ Location
com.skype.polaris (G)	✓	-	-	✓ User agent string, country code
com.tencent.mobileqq (A)	-	-	-	✓ Gateway IP, SQL statement, established connections, network info and quality test
com.google.android.youtube (G)	✓	-	-	✓ Country code, network info
com.facebook.katana (G)	-	✓	-	✓ Gateway IP, GPS data
com.cleanmaster.mguard (A)	✓	-	✓	-
com.snapchat.android (G)	-	-	✓	-
co.vine.android (G)	-	-	✓	-

One interesting example is due to the improper use of third-party SDK. Snapchat [10] uses Flurry [11] SDK to help its developers obtain the usage analytics. Flurry defines log APIs for developers to monitor the runtime behaviours of apps during developing and debugging. It is observed that some real-time user operations are logged using Flurry APIs in the release version. One of such cases, which happens during registration, is demonstrated in Listing 3. It can be inferred that Snapchat first focuses on the email field (Line 2), and then the edit on this filed begins (Line 3). After that, it focuses on the password filed waiting for inputs (Line 4). Once a user starts inputting his/her password, it immediately outputs the corresponding log (Line 5). Even there is no direct leakage of email or password, the information about focusing and editing can be used maliciously to launch other attacks such as keylogger attacks.

Listing 3. FlurryAgent logs in Snapchat showing user interactions during registration.

```
1    W/FlurryAgent(20495):  Event  count  started:  R01_BEGIN_REGISTRATION
2    W/FlurryAgent(20495):  Event  count  started:  R01_FOCUS_ON_EMAIL
3    W/FlurryAgent(20495):  Event  count  started:  R01_EDITED_EMAIL
4    W/FlurryAgent(20495):  Event  count  started:  R01_FOCUS_ON_PASSWORD
5    W/FlurryAgent(20495):  Event  count  started:  R01_EDITED_PASSWORD
```

3.3   User Input Inference

User input inference is a way to obtain users' private information such as account credential by capturing their input. An attacker can apply the input inference to surmise the credential at the time of user inputting. Unfortunately, if the no-root approach is misused, both input timing and input characters are available.

Good Timing of Credential Input. Normally, when a login activity is shown on screen, if the keyboard is invoked at the same time, there is a higher chance that a user is going to input account credential to this activity.

Login activities usually share a common pattern which can be used to detect them. A login activity normally consists of at least two EditText fields for inputting the username and password, respectively. Among the two, the second EditText field conceals the password by representing each input character in a black dot or asterisk. This pattern is reflected in the activity layout which can be obtained in XML format using the shell command "uiautomator". And the keyboard appearance can be captured using the shell command "dumpsys".

We test the good timing detection algorithm with the top 20 finance apps in Google Play. Experiments show that the algorithm can capture all the login activities in 15 apps. The other 5 apps are verified to have no login activities.

Inference of Input Characters. The characters that a user inputs on a touchscreen can be inferred from knowing both of the touch position on screen and the software keyboard layout.

First, let us consider the touch positions. The dispatch destination of each click position is supposed to be the app running on screen only. However, with the dark side of the no-root approach, a malicious app on the same device can access directly the touch coordinates using the shell command "getevent" no matter it is running on screen or not. In this way, the accurate touch position is known by parsing these raw events [12] returned by this command straightly.

Second, let us consider the keyboard layout. The position of each key varies according to different layouts, e.g., "QWERTY" layout. Even for the same layout, the position might be different due to the adjustment by vendors. The information about the input method, e.g., its vendor name and whether it is invoked, is available using "dumpsys". As a result, the combination of touch positions and the keyboard layout can further surmise the input characters.

4 Discussion

After we verify that the no-root approach can work on Android versions from 4.x to 5.x, we reported it to Android in August 2015. Android admitted soon that the no-root approach can work as intended, and so do the exploits on its dark side. Later in October 2015, Android adopted a straightforward solution by removing the ADB client and ADB server, i.e., the ADB binary from the newly released Android 6.0. These two components are responsible for accepting debugging commands and communicating with the ADB daemon, respectively. As a consequence, an Android device can no long be used to debug other Android devices. While it is a simple solution to remove the debug functionality, it is not ideal due to sacrificing much benefit/convenience provided by ADB debugging and no-root apps. A preferred solution should mitigate the ADB loopback exploits while still make it work for benign no-root apps, such as extending the existing permission-based mechanism. We leave this to the future work.

On the other hand, the ignorance of developers and markets is another important cause of the exploits. On the app developers' side, proper coding and configuration would help to protect apps against some malicious exploits. It is important for app developers to clean up sensitive logs when producing release versions. On the app markets' side, it is suggested that app markets enforce effective and specific vetting processes. Google Play has set up an example of using its bouncer [13], which checks for malicious operations and certain vulnerabilities in each app submitted to Google Play and suggests whether or not accept the app in the market. We suggest that Android markets, both official and third-party ones, should check for the usage of logging code, e.g., debug or verbose level log, so as to avoid leaking sensitive information in logs.

5 Related Works

Several ADB based attacks have been identified before. Vidas et al. [14] mentioned in their survey that an untrusted ADB connection via USB could result in security breaches when an attacker is physically close to the target device. Recently, Symantec detected a Windows malware which may infect Android devices with ADB [15] via USB connections. Hwang et al. [16] presented some feasible stealthy attacks which can be performed with ADB capabilities. In this paper, we firstly discover a feasible no-root approach that based on ADB loop-back to achieve extra privilege in Android system without root. The dark-side exploits of this no-root approach and the evaluation on real-world apps are com-plementary to the ADB based attacks identified before in terms of providing a better understanding on how ADB can be misused.

Previous research has shown that some existing no-root applications can be misused. Lin et al. [7] attacked some existing no-root screenshot apps and abused their screenshot functionalities. It was shown that user input can be inferred by analysing the screenshots taken by these apps. In order to prevent the newly-discovered no-root approach from being misused or attacked, we proactively explore its dark side.

Developers' negligence in code regulation was pointed out that a malicious app can read SMS, obtain contacts and access location by selectively reading the system logs in earlier versions of Android [9]. However, since Android 4.1, an app is restricted to read its own logs only. Nonetheless, it is still not a secure way to log sensitive information. Because like one of the dark-side exploits in this paper, the system-wide logs may become available to an installed malicious app. The evaluation on the top-ranked real-world apps shows that many of them still log informative data, which leads to severe privacy leakage.

6   Conclusions

In this paper, we discover a feasible no-root approach leveraging ADB loopback working on Android devices of versions 4.x and 5.x for the first time. To ensure that this no-root approach is not misused in a proactive manner, we investigate its typical dark-side exploits and evaluate them with real-world apps. Finally, we discuss the mitigation that could be adopted by different parties.

Acknowledgement. This material is based on research work supported by the Singapore National Research Foundation under NCR Award Number NRF2014NCR-NCR001-012. We thank Professor Lingyun Ying from Chinese Academy of Sciences for his helpful discussion at the early stage of this work.

References

1. Helium - app sync and backup. https://play.google.com/store/apps/details? id=com.koushikdutta.backup
2. Clockworkmod tether (no root). https://play.google.com/store/apps/details? id=com.koushikdutta.tether
3. No root screenshot it. https://play.google.com/store/apps/details?id=com. edwardkim.android.screenshotitfullnoroot
4. Android debug bridge. http://developer.android.com/tools/help/adb.html
5. Platform versions distrubution. http://developer.android.com/about/dashboards/ index.html
6. Shell permissions on android. https://android.googlesource.com/platform/ frameworks/base/+/android-5.1.0_r5/packages/Shell/AndroidManifest.xml

 7. Lin, C.-C., Li, H., Zhou, X., Wang, X.F.: Screenmilker: How to milk your android screen for secrets. In: NDSS (2014)
 8. Log. http://developer.android.com/reference/android/util/Log.html
 9. Lineberry, A., Richardson, D.L., Wyatt, T.: These aren't the permissions you're looking for (2010). https://www.defcon.org/images/defcon-18/dc-18-presentations/Lineberry/DEFCON-18-Lineberry-Not-The-Permissions-You-Are-Looking-For.pdf
10. Snapchat. https://play.google.com/store/apps/details?id=com.snapchat.android
11. Flurry. http://www.flurry.com/
12. Getevent. https://source.android.com/devices/input/getevent.html
13. Android and security. http://googlemobile.blogspot.sg/2012/02/android-and-security.html
14. Vidas, T., Votipka, D., Christin, N.: All your droid are belong to us: a survey of current android attacks. In: WOOT, pp. 81–90 (2011)
15. Windows malware attempts to infect android devices. http://www.symantec.com/connect/blogs/windows-malware-attempts-infect-android-devices
16. Hwang, S., Lee, S., Kim, Y., Ryu, S.: Bittersweet adb: Attacks and defenses. In: Proceedings of the 10th ACM Symposium on Information, Computer and Communications Security, pp. 579–584 (2015)

Short Papers-Network Security

Improved Classification of Known and Unknown Network Traffic Flows Using Semi-supervised Machine Learning

Timothy Glennan[(✉)], Christopher Leckie, and Sarah M. Erfani

Department of Computing and Information Systems, The University of Melbourne,
Melbourne, Australia
{tglennan,caleckie,sarah.erfani}@unimelb.edu.au

Abstract. Modern network traffic classification approaches apply machine learning techniques to statistical flow properties, allowing accurate classification even when traditional approaches fail. We base our approach to the task on a state-of-the-art semi-supervised classifier to identify known and unknown flows with little labelled training data. We propose a new algorithm for mapping clusters to classes to target classes that were previously difficult to classify. We also apply alternative statistical features. We find our approach has an accuracy of 95.10 %, over 17 % above the technique on which it is based. Additionally, our approach improves the classification performance on every class.

1 Introduction

Network traffic classification is an important task for a range of network-related areas, including network management, surveillance, and security. Traffic classification has traditionally been performed by inspecting port numbers. However, this is often ineffective due to the number of applications using non-unique and non-standard port numbers [1]. Deep-packet inspection avoids reliance on port numbers, but demands an up-to-date database of application signatures and has significant computational complexity, often making the approach unfeasible for real-world use [2, 3].

Machine learning techniques have been gaining popularity for their ability to effectively classify network applications using only statistical flow features [1–3] and without the drawbacks of more traditional approaches. The open problem we address is how to improve the accuracy of traffic classification from applications that have been difficult to classify using only statistical traffic flow properties.

In this paper, we apply a semi-supervised machine learning technique to automatically identify network applications using only statistical traffic flow properties. Our approach is based on a leading semi-supervised traffic classification approach [4], which can handle flows generated by unknown applications. We propose two innovations to this method in order to further increase its effectiveness. First, our approach introduces an alternate algorithm for identifying applications, Second, we propose introducing feature selection into the system model. Based on an empirical evaluation on a standard benchmark dataset, we show that our approach has an accuracy of 95.10 %, an increase

© Springer International Publishing Switzerland 2016
J.K. Liu and R. Steinfeld (Eds.): ACISP 2016, Part II, LNCS 9723, pp. 493–501, 2016.
DOI: 10.1007/978-3-319-40367-0_33

of over 17 % against the technique on which it is based [4]. Additionally, our approach improves the classification performance on every class.

2   Related Work

Current research into traffic classification has shown various supervised, unsupervised, and semi-supervised machine learning techniques to be viable approaches. Supervised machine learning approaches [5, 6] have been shown to achieve particularly high classification effectiveness. However, these approaches can only predict predefined classes found in the training data. Unsupervised learning approaches [7, 8] classify from clusters of unlabelled training flows. While using unlabelled data means they can handle known and unknown classes, mapping clusters to classes remains a key challenge.

Semi-supervised approaches aim to address the problems of both supervised and unsupervised approaches. Erman *et al.* [2] developed an effective semi-supervised approach for classifying network applications, combining K-Means clustering with probabilistic assignment. Using a small set of labelled flows with a larger unlabelled set, clusters with labelled flows can automatically be mapped to classes. Clusters without labelled flows represent unknown classes. The key advantage of this technique is simple class mapping and handling of unknown classes. With few labelled instances, however, clusters are often incorrectly labelled "unknown". A recent extension to this approach by Zhang *et al.* [4] countered this weakness by automatically extending the labelled portion of training data. This was done by identifying correlated flows – flows sharing the same destination IP address and port, and protocol – and sharing labels between them. This approach was shown to significantly increase the labels available and thus better label clusters. Furthermore, applying compound classification to correlated test flows further improved effectiveness. It was shown to outperform standard and state-of-the-art machine learning algorithms, including decision trees, K nearest neighbours, Bayesian networks, and the Erman *et al.* approach.

While the Zhang *et al.* approach is a leading semi-supervised approach for traffic classification, certain traffic classes still proved challenging to identify. We aim to target these classes for an overall more consistently effective classifier.

3   Problem Statement

We are given a set of training flows $T = \{t_i \mid i = 1, 2,\dots n\}$ and a set of testing flows $X = \{x_j \mid j = 1, 2,\dots m\}$, generated on a single network. Each flow represents a bidirectional series of packets between two hosts, sharing the same source and destination addresses, port numbers, and protocol. Each flow has been generated by some known or unknown traffic class c. For each known class c, a subset of T exists such that $T_c = \{L_c \cap U_c\}$ and $\| L_c \| < < \| U_c \|$, where L_c is the set of pre-labelled flows of class c and U_c is the set of unlabelled flows of class c. For any unknown class c, the subset of T containing flows of class c is $T_c = \{U_c\}$. That is, none of its flows are pre-labelled.

From T, we aim to create classifier $f(\mathbf{x}) = c$ such that when a flow $\mathbf{x}$ is given, a traffic class c is predicted. The traffic class c indicates that flow $\mathbf{x}$ was generated by a specific known class, or that it was generated by some unknown classes.

4 Our Proposed Approach

Figure 1 illustrates the details of our approach. The flow label propagation algorithm is first applied to a large training set containing a small number of labelled flows per class. The flow label propagation algorithm uses the correlated flows property of network traffic described in Sect. 2 to automatically increase the number of labelled flows. Feature selection algorithms are then applied to this larger labelled set to identify the strongest features. Next, clustering is performed on all training data, and then labelled flows are used to identify clusters as classes. Finally, the nearest cluster classifier predicts flow classes.

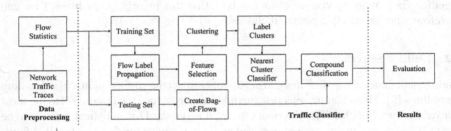

Fig. 1. System model.

This system model is based on Zhang *et al.* [4], with some key alterations. Like [4], this model's main advantage is its ability to appropriately handle flows generated by unknown applications. Creating and identifying "unknown" clusters achieves this. However, we propose an alternative cluster labelling algorithm for increased effectiveness. After flow label propagation, we also introduce feature selection to identify a stronger feature set. Label propagation can greatly increase the amount of labelled data available, allowing feature selection algorithms to work more effectively. Thus this step can again increase the classification success. Below we describe our alternative cluster labelling algorithm, followed by our feature selection approach.

4.1 Fuzzy Cluster Labelling Algorithm

The cluster labelling algorithm introduced below is our proposed alternative to the algorithm used in [2, 4]. Their algorithm is a simple majority vote; the label for some cluster i is the most common label in i. If i has no labelled flows, then it is an unknown cluster. We follow the same principle, but our algorithm has two key differences. First, "unknown" is treated as a traffic class. Second, clusters can be labelled as multiple traffic classes. For this reason we dub the algorithm *fuzzy cluster labelling*.

```
Input: training flows T; set of k clusters trained on T
Output: traffic class labels, labels_i, for each cluster c_i
for i = 1 ← k
    c_ij = number of flows labelled as class j in cluster c_i
    labels_i = [argmax_j(c_ij)]
    foreach traffic class j
      if j not in labels_i and c_ij * threshold > y:
          append j to labels_i
```

Algorithm 1. Fuzzy Cluster Labelling

The algorithm requires a reasonable number of pre-labelled flows per class, which is achieved in our model by first applying the label propagation from [4]. The threshold ensures we assign additional cluster labels in the case of no clear majority. Otherwise we give it just one label. The labels are then naturally decided between during compound classification. The compound classification stage classifies all correlated test flows together via a majority vote of class labels. Using this algorithm, each test flow can therefore vote for multiple potential classes.

4.2 Feature Selection

Irrelevant or unnecessary features can negatively impact the success of machine learning algorithms [9]. Thus, feature selection methods aim to reduce the feature set to the most relevant subset. For classifying network flows, it is standard for statistical features to be used [3]. However, in our semi-supervised context, we have too few pre-labelled flows for feature selection to be effective. This problem is alleviated by first applying flow label propagation to the dataset. Once this is applied, there is a more reasonable pool of labelled data for feature selection algorithms to use. We reduce an initial set of 40 statistical features by applying the extra trees classifier algorithm [10], selected for its efficiency and simplicity, to identify a feature subset.

5   Experimental Evaluation

This section evaluates our proposed method against the Zhang method on which it is based, as this method has been shown to outperform other standard and state-of-the-art approaches.

5.1   Data Set Description

The data used in this experiment originates from a publicly available *wide* (http:// mawi.wide.ad.jp/mawi/) network traffic trace. The data used is a sample from traffic captured in March 2008. NetMate [11] is used to convert packets into flows and compute various features. This dataset was then separated into a training set of approximately 114,000 flows and a testing set of approximately 28,500 flows. While we acknowledge identifying ground truth classes through standard port numbers will introduce some error, this is a common labelling approach used in the literature, and the error introduced is expected to be small [12]. A maximum of 24,000 training flows and 6,000 testing flows were selected at random per class to prevent over-representation. Table 1 shows a complete breakdown of classes used.

Table 1. Traffic class breakdown in the sample of the *wide* dataset used.

Traffic class	# of training flows	# of testing flows
HTTP	24,000	6,000
BitTorrent	2,448	613
DNS	24,000	6,000
SMTP	24,000	6,000
SSH	24,000	6,000
HTTPS	15,370	3,843

5.2 Evaluation Metrics

Two standard metrics are used to evaluate the performance of the proposed method. The first method is accuracy, i.e., the number of correctly classified flows out of all classifications made. This metric is used to evaluate overall classifier performance.

$$Accuracy = \frac{CorrectlyClassifiedFlows}{TotalNumberofFlows} \tag{1}$$

The second metric used is F-measure, i.e., the weighted harmonic mean of precision and recall. Precision is defined as the ratio of flows correctly classified as a class to all flows classified as that class. Recall is defined as the ratio of flows classified as some class to all flows truly belonging to that class.

$$F - Measure = \frac{2 \times Precision \times Recall}{Precision + Recall} \tag{2}$$

The F-Measure is used to evaluate the performance for each class individually.

5.3 Experimental Setup

For each experiment, we use 100 pre-labelled flows per known traffic class (HTTP, BitTorrent, SSH, and HTTPS). We select DNS and SMTP as unknown classes with no pre-labelled flows. We use k-Means as our clustering algorithm. The number of clusters for both Zhang's method and the proposed method is set to $k = 500$, and each experiment is repeated 5 times with results averaged. The large k chosen is appropriate since using a large number of clusters has been shown to result in pure clusters for network traffic [8], and the Zhang *et al.* method has been shown to be robust when varying the number of clusters [4]. The features used in our implementation of the Zhang approach are 20 statistical features described in [4].

5.4   Results of Fuzzy Cluster Labelling

The results of the fuzzy cluster labelling algorithm (with a threshold of 2.5) against the original Zhang *et al.* labelling can be seen in Fig. 2. The same statistical features from [4] were used in both experimental setups. The labelling threshold parameter was varied between 2.0 and 3.0 and the impact was largely negligible.

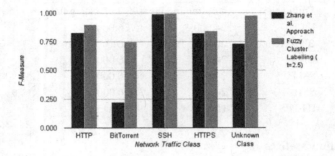

Fig. 2. F-Measure per traffic class when applying alternate cluster labelling methods. (Color figure online)

Our proposed labelling algorithm resulted in an increase in F-Measure for every class. For classes where the Zhang approach performed well, there was always a slight, albeit sometimes insignificant, improvement. For example, the algorithm produced an increase in F-Measure of just 0.071 and 0.021 for HTTP and HTTPS classes respectively. For classes where the Zhang approach did not perform as well, our algorithm made more noticeable improvement. The unknown class improved from 0.733 to 0.980, an increase of 0.247. The BitTorrent class improved from 0.222 to 0.750, an increase of 0.528. We note that the BitTorrent class performed much better in [4] than in our implementation of the Zhang's approach. We attribute this to using different samples of the same dataset and having few training and test instances for this class.

5.5   Results of Fuzzy Labelling and Feature Selection

Applying feature selection reduced an initial set of 40 statistical features to the 17 described in Table 2. Applying both the new feature subset and the proposed clustering algorithm together completes our approach. The combined impact can be seen in Fig. 3. Figure 3(a) shows the overall accuracy found is an increase from 77.77 % to 95.10 %, a significant increase of over 17 % against [4].

The effect on F-Measure in Fig. 3(b) shows that our approach improved the F-Measure for each class when again compared against [4]. The HTTP class increased by 0.087 to an F-Measure of 0.913. The F-Measure for the SSH class was 0.997, and 0.860 for HTTPS. These rose by a very minor 0.002 and 0.043 respectively. The unknown class grew from 0.733 to 0.980, and BitTorrent from 0.225 to 0.821.

Table 2. Final feature set used after feature selection.

Feature category	Description	# of features
Bytes (Forwards)	Minimum, maximum, and standard deviation of packets.	3
Bytes (Backwards)	Mean, maximum, and standard deviation of packets.	3
Inter Packet Time (Forwards)	Minimum, mean, maximum, and standard deviation of inter packet time in the forward direction.	4
Inter Packet Time (Backwards)	Mean, maximum, and standard deviation of inter packet time in the reverse direction.	3
Duration	Duration of the flow.	1
Flag	Whether there was a PSH flag in the forward direction.	1
Headers	Total size of the headers in each direction.	2

Using our alternative feature improved only marginally over the Zhang feature set. However, each class performed as well or better than before. Most significantly, the BitTorrent class grew by a further 0.070. The HTTP and HTTPS classes found minor improvements of 0.013 and 0.016 respectively. The other classes remained as before.

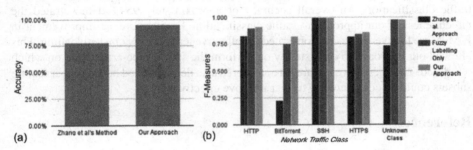

Fig. 3. Overall accuracy and F-Measures of the Zhang *et al.* approach against our approach. (Color figure online)

6   Analysis and Discussion

The results in Sect. 5 demonstrate that our approach can significantly improve traffic classification effectiveness against a state-of-the-art method. The overall accuracy improvement of over 17 % demonstrates the potential of our approach.

The proposed fuzzy cluster labelling algorithm made the most significant impact. There are two reasons for this. First, the Zhang approach ignores unlabelled flows when labelling, while we make use of them. Many of the unlabelled instances are truly of the unknown class, hence our cluster labelling accounts for this. Otherwise there is strong bias towards known classes, even when clusters are overwhelmingly unknown. While this incorrectly treats some unlabelled known class flows as unknown, we counter this error with label propagation, multiple labels, and compound classification. The second reason for improvement is to allow multiple labels per cluster. The labelling method in [2, 4] would label entire clusters based on its most common labelled class. However, there are circumstances when it does not make sense to apply this method. While we expect pure clusters in this domain with a large k [8], a brief analysis showed some clusters had as low as 35 % purity. In these cases, majority labelling fails to represent the cluster, and thus explains why multiple labels allow such improvement. Our results show that a good choice of threshold can improve the performance of every class. This parameter ensures that pure clusters confidently vote once, while less pure clusters are given multiple class votes. The classes that were already classified effectively remained successful. Meanwhile, classes that were previously frequently mislabelled exhibited more significant improvement. Additionally, fuzzy clustering labelling is seen as efficient in terms of computational complexity. Let n represent the number of flows in a cluster, and c represent the number of traffic classes. The total time complexity for our labelling algorithm is thus $O(n + c)$. There are typically very few classes c compared to flows n. Thus, this is approximately equivalent to the $O(n)$ of the method from [2, 4].

7 Conclusion

This paper presented a new take on an existing semi-supervised approach for network traffic classification. An overall accuracy of approximately 95 % demonstrated the effectiveness of our approach to traffic classification. Furthermore, an improvement in F-Measure for every class demonstrated the effectiveness of fuzzy cluster labelling. This allowed our approach to consistently outperform the state-of-the-art method on which it is based. The alternative feature set considered also demonstrated how stronger feature subsets could be considered to further improve effectiveness.

References

1. Karagiannis, T., Broido, A., Faloutsos, M.: Transport layer identification of P2P traffic. In: ACM SIGCOMM Conference on Internet Measurement, pp. 121–134 (2004)
2. Erman, J., et al.: Offline/realtime traffic classification using semi-supervised learning. Perform. Eval. **64**(9), 1194–1213 (2007)
3. Williams, N., Zander, S., Armitage, G.: Evaluating machine learning algorithms for automated network application identification. Center for Advanced Internet Architectures (CAIA), Technical Report B, 60410 (2006)
4. Zhang, J., Chen, C., Xiang, Y., Zhou, W., Vasilakos, A.V.: An effective network traffic classification method with unknown flow detection. IEEE Trans. Netw. Serv. Manage. **10**(2), 133–147 (2013)
5. Erman, J., et al.: Offline/realtime traffic classification using semi-supervised learning. Perform. Eval. **64**(9), 1194–1213 (2005)
6. Auld, T., Moore, A.W., Gull, S.F.: Bayesian neural networks for internet traffic classification. IEEE Trans. Neural Networks **18**(1), 223–239 (2007)

7. McGregor, A., Hall, M., Lorier, P., Brunskill, J.: Flow clustering using machine learning techniques. In: Barakat, C., Pratt, I. (eds.) PAM 2004. LNCS, vol. 3015, pp. 205–214. Springer, Heidelberg (2004)
8. Erman, J., Arlitt, M., Mahanti, A.: Traffic classification using clustering algorithms. In: SIGCOMM Workshop on Mining Network Data, pp. 281–286 (2006)
9. Nguyen, T.T., Armitage, G.: A survey of techniques for internet traffic classification using machine learning. IEEE Comm. Surv. Tutorials 10(4), 56–76 (2008)
10. Scikit-Learn.: http://scikit-learn.org/stable/modules/ensemble.html (as of March 2016)
11. NetMate.: http://sourceforge.net/projects/netmate-meter/ (as of March 2016)
12. Williams, N., Zander, S., Armitage, G.: A preliminary performance comparison of five machine learning algorithms for practical IP traffic flow classification. ACM SIGCOMM Comput. Commun. Rev. 36(5), 5–16 (2006)

Short Papers-Pseudo Random/One-way Function

A Noiseless Key-Homomorphic PRF: Application on Distributed Storage Systems

Jhordany Rodriguez Parra$^{(\boxtimes)}$, Terence Chan, and Siu-Wai Ho

School of Information Technology and Mathematical Sciences,
University of South Australia, Adelaide, Australia
jhordany.rodriguez_parra@mymail.unisa.edu.au,
{Terence.Chan,Siuwai.ho}@unisa.edu.au

Abstract. Key-homomorphic pseudo random functions (KH-PRF) have many practical applications including proxy re-encryption, distributed credential protection systems and updatable encryption. We present a key-homomorphic pseudo random function that is homomorphic with respect to a significant part of the secret key and analyse its security. Previous constructions rely on the learning with errors problem which adds some small error to the homomorphic operations due to the noisy outputs. Our construction, based on elliptic curves, removes the need of adding this noise at the cost of adding a few bits to the secret key for which homomorphism does not follow. The main advantage of our construction is that homomorphism can be applied several times without incurring into errors. In particular, we show how our KH-PRF can be used to provide key updatable encryption to distributed storage networks. Also, by relaxing the security assumptions, our PRF can be modified to be homomorphic with respect to the entire key.

Keywords: Distributed storage systems · Elliptic curves · Key-homomorphic PRFs

1 Introduction

One of the most important cryptographic primitives are the pseudo random functions (PRF). A PRF is a function for which $\mathcal{X}$, $\mathcal{S}$ and $\mathcal{Y}$ are the input, key and output spaces respectively. A PRF $G : \mathcal{X} \times \mathcal{S} \to \mathcal{Y}$ is secure if knowing X but not S, $G(X, S)$ is computationally indistinguishable from random [1]. In this paper we will study a kind of PRF with the following property: If $S_3 = S_1 + S_2$, then $G(X, S_3) = G(X, S_1) + G(X, S_2)$. This is a special case of the definition of key-homomorphic PRF (KH-PRF) given in [2, Definition 3.1]. It was also shown in [2, Section 1.2] that KH-PRFs can be used to implement important cryptographic functions such as secure distributed PRFs, proxy re-encryption and updatable encryption.

This work was supported in part by ARC Discovery Project DP150103658.

J.K. Liu and R. Steinfeld (Eds.): ACISP 2016, Part II, LNCS 9723, pp. 505–513, 2016.
DOI: 10.1007/978-3-319-40367-0_34

The wide range of applications of KH-PRFs has motivated the construction of several candidates for which security has been proven [2,3]. Most of these schemes are based on the learning with errors problem (LWE) [4] which naturally adds some 'noise' to the outputs leading to an 'almost' KH-PRF. To be specific, for some small error e (different in every case), $G(X, S_1 + S_2) = G(X, S_1) + G(X, S_2) + e$. Namely, for some $n \in \mathcal{Z}$ and a large integer q, the outputs are vectors in $\mathcal{Z}_q^n$ and $e \in \mathcal{Z}_3^n$. Since this error is small, the homomorphism can be used at the cost of ignoring the least significant bits of the output. However, in some applications such as distributed storage systems (DSS), the homomorphism might need to be applied several times and it is desirable to have $e = 0$ to avoid eventual errors. Our PRF removes the need of adding noise to provide security at the cost of having a small part of the secret key for which homomorphism does not follow. However, by relaxing the security assumptions, we can obtain a KH-PRF for which homomorphism follows for the whole key.

We show how the noiseless property of our PRF allows to remotely change the key of data stored in a DSS by transmitting only a small token. Notice that the naive approach will require to download the data, de-encrypt it, re-encrypt it with the new key and upload it to the storage network again. We also would like to mention that the noiseless property of our PRF allows to increase the number of key servers in the distributed credential protection system with distributed PRFs described in [2, Sect. 1.2]. We describe our PRF and analyse its security in Sect. 2. Section 3 shows how the noiseless property allows key update in DSS. Finally, conclusion and future work are presented in Sect. 4.

2 Main Results

2.1 Backgrounds

Our contribution is a KH-PRF based on elliptic curves for which homomorphism follows for a significant part of the key. Furthermore, by relaxing the security assumptions, we can obtain a KH-PRF where homomorphism applies to the whole key. We start by recalling some facts about elliptic curves. Let $\mathcal{P}$ denote the set of valid points in the curve. $\mathcal{P}$ is a cyclic group in which addition is defined by the chord and tangent method (see [5]). We use $\oplus$ to denote addition in $\mathcal{P}$. We let b denote the order of the curve. That is, $|\mathcal{P}| = b$. For $a \in \mathcal{Z}_b$, and $P \in \mathcal{P}$ we use $[a]P$ to denote adding P to itself a times. Then, it follows that,

$$[a]P \oplus [c]P = [a + c]P \tag{1}$$

The identity is the point to infinity $\mathcal{O}$. We have that $[b]P = \mathcal{O}$ and for $a \in \mathcal{Z}_b$,

$$[a]P \oplus [a]Q = [a](P \oplus Q) \tag{2}$$

In the following we introduce some required notations:

Points to Vectors: For an elliptic curve defined over $GF(q^\alpha)$, $P = (\bar{X}, \bar{Y})$ is a valid point if $\bar{X} \in GF(q^\alpha)$ and $\bar{Y} \in GF(q^\alpha)$ are such that

$$\bar{Y}^2 = \bar{X}^3 + A\bar{X} + B \tag{3}$$

for previously defined constants A and B. Recall that $\bar{X}$ and $\bar{Y}$ are polynomials with some coefficients $\{\beta_1, \ldots, \beta_\alpha\} \in \mathcal{Z}_q$ and $\{\gamma_1, \ldots, \gamma_\alpha\} \in \mathcal{Z}_q$, respectively. Then, there is a trivial map $\zeta : \mathcal{P} \mapsto \mathcal{Z}_q^{2\alpha}$ defined as

$$\zeta(P = (\bar{X}, \bar{Y})) \triangleq [\beta_1, \ldots, \beta_\alpha, \gamma_1, \ldots, \gamma_\alpha].$$

To simplify our notations, we may use the bold-face symbol $\mathbf{P}$ to denote $\zeta(P)$.

Map to $\mathcal{N}$: For an integer u, let $\pi : \mathcal{Z}_u \to \mathcal{N}$ be a mapping that takes inputs from $\mathcal{Z}_u$ and treats them as natural numbers. Namely, for $1 \leq i \leq u - 1$, $\pi : \mathcal{Z}_u \to \mathcal{N}$ is the mapping from the (ordered) set $\mathcal{A} = \{0, \ldots, u - 1\} \in \mathcal{Z}_u$ to the set $\mathcal{B} = \{0, \ldots, u - 1\} \in \mathcal{N}$ defined as $\pi(A_i) = B_i$. When applied to a vector or matrix $\boldsymbol{T} \in \mathcal{Z}_u^{m \times n}$, the map π is independently applied to each entry of $\boldsymbol{T}$.

Function ω: For any $\boldsymbol{A} \in \mathcal{Z}_q^{2\alpha}$, we define a metric $||\boldsymbol{A}|| \triangleq \sum_{i=1}^{2\alpha} q^{2\alpha - i} \pi(A_i)$. Let $-$ be subtraction in the integers. The map $\omega : \mathcal{Z}_q^{2\alpha} \to \mathcal{P}$ is the map that returns the element $P \in \mathcal{P}$ such that $||(|\zeta(P) - \boldsymbol{A}|)||$ is the smallest.

In the following we provide one implementation for ω based on the observation that the metric $|| \cdot ||$ gives more weight to $\bar{X}$ (The first α entries of the vector) than to $\bar{Y}$. Then, this implementation sets $\bar{X}$ first. Given a vector $\boldsymbol{A} = (A_1, \ldots, A_{2\alpha})$ with entries in $\mathcal{Z}_q$, set $i = 0$.

1. Define $\bar{X}_1 = (A_1, \ldots, A_\alpha + i)$ and $\bar{X}_2 = (A_1, \ldots, A_\alpha - i)$ in $GF(q^\alpha)$. Then, following (3) compute $\bar{Y}_1^* = \bar{X}_1^3 + A\bar{X}_1 + B$ and $\bar{Y}_2^* = \bar{X}_2^3 + A\bar{X}_2 + B$. Notice that, for $i = 1, 2$, a point in the curve $P(\bar{X}, \bar{Y})$ such that $\bar{X} = \bar{X}_i$ only exists if $\bar{Y}_i^*$ is a quadratic residue in $GF(q^\alpha)$. Let $\mathcal{V}$ be the set of quadratic residues in $GF(q^\alpha)$ (We know that approximately half the elements in $GF(q^\alpha)$ belong to $\mathcal{V}$. Also $\mathcal{V}$ is expected to be randomly 'spread' over $GF(q^\alpha)$). Set $\mathcal{U} = \{\bar{Y}^* \in \{\bar{Y}_1^*, \bar{Y}_2^*\} : \bar{Y}^* \in \mathcal{V}\}$. If $\mathcal{U}$ is empty, increase i and repeat step 1. Otherwise go to step 2.
2. Every element $\bar{Y}^* \in \mathcal{U}$ can create two points in the curve. One point for each root of $\bar{Y}^*$ and the already known coordinate from $\{\bar{X}_1, \bar{X}_2\}$. Let $\mathcal{R}$ be the set of these candidate points (Notice that $|\mathcal{R}| \leq 4$). Then,

$$\omega(\boldsymbol{A}) = \arg\min_{P \in \mathcal{R}} ||\zeta(P) - \boldsymbol{A}||$$

Special dot product: Let $b \geq q$. For two vectors $\boldsymbol{A} \in Z_b^n$ and $\boldsymbol{B} \in Z_q^n$ define $\langle \boldsymbol{A}, \boldsymbol{B}^T \rangle_b$ as the dot product where all entries in $\boldsymbol{A}$ and $\boldsymbol{B}$ are treated as natural numbers and the result is reduced module b. In other words,

$$\langle \boldsymbol{A}, \boldsymbol{B} \rangle_b \triangleq (\pi(\boldsymbol{A}) \cdot \pi(\boldsymbol{B}^T)) \bmod b.$$

2.2 Our Construction

Our construction uses an elliptic curve EC defined over $GF(q^\alpha)$. We let $\mathcal{P}$ denote the set of points in EC and $|\mathcal{P}| = b$. First, we define the key of our PRF.

For a public small paramter $\lambda > 0$, the secret key is defined as:

$$S \triangleq (\boldsymbol{A} \in \mathcal{Z}_b^{(2\alpha+1)\lambda}, \theta \in \mathcal{Z}_q, Q \in \mathcal{P}).$$

We first describe 3 values required for the evaluation of our PRF:

1. For $X \in \mathcal{N}$, a public full rank matrix $\boldsymbol{T} \in \mathcal{Z}_q^{2\alpha \times 2\alpha}$ and a public point $\hat{P} \in \mathcal{P}$,

$$P(X) \triangleq \omega(\boldsymbol{R}) \text{ where } \boldsymbol{R} = \langle \zeta([X]\hat{P}), \boldsymbol{T} \rangle_q \tag{4}$$

2. We let $\boldsymbol{P(X)} \triangleq \zeta(P(X))$. Let $\mathbb{P}(\mathbb{X})$ be an expansion of $\boldsymbol{P(X)}$ to $\mathcal{Z}_q^{(2\alpha+1)\lambda}$. For $i = 1, \ldots, 2\alpha$ and $j = 1, \ldots, \lambda$, the first $2\alpha\lambda$ entries are computed as

$$\mathbb{P}(\mathbb{X})_{(j-1)2\alpha+i} \triangleq \begin{cases} \boldsymbol{P(X)}_i & \text{if } (\boldsymbol{P(X)}_i \bmod \lambda) + 1 = j \\ 0 & \text{Otherwise,} \end{cases} \tag{5}$$

and, for a non-homomorphic PRF $\sigma : \mathcal{Z}_q \times \mathcal{Z}_q \to \mathcal{Z}_q$, and $i = 1, \ldots, \lambda$, the last λ elements are defined as

$$\mathbb{P}(\mathbb{X})_{2\alpha\lambda+i} \triangleq \begin{cases} \sigma(X, \theta) & \text{if } (\sigma(X, \theta) \bmod \lambda) + 1 = i \\ 0, & \text{Otherwise,} \end{cases} \tag{6}$$

3. $f(\boldsymbol{P(X)})$ is a function $f : \mathcal{Z}_q^{2\alpha} \to \mathcal{Z}_b \backslash \{0\}$ defined as:

$$f(\boldsymbol{P(X)}) \triangleq \begin{cases} \sigma(\langle \boldsymbol{P(X)}, \boldsymbol{V} \rangle_q, J) \to \mathcal{Z}_b & \text{if } \sigma(\langle \boldsymbol{P(X)}, \boldsymbol{V} \rangle_q, J) \neq 0 \\ 1 & \text{Otherwise,} \end{cases} \tag{7}$$

where J and $\boldsymbol{V}$ are public elements in $\mathcal{Z}_q$ and $\mathcal{Z}_q^{2\alpha}$, respectively.

Finally, our PRF is computed as a function $G : \mathcal{N} \times \mathcal{S} \to \mathcal{P}$ defined as

$$G(X, S) \triangleq [\langle \boldsymbol{A}, \mathbb{P}(\mathbb{X}) \rangle_b] P(X) \oplus [f(\boldsymbol{P(X)})]Q \tag{8}$$

In the following, we will use $\oplus$ to denote the sum of points in the curve. That is, $\bigoplus_{i=1}^n P_i = P_1 \oplus, \ldots, \oplus P_n$. Before proving the homomorphism of our PRF, we define the addition operation in $\mathcal{S}$ (The set of keys):

Definition 1 *(Key Addition). For $i = 1, \ldots, n$, let $S^i = (\boldsymbol{A}^i, \theta^i, Q^i)$ be n different keys. We say that $S^m = S^1 +, \ldots, +S^n$ if*

$$\boldsymbol{A}^m = \sum_{i=1}^n \boldsymbol{A}^i, \quad Q^m = \bigoplus_{i=1}^n Q^i \text{ and } \theta^1 = \ldots = \theta^m$$

Also, for $S \in \mathcal{S}$ and $n \in \mathcal{N}$, then $nS = \sum_{i=1}^n S$.

Lemma 1 *(Key-Homomorphism). For $S^1, \ldots, S^n, S^m$ such that $S^m = \sum_{i=1}^n S^i$ as in* Definition 1

$$G(X, S^m) = \bigoplus_{i=1}^n G(X, S^i) \tag{9}$$

Proof. From the definition of our special dot product. If $\boldsymbol{A}^1, \ldots, \boldsymbol{A}^m$ have entries in $\mathcal{Z}_b$, and if $\boldsymbol{A}^m = \sum_{i=1}^n \boldsymbol{A}^i$, then

$$\langle \boldsymbol{A}^m, \mathbb{P}(\mathbb{X}) \rangle_b = \sum_{i=1}^n \langle \boldsymbol{A}^i, \mathbb{P}(\mathbb{X}) \rangle_b \tag{10}$$

Also, since $Q^m = \bigoplus_{i=1}^n Q^i$ and $f(\boldsymbol{P(X)})$ is fixed, from (2) we have that

$$[f(\boldsymbol{P(X)})]Q^m = [f(\boldsymbol{P(X)})] \bigoplus_{i=1}^n Q^i. \tag{11}$$

From (1) and (2), $\bigoplus_{i=1}^n G(X, S^i) = \bigoplus_{i=1}^n [\langle \boldsymbol{A}^i, \mathbb{P}(\mathbb{X}) \rangle_b]P(X) \oplus \bigoplus_{i=1}^n [f(\boldsymbol{P(X)})]Q^i$ becomes

$$\bigoplus_{i=1}^n G(X, S^i) = [\sum_{i=1}^n \langle \boldsymbol{A}^i, \mathbb{P}(\mathbb{X}) \rangle_b]P(X) \oplus [f(\boldsymbol{P(X)})](\bigoplus_{i=1}^n Q^i)$$
$$= [\langle \boldsymbol{A}^m, \mathbb{P}(\mathbb{X}) \rangle_b]P(X) \oplus [f(\boldsymbol{P(X)})]Q^m. \tag{12}$$

Corollary 1. *Let $\{\alpha_1, \ldots, \alpha_n\} \in \mathcal{Z}_b$ and $X \in \mathcal{N}$. If $S^m = \sum_{i=1}^n \alpha_i S^i$ (sum and multiplication as in Definition 1), then $G(X, S^m) = \sum_{i=1}^n [\alpha_i] G(X, S^i)$*

2.3 · Security Analysis

We use the hardness of the elliptic curve discrete logarithm problem (ECDLP) in order to provide security. ECDLP is defined as follows: Given a point $P \in \mathcal{P}$ and a point $Q = [X]P$, find X. The hardness of the ECDLP has been widely used in security protocols such as key exchange and digital signatures [5]. Due to space constraints, we only provide evidence of the security of our PRF. A more detailed analysis can be found in the full version. From (8), the evaluation of our PRF is:

$$G(X, S) = [\langle \boldsymbol{A}, \mathbb{P}(\mathbb{X}) \rangle_b]P(X) \oplus [f(\boldsymbol{P(X)})]Q \tag{13}$$

where the attacker knows $P(X)$ and $f(\boldsymbol{P(X)})$. Consider the *ith* query from the attacker in a CPA (Chosen plain text attack) security game. Let P^* be a generator of $\mathcal{P}$. Therefore, there exist Ω_1^i and Ω_2^i such that $P(X) = [\Omega_1^i]P^*$ and $Q = [\Omega_2^i]P^*$. Using P^* we can rewrite the evaluation of query i as

$$G(X, S) = [\Omega_1^i(\langle \boldsymbol{A}, \mathbb{P}(\mathbb{X}) \rangle_b) + \Omega_2^i f(\boldsymbol{P(X)})]P^* \tag{14}$$

Notice that Ω_1^i and Ω_2^i are solutions to the ECDLP for $(P^*, P(X))$ and (P^*, Q), respectively. Since Ω_1^i depends on $P(X)$, it will be different for each evaluation of the PRF. Let Ω^i denote the value inside the brackets in (14) for query i. The evaluations of points $X_1, \ldots, X_n$ return $[\Omega^1]P^*, \ldots, [\Omega^n]P^*$ where $\Omega^1, \ldots, \Omega^n$ depend (no linearly) on different values $\Omega_1^1, \ldots, \Omega_1^n$ that are solutions to different instances of the ECDLP. Therefore, the attacker will not be able to efficiently find a relationship between $\Omega^1, \ldots, \Omega^n$.

Consider the situation in which the attacker tries to select queries $X_1, \ldots, X_n$ such that $P(X_1), \ldots, P(X_n)$ allow to find $\Omega_1^1, \ldots, \Omega_1^n$ for some generator P^*. First, notice that due to the computation of (4), the attacker still needs to solve an instance of the ECDLP if he or she wants to obtain a specific $P(X)$. Furthermore, even if such $P(X_1), \ldots, P(X_n)$ are found, $\mathbb{P}(\mathbb{X})$ is not known to the attacker due to the non-homomorphic component θ. Notice that since $P(X_1), \ldots, P(X_n)$ are difficult to find. The size of θ can be small compared to the size of $\boldsymbol{A}$. By keeping θ fixed and public, our PRF is homomorphic with respect to the whole key.

3   Application to Distributed Storage Systems

In this section we show how our noiseless PRF can be used to encrypt content in distributed storage systems (DSS) such that the encryption key can be remotely changed. First, we describe the general DSS paradigm. For specific details, constructions and analysis, we refer to [6].

Assume we want to store a file F in a storage network. Since individual nodes may fail, backup mechanisms are needed. An easy solution is to store exact copies of F in several nodes. However, this approach implies a high storage cost to achieve failures resiliance: Let $|F|$ be the size of F in bits. To guarantee recovery after any r failures, a total of $(r+1)|F|$ bits need to be stored in the storage network. Linear codes for DSS reduce this storage cost as follows: To store F in n nodes, we will let $\boldsymbol{N} = [N_1, \ldots, N_n]$ be a column vector in which for $i = 1, \ldots, n$, N_i denotes the content to be stored in node i. For $r < n$, F is divided into r blocks. Let $\boldsymbol{M} = [M_1, \ldots, M_r]$ be the column vector where every element represents one block. We require that for $i = 1, \ldots, r$, $M_i \in \mathcal{M}$ where $\mathcal{M}$ is a group under addition and for which scalar multiplication is defined. For a public $n \times r$ matrix $\boldsymbol{W}$ with entries in $\mathcal{Z}_{|\mathcal{M}|}$, $\boldsymbol{N}$ (i.e., the content of all r nodes) is defined by

$$\boldsymbol{W} \cdot \boldsymbol{M} = \boldsymbol{N}. \tag{15}$$

Certainly, in order to be able to recover F from any r nodes, we require any r rows of $\boldsymbol{W}$ to be linearly independent. Notice that by varying n and r, we will get different storage costs. The authors in [6] present a complete analysis of the tradeoffs between storage cost and the information to be transferred to repair a failed node (bandwidth cost). For $1 \le i \le n$, let $\{\alpha_{i,1}, \ldots, \alpha_{i,r}\}$ be the ith row of $\boldsymbol{W}$. From the above definition of the code

$$N_i = \sum_{j=1}^{r} \alpha_{i,j} M_j \tag{16}$$

Notice that every element $M_1, \ldots, M_r$ can be a vector itself and we will always be able to recover $\boldsymbol{M}$ (from (15)).

We now consider the case where secrecy is required: Let Eve be a unauthorised user (adversary). Having N_i, Eve can get information about F. For instance, assume Eve knows that either file F_1 or F_2 has been stored in the DSS.

Since W is public, Eve can compute (16) for both F_1 and F_2 and compare her results with N_i. Then, Eve will be able, with high probability, to tell which file was stored. To prevent this from happening, we use encryption.

We will assume that counter mode encryption (CTR) is used to provide secrecy to the DSS. CTR represents the messages to be encrypted as vectors. As it was said before, $M_1, \ldots, M_r$ can be vectors themselves, say of length ℓ. Let $\mathcal{M}^\ell$ denote the set of vectors of length ℓ with entries in $\mathcal{M}$. Thus, F can be written as a $r \times \ell$ matrix where $\{M_1, \ldots, M_r\}$ are the rows. Let $E : \mathcal{M}^\ell \times S \to \mathcal{M}^\ell$ be an encryption function that implements CTR with Underlying PRF $\hat{G} : \mathcal{X} \times S \to \mathcal{M}$. For $i = 1, \ldots, r$,

$$E(M_i^\ell, S) = [M_{i,1} \oplus \bar{G}(X_1, S), \ldots, M_{i,\ell} \oplus \bar{G}(X_\ell, S)] \tag{17}$$

for some publicly known $\{X_1, \ldots, X_\ell\}$. Since our PRF has outputs in $\mathcal{P}$, we require $\{M_1, \ldots, M_r\}$ to be elements in $\mathcal{P}^\ell$. There are several maps from the integers to points in elliptic curves that can be used for this purpose.

Definition 2. Let $G : \mathcal{N}^\ell \times S \to \mathcal{P}^\ell$ be the generalisation of our PRF G to vectors. That is, for $X^\ell \in \mathcal{N}^\ell$ and $S \in \mathcal{S}$, $G(X^\ell, S) = [G(X_1, S), \ldots, G(X_\ell, S)]$

Remark 1. Since addition in $\mathcal{P}^\ell$ is component wise, corollary 1 extends to G.

To provide secrecy to the DSS, instead of providing M in (15) to the storage network, the owner of the file selects a public vector $X^\ell \in \mathcal{X}^\ell$, together with a set of seeds $\{S^1, \ldots, S^r\}$ and computes $C \in \mathcal{P}^{r \times \ell}$ where for $i = 1, \ldots, r$

$$C_i = M_i \oplus G(X^\ell, S^i).$$

Notice that making $S^i = S^j$ for all $i < j \leq r$ will imply using the same random pad to encrypt several messages which is well known to lead to insecure systems. Therefore, we require that for $i < j \leq r$, $S^i \neq S^j$. These seeds can be shared between the source and the authorised users using a common secret K. We will call this key K, the 'general key'. Having computed C, the owner of the file sends C to the DSS. Having C, the DSS uses $W \in \mathcal{Z}_b^{n \times r}$ to compute

$$W \cdot C = N \tag{18}$$

where multiplication is replaced by scalar multiplication of points in $\mathcal{P}$. From (18), the content of node N_i (which is a vector in $\mathcal{P}^\ell$) will be given by

$$N_i = \bigoplus_{j=1}^r [\alpha_{i,j}](M_j \oplus G(X^\ell, S^i)) = \bigoplus_{j=1}^r [\alpha_{i,j}]M_j \oplus \bigoplus_{j=1}^r [\alpha_{i,j}]G(X^\ell, S^i) \tag{19}$$

Let $\{S^1, \ldots, S^r\}$ and $\{\hat{S}^1, \ldots, \hat{S}^r\}$ be the seeds generated by general keys K and $\hat{K}$, respectively. Assume that we want to change K for $\hat{K}$. The source will compute $\{\bar{S}^1, \ldots, \bar{S}^r\}$ such that for $i = 1, \ldots, r$, $\hat{S}^i = S^i + \bar{S}^i$ and will send the token $S^\Delta = \sum_{j=1}^r \alpha_{i,j} \bar{S}^i$ to the storage node. The node computes $G(X^\ell, S^\Delta)$ and changes its content from N_i to $\hat{N}_i$ (the updated content) as follows:

$$\hat{N}_i = N_i \oplus G(X^\ell, S^\Delta).$$

$$= \bigoplus_{j=1}^{r}[\alpha_{i,j}]M_j \oplus \bigoplus_{j=1}^{r}[\alpha_{i,j}]G(X^\ell, S^i) \oplus \bigoplus_{j=1}^{r}[\alpha_{i,j}]G(X^\ell, \bar{S}^i)$$

$$= \bigoplus_{j=1}^{r}[\alpha_{i,j}]M_j \oplus \bigoplus_{j=1}^{r}[\alpha_{i,j}](G(X^\ell, S^i) \oplus G(X^\ell, \bar{S}^i))$$

$$= \bigoplus_{j=1}^{r}[\alpha_{i,j}]M_j \oplus \bigoplus_{j=1}^{r}[\alpha_{i,j}](G(X^\ell, \hat{S}^i)) \tag{20}$$

As it can be seen, the node was able to change the encryption key without knowing the individual components of C. Also, since S^Δ is independent from the plain-text (i.e., M), S^Δ tells nothing about the plain-text. Notice also that S^Δ is pair wise independent with $\{S^1, \ldots, S^r\}$ and $\{\hat{S}^1, \ldots, \hat{S}^r\}$.

Remark 2. After decryption, the users will still need to solve (15) for M. The users may use Gaussian ellimination. If for a known a, $Q = [a]P$ needs to be solved for $P \in \mathcal{P}$ in the last step, the users can look for an integer a^{-1} such that $aa^{-1} \equiv 1 \bmod b$ and do $P = [a^{-1}]Q$. If such an integer does not exist (can happen if b is not prime), they might need to download M_i from one of the nodes that store systematic parts. It is interesting to find structures for W to prevent this from happening.

4 Conclusion and Future Work

We have created the first key-homomorphic PRF without noisy outputs. This KH-PRF has many practical applications for key management including distributed PRFs, proxy re-encryption and updatable encryption. We also showed the benefits of the 'noiseless' property when changing the encryption key of data stored in a a remote distributed storage system. In order to provide security, we added a few bits to the secret key (Namely, θ) for which homomorphism does not follow. However, by relaxing the security assumptions, we can keep θ fixed and our PRF becomes homomorphic with respect to the entire key. When using θ as part of the secret key, it is necessary to keep track of the values of θ as the keys are changed. However, specially for large files, the size of θ is negligible.

Our PRF is based on elliptic curves and therefore, it is slow compared to block ciphers such as AES. However, the homomorphic property allows saving a resource that in some situations, is at least as important as computing power: bandwidth. Our PRF will benefit from any improvements on the efficiency of computations over elliptic curves. Also, it is interesting to know different ways to generate the matrix W such that the decoding is more efficient.

References

1. Goldreich, O., Goldwasser, S., Micali, S.: How to construct random functions. J. ACM **33**(4), 792–807 (1986)

2. Boneh, D., Lewi, K., Montgomery, H., Raghunathan, A.: Key homomorphic PRFs and their applications. In: Canetti, R., Garay, J.A. (eds.) CRYPTO 2013, Part I. LNCS, vol. 8042, pp. 410–428. Springer, Heidelberg (2013)

3. Banerjee, A., Peikert, C.: New and improved key-homomorphic pseudorandom functions. In: Garay, J.A., Gennaro, R. (eds.) CRYPTO 2014, Part I. LNCS, vol. 8616, pp. 353–370. Springer, Heidelberg (2014)

4. Regev, O.: On lattices, learning with errors, random linear codes, cryptography. J. ACM **56**(6), 34:1–34:40 (2009)

5. Costello, C.: Fast formulas for computing cryptographic pairings. Ph.D. dissertation, Information Security Institute. Queensland University of Technology (2012)

6. Dimakis, A., Ramchandran, K., Wu, Y., Suh, C.: A survey on network codes for distributed storage. Proc. IEEE **99**(3), 476–489 (2011)

Author Index

Au, Man Ho I-3, I-20, I-389, I-443, II-207

Bagheri, Nasour II-301
Bai, Bo I-3
Barmawi, Ari Moesriami I-409
Boyd, Colin I-161
Braun, Johannes I-426
Buchmann, Johannes I-426
Bunder, Martin II-258

Cai, Haibin I-265
Carr, Christopher I-161
Castiglione, Aniello I-231, II-37
Castiglione, Arcangelo II-37
Chan, Terence II-505
Chen, Chao I-215
Chen, Huaifeng II-409
Chen, Jiageng II-333
Chen, Rongmao II-3, II-223
Chen, Wei I-20
Chen, Xiaofeng I-361, I-509
Chen, Zehong I-525
Cheng, Yao II-481
Choo, Kim-Kwang Raymond I-265, I-389
Chow, Kam-Pui II-457
Chow, Yang-Wai I-409
Cornea, Tudor I-231
Cui, Xingmin I-40

Deng, Robert H. II-207, II-481
Dobre, Ciprian I-231
Duong, Dung Hoang II-427
Dutta, Avijit I-343

Erfani, Sarah M. II-493

Fang, Junbin I-40, II-333
Feng, Yong I-329
Forler, Christian II-317

Glennan, Timothy II-493
Goh, Yong Kheng I-77
Gosman, Catalin I-231

Großschädl, Johann I-94
Gu, Dawu II-134
Guo, Fuchun I-477, II-3, II-170, II-223

Han, Fengling I-329
Han, Jinguang I-443
Hanaoka, Goichiro II-269
Hanzlik, Lucjan II-467
Hao, Feng I-57
He, Debiao II-73
He, Kai II-207
He, Xiaoyang II-285
Ho, Siu-Wai II-505
Horsch, Moritz I-426
Hou, Lin I-461
Hu, Jiankun II-87
Hu, Wei I-310
Huang, Xinyi I-310
Huang, Zhangjie II-379
Huh, Jun Ho I-128
Hui, Lucas C.K. I-40

Ji, Min I-495
Jia, Chunfu II-153
Jia, Keting II-363
Jiang, Peng II-170
Jiang, Tao I-361
Jiang, Yinhao I-477
Jiang, Zoe L. II-153

Ke Wang, Eric I-40
Khor, Ean Yee II-437
Kim, Hyoungshick I-128
Kluczniak, Kamil II-467
Kunihiro, Noboru II-243, II-269
Kutyłowski, Mirosław II-467

Lai, An Chow I-77
Lai, Jianchang II-223
Lai, Junzuo I-461
Lazaridis, Emmanuel I-77
Leckie, Christopher II-493
Lee, Min Cherng I-77

Li, Bao   II-285
Li, Hui   I-509
Li, Jin   I-509, II-153
Li, Lin   I-94
Li, Ping   II-153
Li, Tong   II-153
Li, Xiangxue   I-293
Li, Yannan   I-389
Li, Yingjiu   II-481
Li, Zhen   I-198
Liang, Kaitai   I-376, I-525, II-103
Lin, Xiaodong   II-120
List, Eik   II-317
Liu, Jianwei   I-310
Liu, Jingwen   I-310, II-87
Liu, Lixian   I-461
Liu, Shigang   I-215
Liu, Weiran   II-87
Liu, Zhe   I-94
Liu, Zheli   II-153
Lou, Wenjing   I-361
Lu, Haibing   I-265
Lu, Jiqiang   II-395
Lu, Rongxing   II-120
Lucks, Stefan   II-317
Luo, Xiapu   I-3, I-20
Luo, Xiling   II-87
Lv, Bo   I-281

Ma, Jianfeng   I-361
Ma, Sha   II-21
Ma, Xiaobo   I-3
Mao, Yijun   II-207
Masucci, Barbara   II-37
McCorry, Patrick   I-57
Mendel, Florian   II-301
Minematsu, Kazuhiko   II-347
Mitra, Robin   I-77
Miyaji, Atsuko   I-376
Morozov, Kirill   I-181
Möser, Malte   I-57
Mu, Yi   I-477, II-3, II-21, II-57, II-170,
    II-187, II-223

Nandi, Mridul   I-343
Nisbet, Alastair   I-115
Nitaj, Abderrahmane   II-258

Ooi, Shih Yin   II-437

Palmieri, Francesco   II-37
Pan, Shiran   I-141, II-446
Pang, Ying Han   II-437
Parampalli, Udaya   II-134
Parra, Jhordany Rodriguez   II-505
Paul, Goutam   I-343
Petzoldt, Albrecht   II-427
Phillips, James G.   I-409
Phuong, Tran Viet Xuan   II-103
Pop, Florin   I-231
Pranata, Ilung   I-409

Qian, Haifeng   I-293
Qin, Bo   I-310
Qin, Lingyue   II-409
Qiu, Xinliang   I-3

Ren, Yili   II-87
Rudolph, Carsten   I-249

Samsudin, Azman   II-333
Santis, Alfredo De   II-37
Sasaki, Yu   II-301
Schlipf, Mario   I-426
Shahandasti, Siamak F.   I-57
Shao, Jun   I-495
Shen, Wuqiang   I-281
Song, Ling   II-379
Song, Youngbae   I-128
Su, Chunhua   I-376, II-333
Sun, Shi-Feng   II-134
Sun, Yang   I-310
Sun, Yujuan   I-293
Susilo, Willy   I-361, I-389, I-409, I-477, II-3,
    II-103, II-223, II-258

Takagi, Tsuyoshi   I-181, II-427
Takayasu, Atsushi   II-243
Tang, Shaohua   I-281
Tang, Yajuan   I-20
Teh, Je Sen   II-333
Tian, Song   II-285
Tonien, Joseph   II-258

van Schyndel, Ron   I-329

Wang, Jingxuan   I-40
Wang, Kunpeng   II-285
Wang, Ning   II-363
Wang, Shulan   I-525
Wang, Ting   I-525

Wang, Xiaofen   II-57
Wang, Xiaoyun   II-409
Wang, Yu   I-215
Wang, Zhen   II-87
Wei, Guiyi   I-495
Wei, Zhuo   I-265
Wen, Qiaoyan   II-170
Weng, Jian   II-207
Wenzel, Jakob   II-317
Woodward, Andrew   I-115
Wu, Qianhong   I-310, I-361, II-87
Wu, Wei   I-198

Xia, Zhe   II-73
Xiang, Yang   I-215
Xiao, Bin   I-20
Xiao, Min   II-73
Xie, Mande   I-495
Xu, Fei   II-457
Xu, Qiuliang   I-94, I-443
Xu, Rui   I-181
Xu, Shengmin   II-21
Xu, Wei   II-87

Yamakawa, Takashi   II-269
Yan, Shen   I-141, II-446
Yang, Guomin   I-409, II-3, II-21, II-103,
    II-187
Yang, Min   II-457

Yang, Qianqian   II-379
Yang, Rupeng   I-443
Yang, Xiaoyun   II-73
Yang, Xuechao   I-329
Yang, Yanjiang   I-181, I-265
Yap, Wun-She   I-77
Yi, Xun   I-329
Yin, Chengyu   I-20
Yiu, S.M.   I-40
Yu, Wei   II-285
Yu, Yong   I-389
Yu, Yu   I-293, II-134
Yu, Zuoxia   I-443
Yuen, Tsz Hon   II-134

Zhang, Kai   I-293
Zhang, Mingwu   II-3
Zhang, Peng   I-525
Zhang, Shiwei   II-187
Zhang, Xinpeng   I-389
Zhang, Yinghui   I-509
Zhao, Shuang   I-3
Zhao, Yuhang   I-141
Zheng, Dong   I-509
Zhou, Jianying   I-181
Zhou, Yuan   I-293
Zhu, Wen-Tao   I-141, II-446
Zou, Wei   I-3
Zuo, Cong   I-495